ANNOUNCING
NOW RE.

The edition of *The Complete Wι*

Volume I *Behold Your King:*
     The Complete Poetical Works of Frances Ridley Havergal

Volume II *Whose I Am and Whom I Serve:*
     Prose Works of Frances Ridley Havergal

Volume III *Loving Messages for the Little Ones:*
     Works for Children by Frances Ridley Havergal

Volume IV *Love for Love: Frances Ridley Havergal:*
     Memorials, Letters and Biographical Works

Volume V *Songs of Truth and Love:*
     Music by Frances Ridley Havergal and William Henry Havergal

David L. Chalkley, Editor   Dr. Glen T. Wegge, Music Editor

The Music of Frances Ridley Havergal by Glen T. Wegge, Ph.D.

This Companion Volume to the Havergal edition is a valuable presentation of F.R.H.'s extant scores. Except for a very few of her hymntunes published in hymnbooks, most or nearly all of F.R.H.'s scores have been very little—if any at all—seen, or even known of, for nearly a century. What a valuable body of music has been unknown for so long and is now made available to many. Dr. Wegge completed his Ph.D. in Music Theory at Indiana University at Bloomington, and his diligence and thoroughness in this volume are obvious. First an analysis of F.R.H.'s compositions is given, an essay that both addresses the most advanced musicians and also reaches those who are untrained in music; then all the extant scores that have been found are newly typeset, with complete texts for each score and extensive indices at the end of the book. This volume presents F.R.H.'s music in newly typeset scores diligently prepared by Dr. Wegge, and Volume V of the Havergal edition presents the scores in facsimile, the original 19th century scores. (The essay—a dissertation—analysing her scores is given the same both in this Companion Volume and in Volume V of the Havergal edition.)

    Dr. Wegge is also preparing all of these scores for publication in performance folio editions.

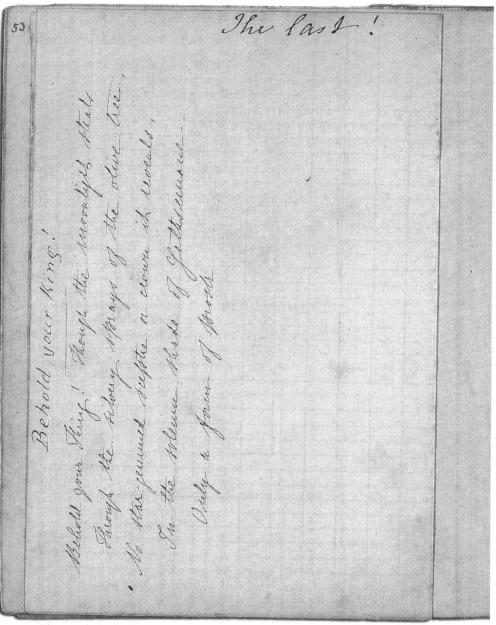

This rough draft of "Behold your King" was found in the last Manuscript Book Nº IX. The poem was written on the back of a printed sheet. On the facing page to the left is the fair copy begun by Frances, left uncompleted. The notations "The very last"

54

Behold your King! Through the moonlight pale
Through the silvery shade of the olive tree
No flargemmed sceptre or crown it reveals
In the solemn shade of Gethsemane.
Only a form of prostrate grief,
~~Fallen~~, crushed, like a broken leaf!
O think of His sorrow! ~~& you~~ that we may know
The depth of love in the depth of woe.

Behold your King! Is it nothing to you
That the crimson tokens of agony
From the kingly brow must fall like dew
Through the shuddering shades of Gethsemane?
Jesus Himself the Prince of Life,
Bows in mysterious mortal strife;
O think of His sorrow! ~~& you shall~~ that we may know
The unknown love in the unknown woe.
Behold your King! With His sorrow crowned,
Alone, alone in the valley is He!
The shadows of death are gathering round,
And the Cross must follow Gethsemane.
Darker & darker the gloom must fall!
Filled is the Cup, He must drink it all!
O think of His sorrow ~~& you shall know~~ that we may know
~~The glory of love in the gloom of woe.~~
His wondrous love in His wondrous woe.

The very last

and "The last!" were written later, likely by her sister Maria. See pages 640–641 of
this book. Thus this was her last finished poem.

Behold your King.

'Behold, and see if there be any sorrow like unto My sorrow.'—LAMENTATIONS 1:12.

BEHOLD your King! Though the moonlight steals
  Through the silvery sprays of the olive tree,
No star-gemmed sceptre or crown it reveals,
  In the solemn shade of Gethsemane.
      Only a form of prostrate grief,
      Fallen, crushed, like a broken leaf!
Oh, think of His sorrow! that we may know
The depth of love in the depth of woe.

Behold your King! Is it nothing to you,
  That the crimson tokens of agony
From the kingly brow must fall like dew,
  Through the shuddering shades of Gethsemane?
      Jesus Himself, the Prince of Life,
      Bows in mysterious mortal strife;
Oh, think of His sorrow! that we may know
The unknown love in the unknown woe.

Behold your King, with His sorrow crowned,
  Alone, alone in the valley is He!
The shadows of death are gathering round,
  And the Cross must follow Gethsemane.
      Darker and darker the gloom must fall,
      Filled is the Cup, He must drink it all!
Oh, think of His sorrow! that we may know
His wondrous love in His wondrous woe.

F. R. H. Good Friday, 1879.

THE POETICAL WORKS

OF

FRANCES RIDLEY HAVERGAL.

The Definitive Nisbet Edition of 1884
With Also Further Poems, Etc.

Taken from *The Complete Works of Frances Ridley Havergal.*

" Knowing her intense desire that Christ should be magnified, whether
by her life or in her death, may it be to His glory
that in these pages she, being dead,
'Yet speaketh!'"

THE POETRY OF FRANCES RIDLEY HAVERGAL
Copyright © 2016 by
The Havergal Trust

ISBN 978-1-937236-50-2   Library of Congress: 2016918251

Cover Design by Glen T. Wegge.

Havergal, Frances Ridley
The Poetry of Frances Ridley Havergal taken from the edition of the complete
works of Frances Ridley Havergal / Frances Ridley Havergal.

1. Havergal, Frances Ridley, 1836–1879. 2. Christian Life. 3. Christian Poetry,
English. 4. Music. I. Title

Printed in the United States of America.

This book is printed on acid-free paper.

This is taken from the new edition of *The Complete Works of Frances Ridley
Havergal* edited by David L. Chalkley, and Dr. Glen T. Wegge, Music Editor.

In all that she did, and in all that she wrote, Frances Ridley Havergal's one over-riding desire was—as Colossians 1:18 says—"that in all things he [*her Lord*] might have the pre-eminence." She saw herself as an instrument in her Saviour's hand, writing for His sake, His glory alone. Indeed the words of Psalm 45:1 were true of her: "My heart is inditing a good matter: I speak of the things which I have made touching the King: my tongue is the pen of a ready writer."

The truth of Christ, which she so loved, and which He used her to present to others, is what is relevant and important, not Frances herself. Understanding the truth of this, you don't first of all think "what a wonderful, fine lady she was" but "what a Saviour ! she had." Jesus Christ alone was changing her from what she was, to become daily more like Himself. Frances would not want anyone to look solely or primarily at her, but she would want all to see her Lord and Saviour. He was her only beauty, righteousness, wisdom, her all. So as you embark on reading, may you too see the Lord Jesus Christ. To see her King is what she would have wanted, the true conclusion of her works and life, and of any genuine disciple's works and life. The Lamb is all the glory in Emmanuel's land, the kingdom of God.

The purpose of this work is ministry, and any money received by the Havergal Trust from sales of these books is to be applied to continue the work of the Trust, all revenues being applied to cover true costs of production and distribution and then to publish and distribute more books more widely, with very affordable prices, with no financial profit to any involved beyond fair market compensation for time and labor. The purpose of the Trust is to preserve far into the future (if our Lord does not return sooner) works by and about F.R.H., to make available to many these works, and to publish works by other authors similar to Havergal.

While most of the Havergal edition is made of public domain works published before 1923, throughout the edition are numerous items of new work in 2003–2011.

Frances Ridley Havergal used language clearly, specifically, powerfully, precisely, and beautifully, and no alteration of any of her works should be done. At the beginning of the 21st century her words are as simple and fresh as they were when she was here, and they should be left precisely as she wrote them without any change.

Many valuable, important works have been gutted with a pretence of improving or clarifying the language, when the language of Bonar, Spurgeon, Chambers, and others should be left alone in its original clarity, beauty, and power. F.R.H.'s sentences—and very words—have a special power, clarity, beauty, sweetness, and precision which cannot be improved nor even matched—only harmed and distorted—by any changes. Similarly, C. H. Spurgeon, J. C. Ryle, John Owen, John Flavel, Thomas Watson, George Whitefield, Jonathan Edwards, Robert Murray M'Cheyne, and many other similar authors should be left alone in their precise words they originally wrote: any "improvement" of their precise words improves nothing, harms and distorts what they really said, and very often if not always guts what they meant and invites things they never meant. This is far worse than "improving" paintings by Rembrandt, Vermeer, Monet (which would be derided by anyone serious about art), or "improving" scores by Bach, Beethoven, or Rachmaninoff (any true musician cleaves to the original scores with absolute fidelity to the tiniest notated details), and serious people would not accept such against Shakespeare, Nathaniel Hawthorne, Goethe, nor such secular authors. It is a remarkable distortion for an editor to impose "trust me, I know better" rather than the original author.

The photographs and illustrations should also be left just as they are, not "updated," "enhanced," nor changed in any way. ("Improving" Frances does not improve her.)

<u>Many</u> pieces such as "One Hour with Jesus," any of the poems, or other parts of this edition would be very beneficial to print in bulletins, periodicals, and other formats.

The Havergal Trust   P.O.Box 649   Kirksville, Missouri 63501

A NOTE TO THE READER

Serious effort has been made to publish this edition of *The Complete Works of Frances Ridley Havergal* very closely to the original texts of F.R.H. When clear mistakes had been made in the original books, they were corrected without comment, and other, exceptional changes were made only when there was very good reason. Details of spelling and punctuation were preserved as they were found in the original works.

There were many inconsistencies in the original texts. For example, among different books, or even within the same book on occasion, "labour" and "endeavour" might also be spelled "labor" and "endeavor." Even among the original 19th century Havergal books published by James Nisbet & Co. (F.R.H.'s primary publisher), there is much inconsistency in the way quotation marks were done, consistent within the same book but different from one Nisbet book to another. The British way is to place quotations within single quotation marks, and to place quotations in quotations within double quotation marks: 'Jesus says, and says to you, "Come, oh come, to Me."' The American way is the reverse: "Jesus says, and says to you, 'Come, oh come, to Me.'" As this edition was typeset in 2004, the British way of quotation marks was used for the first item, the definitive, remarkably fine Nisbet edition of *The Poetical Works of Frances Ridley Havergal*, because this original volume used the British style of quotation marks. As we proceeded beyond Nisbet's *Poetical Works*, we saw that various original books alternated between the British and American styles, both among different books by the same publisher Nisbet, and also among other contemporary publishers of F.R.H. in the United Kingdom (Home Words Publishing Co. in London, Marcus Ward in Belfast, and others). Even a manuscript in Frances' own handwriting used the American way of quotation marks. Because there was a need for consistency (not an appearance of randomness or chaos), and because comparatively few are likely to see the pages of the original books, all the quotation marks in this edition are given in the American way, except for Nisbet's *Poetical Works*. Besides quotation marks, there were several other details that we would have done differently ourselves now in the 21st century, which we left the same as we found them in the original books.

If, in reading through these volumes, there is an *appearance* of randomness in the way the various works appear printed on the pages, we would ask that the reader please bear in mind that this edition was typeset using the *original* works: numerous volumes of poetry, prose (including biographies, sermons by Frances' father and others, etc.), and music by a number of different authors and publishers. As much as was practicable, considerable effort was made to make these works in this new edition "mirror" the original works—title pages, contents pages, etc.—even though we knew it is unlikely that the vast majority of readers will ever actually *see* these original works.

The desire and earnest effort was that this edition be an "urtext" edition, cleaving very closely to the original text. Exceptions were made when there was good reason, but these were rare. Perhaps the careful reader will also notice that most of the punctuation marks within the text of the Havergal edition have spacing inserted between them and adjacent letters and/or additional punctuation marks, reflecting typesetting practices of the 19th century. Significant effort was expended to accomplish this, the reason being, again, to cleave as closely as possible to the original text, as well as to give the finished version as much of an authentic look as practicable.

The important matter is, that we sought not to "improve" Frances (and her father, her sisters, and the others in this edition) but to present her as she originally wrote.

David Chalkley, Thomas Sadowski

This was F.R.H.'s personal seal.

Explanatory Note: This volume, prepared initially to be a Kindle book, has 1. the sterling collection of the Nisbet edition of *The Poetical Works of Frances Ridley Havergal* (London, James Nisbet & Co., 1884), and 2. poems by F.R.H. not found in Nisbet's *Poetical Works*. Most of this book is a copy of another volume, entitled *Behold Your King: The Complete Poetical Works of Frances Ridley Havergal*, which is Volume I of *The Complete Works of Frances Ridley Havergal*. That Volume I has all of the items in this volume, plus F.R.H.'s three compilations entitled *Echoes from the Word, Royal Gems and Wayside Chimes*, and *Red Letter Days* (calendar year books prepared by Frances, in which she uses selections—either excerpts or whole poems—from her own poetry: nearly all of those selections are given in the pages of this volume), and other items. This volume has nearly every piece of poetry by her that has been found in research for the Havergal edition, but Volume I of her *Complete Works* is a more thorough presentation with also other relevant items and more meticulous, precise details. David L. Chalkley and Dr. Glen T. Wegge, March 30, 2017

A personal note: The seed of the Havergal work was planted in me in late 1996 or early 1997. This work is the Lord's provision, so wonderfully and compassionately provided by Him. Countless details, far more than I realize, of His love, provision, protection, guidance, blessing in this work. The Lamb is all the glory in Emmanuel's land, the kingdom of God. David Chalkley, October 16, 2016

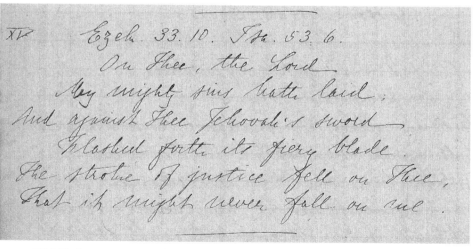

F.R.H.'s fair copy autograph of one of her "Verses on Texts" written in April, 1877, the single verse on Ezekiel 33:10 and Isaiah 53:6, on page 170 in her Manuscript Book N° VIII begun November, 1873. See page 563 of this book.

CONTENTS.

*F.R.H.'s fair copy autograph of her single-verse poem on Psalm 37:7 (on a margin
reading), one of her "Verses on Texts," found in her Manuscript Book Nº VIII. See page
560 of Volume I of the Havergal edition. See also pages 559 and 589 of this Volume II.*

IV Psa.37.7. (margin)
Rest, and be silent ! For, faithfully listening,
  Patiently waiting, thine eyes shall behold
Pearls in the waters of quietness glistening,
  Treasures of promise that He shall unfold.
Rest, & be silent ! for Jesus is here,
Calming & stilling each ripple of fear.

LIST OF ILLUSTRATIONS

Note: Not all, but many of the illustration pages in this book were caused by the need to keep the correct left-page and right-page orientations. Though many were caused by this, these illustration pages were valuable, needful, or necessary, and twice as many pages could be filled with valuable, relevant illustrations.

PAGE

Please see the Explanatory note on page XIII of this book.

The Complete Works of Frances Ridley Havergal

PREFACE TO VOLUME I.

Behold Your King: The Complete Poetical Works of Frances Ridley Havergal

All things were created by the Lord, to His glory and our benefit. Sin has greatly marred or distorted much of what He created and compassionately gave to us. All of the Lord's gifts were given by Him to us to point us to Himself, and He is Himself His own best gift. Language, mathematics, music, the physical creation—all things—are His creation, truly reflective of Him, in which He is greatly glorified. God gave us language for Him to communicate in love to us His truth, and for us to communicate to Him and to each other. The purpose of language is the communication of truth. Poetry is the most artistic, richest (and most complex and difficult to say) part of language, and is the part of language nearest to music, at the edge or border where music and language meet.

Next to George Herbert and fully at his level, Frances Ridley Havergal's poetry is among the finest theological verse given to us in the English language (and what else is relevant ? than to see the Lord and His truth and glory—though He is shown in Shakespeare and Goethe also), with few if any other poets having a similar level of ideas and beautiful presentation. Her gift in poetry was clearly given from the Lord and diligently used for His glory and our enrichment. In the way Frances spoke, wrote, sang, played the keyboard, there was both a great richness of truthful ideas—truth—and also a special sweetness of presentation of that content. Full of truth and life, sweetly and so well presented. Havergal's poetry and prose have a special sweetness but never saccharine, with power, similar to the special sweetness and power in the way Handel sang or Bach played the violin, and like them the content was the more important part, the presentation being the compassionate, effective means to open and enter others' hearts and minds to present the content.

Frances Ridley Havergal lived forty-two and a half years. She glowed the Lord Jesus Christ and His truth, and her life profoundly benefitted many who knew her and many who later read books or pamphlets by her or sang her hymns. At the start of the 21st century, very few recognize her name, and most who do remember her name only know of her as a hymn-writer. At the time of her death, she was very widely known and greatly valued on both sides of the

Atlantic, and likely four million of her books and booklets were published between 1870 and 1900. There is true gold in her writings, help and enrichment to disciples.

She was born in 1836, the sixth and last child of Rev. William Henry and Jane Head Havergal. As a child she was called "little quicksilver." Her mother's death, when Frances was 11, very deeply affected her. She was brought to a saving knowledge of Christ when she was 14, and though she had attended church and read the Bible for years, now she had the light and life of Christ she had not known before.

Though her formal education ended when Frances was 17 (concluding with one term at a girls' school in Düsseldorf, Germany, where she was awarded top prize, never previously done at the school), she was a true scholar and student the rest of her life. She had a rare level of gifts (at or near the level of John Milton), and she had rare diligence with her gifts. She was utterly fluent in German and French, and nearly fluent in Italian. Her tutor (a pastor in Switzerland) said that she read and understood the German divines and reformers with marvellous speed and perception, swallowing whole whatever he gave her to read (in German or Latin). Today few—almost none—realize the rare gifts she had in music, and the importance of her music. Frances' knowledge was only a means by which to know better her Saviour, and to glorify Him and to bring His truth to others. She read the original Hebrew and Greek texts, not as a dilettante but with real proficiency, diligence, love. Her sister Maria wrote in *Memorials of Frances Ridley Havergal* and in *Lilies and Shamrocks* that she memorized all the New Testament except the Book of Acts, all the Minor Prophets, Isaiah, and all the Psalms. (Maria was accurate, would not have overstated any more than Frances, and sooner understated by leaving out details—books not completed, and various chapters memorized.) She loved the Word of God, and was intimately familiar with every page, searching and underlining and glowing till the end.

Much of her life was very crowded with so much to do, various ministries and projects, the care of her step-mother, very important things to complete, and she was many times rendered unable to work by severe illness or weakness and recovery. The love of Christ was her life, and she lived as she wrote, "ever, *only*, ALL for Thee." On June 3, 1879, she entered into His presence. Ten minutes before she died, she sang the first verse of a hymn by Mary Jane Walker, set to music by Frances:

> Jesus, I will trust Thee, trust Thee with my soul;
> Guilty, lost, and helpless, Thou canst make me whole.
> There is none in heaven or on earth like Thee:
> Thou hast died for sinners—therefore, Lord, for me.

This first volume in *The Complete Works of Frances Ridley Havergal* presents virtually all of her poetry now extant.

Though Frances had a few other publishers who printed smaller items (S. W. Partridge & Co., C. Caswell, J. C. Parlane, Charles Bullock, and Hutchings & Romer for music), James Nisbet & Co. was by far the foremost and primary publisher of her works in her lifetime and after her death. The Nisbet editions are almost always definitive. Frances was directly involved in the final preparations for press when she lived, and in the *The Poetical Works of Frances Ridley Havergal* posthumously published by Nisbet, her sister Maria and her niece and god-daughter Frances Anna Shaw directly oversaw the edition with original manuscripts (rough drafts and fair copies in F.R.H.'s own hand), intimate familiarity, and true diligence. The Nisbet edition of *Poetical Works* contains almost everything.

Echoes from the Word and the *Home Words Birthday Book* were prepared by Frances late in her life, published posthumously by her friend, Rev. Charles Bullock.

Frances completed *Red Letter Days* shortly before her final sickness, published by Marcus Ward & Co.: this volume was likely encouraged by her niece's previously published *Links of Memory* (for which F.R.H. wrote a Preface, also published by Marcus Ward). Ward's *Mottoes for the Months* was among the better posthumous collections, and definitely Nisbet's *Three-fold Praise* and *Fulness of Joy* are worthy of note. A number of posthumous small collections only gave parts of poems or even single stanzas, and most of these collections seemed unsubstantial or feeble.

After poems not found in Nisbet's *Poetical Works* and "Notes about Various Collections of Havergal's Poems," prefaces and excerpts from smaller volumes are given. *Streamlets of Song for the Young* was compiled by Miriam Crane, Frances' oldest sister (aged 19 when Frances was born), who began to tutor her when she was two and a half, and the list of Miriam's selection is worthy of note.

Nisbet's edition of the *Poetical Works* is definitive. In that edition is a vast treasure, a gold-mine scattered (or, rather, stuffed) with big chunks of gold. A miner can have a generous pile of "special favorites" and then find the pile keeps growing. Many know "Take my life," "I gave My life for thee," "Like a river glorious," and a few others, but for a century extremely few have realized that there are hundreds more poems by Havergal similarly rich and beneficial, true worship, from Christ alone, to Him alone.

Mr. Stanley Ward was asked to select 100 poems by Havergal for *Like a River Glorious* (an introductory seed volume to the edition of F.R.H.'s *Complete Works*), and he wrote at the front of his list:

My dear David, What a job hast thou given me! Not that it is irksome; but how does one select a mere "one hundred" from such a chest of gems? So, I have done as you ask . . . . Yet I confess that, if called upon again at a later date, I might well do differently; for the jewels shine with varying lustre according to changing circumstances.

One thing Frances would desire, and that is that her verses would bring glory to our Saviour alone, in doctrine and life.

Your . . . friend in Christ, Stanley Ward

This volume of her *Complete Poetical Works* has very nearly all her poems (there are very likely or almost surely a few more in manuscript not yet found). In this volume, one can, like a jeweller, choose from a large chest of the finest gems to make many bracelets, necklaces, and other pieces; like a florist with a great, expansive garden with so many of the finest flowers, you can make countless bouquets. Each gem, each flower, each poem, is full of truth, truly valuable and important, an offering to the Lord and a benefit to His people, truly to His glory and the enrichment and help of His people.

As her sister Maria wrote, "Knowing her intense desire that Christ should be magnified, whether by her life or in her death, may it be to His glory that in these pages she, being dead, 'Yet speaketh!'"

The reader is also encouraged to find and obtain the small volume *The Temple* by George Herbert (1593–1633), a book of poetry Frances truly loved, now so very little known among believers. Before I knew F.R.H., I profoundly loved and valued George Herbert, and far into my work on her, I saw that she valued him similarly as I did. I long thought that Herbert was the most important—or most valuable—poet in the English language, and that Frances was second after him. Around 2004 or so, five or six years after I began to work on Havergal, I—very unexpectedly to me—came to the conclusion that F.R.H. was fully as valuable as G.H., fully at the level of Herbert in both her ideas and the presentation of her ideas. The two are quite different, like Bach and Schubert. Frances is often or usually more readily or easily accessible. A saving knowledge of the Lord Jesus Christ is necessary to understand each of them: without knowing Him, a reader cannot really understand adequately either of them.

Near the end of this book is a section of "Grateful Acknowledgements," a list of people to whom sincere thanks are expressed, who very importantly helped and enabled the completion of this book and the edition of Havergal's *Complete Works*. This researcher is heartfully grateful to them.

Thanks be to God for His indescribable gift to us in Christ.

David Chalkley

The German poet, playwright, and novelist Goethe apparently had a remarkable ability to take up, set down, and take up again the work he was writing, at will stopping and resuming when and as he wanted. Using a phrase F.R.H. said in a quotation given on the next page, Goethe seemed to have his chest of gold in his possession to use as he wanted. Frances was not at all so. She waited on the Lord, and received from Him her works, "piece by piece just when He will and as much as He will, and no more." Her life and her written works were (to use the statement attributed to the great scientist Johann Kepler) "thinking God's thoughts after Him"; as I Corinthians 2:16 and Philippians 2:5 say, she had the mind of Christ. She wanted every trace of herself and all she had to be His, to be and do as He said in the two commandments (Matthew 22:37–40), to love Him with all her being, and to love her neighbor as herself.

Frances Ridley Havergal wrote this in a letter in February, 1868, when she was 31:

> . . . I have not had a single poem come to me for some time, till last night, when one shot into my mind. All my best have come in that way, Minerva fashion, full grown. It is so curious, one minute I have not an idea of writing anything, the next I *have* a poem; it is *mine*, I see it all, except laying out rhymes and metre, which is then easy work! I rarely write anything which has not come thus.[1]

Her poems were given to her. In August, 1870, she wrote this in a letter to her close colleague and dear friend, Charles Busbridge Snepp:

> I shall trust you more than ever, because you tell me candidly my hymn won't do! I am afraid it is no use hoping that I shall be able to write a better. I will tell you why; I cannot write, and never yet have written beyond my own personal experience. I need to have felt a theme and lived into it before I can write about it. And the better a hymn or poem of mine is, the more the feeling from which it arose generally exceeded it; it is only when anything is burning in my heart that I write my best, though I can express but little of it.[2]

In *Memorials of Frances Ridley Havergal*, her sister Maria quotes parts of two letters by F.R.H.:

---

[1] *Memorials of Frances Ridley Havergal* by her sister, Maria Vernon Graham Havergal (London: James Nisbet & Co., 1880), page 93 of the original book, page 28 of Volume IV of the Havergal edition, *Love for Love: Frances Ridley Havergal: Memorials, Letters and Biographical Works.*

[2] *Letters by the Late Frances Ridley Havergal* edited by her sister, Maria Vernon Graham Havergal (London: James Nisbet & Co., 1886), pages 390–391 of the original book, page 257 of Volume IV of the Havergal edition.

March 19, 1874.

Dear Mr . W——,

. . . I can never set myself to write verse. I believe my King suggests a thought and whispers me a musical line or two, and then I look up and thank Him delightedly, and go on with it. That is how the hymns and poems come. Just now there is silence. I have not had the least stir of music in my mind since I wrote that tiny consecration hymn, a most unusually long interval; and till He sends it there will be none. I am always ready to welcome it and work it when it comes, but I never press for it. . . .[3]

Maria wrote, "And the following letter confirms this statement."

Dear Mr . W——,

I can't make you quite understand me! You say "F. R. H. could do 'Satisfied' grandly"! *No*, she couldn't! Not unless He gave it me line by line! That is how verses come. The Master has not put a chest of poetic gold into my possession and said "Now use it as you like!" But He keeps the gold, and gives it me piece by piece just when He will and as much as He will, and no more. Some day perhaps He will send me a bright line of verse on "Satisfied" ringing through my mind, and then I shall look up and thank Him, and say, "Now, dear Master, give me another to rhyme with it, and then another"; and then perhaps He will send it all in one flow of musical thoughts, but more likely one at a time, that I may be kept asking Him for every line. There, that is the process, and you see there is no "I can do it" at all. That isn't His way with me. I often smile to myself when people talk about "gifted pen" or "clever verses," etc.; because they don't know that it is neither, but something really much nicer than being "talented" or "clever."[4]

Maria next wrote, "Nearly every poem would verify the above."

Later in *Memorials*, Maria quoted this that Frances wrote to a friend (undated, likely part of a letter):

It does seem wonderful that God should so use and bless my hymns; and yet it really does seem as if the seal of His own blessing were set upon them, for so many testimonies have reached me. Writing is praying, with me, for I never seem to write even a verse by myself, and feel like a little child writing;

---

[3] *Memorials of Frances Ridley Havergal* by Maria Vernon Graham Havergal (London: James Nisbet & Co., 1880), pages 135–136 of the original book, page 38 of Volume IV of the Havergal edition.

[4] *Ibid.*, page 136 of the original book, page 38 of Volume IV.

you know a child would look up at every sentence and say "And what shall I say next?" That is just what I do; I ask that at every line He would give me, not merely thoughts and power, but also every word, even the very rhymes. Very often I have a most distinct and happy consciousness of direct answers.[5]

Read her poem "On the Last Leaf" on pages 80–82 of this book.

The next quotation similarly shows that she realized that both her gifts to write poetry and also the very poems and lines were given to her by God. This is not remotely a claim of Scriptural inspiration nor of infallibility (she clearly thought and said that there were weak places in her poetry), but a realization of the Giver and source of her work, and of her happy dependence upon Him.

. . . . I have a curiously vivid sense, not merely of my verse faculty in general being *given* me, but of every separate poem or hymn, nay every line, being *given*. I never write the simplest thing now without prayer for help. I suppose this sense arises from the fact that I cannot write exactly at will. It is peculiarly pleasant thus to take every thought, every verse as a direct gift; and it is not a matter of effort, it is purely involuntary, and I feel it so.[6]

She seems to have very often had little or no awareness of the value and richness of the poems that she was given. She wrote this in a letter to Dr. John Tinson Wrenford in November, 1876:

. . . . I think "The Thoughts of God," printed in *The Sunday Magazine*, is the very best poem I ever wrote; but I have not heard one word about its doing anybody any real good. It's generally something that I don't think worth copying out or getting printed (like "I did this for thee," and "Take my life"), that God sees fit to use.[7]

Frances wrote this in a letter dated August 24, 1867:

---

[5] *Memorials of Frances Ridley Havergal* by Maria V.G. Havergal, pages 104–105 of the original book, page 31 of Volume IV of the Havergal edition.

[6] *Letters by the Late Frances Ridley Havergal*, page 59 of the original book, page 162 of Volume IV of the Havergal edition.

[7] *Memorials of Frances Ridley Havergal* by Maria V. G. Havergal, page 220 of the original book, page 59 of Volume IV of the Havergal edition. The poem "The Thoughts of God" is found on pages 587–599 of this book.

. . . I have a singular difficulty in alterations. Most of my verses have been published exactly as they were first written on the backs of old letters or on a slate. I never make a rough sketch—can't do it. . . .[8]

In another letter, written to her sister Maria and dated November 13, 1875, she wrote this:

In answer to your question about *Reality*, I find it was written at Whitby on the very evening of N.'s prayer.

Dear mother likes *Reality* better than anything I ever wrote! she gushed over it, till it actually made the tears come into my own eyes! I didn't see anything in the verses myself, but mother says "it's perfect"! [9]

Her sister Maria wrote in a "Journal of a Visit to Aix-Les-Bains and Switzerland in 1882" that,

"Miss G. not only told me of the liftings she received by F.'s works, but the marvellous power some of her thoughts have had with infidels. She gave me particulars of one most learned man who was staggered by the genius, the master thought of F.'s argument in her *Thoughts of God*." [10]

Her poetry is very musical, exceptionally and finely so, full of rhythms and cadences and musical aspects. "The Scripture cannot be broken" is a fine example, though so many other poems by her exemplify music in the words. Poetry is the part of language closest to music, at the edge or border where language and music meet, and Frances' poetry reflects her deep, profound musicianship. Her first published book was a collection of poems entitled *The Ministry of Song* (no notes nor staves, full of music), and her 1878 volume of poetry *Loyal Responses* (also words only, full of music) had the sub-title "Daily Melodies for the King's Minstrels." Just as Havergal's poem "Seulement pour Toi" ("Only for Thee") needs (requires) a

---

[8] *Letters by the Late Frances Ridley Havergal* edited by her sister Maria Vernon Graham Havergal (London: James Nisbet & Co., 1886), original book page 377 in the Appendix II, page 253 of Volume IV of the Havergal edition.

[9] *Ibid.*, page 241 of the original book, page 214 of Volume IV of the Havergal edition. "Dear mother" was their step-mother, Caroline Anne Cooke Havergal. This poem "Reality" is found on pages 608–610 of this book.

[10] *The Autobiography of Maria Vernon Graham Havergal* (London: James Nisbet & Co., 1887), pages 183–184 of the original book, page 539 of Volume IV of the Havergal edition. This poem "The Thoughts of God" is found on pages 587–599 of this book.

person with an advanced knowledge of French to see the beauty and power of that French poem, similarly a true musician can see rich details in the warp and woof of Frances' poetry and other works which are very reflective of a true musician, which others who are not musicians might easily miss. Apart from her performance and compositions, which were so valuable for those who heard her, she was a musician to the core, and her musical gifts enrich her other works, her poetry and prose.

Her works, both poetry and prose, are notably consistent in the fineness of both the ideas and the presentation of the ideas. The content of the ideas is more important than the presentation of the ideas, though both content and presentation are so very important.

There is a special beauty in her poetry (and also in her prose and in her music scores), true art and true beauty, both in her presentation of the ideas and in the content of the ideas. There is such rich truth presented in her poems. Numerous examples of this could be given, but "Just when Thou wilt" (pages 556—557 of this book) and "The Song of a Summer Stream" (pages 163—164 of this book) are two suggested examples to read now.

In a letter to her friend—and a fine poet—Julia Kirchhoffer, on April 9, 1876, Frances wrote this about poetry:

> I have an idea that metre answers to key in music, and that one may introduce modulation of metre exactly as one introduces modulation of key, and with similar mental effect. I have tried it in several recent longish poems, using different metres for different parts, and modulating from one into the other instead of passing directly. You will see what I mean in "The Sowers," where, instead of jumping direct into the rather jubilant metre of the last part, I work up to it through "One by one no longer," etc.[11]

Another example is a phrase that she wrote in a letter, "musical thoughts," when she was referring not to composing music but to writing poetry. [12]

---

[11] *Memorials of Frances Ridley Havergal* by Maria V. G. Havergal, page 197 of the original book, page 53 of Volume IV of the Havergal edition. "The Sowers" is found on pages 407–418 of this book.

[12] *Memorials*, page 136 of the original book, page 38 of Volume IV of the Havergal edition. See the second quotation on page XXV (three pages ago).

2 Elm Row
Hampstead.

This was a preparatory sketch of F.R.H. by T. J. Hughes before his fine portrait of Frances, shown on page xviii. T. J. Hughes' address was 2 Elm Row, Hampstead, London. (See the caption on page xvii.)

Her sister Maria wrote: "With the utmost skill, no artist or photograph gives a real idea of her lighted up expression. Is it because soul cannot be represented any more than a sunbeam? And my pen fails, too, in giving an idea to strangers of her sunny ways, merrily playing with children, and heartily enjoying all things. But her deep sympathy with others' joys and sorrows, and her loyal longings that all should know the 'joy unspeakable and full of glory,' were the secret of her influence with others." (Chapter XI in Memorials of Frances Ridley Havergal *by Maria V. G. Havergal, the first item in Volume IV of this Havergal edition.)*

"Whose I am, and

Jesus, Master, whose I am
    Purchased Thine alone to be,
By thy blood, O spotless Lamb,
    Shed so willingly for me;
Let my heart be all thine own,
Let me live to Thee alone.

Other lords have long held sway;
    Now, Thy name alone to bear,
Thy dear voice alone obey,
    Is my daily, hourly prayer.
Whom have I in heaven but Thee?
Nothing else my joy can be

Jesus, Master! I am Thine;
    Keep me faithful, keep me near;
Let thy presence in me shine
    All my homeward way to cheer,
Jesus! at thy feet I fall,
Oh, be Thou my All in all!

These two poems, hymns, were published in F.R.H.'s first published book, The Ministry of Song, *in 1869. These are the fair copy autographs in her own handwriting, in her Manuscript Book Nº IV (for poems). See pages 22–23 of this book. She had earlier written for those*

"Whom I serve".   Acts 27. 23.

Jesus, Master! whom I serve,
   Though so feebly & so ill,
Strengthen hand & heart & nerve
   All Thy bidding to fulfil.
Open Thou mine eyes to see
All the work Thou hast for me.

Lord! Thou needest not, I know,
   Service such as I can bring,
Yet I long to prove & show
   Full allegiance to my King.
Thou an * honour art to me,
Let me be a praise to Thee.

Jesus, Master! wilt Thou use
   One who owes Thee more than all?
As Thou wilt! I would not choose,
   Only let me hear thy call.
Jesus! let me always be
In thy service glad and free.

Dec. 1865.   * See marginal
              reading of 1 Pet. 2. 7.

30

lines 2–4 of the second stanza, "Now it is my hourly prayer / Only thy dear voice to obey / Only thy dear name to bear." The new lines on paper covering over the earlier lines were her finalized text that she published.

This is Frances' rough draft of the poem on pages 639–640 of this book. On the next, facing page is her "fair copy" autograph of the same poem. Apparently after she wrote the fair copy, she later made changes, removing words in the rough draft: the changes with removal of the words crossed out became her finalized text. Frances kept manuscript books, in which she wrote out in fair copy manuscripts her poems, usually after

The Scripture cannot be broken.

Upon the Word I rest,
 Each pilgrim day;
This golden staff is best
 For all the way.
What Jesus Christ Himself hath sealed and spoken,
Can not betray or bend, cannot be broken:
 Upon the Word I rest,
 So strong, so sure,
 So full of comfort blest,
 So sweet, so pure!
The changeless charter of our great salvation,
For faith and hope and joy our broad foundation.
 Upon the Word I stand!
 That cannot die!
 Christ seals it in my hand
 He cannot lie!
The Word that faileth not, that changeth never:
Oh Christ we rest upon Thy word for ever!
Chorus. The Master hath said it, rejoicing in this,
 We ask not for sign or for token;
 His word is enough for our confident bliss—
 "The scripture cannot be broken!"

 F. R. H.

she finalized them. Frances wrote this poem in April, 1879, before she died unexpectedly early on June 3, 1879. The rough draft and fair copy manuscripts were found in her last manuscript book, which had this written in her hand on the front page: "Manuscript Book. No IX. Begun Feb. 24. 1878. 'I will direct their work in truth.'" Faintly after the quotation is written "Isa. 61.8."

This photograph of F.R.H. was taken by the photographers Elliott & Fry in London on Saturday, February 1, 1879, shortly after her 42nd birthday.

THE

POETICAL WORKS

OF

FRANCES RIDLEY HAVERGAL

London

James Nisbet & Co. Limited

21 Berners Street, W.

When thy days on earth are past,
Christ will call thee home at last,
His redeeming love to praise,
Who hath strengthened all thy days.

Frances R. Havergal

Engraved by W. Ridgway from a Photograph by Elliott & Fry.

The frontispiece of the definitively fine The Poetical Works of Frances Ridley Havergal *published by James Nisbet & Co. in 1884.*

PREFATORY NOTE

It is in answer to many requests that the various poems, hymns, and song of Frances Ridley Havergal are comprised in this library edition. It will be obvious, there was some difficulty in selecting the order of their sequence. We doubt not that the dear author's own arrangement in 'Ministry of Song,' 'Under the Surface,' and 'Loyal Responses' will be generally preferred, and consequently they remain intact. To group successfully poetic aspirations of such varied circumstances and ideas, ranging from the sweet simplicities of her songs for the little ones, to those higher soarings which seem to culminate in 'The Thoughts of God,' was indeed a problem. And it is due to my dear sister's memory to state distinctly that *she* never contemplated the publication of many impromptu verses, written to gratify young friends, or in the utterance of rapid imaginings. When F. R. H. was arranging a selection for the first illustrated volume, 'Life Mosaic,' she submitted her poems to her poet friend, the Rev. R. Wilton, earnestly soliciting him to prune away with unsparing keenness 'any of my weaker poems.' And we are aware that other poet critics would prefer only the finer chords to be lasting echoes of F. R. H.

But there are many, oh, so many, who lovingly treasure even the spray of her pen, as well as the nobler waves of thought, and so we open and unseal all the manuscripts in her study drawers. For some of her simpler utterances seem to go at once to the heart of those in humbler life, and their intellect can better grasp such thoughts than the loftier flights of her imagination. By them it is not as a feast of intellect, but as heart cheer for home sorrows, that F. R. H.'s lowliest lays are prized.

The arrangement is subjective, not chronological. But in the Index [page v of this book] will be found the dates and places of her poems; we are aware this is unusual, but it would seem as if her sunny presence and springing footsteps may thus still linger in our midst. It is with pleasure that I entrust to my dear niece, Frances Anna Shaw, the entire arrangement and revision of this complete and final edition. It was no slight labour to prepare the various dates and subdivide the numerous subjects into their present order. In shattered health, I thankfully accept my niece's skilful labour. And we would bring these pages with loyal loving hand to the very feet of F. R. H.'s Master and King, re-echoing words, which seem to float down from the golden heights where now my sister stands amid the upper choir, joining the service of high praise in the 'Eternal Land:'

> 'I have no word to bring
> Worthy of Thee, my King,
> And yet one anthem in Thy praise
> I long, I long to raise.'

'*One* anthem'? Have they not been countless? has not her silver refrain echoed and re-echoed till many an isolated and trembling one has taken up in a gathering and rejoicing chorus, 'Unto Him that loved us, and washed us from our sins in His own blood, and hath made us kings and priests unto God and His Father; to Him be glory and dominion for ever and ever. Amen.'

And does not F. R. H.'s earliest prelude become a fitting closing chord to her life and poems,—

> 'AMID the broken waters of our ever-restless thought,
> Oh be my verse an answering gleam from higher radiance caught;
> That where through dark o'erarching boughs of sorrow, doubt, and sin,
> The glorious Star of Bethlehem upon the flood looks in,
> Its tiny trembling ray may bid some downcast vision turn
> To that enkindling Light, for which all earthly shadows yearn.
> Oh be my verse a hidden stream, which silently may flow
> Where drooping leaf and thirsty flower in lonely valleys grow;
> And often by its shady course to pilgrim hearts be brought
> The quiet and refreshment of an upward-pointing thought;
> Till, blending with the broad bright stream of sanctified endeavour,
> God's glory be its ocean home, the end it seeketh ever.'

MARIA V. G. HAVERGAL.

Ellen A. B. La Barte

with love from

F. R. Havergal's sister

J. Miriam Crane.

Lynwood

Weston-super-mare.

24. February 1892.

This inscription was found in the front of a copy of The Poetical Works of Frances Ridley Havergal *published by James Nisbet & Co. Miriam (1817–1898, nineteen when Frances was born) tutored Frances when she was two and a half.*

Contents.

THE MINISTRY OF SONG.

EARLY POEMS.

MISCELLANEOUS POEMS.

ENIGMAS AND CHARADES.

ANSWERS TO ENIGMAS.

ANSWERS TO CHARADES.

CHORDS FOR CHILDREN.

VERSES ON TEXTS.

'UNDER HIS SHADOW.'

CLOSING CHORDS.

This portrait on the following page was made in Frances' last year, when she was visiting friends in London, in February 1879 (after her 42nd birthday on December 14). There are strong reasons to think that this portrait is in no way flattering but gives an accurate copy of how she looked at that time. Ira Sankey, D. L. Moody's song leader, visited her weeks before her very unexpected early death, and he later commented on how young she looked; others also commented on how she looked younger than her age in years. Both Frances and her family would have accepted only an accurate, realistic, truthful portrait, never a flattering one. The brooch was a gift to her from her father, having Frances' personal emblem, a harp; this was one of very few pieces of jewelry she kept, clearly special to her, and she had months earlier sold nearly all her other jewelry, to give the proceeds to the support of foreign missions (she added the monetary value of this brooch to the other jewelry that she donated). She was full of life and love, glowing Christ, and those who knew her or saw and heard her realized what can scarcely be conveyed on paper. In this way her sister Miriam wrote of how she sang "in quick tune, and with the spirit which only those who heard her can imagine" (from the small book *Footprints and Living Songs*, the essay on Frances' hymns by Miriam Crane). Her sister Maria Vernon Graham Havergal was quoted in the following notice printed in the newspaper *The Christian* for July 3, 1879: "THE LATE MISS F. RIDLEY HAVERGAL.—Mr. T. J. Hughes, of 2 Elm Row, Hampstead [London], has shown us a portrait in chalk for which Miss Havergal sat to him several times. This likeness is recommended by her sister, Miss M. V. G. Havergal, as being so life-like. Orders for photographic copies, at a guinea each, may be sent to Mr. Hughes."

David Chalkley

THE LATE MISS F. RIDLEY HAVERGAL.—Mr. T. J. Hughes, of 2, Elm-row, Hampstead, has shown us a portrait in chalk for which Miss Havergal sat to him several times. This likeness is recommended by her sister, Miss M. V. G. Havergal, as being so life-like. Orders for photographic copies, at a guinea each, may be sent to Mr. Hughes.

The Ministry of Song.

Frances Ridley Havergal's first published book was *The Ministry of Song*, published in 1869 by the Christian Book Society of London. Her original inscription was "To My Father." Her father, Rev. William Henry Havergal, died in 1870, and the inscription "To my Father's Memory." was placed at the front of the book when James Nisbet & Co. published *The Ministry of Song* in 1871. This is a facsimile copy of the inscription in this place in Nisbet's *The Poetical Works of Frances Ridley Havergal*.

The Ministry of Song.

Prelude.

AMID the broken waters of our ever-restless thought,
Oh be my verse an answering gleam from higher radiance caught;
That where through dark o'erarching boughs of sorrow, doubt, and sin,
The glorious Star of Bethlehem upon the flood looks in,
Its tiny trembling ray may bid some downcast vision turn
To that enkindling Light, for which all earthly shadows yearn.
Oh be my verse a hidden stream, which silently may flow
Where drooping leaf and thirsty flower in lonely valleys grow;
And often by its shady course to pilgrim hearts be brought
The quiet and refreshment of an upward-pointing thought;
Till, blending with the broad bright stream of sanctified endeavour,
God's glory be its ocean home, the end it seeketh ever.

The Ministry of Song.

IN God's great field of labour
    All work is not the same;
He hath a service for each one
    Who loves His holy name.
And you, to whom the secrets
    Of all sweet sounds are known,
Rise up! for He hath called you
    To a mission of your own.
And, rightly to fulfil it,
    His grace can make you strong,
Who to your charge hath given
    The Ministry of Song.

Sing to the little children,
    And they will listen well;
Sing grand and holy music,
    For they can feel its spell.

Tell them the tale of Jephthah;
    Then sing them what he said,—
'Deeper and deeper still,' and watch
    How the little cheek grows red,
And the little breath comes quicker:
    They will ne'er forget the tale,
Which the song has fastened surely,
    As with a golden nail.

I remember, late one evening,
    How the music stopped, for, hark!
Charlie's nursery door was open,
    He was calling in the dark,—
'Oh no! I am not frightened,
    And I do not want a light;
But I cannot sleep for thinking
    Of the song you sang last night.
Something about a "valley,"
    And "make rough places plain,"
And "Comfort ye;" so beautiful!
    Oh, sing it me again!'

Sing at the cottage bedside;
    They have no music there,
And the voice of praise is silent
    After the voice of prayer.
Sing of the gentle Saviour
    In the simplest hymns you know,
And the pain-dimmed eye will brighten
    As the soothing verses flow.
Better than loudest plaudits
    The murmured thanks of such,
For the King will stoop to crown them
    With His gracious 'Inasmuch.'

Sing, where the full-toned organ
    Resounds through aisle and nave,
And the choral praise ascendeth
    In concord sweet and grave.
Sing, where the village voices
    Fall harshly on your ear;

And, while more earnestly you join,
    Less discord you will hear.
The noblest and the humblest
    Alike are 'common praise,'
And not for human ear alone
    The psalm and hymn we raise.

Sing in the deepening twilight,
    When the shadow of eve is nigh,
And her purple and golden pinions
    Fold o'er the western sky.
Sing in the silver silence,
    While the first moonbeams fall;
So shall your power be greater
    Over the hearts of all.
Sing till you bear them with you
    Into a holy calm,
And the sacred tones have scattered
    Manna, and myrrh, and balm.

Sing! that your song may gladden;
    Sing like the happy rills,
Leaping in sparkling blessing
    Fresh from the breezy hills.
Sing! that your song may silence
    The folly and the jest,
And the 'idle word' be banished
    As an unwelcome guest.
Sing! that your song may echo
    After the strain is past,
A link of the love-wrought cable
    That holds some vessel fast.

Sing to the tired and anxious
    It is yours to fling a ray,
Passing indeed, but cheering,
    Across the rugged way.
Sing to God's holy servants,
    Weary with loving toil,
Spent with their faithful labour
    On oft ungrateful soil.

The chalice of your music
    All reverently bear,
For with the blessèd angels
    Such ministry you share.

When you long to bear the Message
    Home to some troubled breast,
Then sing with loving fervour,
    'Come unto Him, and rest.'
Or would you whisper comfort,
    Where words bring no relief,
Sing how 'He was despisèd,
    Acquainted with our grief.'
And, aided by His blessing,
    The song may win its way
Where speech had no admittance,
    And change the night to day.

Sing, when His mighty mercies
    And marvellous love you feel,
And the deep joy of gratitude
    Springs freshly as you kneel;
When words, like morning starlight,
    Melt powerless,—rise and sing!
And bring your sweetest music
    To Him your gracious King.
Pour out your song before Him
    To whom our best is due;
Remember, He who hears your prayer
    Will hear your praises too.

Sing on in grateful gladness!
    Rejoice in this good thing
Which the Lord thy God hath given thee,
    The happy power to sing.
But yield to Him, the Sovereign,
    To whom all gifts belong,
In fullest consecration,
    Your Ministry of Song,

Until His mercy grant you
    That resurrection voice,
Whose only ministry shall be,
    To praise Him and rejoice.

Our Hidden Leaves.

OH the hidden leaves of Life!
    Closely folded in the heart;
Leaves where Memory's golden finger,
Slowly pointing, loves to linger;
    Leaves that bid the old tears start.

Leaves where Hope would read the future,
    Sibylline, and charged with fate:
Leaves which calm Submission closeth,
While her tearless eye reposeth
    On the legend, 'Trust, and wait!'

Leaves which grave Experience ponders,
    Soundings for her pilot-charts;
Leaves which God Himself is storing,
Records which we read, adoring
    Him who writes on human hearts.

All our own, our treasured secrets,
    Indestructible archives!
None can copy, none can steal them,
Death itself shall not reveal them,
    Sacred manuscripts of lives.

Some are filled with fairy pictures,
    Half imagined and half seen;
Radiant faces, fretted towers,
Sunset colours, starry flowers,
    Wondrous arabesques between.

Some are traced with liquid sunbeams,
    Some with fire, and some with tears;
Some with crimson dyes are glowing,
From a smitten life-rock flowing
    Through the wilderness of years.

Some are crossed with later writing,
    Palimpsests of earliest days;
Old remembrance faintly gleaming
Through the thinking and the dreaming
    Outlines dim in noontide haze.

One lies open, all unwritten,
    To the glance of careless sight;
Yet it bears a shining story,
Traced in phosphorescent glory,
    Only legible by night.

One is dark with hieroglyphics
    Of some dynasty of grief:
Only God, and just one other,
Dearest friend, or truest brother,
    Ever read that hidden leaf.

Many a leaf is undeciphered,
    Writ in languages unknown;
O'er the strange inscription bending,
(Every clue in darkness ending,)
    Finding no 'Rosetta Stone,'

Still we study, always failing!
    God can read it, we must wait;
Wait, until He teach the mystery,
Then the wisdom-woven history
    Faith shall read, and Love translate.

Leaflets now unpaged and scattered
    Time's great library receives;
When eternity shall bind them,
Golden volumes we shall find them,
    God's light falling on the leaves.

Threefold Praise.

HAYDN—MENDELSSOHN—HANDEL

'We bless Thee for our creation, preservation, and all the blessings of this
life; but above all, for Thine inestimable love in the redemption of the world
by our Lord Jesus Christ.'

PART I.

'We bless Thee for our creation.'

Haydn's 'Creation.'

WHAT is the first and simplest praise,
    The universal debt,
Which yet the thoughtless heart of man
    So quickly may forget?
'We bless Thee for creation!'
    So taught the noble band
Who left a sound and holy form,
    For ages yet to stand,
Rich legacy of praise and prayer,
    Laid up through ages past,
Strong witness for the truth of God:
    Oh, may we hold it fast!

'We bless Thee for creation!'
    So are we blithely taught
By Haydn's joyous spirit;
    Such was the praise he brought.
A praise all morning sunshine,
    And sparklers of the spring,
O'er which the long life-shadows
    No chastening softness fling.

A praise of early freshness,
    Of carol and of trill,
Re-echoing all the music
    Of valley and of rill.
A praise that we are sharing
    With every singing breeze,

With nightingales and linnets,
    With waterfalls and trees;
With anthems of the flowers
    Too delicate and sweet
For all their fairy minstrelsy
    Our mortal ears to greet.

A mighty song of blessing
    Archangels too uplift,
For their own bright existence,
    A grand and glorious gift.
But such their full life-chalice,
    So sparkling and so pure,
And such their vivid sense of joy
    Sweet, solid, and secure,
We cannot write the harmonies
    To such a song of bliss,
We only catch the melody,
    And sing, content with this.

We are but little children,
    And earth a broken toy;
We do not know the treasures
    In our Father's house of joy.
Thanksgivings for creation
    We ignorantly raise;
We know not yet the thousandth part
    Of that for which we praise.

Yet, praise Him for creation!
    Nor cease the happy song,
But this our Hallelujah
    Through all our life prolong;
'T will mingle with the chorus
    Before the heavenly throne,
Where what it truly is TO BE
    Shall first be fully known.

PART II.

'. . . preservation, and all the blessings of this life.'

Mendelssohn's 'Elijah.'

O FELIX! happy in thy varied store
Of harmonies undreamt before,
    How different was the gift
    Of praise 'twas thine to pour,
Whether in stately calm, or tempest strong and swift!

    Mark the day,
    In mourning robe of grey,
Of shrouded mountain and of storm-swept vale,
And purple pall spread o'er the distance pale,
    While thunderous masses wildly drift
In lurid gloom and grandeur: then a swift
And dazzling ray bursts through a sudden rift;
The dark waves glitter as the storms subside,
And all is light and glory at the eventide.

    O sunlight of thanksgiving! Who that knows
    Its bright forth-breaking after dreariest days,
    Would change the after-thought of woes
    For memory's loveliest light that glows,
If so he must forego one note of that sweet praise?

    For not the song
    Which knows no minor cadence, sad and long;
    And not the tide
    Whose emerald and silver pride
Was never dashed in wild and writhing fray,
Where grim and giant rocks hurl back the spray;
    And not the crystal atmosphere,
    That carves each outline sharp and clear
Upon a sapphire sky: not these, not these,
Nor aught existing but to charm and please,
Without acknowledging life's mystery,
    And all the mighty reign
    Of yearning and of pain
That fills its half-read history,

Fit music can supply
To lift the wandering heart on high
To that Preserving Love, which rules all change,
And gives 'all blessings of this life,' so dream-like and so strange.

And his was praise
Deeper and truer, such as those may raise
Who know both shade and sunlight, and whose life
Hath learnt victorious strife
Of courage and of trust and hope still dear,
With passion and with grief, with danger and with fear.

————

Upriseth now a cry,
Plaintive and piercing, to the brazen sky:
Help, Lord! the harvest days are gone;
Help, Lord! for other help is none;
The infant children cry for bread,
And no man breaketh it. The suckling's tongue for thirst
Now cleaveth to his mouth. Our land is cursed;
Our wasted Zion mourns, in vain her hands are spread.

A mother's tale of grief,
Of sudden blight upon the chief,
The *only* flower of love that cheered her widowed need:
O loneliest! O desolate indeed!
Were it not mockery to whisper here
A word of hope and cheer?

A mountain brow, an awe-struck crowd,
The prayer-sent flame, the prayer-sent cloud,
A mighty faith, a more than kingly power,
Changed for depression's darkest hour,
For one lone shadow in the desert sought,
A fainting frame, a spirit overwrought,
A sense of labour vain, and strength all spent for nought.

Death hovering near,
With visible terror-spear
Of famine, or a murder-stainèd sword,

A stricken land forsaken of her Lord;
　　While bowed with doubled fear,
　　The faithful few appear;
O sorrows manifold outpoured!
Is blessing built upon such dark foundation;
And can a temple rising from such woe,
Rising upon such mournful crypts below,
Be filled with light and joy and sounding adoration?

O strange mosaic! wondrously inlaid
　　Are all its depths of shade,
With beauteous stones of promise, marbles fair
Of trust and calm, and flashing brightly, there
The precious gems of praise are set, and shine
Resplendent with a light that almost seems Divine.

　　Thanks be to God!
　　The thirsty land He laveth,
　　The perishing He saveth;
　　The floods lift up their voices,
　　The answering earth rejoices.
Thanks be to Him, and never-ending laud,
For this new token of His bounteous love,
Who reigns in might the waterfloods above:
　　The gathering waters rush along;
And leaps the exultant shout, one cataract of song,
　　Thanks be to God!

　　Thus joyously we sing;
Nor is this all the praise we bring.
We need not wait for earthquake, storm, and fire
　　To lift our praises higher;
Nor wait for heaven-dawn ere we join the hymn
　　Of throne-surrounding cherubim;
For even on earth their anthem hath begun,
To Him, the Mighty and the Holy One.

We know the still small Voice in many a word
Of guidance, and command, and promise heard;
And, knowing it, we bow before His feet,

With love and awe the seraph-strain repeat,
 Holy, Holy, Holy! God the Lord!
His glory fills the earth, His name be all-adored.

O Lord, our Lord! how excellent Thy name
 Throughout this universal frame!
 Therefore Thy children rest
 Beneath the shadow of Thy wings,
 A shelter safe and blest;
 And tune their often tremulous strings
Thy love to praise, Thy glory to proclaim,
The Merciful, the Gracious One, eternally The Same.

Part III.

'. . . but above all, for Thine inestimable love in the redemption of the world by our Lord Jesus Christ.'

Handel's 'Messiah.'

Hush! for a master harp is tuned again,
 In truest unison with choirs above,
For prelude to a loftier, sweeter strain,
 The praise of God's inestimable love;
Who sent redemption to a world of woe,
That all a Father's heart His banished ones might know.

Hush! while on silvery wing of holiest song
 Floats forth the old, dear story of our peace,
His coming, the Desire of Ages long,
 To wear our chains, and win our glad release.
Our wondering joy, to hear such tidings blest,
Is crowned with 'Come to Him, and He will give you rest.'

Rest, by His sorrow! Bruisèd for our sin,
 Behold the Lamb of God! His death our life.
Now lift your heads, ye gates! He entereth in,
 Christ risen indeed, and Conqueror in the strife.
Thanks, thanks to Him who won, and Him who gave
Such victory of love, such triumph o'er the grave.

Hark! 'Hallelujah!' O sublimest strain!
    Is it prophetic echo of the day
When He, our Saviour and our King, shall reign,
    And all the earth shall own His righteous sway?
Lift heart and voice, and swell the mighty chords,
While hallelujahs peal, to Him, the Lord of lords!

'Worthy of all adoration,
    Is the Lamb that once was slain,'
Cry, in raptured exultation,
His redeemed from every nation;
    Angel myriads join the strain,
Sounding from their sinless strings
Glory to the King of kings:
Harping, with their harps of gold,
Praise which never can be told.

Hallelujahs full and swelling
    Rise around His throne of might,
All our highest laud excelling,
Holy and immortal, dwelling
    In the unapproachèd light,
He is worthy to receive
All that heaven and earth can give;
Blessing, honour, glory, might,
All are His by glorious right.

As the sound of many waters
    Let the full Amen arise!
HALLELUJAH! Ceasing never,
Sounding through the great FOR EVER,
    Linking all its harmonies;
Through eternities of bliss,
Lord, our rapture shall be this;
And our endless life shall be
One AMEN of praise to Thee.

Not Yet.

JOHN 13:7.

NOT yet thou knowest what I do,
　　O feeble child of earth,
Whose life is but to angel view
　　The morning of thy birth!
The smallest leaf, the simplest flower,
　　The wild bee's honey-cell,
Have lessons of My love and power
　　Too hard for thee to spell.

Thou knowest not how I uphold
　　The little thou dost scan;
And how much less canst thou unfold
　　My universal plan,
Where all thy mind can grasp of space
　　Is but a grain of sand;—
The time thy boldest thought can trace,
　　One ripple on the strand!

Not yet thou knowest what I do,
　　In this wild, warring world,
Whose prince doth still triumphant view
　　Confusion's flag unfurled;
Nor how each proud and daring thought
　　Is subject to My will,
Each strong and secret purpose brought
　　My counsel to fulfil.

Not yet thou knowest how I bid
　　Each passing hour entwine
Its grief or joy, its hope or fear,
　　In one great love-design;
Nor how I lead thee through the night,
　　By many a various way,
Still upward to unclouded light,
　　And onward to the day.

Not yet thou knowest what I do
   Within thine own weak breast,
To mould thee to My image true,
   And fit thee for My rest.
But yield thee to My loving skill;
   The veilèd work of grace,
From day to day progressing still,
   It is not thine to trace.

Yes, walk by faith and not by sight,
   Fast clinging to My hand;
Content to feel My love and might,
   Not yet to understand.
A little while thy course pursue,
   Till grace to glory grow;
Then what I am, and what I do,
   Hereafter thou shalt know.

Thanksgiving.

THANKS be to God! to whom earth owes
   Sunshine and breeze,
The heath-clad hill, the vale's repose,
   Streamlet and seas,
The snowdrop and the summer rose,
   The many-voicèd trees.

Thanks for the darkness that reveals
   Night's starry dower;
And for the sable cloud that heals
   Each fevered flower;
And for the rushing storm that peals
   Our weakness and Thy power.

Thanks for the sweetly-lingering might
   In music's tone;
For paths of knowledge, whose calm light
   Is all Thine own;
For thoughts that at the Infinite
   Fold their bright wings alone.

Yet thanks that silence oft may flow
    In dewlike store;
Thanks for the mysteries that show
    How small our lore;
Thanks that we here so little know,
    And trust Thee all the more!

Thanks for the gladness that entwines
    Our path below;
Each sunrise that incarnadines
    The cold, still snow;
Thanks for the light of love which shines
    With brightest earthly glow.

Thanks for the sickness and the grief
    Which none may flee;
For loved ones standing now around
    The crystal sea;
And for the weariness of heart
    Which only rests in Thee.

Thanks for Thine own thrice-blessèd Word,
    And Sabbath rest;
Thanks for the hope of glory stored
    In mansions blest;
Thanks for the Spirit's comfort poured
    Into the trembling breast.

Thanks, more than thanks, to Him ascend,
    Who died to win
Our life, and every trophy rend
    From Death and Sin;
Till, when the thanks of Earth shall end,
    The thanks of Heaven begin.

NOTE.—It may be well to say, that these verses were in print before the writer either
saw or heard of the beautiful little poem by Adelaide Proctor on the same theme.

Life-Crystals.

The world is full of crystals. Swift, or slow,
Or dark, or bright their varying formation;
From pure calm heights of fair untrodden snow
To fire-wrought depths of earliest creation.
And life is full of crystals; forming still
In myriad-shaped results from good and seeming ill.

Yes! forming everywhere; in busiest street,
In noisiest throng. Oh how it would astound us,
The strange soul-chemistry of some we meet
In slight and passing talk! For all around us,
Deep inner silence broods o'er gems to be.
Now, in three visioned hearts trace out the work with me!

A heart that wonderingly received the flow
Of marvels and of mysteries of being,
Of sympathies and tensions, joy and woe;
Each earnestly from baser substance freeing:
A great life-mixture, full, and deep, and strong:
A sudden touch, and lo! it crystallized in song.

Then forth it flashed among the souls of men
Its own prismatic radiance, brightly sealing
A several rainbow for each several ken;
The secrets of the distant stars revealing;
Reflecting many a heart's clear rays unknown,
And, freely shedding light, it analyzed their own.

A heart from which all joy had ebbed away,
And grief poured in a flood of burning anguish,
Then sealed the molten glow; till, day by day,
The fires without, within, begin to languish:
Then 'afterward' came coolness; all was well,
And from the broken crust a shining crystal fell.

A mourner found, and fastened on her breast
The soft-hued gem, the prized by mourners only;

With sense of treasure gained she sought her rest,
No longer wandering in the twilight lonely;
The sorrow-crystal glittering in the dark,
While faith and hope shone out to greet its starry spark.

A heart where emptiness seemed emptier made
By colourless remains of tasteless pleasure;
ONE came, and pitying the hollow shade,
Poured in His own strong love in fullest measure;
Then shadowed it with silent falling night,
And stilled it with the solemn Presence of His might.

A little while, then found the Master there
Love-crystals, sparkling in the joyous morning;
He stooped to gaze, and smiled to own them fair,
A treasured choice for His own rich adorning;
Then set them in His diadem above,
To mingle evermore with His own light and love.

Not Your Own.

'Not your own!' but His ye are,
    Who hath paid a price untold
For your life, exceeding far
    All earth's store of gems and gold.
With the precious blood of Christ,
Ransom treasure all unpriced,
Full redemption is procured,
Full salvation is assured.

'Not your own!' but His by right,
    His peculiar treasure now,
Fair and precious in His sight,
    Purchased jewels for His brow.
He will keep what thus He sought,
Safely guard the dearly bought,
Cherish that which He did choose,
Always love and never lose.

'Not your own!' but His, the King,
   His, the Lord of earth and sky,
His, to whom archangels bring
   Homage deep and praises high.
What can royal birth bestow?
Or the proudest titles show?
Can such dignity be known
As the glorious name, 'His own!'

'Not your own!' To Him ye owe
   All your life and all your love;
Live, that ye His praise may show,
   Who is yet all praise above.
Every day and every hour,
Every gift and every power,
Consecrate to Him alone,
Who hath claimed you for His own.

Teach us, Master, how to give
   All we have and are to Thee;
Grant us, Saviour, while we live,
   Wholly, only, Thine to be.
Henceforth be our calling high
Thee to serve and glorify;
Ours no longer, but Thine own,
Thine for ever, Thine alone!

Wounded.

Only a look and a motion that nobody saw or heard,
Past in a moment and over, with never the sound of a word;
Streams of converse around me smoothly and cheerily flow,
But a terrible stab has been given, a silent and staggering blow.

Guesses the hand that gave it hardly a tithe of the smart,
Nothing at all of the anguish that fiercely leapt up in my heart,
Scorching and scathing its peace, while a tremulous nerve to the brain
Flashed up a telegram sudden, a message of quivering pain.

They must be merry without me, for how can I sing to-night?
They will only think I am tired, and thoughtfully shade the light;
Finger and voice would fail while the wound is open and sore;
Bleeding away the strength I had gathered for days before.

Only a look and a motion! Yes, but we little know
How from each dwarf-like 'only' a giant of power may grow;
The thundering avalanche crushes, loosened by only a breath,
And only a colourless drop may be laden with sudden death.

Only a word of command, but it loses or wins the field;
Only a stroke of the pen, but a heart is broken or healed;
Only a step may sever, pole-wide, future and past;
Only a touch may rivet links which for life shall last.

Only a look and a motion! Why was the wound so deep?
Were it no echo of sorrow, hushed for a while to sleep,
Were it no shadow of fear, far o'er the future thrown,
Slight were the suffering now, if it bore on the present alone.

Ah! I would smile it away, but 'tis all too fresh and too keen;
Perhaps I may some day recall it as if it had never been;
Now I can only be still, and endure where I cannot cope,
Praying for meekness and patience, praying for faith and hope.

Is it an answer already that words to my mind are brought,
Floating like shining lilies on waters of gloomiest thought?
Simple and short is the sentence, but oh! what it comprehends!
'*Those with which I was wounded, in the house of My friends.*'

Floating still on my heart, while I listen again and again,
Stilling the anxious throbbing, soothing the icy pain,
Proving its sacred mission healing and balm to bring.
'Coming?' Yes, if you want me! Yes, I am ready to sing.

Whose I Am.

JESUS, Master, whose I am,
    Purchased Thine alone to be,
By Thy blood, O spotless Lamb,
    Shed so willingly for me;

Let my heart be all Thine own,
Let me live to Thee alone.

Other lords have long held sway;
   Now, Thy name alone to bear,
Thy dear voice alone obey,
   Is my daily, hourly prayer.
Whom have I in heaven but Thee?
Nothing else my joy can be.

Jesus, Master! I am Thine;
   Keep me faithful, keep me near;
Let Thy presence in me shine
   All my homeward way to cheer.
Jesus! at Thy feet I fall,
Oh, be Thou my All-in-all.

Whom I Serve.

Jesus, Master, whom I serve,
   Though so feebly and so ill,
Strengthen hand and heart and nerve
   All Thy bidding to fulfil;
Open Thou mine eyes to see
All the work Thou hast for me.

Lord, Thou needest not, I know,
   Service such as I can bring;
Yet I long to prove and show
   Full allegiance to my King.
Thou an honour[1] art to me,
Let me be a praise to Thee.

Jesus, Master! wilt Thou use
   One who owes Thee more than all?
As Thou wilt! I would not choose,
   Only let me hear Thy call.
Jesus! let me always be
In Thy service glad and free.

[1] See marginal reading of 1 Peter 2:7.

Peace.

Is this the Peace of God, this strange, sweet calm?
The weary day is at its zenith still,
Yet 'tis as if beside some cool, clear rill,
    Through shadowy stillness rose an evening psalm,
And all the noise of life were hushed away,
And tranquil gladness reigned with gently soothing sway.

It was not so just now. I turned aside
With aching head, and heart most sorely bowed;
Around me cares and griefs in crushing crowd,
    While inly rose the sense, in swelling tide,
Of weakness, insufficiency, and sin,
And fear, and gloom, and doubt, in mighty flood rolled in.

That rushing flood I had no strength to meet,
Nor power to flee: my present, future, past,
My self, my sorrow, and my sin I cast
    In utter helplessness at Jesu's feet;
Then bent me to the storm, if such His will.
He saw the winds and waves, and whispered, ' Peace, be still!'

And there was calm! O Saviour, I have proved
That Thou to help and save art *really* near:
How else this quiet rest from grief, and fear,
    And all distress? The cross is not removed,
I must go forth to bear it as before,
But, leaning on Thine arm, I dread its weight no more.

Is it indeed Thy Peace? I have not tried
To analyze my faith, dissect my trust,
Or measure if belief be full and just,
    And therefore claim Thy Peace. But Thou hast died.
I know that this is true, and true for me,
And, knowing it, I come, and cast my all on Thee.

It is not that I feel less weak, but Thou
Wilt be my strength; it is not that I see
Less sin, but more of pardoning love with Thee,

And all-sufficient grace. Enough! And now
All fluttering thought is stilled, I only rest,
And feel that Thou art near, and know that I am blest.

God's Message.

To him that is far off.

Peace, peace!
To him that is far away.
Turn, O wanderer! why wilt thou die,
When the peace is made that shall bring thee nigh?
Listen, O rebel! the heralds proclaim
The King's own peace through a Saviour's name;
Then yield thee to-day.

Peace, peace!
The word of the Lord to thee.
Peace, for thy passion and restless pride,
For thy endless cravings all unsupplied,
Peace for thy weary and sin-worn breast;
He knows the need who has promised rest,
And the gift is free.

Peace, peace!
Through Him who for all hath died!
Wider the terms than thy deepest guilt,
Or in vain were the blood of our Surety spilt:
Even *because* thou art far away
To thee is the message of peace to-day,
Peace through the Crucified.

And to him that is near.

Peace, peace!
Yea, peace to him that is near.
The crown is set on the Victor's brow,
For thy warfare is accomplished now;
And for thee eternal peace is made
By the Lord on whom thy sins were laid:
Then why shouldst thou fear?

Peace, peace!
Wrought by the Spirit of Might.
In thy deepest sorrow and sorest strife,
In the changes and chances of mortal life,
It is thine, belovèd! Christ's own bequest,
Which vainly the Tempter shall strive to wrest;
It is now thy right.

Peace, peace!
Look for its bright increase;
Deepening, widening, year by year,
Like a sunlit river, strong, calm, and clear;
Lean on His love through this earthly vale,
For His word and His work shall never fail,
And 'He is our Peace.'

'A Great Mystery.'

THERE is a hush in earth and sky,
The ear is free to list aright
In darkness, veiling from the eye
The many-coloured spells of light.

Not heralded by fire and storm,
In shadowy outline dimly seen,
Comes through the gloom a glorious Form,
The once despisèd Nazarene.

Through waiting silence, voiceless shade,
A still, small Voice so clearly floats,
A listening lifetime were o'erpaid
By one sweet echo of such notes.

'Fear not, belovèd! thou art Mine,
For I have given My life for thee;
By name I call thee, rise and shine,
Be praise and glory unto Me.

'In Me all spotless and complete,
And in My comeliness most fair

Art thou; to Me thy voice is sweet,
    Prevailing in thy feeblest prayer.

'Thy life is hid in God with Me,
    I stoop to dwell within thy breast;
My joy for ever thou shalt be,
    And in My love for thee I rest.

'O Prince's daughter, whom I see
    In bridal garments, pure as light,
Betrothed for ever unto Me,
    On thee My own new name I write.'

Lo! 'neath the stars' uncertain ray
    In flowing mantle glistening fair,
One, lowly bending, turns away
    From that sweet voice in cold despair.

Is it Humility, who sees
    Herself unworthy of such grace,
Who dares not hope her Lord to please,
    Who dares not look upon His face?

Nay, where that mantle fleeting gleams
    'Tis Unbelief who turns aside,
Who rather rests in self-spun dreams,
    Than trust the love of Him who died.

Faith casts away the fair disguise,
    She will not doubt her Master's voice,
And droop when He hath bid her rise,
    Or mourn when He hath said, 'Rejoice!'

Her stained and soilèd robes she leaves,
    And Christ's own shining raiment takes;
What His love gives, her love receives,
    And meek and trustful answer makes:

'Behold the handmaid of the Lord!
    Thou callest, and I come to Thee:
According to Thy faithful word,
    O Master, be it unto me!

'Thy love I cannot comprehend,
    I only know Thy word is true,
And that Thou lovest to the end
    Each whom to Thee the Father drew.

'Oh! take the heart I could not give
    Without Thy strength-bestowing call;
In Thee, and for Thee, let me live,
    For I am nothing, Thou art all.'

Be Not Weary.

Yes! He knows the way is dreary,
    Knows the weakness of our frame,
Knows that hand and heart are weary;
    He, 'in all points,' felt the same.
He is near to help and bless;
Be not weary, onward press.

Look to Him who once was willing
    All His glory to resign,
That, for thee the law fulfilling,
    All His merit might be thine.
Strive to follow day by day
Where His footsteps mark the way.

Look to Him, the Lord of Glory,
    Tasting death to win thy life;
Gazing on 'that wondrous story,'
    Canst thou falter in the strife?
Is it not new life to know
That the Lord hath loved thee so?

Look to Him who ever liveth,
    Interceding for His own:
Seek, yea, claim the grace He giveth
    Freely from His priestly throne.
Will He not thy strength renew
With His Spirit's quickening dew?

Look to Him, and faith shall brighten,
    Hope shall soar, and love shall burn;
Peace once more thy heart shall lighten
    Rise! He calleth thee, return!
Be not weary on thy way,
Jesus is thy strength and stay.

The Great Teacher.

I LOVE to feel that I am taught,
    And, as a little child,
To note the lessons I have learnt
    In passing through the wild.
For I am sure God teaches me,
    And His own gracious hand
Each varying page before me spreads,
    By love and wisdom planned.

I often think I cannot spell
    The lesson I must learn,
And then, in weariness and doubt,
    I pray the page may turn;
But time goes on, and soon I find
    I was learning all the while;
And words which seemed most dimly traced
    Shine out with rainbow smile.

Or sometimes strangely I forget,
    And, learning o'er and o'er,
A lesson all with tear-drops wet,
    Which I had learnt before.
He chides me not, but waits awhile,
    Then wipes my heavy eyes:
Oh what a Teacher is our God,
    So patient and so wise!

Dark silent hours of study fall,
    And I can scarcely see;
Then one beside me whispers low
    What is so hard to me.

'Tis easier then! I am so glad
    I am not taught alone;
It is such help to overhear
    A lesson like my own.

Sometimes the Master gives to me
    A strange new alphabet;
I wonder what its use will be,
    Or why it need be set.
And then I find this tongue alone
    Some stranger ear can reach,
One whom He may commission me
    For Him to train or teach.

If others sadly bring to me
    A lesson hard and new,
I often find that helping them
    Has made me learn it too.
Or, had I learnt it long before,
    My toil is overpaid,
If so one tearful eye may see
    One lesson plainer made.

We do not see our Teacher's face,
    We do not hear His voice;
And yet we know that He is near,
    We feel it, and rejoice.
There is a music round our hearts,
    Set in no mortal key;
There is a Presence with our souls,
    We know that it is He.

His loving teaching cannot fail;
    And we shall know at last
Each task that seemed so hard and strange,
    When learning time is past.
Oh! may we learn to love Him more,
    By every opening page,
By every lesson He shall mark
    With daily ripening age.

And then, to 'know as we are known'
    Shall be our glorious prize,
To see the Teacher who hath been
    So patient and so wise.
O joy untold! Yet not alone
    Shall ours the gladness be;
The travail of His soul in us
    Our Saviour-God shall see.

Auntie's Lessons.

THEY said their texts, and their hymns they sang,
    On that sunny Sabbath-day;
And yet there was time ere the church-bell rang,
    So I bid them trot away.
And leave me to rest and read alone,
Where the ash-tree's shade o'er the lawn was thrown.

But oh! 'twas a cry and a pleading sore,
    'O Auntie! we will not tease,
But tell us one Sunday story more;
We will sit so still on the grassy floor;
Tell us the one you told before
    Of little black Mumu, please,
Whom, deaf and dumb, and sick and lone,
    The good ship brought to Sierra Leone.'

Willie begged loud, and Francie low,
    And Alice, who could resist her?
Certainly not myself, and so
The story was just beginning, when lo!
    To the rescue came my sister.
'*I* will tell you a story to-day;
Aunt Fanny has all her own lessons to say!'

Wonderful notion, and not at all clear!
    Alfred looked quite astounded.
Who in the world *my* lessons could hear?

They guessed at every one far and near,
    'Twas a mystery unbounded.
They settled at last that it must be
Grandpapa Havergal over the sea.

Then merry eyes grew grave and wise,
    On tiptoe Alice trod;
She had a better thought than they,
And whispered low, 'Does Auntie say
    Her lessons all to God?'
How little the import deep she knew
Of those baby-words, so sweet and true!

Little she knew what they enfold!—
    A treasure of happy thought;
A tiny casket of virgin gold,
    With jewels of comfort fraught.
Great men's wisdom may pass away,
Dear Alice's words in my heart will stay.

Rest.

'Thou hast made us for Thyself, and the heart never resteth till it findeth rest in Thee.'—*St. Augustine.*

Made for Thyself, O God!
Made for Thy love, Thy service, Thy delight;
Made to show forth Thy wisdom, grace, and might;
Made for Thy praise, whom veiled archangels laud;
Oh strange and glorious thought, that we may be
    A joy to Thee!

Yet the heart turns away
From this grand destiny of bliss, and deems
'Twas made for its poor self, for passing dreams,
Chasing illusions melting day by day;
Till *for ourselves* we read on this world's best,
    'This is not rest!'

Nor can the vain toil cease,
Till in the shadowy maze of life we meet
One who can guide our aching, wayward feet
To find Himself, our Way, our Life, our Peace.
In Him the long unrest is soothed and stilled;
Our hearts are filled.

O rest, so true, so sweet!
(Would it were shared by all the weary world!)
'Neath shadowing banner of His love unfurled,
We bend to kiss the Master's piercèd feet;
Then lean our love upon His loving breast,
And know God's rest.

One Question, Many Answers.

'WHAT wouldst thou be?'
The question hath wakened wild thoughts in me,
And a thousand responses, like ghosts from their graves,
Arise from my soul's unexplored deep caves,
The echoes of every varying mood
Of a wayward spirit all unsubdued;
The voices which thrill through my inmost breast
May tell me of gladness, but not of rest.
What wouldst thou be?
'Tis well that the answer is not for me.

'What wouldst thou be?'
An eagle soaring rejoicingly.
One who may rise on the lightning's wing,
Till our wide, wide world seem a tiny thing;
Who may stand on the confines of boundless space,
And the giant form of the universe trace,
While its full grand harmonies swell around,
And grasp it all with mind profound.
Such would I be,
Only stayed by infinity.

'What wouldst thou be?'
A bright incarnation of melody.
One whose soul is a fairy lute,
Waking such tones as bid all be mute,
Breathing such notes as may silence woe,
Pouring such strains as make joy o'erflow,
Speaking in music the heart's deep emotion,
Soothing and sweet as the shell of the ocean.
　　　Such would I be,
Like a fountain of music, all pure and free.

'What wouldst thou be?'
A living blossom of poesy.
A soul of mingled power and light,
Evoking images rare and bright,
Fair and pure as an angel's dream;
Touching all with a heavenly gleam;
And royally claiming from poet-throne
Earth's treasure of beauty as all mine own.
　　　Such would I be—
My childhood's dream in reality!

'What wouldst thou be?'
A wondrous magnet to all I see.
A spirit whose power may touch and bind
With unconscious influence every mind;
Whose presence brings, like some fabled wand,
The love which a monarch may not command.
As the spring awakens from cold repose
The bloomless brier, the sweet wild rose.
　　　Such would I be,
With the love of all to encircle me.

'What wouldst thou be?'
A wavelet just rising from life's wide sea.
I would I were once again a child,
Like a laughing floweret on mountains wild;
In the fairy realms of fancy dwelling,
The golden moments for sunbeams selling;

Ever counting on bright to-morrows,
And knowing nought of unspoken sorrows.
    Such would I be,
A sparkling cascade of untiring glee.

    'What wouldst thou be?'
A blessing to each one surrounding me;
A chalice of dew to the weary heart,
A sunbeam of joy bidding sorrow depart,
To the storm-tossed vessel a beacon light,
A nightingale song in the darkest night,
A beckoning hand to a far-off goal,
An angel of love to each friendless soul:
    Such would I be.
Oh that *such* happiness were for me!

    'What wouldst thou be?'
With these alone were no rest for me.
I would be my Saviour's loving child,
With a heart set free from its passions wild,
Rejoicing in Him and His own sweet ways;
An echo of heaven's unceasing praise,
A mirror here of His light and love,
And a polished gem in His crown above.
    Such would I be,
Thine, O Saviour, and one with Thee!

Content.

    '"WHAT wouldst thou be?"
A wavelet just rising from life's wide sea.
I would I were once again a child,
Like a laughing floweret on mountains wild;
In the fairy realms of fancy dwelling,
The golden moments for sunbeams selling;
Ever counting on bright to-morrows,
And knowing nought of unspoken sorrows.
    Such would I be,
A sparkling cascade of untiring glee.'

1860

.   .   .   .

    Not so, not so!
For longings change as the full years flow.
When I had but taken a step or two
From the fairy regions still in view;
While their playful breezes fanned me still
At every pause on the steeper hill,
And the blossoms showered from every shoot,
Showered and fell, and yet no fruit,—
    It was grief and pain
That I never could be a child again.

    Not so, not so!
Back to my life-dawn I would not go.
A little is lost, but more is won,
As the sterner work of the day is done.
We forget that the troubles of childish days
Were once gigantic in morning haze.
There is less of fancy, but more of truth,
For we lose the mists with the dew of youth;
    And a rose is born
On many a spray which seemed only thorn.

    Not so, not so!
While the years of childhood glided slow,
There was all to receive and nothing to give:
Is it not better for others to live?
And happier far than merriest games
Is the joy of our new and nobler aims:
Then fair fresh flowers, *now* lasting gems;
Then wreaths for a day, but *now* diadems,
    For ever to shine,
Bright in the radiance of Love Divine.

    Not so, not so!
I would not again be a child, I know!
But were it not pleasant again to stand
On the border-line of that fairy land,—

Feeling so buoyant and blithe and strong,
Fearing no slip as we bound along,
Halting at will in the sunshine to bask,
Deeming the journey an easy task,
    While Courage and Hope
Smooth with 'Come, see, and conquer' each emerald slope?

    Not so, not so!
Less leaping flame, but a deeper glow!
There is more of sorrow, but more of joy,
Less glittering ore, but less alloy;
There is more of pain, but more of balm,
And less of pleasure, but more of calm;
Many a hope all spent and dead,
But higher and brighter hopes instead;
    Less risked, more won;
Less planned and dreamed, but perhaps more done.

    Not so, not so!
Not in stature and learning alone we grow.
Though we no more look from year to year
For power of mind more strong and clear,
Though the table-land of life we tread,
No widening view before we spread,
No sunlit summits to lure ambition,
But only the path of a daily mission,
    We would not turn
Where the will-o'-the-wisps of our young dreams burn.

    Then be it so!
For in better things we yet may grow.
Onward and upward still our way,
With the joy of progress from day to day;
Nearer and nearer every year
To the visions and hopes most true and dear;
Children still of a Father's love,
Children still of a home above!
    Thus we look back,
Without a sigh, o'er the lengthening track.

Misunderstood.

'PEOPLE do not understand me,
    Their ideas are not like mine;
All advances seem to land me
    Still outside their guarded shrine.'

So you turn from simple joyance,
    Losing many a mutual good,
Weary with the chill annoyance
    So to be misunderstood.

Let me try to lift the curtain
    Hiding other hearts from view;
You complain, but are you certain
    That the fault is not with you?

In the sunny summer hours,
    Sitting in your quiet room,
Can you wonder if the flowers
    Breathe for you no sweet perfume?

True, you see them bright and pearly
    With the jewelry of morn;
But their fragrance, fresh and early,
    Is not through your window borne.

You must go to them, and stooping,
    Cull the blossoms where they live;
On your bosom gently drooping,
    All their treasure they will give.

Who would guess what fragrance lingers
    In verbena's pale green show!
Press the leaflet in your fingers,
    All its sweetness you will know.

Few the harps Æolian, sending
    Unsought music on the wind:
Else must love and skill be blending
    Music's full response to find.

'But my key-note,' are you thinking,
'Will not modulate to theirs?'
Seek! and subtle chords enlinking,
Soon shall blend the differing airs.

Fairly sought, some point of contact
There must be with every mind;
And, perchance, the closest compact
Where we least expect we find.

Perhaps the heart you meet so coldly
Burns with deepest lava-glow;
Wisely pierce the crust, and boldly,
And a fervid stream shall flow.

Dialects of love are many,
Though the language be but one;
Study all you can, or any,
While life's precious school-hours run.

Closed the heart-door of thy brother,
All its treasure long concealed?
One key fails, then try another,
Soon the rusty lock shall yield.

Few have not some hidden trial,
And could sympathize with thine;
Do not take it as denial
That you see no outward sign.

Silence is no certain token
That no secret grief is there;
Sorrow which is never spoken
Is the heaviest load to bear.

Seldom can the heart be lonely,
If it seek a lonelier still,
Self-forgetting, seeking only
Emptier cups of love to fill.

'Twill not be a fruitless labour,
    Overcome this ill with good;
Try to understand your neighbour,
    And you will be understood.

Sunbeams in the Wood.

MARK ye not the sunbeams glancing
    Through the cool green shade,
On the waving fern-leaves dancing,
    In the quiet glade?

See you how they change and quiver
    Where the broad oaks rise,
Rippling like a golden river
    From their fountain skies?

On the grey old timber resting
    Like a sleeping dove,
Like a fairy grandchild nesting
    In an old man's love.

On the dusty pathway tracing
    Arabesques with golden style;
Light and shadow interlacing,
    Like a tearful smile.

Many a hidden leaf revealing,
    Many an unseen flower;
Like a maiden lightly stealing
    Past each secret bower.

Oh! how beautiful they make it
    Everywhere they fall;
Sunbeams! why will ye forsake it
    At pale Evening's call?

In the arching thickets linger,
    In the woodland aisle,
Gilding them with trembling finger,
    Yet a little while.

Then, your last calm radiance pouring,
    Bid the earth good-night;
Like a sainted spirit soaring
    To a home of light.

The Star Shower.

NOVEMBER 14, 1866.

OH! to raise a mighty shout,
And bid the sleepers all come out!
No dreamer's fancy, fair and high,
Could image forth a grander sky.
And oh for eyes of swifter power
To follow fast the starry shower!
Oh for a sweep of vision clear
To grasp at once a hemisphere!

The solemn old chorale of Night,
With fullest chords of awful might,
Re-echoes still in stately march
Throughout the glowing heavenly arch:
But harmonies all new and rare
Are intermingling everywhere,
Fantastic, fitful, fresh, and free;
A sparkling wealth of melody,
A carol of sublimest glee,
Is bursting from the starry chorus,
In dazzling exultation o'er us.
O wondrous sight! so swift, so bright,
Like sudden thrills of strange delight;
As if the stars were all at play,
And kept ecstatic holiday;
As if it were a jubilee
Of glad millenniums fully told,
Or universal sympathy
With some new-dawning age of gold.

Flashing from the lordly Lion,
Flaming under bright Procyon,

From the farthest east up-ranging,
Past the blessed orb[1] unchanging;
Ursa's brilliance far out-gleaming,
From the very zenith streaming;
Rushing, as in joy delirious,
To the pure white ray of Sirius;
Past Orion's belted splendour,
Past Capella, clear and tender;
Lightening dusky Polar regions,
Brightening pale encircling legions;
Lines of fiery glitter tracing,
Parting, meeting, interlacing;
Paling every constellation
With their radiant revelation!
All we heard of meteor glory
Is a true and sober story;
Who will not for life remember
This night grandeur of November?

———————

'Tis over now, the once-seen, dream-like sight!
With gradual hand the clear and breezy dawn
Hath o'er the marvels of the meteor night
A veil of light impenetrable drawn.
And earth is sweeping on through starless space,
Nor may we once look back, the shining field to trace.

Ere next the glittering stranger-throng we meet,
How many a star of life will seek the west!
Our century's dying pulse will faintly beat;
The toilers of to-day will be at rest;
And little ones, who now but laugh and play,
Will weary in the heat and burden of the day.

Oh, is there nothing beautiful and glad
But bears a message of decay and change?

———

[1] 'That admirable Polar Star, which is a *blessing* to astronomers.'—*Professor Airy's Popular Lectures on Astronomy.*

So be it! Though we call it stern and sad,
Viewed by the torch of Love, it is not strange.
'Tis mercy that in Nature's *every* strain
Deep warning tones peal out, in solemn sweet refrain.

And have not all created things a voice
For those who listen farther,—whispers low
To bid the children of the light rejoice
In burning hopes they yet but dimly know?
What will it be, all earthly darkness o'er,
To shine as stars of God for ever—evermore!

Treasure Trove.

I PLAYED with the whispering rushes,
 By a river of reverie,
Flowing so quietly onward
 Into an unknown sea.

And I watched the dreamy current,
 Till to my feet it brought,
Glistening among the pebbles,
 The pearl of a fair new thought.

New! yet many another,
 Leaning over the stream,
May have welcomed its sudden shining,
 And gazed on its gentle gleam.

Long it must have been lying,
 Yet it is new to me.
Oh the treasures around us,
 If we could only see!

I have broken the smooth dark water
 Into ripples and circles bright,
Lifting my pearl from the pebbles,
 Bearing away its light.

I am so glad to have found it!
   I shall treasure it safely a while,
It will brighten the niche that is darkest
   In my spirit's loneliest aisle.

And then, it may be, a dear one
   Will wear it, a long, long time,
Fastened firm on her bosom,
   In a setting of silver rhyme.

Coming Summer.

WHAT will the summer bring?
   Sunshine and flowers,
Brightness and melody,
   Golden-voiced hours;
Rose-gleaming mornings
   Vocal with praise;
Crimson-flushed evening,
   Nightingale lays.

What may the summer bring?
   Gladness and mirth,
Laughter and song,
   For the children of earth;
Smiles for the old man,
   Joy for the strong,
Glee for the little ones
   All the day long.

What will the summer bring?
   Coolness and shade,
Eloquent stillness
   In thicket and glade;
Whispering breezes,
   Fragrance oppressed;
Lingering twilight
   Soothing to rest.

What may the summer bring?
　　Freshness and calm
To the care-worn and troubled,
　　Beauty and balm.
O toil-weary spirit,
　　Rest thee anew,
For the heat of the world-race
　　Summer hath dew!

What will the summer bring?
　　Sultry noon hours,
Lurid horizons,
　　Frowning cloud-towers!
Loud-crashing thunders,
　　Tempest and hail,
Death-bearing lightnings,
　　It brings without fail.

What may the summer bring?
　　Dimness and woe,
Blackness of sorrow
　　Its bright days may know;
Flowers may be wormwood,
　　Verdure a pall,
The shadow of death
　　On the fairest may fall.

Is it not ever so?
　　Where shall we find
Light that may cast
　　No shadow behind?
Calm that no tempest
　　May darkly await?
Joy that no sorrow
　　May swiftly abate?

Will the story of summer
　　Be written in light,
Or traced in the darkness
　　Of storm-cloud and night?

We know not—we *would* not know
    Why should we quail?
Summer, we welcome thee!
    Summer, all hail!

September 1868.

An April burst of beauty,
    And a May like the Mays of old,
And a glow of summer gladness
    While June her long days told;
And a hush of golden silence
    All through the bright July,
Without one peal of thunder,
    Or a storm-wreath in the sky;
And a fiery reign of August,
    Till the moon was on the wane;
And then short clouded evenings,
    And a long and chilling rain.
I thought the summer was over,
    And the whole year's glory spent,
And that nothing but fog and drizzle
    Could be for Autumn meant;—
Nothing but dead leaves, falling
    Wet on the dark, damp mould,
Less and less of the sunshine,
    More and more of the cold.

But oh! the golden day-time;
    And oh! the silver nights;
And the scarlet touch on the fir trunks
    Of the calm, grand sunset lights;
And the morning's bright revealings,
    Lifting the pearly mist,
Like a bridal veil, from the valley
    That the sun hath claimed and kissed;
And oh! the noontide shadows
    Longer and longer now,

On the river margin resting,
    Like the tress on a thoughtful brow.
Rich fruitage bends the branches
    With amber, and rose, and gold,
O'er the purple and crimson asters,
    And geraniums gay and bold.

The day is warm and glowing,
    But the night is cool and sweet,
And we fear no smiting arrows
    Of fierce and fatal heat.
The leaves are only dropping,
    Like flakes of a sunset cloud,
And the robin's song is clearer
    Than Spring's own minstrel-crowd.
A soft new robe of greenness
    Decks every sunny mead,
And we own that bright September
    Is beautiful indeed.

Is thy life-summer passing?
    Think not thy joys are o'er!
Thou hast not seen what Autumn
    For thee may have in store.
Calmer than breezy April,
    Cooler than August blaze,
The fairest time of all may be
    September's golden days.
Press on, though summer waneth,
    And falter not, nor fear,
For God can make the Autumn
    The glory of the year.

Early Faith.

Whom hear we tell of all the joy which loving Faith can bring,
The ever-widening glories reached on her strong seraph wing?
Is it not oftenest they who long have wrestled with temptation,
Or passed through fiery baptisms of mighty tribulation?

Perhaps, in life's great tapestry, the darkest scenes are where
The golden threads of Faith glance forth most radiant and fair;
And gazing on the coming years, which unknown griefs may bring,
We hail the lamp which o'er them all shall heavenly lustre fling.

Thank God! there is at eventide a gleam of ruby light,
A star of love amid the gloom of sorrow's lingering night,
An ivy-wreath upon the tomb, a haven in the blast,
A staff for weary, trembling ones, when youth and health are past.

But shall we seek the diamonds in the lone and dusky mine,
When 'mid the sunny sands of *youth* they wait to flash and shine?
Neglect the fountain of Christ's joy till woe-streams darkly flow,
Nor seek a Father's smile until the world's cold frown we know?

Nay! be our faith the rosy crown on morn's unwrinkled brow,
The sparkling dewdrop on the grass, the blossom on the bough;
The gleam of pearly light within the snowy-bosomed shell;
An added power of loveliness in beauty's every spell.

Oh, let it be the sunlight of the pleasant summer hours,
That calls to pure and radiant birth unnumbered fragrant flowers;
That bathes in golden joyance every anthem-murmuring tree,
And spreads a robe of glory o'er the silver-crested sea.

Oh, let it be the key-note of the symphony of gladness,
Which wots[1] not of the broken lyre, the requiem of sadness:
For they who melodies of heaven in hours of brightness know,
Will modulate sweet harmony from earth's discordant woe.

Our Father.

'OH that I loved the Father
　　With depth of conscious love,
As stedfast, bright, and burning,
　　As seraphim above!
But how can I be deeming
　　Myself a loving child,
When here, and there, and everywhere,
　　My thoughts are wandering wild?

[1] wots: knows

'It is my chief desire
    To know Him more and more,
To follow Him more fully
    Than I have done before:
My eyes are dim with longing
    To see the Lord above;
But oh! I fear from year to year,
    I do not truly love.

'For when I try to follow
    The mazes of my soul,
I find no settled fire of love
    Illumining the whole;
'Tis all uncertain twilight,
    No clear and vivid glow:
Would I could bring to God my King
    The perfect love I owe!'

The gift is great and holy,
    'Twill not be sought in vain;
But look up for a moment
    From present doubt and pain,
And calmly tell me *how* you love
    The dearest ones below?
'This love,' say you, 'is deep and true!'
    But tell me how you know?

How do you love your father?
    'Oh, in a thousand ways!
I think there's no one like him,
    So worthy of my praise.
I tell him all my troubles,
    And ask him what to do;
I know that he will give to me
    His counsel kind and true.

'Then every little service
    Of hand, or pen, or voice,
Becomes, if he has asked it,
    The service of my choice.

And from my own desires
   'Tis not so hard to part,
If once I know I follow so
   His wiser will and heart.

' I know the flush of pleasure
   That o'er my spirit came,
When far from home with strangers,
   They caught my father's name;
And for his sake the greeting
   Was mutual and sweet,
For if they knew my father too,
   How glad we were to meet!

' And when I heard them praising
   His music and his skill,
His words of holy teaching,
   Life-preaching, holier still,
How eagerly I listened
   To every word that fell!
'Twas joy to hear that name so dear
   Both known and loved so well.

' Once I was ill and suffering
   Upon a foreign shore,
And longed to see my father,
   As I never longed before.
He came: his arm around me;
   I leant upon his breast;
I did not long to feel more strong,
   So sweet that childlike rest.

' The thought of home is pleasant,
   Yet I should hardly care
To leave my present fair abode,
   Unless I knew him there.
All other love and pleasure
   Can never crown the place,
A home to me it cannot be
   Without my father's face.'

This is no fancy drawing,
    But every line is true,
And you have traced as strong a love
    As ever daughter knew.
But though its fond expression
    Is rather lived than told,
You do not say from day to day,
    'I fear my love is cold!'

You do not think about it;
    'Tis never in your thought—
'I wonder if I love him
    As deeply as I ought?
I know his approbation
    Outweighs all other meed,
That his employ is always joy
    But do I love indeed?'

Now let your own words teach you
    The higher, holier claim
Of Him, who condescends to bear
    A Father's gracious name.
No mystic inspiration,
    No throbbings forced and wild
He asks, but just the loving trust
    Of a glad and grateful child.

The rare and precious moments
    Of realizing thrill
Are but love's blissful blossom,
    To brighten, not to fill
The storehouse and the garner
    With ripe and pleasant fruit;
And not alone by these is shown
    The true and holy root.

What if your own dear father
    Were summoned to his rest!
One lives, by whom that bitterest grief
    Could well be soothed and blessed.

Like balm upon your sharpest woe
    His still small voice would fall;
His touch would heal, you could not feel
    That you had lost your all.

But what if He, the Lord of life,
    Could ever pass away!
What if *His* name were blotted out
    And you could know to-day
There was *no* heavenly Father,
    No Saviour dear and true,
No throne of grace, no resting-place,
    No living God for you!

We need not dwell in horror
    On what can never be,
Such endless desolation,
    Such undreamt misery.
Our reason could not bear it,
    And all the love of earth,
In fullest bliss, compared with this,
    Were nothing, *nothing* worth.

Then bring your poor affection,
    And try it by this test;
The hidden depth is fathomed,
    You see you love Him *best!*
'Tis but a feeble echo
    Of His great love to you,
Yet in His ear each note is dear,
    Its harmony is true.

It is an uncut jewel,
    All earth-encrusted now,
But He will make it glorious,
    And set it on His brow:
'Tis but a tiny glimmer,
    Lit from the light above,
But it shall blaze through endless days,
    A star of perfect love.

Disappointment.

OUR yet unfinished story
    Is tending all to this:
To God the greatest glory,
    To us the greatest bliss.

If all things work together
    For ends so grand and blest,
What need to wonder whether
    Each in itself is best!

If some things were omitted
    Or altered as we would,
The whole might be unfitted
    To work for perfect good.

Our plans may be disjointed,
    But we may calmly rest;
What God has once appointed
    Is better than our best.

We cannot see before us,
    But our all-seeing Friend
Is always watching o'er us,
    And knows the very end.

What though we seem to stumble?
    He will not let us fall;
And learning to be humble
    Is not lost time at all.

What though we fondly reckoned
    A smoother way to go
Than where His hand has beckoned?
    It will be better so.

What only seemed a barrier
    A stepping-stone shall be;
Our God is no long tarrier,
    A present help is He.

And when amid our blindness
   His disappointments fall,
We trust His loving-kindness
   Whose wisdom sends them all.

They are the purple fringes
   That hide His glorious feet;
They are the fire-wrought hinges;
   Where truth and mercy meet.

By them the golden portal
   Of Providence shall ope,
And lift to praise immortal
   The songs of faith and hope.

From broken alabaster
   Was deathless fragrance shed,
The spikenard flowed the faster
   Upon the Saviour's head.

No shattered box of ointment
   We ever need regret,
For out of disappointment
   Flow sweetest odours yet.

The discord that involveth
   Some startling change of key,
The Master's hand resolveth
   In richest harmony.

We hush our children's laughter,
   When sunset hues grow pale;
Then, in the silence after,
   They hear the nightingale.

We mourned the lamp declining,
   That glimmered at our side;—
The glorious starlight shining
   Has proved a surer guide.

Then tremble not and shrink not
   When Disappointment nears;

Be trustful still, and think not
     To realize all fears.

While we are meekly kneeling,
     We shall behold her rise,
Our Father's love revealing
     An angel in disguise.

The Song Chalice.

'You bear the chalice.' Is it so, my friend?
     Have I indeed a chalice of sweet song,
     With underflow of harmony made strong
New calm of strength through throbbing veins to send?
I did not form or fill,—I do but spend
     That which the Master poured into my soul,
     His dewdrops caught in a poor earthen bowl,
That service so with praise might meekly blend.
May He who taught the morning stars to sing,
     Aye keep my chalice cool, and pure, and sweet,
And grant me so with loving hand to bring
     Refreshment to His weary ones,—to meet
Their thirst with water from God's music-spring;
     And, bearing thus, to pour it at His feet.

Silent in Love.

'He will rest [1] in his love.' ZEPHANIAH 3:17.

Love culminates in bliss when it doth reach
     A white, unflickering, fear-consuming glow;
     And, knowing it is known as it doth know,
Needs no assuring word or soothing speech.
It craves but silent nearness, so to rest,
     No sound, no movement, love not heard but felt,
     Longer and longer still, till time should melt,
A snow-flake on the eternal ocean's breast.

[1] Marginal reading—'be silent.'

Have moments of this silence starred thy past,
Made memory a glory-haunted place,
Taught all the joy that mortal ken can trace?
     By greater light 'tis but a shadow cast;—
So shall the Lord thy God rejoice o'er thee,
And in His love will rest, and silent be.

Light and Shade.

LIGHT! emblem of all good and joy!
     Shade! emblem of all ill!
And yet in this strange mingled life,
     We need the shadow still.
A lamp with softly shaded light,
To soothe and spare the tender sight,
               Will only throw
               A brighter glow
Upon our books and work below.

We could not bear unchanging day,
     However fair its light;
Ere long the wearied eye would hail,
As boon untold, the evening pale,
     The solace of the night.
And who would prize our summer glow
If winter gloom we did not know?
               Or rightly praise
               The glad spring rays
Who never saw our rainy days?

How grateful in Arabian plain
     Of white and sparkling sand,
The shadow of a mighty rock
     Across the weary land!
And where the tropic glories rise,
Responsive to the fiery skies,
               We could not dare
               To meet the glare,
Or blindness were our bitter share.

Where is the soul so meek and pure,
    Who through his earthly days
Life's fullest sunshine could endure,
    In clear and cloudless blaze!
The sympathetic eye would dim,
And others pine unmarked by him,
            Were no chill shade
            Around him laid,
And light of joy could never fade.

He, who the light-commanding word
    Erst spake, and formed the eye,
Knows what that wondrous eye can bear,
And tempers with providing care,
By cloud and night, all hurtful glare,
    By shadows ever nigh.
So in all wise and loving ways
He blends the shadows of our days,
            To win our sight
            From scenes of night,
To seek the 'True and Only Light.'

We need some shadow o'er our bliss,
    Lest we forget the Giver:
So, often in our deepest joy
    There comes a solemn quiver;
We could not tell from whence it came,
    The subtle cause we cannot name;
            Its twilight fall
            May well recall
Calm thought of Him who gave us all.

There are who all undazzled tread
    Awhile the sunniest plain;
But they have sought the blessèd shade
By one great Rock of Ages made,
    A sure, safe rest to gain.
Unshaded light of earth soon blinds
To light of heaven sincerest minds:

O envy not
A cloudless lot!
We ask indeed we know not what.

So is it here, so is it now!
Not always will it be!
There is a land that needs no shade,
A morn will rise which cannot fade,
And we, like flame-robed angels made,
That glory soon may see.
No cloud upon its radiant joy,
No shadow o'er its bright employ,
No sleep, no night,
But perfect sight,
The Lord our Everlasting Light.

No Thorn Without a Rose.

'There is no rose without a thorn!'
Who has not found this true,
And known that griefs of gladness born
Our footsteps still pursue?

That in the grandest harmony
The strangest discords rise;
The brightest bow we only trace
Upon the darkest skies!

No thornless rose! So, more and more,
Our pleasant hopes are laid
Where waves this sable legend o'er
A still sepulchral shade.

But Faith and Love, with angel-might,
Break up life's dismal tomb,
Transmuting into golden light
The words of leaden gloom.

Reversing all this funeral pall,
White raiment they disclose;

Their happy song floats full and long,
  'No thorn without a rose!

'No shadow, but its sister light
  Not far away must burn!
No weary night, but morning bright
  Shall follow in its turn.

'No chilly snow, but safe below
  A million buds are sleeping;
No wintry days, but fair spring rays
  Are swiftly onward sweeping.

'With fiercest glare of summer air
  Comes fullest leafy shade;
And ruddy fruit bends every shoot,
  Because the blossoms fade.

'No note of sorrow but shall melt
  In sweetest chord unguessed;
No labour all too pressing felt,
  But ends in quiet rest.

'No sigh but from the harps above
  Soft echoing tones shall win;
No heart-wound but the Lord of Love
  Shall pour His comfort in.

'No withered hope, while loving best
  Thy Father's chosen way;
No anxious care, for He will bear
  Thy burdens every day.

'Thy claim to rest on Jesu's breast
  All weariness shall be,
And pain thy portal to His heart
  Of boundless sympathy.

'No conflict, but the King's own hand
  Shall end the glorious strife;
No death, but leads thee to the land
  Of everlasting life.'

Sweet seraph voices, Faith and Love!
    Sing on within our hearts
This strain of music from above,
    Till we have learnt our parts:

Until we see your alchemy
    On all that years disclose,
And, taught by you, still find it true,
    'No thorn without a rose!'

Yesterday, To-day, and For Ever.

A Greek acrostic, thrice tripled.

Αει.[1]

A H! the weary cares and fears,
E arnest yearnings through the years!
I s it not a vale of tears?

A h! the love we gladly greet
E ver now is incomplete;
I f the melody be sweet,

A nd the harmony be true,
E arlier loss is more in view,
I ll forebodings shadow through.

———

A fter wintry frost and rime,
E ven now, the heavenly chime
I s a pledge of summer time.

A nchorage within the veil,
E ver stedfast, cannot fail,
I f the wildest storms assail.

A ngel songs of love are clearer,
E arth is brighter, death is dearer,
I f the heavenly home be nearer.

———

[1] For ever.

A ll in perfect union brought,
E very link which *God* has wrought
I n the chains of loving thought:

A ll our dear ones, far asunder,
E ach shall join the anthem-thunder
I n our future joy and wonder.

A ll shall come where nought shall sever,
E ndless meeting, parting never,
I n God's house to dwell for ever.

Christ's Recall.

RETURN!
O wanderer from My side!
Soon droops each blossom of the darkening wild,
Soon melts each meteor which thy steps beguiled,
Soon is the cistern dry which thou hast hewn,
And thou wilt weep in bitterness full soon.
Return! ere gathering night shall shroud the way
Thy footsteps yet may tread, in this accepted day.

Return!
O erring, yet beloved!
I wait to bind thy bleeding feet, for keen
And rankling are the thorns where thou hast been;
I wait to give thee pardon, love, and rest;
Is not My joy to see thee safe and blest?
Return! I wait to hear once more thy voice,
To welcome thee anew, and bid thy heart rejoice.

Return!
O fallen, yet not lost!
Canst thou forget the life for thee laid down,
The taunts, the scourging, and the thorny crown?
When o'er thee first My spotless robe I spread,
And poured the oil of joy upon thy head,
How did thy wakening heart within thee burn!
Canst thou remember all, and wilt thou not return?

Return!
O chosen of My love!
Fear not to meet thy beckoning Saviour's view;
Long ere I called thee by thy name, I knew
That very treacherously thou wouldst deal;
Now I have seen thy ways, yet I will heal.
Return! Wilt thou yet linger far from Me?
My wrath is turned away, I have redeemèd thee.

Faith's Question.

To whom, O Saviour, shall we go
    For life, and joy, and light?
No help, no comfort from below,
No lasting gladness we may know,
    No hope may bless our sight.
Our souls are weary and athirst,
But earth is iron-bound and cursed,
And nothing she may yield can stay
The restless yearnings day by day;
Yet, without *Thee*, Redeemer blest,
We *would* not, if we *could*, find rest.

To whom, O Saviour, shall we go?
    We gaze around in vain.
Though pleasure's fairy lute be strung,
And mirth's enchaining lay be sung,
    We dare not trust the strain.
The touch of sorrow or of sin
Hath saddened all, without, within;
What here we fondly love and prize,
However beauteous be its guise,
Has passed, is passing, or may pass,
Like frost-fringe on the autumn grass.

To whom, O Saviour, shall we go?
    Our spirits dimly wait
In the dungeon of our mortal frame;
And only one of direful name
    Can force its sin-barred gate.

Our loved ones can but greet us through
The prison gate, from which we view
All outward things. They enter not:
Thou, Thou alone, canst cheer our lot.
O Christ, we long for Thee to dwell
Within our solitary cell!

To whom, O Saviour, shall we go?
   Unless Thy voice we hear,
All tuneless falls the sweetest song,
And lonely seems the busiest throng
   Unless we feel Thee near.
We dare not think what earth would be,
Thou Heaven-Creator, but for Thee;
A howling chaos, wild and dark—
One flood of horror, while no ark,
Upborne above the gloom-piled wave,
From one great death-abyss might save.

To whom, O Saviour, shall we go?
   The Tempter's power is great;
E'en in our hearts is evil bound,
And, lurking stealthily around,
   Still for our souls doth wait.
Thou tempted One, whose suffering heart
In all our sorrows bore a part,
Whose life-blood only could atone,
Too weak are we to stand alone;
And nothing but Thy shield of light
Can guard us in the dreaded fight.

To whom, O Saviour, shall we go?
   The night of death draws near;
Its shadow must be passed alone,
No friend can with our souls go down
   The untried way to cheer.
Thou hast the words of endless life;
Thou givest victory in the strife;
Thou only art the changeless Friend,
On whom for aye we may depend:
In life, in death, alike we flee,
O Saviour of the world, to THEE.

'I Did This for Thee! What Hast Thou Done for Me?'

(MOTTO PLACED UNDER A PICTURE OF OUR SAVIOUR IN THE STUDY OF A GERMAN DIVINE.)

I GAVE My life for thee,	Galatians 2:20.
My precious blood I shed,	1 Peter 1:19.
That thou might'st ransomed be,	Ephesians 1:7.
And quickened from the dead.	Ephesians 2:1.
I gave My life for thee;	Titus 2:14.
What hast thou given for Me?	John 21:15–17.
I spent long years for thee	1 Timothy 1:15.
In weariness and woe,	Isaiah 53:3.
That an eternity	John 17:24.
Of joy thou mightest know.	John 16:22.
I spent long years for thee;	John 1:10, 11.
Hast thou spent *one* for Me?	1 Peter 4:2.
My Father's home of light,	John 17:5.
My rainbow-circled throne,	Revelation 4:3.
I left, for earthly night,	Philippians 2:7.
For wanderings sad and lone.	Matthew 8:20.
I left it all for thee;	2 Corinthians 8:9.
Hast thou left aught for Me?	Luke 10:29.
I suffered much for thee,	Isaiah 53:5.
More than thy tongue may tell,	Matthew 26:39.
Of bitterest agony,	Luke 22:44.
To rescue thee from hell.	Romans 5:9.
I suffered much for thee;	1 Peter 2:21–24.
What canst thou bear for Me?	Romans 8:17, 18.
And I have brought to thee,	John 4:10, 14.
Down from My home above,	John 3:13.
Salvation full and free,	Revelation 21:6.
My pardon and My love.	Acts 5:31.
Great gifts I brought to thee;	Psalm 68:18.
What hast thou brought to Me?	Romans 12:1.

Oh, let thy life be given,	Romans 6:13.
Thy years for Him be spent,	2 Corinthians 5:15.
World-fetters all be riven,	Philippians 3:8.
And joy with suffering blent;	1 Peter 4:13–16.
I gave Myself for thee:	Ephesians 5:2.
Give thou *thyself* to Me!	Proverbs 23:26.

Isaiah 33:17.

THINE eyes shall see! Yes, thine, who, blind erewhile,
   Now trembling towards the new-found light dost flee,
Leave doubting, and look up with trustful smile—
      Thine eyes shall see!

Thine *eyes* shall see! Not in some dream Elysian,
   Not in thy fancy, glowing though it be,
Not e'en in faith, but in unveilèd vision,
      Thine *eyes* shall see!

Thine eyes *shall* see! Not on thyself depend
   God's promises, the faithful, firm, and free;
Ere they shall fail, earth, heaven itself, must end:
      Thine eyes *shall* see!

Thine eyes shall *see!* Not in a swift glance cast,
   Gleaning one ray to brighten memory,
But while a glad eternity shall last,
      Thine eyes shall *see!*

Thine eyes shall see *the* King! The very same
   Whose love shone forth upon the curseful tree,
Who bore thy guilt, who calleth thee by name;
      Thine eyes shall see!

Thine eyes shall see the *King!* the mighty One,
   The many-crowned, the Light-enrobed; and He
Shall bid thee share the kingdom He hath won,
      Thine eyes shall see!

And *in His beauty!* Stay thee, mortal song,
  The 'altogether lovely' One must be
Unspeakable in glory,—yet ere long
      Thine eyes shall see!

Yes! though the land be 'very far' away,
  A step, a moment, ends the toil for thee;
Then, changing grief for gladness, night for day,
      Thine eyes shall see!

God the Provider.

'My God shall supply all your need, according to His riches in glory by Christ Jesus.'—
PHILIPPIANS 4:19.

Who shall tell our untold need,
  Deeply felt, though scarcely known!
Who the hungering soul can feed,
  Guard, and guide, but God alone?
Blessèd promise! while we see
Earthly friends must powerless be,
Earthly fountains quickly dry:
'*God*' shall all your need supply.

He hath said it! so we know
  Nothing less can we receive.
Oh that thankful love may glow
  While we restfully believe,—
Ask not *how,* but trust Him still;
Ask not *when,* but wait His will:
Simply on His word rely,
God '*shall*' all your need supply.

Through the whole of life's long way,
  Outward, inward need we trace;
Need arising day by day,
  Patience, wisdom, strength, and grace.
Needing Jesus most of all,
Full of need, on Him we call;
Then how gracious His reply,
God shall '*all*' your need supply!

Great our need, but greater far
   Is our Father's loving power;
He upholds each mighty star,
   He unfolds each tiny flower.
He who numbers every hair,
Earnest of His faithful care,
Gave His Son for us to die;
God shall all *'your'* need supply.

Yet we often vainly plead
   For a fancied good denied,
What we deemed a pressing need
   Still remaining unsupplied.
Yet from dangers all concealed,
Thus our wisest Friend doth shield;
No *good* thing will He deny,
God shall all your *'need'* supply.

Can we count redemption's treasure,
   Scan the glory of God's love?
Such shall be the boundless measure
   Of His blessings from above.
All we ask or think, and more,
He will give in bounteous store,—
He can fill and satisfy!
God shall all your need *'supply.'*[1]

One the channel, deep and broad,
   From the Fountain of the Throne,
Christ the Saviour, Son of God,
   Blessings flow through Him alone.
He, the Faithful and the True,
Brings us mercies ever new:
Till we reach His home on high,
'God shall all your need supply.'

---

[1] The Greek word is much stronger than the English,—πληρώσει—'will supply to the full,' 'fill up,' 'satisfy.'

Wait Patiently for Him.

GOD doth not bid thee wait
To disappoint at last;
A golden promise, fair and great,
In precept-mould is cast.
Soon shall the morning gild
The dark horizon-rim,
Thy heart's desire shall be fulfilled,
' *Wait* patiently for Him.'

The weary waiting times
Are but the muffled peals
Low precluding celestial chimes,
That hail His chariot-wheels.
Trust Him to tune thy voice
To blend with seraphim;
His 'Wait' shall issue in 'Rejoice!'
'Wait *patiently* for Him.'

He doth not bid thee wait,
Like drift-wood on the wave,
For fickle chance or fixèd fate
To ruin or to save.
Thine eyes shall surely see,
No distant hope or dim,
The Lord thy God arise for thee:
'Wait patiently *for Him.*'

This Same Jesus.

Acts 1:11.

'THIS same Jesus!' Oh! how sweetly
Fall those words upon the ear,
Like a swell of far off music,
In a nightwatch still and drear!

He who healed the hopeless leper,
    He who dried the widow's tear;
He who changed to health and gladness
    Helpless suffering, trembling fear;

He who wandered, poor and homeless,
    By the stormy Galilee;
He who on the night-robed mountain
    Bent in prayer the wearied knee;

He who spake as none had spoken,
    Angel-wisdom far above,
All-forgiving, ne'er upbraiding,
    Full of tenderness and love;

He who gently called the weary,
    'Come and I will give you rest!'
He who loved the little children,
    Took them in His arms and blest;

He, the lonely Man of sorrows,
    'Neath our sin-curse bending low;
By His faithless friends forsaken
    In the darkest hours of woe;—

'This *same* Jesus!' When the vision
    Of that last and awful day
Bursts upon the prostrate spirit,
    Like a midnight lightning ray;

When, else dimly apprehended,
    All its terrors seem revealed,
Trumpet knell and fiery heavens,
    And the books of doom unsealed;

Then, we lift our hearts adoring
    'This same Jesus,' loved and known,
Him, our own most gracious Saviour,
    Seated on the great white Throne;

He Himself, and 'not another,'
    He for whom our heart-love yearned

Through long years of twilight waiting,
　　To His ransomed ones returned!

For this word, O Lord, we bless Thee,
　　Bless our Master's changeless name;
Yesterday, to-day, for ever,
　　Jesus Christ is still the Same.

Mary's Birthday.

SHE is at rest,
In God's own presence blest,
Whom, while with us, this day we loved to greet;
　　Her birthdays o'er,
　　She counts the years no more;
Time's footfall is not heard along the golden street.

　　When we would raise
　　A hymn of birthday praise,
The music of our hearts is faint and low;
　　Fear, doubt, and sin
　　Make dissonance within;
And pure soul-melody no child of earth may know.

　　That strange 'new song,'
　　Amid a white-robed throng,
Is gushing from her harp in living tone;
　　Her seraph voice,
　　Tuned only to rejoice,
Floats upward to the emerald-archèd throne.[1]

　　No passing cloud
　　Her loveliness may shroud,
The beauty of her youth may never fade;
　　No line of care
　　Her sealèd brow may wear,
The joy-gleam of her eye no dimness e'er may shade.

[1] Revelation 4:3.

No stain is there
Upon the robes they wear,
Within the gates of pearl which she hath passed;
Like woven light,
All beautiful and bright,
Eternity upon those robes no shade may cast.

No sin-born thought
May in that home be wrought,
To trouble the clear fountain of her heart;
No tear, no sigh,
No pain, no death, be nigh
Where she hath entered in, no more to 'know in part.'

Her faith is sight,
Her hope is full delight,
The shadowy veil of time is rent in twain:
Her untold bliss—
What thought can follow this!
To her to live was Christ, to die indeed is gain.

Her eyes have seen
The King, no veil between,
In blood-dipped vesture gloriously arrayed:
No earth-breathed haze
Can dim that rapturous gaze;
She sees Him face to face on whom her guilt was laid.

A little while,
And they whose loving smile
Had melted 'neath the touch of lonely woe,
Shall reach her home,
Beyond the star-built dome;
Her anthem they shall swell, her joy they too shall know.

Daily Strength.

'As thy days thy strength shall be!'
This should be enough for thee;
He who knows thy frame will spare
Burdens more than thou canst bear.

When thy days are veiled in night,
Christ shall give thee heavenly light;
Seem they wearisome and long,
Yet in Him thou shalt be strong.

Cold and wintry though they prove,
Thine the sunshine of His love,
Or, with fervid heat oppressed,
In His shadow thou shalt rest.

When thy days on earth are past,
Christ shall call thee home at last,
His redeeming love to praise,
Who hath strengthened all thy days.

The Right Way.

LORD, is it still the right way, though I cannot see Thy face,
Though I do not feel Thy presence and Thine all-sustaining grace?
Can even this be leading through the bleak and sunless wild
To the City of Thy holy rest, the mansions undefiled?

Lord, is it still the right way? A while ago I passed
Where every step seemed thornier and harder than the last;
Where bitterest disappointment and inly aching sorrow
Carved day by day a weary cross, renewed with every morrow.

The heaviest end of that strange cross I knew was laid on Thee;
So I could still press on, secure of Thy deep sympathy.
Our upward path may well be steep, else how were patience tried?
I knew it was the right way, for it led me to Thy side.

But now I wait alone amid dim shadows dank and chill;
All moves and changes round me, but I seem standing still;
Or every feeble footstep I urge towards the light
Seems but to lead me farther into the silent night.

I cannot hear Thy voice, Lord! dost Thou still hear my cry?
I cling to Thine assurance that Thou art ever nigh;
I know that Thou art faithful; I trust, but cannot see
That it is still the right way by which Thou leadest me.

I think I could go forward with brave and joyful heart,
Though every step should pierce me with unknown fiery smart,
If only I might see Thee, if I might gaze above
On all the cloudless glory of the sunshine of Thy love.

Is it really leading onwards? When the shadows flee away,
Shall I find this path has brought me more near to perfect day?
Or am I left to wander thus that I may stretch my hand
To some still wearier traveller in this same shadow-land.

Is this Thy chosen training for some future task unknown?
Is it that I may learn to rest upon Thy word alone?
Whate'er it be, oh! leave me not, fulfil Thou every hour
The purpose of Thy goodness, and the work of faith with power.

I lay my prayer before Thee, and, trusting in Thy word,
Though all is silence in my heart, I know that Thou hast heard.
To that blest City lead me, Lord (still choosing all my way),
Where faith melts into vision as the starlight into day.

Thy Will Be Done.

'Understanding *what* the will of the Lord is.'—EPHESIANS 5:17.

WITH quivering heart and trembling will
    The word hath passed thy lips,
Within the shadow, cold and still,
    Of some fair joy's eclipse.
'Thy will be done!' Thy God hath heard,
And He will crown that faith-framed word.

Thy prayer shall be fulfilled: but how?
    His thoughts are not as thine;
While thou wouldst only weep and bow,
    He saith, 'Arise and shine!'
Thy thoughts were all of grief and night,
But His of boundless joy and light.

Thy Father reigns supreme above:
    The glory of His name
Is Grace and Wisdom, Truth and Love,
    His will must be the same.
And thou hast asked all joys in one,
In whispering forth, 'Thy will be done.'

His will—each soul to sanctify
    Redeeming might hath won; [1]
His will—that thou shouldst never die,
    Believing on His Son; [2]
His will—that thou, through earthly strife,
Shouldst rise to everlasting life. [3]

That one unchanging song of praise
    Should from our hearts arise; [4]
That we should know His wondrous ways,
    Though hidden from the wise; [5]
That we, so sinful and so base,
Should know the glory of His grace. [6]

His will—to grant the yearning prayer
    For dear ones far away, [7]
That they His grace and love may share,
    And tread His pleasant way;
That in the Father and the Son
All perfect we may be in one. [8]

His will—the little flock to bring
    Into His royal fold,
To reign for ever with their King, [9]
    His beauty to behold. [10]
Sin's fell dominion crushed for aye,
Sorrow and sighing fled away.

---

[1] 1 Thessalonians 4:3.
[2] John 6:40.
[3] John 6:39.
[4] 1 Thessalonians 5:18.
[5] Matthew 11:25, 26.
[6] Ephesians 1:5, 6, 11, 12.
[7] 1 John 5:14–16.
[8] John 17:23, 24.
[9] Luke 12:32.
[10] Isaiah 33:17.

This thou hast asked! And shall the prayer
　　Float upward on a sigh?
No song were sweet enough to bear
　　Such glad desires on high!
But God thy Father shall fulfil,
In thee and for thee, all His will.

'The Things Which Are Behind.'

LEAVE behind earth's empty pleasure,
　　Fleeting hope and changeful love;
Leave its soon-corroding treasure:
　　There are better things above.

Leave, oh, leave thy fond aspirings,
　　Bid thy restless heart be still;
Cease, oh, cease thy vain desirings,
　　Only seek thy Father's will.

Leave behind thy faithless sorrow,
　　And thine every anxious care;
He who only knows the morrow
　　Can for thee its burden bear.

Leave behind the doubting spirit,
　　And thy crushing load of sin;
By thy mighty Saviour's merit,
　　Life eternal thou shalt win.

Leave the darkness gathering o'er thee,
　　Leave the shadow-land behind;
Realms of glory lie before thee;
　　Enter in, and welcome find.

'Now I See.'

JOHN 9:25.

'Now I see!' But not the parting
　　Of the melting earth and sky,

Not a vision dread and startling,
    Forcing one despairing cry.
But I see the solemn saying,
    All have sinned, and all must die;
Holy precepts disobeying,
    Guilty all the world must lie.
Bending, silenced, to the dust,
Now I see that God is just.

'Now I see!' But not the glory,
    Not the face of Him I love,
Not the full and burning story
    Of the mysteries above.
But I see what God hath spoken,
    How His well-belovèd Son
Kept the laws which man hath broken,
    Died for sins which man hath done;
Dying, rising, throned above!
'Now I see' that God is Love.

Everlasting Love.

'Yea, I have loved thee with an everlasting love, *therefore* with loving-kindness have I drawn thee.'—JEREMIAH 31:3 'No man can come to Me except the Father which hath sent Me draw him.'—JOHN 6:44.

'GOD's everlasting love! What wouldst thou more?'
O true and tender friend, well hast thou spoken.
My heart was restless, weary, sad, and sore,
And longed and listened for some heaven-sent token:
And, like a child that knows not why it cried,
'Mid God's full promises it moaned, 'Unsatisfied!'

Yet there it stands. O love surpassing thought,
So bright, so grand, so clear, so true, so glorious;
Love infinite, love tender, love unsought,
Love changeless, love rejoicing, love victorious!
And this great love for us in boundless store:
God's everlasting love! What would we more?

Yes, one thing more! To know it ours indeed,
To add the conscious joy of full possession.
O tender grace that stoops to every need!
This everlasting love hath found expression
In loving-kindness, which hath gently drawn
The heart that else astray too willingly had gone.

From no less fountain such a stream could flow,
No other root could yield so fair a flower:
Had He not loved, He had not drawn us so;
Had He not drawn, we had nor will nor power
To rise, to come;—the Saviour had passed by
Where we in blindness sat without one care or cry.

We thirst for *God,* our treasure *is* above;
Earth has no gift our one desire to meet,
And that desire is pledge of His own love.
Sweet question; with no answer! oh *how* sweet!
My heart in chiming gladness o'er and o'er
Sings on—'God's everlasting love! What wouldst
    thou more?'

'Master, Say On!'

MASTER, speak! Thy servant heareth,
    Waiting for Thy gracious word,
Longing for Thy voice that cheereth;
    Master! let it now be heard.
I am listening, Lord, for Thee;
What hast Thou to say to me?

Master, speak in love and power:
    Crown the mercies of the day,
In this quiet evening hour
    Of the moonrise o'er the bay,
With the music of Thy voice;
Speak! and bid Thy child rejoice.

Often through my heart is pealing
　　Many another voice than Thine,
Many an unwilled echo stealing
　　From the walls of this Thy shrine:
Let Thy longed-for accents fall;
Master, speak! and silence all.

Master, speak! I do not doubt Thee,
　　Though so tearfully I plead;
Saviour, Shepherd! oh, without Thee
　　Life would be a blank indeed!
But I long for fuller light,
Deeper love, and clearer sight.

Resting on the 'faithful saying,'
　　Trusting what Thy gospel saith,
On Thy written promise staying
　　All my hope in life and death,
Yet I long for something more
From Thy love's exhaustless store.

Speak to me by name, O Master,
　　Let me *know* it is to me;
Speak, that I may follow faster,
　　With a step more firm and free,
Where the Shepherd leads the flock,
In the shadow of the Rock.

Master, speak! I kneel before Thee,
　　Listening, longing, waiting still;
Oh, how long shall I implore Thee
　　This petition to fulfil!
Hast Thou not one word for me?
Must my prayer unanswered be?

Master, speak! Though least and lowest,
　　Let me not unheard depart;
Master, speak! for oh, Thou knowest
　　All the yearning of my heart,
Knowest all its truest need;
Speak! and make me blest indeed.

Master, speak! and make me ready,
When Thy voice is truly heard,
With obedience glad and steady
Still to follow every word.
I am listening, Lord, for Thee;
Master, speak, oh, speak to me!

Remote Results.

WHERE are the countless crystals,
So perfect and so bright,
That robed in softest ermine
The winter day and night?
Not lost! for, life to many a root,
They rise again in flower and fruit.

Where are the mighty forests,
And giant ferns of old,
That in primeval silence
Strange leaf and frond unrolled?
Not lost! for now they shine and blaze,
The light and warmth of Christmas days.

Where are our early lessons,
The teachings of our youth,
The countless words forgotten
Of knowledge and of truth?
Not lost! for they are living still,
As power to think, and do, and will.

Where is the seed we scatter,
With weak and trembling hand,
Beside the gloomy waters,
Or on the arid land?
Not lost! for after many days
Our prayer and toil shall turn to praise.

Where are the days of sorrow,
And lonely hours of pain,

When work is interrupted,
              Or planned and willed in vain?
Not lost! it is the thorniest shoot
That bears the Master's pleasant fruit.

Where, where are all God's lessons,
              His teachings dark or bright?
Not lost! but only hidden,
              Till, in eternal light,
We see, while at His feet we fall,
The reasons and results of all.

On the Last Leaf. [1]

FINISHED at last!
Yet for five years past
My book on the dusty shelf hath lain,
And I hardly thought that ever again
My thoughts would follow the pleasant chime
Of musical measure and ringing rhyme.

I remember well when I laid it by,
Closed with a sort of requiem sigh.
Spring in her beauty had swept along,
And left my spirit all full of song:
The wakening depths of my heart were stirred,
Voices within and without I heard,
              Whispering me
              That I might be
A messenger of peace and pleasure;
       That in my careless minstrelsy
Lay something of poetic treasure,
Which, wrought with care, I yet some day
At all my loved ones' feet might lay.
Perhaps 'twas a vain and foolish dream,
A fancy-lit, illusive gleam!

---

[1] Written at the close of a manuscript volume.

And yet I cannot quite believe
That such bright impulse could deceive.
I felt I had so much to say,
Such pleasant thoughts from day to day,
Sang, lark-like, with each morning ray,
Or murmured low in twilight grey,
    Like distant curfew pealing.
And then, for each, fair Fancy brought
A robe of language ready wrought,
The smile of every wingèd thought
    Half veiling, half revealing.
And I only waited, with longing gaze,
For the golden leisure of summer days,
Which I thought to crown with happiest lays.

God thought not so! Ah no, He knew
There was other work for me to do,
There were other lessons for me to learn:
Another voice fell, low and stern,
    Upon the too reluctant ear.
Before the solemn voice of Pain
My visions fled, nor came again,
With all their glad and lovely train,
    My summer-tide to cheer.

Well is it when, at high command
Of wisest Love, she takes her stand
    At the heart's busy portal,
And warns away each noisy guest
Whose presence chases calm and rest,
Our powers, the brightest and the best,
    Proclaiming weak and mortal.
That so the way may be more clear
    For Him, the Prince of Peace, to come,
That which is left all void and drear
    To make His palace and His home.

And so the song of my heart was hushed,
    And the chiming thoughts were stilled:

Summer flew by, but the hope was crushed,
Swiftly onward my life-tide rushed,
    But my book remained unfilled.
For an aching head and a weary frame,
Poetry is but an empty name.
Yet I am sure it was better so,
I *trusted* then, and now I *know*.

For ever, I think, the gift is fled
    Which once I fancied mine:
So be it! A 'name' is not for me;
Loving and loved I would rather be,
With power to cheer and sympathize,
Bearing new light for tear-dimmed eyes;
    But I do not care to shine.

So if aught I write may tend to this,
My fairest hope of earthly bliss,
    Content with humblest rhyme I'll be;
And, striving less and trusting more,
All simple, earnest thoughts outpour,
    Such as my God may give to me.

How Should They Know Me?

THERE are those who deem they know me well,
    And smile as I tell them 'nay!'
Who think they may clearly and carelessly tell
Each living drop in my heart's deep well,
And lightly enter its inmost cell;
    But little (how little!) know they!

How should they know me? My soul is a maze
    Where I wander alone, alone;
Never a footfall there was heard,
Never a mortal hand hath stirred
The silence-curtain that hangs between
Outer and inner, nor eye hath seen
    What is only and ever my own.

They have entered indeed the vestibule,
      For its gate is opened wide,
High as the roof, and I welcome all
Who will visit my warm reception-hall,
And utter a long and loving call
      To some who are yet outside.

I would lead each guest to a place of rest;
      All should be calm and bright;
Then a lulling flow of melody,
And a crystal draught of sympathy,
And odorous blossoms of kindly thought,
With golden fruit of deed, be brought
      From the chambers out of sight.

Some I would take with a cordial hand,
      And lead them round the walls;
Showing them many a storied screen,
Many a portrait, many a scene,
Deep-cut carving, and outlined scroll;
Passing quickly where shadows roll,
      Slowly where sunshine falls.

They do not know and they cannot see
      That strong-hinged, low-arched door,
Though I am passing in and out,
From gloom within to light without,
Or from gloom without to light within;
None can ever an entrance win,
      None! for evermore.

It is a weird and wondrous realm,
      Where I often hold my breath
At the unseen things which there I see,
At the mighty shapes which beckon to me,
At the visions of woe and ecstasy,
      At the greetings of life and death.

They rise, they pass, they melt away,
      In an ever-changing train;

I cannot hold them or tell their stay,
Or measure the time of their fleeting sway;
As grim as night, and as fair as day,
    They vanish and come again.

I wander on through the strange domain,
    Marvelling ever and aye;
Marvelling how around my feet
All the opposites seem to meet,
The dark, the light, the chill, the glow,
The storm, the calm, the fire, the snow,—
How can it be? I do not know.
    Then how, oh how, can they?

What am I, and how? If reply there be,
    In unsearchable chaos 'tis cast.
Though the soaring spirit of restless man
Might the boundary line of the universe scan,
And measure and map its measureless plan,
    The gift of self-knowledge were last!

Making Poetry.

Little one, what are you doing,
    Sitting on the window-seat?
Laughing to yourself, and writing,
Some right merry thought inditing,
    Balancing with swinging feet.

' 'Tis some poetry I'm making,
    Though I never tried before:
Four whole lines! I'll read them to you.
Do you think them funny, do you?
    Shall I try to make some more?

' I should like to be a poet,
    Writing verses every day;
Then to you I'd always bring them,
You should make a tune and sing them;
    'Twould be pleasanter than play.'

Think you, darling, nought is needed
 But the paper and the ink,
And a pen to trace so lightly,
While the eye is beaming brightly,
 All the pretty things we think?

There's a secret,—can you trust me?
 Do not ask me what it is!
Perhaps some day you too will know it,
If you live to be a poet,
 All its agony and bliss.

Poetry is not a trifle,
 Lightly thought and lightly made;
Not a fair and scentless flower,
Gaily cultured for an hour,
 Then as gaily left to fade.

'Tis not stringing rhymes together
 In a pleasant true accord;
Not the music of the metre,
Not the happy fancies, sweeter
 Than a flower-bell, honey-stored.

'Tis the essence of existence,
 Rarely rising to the light;
And the songs that echo longest,
Deepest, fullest, truest, strongest,
 With your life-blood you will write.

With your life-blood. None will know it,
 You will never tell them how.
Smile! and they will never guess it:
Laugh! and you will not confess it
 By your paler cheek and brow.

There must be the tightest tension
 Ere the tone be full and true;
Shallow lakelets of emotion
Are not like the spirit-ocean,
 Which reflects the purest blue.

Every lesson you shall utter,
   If the charge indeed be yours,
First is gained by earnest learning,
Carved in letters deep and burning
   On a heart that long endures.

Day by day that wondrous tablet
   Your life-poem shall receive,
By the hand of Joy or Sorrow;
But the pen can never borrow
   Half the records that they leave.

You will only give a transcript
   Of a life-line here and there,
Only just a spray-wreath springing
From the hidden depths, and flinging
   Broken rainbows on the air.

Still, if you but copy truly,
   'T will be poetry indeed,
Echoing many a heart's vibration,
Rather love than admiration
   Earning as your priceless meed.

Will you seek it? Will you brave it?
   'Tis a strange and solemn thing,
Learning long, before your teaching,
Listening long, before your preaching,
   Suffering before you sing.

The Cascade.

WHO saith that Poetry is not in thee,
Thou wild cascade, bright, beautiful, and free?
Who saith that thine own sunny gleaming waters
Are not among 'sweet Poesie's' fair daughters?
No Poetry in thee? then tell, oh tell,
Where is the home where she delights to dwell?
But what is Poetry? Some aerial sprite,

Clothed in a dazzling robe of wavy light,
Whose magic touch unlocks the gates of joy
In dreamland to some vision-haunted boy?
Or is she but a breath from Eden-bowers,
Charged with the fragrance of their shining flowers,
Which, passing o'er the harp-strings of the soul,
Awakes new melody, whose echoes roll
In waves of spirit-music through the heart,
Till tears and smiles in mingling sweetness start?
It may be so, but still she seems to me
Most like a God-sent sunlight, rich and free,
Bathing the tiniest leaf in molten gold,
Bidding each flower some secret charm unfold,
Weaving a veil of loveliness for earth,
Calling all fairy forms to wondrous birth.

Our sweet soul-Artist! Many a fair surprise
Her colour-treasures bring to waiting eyes;
Her pictures, sudden seen, oft seem to dwell
Like pearls within the rugged ocean shell,
They tell of something purer and more fair
Than earth can boast, and gleam forth everywhere,
Star-glimpses through the trees, or flashes bright
Of meteor glory in a northern night.

Our sweet soul-Harpist! linking winds with sighs,
And blending both with spirit-melodies,
And adding chords that come we know not whence,
Dream-echoes mingling with the wakeful sense.
O strange, O beautiful! though all unknown,
The music-fount of every lovely tone,
The colour-fount of every lovely thought,
By this bright ministrant so freely brought,
Save that we own their true and soothing might
One of His perfect gifts, whose names are Love and Light.

Oh! she is often where we least surmise,
And scorns the dimness of our heavy eyes;
We catch the ruby sparkles of her wing,
And she is gone like dewdrops of the spring;

Again, to glad us with her smile she stays,
And shows her brightness to our loving gaze.
No cave so dark but she may gain its porch,
And gild the shadows with her quenchless torch;
No dell so silent but her pealing voice
Can bid a leafy orchestra rejoice;
No waste so lonely but she there may hold
Her gorgeous court in splendour all untold.
And where those waters murmur as they leap,
A song of gentleness, and calm, and sleep,
Within the sounding music of their tone
I hear a voice, and know it is her own.

And where the fair, fond sunbeams blithely play
Amid the hazy wreaths of dancing spray,
A form of fairy grace shines forth to me;
I hail the vision, for I know 'tis she.
She loves that changeful, yet unchanging foam,
Within its arching bowers she finds a home,
And reads beneath its roof of fleeting snow
The secrets of the shadowy depth below.
Then who shall say that she is not in thee,
Thou wild cascade, bright, beautiful, and free!

Constance De V—.

AN EPISODE IN THE LIFE OF CHARLES MAURICE, PRINCE DE TALLEYRAND.

YE maidens of Old England!
   The joyous and the free,
The loving and the loved of all,
   Wherever ye may be;
Who wander through the ferny dell,
   And o'er the breezy hill,
And glide along the woodland path
   All at your own sweet will;
Who know the many joys of home,
   The song, the smile, the mirth,
The happy things which God has given
   To brighten this our earth:

Comes there a sigh, a longing thought,
   In lonely musing hours?
Deem ye there is a fairer realm,
   A purer faith than ours?
O cast away the yearning dream,
   And listen, while I tell
Of one who knew no other home
   Than her own convent cell.

I.

The rain comes down relentlessly,
   The sky is robed in grey,
Oh, Paris is a dreary place
   On such a dreary day!
But dreariest of the darkening streets,
   Where the loud rain doth fall,
Is that where looms the convent tower,
   Where frowns the convent wall.

II.

A boyish step is passing
   Beneath the dripping eaves,
With monkish lore beladen,
   With musty Latin leaves.
Ah, Charles Maurice, the young abbé,
   Thou art of princely birth!
For thee shall dawn a brighter day,
A strange high part be thine to play,
With wondrous tact to guide and sway
   The great ones of the earth!

III.

But the still-increasing torrents
   Will spoil the ancient tomes,
And woe betide Charles Maurice
   From the wrath of cowlèd gnomes!

So he seeks a low-bent archway
    Within the grim old wall,
Where never the laughing footstep
    Of a sunbeam dares to fall.

IV.

Anon he wraps the volumes
    In the folds of his hooded gown;
Then starts to hear, though he knows no fear,
A sound which tells him life is near—
    That he is not alone.
He turns—the passage is dark as night,
    He listens—but all is still,
Save the raindrops in monotonous march,
And the ceaseless drip from the mouldering arch,
    On the stone so damp and chill.

V.

'*Qui vive?*' he cries right gaily,
    Through the cavernous entry's gloom;
But a low, faint cry is the sole reply,
As the voice of one who is come to lie
    On the brink of a yawning tomb.
Oh, where is the true-hearted lad,
    Who at the call of sorrow
But in his thoughtlessness is glad
To help the weak and cheer the sad,
    And promise a brighter morrow?

VI.

The cry was one of weakness—
    Of weariness unblest;
And a pulse of gentle sympathy
    Makes music in his breast.
Through the dark way he gropeth
    To the iron-studded door,
Behind whose oaken grimness
Some dwell in cloistral dimness
    Who may pass out no more.

VII.

There, in the glimmering darkness,
      He deems he can descry
A small and sable-robèd form
      On the cold doorstep lie.
The form is that of maidenhood;
      And, in that boyish heart,
It wakes a helpful tenderness,
Like that which, hidden, yet doth bless
Through a loved brother's fond caress,
      Ere childhood's hours depart.

VIII.

'What is it?' said Charles Maurice,
      In a softly pitying tone;
'What dost thou fear? why art thou here?
      And why that weary moan?'
Then, lifting her with gentle arm,
      He bore her where the light
Fell on a girlish face so fair,
It seemed a seraph light to wear,
But for the sorrow mantling there,
      And the glance of wild affright.

IX.

Why should I paint her beauty?
      Have ye not often tried
To tell of rosy lip and cheek,
Of starlit eyes that shine and speak,
Of cloudlike locks that vainly seek
      The snowy brow to hide?
And feel ye not, when all is said
      That words can ever say,
The fount of beauty still is sealed—
The loveliness is not revealed
      To those who list the lay.

X.

Oh, words can never satisfy—
     They are too hard and real;
The subtle charm they cannot show
By which the Beautiful we know,
     The Beautiful we feel.
Perchance they speak the form, the mind,
     And draw the likeness well;
But at the closèd entrance gate
All reverently they bend and wait
     Where, 'neath the marble-arching dome,
In crystal-windowed palace-home,
     The soul itself doth dwell.

XI.

And who may tell how lovely
     The gentle Constance seemed,
When through such clouds of sorrow
     Her meteor beauty gleamed!
What wonder that all speechless,
     As in a trance of gladness,
The young abbé stood wonderingly,
     Before such radiant sadness?

XII.

For the look of hopeless terror
     Was softened as she raised
Those orbs of strange, quick brightness,
     And on Charles Maurice gazed.
She saw the pledge of kindness
     Traced on that high fair brow;—
'Oh, no! thou never wilt betray,
But aid thou canst not; say, oh say,
Am I not lost? There is no way
     Of safe return, I know.'

XIII.

Then the trembling hands she folded
    Over the burning cheek,
A wild and woe-born sobbing
    Forbade the lips to speak;
Till quiet words of sympathy,
    So softly breathed and low,
And the touch of that young hand on hers,
    Soon bade her story flow.

XIV.

'I was a very little child,
    Not old enough to know,
Perhaps kind looks had on me smiled,
    But I forget them now,
When I was brought to live so coldly here,
Where all goes on the same through weary month
    and year.

XV.

'I did not know how lovely all
    The world without must be;
The sunbeams on the convent wall
    Were quite enough for me;
But others came who knew, and then they told
Of all that I had dreamt, but never might behold.

XVI.

'They told me of the mountains tall,
    Where they might freely roam;
They told me of the waterfall,
    With music in its foam;
They told me of wide fields and opening flowers,
Of sloping mossy banks and glowing autumn bowers.

XVII.

'Of other things they told me, too,
　　More beautiful to them,
Of gleaming halls where sparklets flew
　　From many a radiant gem;
And then they told of mirth, and dance, and song.
Would I had never heard, that I might never long!

XVIII.

'They said the sky was just as blue
　　Above the convent towers,
As where the arching forests threw
　　A shade o'er summer flowers;
But I grew weary of that dazzling sky,
And longed to wander forth, e'en if it were to die.

XIX.

'I did not want to change my lot,
　　I knew it might not be;
I only longed to have one spot
　　All bright with memory.
To gaze just once upon the world I tried,
And then I would return to be Heaven's lonely bride.

XX.

'But, oh, I heard no sounds of mirth,
　　No beauty I could see;
I could not find the lovely earth,
　　It was not made for me.
And now my punishment indeed is sore,
My only home hath closed on me its iron door.'

XXI.

Yes! in her fevered restlessness
　　She left her unwatched cell,
When all around were summoned
　　By the deep-voiced matin-bell.

And in the damp-stoned cloisters
 To rest awhile she thought,
Where cold, fresh air might round her play,
The burning fever pass away,
And coolness of the early day
 To her hot brow be brought.

XXII.

Strange carelessness! no massy bar
 Across the gate was thrown!
She deemed that world of beauty near;
She gazed around in haste and fear,
Oh, none were there to see and hear—
 The timid bird has flown!
But the rain came down relentlessly,
 The sky was robed in grey;
All dreary seemed the narrow street,
And nothing bright or fair might meet
Her of the white and trembling feet;
No loveliness is there to greet
 That wandering star to-day.

XXIII.

Then, bowed with shame and weakness,
 And disappointed hope
She only reached the heavy door
To find it firmly closed once more;
Ah, who shall help, and who restore,
 And who that door shall ope?
The strong young arm of Charles Maurice
 Tries once and yet again,
But the weighty portal baffles him:
 Ah! is it all in vain?

XXIV.

But Constance darts one upward glance
 Of blent despair and trust;

There is no bolt, for daylight gleams
Between the scarcely-meeting beams:
Some unknown obstacle there seems,
     And conquer it he must.
He strains his utmost strength, the sweat
     Is beading on his brow;
It creaks—it yields! O Constance, smile,
     The door is open now!

XXV.

From her cheek the flush hath faded,
     As fades the evening glow,
In pristine whiteness leaving
     The rosy Alpine snow.
And like a breeze of twilight
     The aspen-leaves among,
A whisper falls upon his ear
     From quivering lip and tongue:

XXVI.

'Farewell! Oh, thou hast saved me!'
     And the hand so white and cold,
With lingering clasp of gratitude,
     Her wordless thanks hath told.
One moment on that small, fair hand
     His youthful lips are pressed;
There is a reverence in his eye,
For grief and beauty both are nigh;
She passes like a spirit by,
     To seek her cheerless rest.

XXVII.

They are parted, like the dewdrops
     That linger in the smile
Of a storm-begotten rainbow,
     But for a little while:
Then one in lonely dimness
     To earth may soon descend;

And one with the bright sky above,
   Though all unseen, may blend.

XXVIII.

The young abbé hath paused in vain
   To hear her footstep pass;
'Twas lighter than the noiseless fall
   Of rose-leaf on the grass.
No sound is heard but the pattering rain,
   And he slowly turns away,
With the brown old books beneath his gown,
To meet his abbot's gathering frown,
   For loitering on the way.

XXIX.

Think you he conned the loveless lore
   Without a thoughtful sigh
For the loveliness in sorrow,
   Which passed so trance-like by?
Among the missal borders
   Was no such angel-face;
And such, once seen, fade not away;
Their image shines without decay,
When on the canvas of the heart,
With untaught skill, yet mystic art,
   Each line of light we trace.

XXX.

The wing of Time seems broken now,
   So tardy is his flight;
He deems by day that she is dead,
   He dreams she lives, by night.
Till quick anxiety hath found
   A messenger to bear
The tidings that he strove to frame,
   From woven hope and fear.

XXXI.

What wonder that he heard not
    Her footfall on the stone!
She sank beneath the cloister wall,
    Unheeded and alone;
And ere Charles Maurice stood again
    Beneath the open sky,
For ever on the things of earth
    She closed her weary eye.

XXXII.

Constance, the beautiful, hath left
    Her dismal convent cell;
She hath not known one hope fulfilled,
One granted joy, one longing stilled.
For her the melody of life
Was but one chord of inward strife,
    Was but one ruthless knell.
Her heart bedimmed with sameness,
    Her only wish denied,
Oh, what a mockery it were
Her lot should such a title bear,
    'Heaven's own appointed bride!'

XXXIII.

Why should her early spring-time
    Be quenched in wintry gloom?
Was it not merciful and wise
To call her spirit to the skies
    From such a living tomb?
How might that gentle maiden
    Have scattered joy around,
And made the earth a brighter place,
For all her radiance and grace!
But now, unsorrowed and unknown,
Her only memory is a stone
    Within the convent bound.

Fairy Homes.

I'VE found at last the hiding-place
  Where the fairy people dwell,
And to win the secrets of their race
  I hold the long-sought spell.

With the woodland fairies I can talk,
  I can list their silvery lays;
Oh! pleasant in a lonely walk
  Is the company of fays.

No fabled fancy 'tis to me,
  For in every floweret's bell
Is a tiny chamber, where I see
  A gentle fairy dwell.

And at my bidding forth they come,
  To soothe me or to cheer,
And to tell me tales of fairydom
  With voices soft and clear.

Full many a beauteous lesson, too,
  Their rosy lips can teach;
Great men would wonder if they knew
  How well the fairies preach!

When thoughts of sorrow sadden me,
  They seem to sympathize,
And gaze upon me lovingly,
  With tender earnest eyes;

But when a tide of joyous glee
  Is bringing song and smile,
Then brightly they look up to me,
  And laugh with me awhile.

Oh! lovely are the floweret homes
  Of these sweet summer fays;
God's thoughts of beauty taking form
  To gladden mortal gaze.

More Music.

OH for a burst of song,
Exultant, deep, and strong,
One gush of music's billowy might,
To bear my soul away
Into the realms of day,
From these dim glacier-caves of Life's cold night!

Oh for a sunset strain
Wafted o'er slumberous main,
To enter, spirit-like, my prisoned heart,
And there, with viewless hand,
Unloose each mortal band,
That in the songs of heaven I too might learn a part.

The sweetest music here
Calls forth the quiet tear,
For grief and gladness flow in blended stream;
Oh for the joyous day,
(Can it be far away?)
When one great Alleluia song shall chase Life's tuneless dream!

Travelling Thoughts.

ON BOARD THE STEAMER LA FRANCE, JANUARY 26, 1866.

A STILL grey haze around us,
Behind, a foreign shore,
A still grey deep beneath us,
And Dover cliffs before.
Not one within a hundred miles
Whose name I ever heard,
None who would care to speak to me
A passing friendly word:
Yet not a shadow crosseth me
Of loneliness or fear;
I bless the Omnipresent One,
I know that God is here.

All whom I love are scattered:
    And many a month and mile
Rise, mountain-like, before, behind,
    Between me and their smile.
Oh that the love I bear them
    Might blossom into skill
To comfort and to brighten,
    And all with gladness fill!
Ah! helpless love! Yet 'tis a joy
    To turn each wish to prayer,
And, where each loved one sojourneth,
    To know that God is there.

The nearest and the dearest
    Are where the rushing Rhine
Bends northward from the Drachenfels,
    From castle, rock, and vine;
Where long-lined chestnut shadows
    Make tracery below,
And the moss-framed window challenges
    The might of frost and snow.
Lit rather by the dawn of heaven
    Than earthly sunset glow,
That passing home of faith and prayer!
    Oh, God is there, I know!

From thence the wing of loving thought
    Speeds on where Severn flows,
And hovers o'er as fair a scene
    As our fair England knows;
The home of summer roses,
    Of winter mirth and glee,—
Long may that home unbroken,
    That mirth unsilenced be!
The blessings of unbounded grace
    I pray Him to bestow,
And trust Him for the coming years,
    For He is there, I know.

Now westward sweeps the vision
    Across the Irish Sea,
And echoes low of sisters' love
    Come back again to me.
A beacon bright in stormy night
    Of error, rage, and wrong,
That home of love and truth shall cast
    Its radiance pure and strong.
They tell of rumours strange and dark;
    But oh! no need to fear!
God will not leave His own, I know,
    His guardian hand is near.

Another scene by gentle Ouse
    Must aye be dear to me,
Though all are not together now,
    And one is on the sea.
And where a grey cathedral tower
    Uprises broad and high,
A home is made in cloistral shade,
    Beside the winding Wye.
To seek the richest boons for these,
    Why should the heart be slow?
One Shepherd, Chief, and Great, and Good,
    Is watching there, I know.

Then, in a busy city,
    A crypt all dark and lone,
A name engraven on our hearts
    Is traced upon a stone.
Not *there* the sainted spirit!
    She dwells in holy light,
Within the pearl-raised portals,
    With those who walk in white.
May all her children follow
    The path she meekly trod,
And reach the home she rests in now,
    And dwell, like her, with God.

New Year's Wishes.

A PEARL-STREWN pathway of untold gladness,
Flecked by no gloom, by no weary sadness,
  Such be the year to thee!
A crystal rivulet, sunlight flinging,
Awakening blossoms, and joyously singing
  Its own calm melody.

A symphony soft, and sweet, and low,
Like the gentlest music the angels know
  In their moments of deepest joy;
'Mid earth's wild clamour thy spirit telling
Of beauty and holiness, upward swelling,
  And mingling with the sky.

A radiant, fadeless Eden flower,
Unfolding in loveliness hour by hour,
  Like a wing-veiled seraph's face;—
Such be the opening year to thee,
Shrouded though all its moments be,
  Unknown as the bounds of space.

Blessings unspoken this year be thine!
Each day in its rainbow flight entwine
  New gems in thy joy-wreathed crown;
May each in the smile of Him be bright,
Who is changeless Love and unfading Light,
Till the glory seem to thy trancèd sight
  As heaven to earth come down.

Bonnie Wee Eric.

BONNIE wee Eric! I have sat beside the evening fire,
And listened to the leaping flame still darting keenly higher,
And all the while a lisping voice and eyes of sunny blue
Out-whispered the flame-whisper, and outshone the flicker too.

Bonnie wee Eric! To his home thoughts pleasantly return,
To long fair evenings in the land of ben and brae and burn;
Sweet northern words, so tunefully upon our Saxon flung,
As if a mountain breeze swept by where fairy bells are hung.

But sweeter than all fairy bells of quaint sweet minstrel tongue,
Rang out wee Eric's gentlest tone when o'er his cot I hung,
And told him in the sunset glow once more the old dear story
Of Him who walked the earth that we might walk with Him in glory.

'He loves the little children so;—does darling Eric love Him?'
I think the angels must have smiled a rainbow-smile above him,
Yet hardly brighter than his own, that lit the answer true,
'Jesus, the kind good Jesus! Me do, oh yes, me do!'

Bonnie wee Eric! How the thought of heaven is full of joy,
And death has not a shadow for the merry healthful boy!
To hear about the happy home he gladly turns away
From picture books, or Noah's ark, or any game of play.

'Mamma, some day me die, and then the angels take me home
To Jesus, and me sing to Him;—Papa and you too come.'
So brightly said! 'But, Eric, would you really *like* to die?'
She answered him; 'then, darling, tell mamma the reason why?'

And then the sunny eyes looked up, and seemed at once to be
Filled with a happy solemn light, like sunrise on the sea;
He said—'Yes, me *would* like to die, *for me know where me going!*'
What saint-like longing, baby lips! and oh! what blessèd knowing!

The lesson of the 'little child' is sweetly learnt from him;
No questioning, no anxious faith all tremulous and dim,
No drowsy love that hardly knows if it be love indeed;
Not 'think' or 'hope,' but—'Oh me *do*,'—'me *know*,'—his simple creed.

Bonnie wee Eric! Hardly launched on this world's troubled sea,
We know the little bark is safe whate'er its course may be,
And short or long, or fair or rough, our hearts are glad in knowing
It will be onward, heavenward still, for he '*knows where he's going.*'

My Sweet Woodruff.

No more the flowers of spring are seen,
And silence fills the summer noon;
The woods have lost the fresh bright green
      Of May and June.

But yesterday I found a flower,
Deep sheltered from the withering rays,
Which might have known the sun and shower
      Of April days.

I did not think again to find
Such tender relic of the spring;
It thrilled such gladness through my mind,
      I needs must sing.

My girlhood's spring has passed for aye,
With many a fairy tint and tone;
The heat and burden of the day
      Are better known.

But by my summer path has sprung
A flower of happy love, as fair
As e'er a subtle fragrance flung
      On spring's clear air.

I hardly thought to feel again
Such dewy freshness in my heart,
And so one little loving strain
      Must upward start.

There was spring-sunshine in my eyes,
I had such joy in finding you
So full of all I love and prize,
      So dear and true.

My heart is richer far to-day
Than when I came a week ago;
How near to me such treasure lay
      I did not know!

The long parenthesis is o'er,
And now, in letters all of light,
The story of our love once more
      We both may write.

I have no words to breathe the praise
Which now for this 'good gift' I owe;
A wordless anthem I must raise,
      But HE will know.

Our Gem Wreath.

HEARD ye the sounds of joyous glee,
And the notes of merry minstrelsy,
And the purling of low, sweet words which start
From the silent depths of a loving heart;
And the gushing laugh, and the rippling song,
As the summer days sped swift along?
    Saw ye the gleam of sunny hair,
And the glancing of forms yet young and fair,
And the dancing light of happy eyes,
And smiles like the rosy morning skies
Saw ye and heard? and would ye not know
What made such mirth and music flow?

There were maidens five, as blithe and free
As the curbless waves of the open sea:
They met;—ye may liken their early greeting
To the dewdrops on a rose-leaf meeting;
Then many a day flew uncounted by,
With Love like an angel hovering nigh,
While the ruby light of his sparkling wing
Flung a tint of joy on everything.
'In books, or works, or healthful play,'
As the merriest lips would often say,
Or in strange attempts to weave a spell
Which might bid the Muses among them dwell,
Or in a stream of mingled song,

Some of their hours have passed along;
Bearing the sound of each pleasant lay,
And the echo of many a laugh, away.
    When the burning day is on the wane,
They wander through some darkening lane,
In quieter converse lingering awhile
'Neath the arching roof of its shadowy aisle.
    Where the latest sunbeams kiss the brow
Of Malvern's Beacon, see them now;
Springing o'er moss-bed, and rock, and stone,
As though the green earth were all their own;
And singing forth to the fair wide scene,
In a loyal chorus, '*God save the Queen!*'
    Again, from out the busy street,
They pass with gladly reverent feet
Within the old cathedral's shade;
And feel the sacred silence laid
Upon the lips, upon the heart,
By time and place thus 'set apart.'
Then the anthem fills the glorious fane,[1]
Till its solemn tones float back again,
Round arch and column the sound enwreathing,
Till they seem with holy music breathing,—
Music and love; while the choral praise
Images better and holier days.
    Yet once again;—with low bent head,
They are kneeling where the Feast is spread;
Not one is absent, all are there,
Its silent blessedness to share.
Well may a bond of love be felt,
When thus together they have knelt.

Would ye know the maidens five, oh say?
The meek, the merry, the grave, the gay:
Each jewel of all the sunlit cluster
Shines with its own unborrowed lustre;—
Then listen and gaze, while each shall pass,
As a half-seen vision in magic glass.

---

[1] fane: temple

I.

A quiet summer evening, when the daybeams' heat and glare
Have passed away, and coolness comes upon the cloudless air,
And the soft grey twilight wakes the stars to glisten o'er the hill,
And the only vesper-chime is rung by one low-murmuring rill:

Like such an evening is the soul of that one dark-eyed maid,
Amid earth's restless turmoil like a calm and pleasant shade;
So soothing and so gently sweet her words of deep love fall
Upon the wearied spirit, like the ringdove's forest call.

Well hath she learnt to sympathize with every hope and fear,
Well hath she learnt the sorrowing heart to brighten and to cheer;
Long years of weary weakness have not passed away in vain,
If the holy art of sympathy they taught her to attain.

Her fairy footstep falleth as a noiseless flake of snow,
So violet-like and still that we her presence hardly know;
But like a gleaming vessel-path, far glittering through the night,
She leaves a memory behind of soft and silvery light.

Within the crystal cavern of retirement ye find
That gem of inward radiance, her 'meek and quiet' mind;
Not like the flashing topaz, or the ruby's gorgeous glow,
She is a precious AMETHYST, whose value well we know.

II.

Now turn we to that merry maiden,
With azure eye, and smooth bright hair;
A lily blossom, fragrance-laden,
    Is not more fair.

A dewdrop to the thirsty flower,
A sun-ray gilding every cloud,
A rainbow when the thunder-shower
    Is rushing loud;

A spirit full of pleasant brightness,
That speaks from lip, and cheek, and brow,
To whose glad spell of cheering lightness
    E'en grief must bow.

Her hand hath learnt with wondrous power
Scenes of rare loveliness to trace,
And picture forms with airy dower
    Of beauteous grace.

The breath of flattery hath not tainted
Her simple thought with pride's dark stain:
Because her leaves are richly painted,
    Is the rose vain?

Then, as an orient EMERALD shining,
Long may her loveliness be set
Among the sister-gems, entwining
    Our coronet.

III.

Say, who shall form the vision-centre now?
She of the large, soft eye, and pensive smile,
She of the earnest gaze, and thoughtful brow:
Who would not love to read her looks awhile,
Or list that often silent voice, whose flow
Like distant waterfall is heard, so sweet and low?

Not many summers o'er her youth have cast
Their varying sun and shade, and we might deem
No breath of sadness o'er her soul had passed,
But for that orb subdued, like some lone stream,
Where the sad willows rest in shadowy love,
While its blue depth reflects the sunlit heaven above.

All calmness, yet deep sorrow she hath known,
Dimming the star of hope which shone so clear,
The song of life hath changed its joyous tone,
The pearl of life hath melted to a tear;
But star and song shall rise in brighter day,
And hers that priceless Pearl which none may take away.

Her sorrow, all unspoken, doth but twine
Our earnest love more changelessly around her;
While we look onward, upward, for the time
When Joy's fair garland shall again have crowned her,

Who as the PEARL of all our wreath is gleaming,
In mild and moonlit radiance softly 'mid us beaming.

IV.

Like a flash of meteor light,
Strangely gladdening and bright,
Is the youngest of the band,
Making every heart expand.

Like a petrel on the wave,
What to her though tempests rave?
She will skim each foamy crest,
Making all around her blest.

Like a song-bird of the spring,
She is ever on the wing;
Carolling in blithest glee,
Like the wild breeze, fresh and free.

Like a beautiful gazelle
Bounding over hill and dell;
Like the scented hawthorn-flowers,
Ever scattering blossom-showers.

Can a star of light be found,
Shedding aught but light around?
Joy and gladness must be nigh,
Where her starry pinions fly.

Clear and open as the day,
All may trust her glancing ray,
All must love its rainbow light:
Is she not a DIAMOND bright?

V.

And the last maiden,—what is she?
She sees not herself as others see,
  From an outward point of view;
She only knows the scenes within,
The weary conflict, and the sin,

The strivings a better life to win,
    And the gleams of gladness too.

But little she knows of the secret cells,
Where in lonely twilight the spirit dwells
    In an ever mysterious home,
Where music, and beauty, and sweet perfume,
Grim storms, and the blackness of the tomb,
In morning brightness, and midnight gloom,
    In an untracked labyrinth roam.

How many a chamber within is sealed!
How wondrous the little that is revealed
    In a scarce-caught whispering tone!
Strange thoughts come forth to her outer gaze,
Wild fancies flash with spectral rays,
And feelings glow with uncertain blaze;
    But their fountain is all unknown.

Ah! she would long to glean a ray
From each lovely gem of this summer lay,
    For her own are faint and few.
The tremulous OPAL's changeful light
May emblem her, now dark, now bright,
Yet blending in love with each sister sprite
    In a union fond and true.

———

Such are the five, as now they seem
In the golden haze of Memory's dream.
But the future! who may lift the veil
And read its yet unwritten tale!
The rose, or the thorn, the sun, the cloud,
The gleeful heart, or the spirit bowed,
The song of joy, or the wail of woe,
Which shall be theirs, we may not know.
Then sorrow and joy alike we leave
    In the Hand which doeth all things well,
And calmly from that Hand receive
    All that each coming year may tell.

Our jewel-garland lives by Him;
    We would not ask of Life or Death,
Who first shall break its shining rim;
    It shall be as the Master saith:
He only shall untwine the bond,
So fair and faithful, fresh and fond.
But oh that each who glistens now
    In this verse-woven coronet,
Upon the Saviour's thorn-wreathed brow
    May as a living gem be set!
Then never shall their light grow dim;
Redeemed and sanctified by Him,
Their life and love in blended rays
Shall shine in everlasting praise.

My Name [1]

FROM childish days I never heard
    My own baptismal name;
Too small, too slight, too full of glee
Aught else but 'Little Fan' to be,
The stately 'Frances' not in me
    Could any fitness claim.

Now, in the crowded halls of life,
    May it be mine to bring
Some gentle stir of the heated air,
Some coolness falling fresh and fair,
    Like a passing angel's wing.

My father's name,—oh how I love
    Its else unwonted look!
For his dear sake right dear I hold
Each letter, changed, as he has told,
Long since from early Saxon mould—
    'The rising of the brook.' [2]

---

[1] Suggested by the question, 'What does the letter R in your initials (F. R. H.) represent?'
[2] 'Heavergill'—the heaving or rising of the brook, or gill.

Of music, holiness, and love
  That name will always tell,
While sacred chant and anthem rise,
Or mourners live whose deepest sighs
To echoes of a Father's will
He tuned, or child, or grandchild still
  On his bright memory dwell.

But 'what the R doth represent,'
  I value and revere;
A diamond clasp it seems to be
On golden chains enlinking me
In loyal love to England's hope,
Bulwark 'gainst infidel and Pope,
  The Church I hold so dear.

Three hundred years ago was one
  Who held with stedfast hand
That chalice of the truth of God,
And poured its crystal stream abroad
  Upon the thirsting land.

The moderate, the wise, the calm,
  The learned, brave, and good, [1]
A guardian of the sacred ark,
A burning light in places dark,
For cruel, changeless Rome a mark,
  Our Bishop RIDLEY stood.

The vengeance of that foe nought else
  But fiery doom could still:
Too surely fell the lightning stroke
Upon that noble English oak,
Whose acorn-memory survives
In forest ranks of earnest lives,
  And martyr-souls in will.

---

[1] 'A man beautified with such excellent qualities, so ghostly inspired and godly learned, and now written doubtless in the book of life with the blessed saints of the Almighty, crowned and throned amongst the glorious company of martyrs.'—*Foxe's Acts and Monuments.*

Rome offered life for faith laid down:
　　Such ransom paid not he!
'As long as breath is in this frame,
My Lord and Saviour Christ His name
And His known truth I'll not deny:'
He said (and raised his head on high),
　　'God's will be done in me.'[1]

He knelt and prayed, and kissed the stake,
　　And blessed his Master's name
That he was called His cross to take,
And counted worthy for His sake
　　To suffer death and shame.[2]

Though fierce the fire and long the pain,
　　The martyr's God was nigh;
Till from that awful underglow
Of torture terrible and slow,
Above the weeping round about,
Once more the powerful voice rang out
　　His Saviour's own last cry.

Oh faithful unto death! the crown
　　Was shining on thy brow,
Before the ruddy embers paling,
And sobbing after-gusts of wailing
Had died away, and left in silence
That truest shrine of British Islands,
　　That spot so sacred now!

In dear old England shineth yet
　　The candle lit that day;
Right clear and strong its flames arise,
Undimmed, unchanged, toward the skies,
By God's good grace it never dies,
　　A living torch for aye.

---

[1] See Works of Bishop Ridley, Parker Society, pp. 295 and 296.

[2] Ibid.

'Tis said that while he calmly stood
  And waited for the flame,
He gave each trifle that he had,
True relic-treasure, dear and sad,
  To each who cared to claim.
I was not there to ask a share,
But reverently for ever wear
  That noble martyr's *name*.

Faith and Reason.

REASON unstrings the harp to see
  Wherein the music dwells;
Faith pours a Hallelujah song,
  And heavenly rapture swells.
While Reason strives to count the drops
  That lave our narrow strand,
Faith launches o'er the mighty deep,
  To see a better land.

One is the foot that slowly treads
  Where darkling mists enshroud;
The other is the wing that cleaves
  Each heaven-obscuring cloud.
Reason, the eye which sees but that
  On which its glance is cast;
Faith is the thought that blends in one
  The Future and the Past.

In hours of darkness, Reason waits,
  Like those in days of yore,
Who rose not from their night-bound place,
  On dark Egyptian shore.
But Faith more firmly clasps the hand
  Which led her all the day,
And when the wished for morning dawns,
  Is farther on her way.

By Reason's alchemy in vain
　　Is golden treasure planned;
Faith meekly takes a priceless crown,
　　Won by no mortal hand.
While Reason is the labouring oar
　　That smites the wrathful seas,
Faith is the snowy sail spread out
　　To catch the freshening breeze.

Reason, the telescope that scans
　　A universe of light;
But Faith, the angel who may dwell
　　Among those regions bright.
Reason, a lonely towering elm,
　　May fall before the blast;
Faith, like the ivy on the rock,
　　Is safe in clinging fast.

While Reason, like a Levite, waits
　　Where priest and people meet,
Faith, by a ' new and living way,'
　　Hath gained the mercy-seat.
While Reason but returns to tell
　　That this is not our rest,
Faith, like a weary dove, hath sought
　　A gracious Saviour's breast.

Yet both are surely precious gifts
　　From Him who leads us home;
Though in the wilds Himself hath trod
　　A little while we roam.
And, linked within the soul that knows
　　A living, loving Lord,
Faith strikes the key-note, Reason then
　　Fills up the full-toned chord.

Faith is the upward-pointing spire
　　O'er life's great temple springing,
From which the chimes of love float forth
　　Celestially ringing;

While Reason stands below upon
    The consecrated ground,
And, like a mighty buttress, clasps
    The wide foundation round.

Faith is the bride that stands enrobed
    In white and pure array;
Reason, the handmaid who may share
    The gladness of the day.
Faith leads the way, and Reason learns
    To follow in her train;
Till, step by step, the goal is reached
    And death is glorious gain.

Lynton.

WHY does it seem familiar ground?
    I was never here before;
I never saw this fairy dream
Of wood and wave, of rock and stream,
Nor watched the snowy foam-line gleam
    On Devon's bay-loved shore.

It feels as weird and strange as though
    My spirit had been here;
And in the mists of long ago
An outline wavers to and fro,
Now colourless, now all aglow,
    Now faint, now wondrous clear.

I know it now—the tender spell
    On all this pleasant scene;
For memory's first pale flickering light
Falls on a long-forgotten night,
Though conscious lifetime, dark and bright,
    Lies all outstretched between.

The dearest name I ever spoke
    Was on my lips that eve;

We gave her 'welcome home' once more,
Unknown, the last short absence o'er;
And now, she is but 'gone before'
    The palm-branch to receive.

I know it now,—*she* told me all;
    I sat upon her knee,
And heard about the cliff so tall,
The craggy path, the rocky wall,
The ever-chanting waterfall,
    The silver autumn sea:

The steep and dangerous way above,
    The winding dell beneath;
The rushing Lyn, the shadowy trees,
The hills that breast the Channel-breeze,
The white ships bound for western seas;
    One shining marvel-wreath!

A little picture she had brought
    Of Lynton's lovely vale:
I fastened it upon my wall,
Half deeming I had seen it all;
While colours came at fancy's call
    To deck those outlines pale.

Hers then the charm, so strangely sweet,
    Which made me sit and gaze;
'Tis like a breeze from far-off hills,
Or midnight anthem of wild rills,
That cools the fever-fire which fills
    Our hot and hurried days.

It may be that the parting time
    Has more than half gone by,
That ere another twenty years
Have mingled all their smiles and tears,
We may have passed all griefs and fears,
And her dear welcome greet our ears
    To her blest home on high.

Oh, might it be! That far-off land
  Is all unseen as yet:
But when we pass its portals fair,
It may be that some glory there
Sweetly familiar shall appear,
Because we heard it whispered here
By that soft voice, whose accents dear
  We never can forget.

A Birthday Greeting to My Father.

1860

'Tis fully known to ONE, by us yet dimly seen,
  The blessing thou HAST BEEN;
Yet speaks the silent love of many a mourning heart
  The blessing that thou ART;
While traced on coming years, in faith and hope we see,
  'A blessing thou SHALT BE';
Then here in holy labour, there in holier rest,
  BLESSING, thou SHALT BE BLESSED.

A Lull in Life.

'And He said unto them, Come ye yourselves apart into a desert place, and
rest awhile: for there were many coming and going, and they had no leisure so
much as to eat.'—MARK 6:31.

OH for 'a desert place' with only the Master's smile!
Oh for the 'coming apart' with only His 'rest awhile!'
Many are 'coming and going' with busy and restless feet,
And the soul is hungering now, with 'no leisure so much as to eat.'

Dear is my wealth of love from many and valued friends,
Best of the earthly gifts that a bounteous Father sends;
Pleasant the counsel sweet, and the interchange of thought,
Welcome the twilight hour with musical brightness fraught.

Dear is the work He gives in many a varied way,
Little enough in itself, yet something for every day,—
Something by pen for the distant, by hand or voice for the near,
Whether to soothe or teach, whether to aid or cheer.

Not that I lightly prize the treasure of valued friends,
Not that I turn aside from the work the Master sends,
Yet I have longed for a pause in the rush and whirl of time,
Longed for silence to fall instead of its merriest chime:

Longed for a hush to group the harmonies of thought
Round each melodious strain that the harp of life hath caught,
And time for the fitful breeze Æolian chords to bring,
Waking the music that slept, mute in the tensionless string:

Longed for a calm to let the circles die away
That tremble over the heart, breaking the heavenly ray,
And to leave its wavering mirror true to the Star above,
Brightened and stilled to its depths with the quiet of 'perfect love':

Longed for a sabbath of life, a time of renewing of youth,
For a full-orbed leisure to shine on the fountains of holy truth;
And to fill my chalice anew with its waters fresh and sweet,
While resting in silent love at the Master's glorious feet.

There are songs which only flow in the loneliest shades of night,
There are flowers which cannot grow in a blaze of tropical light,
There are crystals which cannot form till the vessel be cooled and stilled;
Crystal, and flower, and song, given as God hath willed.

There is work which cannot be done in the swell of a hurrying tide,
But my hand is not on the helm to turn my bark aside;
Yet I cast a longing eye on the hidden and waveless pool,
Under the shadowing rock, currentless, clear, and cool.

Well! I will wait in the crowd till He shall call me apart,
Till the silence fall which shall waken the music of mind and heart;
Patiently wait till He give the work of my secret choice,
Blending the song of life with the thrill of the Master's voice.

Adoration.

O MASTER, at Thy feet
I bow in rapture sweet!
Before me, as in darkening glass,
Some glorious outlines pass,
Of love, and truth, and holiness, and power;
I own them Thine, O Christ, and bless Thee for this hour.

O full of truth and grace,
Smile of Jehovah's face,
O tenderest heart of love untold!
Who may Thy praise unfold?
Thee, Saviour, Lord of lords and King of kings,
Well may adoring seraphs hymn with veiling wings.

I have no words to bring
Worthy of Thee, my King,
And yet one anthem in Thy praise
I long, I long to raise;
The heart is full, the eye entranced above,
But words all melt away in silent awe and love.

How can the lip be dumb,
The hand all still and numb,
When Thee the heart doth see and own
Her Lord and God alone?
Tune for Thyself the music of my days,
And open Thou my lips that I may show Thy praise.

Yea, let my whole life be
One anthem unto Thee,
And let the praise of lip and life
Outring all sin and strife.
O Jesus, Master! be Thy name supreme
For heaven and earth the one, the grand, the eternal theme.

" WHAT I DO, THOU KNOWEST NOT NOW, BUT THOU SHALT KNOW HEREAFTER."

We shall know why the Cross was so hard
    to bear,
In the day when the Crowns are won ;
Why the "marching time" was so long
    and sore,
In the Land where the march is done !

We shall know why the Master came in
    the night,
And called us to follow Him ;
Up the blood-stained Way, amid storm
    and blast,
Where the shadows were long and dim !

We shall know why the Lord oft hid His Face,
And left us so sad and lone ;
In the Land, where the soul will in
    rapture gaze,
On the Blessed Three in One !

We shall know, why our streams of
    earthly joy,
So often ceased their flow ;
In the Land, where the River of Life
    rolls on,
'Neath the beams of the " *Emerald Bow !* "

We shall know why the Shepherd leads
    His flock,
O'er a barren and lonely way ;
In the Land, where the " *shadows* " can
    fall no more,
In the Land of Unclouded Day !

Harriet Kinnaway.

This poem by Harriet Kinnaway was found among Havergal manuscripts and pa-
pers. See F.R.H.'s poem "Not Yet" on pages 16–17 of this book.

Early Poems

'I Leave It All with Thee.'

YES, I will leave it all with Thee,
And only ask that I may be
Submissive to Thy loving will,
Confiding, waiting, trusting still.
Thou every fond desire dost know
Which in my inmost heart doth glow;
Thou hearest every secret sigh
When silent sorrow's power is nigh.
Omniscience alone may tell
The thoughts which in my spirit dwell;
But 'tis a soothing word to me,
'My Father every thought can see.'
He knows them all—the hopes—the fears—
Confided not to mortal ears.
He knows the deep intensity
Of feelings wakened now in me.
And if He knows them, 'tis enough!
I need not fear a stern rebuff;
There's sympathy within His breast,
On which my weary heart can rest.
Nor is there sympathy alone,
Almighty is my Father's throne,
And He can grant me each desire;
His gracious hand may never tire.
He *can*. But *will* He? Trust Him yet,
My faithless soul! Can I forget
That He hath passed His word of old—
'Not one good thing will He withhold
From them, the children of My love,
Whose hearts are set on things above'?
Not one good thing! But can I see
What may be good, what ill for me?

Can I unbar the massy gate
Which hides from me the way I take?
But His eye turneth night to day,
E'en like the lightning's piercing ray;
Then here is my security,
That God my truest good doth see.
That joy which earnestly I crave,
O'er which my fondest hopes now wave,
Might prove to me the shade of death!
That healing breeze—the Simoom's breath,[1]
If so—it never will be mine.
At such a loss shall I repine?
No! let me rather praise the Hand
Which looseneth the dangerous band.
But if it be a heaven-born plant,
For whose sweet flowers my soul doth pant
If heavenly gladness it shall bring,
And raise my soul on angel wing,
Till nearer Thee each day I live,—
Oh, then that blessing Thou wilt give.
The joy scarce hoped for shall be mine,
A deeply grateful heart be Thine!
Then I will leave it all with Thee!
My Father, grant that I may be
Submissive to Thine own good will,
Confiding, waiting, loving still!

Matthew 14:23.

IT is the quiet evening time, the sun is in the west,
And earth enrobed in purple glow awaits her nightly rest;
The shadows of the mountain peaks are lengthening o'er the sea,
And the flowerets close their eyelids on the shore of Galilee.
The multitude are gone away, their restless hum doth cease,
The birds have hushed their music, and all is calm and peace;
But on the lowly mountain side is One, whose beauteous brow
The impress bears of sorrow and of weariness e'en now.
The livelong day in deeds of love and power He hath spent,
And with them words of grace and life hath ever sweetly blent.

---

[1] Simoom: a deadly, hot, dry wind in the Sahara, Arabia, and parts of the Middle East. This violent wind, arising quickly and unpredictably from mid-June to mid-August, blows sand, is very hot and dry, and kills whatever is in its path.

Now He hath gained the mountain top, He standeth all alone,
No mortal may be near Him in that hour of prayer unknown.
He prayeth.—But for whom? For Himself He needeth nought;
Nor strength, nor peace, nor pardon, where of sin there is no spot;
But 'tis for us in powerful prayer He spendeth all the night,
That His own loved ones may be kept and strengthened in the fight;
That they may all be sanctified, and perfect made in one;
That they His glory may behold where they shall need no sun;
That in eternal gladness they may be His glorious bride:
It is for this that He hath climbed the lonely mountain side.
It is for this that He denies His weary head the rest
Which e'en the foxes in their holes, and birds have in their nest.
The echo of that prayer hath died upon the rocky hill,
But on a higher, holier mount that Voice is pleading still;
For while one weary child of His yet wanders here below,
While yet one thirsting soul desires His peace and love to know,
And while one fainting spirit seeks His holiness to share,
The Saviour's loving heart shall pour a tide of mighty prayer;
Yes! till each ransomed one hath gained His home of joy and peace,
That Fount of Blessings all untold shall never, never cease.

Matthew 26:30.

'And when they had sung an hymn, they went out.'

THE sun hath gilded Judah's hills
    With his last gorgeous beam;
Ghost-like the still grey mists arise
    From Jordan's sacred stream.
The stars, bright flowers of the sky,
    Unfold their beauties now,
And gaze on Salem's marble fane,[1]
    By Olivet's dark brow.
In David's city sound is hushed
    And tread of busy feet,
For solemnly his sons have met
    The paschal lamb to eat.
But list! the silence of the hour
    Is broken; the still air

[1] fane: temple

A melody hath caught which far
    Its viewless pinions bear.
Unwonted sweetness hath the strain,
    And as its numbers flow,
More tender and more touching yet
    Its harmony doth grow.
Not royal David's tuneful harp
    Such thrilling power had known
To wake deep echoes in the soul,
    As its scarce earthly tone.
Within an 'upper room' are met
    A small, yet faithful band,
On whom a deep yet chastened grief
    Hath laid its softening hand.
Among them there is One who wears
    A more than mortal mien,
'Tis He on whom in all distress
    The weary one may lean.
Mysterious sadness, on that brow
    So pure and calm, doth lie;
And untold stores of deepest love
    Are beaming from His eye.
What wonder if the strain was sweet
    Above all other lays?
Seraphic well might seem the hymn
    Which Jesu's voice did raise.
The angels hush their lyres, and bend
    To hear the thrilling tone,
And heaven is silent,—with that song
    They mingle not their own.
The sorrowing ones around have heard
    Their blessèd Master tell,
That He with them no longer now
    As heretofore may dwell.
And they have sadly shared with Him
    The last, last evening meal,
And heard the last sweet comfort which
    Their mourning hearts may heal.
They do not know the fearful storm
    Which on His head must burst;

They know not all—He hath not told
   His loving ones the worst.
How could He? E'en an angel's mind
   Could never comprehend
The weight of woe, 'neath which for us
   The Saviour's head must bend;
Ere long the voice, which waketh now
   Such touching melody,
Shall cry, 'My God, My God, oh why
   Hast Thou forsaken Me?'
The hour is come; but ere they meet
   Its terrors,—yet once more
Their voices blend with His who sang
   As none e'er sang before.
Why do they linger on that note?
   Why thus the sound prolong?
Ah! 'twas the last! 'Tis ended now,
   That strangely solemn song.
And forth they go:—the song is past;
   But, like the rose-leaf, still,
Whose fragrance doth not die away,
   Its soft low echoes thrill
Through many a soul, and there awake
   New strains of glowing praise
To Him who, on that fateful eve,
   That last sweet hymn did raise.

'Leaving Us an Example, that Ye Should Follow His Steps.'

O Jesu, Thou didst leave Thy glorious home,
   Of brightness more than mortal eye could bear,
And joys ineffable, alone to roam
Through earth's dark wilderness in grief and want and care.
   Thou didst exchange the praise of seraph voices
   For sin-made discords and the wail of pain,
The anthems swelling high where each in Thee rejoices
For fierce revilings in the world where unbelief doth reign.

Yes, Thou didst leave Thy bliss-encircled dwelling,
    Of joy and holiness and perfect love,
And camest to this world of sorrow, telling
    Each weary one the way to realms of rest above.
Mark we Thy walk along the holy way,—
    Each step is graven, that all the path may trace
Which leads where Thou art gone,—and never may
    The powers of darkness one bright step erase!
And Thou hast left a solemn word behind Thee,
    Solemn, yet fraught with blessing;—would we learn
How we may gain Thy dwelling, and there find Thee?
    Thou sayest, 'Follow Me.' Be this our great concern
And oh how blessèd thus to mark each hour
    The footsteps of our Saviour, and to know
That in them we are treading,—then each flower
Of hope seems fairer, and each joy doth yet more brightly glow.
    Oh that I always followed Him alone!
        I know that I am His, for I have bowed
In peaceful faith before my Saviour's throne,
    And gladly there to Him my life, my all, have vowed.
And He hath pardoned me, and washed away
    Each stain of guilt, and bade me quickly rise
And follow Him each moment of each day;
And He hath set a crown of life and joy before mine eyes.
    How can I turn aside and wound the love
        That gave Himself to bleed and die for me!
How can I stray, and grieve the holy Dove
    Who lights my soul, opening mine eyes to see!
O Saviour, fix my wayward, wandering heart
    Upon Thyself, that I may closely cling
To Thy blest side, and never more depart
From Thee, my loved Redeemer, Thee, my heart's own King.
    And grant me daily grace to follow Thee
        Through joy and pleasure, or through grief and sadness,
Until an entrance is vouchsafed to me
    In Thy bright home of holiness and gladness.

Our English Sabbaths.

O ENGLAND, thou art beautiful, and very dear to me,
And the spirit of thy noble sons is high and pure and free;
Full many a jewel sparkles clear in the crown upon thy brow,
But *one* is gleaming fairest in that glorious garland now.

It gleameth with a holy light, too pure for sinful earth,
In the twilight of this shadow-land it hath not had its birth;
'Tis polished by no mortal hand, its radiance is its own,
And it mingleth with the glory of the Father's dazzling throne.

Oh, gaze upon its beauty, reflecting yet the light
Of Eden's spotless, shadeless hours, in this our sin-made night;
Oh, gaze again, and thou shalt see, in that all-beauteous ray,
A gleam of that celestial morn which ne'er may fade away!

It is a gem of untold worth, it is a golden mine,
The pledge of an inheritance,—a gift of love Divine;
A monarch may not buy it,—oh, then let it not be sold!
Oh, England, dear old England, this, thy priceless treasure, hold!

Thy Sabbath is this treasure, a fount of ceaseless blessing,
And thou art rich and powerful, this glorious gift possessing;
Oh, heed not those who craftily would bid thee cast away
The diamond hours of Sabbath rest, no pleasure can repay.

There is a cloud o'er other lands, though fair their mountains be,
And beautiful their sunny plains, re-echoing with glee;
But on our Sabbath-loving heart it casts a saddening gloom,
While the mirth of all their songs is as the music of the tomb.

They know no holy Sabbath rest; and yet, above, around,
The trees are waving solemnly with a deep and holy sound;
And the flowers smile to greet His day, and the streams more softly roll,
And all things speak of God to the silent listening soul.

They heed it not! with song and glee the hallowed hours are passed;
The blessings which the Sabbath brings, aside are lightly cast;
And 'neath the sparkling wavelets of unsanctified delight
Is a dark, deep stream of weary toil from morn to welcome night.

There are some who listen eagerly while told of Sabbath rest,
As a thirsting desert pilgrim hears of Araby the blest;
'Mid their changeless seven days' labour they drop a hopeless tear,
'Oh, would to God that we might have an English Sabbath here!'

Sad is their lot! but there are those within our own dear land
Who would forge for us such fetters, and burst our golden band,
Who sin in deeper bondage yet, while striving to be free
And know not that our Father's law is truest Liberty!

Colossians 3:2.

WHY do we cling to earth? Its sweetest pleasures
Are transient as the snowflake of the spring;
Like early mist its most abiding treasures,
Or foam of ocean wave. To earth why do we cling?

Why do we cling to earth? Is it the fleeting brightness
Of her gay robes? fair fields, green forest trees,
Grand mountains, lovely dells, or gleaming whiteness
Of silent snow? To heavenly beauties what are these?

Lovely, most lovely are earth's radiant flowers,
Her very smiles of joy, aye chasing gloom;
But soon they wither in her happiest bowers:
In heaven doth the Rose of Sharon ever bloom!

And beautiful the gleaming wavelet dancing,
And wild cascade, rejoicing to be free,
And pure, cool fountains through the green shades glancing:
In heaven the living streams well forth eternally!

Most glorious is the glowing sun on high,
The moon's soft brilliance crowning the still night,
The million starry diamonds of the sky:
In heaven is God Himself the source of perfect light!

Sweet is earth's music! whether o'er us stealeth
The lyre's calm melody, or blackbird's untaught lay,
Or harmony through shadowy aisles full pealeth:
In heaven new songs of rapture angel harps essay!

What though the eastern monarch's robes are gleaming
With gold and orient gems, each gorgeous hue
With more than rainbow brightness in them beaming;
The robes of heaven are woven light, and ever new.

All these are beautiful; and we may love them
As His good gifts; but oh! they pass away:
Then cling not to them; seek, far, far above them
The joys ineffable, which fade not, nor decay.

But cling we to earth's honours? What delusion!
Immortal souls they ne'er may satisfy;
How mean, how small e'en tenfold their profusion
Beside heaven's glorious crown and palm of victory.

Hath love of knowledge cast her fetters o'er us?
Here we know nothing! But in heaven's bright day
The lore of ages will be spread before us,—
Yes, of eternity! illumed with truth's pure ray.

Have we dear friends our fond affections chaining
To scenes of earth? But they *may* change, *must* die.
In heaven the purest love is ever reigning,
Far more abiding than the pillars of the sky.

Do we seek happiness? No mirage fleeteth
More quickly than all happiness below,—
But oh! no heart may dream the joy which meeteth
The soul which wakes in heaven, its bliss here none can know.

Is holiness our heart's intense desire?
Then every glance from earth must turn away.
In heaven all sinless is each voice, each lyre;
Heaven's holiness is perfect, endless as its day.

Yes, beauty, light, and music are above;
There honour, wisdom, knowledge, all are given;
There is the home of friendship and of love,
And happiness and holiness, twin flowers of heaven.

But more, far more than all! 'Tis God's own dwelling,
Thrice blessèd thought! ever with Him to be!
Eternity would be too short for telling
The bliss of even one unveilèd glimpse of Thee.

To see, and know, and love, and praise for ever
The Saviour who hath died that we might live,
Where sorrow, pain, and death may enter never!
And ever learn new cause new songs of praise to give!

Oh, what a prospect! How, how can we cling
To earth's dark dream, when such a hope is given?
Oh may we from this hour, on faith-plumed wing,
No longer cling to earth, but soar to yon bright heaven!

Clouds in Prospect.

Oh pleasant have the hours of my early childhood been,
When all around me seemed enrobed in brightly glittering sheen;
When a thousand rainbow tints were in every simple flower,
And a thousand new delights came with every sunny hour;
When I thought the merry birds trilled their carols all for me,
And with heart and voice I joined in their joyous melody;
When all heedless of the darkening storm, I loved the purple cloud,
And listened with delight to the thunder pealing loud.
In those happy days of childhood, I did not think or see
That many trials might be waiting even then for me;
But now, though yet I meet them not, I know that they must stand
In many a varied shape and form, unseen on every hand.
As yet from heavy troubles, thank God, I have been free;
Oh, surely there are few who have what is vouchsafed to me!
But one eclipse hath shadowed o'er my childhood's sunny hours,
And now its sharpness seemeth past, that thorn 'mid many flowers.
But still the saddening feeling cometh oftener than before,
That many a future sorrow e'en for me may be in store;
For all around me seem to have some wearying care or grief,
From which they scarcely dare to hope on earth to find relief.
And my memory loves to dwell upon the merry careless hours,
When I thought the world a thornless garden full of lovely flowers.

Earth's Shadow.

I HAVE but passed the first short stage
Of life, and yet I'm growing weary;
For every step towards riper age
The way becomes more dreary.

I look behind;—few years ago
The world seemed full of fairy flowers,—
I loved them; for I did not know
How sin pervades Earth's loveliest bowers.

Like Italy's fair sunny vales
With unknown deathly vapours teeming—
Or like Sahara's sand-charged gales
Beneath a sun unclouded beaming,—

Such is our Earth. Roam where you will,
Seems loveliness the eye entrancing;
The silent glen, the breezy hill,
The sun-tipped wavelet blithely dancing.

But gaze again. Each zephyr's breath
Uplifts a veil, dark truths revealing;
For all is stained with sin, and death
The fairest buds is grimly sealing.

That sense of sin! It casts a cloud
O'er all Earth's scenes of glee and pleasure:
Is nought then pure amid her crowd
Of joys? nought spotless of her treasure?

Nought, nought! cries Echo. How I love
The spirit which to me is given!
My priceless gem, my cherished dove,
My sweetest, dearest gift of heaven.

How oft I've sought for solace in
My own loved soul in hours of sadness;
Oh, how I love it! It has been
My more than friend, my fount of gladness.

But oh, 'tis sinful! Even here
My simple joy and love are ending;
How can the mind to me be dear
Where sin with every thought is blending?

If e'en my Eden is not pure,
How *can* my heart's love rest below?
Say, will the passage-bird endure
To tarry 'mid the northern snow?

It cannot rest! Like early dew
A pure warm Sun hath called it higher
Where sin is not; where, holy too,
E'en *I* may tune a sinless lyre.

Aspirations.

Oн to be nearer Thee, my Saviour,
  Oh to be filled with Thy sweet grace,
Oh to abide in Thine own favour,
  Oh to behold Thy glorious face.

Oh to be ever upward gazing,
  Glad with the sunshine of Thy love;
Oh to be ever, ever praising,
  Echoing here the songs above.

Oh to be never, never weary
  E'en in the dark affray of sin;
Oh to press on through conflicts dreary,
  One of Thine own dear smiles to win.

Oh to desire to spread Thy glory,
  Seeking it as my only aim;
Oh to be taught Thy strange sweet story
  Worthily, fully to proclaim.

Oh to go onward, self forgetting,
  Willing to take the lowest place;
Oh to go upward, never letting
  Pride of the heart my glance abase.

Oh to become each day more lowly,
    More of Thine own blest image gain;
Oh to be made, as Thou art, holy,
    Oh to be freed from sin's dread chain.

Oh to be listening every hour
    The more than music of Thy voice;
Feeling its soothing quickening power,
    Bidding the silenced heart rejoice!

Sunset.

(Impromptu during a walk with E. Clay.)

How pleasant 'tis at eventide
    To walk with friends we love;
And think and speak of Him who died,
    And who now reigns above.

Is there a subject half so sweet,
    On which our thoughts could dwell?
No, 'tis a theme for angels meet,
    Though we of it may tell.

The beauties that around we see,
    On this calm lovely eve,
Show forth His love to you and me,
    If we this love believe.

The sunset paints the western sky
    With colours fair and bright;
But we will raise our wondering eye
    To scenes of heavenly light.

The clouds that round their monarch stay
    A light and radiance gain;
While those which tarry far away
    Such brightness ne'er attain.

So those who, in this wilderness,
    Still near their Master stay,

The beauty gain of holiness,
    Of heaven's own light a ray.

Now, soon the darkening shades of night
    Will o'er these scenes be thrown,
The sun's last ray of golden light
    Will far away be flown.

Then hasten to our heavenly home,
    That land more fair, more bright;
Where shades of darkness never come,
    Where there is no more night.

The Spirit's Longings.

WHEN the loveliest flowers are waking,
    Whispering thoughts of silent joy,
And the lark, his nest forsaking,
    Carols in the beaming sky;
When her mantle Beauty flings
Over Nature's gladsome things:
Yet the soul it doth not fill,
Something seeks it fairer still.

When the crystal streams are glancing
    From the Fount of Poesy,
Mingling with the all-entrancing
    Sweetness of calm melody:
When the spirit, thirsting long,
Feels the wondrous power of song,
Yet it yearns for something more,
Something which may be in store.

When the heart is warmly glowing
    Toward the dearest ones around,
And, with joyous love o'erflowing,
    Fancies happiness is found,
Softly hushing noisy mirth,
Finds the purest joy of earth;

Even then it must aspire,
Ever seeking something higher.

When the weary spirit turneth
    From the dark low earth away,
And with contrite sorrow mourneth
    Till the shadows flee away;
When the soul on Jesus' breast
Sinks in lowly peaceful rest,—
Then its yearnings all are stilled,
And with perfect bliss 'tis filled.

The Old and the New Earth.

WHEN the first bright dawn of a Sabbath-day
O'er the purple hills of the far east gleamed;
When in pristine loveliness Eden lay,
And the fairest spot of the fair earth seemed;
When the first sweet lay of the nightingale
Rang in liquid music o'er every hill,
And the verdant waste of the new-formed vale
Heard the first wild song of the sparkling rill;
When in first fresh beauty the young flowers stood,
And their leafy banners the trees unfurled;
When the Maker of all called it 'very good,'—
I would I had seen our beautiful world.

When the dwelling bright of the Shining Ones,
The abode of Him who is Love and Light,
Heard the joyous song of God's holy sons,
As the new-born world met their ravished sight;
When the morning stars caught the cadence sweet,
And took up the strain of the heavenly song,
And each bright one joined from his glorious seat
In the chorus swelling so loud and long;
Praising Him who made by His mighty Word
The new earth in beauty and purity;—
I would that the echo I might have heard
Of their thrilling celestial melody.

When in Eden's lovely and thornless bowers,
All unstained by sin, our first parents dwelt;
When on wings of joy flew their sunny hours,
And the touch of sorrow they had not felt;
When their sole companions were seraphs bright,
And their sweetest music the angels' lays;
When a gleam of heaven's own glorious light
Might often meet their enraptured gaze;
When while dwelling here Love was still their guide,
And the dreaded angel, Death, did not wait
To unlock for them heaven's portals wide;—
I would I had shared in their blissful state.

But the time will come, when, all purified
From its ev'ry spot by a fiery flood,
Our earth shall hear, as recedes the tide
Once again the words, 'It is *very good.*'
When the song of the stars shall be heard again
O'er their sister joying, the holy earth;
When the purest love shall for ever reign,
And immortal joys have their blissful birth;
There shall be no sorrow and no more sin,
Pain shall pass away, Death himself shall die,
To that fairer Eden may we go in,
And entering, dwell there eternally.

Thoughts Awakened by Astley Bells.

Sweet Astley bells! your distant chime,
    So tuneful, yet so sad,
Recalls my childhood's earliest time:
    I sigh, and yet am glad.

My thoughts return, on swift unsteady wings,
    Along the trodden path whose misty light
Revealed dim visions of unspoken things,
        Passing, yet bright.
Oh, years have glided by so fast,
That twenty-one have almost past,

And now those softened bells,
  With wondrous spells,
Have called the solemn train of bygone times
Back from Eternity's mysterious chimes.
    They come, a fearful crowd,
        And gaze with spectral eyes;
      Before this witness cloud
          My spirit silent lies:
No sound is there, yet strange wild echoes thrill
The inmost caverns of my soul, where all seemed waste
    and still.

          Scenes arise before me
              Fairer than the light,
          Visions hover o'er me
              Darker than the night;
          While my spirit haileth
              Those with fond delight,
          Yet at these it quaileth,
              Shrouded in affright.
For the past years press me closer round,
    And I cannot bear their gaze;
With a brazen fetter I am bound,
While their deep reproachful voices sound
    And their piercing eyebeams blaze.
They speak of thoughtless words and wasted hours,
    Of hopes forgotten, resolutions broken;
Their breath recalls once bright, now faded flowers,
    Their tones bring back the words which sainted lips
        have spoken.
Again is heard that spirit-wakening bell;
    Each stroke is branding deep my heavy heart,
Like some inevitable knell,
    Saying, 'Thou too must soon depart.'
And 'tis a knell! My youth is past,
    That very chime hath told me so!
This year hath been the last, the last;
    My spring is gone, I know!

The sound hath melted o'er the hill,
 And all is still!
  Again the peal is ringing,
  Like angel voices singing,—
   'May there not be
   A summer yet for thee?
Without the chilling frosts of spring,
 Without the piercing wind,
Without the yet unclothèd spray,
 These thou hast left behind!
What though the rainbow fade away?
 The light which gave it birth
Is still the same; and e'en the cloud
 May bless the thirsty earth.
What though the blossom fall and die?
 The flower is not the root;
A summer's sun may ripen yet
 The Master's pleasant fruit.
What though by many a sinful fall
 Thy garments be defiled?
A Saviour's blood can cleanse them all;
 Fear not, thou art His child!
Arise! to follow in His track,
 His lowly ones to cheer;
And on an upward path, look back
 With every brightening year.
Arise! and on thy future way
 His blessing with thee be,
His presence be thy staff and stay
 Till thou His glory see.
What though thy heart distrust thy strength?
 The way may not be long,
And He will bring thee home at length
 To learn His own new song.'

Sweet Astley bells! your distant chime,
 So tuneful, though so sad,
Speaks of a holier, happier time:
 I sigh, and yet am glad.

'Pray for Me.'

WHEN the early morn awaketh,
    Veiled in mist, or robed in fire;
When the evening ray forsaketh
    Golden cloud and gleaming spire,—
Thy request shall sacred be
In the shrine of memory,
And for thee my prayer shall rise
Far beyond the silent skies.

When the Sabbath calm is sleeping
    Like a moonbeam everywhere;
When the solemn feast-day keeping,
    Upward float our praise and prayer;
When in holy love and fear
To our Father we draw near,—
Many a wingèd hope for thee
To His ear shall wafted be.

When we hear the loud thought-chorus,
    While the Old Year's knell is tolled;
When the Future looms before us,
    And the Past seems all unrolled;
When each moment fleeteth by,
Like a deep mysterious sigh,—
Then, oh then, my heart shall be
Lifted earnestly for thee:

Lifted—that our God may lead thee
    All the way that thou shouldst go,
With His daily manna feed thee,
    Every needful good bestow;
That the dearest ones to thee
Near and dear to Him may be;
That His smile on thee may rest,
In His presence calmly blest:

Lifted—that our holy Saviour
    More and more to thee may show

All the wondrous grace and favour
　　He hath suffered to bestow;
That His love may be thy shield
In Temptation's battle-field;
And His sympathy thy light
In Affliction's darkest night:

That the Comforter, descending
　　In His sanctifying power,
Peace and hope and gladness blending,
　　On thy waiting soul may shower;
That our Triune God may shed
Every blessing on thy head,
Till thou enter in and see
All He hath prepared for thee.

On the Death of Captain Allan Gardiner.

The First Missionary to Patagonia.

In desolate wild grandeur all around,
　　Dark rocky spires are tow'ring to the sky,
While through the caverns echoes far the sound
Of winds, which o'er Antarctic seas sweep fitfully.

The ocean waves with deep and hollow tone
　　Combat the haughty cliffs in fierce affray,
Then back returning with a sullen moan,
Sink, till again they dash, their warrior spray.

No flowerets spring that barren land to cheer,
　　No waving trees salute that stormy sky
With graceful bend; scarce grass and herbs appear,
Or aught of greenery, to soothe the wearied eye.

O who in such a dreary clime could dwell?
　　Who would abide on such a desert shore?
Save the wild natives, who, our sailors tell,
No Saviour know, no Deity supreme adore.

But list awhile! Who breathed that deep-drawn sigh?
    Whence came it? Hark again! A voice of prayer,
  Mingled with heavenly praises, rose on high,
As with sweet incense hallowing the chilly air.

Alone, no earthly friend or brother near,
    A human form lies on that bleak, bleak strand:
  Sunken his eye, and wan his cheeks appear,
For famine pale has laid on him her withering hand.

Nor food nor water six long weary days
    Have passed those pallid lips, yet not a plaint
  From him may fall, but notes of joyful praise;
Sustained with bread of life his soul can never faint:

For Jesus whispers comfort to his soul,
    And smooths his pillow, though so cold and hard;
  He hears no wind, he sees no surges roll,
He only hears his Master, sees his bright reward.

Another sigh, his happy soul hath flown
    From its frail dwelling, where so long it lay
  Pinioned, his painful toils at length are done,
And angels welcome him to dwell in endless day.

Wherefore left he his lovely native isle?
    Wherefore his life, his all thus sacrifice?
  Did he for pleasure undertake such toil?
Was it for sordid gold, which men so highly prize?

No! higher motives filled that noble breast;
    He sacrificed his all from Christian love,
  He went to tell of peace and heavenly rest,
To teach those heathen of a gracious God above.

And shall we blame him, who devoted thus
    To his great Master's name his freshest days?
  Despise that bright example left to us,
And on his memory strive to cast a gloomy haze?

Shame, shame on those who dare aspersions fling
   On Gardiner's honoured name! They know it's true
  Right well he served his Saviour and his King;
And they who love the Master, love the servant too.

But now he rests in peace, his labours past;
   Nothing can vex that noble spirit more,
  For he hath gained his distant port at last,
The waves have only carried him to that blest shore.

No laurels bloomed on that pale dying brow,
   No earthly honours clustered round that bed;
  But victor-wreaths of life encircle now,
And a bright crown adorns, that mission martyr's head!

'Thank God.'

'For nine-and-twenty years the rainbow-pinioned Spring
   Hath kissed the young lips of her smiling flowers;
For nine-and-twenty years hath Autumn's golden ring
   Encircled the fair fruit in all her bowers.

'Yes, nine-and-twenty years have darkly, sadly passed
   Since last the light of heaven 'twas mine to see;
All aid has failed! Thy skill my only hope, my last!
   Good Hofrath, can there yet be hope for me?'

Say, hath a passing angel left in that kind face
   The mirrored image of his own sweet smile,
To the great good man's reverend beauty adding grace?
   It may be so! listen! he speaks awhile.

'There is yet hope for thee! If God vouchsafe to bless,
   Thou yet again may'st see the blessèd summer light!
Though there's a thorny hedge of pain, yet may access
   Be gained thee to thy Eden of glad sight!'

The time is come, the operation o'er; yet he must wait
   One moment longer, with unopened eye,—
The Hofrath writes (oh, what will be his fate?),
   Now, blind one, read!—'Thank God!' his joyous cry.

What words may tell the unknown joy of that glad heart?
    Words cannot paint a bliss so deeply felt;
Like flakes of spring-snow, like the lightning's passing dart,
    Half-formed in glowing happiness they melt.

'Thank God!' Yes, after nine-and-twenty years of night,
    At length awakes for him the radiant day,
And the first word which he doth read with glad new sight
    Is 'Thank God!' Thanks, praise to Him alway!

E'en had the first-seen sunbeam not upborne his mind
    In praise to Him who said, 'Let there be light,'[1]
The Hofrath's beautiful device must surely find
    A deep response, and heavenward turn his sight.

It was a lovely thought, to place the sweet-toned lyre
    At once within the joy-unnervèd hand;
May blessings rest on him, and may the angel choir
    Around him breathe the songs of their bright Fatherland.

[1] An incident at Gräfrath, related by a patient of the skilful oculist, Dr. de Leuve.

The Maidens of England.

ON THE PRESENTATION OF A BIBLE TO THEIR PRINCESS ROYAL.

ERE the pathless ocean waters
    Bear thee far from England's shore,
Come we, England's youthful daughters,
    Warmly greeting thee once more.

Rarest jewels, lustre flinging,
    Grace thy royal diadem;
Yet we come, an offering bringing
    Richer than its richest gem.

While with prayerful love unspoken,
    Princess! glows each maiden heart,
Deign to take this sacred token,
    Brightest lamp and surest chart.

May its holy precepts guide thee
    In each hour of joy or sadness;
Yet may he who stands beside thee
    Share with thee unfading gladness.

Ever on thy pathway shining,
    Living stars 'mid earthly night,
May its peace and grace entwining
    Gird thee with a robe of light.

Rose of England! fragrance breathing,
    To thy far new home depart,
Round thy early bloom enwreathing
    All the love of England's heart.

Be thy gladness ever vernal
    'Mid the wintry scenes below,
Till a crown of life eternal
    Gleams upon thy royal brow!

Father, be Thou ever near her!
    Saviour, fill her with Thy love!
Let Thy constant presence cheer her,
    Joy-imparting Holy Dove!

'No, Not a Star.'

(ANSWER TO A REMARK.)

No, not a *star!* that is a name too beautiful and bright
For any earthly lay to wear, in this our lingering night;
But 'mid the broken waters of our ever-restless thought,
My verse should be an answering gleam from higher radiance caught;
That when through dark o'erarching boughs of sorrow, doubt, and sin,
The glorious Star of Bethlehem upon the flood looks in,
Its tiny trembling ray may bid some downcast vision turn
To that enkindling Light, for which all earthly shadows yearn.

No, not a *rainbow!* though upon the tearful cloud it trace
Sweet messages of sparing love, of changeless truth and grace.

The daughter of its meekest hue I would my verse might prove,
The leaf-veiled violet, that wins so many a childish love;
For little hearts no wounding thorn or poison-cup to bear,
But pleasant fragrance and delight to greet them everywhere.
I grieve not though each blossom fall with swiftly ripening spring,
If o'er one eager face a smile of gladness it may fling.

No, not a *fountain!* though it seem to spread white angel-wings,
And soar aloft in spirit guise, no gentle help it brings;
It lives for its own loveliness alone, then seeks once more
The chilly bosom of the rock it slumbered in before.
Oh, be my verse a hidden stream which silently may flow
Where drooping leaf and thirsty flower in lonely valleys grow;
Till, blending with the broad bright stream of sanctified endeavour,
God's glory be its ocean home, the end it seeketh ever!

"None of self, and all of Thee."

CHRIST.

Galatians ii. 20.

DEMROSE AND SONS, LONDON AND DERBY.
Price 3s. per 100, 5d. per dozen, post free.

THE ALTERED MOTTO.

Oh! the bitter shame and sorrow,
     That a time could ever be
When I let the Saviour's pity
Plead in vain, and proudly answered:
     "All of self, and none of Thee."

Yet He found me; I beheld Him
     Bleeding on the accursed tree,
Heard Him pray: "Forgive them, Father!"
And my wistful heart said faintly:
     "Some of self, and some of Thee."

Day by day His tender mercy
     Healing, helping, full and free,
Sweet and strong, and ah! so patient!
Brought me lower, while I whispered:
     "Less of self, and more of Thee."

Higher than the highest heavens,
     Deeper than the deepest sea,
Lord, Thy love at last hath conquered;
Grant me now my soul's desire:
     "None of self, and all of Thee."
                         TH. MONOD.

This card or small leaflet was found among Havergal manuscripts and papers. A number of F.R.H.'s poems were similarly printed to distribute, a good means to give rich truths to many people, both friends and strangers. See also pages 672–675 of this book.

Answers to Charades & Enigmas.

Enigmas by Sabrina 1857.
20. Sere – Seir – Seer – Sear (scared)
21. Bacon. 22. Lava

Charades by Sabrina 1857
21. Cutlass   24. Nightingale
22. Carpet   25. Sunday
23. Or·i·on

Enigmas by Zoide 1857
6. Needles   9. Trunk
7. Lines   10. Malice
8. Table   11. Scrape·crape Vce

Charades by Fanny R. H. 1858
2. Ivan·hoe   5. Words – worth
3. Ice·land   6. Hare·ball
4. Hem·lock   7. Par·son·age

Turn over.

Enigmas by Fanny R. H. 1858
6. Spring   9. Ice
7. Lock   10. Gas
8. Pole

Charades by Zoide 1857
13. Dande(y)lion   14. Gladstone

Enigmas by Fanny R. H. 1860
1. Shadow.   4. Enigma Riddle
2. Arch.   5. Wheels.
3. Melodies.   6. Perch.

Enigmas by Fanny R. H. 1860.
1. Ball.
2. Box.

Charades by Fanny R. H. 1860.
1. Bar·gain
2. Gentleman
3. Palmerston

Charades by Fanny R. H. 1860
1. Lark·spur.   2. Ram·pant.

This is a list of answers to Enigmas and Charades by F.R.H., in her handwriting. She used the pen names of "Sabrina" and "Zoide" for a number of these poems.

Miscellaneous Poems.

The Queen of the Sea.

O SEA, calm, sleeping Sea! awake, and tell
What o'er thee hath cast this soothing spell?

'Brightly the young moon is beaming
    From her purple throne,
On my waveless breast is gleaming
    Radiance all her own.
I have hushed each booming billow,
    For her peerless royal brow
Resteth on my glistening pillow
    Like a sleeping angel now.'

O Sea, glad and playful Sea! what meanest thou?
What do thy white-winged wavelets carol now?

'Merrily they all are singing,
    For with golden hand,
Silver fetters she is flinging
    O'er my fairy band.
'Neath them blithely are they dancing,
    And her jewels rare and bright
In their waving crests are glancing—
    Liquid diamonds of light.'

O Sea, wild, raging Sea! what horrors dire
Have raised thy maniac wrath, thy frenzied ire?

'Seest thou not the lightning flashing
    From yon lurid cloud?
Fiercely are my billows dashing,
    Foaming, roaring loud,
For the frowning sky is veiling
    Darkly o'er their beauteous Queen:
Fury mingleth with their wailing
    Till her face again be seen.'

Two Points of View.

TERRIBLE waves! In fierce, unearthly chorus
    Ye threaten the frail vessel to entomb;
Still darker than the fearful storm-cloud o'er us,
    Your yawning gulfs of death-portending gloom.

Beautiful waves! In joyous freedom dancing,
    Ye burst like living things upon the strand;
Your snowy crests in the pure sunlight glancing,
    Flash like a vision bright of fairy-land.

Oh, such are trials! All Earth's sons and daughters
    Feel in them awful messengers of ire,
More dark and dread than ocean's troubled waters;
    Death, and not Life, their horrors aye inspire.

Not so in Heaven! On that shore of gladness
    Each past grief seems a blessing, and each pain
Hath lost the midnight hues of earthborn sadness,—
    The once-dark waves gleam bright—each loss appears
        a gain.

Morning Song.

(FROM THE GERMAN.)

THE dawning day is beaming,
    The long night flies away,
The gates of light are gleaming,
    Oped by the rosy ray.
Thou beauteous light of earth, all hail!
Let not thy cheering presence fail!

Above all goodness dwelleth;
    Where, at the fount of light,
The angel-chorus swelleth,
    There it is ever bright!
Though here in darksome vale we stray,
'Tis lighted by that glorious ray.

Thy light and blessing sending
　From Thine own radiant side,
While here our dark paths wending,
　Be Thou our guard and guide.
Lift up the brightness of Thy face!
Forsake not, Lord, Thy chosen race!

Evening Song.

(FROM THE GERMAN.)

EVENING now is closing
　Over vale and hill;
Peacefully reposing,
　All the world is still.

But the brooklet, pouring
　Where the tall rocks close,
With its restless roaring
　Ever, ever flows.

Evening is not bringing
　To its waters peace,
And no sweet bell ringing,
　Bids its turmoil cease.

In its restless striving
　I behold my own,—
True repose deriving
　From my God alone.

Peace.

A SHOUT of gladness is heard afar;
They are greeting a glowing triumphal car;
And the nations bend to the gentle sway
Of white-robed Peace, with her olive spray.
She is come! and the tongues of ten thousand bells
Re-echo the shout through our island dells.

She is come! Like a star from the darksome wave
Arising, o'er many an unknown grave;
Like the moon, when her sad eclipse is past,
Her silver fetters o'er earth doth cast;
Like the sun, dispelling with ardent might
The gloomy spectres and shades of night.

She is come! Like the falling of cool, sweet dew,
Like a buried flower which Spring doth renew;
Like the burst of a rivulet's laughing waves
From the death-like glacier's awful caves;
As a pearl gleams forth from its dark, rough shell,
She is come! and her song is War's funeral knell.

She is come! with her lyre all newly strung
For the lay which the Bethlehem angels sung:
Glad harmony dwells in its every tone,
Triumphantly ruling the song alone;
For discord hath melted before her sway,
Like as snow-wreath yields to the warm spring ray.

She is come! with her diamond-gleaming zone,
To bind Earth's children before her throne,
And her flowing mantle, which every trace
Of War's wild fury shall soon erase;
Her golden crown is returning wealth,
And her balmy breath is the nation's health.

She is come! with blessings for each and all,
For the rich and poor, for the great and small,
For our own loved Queen, in her royal chair,
For the poor man toiling for daily fare,
For the senate-hall, for the busy mart,
For the striving mind, for the loving heart.

She is come! As an angel from Heaven above,
With her smile of joy and her look of love;
Each grim foreboding to chase away,
Each tenderly anxious fear to allay;
To bid the death-thunder of War to cease:
Then hail to the long, long sighed for Peace!

She is come! But e'en 'neath her radiant sway
There are those who sorrow each weary day;
Who weep for the noble, the loved, the brave,
That are resting now in an Eastern grave:
Then oh! for them let our prayers ascend,
To the orphan's Father, the widow's Friend.

She is come! Then our anthems shall loudly rise
To the gracious Ruler of earth and skies,
Who hath poured on us from His chalice of love
A sparkling drop of the Peace above;
And hath stilled the dark billows of War with a word!
Yes! our grateful songs shall be widely heard.

She is come! But oh! she may pass away,
Like the fleeting brightness of April's ray,
And War's fierce tempest arise once more!
Then in faith let us 'onward and upward' soar,
Where the many jarrings of earth shall cease,
In the glorious reign of the Prince of Peace.

Fragments.

I WANDER in fancy far away
To scenes of many a summer day,
    Beautiful even now
In the pale and wan November ray,
When Nature lays her cooling hand
On the hot and aching brow,
And quiets the throbbing heart with a touch,
    And whispers much,
In her own dear musical tone,
    Of rest and calm,
    And peace and balm,
Till the heart is tuned to her own sweet psalm,
    And feels no more alone.
Oh, the healing she has brought!
Oh, the cures that she has wrought!
Only engage her as nurse and physician,

And let her fulfil her miraculous mission,
     And you will find
     That she leaves behind
All the wonders of homœopathy.
     Oh! I could tell,
     For I know so well,
How the unstrung nerves are tuned again,
And the load rolls off from the tired brain,
And strength comes back to the languid frame,
And existence hardly seems the same.
Her process is surer far and shorter,
When out of reach of bricks and mortar!
When all her gentle remedies
Are brought to bear, till the work is done.

     Oh! give to me
A pierless and paradeless sea,
With a shore as God made it, grand and free,
And not a mere triumph of masonry;
     Where the thundering shocks,
     And the Titan play
     Of the wild white spray,
Which dies on the shingly beach,
     With a golden reach
     Of fair smooth sand,
     Laid by the hand
     Of the lulling tide,
Inviting many a stroll or ride.
     Oh, for the pure and lovely shell!
     Oh, for the crimson frond!
Witness of all fair forms that dwell
In the marvellous deep below and beyond,
     Where living flowers
     From mermaids' bowers,
     Many a living star,
     Many a crystal, many a spar,
Where Nature distributes all her treasures,
And all her special sea-side pleasures.

Oh! give me the rocks of Ilfracombe,
With their witchery of gleam and gloom,

With the crystal pools in the tide-swept cave,
Where myriad fairy forests wave,
And the delicate fringes of crimson and green,
Purple and amber, ruby and rose,
With snowy gleaming shells between,
And marvellous forms of life are seen,
While the musical tide still ebbs and flows;
Where not a step but brings to view
Something exquisite, something rare,
Something marvellously fair,
    Always beautiful, always new.

    .   .   .   .   .

My heart is wandering still
At its strange and wayward will.
Oh, for the Glen of the Waters' Meet,
    Where the merry Lyn leaps down
    To that loveliest vale below,
    And hastens to join the Channel flow;
Where the Lynton cliffs, without a frown,
    Majestically crown
This mingling of sublime and sweet.
And oh, for the mighty roar
At the foot of Penmaenmawr!
    Or an autumn storm
    On the Greater Orme,
Where the giant breakers hurl their spray
    At the mountain's mighty breast,
And the wild wind, mingling in the fray,
Seizes and whirls it high and away
    Over the proud rock's crest;
    While the maddened waves
    Rush into the caves
With thunder and growl, and rush back again,
As if the assault had been all in vain,
But only to gather in awful might
For a tenfold struggle of fiercer fight.
Who would have time for a thought of care,
Or a fit of the blues, if standing there!
    Away! away! to the bracing North,
    To the grand old seas
    Of the Hebrides,

To the sunny Clyde, or the silver Forth,
Purple heather above, and shadowy loch below,
Golden glory of furze, and a far-off wealth of snow,
Violet peaks afar, and dark green pines anear,
And long bright evenings so soft and clear,
And concert halls of birdies sweet
Trill and carol so blithely meet;—
Treasures untold, their myriad gleam
Is far beyond a poet's dream.

The Wandering Sunbeam.

It wandered far, that Sunbeam bright,
To mortal eyes of purest light,—
And, gladdening all o'er whom it beamed,
A seraph's smile of joy it seemed.
But farther yet it longed to soar,
Where earthly darkness dims no more,
To visit that abode of light,
Too dazzling far for human sight.
On glowing wing through space it flew,
Till Heaven's own glory was in view,
And through the pearly gates it passed,
Which only light, not shadow, cast.
Then burst upon the wondering Ray
The radiance fair of perfect Day.
A beauteous seraph passed along,
The Sunbeam heard the thrilling song;
But quickly ceased the gladsome lay,
The swift-winged seraph fled away!
What might that haste, that strange fear mean?
What dreaded spectre had he seen?
'An earth-born cloud of darksome Night
Hath dared to scale the walls of light;
O'er yon fair hill a shade is thrown,
Which only in those worlds is known
Which far from Heaven's pure boundaries lie,
To Chaos' gloomy realm more nigh.'
Thus spake he to a marvelling throng,

But gazed not on the Sunbeam long:
An angel's eye was far too pure
E'en that fair Sunray to endure.
Nor long remained it there to tell
In what strange darkness Earth must dwell,
Too gross with beams of heavenly birth
To mix, yet to return to Earth
Too glorious, since its joyful gaze
Had met those all-effulgent rays.
Half way to Earth it flew, and there,
While yet its wing Heaven's radiance bare,
It rested, and became a star,
To tell Earth's children from afar,
How infinitely pure and bright
Is Heaven's eternal shadeless light.

May Day.

O HASTE, O haste to the fields away!
    For dawneth now the month of May;
O leave the city's crowded street,
    And haste ye now sweet May to greet.

For May is come on fairy wings,
    And thousand beauties with her brings;
The fairest month of all the year,
    Oh, well can she the sad heart cheer.

Nature her jewelry displays,
    Unfolds her gems to meet our gaze;
Bright leaves and buds of *emerald* hue,
    Forget-me-nots of *sapphire* blue.

The *pearly* lily's drooping bells,
    Listen! a tale it sweetly tells:
'If God so clothe the lilies fair,
    Much more may ye trust in His care.'

The *turquoise* gentianella bright,
    The shining king-cup's golden light,

Carnation's *ruby* hues behold,
    And *silvery* daisy set with *gold*.

Of these we'll twine a garland gay,
    Meet for the brow of beauteous May;
And see, they gain a brighter hue
    By glittering drops of *diamond* dew.

Now hark! what sound so sweetly floats
    Upon the breeze? The cuckoo's notes!
How far they come to welcome May,
    And pour for us the simple lay!

Forest Voices.

THE forest hath its voices,
    Whose sweetness aye rejoices,
Or soothes the spirit wondrously;
    Borne on their leafy wings,
    They tell of quiet things
And mingle in strange harmony.

There is a murmuring song,
    A cadence soft and long,
Evoking dreams of still delight;
    There is a clarion note,
    Whose blithesome echoes float,
Chasing the darkling spells of grief and night.

There is a whispering sound
    Within the forest-bound,
Telling the heart of things unseen;
    That nameless holy thrill
    Passeth o'er vale and hill
And through the dark and lone ravine.

It is a harp sublime
    With ever-varying chime,
Awakening feelings ever new;
    For, tuned by Him who made
    The all-harmonious shade,
Each forest-voice is sweet and true.

The Shower.

ON every budding leaf and flower,
 The sweet, soft rain of spring
Comes down in a soft and gentle shower,
 Like a whispering angel-wing.

The shower hath bow'd the proud red rose
 With many a fragrant tear,
It hath wakened the harebell's long repose,
 The wanderer now to cheer.

It hath given the woodbine strength to cling
 To the strong elm's rugged bough;
And the wakeful pimpernel folds its wing,
 And quietly slumbers now.

It hath watered the seeds in their cold dark bed,
 And they burst through the prisoning clay.
To the lingering buds it hath gently said,
 'Unfold to the bright sun-ray.'

Among the leaves of the forest-tree
 Its gentle footsteps go,
And they murmur thanks so pleasantly
 In an anthem soft and low.

———

Showers there are for the thirsty soul,
 A sweet and refreshing dew,
The Spirit who makes the wounded whole,
 And the evil heart makes new.

He will teach the trembling one to cling
 To an Arm of love and might;
And the earth-stained soul 'neath His holy wing
 Shall again be pure and white.

The weary heart with its wild unrest
 He can hush to a trustful calm;
To the spirit crushed and sorely pressed
 He comes with His healing balm.

He comes to the soul in its sin-wrought tomb,
    And rent are the chains of death!
Then His own sweet graces awake and bloom
    Beneath His living breath.

Yes! the Spirit shall teach the heart to sing,
    And shall tune its long silent lyre,
And He who shall meeten it praise to bring
    In the sinless, white-robed choir.

Come then, O Spirit, as once of yore,
    Come in Thy quickening might!
Come, on Thy waiting Church to pour
    Thy life, Thy grace, Thy light.

Tiny Tokens.

I.

THE murmur of a waterfall
    A mile away,
The rustle when a robin lights
    Upon a spray,
The lapping of a lowland stream
    On dipping boughs,
The sound of grazing from a herd
    Of gentle cows,
The echo from a wooded hill
    Of cuckoo's call,
The quiver through the meadow grass
    At evening fall:—
Too subtle are these harmonies
    For pen and rule,
Such music is not understood
    By any school:
But when the brain is overwrought,
    It hath a spell,
Beyond all human skill and power,
    To make it well.

II.

The memory of a kindly word
    For long gone by,
The fragrance of a fading flower
    Sent lovingly,
The gleaming of a sudden smile
    Or sudden tear,
The warmer pressure of the hand,
    The tone of cheer,
The hush that means 'I cannot speak,
    But I have heard!'
The note that only bears a verse
    From God's own Word:—
Such tiny things we hardly count
    As ministry;
The givers deeming they have shown
    Scant sympathy:
But when the heart is overwrought,
    Oh, who can tell
The power of such tiny things
    To make it well!

April.

O THE wealth of pearly blossom, O the woodland's emerald gleam!
O the welcome, welcome sunshine on the diamond-sparkling stream!
O the carol from the hawthorn and the trill from dazzling blue!
O the glory of the spring-time, making all things bright and new!
    O the rosy eve's surrender
    To the Easter moonlight tender!
    O the early morning splendour,
        Fresh and fragrant, cool and clear,
        In the rising of the year!
O the gladness of the children after all the dismal days,
In the freedom and the beauty and the heart-rejoicing rays!
Do we chill the gleeful spirit, check the pulses bounding fast,
By the mournful doubt suggested: 'Ah, but, darling, *will it last?*'

Though we know there may be tempests, and we know there will be showers,
Yet we know they only hasten summer's richer crown of flowers.
Blossom leads to golden fruitage, bursting bud to foliage soon;
April's pleasant gleam shall strengthen to the glorious glow of June.
   April leads to joyous May-time,
   With its ever-lengthening day-time:
   This again to joyous hay-time,
    When the harvest-home is near,
    In the zenith of the year.
So we only tell the children of the sunnier days in store,
Of the treasures and the beauties that shall open more and more.
So the silver carol rises, for the winter-time is past!
When the summer days are coming, need we ask if spring shall last?

O the gladness of the spirit, when the true and Only Light
Pours in radiant resplendence, making all things new and bright!
When the love of Jesus shineth in its overcoming power,
When the secret sweet communion hallows every passing hour.
   O the calm and happy resting,
   Free from every fear molesting!
   O the Christ-victorious breasting
    Of the tempter's varied art,
    In the spring-time of the heart!
O the freedom and the fervour after all the faithless days!
O the ever-new thanksgiving and the ever-flowing praise!
Shall we tempt the gaze from Jesus, and a doubting shadow cast,
Satan's own dark word suggesting by the whisper '"*If*" it last'?

Though we know there must be trials and there will be tears below,
Yet we know His glorious purpose, and His promises we know!
Only ask—'What saith the Master?' and believe His word alone,
That 'from glory unto glory' He shall lead, shall change His own.
   Ever more and more bestowing,
   Love and joy in riper glowing,
   Faith increasing, graces growing—
    Such His promises to you!
    He is faithful, He is true!
Each Amen becomes an anthem, for we know He will fulfil
All the purpose of His goodness, all the splendour of His will.
Only trust the living Saviour, only trust Him all the way,
And your springtide path shall brighten to the perfect summer day!

The Song of a Summer Stream.

A FEW months ago
I was singing through the snow,
Though the dead brown boughs gave no hope of summer shoots,
And my persevering fall
Seemed to be no use at all,
For the hard, hard frost would not let me reach the roots.

Then the mists hung chill
All along the wooded hill,
And the cold, sad fog through my lonely dingles crept;
I was glad I had no power
To awake one tender flower
To a sure, swift doom! I would rather that it slept.

Still I sang all alone
In the sweet old summer tone,
For the strong white ice could not hush me for a day;
Though no other voice was heard
But the bitter breeze that whirred
Past the gaunt, grey trunks on its wild and angry way.

So the dim days sped,
While everything seemed dead,
And my own poor flow seemed the only living sign;
And the keen stars shone
When the freezing night came on,
From the far, far heights, all so cold and crystalline.

A few months ago
I was singing through the snow!
But now the blessed sunshine is filling all the land,
And the memories are lost
Of the winter fog and frost,
In the presence of the Summer with her full and glowing hand.

Now the woodlark comes to drink
At my cool and pearly brink,
And the ladyfern is bending to kiss my rainbow foam;
And the wild-rose buds entwine
With the dark-leaved bramble-vine,
And the centuried oak is green around the bright-eyed squirrel's home.

O the full and glad content,
That my little song is blent
With the all-melodious mingling of the choristers around!
I no longer sing alone
Through a chill surrounding moan,
For the very air is trembling with its wealth of summer sound.

Though the hope seemed long deferred,
Ere the south wind's whisper heard
Gave a promise of the passing of the weary winter days,
Yet the blessing was secure,
For the summer time was sure
When the lonely songs are gathered in the mighty choir of praise.

An Autumn Holiday.

I DON'T want to think about 'the meaning,'
    I don't want to think fine thoughts at all!
On the great heather cushions leaning,
    I'm watching the sunset, that is all!

Why should I puzzle and tease with questions,
    When Nature shows me her picture-book?
I will leave her to make her own suggestions,
    And just do nothing but sit and look.

I have finished the work of a busy season,
    And I want to quiet a busy brain,
Now is the time for rest (in reason),
    Before I begin a new campaign.

And oh it is rest, and most delicious,
    To know that I need not speak a word;
By only the midges (most officious!)
    Could anything here be overheard.

Isn't it nice! The bracken browning
    Is almost gold in the autumn glow,
And the silver birch, with the same fair crowning,
    Gleams like a streak of glistening snow.

The sweet south air is so soft and quiet,
   Stealing along through the fern to me,
After the most uncivil riot
   Of his cousin from over the western sea.

The broad blaze hides all the fresh-foldings,
   Under the flood of sunset light,
And touches anew all the quarry mouldings
   Of the eastern hills with its gilding bright.

The clouds are hanging a cool grey curtain,
   Up in the north till the sun gets low;
Only biding their time, and certain
   Then to flaunt in a crimson show.

Slowly, slowly the sun is sinking,
   Silence and glory are everywhere!
No more writing, and no more thinking!
   Only rest in the golden air!

The Song of Love.

I PASSED along the meadows fair,
The lark's loud carol filled the air,
   A living song up-soaring.
A wanderer passed along, and sang
A song that all the lark's outrang,
   His very soul outpouring.
     'Still onward to my quiet home,
       With yearning, glad endeavour,
     Still singing all the way I roam
       A song of love for ever.'

I passed along the forest green,
And heard a song ring out between
   The leafy aisles o'erarching.
The music filled the silent shade,
The singer passed through glen and glade,
   With steady footstep marching.
     'Still onward to my quiet home,
       With yearning, glad endeavour,

Still singing all the way I roam
A song of love for ever.'

I lingered by the river side,
And watched a tiny vessel glide,
   And saw the white sails glisten:
The helm was in the wanderer's hand,
The same clear music reached the strand,
   And bid my whole soul listen.
     'Still onward to my quiet home,
       With yearning, glad endeavour,
     Still singing all the way I roam
      A song of love for ever.'

I passed the quiet churchyard bound,
And stood beside a new-made mound
   In silent sunset glory;
The flowering grasses, fresh and fair,
Waved lightly in the golden air,
   And softly told the story.
     'He resteth in his blessèd home,
       Whence nothing now can sever,
     Still singing, though no more to roam,
      His song of love for ever.'

The Awakening.

So it has come to you, dear,
   Come so soon!
Come in the sunshine early,
Come in the morning pearly,
   Not in the blaze of noon.

Yes, it has come to you, dear,
   Strange and sweet;
Come ere the merry May-time
Melts to the glowing hay-time,
   Hushed in the sultry heat.

Come—with mysterious shadow,
    Weird and new,—
Come with a magic lustre
Hung on the shining cluster
    Ripening fast for you.

Come! and the exquisite minor,
    Rich and deep,
Swells with Æolian blending
Chords of the spirit, ending
    Boyhood's enchanted sleep.

Sleep that is past for ever!
    Is it gain?
What does the waking seem like?
Love that is only dream-like
    Sings not a truthful strain.

Hearts that have roused and listened
    Never more,
(Though they may miss the crossed tones,
Though they may mourn the lost tones,)
    Sleep as they slept before.

Come! and the great transition
    Now is past!
Never again the boy-life,
Only the pain—and joy-life,
    More of the first than last.

Come! and they do not guess it,
    Why such a change!
Why should the mirth and riot
Tone into manly quiet!
    Is it not passing strange?

Come! 'Tis a night of wonder
    At this call.
Characters cabalistic,
Writings all dim and mystic
    Tremble upon the wall.

Come! am I glad or sorry?
Wait and see!
Wait for God's silent moulding,
Wait for His full unfolding,
Wait for the days to be.

The Poet's Zenith.

NIGHT is heavy on the valley where the river mist is chill,
Heavy, where the cloud pavilion closes round the silent hill;
Every tiny light that glimmered from the windows near and far,
One by one in sudden darkness has vanished like a lonely star.
All but *one*, and that is shining where the midnight air creeps in,
Cooling with its clammy touch a burning brow and fingers thin;
Brow inscribed by graving tool of thought in life's deep colours dipped,
Fingers that are resting proudly on unfinished manuscript.
'Finished! 'Tis my best, I take it,—best that bears my name as yet;
I am weary, but 'tis worth it, now my signature is set.
How the closing verses thrilled me! seemed that they were hardly mine,
Flashing up in bright succession at my summons line by line.
It has been as though my spirit leapt beyond herself, and left
Half her being yet entangled in a sombre earthly weft,
While her essence soared unfearing upward to the Infinite,
With a new and sudden power, with a new and sudden light.
Year by year have many listened to the truths I sought to teach,
But the work this night sees ended, many more shall surely reach.
It is farther, farther reaching, fond ideals nearing more
Than the last, yet that was stronger than the one that came before.
Finished! but I know my power, know that I have more to say,
Know that better work and deeper shall be done another day.'

Was it so? The hair grew greyer, but the eye retained its light;
Year by year his shining fire-notes fell into the human night,
And his audience grew larger, more and more the souls he stirred,
Till the Poet's name had risen to become a household word.
Yet a whisper rose and mingled with the shoutings of his fame:
'This or that is splendid, adding lustre to a lustrous name,
Some for tenderness and sweetness, some for favour and for force;
All his later works are fine, and so we read them—oh, of course!

But the focus of his power, in the poem we love best,
Stands alone for depth and beauty, far outweighing all the rest.
There's a vividness, a glory, something felt though not defined,
Making one forget the poet in that light and truth combined.
Not an old man, and experience adding treasure for his mint!
Yet his golden coin seems bearing less imperial imprint.
It is heresy, we know it, for his verse is all so good,
But why *does* he never write as once he did and surely could?'

Well, the fatal whisper reached him, floated like a seed of grief,
Thistle-down, that soon upspringing, wounded him with thorny leaf;
Slowly, surely, came the knowledge that the springtide of his power
All unknown had reached its *zenith* in the rapture of an hour;
That the ebbing and the flowing never reached the shining mark
Where the wave of life rose highest in that midnight still and dark.

Mischief Making.

I.

ONLY a tiny dropping
    From a tiny hidden leak;
But the flow is never stopping,
    And the flaw is far to seek.

Only some trickling water,
    Nothing at all at first;
But it grows to a valley-slaughter,
    For the reservoir has burst!

The wild flood once in motion,
    Who shall arrest its course?
As well restrain the ocean
    As that ungoverned force!

Mourn for the desolations,
    And help the ruined men,
Till next spring's fair creations
    Make the valley smile again.

Help with a free, pure pity,
    For your hands in this are clean,
You dwelt in the far-off city,
    With many a mile between.

You did not watch the flowing
    Of the treacherous, trickling rill;
You did not aid the growing
    Of the tiny rifts in the hill.

What if you had? I leave it,
    It is too dark a thought;
How could the heart conceive it?
    How came it, all unsought?

                    II.

A look of great affliction,
    As you tell what one told you,
With a feeble contradiction,
    Or a 'hope it is not true!'

A story quite too meagre
    For naming any more,
Only your friend seems eager
    To know a little more.

No doubt of explanation,
    If all was known, you see;
One might get information
    From Mrs. A. or B.

Only some simple queries
    Passed on from tongue to tongue,
Though the ever-growing series
    Has out of nothing sprung.

Only a faint suggestion,
    Only a doubtful hint,
Only a leading question
    With a special tone or tint.

Only a low 'I wonder!'
    Nothing unfair at all;
But the whisper grows to thunder,
    And a scathing bolt may fall;

And a good ship is dismasted,
    And hearts are like to break,
And a Christian life is blasted,
    For a scarcely-guessed mistake!

The Lorely.

AH, where are the echoes of gladness
    Which dwell in my listening mind?
What meaneth the whisper of sadness,
    Like the moan of the autumn wind?

I am chained by an often told story,
    Come down from the olden time
When fairydom saw its glory,
    A haunting, saddening chime.

The air is still and darkling,
    And silently flows the Rhine,
The mountain peaks are sparkling,
    Where sunset rays yet shine.

A strangely beauteous maiden
    Sits high on the grim rock there
Her arms are with rich gems laden
    She combeth her golden hair.

With a golden comb she is combing,
    And sings an enchanted song,
And wondrously through the gloaming
    That melody floats along.

Then a wild weird sorrow amazeth
    The boatman in gliding skiff,
While upward alone he gazeth
    He sees not the fatal cliff.

The wave-bells a knell are ringing,
    For the Rhine his prey hath won,
And that with her syren-singing
    Hath the Sprite of the Lorely done.

For Denmark, ho!

FOR Denmark, ho!
    Is the cry, we know,
And the shout,—Arise, arise!
    They are struggling long
    'Gainst might and wrong,
The valiant weak, with the craven strong,
    Their homes the invader's prize.

A fair fresh Rose,
    From her northern snows,
Is worn on England's heart,
    And shall England see
    Her parent tree
Crushed by malice? It shall not be,—
    Ours be the helper's part.

Let a voice of might
    For the just and right
Resound o'er sea and land;
    Let the olive fade
    Ere we fail in aid,
And the far-seen gleams of a half-drawn blade
    Flash from our ready hand.

My Singing Lesson.

ABSTRACT.

HERE beginneth—chapter the first of a series,
To be followed by manifold notes and queries;
So novel the queries, so trying the notes,
I think I must have the queerest of throats,

And most notable dullness, or else long ago
The Signor had given up teaching, I trow.
I wonder if ever before he has taught
A pupil who can't do a thing as she ought!

The voice has machinery—(now to be serious),
Invisible, delicate, strange, and mysterious.
A wonderful organ-pipe firstly we trace,
Which is small in a tenor and wide in a bass;
Below an Æolian harp is provided,
Through whose fairy-like fibres the air will be guided.
Above is an orifice, larger or small
As the singer desires to rise or to fall;
Expand and depress it to deepen your roar,
But raise and contract it when high you would soar.
Alas for the player, the pipes, and the keys,
If the bellows give out an inadequate breeze!
So this is the method of getting up steam,
The one motive power for song or for scream:
Slowly and deeply, and just like a sigh,
Fill the whole chest with a mighty supply;
Through the mouth only, and not through the nose,
And the lungs must condense it ere farther it goes
(*How* to condense it, I really don't know,
And very much hope the next lesson will show).
Then, forced from each side, through the larynx it comes,
And reaches the region of molars and gums,
And half of the sound will be ruined or lost
If by any impediment here it is crossed.
On the soft of the palate beware lest it strike,
The effect would be such as your ear would not like.
And arch not the tongue, or the terrified note
Will straightway be driven back into the throat.
Look well to your trigger, nor hasten to pull it:
Once hear the report and you've done with your bullet.
In the feminine voice there are registers three,
Which upper, and middle, and lower must be;
And each has a sounding-board all of its own,
The chest, lips, and head, to reverberate tone.

But in cavities nasal it never must ring,
Or no one is likely to wish you to sing.
And if on this subject you waver in doubt,
By listening and feeling the truth will come out.
The lips, by the bye, will have plenty to do
In forming the vowels Italian and true;
Eschewing the English, uncertain and hideous,
With an *O* and a *U* that are simply amphibious,
In flexible freedom let both work together,
And the under one must not be stiffened like leather.

Here endeth the substance of what I remember,
Indited this twenty-sixth day of November.

To the Choir of Llangryffyth.

(OR WHOMSOEVER IT MAY CONCERN.)

WE nowadays hear of all sorts of progression
In science or politics, custom or view,
In business, or fashion. Perhaps the precession
Of equinoxes has something to do
With the rate at which we are going. 'Tis true
That progress is now and then retrogression,
And the new is the old when the old is the new.
So they breakfast at one and they lunch at four,
And are sitting at dinner at half-past nine,
And go to bed when the night is o'er,
And get up when the day begins to decline.
If they only progress in the same direction,
A few more years will bring it all right;
They will rise in the morning, not dreading detection,
And return to the habit of sleeping at night.

Though the world of fashion progresses so fleetly,
The church at Llangryffyth outdoes it completely;
For at twelve o'clock, nay, ten minutes past,
By a watch that was certainly not too fast,
The choir exhorted our souls to awake,
And slumber and sleepiness off to shake,

And then and there from our beds to rise,
Exactly as if we were rubbing our eyes.
A little bit later were more apropos,
For afternoon drowsiness lazy and slow
Might make an excuse for a timely suggestion.
Then, further, the sun was brought into the question,
As if he were rising at that time of day,
Instead of completing the half of his way.
Nor these incongruities only appeared:
We thought that good Welshmen the Sabbath revered,
And that '*daily duties*' aside were laid
That respect to our Holy Day might be paid;
Resting, not '*running*' the trodden ways
Of the cares and business of other days.
But here at Llangryffyth the choir advise,
With the Fourth Commandment plain under their eyes
To 'awake' (ten minutes past twelve!) 'with the sun,'
And our '*daily stage of duty run.*'
What would the good old Bishop have said
(Who sang the sweet verses upon his bed,
Day by day as the morning broke,
And the busy week-day world awoke)
Of the common sense of those who bring
Such meaningless praise to the Heavenly King!
O choir of Llangryffyth, your office high
Is to 'teach and admonish,' and edify,—
To wield an influence deep and strong,
The heart to touch and the soul to raise,—
In God's own temple to lift the song,
To bring a tribute of holy praise
Before the Lord, who entrusts to you
His gift of music, so high and true!
Be it yours the preacher's words to meet,
He choosing wisely, ye singing sweet
Of the bright inheritance kept above,[1]
Of the Living Water, the Fount of love.[2]

---

[1] The morning text—1 Peter 1:4: 'An inheritance reserved.'
[2] The evening text—Revelation 22:17: 'Let him take the Water of Life.'

May He who gave you voice and skill
So tune your hearts that ye may indeed
Your ministry of song fulfil,
And 'with understanding' His praises lead.

P.S.—It *might* be as well if the whole congregation
Could join in the Canticles' grand adoration,
But the few that try at your speed, you will find,
Are speedily distanced and left behind.
It *might* be as well for the Kyrie to bear
Some slight resemblance to penitent prayer;
Not tripping it off in cheerful repeat
To a pretty tune with a lively beat.
It *might* be as well in the hymns if we could
Take breath where the writers intended we should,
Not hunting and racing the sense to death
By aiming at singing a verse in a breath.

The Turned Lesson.

'I THOUGHT I knew it!' she said,
    'I thought I had learnt it quite!'
But the gentle Teacher shook her head,
    With a grave yet loving light
In the eyes that fell on the upturned face,
        As she gave the book
With the mark still set in the self-same place.

'I thought I knew it!' she said;
    And a heavy tear fell down,
As she turned away with bending head,
    Yet not for reproof or frown,
Not for the lesson to learn again,
        Or the play-hour lost;—
It was something else that gave the pain.

She could not have put it in words,
    But the Teacher understood,
As God understands the chirp of the birds
    In the depth of an autumn wood.

And a quiet touch on the reddening cheek
    Was quite enough;
No need to question, no need to speak.

Then the gentle voice was heard,
    'Now I will try you again!'
And the lesson was mastered,—every word!
    Was it not worth the pain?
Was it not kinder the task to turn,
    Than to let it pass,
As a lost, lost leaf that she did not learn?

Is it not often so,
    That we only learn in part,
And the Master's testing-time may show
    That it was not quite 'by heart'?
Then He gives, in His wise and patient grace,
    That lesson again
With the mark still set in the self-same place.

Only, stay by His side
    Till the page is really known,
It may be we failed because we tried
    To learn it all alone.
And now that He would not let us lose
    One lesson of love
(For He knows the loss)—can we refuse?

But oh! how *could* we dream
    That we knew it all so well?
Reading so fluently, as we deem,
    What we could not even spell!
And oh! how could we grieve once more
    That patient One
Who has turned so many a task before?

That waiting One, who now
    Is letting us try again;
Watching us with the patient brow
    That bore the wreath of pain;

Thoroughly teaching what He would teach,
　　Line upon line,
Thoroughly doing His work in each.

Then let our hearts ' be still,'
　　Though our task is turned to-day.
Oh let Him teach us what He will,
　　In His own gracious way,
Till, sitting only at Jesu's feet,
　　As we learn each line,
The hardest is found all clear and sweet!

Leaning Over the Waterfall.

A young lady, aged 20, fell over the rocks at the Swallow Waterfall in the summer of 1873, and was lost to sight in a moment. The body was not recovered till four hours afterwards.

LEANING over the waterfall!
　　Lured by the fairy sight,
Heeding not the warning call,
　　Watching the foam and the flow,
Smooth and dark, or swift and bright,
Here in the shade and there in the light!
　　Oh, who could know
The coming sorrow, the nearing woe!

Leaning over the waterfall!
　　Only a day before
She had spoken of Jesu's wondrous call,
　　As He trod the waves of Galilee.
They asked, as she gazed from the sunset shore,
'If He walked that water, what would you do?'
Then fell the answer, glad and true,
　　'If He beckoned me,
I would go to Him on the pathless sea.'

Leaning over the waterfall
　　Only a moment before!
And then the slip, the helpless call,
　　The plunge unheard in the pauseless roar
　　By the startled watchers on the shore;

And the feet that stood by the waterfall,
      So fair and free,
Are standing with Christ by the crystal sea.

Leaning over the waterfall!
      Have you not often leant
(What should hinder? or what appall?)
Freely, fearlessly, over the brink,
      Merrily glancing adown the stream,
      Or gazing wrapt in a musical dream
At the lovely waters? But pause and think—
      Who kept *your* feet,
And suffered you not such death to meet?

Leaning over the waterfall!
      What if *your* feet had slipped?
Never a moment of power to call,
      Never a hand in time to save
      From the terrible rush of the ruthless wave!
Hearken! would it be ill or well
      If thus *you* fell?
Hearken! would it be heaven or hell?

Leaning over the waterfall!
      Listen, and learn, and lean!
Listen to Him whose loving call
      Soundeth deep in your heart to-day!
      Learn of Jesus, the only way,
How to be holy, how to be blest!
      Lean on His breast,
And yours shall be safety and joy and rest.

The Seed of Song.

THE seed of a song was cast
      On the listening hearts around,
      And the sweetly winning sound
In a few short minutes passed.
But a song of perfect praise,
      And a song of perfect love

Was the harvest after many days,
Beneath the everlasting rays
    Of the summer-time above.

The seed of a single word
    Fell among the furrows deep,
    In their silent, wintry sleep,
And the sower never an echo heard.
But the 'Come!' was not in vain,
    For that germ of Life and Love,
And the blessèd Spirit's quickening rain,
Made a golden sheaf of precious grain
    For the Harvest Home above.

Will you not sow that song?
    Will you not drop that word
    Till the coldest hearts be stirred
From their slumber deep and long?
Then your harvest shall abound
    With rejoicing full and grand,
Where the heavenly summer-songs resound,
And the fruits of faithful work are found,
    In the Glorious Holy Land.

Finis.

I HAVE filled my book,
    In odds and ends of time,
With fancies and reveries
    And careless scraps of rhyme.

It is,—and yet it is not
    A transcript of my soul;
For the passing gleams of light,
    And the passing clouds that roll—

Like an unwilled photograph,
    Have printed their image clear;
And the echo of many a laugh
    And of many a sigh is here.

But words are cold, dead things,
   And little they tell of the heart,
     Or the burning glow
     Of the fount below,
   Whence the glance and the cheek-flush start.

I feel there is more within
   Than may lightly be revealed;
What the spirit itself hath but dimly seen
   To the pen may well be sealed.

Yes, I have filled my book,
   And another will soon begin:
But no venturous guess may say
   What shall be traced within!

Shall its songs be all of joy,
   Or of deepest and keenest woe?
I dare not anticipate,
   And I'm glad that I do not know.

Shall its yet unwritten page
   Be filled by *my* restless hand?
Or shall I be called away
   To the shores of the Silent Land?

One thing I would hope and pray,
   That its record may brighter shine,
That an onward and upward course
   May be traced in every line.

And that some of its words may cheer
   Some troubled and weary soul,
Or point as a waymark clear
   To the distant yet nearing goal.

Then I shall not begrudge my thoughts
   Their robing of careless rhyme;
Or deem them a useless waste
   Of the priceless gift of Time.

120

1057

And see, above their door the Saint
Is rudely carved in stone.

XXI. BY SABRINA.

THE veiling shades of night departed,—
On Lebanon's heights was a rosy glow,
When the serried ranks of the lion-hearted
Prepared for my *first* at the Moslem foe.
A voice was heard, like a clarion proud,
Forth, forth, to battle, to glory go!—
To my lovely *second* I solemnly vowed
To crush the insolent Moslem foe.
And forth they went; but the voice was still'd;
A stroke of my *whole* had laid him low;
By other hands was the vow fulfill'd,
For they tamed the pride of the Moslem foe.

XXII. BY THE SAME.

FROM his ruby pavilion Phœbus arose,
And look'd down from his shining *first*;
And the earth at his glance from her calm repose
Into beauty and gladness burst.
But the clouds of sorrow he could not chase,
Nor the gleaming tears upon Katie's face.
On a merry ride to the busy town
In my *first* she too surely had reckon'd;
Disappointed and angry she flung herself down
On my *whole*; but, alas, in my *second*!
So I told her, my *second* you never can be
While such haughty tempers so often I see.

XXIII. BY THE SAME.

MY *first* gleams bright 'mid azure shields,
Or rich emblazon'd argent fields.
If you too often use my *second*
An egotist you will be reckon'd.

121

My *third*,—it is a battle-cry;
And be it yours in every high,
And good, and noble end and aim;
As such it is the road to fame.
My belted *whole* you may descry
Illumining the southern sky.

XXIV. BY THE SAME.

MY *first* had spread her darksome wing
O'er all the loveliness of spring;
My *third* arose with mournful wail,
The young leaves told their *first* sad tale,
The old oak groan'd, the flow'rets sigh'd,
The hawthorn bloom was scatter'd wide:
But ere my gloomy *first* had pass'd,
When silent was my *third* at last,
My whole awoke the moonlight dell
To list the sweet tale she could tell,
Then mingled, in strange harmony,
Silence and sweetest melody.
"Your *second*? why such strange omission?"
'Tis but a tiny preposition.

XXV. BY THE SAME.

ARISE, my *first*! In peerless radiance beaming,
A veil of glory thou dost weave for earth;
The ocean waves to welcome thee are gleaming,
For thou alone to Beauty givest birth.
Shine forth, my *second*! Freshly now is flowing
The busy stream of life and labour, too;
Each heart with ardour, base or noble, glowing,
Till thou shalt close, aresting all they do.
All hail, my *whole*! thou comest with rich pleasure,
An Angel from the Land of pure delight,
The great man's blessing and the poor man's treasure,
Our earnest of the day which knows no night.

These Charades by "Sabrina" were written by F.R.H. See page 148 of this book. These were loose pages from an un-identified book, found among Havergal manuscripts and papers. These are Charades No. 1, No. 3, No. 2, 13, and 12, on pages 198–199 and 204–205.

Enigmas and Charades.

Enigma No. 1.

AN army of Cyclops, fair reader, are we,
Yet your servants especially ought we to be;
The outposts of England, 'mid ocean's roar,
We have stood since the deluge, and perhaps before.

From Parry, and Cook, and Columbus too,
A vote of thanks to ourselves is due;
But to Solomon's ships, when to Ophir sent,
Our aid, not asked, was of course not lent.

To Matilda of Flanders' assistance we came,
When she toiled to emblazon the Conqueror's fame;
And the lasting memorials we are seen,
In a summer clime, of a swarthier queen.

The records of ancient days we bear,
And Time to erase us doth not dare,
Yet the poorest girl in our native land
Hath held us fast in her weary hand.

We steadily turn from the tropical glow
To the dreary regions of ice and snow,
For we're firmly bound with a magic spell,
Which none may loose, or its meaning tell.

Woe to the man who hath dared to wed
A woman who us and our use hath fled!
If you find us out, you may claim to be
As bright and as sharp as ever are we!

Enigma No. 2.

A WHIMSICAL set we must often seem,
Of crotchets as full as an organist's dream;
If we were abolished, there'd straightway be
A piscatorian jubilee.

We are frequently clothed in a snowy array
As a maiden fair on her bridal day;
Yet we're often black as the blackest night,
E'en when we're lauding the soft moonlight.
The depths of the ocean we faithfully show;
On us hundreds of miles you may swiftly go;
We measure the distance from place to place,
And encircle the globe in our wide embrace.
Woe, woe to the soldier who dares to fly
From us when the hour of battle is nigh!
Yet the gardener himself, in his peaceful trade,
For planting his cabbages needs our aid.
If a lady endeavours her age to hide,
We ruthlessly publish it far and wide
Wherever she ventures to show her head;
Yet in us her destiny oft is read.
In the heart of a friend long, long forsaken
A few of ourselves may deep gladness awaken,
Yet ours is a many-stringed, changeful lyre,
For dismay and despair we may often inspire.
We're essential to poets, to artists, musicians,
To all washerwomen, and mathematicians;
It required a Euclid to tell what we be,
Yet us at this moment, fair reader, you see.

Enigma No. 3.

I AM a native of many a land,
Of Norway's forests, of India's strand;
And beautiful England's smiles and tears
Have ripened and watered my early years.
I am found near the lowliest cottage fire,
And I dwell in the solemn cathedral choir,
The royal hall I am sure to grace,
And always in Parliament find a place;
Around me oft gather the great of the land,
In front of the Queen I audaciously stand;
And Arthur himself, in days of yore,
Owed half his renown to me or more.

As a quadruped oftenest I have been,
One-legged, or three-footed, or legless I'm seen.
The schoolboy I help through his hard calculation
When working a question in multiplication.
Since the era of Moses (who, truth to speak,
In a manner unfitting his character meek,
Most shamefully used me), till quite of late,
I've always been sober, and still, and sedate;
But now I am playing such wondrous vagaries,
That whether Beelzebub, witches, or fairies,
Electric attraction, or galvanic power,
Have thus turned my head, up to this present hour,
The wisest and cleverest brains of the day,
Quite out of their depth, are unable to say.
In olden days to my care were confided
The laws by which monarchs and subjects were guided;
The records of feats of chivalry,
Or of deeds of blood, were preserved by me:
But now having leaves, though, alas! no flower,
I bear what must pass in a single hour.

Enigma No. 4.

Of a useful *whole* I'm the most useful part;
I've a good circulation, for I've a heart;
I have two or three garments or outer clothes;
I am closely allied to a lip and nose;
Rags, and parchments, and jewels rare,
Rubbish and treasures within me I bear;
The tiniest leaf I produce I can nip
With a dexterous finger and thumb at my tip;
Though I'm often as tall as a spire to view,
If you travel far I accompany you;
I am the Indian's light canoe:
To puzzle you more, I'm an aquaduct too;
I'm part of a garment of olden time,
And part of a beast of a southern clime;
And finally, now, to crown the whole,
I am your body, but not your soul!

Enigma No. 5.

A TERM for autumn leaves when all their lovely tints are fled;
A mountain in Arabia, lifting high its rocky head;
What witches and astrologers pretend they truly are;
A state from which I greatly hope your conscience still is far:
Those four are all alike, you'll see, in mere pronunciation,
But diverse in orthography and in signification.
Transpose the second, you will gain the title of a king,
And what you would be sure to do if he should enter in;
Transpose the fourth, you'll see at once how ancient warriors treated
The cities of the enemy, with passion overheated;
Transpose the third, and lo! the first will straightway be revealed.
Now, reader, I shall like to see this mystery unsealed.

Enigma No. 6.

SEVENTEEN hundred and sixty yards,
A maiden's name and a term at cards,
A halting leg, something stronger than beer,
A river to many a student dear,
A fragrant tree, and a foreign fruit,
A government coach on a postal route,
Honiton, Brussels, or Valenciennes,
A spice preceding bishops and deans,
A sin of the tongue, and the stronger sex,
The state of the sea when no tempests vex,
What you look for three or four times a day,
What the Prince of Wales to the crown will lay,
Three Scripture names, and a region wide,
What an archer takes his shaft to guide:
With six little letters all these are framed;
When each you have duly and rightly named,
They form what I hope you will never dare
Against friend or foe in your heart to bear.

Enigma No. 7.

If you get into me, I have no sort of doubt,
But that you will endeavour forthwith to get out;
Behead me, and then I'm the lone widow's weeds;
Behead me again, and I'm tiny round seeds;
Repeat yet again the above operation,
And I am renowned for my quick imitation,
My mischievous habits, and horrid grimaces,—
You're myself, if you practise unnatural graces.

Enigma No. 8.

What was I? Such a clever friar,
I barely 'scaped the witches' pyre;
Yet doth philosophy in me
One of her bright admirers see;
And forms of classic beauty grew
Beneath my hand to nature true;
Each wondrous magic lantern show
To me the happy children owe;
With Schwartz contesting, I should mention
The honour of his great invention.
What am I? What you may despise,
For I am little more than grease,
And yet I am an annual prize
For matrimonial love and peace.
In every scrape or awkward plight
I hope to save me you'll be able.
I am the ploughboy's great delight,
And often grace his Sunday table.
From dreams of mire and sweet repose
To streaky excellence I rose;
And, following still the chimney sweep,
I learned to smoke instead of sleep.

Enigma No. 9.

IN fiery caverns was my glowing birth,
The great laboratories of the earth;
Thence issuing, with devastating power,
Entombing cities in a single hour;
The vineyards of bright Sicily have been
Of my o'erwhelming might too oft the dreary scene.

Yet I encircle many a fair white arm,
Or holding ink and pens give no alarm;
Though none may stay my incandescent course
Till Neptune doth oppose his briny force.
Mysterious child of subterranean fires,
Strange relics I preserve of fair Italia's sires.

Enigma No. 10.

THE royal sun with his orbèd flame
To be myself I modestly claim;
And yet, though strange, it is perfectly true,
I am at this moment within your shoe.
Have you a delicate hand to show?
Its symmetry partly to me you owe;
And I cannot think how you can possibly see
If deprived in another part of me.
The ancient dame, with her spectacled nose,
By my strange contortions I often pose,
As I glide away from her busy hand
To rejoice the juvenile feline band.
I am a being of direful power,
And many I haste to their last dread hour;
Yet the tiny child on his feeble feet
Is gladdened and charmed by my motions fleet.
I am said to whistle, though not to sigh;
Merriment often to hundreds I bring.
On due inquiry I think you will find
That twenty people in me have dined;
Yet when at dinner you take your seat
I'm sometimes the very first thing you eat.

Who patronise me? The college youth,
Loving me better than books in truth;
The friends of science, the friends of strife,
The duellist seeking his fellow's life,
Of sharpers and blacklegs not a few,
Equine doctors frequently too,
The conjuror showing his skilful tricks,
In the list the graceful and fair we mix;
And last, not least, our gracious Queen
My patroness certainly ever hath been.

Enigma No. 11.

I AM a reward, and a punishment too,
What you may give, and what you may do,
Animal, mineral, both I may be,
Vegetable oftenest perhaps of the three.
Once, I know, as the story goes,
I was the cause of a bridegroom's woes;
But often since I have dimmed the life
Of a wearily-sighing neglected wife.
Never a court without me was seen,
Never a vestry either, I ween,
Never a coach, and never a train,
Tho' sometimes a hindrance the latter to gain.
Famous I am for a long dark way,
Dismal as night in the brightest day.
From the depths of my bosom may rise and float
Many a soft and melodious note;
Why should ye marvel? The rich and fair,
The gay and gorgeous are often there.
Wherever the sweetest of sounds goes forth
Through the radiant south or the dreary north,
A tale of me will be surely told,
Or false were the words of a prophecy old.
A little one longs to begin to do good,
I sometimes help it; and always could;
Yet the hardened man and the cruel boy
May find in me a savage joy.

Give me, and oh, what a monster you'll be;
Refuse me, 'was e'er such a niggard as he;'
Hire me, then you are rich, I conclude;
Mount me, and then you may view and be viewed;
Open me, perhaps you are even a thief,
Perhaps 'twas by way of consoling your grief;
Plant me, I see you are neat in your taste;
Enter me—nervousness, flurry, and haste
Won't at all suit, so I pray you take heed,
Or counsel will into me put you indeed.

Enigma No. 12.

Lives there a poet, old or young,
    Who has not sung my praise?
For ever silent be his tongue,
    Forgotten be his lays!

I have a father dark and stern,
    A daughter bright and gay;
I weep upon his funeral urn,
    I die beneath her sway.

And yet that father binds me fast,
    Hushing my low sweet voice;
That daughter sets me free at last,
    And bids me still rejoice.

Deceitful I am said to be,
    A thing of treacherous smiles,
And many meet their end in me,
    Wreck'd by my sunny wiles.

Yet health and cure 'tis mine to give
    To many a sickly frame;
An antelope of Africa
    Usurps my well-known name.

I'm born beneath the cold hard ground,
    Yet life and joy I bring,
With song and mirth to all around,
    Upon my emerald wing.

I help to measure Time's swift flight;
Tide has to do with me;
In guns and traps behold my might:
O say what can I be?

Enigma No. 13.

THAT I'm very well-known to all metaphysicians 'tis true,
Whose brains I attempted to clear, being one of the crew;
A secret of wonderful power in me was conceal'd,
Which firstly by love, but by treachery next was revealed;
I never am mentioned as living, though oft in the city,
When said to be dead, much impatience I rouse, but no pity;
To some navigation I lend indispensable hand,
Yet I'm not of the slightest utility saving inland.
I frequently act as a guardian, though I must own
My wards to attain their majority never were known;
The brow of the maiden to me owes the half of its charms,
And yet, strange to say, I'm a part of death-dealing firearms.
I've a slim coadjutor who with me my secret possesses,
My master he is, for he knows all my inmost recesses;
My safety and faithfulness vanish if once one can gain him,
Yet I'm perfectly useless without him, so prithee retain him.
The apple Eve gathered was never supposed to be me,
And yet if you pick me, beware of the powers that be;
By a figure of speech I'm said to be silver or golden,
Though to metals far baser I really am much more beholden.
Of loved ones far distant I'm often the fondly kept token,
Memorial and echo of harpstrings which death had long broken.

Enigma No. 14.

I MAY be tall, and slender, and round,
Or perfectly square, and as flat as the ground;
No edifice ever without me is raised,
And yet, when 'tis finished, I never am praised.

The bears themselves, with a grim delight,
Hail me as an old acquaintance quite;

And a smaller quadruped lays its claim
With a feline addition to bear my name.

Glows there a heart in the English breast
Which beats for the injured and long oppressed?
At the thought of me it will rise and swell;
For each free-soul'd patriot knows me well.

Where may you find me? In sunny Kent,
Where the hop-pickers sing, while on labour intent
Or in realms of ice and eternal snow,
'Neath the gorgeous aurora's crimson glow.

In celestial regions I'm certainly found,
And wherever on earth there's an acre of ground;
Where his lordship's chariot proudly speeds,
I ever am close to the high-bred steeds.

I have stood very near to the triple crown,
Yet I'm seen in the back streets of every town;
On the festal day of a short-lived queen
The chief attraction I've ever been.

Attraction, said I? You little know
How much to my power of attraction you owe!
All the gold, and the pearls, the silk, sugar, and tea
That are borne to your homes o'er the pathless sea.

I may quietly stand by your drawing-room fire,
Bearing a comfort you often desire!
Or stretch my bold arm o'er the surging wave,
Some wretch from its billowy depths to save.

Enigma No. 15.

WHERE will ye seek me? The Andes rise
        Silently grand beneath tropical skies;
        And far Himalaya's crowns of snow
Gleam o'er the burning plains below;

I dwell with each, for the mountain air
Certainly suits me everywhere.
Know ye the silent and death-like realm,
Where winter hath donn'd his glassy helm,
And conquering rules o'er land and sea?
Beneath his throne is the home for me.
Ye may seek in the gay and brilliant throng,
Where the hours fleet by in dance and song;
There, martyr-like, I'm sure to be,
Though to venture there may be death to me.
Yet I'm never afraid of catching cold
(Like some young ladies) however bold.
'Tis a wonder my mother should let me go,
But she is remarkably yielding, I know;
And many who tried us both can say,
She yields directly when I give way.
My character's quite the more solid, I state,
But she is a person of greater weight.
Though never convicted of any crime
'Tis perfectly true that, for months at a time,
I am starved in a dungeon all damp and bare,
With hardly the half of a prisoner's fare.
I'm rather a traveller, I may tell,
And know the Atlantic routes quite well;
Sometimes on my own account I go,
Sometimes whether I will or no.
When will ye seek me? The sultry glow
Of a summer noon is the time, I trow,
When the burning pavement and dusty street
Make you long for a rest for your aching feet.
I have done in my time some wonderful things;
Have been made the dwelling-place of kings;
Have baffled the general's proud careering;
Have outdone Stephenson's engineering.
I nevertheless can condescend
To Monsieur Soyer my aid to lend;
Or, better still, can bring mirth and joy
To the heart of the sturdy village boy.

Enigma No. 16.

PRIMEVAL woods my parent's birth
Beheld, where no loud axe was heard,
Where through a solitary earth
No voice the leafy echoes stirred;
But I was born in gloominess profound,
In sable swaddling clothes the child of light was bound.

Released at length by human skill,
From long confinement forth I sped,
And in each city's highway still
I linger far beneath your tread;
Though there are times when, grovelling thus no more,
Beyond the clouds of earth, a prisoner still, I soar.

No eye my subtle form may see,
Till, coming forth to light,
A slow consumption wasteth me
In man's unpitying sight.
Yet when from durance vile I swift escape,
All feel my baleful presence, though none see my shape.

I smile upon the giddy scene
Of mirth, and revelry, and song;
Yet in the sacred courts have been
Devotion's handmaid long;
With darkness waging constant strife and sure,
I ever shun the day-beams though so bright and pure.

Though none have ever heard my voice,
Yet words of gladness traced in me
Have bid full many a heart rejoice,
When England's flag waved high and free.
And with the song of victory sweetly blended
The full deep hymn of praise that war's dark storm was ended.

Enigma No. 17.

I AM the child of the brightest thing
Which may gladden mortal eyes,

Yet the silent sweep of my dusky wing
Over my mother may dimness fling,
   And smiling she faints and dies.

I move, I dance, I fall, I fly,
   Yet anon I may calmly sleep;
I mark the bright-winged hours flit by,
Your ingenuity perhaps I try;
   I am long, or short, or deep.

I have been hailed as a boon untold,
   Or dreaded and shunned ere now;
The earth in my wide embrace I fold,
The mountain regions are my stronghold,
   Yet I steadily follow the plough.

I may rest a while in the minster pile,
   Or beneath the old oak tree;
Often with trackless step I pass
O'er the whispering corn and the waving grass,
   Or tread the changeful sea.

All the day through I follow you,
   Yet beware how you follow me;
For each child of man I may oft beguile,
And cloud the light of his sunniest smile,
   Till for ever away I flee.

Enigma No. 18.

Ye have seen me in the skies,
Yet beneath the ground I rise;
Sometimes far above your head,
Sometimes deep below your tread.

Where the forest boughs entwine,
Baffling still the gay sunshine;
Gaze aloft, and you will see
In myself their tracery.

Laughing eye and dimpling smile
May be even me awhile;
Playful words, like javelins thrown,
As myself you often own.

Many a sunny stream ye trace,
Rippling in my calm embrace;
Still I watch the secret shrine
Of the rich and ruddy wine.

Nave, and choir, and aisle, I trow,
All to me their glories owe;
Even a seraph form by me,
Greater, fairer yet may be.

Many a loved one may be laid
In my sadly solemn shade;
On your brow I now may dwell,
While your lips my name will tell.

Enigma No. 19.

SAY, know ye not the pilgrim band,
    Who wander far and wide,
And greeting find in every land
    Wherever they abide?

They meet full many a friend I wot,
    Who fain would have them stay;
To such they cling, and leave them not,
    Yet still go on their way.

Each bears a staff and often twain,
    And need they many a rest;
The oldest oft seems young again,
    And perhaps we love them best.

They speak a language passing sweet,
    With heart-lore richly fraught;
But oh! to some they daily meet
    Their eloquence is nought.

Yet strange the laws their speech obeys,
    Who drink its mystic tone
May find within each simplest phrase
    A meaning all their own.

Some deem they tell of long past years,
    When they were girls and boys;
Some only hear of bygone tears,
    And some of present joys.

Some hear them speak of One who sent
    That welcome pilgrim band,
And bless the love that freely lent
    Such boon to every land.

Enigma No. 20.

OH, haughty Thebes! In shadowy days of yore,
Where history faintly blends with mythologic lore,
I was thy hidden terror, yet, revealed,
I traced a stain of woe upon thy glittering shield.

Fair Palestine! I was put forth in thee
Amid a scene of gay festivity;
Yet brought by me a sullen frown, I ween,
Was on the brow of my originator seen.

'Tis mine to give thee strange and needless toil,
For Gordian knots I weave in many a tangled coil
I shun publicity, for I declare,
That if you speak my name, I vanish into air.

Enigma No. 21.

    THOUGH constantly we're in the mire,
    We shine and sparkle with our fire;
    Part of the verb 'to speak' we need,
    And yet no words from us proceed.
    The annals of the Inquisition
    Reveal too well our awful mission;

In what they call the 'good old days,'
Our patronesses won high praise.
It is our business to convey
Men, beasts, and chattels day by day;
You often bear us near your heart,
And would be loth from us to part.
Though never weary with our speed,
Full often we are tired indeed;
A tribe of insects, most minute,
Receive from us a name to suit.
Long since we used to condescend
Our aid in cookery to lend.
We guide the vessel in its course,
And multiply your puny force.

Charade No. 1.

THE veiling shades of night departed,
   On Lebanon's heights was a rosy glow,
When the serried ranks of the Lion-hearted
   Prepared for my *first* at the Moslem foe.
A voice was heard, like a clarion proud,
   Forth, forth to battle, to glory go!
To my lovely *second* I solemnly vowed
   To crush the insolent Moslem foe.
And forth they went, but the voice was stilled,—
   A stroke of my *whole* had laid him low;
By other hands was the vow fulfilled,
   For they tamed the pride of the Moslem foe.

Charade No. 2.

MY *first* gleams bright 'mid azure shields,
On rich emblazoned argent fields.
If you too often use my *second*,
An egotist you will be reckoned.
My *third*, it is a battle-cry;
And be it yours in every high,

And good, and noble end and aim,
As such it is the road to fame.
My belted *whole* you may descry
Illumining the southern sky.

Charade No. 3.

FROM his ruby pavilion Phœbus arose,
　　And looked down from his shining *first,*
And the earth at his glance, from her calm repose
　　Into beauty and gladness burst,
But the clouds of sorrow he could not chase,
Nor the gleaming tears upon Katie's face.

On a merry ride to the busy town
　　In my *first* she too surely had reckoned,
Disappointed and angry she flung herself down
　　On my *whole:* but alas, in my *second;*
So I told her, my *second* you never can be
While such haughty tempers so often I see.

Charade No. 4.

HURRAH for merry England!
　　For good Saint George hurrah!
For Richard of the Lion Heart,
　　The noble and the gay,
Returns from long captivity,
　　And 'tis a festal day.

With chivalry and minstrelsy
　　The hours shall speed along,
Where meet the beauteous and the brave,
　　The gentle and the strong.
(I would my *first* had gazed upon
　　The gladly loyal throng.)

The warriors of Palestine,
　　Who led my *second* well

When on the ranks of Saladin
    Like avalanche they fell,
Now in the tournament alone
    A fancied foe repel.

The Saxon serf may lay aside
    His clumsy *third,* I trow;
And leave it in the silent field,
    With cool and sweatless brow;
For what has he to do to-day
    With weary spade and plough?

But who is he, the Saxon youth,
    With royal Saxon bride,
Who Saracen and Templar hath
    Successfully defied?
He is my famous *whole,* I ween,
    The valiant and the tried.

Charade No. 5.

MY *second* could never produce my *first,*
Though its opposite frequently may;
'Tis a thing that's trampled upon and cursed,
So tell me its name, I pray.

In my *whole* both my *second* and *first* you would see,
With more of the latter than pleasant;
A treat I consider this latter to be,
Though, like all earthly good, evanescent.

Above my *second* 'tis commonly borne,
Though carefully kept below it;
Full many a home it has caused to mourn,
And the newspaper accidents show it.

When my *second* is looking its dullest and worst,
And my *whole* must be dreary indeed,
Like a hard-hearted tyrant comes forth my *first,*
With whom it were vain to plead.

Charade No. 6.

WHERE the tall pine-forest made
Deepest, darkest, holiest shade,
Came Nesota, sorrow-laden,
She, the lovely Indian maiden.
Came, ere she had waited long,
Karanò, the swift, the strong;
He, who bowed to nought beside,
Bent to her in lowly pride;
Bent, until his lofty brow,
Loftiest of the tribes around,
Touched the greensward hallowed now,
Where her *first* had kissed the ground.

'Karanò! arise and fly!
Hands of power and wrath are nigh,
From thy side shall I be driven,
Like a willow lightning-riven.
Karanò, ere thou depart,
Lay this *second* on thy heart,
Token of Nesota's love,
From thy own, thy stricken dove.'
Trembling in his hand she laid
My shining *second,* then farewell!
She is gone, through bush and blade,
Fleetly as a wild gazelle.

Karanò, the swift, the strong,
Baffles all pursuers long,
Till the moon is on the wane;
Then a red deer they have slain.
To the treacherous banquet led,
When the new moon's feast is spread,
They have mingled in his bowl,
Secretly, my deadly *whole.*
Karanò hath found repose
Where my *whole* doth darkly wave,
And the tall pine-forests close
O'er Nesota's quiet grave.

Charade No. 7.

My *whole,* the poet of flood and fell,
    Of valley and breezy hill,
Has passed from the scenes he loved so well,
    And none his place may fill.
In his *first,* with their simple and childlike grace,
    Of his *second* an index all may trace.

Charade No. 8.

Soon the hour of dawn shall pass,
Clear and loud the lark is singing;
Swiftly through the waving grass
Now my bright-eyed *first* is springing.

Down the still and shadowy dale
Floats my *second,* sweetly telling,
'Morning lifts her misty veil,
Spectral darkness soon dispelling.'

Far remote from beaten way,
Now my dewy *whole* is bending;
And where summer breezes play
Sweetness to their breath is lending.

Charade No. 9.

Distant from the noisy town
Sits my *first* and *next* alone,
In my ivy-wreathen *whole,*
Loved and blessed by many a soul.

More than on my *first,* I ween,
With his brethren he hath been;
But my *third* hath touched his brow,
And he waits in silence now;

Hoping soon to see the day
When his *second,* far away,

May replace his trembling voice:
This shall make his *third* rejoice.

Charade No. 10.

My *first* dwells in the torrid zone,
　　Its beauty and its boon,
Yet this the Esquimaux must own
　　Beneath an Arctic moon.

He who would do it is untrue,
　　Though all in every land
To bear it off in strife desire,
　　It always is at hand.

My *first* and *next* in days of yore
　　Went forth in lowly guise:
A staff was theirs, but little store
　　Of what the world would prize.

Yet one, alas! in later days,
　　With murder on his brow,
Revealed how far in guilty ways
　　A child of earth may go.

My *last* I think you'll quickly name
　　In half a minute more;
Are twenty hundreds quite the same
　　As just a hundred score?

For if you say what each would be,
　　The name you will have got;
And yet, reversing, you will see
　　That surely it is *not*.

My *whole* I leave without debate,
　　For 'tis not woman's mission
To criticise the wise and great
　　And play the politician.

Charade No. 11.

AWAKE, ye sleepers!
My *first* hath sung his loud reveille,
And wakened through the glistening dale
 The early reapers.

 Why will ye linger?
Is it no *second* that ye hear
The morning hymn, so glad and clear,
 Of that wise singer?

 Come forth, nor tarry!
And track the busy-wingèd bee,
Who from my *whole* right joyously
 Sweet spoil doth carry.

Charade No. 12.

ARISE, my *first*! In peerless radiance beaming,
A veil of glory thou dost weave for earth:
The ocean waves to welcome thee are gleaming,
For thou alone to Beauty givest birth.

Shine forth, my *second*! Freshly now is flowing
The busy stream of life, and labour too;
Each heart with ardour, base or noble glowing,
Till thou shalt close, arresting all they do.

All hail, my *whole*! thou comest with rich pleasure
An angel from the land of pure delight,
The great man's blessing, and the poor man's treasure,
Our earnest of the day which knows no night.

Charade No. 13.

My *first* had spread her darksome wing
O'er all the loveliness of spring;
My *third* arose with mournful wail—
The young leaves told their first sad tale,
The old oak groaned, the flowerets sighed,
The hawthorn bloom was scattered wide:

But ere my gloomy *first* had passed,
When silent was my *third* at last,
My *whole* awoke the moonlight dell
To list the sweet tale she could tell;
Then mingled, in strange harmony,
Silence and sweetest melody.
'Your *second,* why such strange omission?'
'Tis but a tiny preposition.

Charade No. 14.

HEARD ye the long, low roar
Blend with the sea-mew's cry?
Saw ye the nearing shore
Where the white foam-wreaths lie?
O wait, seaman, wait while the tempest shall last,
For my *first* is a danger thou hast not passed.

How shall the seaman wait?
There stands his white-walled home,
From its blithely opened gate
Never more need he roam.
My *second* he brings from a distant realm,
And leaves he for ever the weary helm.

On! for the tide ebbs fast!
On! for the night grows dark,
But the cold wave-arms are cast
Round the seaman's sinking bark.
He makes my *whole* with the angry sea,—
Thine be the gold, so my life go free!

Charade No. 15.

My *whole* is but a species of my *third,*
Yet has my *third* no right to such a name
Unless my *first* and *second* form a word,
To which he lays an undisputed claim;
But if my *whole* renounce my *first* and *second,*
My *first* indeed he may, but not my *whole,* be reckoned.

Charade No. 16.

THE all-victorious Roman
    Hath raised his eagles high,
The Carthaginian foeman
    Right proudly to defy.

Forth marched in noble daring
    The leader of the day,
A mighty *second* bearing
    In all the stern affray.

Ye glorious ranks, assemble!
    'Push on, my *first*,' he cried,
'And soon their *whole* shall tremble,
    And crushed shall be their pride.'

Charade No. 17.

ENTER my *first* with a studied grace,
Conceit in his head, and a smirk on his face;
Of fashion he deems himself quite the top,
And he's scented like any perfumer's shop;
So among the ladies he's surely reckoned,
For the evening at least, to be quite my *second.*
But oh! what a fall for the brilliant star!
A lady's whisper is heard too far:
'Of all the flowers that ever were,
The only one I to him compare
Is my scentless *whole,* with its gaudy stare.'
Not quite rightly spelt, but comparison rare.

Charade No. 18.

A BRIGHT and joyous frame of mind,
With Cephas properly combined,
Produce, I'll boldly dare to say,
A statesman of the present day.

The first part of a manuscript score, in F.R.H.'s hand. See page 235 of this book.

A black-and-white copy of a color oil portrait of Frances painted by Solomon Cole in 1845, when she was eight years old.

Chords for Children.

Sunday Bells.[1]

O SWEET Sabbath bells!
A message of musical chiming
Ye bring us from God, and we know what you say;
Now rising, now falling,
So tunefully calling
His children to seek Him, and praise Him to-day.

The day we love best!
The brightest and best of the seven,
The pearl of the week, and the light of our way;
We hold it a treasure,
And count it a pleasure,
To welcome its dawning and praise Him to-day.

O sweet Sabbath rest!
The gift of our Father in heaven;
A herald sent down from the home far away,
With peace for the weary,
And joy for the dreary:
Then, oh! let us thank Him, and praise Him to-day.

Rejoice and be glad!
'Tis the day of our Saviour and Brother,
The Life that is risen, the Truth and the Way;
Salvation He brought us
When wand'ring He sought us,
With blood He hath bought us: then praise Him to-day.

[1] From 'Sacred Songs for Little Singers,' Novello & Co.

Flowers.

BUDS and bells! Sweet April pleasures,
    Springing all around,
White and gold and crimson treasures,
    From the cold, unlovely ground!
He who gave them grace and hue
    Made the little children too!

When the weary little flowers
    Close their starry eyes,
By the dark and dewy hours
    Strength and freshness God supplies.
He who sends the gentle dew
    Cares for little children too!

Then He gives the pleasant weather,
    Sunshine warm and free,
Making all things glad together,
    Kind to them and kind to me.
Lovely flowers! He loveth you,
    And the little children too!

Though we cannot hear you singing
    Softly chiming lays,
Surely God can see you bringing
    Silent songs of wordless praise!
Hears your anthem, sweet and true,
    Hears the little children too!

Evening Prayer.

Now the light has gone away,
Saviour, listen while I pray,
Asking Thee to watch and keep,
And to send me quiet sleep.

Jesus, Saviour, wash away
All that has been wrong to-day,
Help me every day to be
Good and gentle, more like Thee.

Let my near and dear ones be
Always near and dear to Thee;
Oh, bring me and all I love
To Thy happy home above!

Now my evening praise I give:
Thou didst die that I might live,
All my blessings come from Thee;
Oh, how good Thou art to me!

Thou, my best and kindest Friend,
Thou wilt love me to the end!
Let me love Thee more and more,
Always better than before!

Stars.

THE golden glow is paling
    Between the cloudy bars;
I'm watching in the twilight
    To see the little stars.
I wish that they would sing to-night
    Their song of long ago;[1]
If we were only nearer them,
    What might we hear and know!

Are they the eyes of Angels,
    That always wake to keep
A loving watch above us,
    While we are fast asleep?
Or are they lamps that God has lit
    From His own glorious light,
To guide the little children's souls
    Whom He will call to-night?

We hardly see them twinkle
    In any summer night,
But in the winter evenings
    They sparkle clear and bright.

----

[1] 'When the morning stars sang together.'—JOB 38:7.

Is this to tell the little ones,
 So hungry, cold, and sad,
That there's a shining home for them,
 Where all is warm and glad?

More beautiful and glorious,
 And never cold and far,
Is He who always loves them,
 The Bright and Morning Star.
I wish those little children knew
 That holy, happy light!
Lord Jesus, shine on them, I pray,
 And make them glad to-night.

My Little Tree.

THEY tell me that my little tree
Is only just my age, but see,—
Already ripe and rosy fruit
Is peeping under every shoot!
How little have I brought,
But withered leaves of foolish thought;
And angry words, like thorn,
How many have I borne!

No fruit my little tree can bring
Without the gentle rain of spring;
Nor could it ever ripen one,
Without the glowing summer sun:
O Father! shed on me
Thy Holy Spirit from above,
That I may bring to Thee
The golden fruit of love.

Let sunshine of Thy grace increase
The pleasant fruit of joy and peace,
With purple gleam of gentleness,
That most of all my home may bless;
While faith and goodness meet
In ruby ripeness rich and sweet,

Let these in me be found,
And evermore abound.

Thy Kingdom Come.

GOD of heaven! hear our singing;
 Only little ones are we,
Yet a great petition bringing,
 Father, now we come to Thee.

Let Thy kingdom come, we pray Thee,
 Let the world in Thee find rest;
Let all know Thee, and obey Thee,
 Loving, praising, blessing, blessed!

Let the sweet and joyful story
 Of the Saviour's wondrous love,
Wake on earth a song of glory,
 Like the angels' song above.

Father, send the glorious hour,
 Every heart be Thine alone!
For the kingdom, and the power,
 And the glory are Thine own.

The Moon.

'The moon walking in brightness.'—JOB 31:26.

NOT long ago the moon was dark,
 No light she gave or gained;
She did not look upon the sun,
 So all her glory waned.
Now through the sky so broad and high,
 In robe of shining whiteness,
Among the solemn stars of God,
 She walks in brightness.

Look up to Him who is the Sun,
 The true and Only Light,

And seek the glory of His face,
　His smile so dear and bright.
Then making gladness all around,
　By gentleness and rightness,
You, too, shall shine with light divine,
　And walk in brightness.

Jessie's Friend.

Little Jessie, darling pet,
　Do you want a Friend?
One who never will forget,
　Loving to the end;
One whom you can tell when sad
　Everything that grieves;
One who loves to make you glad,
　One who never leaves.

Such a loving Friend is ours,
　Near us all the day,
Helping us in lesson hours,
　Smiling on our play;
Keeping us from doing wrong,
　Guarding everywhere,
Listening to each happy song
　And each little prayer.

Jessie, if you only knew
　What He is to me,
Surely you would seek Him too,
　You would ' come and see.'
Come, and you will find it true,
　Happy you will be;
Jesus says, and says to you,
　' Come, oh come to Me.'

The Bower.

WILL you come out and see
My pretty bower with me,
My sweet little house that lilac boughs have made;
With windows up on high,
Through which I see the sky,
And look up to Him who made the pleasant shade?

The sunbeams come and go
So brightly to and fro,
Like angels of light, too dazzling to be seen!
They weave a curtain fair
About my doorway there,
And paint all my walls with shining gold and green.

I have sweet music too,
And lovely songs for you,
To hear in my house among the lilac leaves;
For breezes softly play,
And robins sing all day:
I think this is praise that God on high receives.

Trust.

SADLY bend the flowers
In the heavy rain;
After beating showers,
Sunbeams come again.
Little birds are silent
All the dark night through;
When the morning dawneth,
Their songs are sweet and new.

When a sudden sorrow
Comes like cloud and night,
Wait for God's to-morrow;
All will then be bright.
Only wait and trust Him
Just a little while;
After evening tear-drops
Shall come the morning smile.

The Dying Sister.

DARLING boy,
Sister's joy,
With your loving smile,
Kiss me now,
On my brow,
Stay with me awhile!
He who has lovèd me,
He whom I longed to see,
Calls me away;
I must not stay.

He is near,
True and dear,
Darling, do not cry!
Jesus too
Loveth you,
Loves you more than I.
Kneel by my pillow here,
Tell Him the sorrow, dear;
He is so kind,
This you will find.

Angels bright,
Robed in light,
In that happy home,
Singing wait
At the gate,
Till He bids me come.
Soon, brother, I shall see
Him who has died for me;
I am so glad,
Yet you are sad.

Hymn and prayer
We did share,
Many an evening past;
Jesus heard
Every word,
This may be the last.

Ere next the light grows dim,
I may be there with Him.
Praising Him too,
Waiting for you!

The Angels' Song.

Now let us sing the Angels' Song,
That rang so sweet and clear,
When heavenly light and music fell
On earthly eye and ear,—
To Him we sing, our Saviour King,
Who always deigns to hear:
'Glory to God! and peace on earth.'

He came to tell the Father's love,
His goodness, truth, and grace;
To show the brightness of His smile,
The glory of His face;
With His own light, so full and bright,
The shades of death to chase.
'Glory to God! and peace on earth.'

He came to bring the weary ones
True peace and perfect rest;
To take away the guilt and sin
Which darkened and distressed;
That great and small might hear His call,
And all in Him be blessed.
'Glory to God! and peace on earth.'

He came to bring a glorious gift,
'Goodwill to men';—and why?
Because He loved us, Jesus came
For us to live and die.
Then, sweet and long, the Angels' Song
Again we raise on high:
'Glory to God! and peace on earth.'

Who Will Take Care of Me?

WRITTEN FOR EMILY F. W. W. SNEPP.

WHO will take care of me? darling, you say!
　　Lovingly, tenderly watched as you are!
Listen! I give you the answer to-day,
　　ONE who is never forgetful or far!

He will take care of you! all through the day,
　　Jesus is near you to keep you from ill;
Walking or resting, at lessons or play,
　　Jesus is with you and watching you still.

He will take care of you! all through the night,
　　Jesus, the Shepherd, His little one keeps;
Darkness to Him is the same as the light;
　　He never slumbers and He never sleeps.

He will take care of you! all through the year,
　　Crowning each day with His kindness and love,
Sending you blessing and shielding from fear,
　　Leading you on to the bright home above.

He will take care of you! yes, to the end!
　　Nothing can alter His love to His own.
Darling, be glad that you have such a Friend,
　　He will not leave you one moment alone!

Something to Do.

'SOMETHING to do, mamma, something to do!'
　　Who has not heard the cry?
　　Something to plan and something to try!
Something to do when the sky is blue,
　　And the sun is clear and high;
Something to do on a rainy day,
Tired of lessons or tired of play;
Something to do in the morning walk,
Better than merely to stroll and talk.
For the fidgety feet, oh, something to do,

For the mischievous fingers something too;
For the busy thought in the little brain,
    For the longing love of the little heart,
Something easy, and nice, and plain;
    Something in which they can all take part;
Something better than breakable toys,
Something for girls and something for boys!
I know, I know, and I'll tell you too,
Something for all of you now to do!

————

First, you must listen! Do you know
Where the poor sick children go?
Think of hundreds all together
In the pleasant summer weather,
Lying sadly day by day,
Having pain instead of play;
No dear mother sitting near,
    No papa to kiss good-night;
Brothers, sisters, playmates dear,
    All away and out of sight.
Little feet that cannot go
Where the pink-tipped daisies grow;
Little eyes that never see
Bud or blossom, bird or tree;
Little hands that folded lie
As the weary weeks go by.
What if you could send them flowers,
Brightening up the dismal hours?

Then the hospitals for others,
For the fathers and the mothers;
Where the weary sufferers lie,
    While the weeks go slowly past,
    Some with hope of cure at last,
Some to suffer till they die.
Now, while you are scampering free,
In your happy spring-tide glee,
They are lying sadly there,
Weak and sick—oh, don't you care?

Don't you want to cheer each one?
Don't you wish it could be done?

Then the poor old people too,
    In the dreary workhouse-room,
Nothing all day long to do,
    Nothing to light up the gloom!
Older, weaker, every day,
All their children gone away;
Nothing pleasant, nothing bright,
For the dimming, aching sight.
Would it not be nice to send
Nosegays by some loving friend?

Then if you could only see
    Where so many thousands live,
All in sin and misery,
Dirt and noise and poverty,
    What, oh, what would you not give,
Just some little thing to do
    That might do a little good!
Don't you want to help them too?
    I will tell you how you could!
Gather flowers for Jesus' sake,
For a loving hand to take
Into all those dreadful places,
Bringing smiles to haggard faces,
Bringing tears to hardened eyes;
Bringing back the memories
Of the home so long ago
Left for wickedness and woe,
Of the time, so far away,
When they learned to sing and pray.
Oh, you cannot guess the power
Of a little simple flower!

––––––––

And yet the message they should bear,
Of God our Father's love and care,

Is never really read aright
Without the Holy Spirit's light;—
Without the voice of Jesus, heard
In His own sweet and mighty word.
And so we *never* send the flowers
With only messages of ours;
But every group of buds and bells
The story of salvation tells.
Let every little nosegay bring
Not only fragrance of the spring,
But sweeter fragrance of His Name,
     Who saves and pardons, soothes and heals,
The living Saviour, still the Same,
     Who every pain and sorrow feels.
The little texts are sweeter far
Than lily-bell or primrose star;
And He will help you just to choose
The very words that He will use.
     To find them out and make a list
Of promise-words, so strong and bright,
So full of comfort and of light,
     That all their meaning *can't* be missed!
Think how every one may be
     God's own message from above
To some little girl or boy,
Changing sadness into joy,
Soothing some one's dreadful pain,
Making some one glad again,
     With His comfort and His love!
Calling them to Jesus' feet,
Showing them what He has done!
Darlings, will it not be sweet
     If He blesses only one?
Only *one?* Nay, ask Him still,
     Ask Him *every one* to bless!
He can do it, and He will;
Do not let us ask Him less!

———

Now then, set to work at once,
If you're not a thorough dunce!
Cut the little holders squarely,
    Keep the edges smooth and straight:
Now the paint-box: artists bold!
    Paint the borders firm and fairly
With your prettiest red or gold!
    Easy this, at any rate.
Now for writing—clearest, neatest,
    (Or it may be gently hinted,
    Better still if neatly printed.)
Tracing words the strongest, sweetest,—
Words that must and will avail,
Though the loveliest blossoms fail.
Then away, away, the first fine day!
Follow the breeze that is out at play,
Follow the bird and follow the bee,
Follow the butterfly flitting free,
    For I think they know
Where the sweetest wildflowers grow;
Bluebells in the shady dingle,
Where the violet-odours mingle;
Where the fairy primrose lamp
    Seems to light the hawthorn shade;
Orchis in the meadow damp,
    Cowslip in the sunny glade.
(But not the pale anemone,
For that will fade so speedily.)
Hedge and coppice, lane and field,
Gather all the store they yield!
Buttercups and daisies too,
Though so little prized by you,
Will be gold and silver treasure,
In their power of giving pleasure
To the poor in city alleys,
Far away from hills and valleys,
Who have never seen them grow
Since their childhood, long ago;

Or to children pale and small,
Who never saw them grow at all!
And don't forget the fair green leaves
    That have their own sweet tales to tell,
And waving grass that humbly weaves
    The emerald robe of bank and dell.
Is there some one at home who cannot go
To gather the flowers as they grow?
Then there is plenty for her to do
In making the nosegays up for you;
Getting them ready to travel away,
In time for the work of the coming day.

But oh, how busy you will be
    When the packing must be done!
Oh, the bustle and the glee,
    Will it not be famous fun?
And when the box is gone away,
    The pleasure need not all be past
    I think it will not be the last!
Just set to work another day!
    And send some more
    From the beautiful store
Which God keeps sending you fresh and new,
    And thank Him too
That He has given you 'SOMETHING TO DO!'

Loving Messages for the Little Ones.[1]

EVERY little flower that grows,
    Every little grassy blade,
Every little dewdrop, shows
    Jesus cares for all He made.
Jesus loves, and Jesus knows!
    So you need not be afraid!

[1] Six floral cards for Caswell.

FAIR the blossoms opening early!
    For the dew
Fell upon them, cool and pearly,
    Brightening every hue.
Like a little thirsty flower,
    Lift your face,
Seek the gentle, holy shower
    Of the Spirit's grace.

GRACE and glory! They are yours
    Through the Saviour's dying love;
For His own sweet word endures
    Longer than the stars above.
It shall never pass away,
So trust His living love to-day.

HAVE you not a song for Jesus?
    All the little buds and flowers,
All the merry birds and breezes,
    All the sunbeams and the showers,
Praise Him in their own sweet way!
What have you to sing to-day?
Bring your happiest songs, and sing
For your Saviour and your King.

KNOWING Christ was crucified,
    Knowing that He loves you now
Just as much as when He died
    With the thorns upon His brow,—
Stay and think! oh, should not you,
Love this blessèd Saviour too?

OPENING flowers I send to you
With a message sweet and true.
They may fade, but Jesus lives,—
Peace and grace and joy He gives.
Come to Him and you will know
What He waiteth to bestow!

F. R. H.'s Thanks.

FOR A PENCIL-CASE FROM HER BIBLE-CLASS.

O THOU who gatherest with loving arm
The tender lambs, who in each dark alarm
Wilt fold them safely,—listen to my prayer
Borne upwards on the silent morning air!
O Saviour, e'en to these extend Thy love,
And let them know its sweetness,—from above
Pour down on them Thy Spirit's quickening showers
That they may flourish as sweet heaven-born flowers!
O let Thy smile beam on them, let them be
For ever gladdened with its radiancy!
May they reflect Thine image pure and bright
As burnished silver, spotless in Thy sight;
Cleansed by Thy blood from every sinful stain,
Let not its free stream pour for them in vain.
When Thou in glory at the last Great Day
Shalt come, when earth and heaven shall flee away,
When, waking at the archangel's clarion sound,
The sleeping ones arise, and gather round
The great tribunal, then let each one here
At Thy right hand redeemed and saved appear,
And in the Book of Life let each one be
Inscribed as in eternal lines by Thee!
O Saviour, let *each* name be *written* there,
Not one be wanting in those pages gleaming!
Hear, Shepherd of the lambs, this fervent prayer,
For ever be Thy blessings o'er them streaming!

F. R. H.'s Thanks.

WITH A COPY OF 'SONGS OF GRACE AND GLORY,' TO CLARA O., FOR THIRTY
BUNCHES OF ASTLEY VIOLETS.

SWEET flowers of Spring,
All fresh and fair to see,
　　You sent to me;
Sweet holy ' Songs of Grace
　　And Glory,' too,
　　I send to you.

Grace all-sufficient may
　　You find, and know
　　On earth below,
Till God's own glory crown
　　Your faith and love,
　　In heaven above.

Inscription in a Copy of 'Life's Morning.'

By Him ' Life's *Morning* ' lovelit be,
Who loved, and lived and died for thee:
So shall thy *Noontide* never know
Earth's burning thirst, or withering glow:
And thou shalt fear no gathering night;
At *Eventide* it shall be light.

Little Nora.

FAR off upon a western shore,
　　Where wildest billows roam,
Beneath the great grim rocks there stands
　　A tiny cabin home;

And in it dwells a little one,
　　With eyes of laughing blue,
And lips as red as any rose
　　With early sparkling dew.

Her father was a fisher, and
  Went out with every tide,
While Nora sat and watched alone
  By her sick mother's side.

It was a weary thing to sit
  For many a long, long day,
Without a ramble on the beach,
  Or e'en a thought of play;

But Nora did not think it hard,
  She loved her mother so,
And in a thousand ways she tried
  Her earnest love to show.

One day she left the cabin door,
  And walked a long, long way—
Now high upon the breezy cliffs,
  Now close to ocean spray.

She went to seek some remedy
  To ease her mother's pain,
Tho' little hope there was that she
  Could e'er be well again.

The ruby clouds have curtained o'er
  The golden glowing west,
Where 'neath the white-winged wavelets now
  The sun hath gone to rest;

But little Nora comes not yet!
  The mother's fears arise,
The evening breeze brings nothing save
  The seabird's mournful cries.

The twilight hour is passing fast
  In weariness and pain,
She waits and listens for her child,
  As yet she waits in vain.

Hark, hark! a bounding step is heard
   Along the pebbly shore,
And now a tiny hand is laid
   Upon the cabin door;

'Oh, mother, darling mother, I
   Have such good news to tell!
Far more than medicine I have brought
   To make you glad and well!'

More brightly gleamed her joyous eye,
   And rosier grew her cheek,
While forth she poured the happy words,
   As fast as tongue could speak.

'I bought the medicine, mother dear,
   And turned to come away,
When by me stood a kind grave man,
   And gently bade me stay;

'And then he spoke sweet words to me,
   About the Saviour's love,
And of the glorious home where all
   His children meet above.

'He told me Jesus loved us so
   That He came down to die,
And suffered all instead of us;—
   And then it made me cry:

'He said His blood was quite enough
   To wash our sins away,
And make us fit for Heaven at once
   If we should die to-day.

'So, mother dear, we shall not need
   To purgatory go;
If Jesus has forgiven all,
   That is enough, you know!'

The rosy glow had rested on
   The mother's whitening cheek;

'Twas fading now, and Nora ceased—
      Then came a long wild shriek,—

'Oh, mother, speak to me once more,—
      Oh, is she really dead?'
'Twas even so, the hand was cold,
      And stilled the throbbing head;

Yes, even while those blessèd words
      Like angel-music fell,
Her weary spirit passed away,
      But whither! who may tell?

Oh, bitter were the tears which fell
      From little Nora's eye,
And many a day and night had passed
      Ere they again were dry.

But bitterest were they when she thought,
      'Oh, I can never tell
If with that blessèd Saviour now,
      Sweet mother, thou dost dwell!

'Ah! had I only sooner known
      What I have heard to-day,
I would have told her more of Him
      Before she went away;

'For perhaps she did not hear me then,
      So she could never know
The way that Jesus Christ has made
      To His bright home to go.

'I love Him, yes, I'm sure I do,
      Then He will take me home
To be with Him for evermore,
      Where sorrow cannot come;

'But oh, I cannot bear to think,
      When I His glory see,
And rest within the Saviour's arms—
      Where will my mother be?'

Dear children, you have learnt the way
    To that bright home above,
You have been told of Jesus and
    His deep and tender love;

In Ireland there are little ones
    Whose hearts are very sad,
Oh, won't you try and send to them
    Sweet words to make them glad?

'Come Over and Help Us.'

THE IRISH CHILD'S CRY.

OH, children of England, beyond the blue sea,
Your poor little brothers and sisters are we;
'Tis not much affection or pity we find,
But we hear you are loving and gentle and kind;
So will you not listen a minute or two,
While we tell you a tale that is all of it true?

We live in a cabin, dark, smoky, and poor;
At night we lie down on the hard dirty floor;
Our clothes are oft tattered, and shoes we have none;
Our food we must beg, as we always have done;
So cold and so hungry, and wretched are we,
It would make you quite sad if you only could see.

There's no one to teach us poor children to read;
There's no one to help us, and no one to lead;
There's no one at all that will tell us the way
To be happy or safe, or teach us to pray:
To the bright place above us we all want to go,
But we cannot,—for how to get there we don't know.

They tell us the Virgin will hear if we call,
But sure in one minute she can't hear us all.
And the saints are too busy in Heaven, we hear;
Then often the priests make us tremble with fear
At the fire of purgatory, which, as they tell,
Is almost as dreadful as going to hell.

Oh, will you not help us, and send us a ray
Of the light of the Gospel, to brighten our way?
Oh, will you not tell us the beautiful story
Of Jesus, who came from His dwelling of glory
To save little children, and not only you,
But even the poor ragged Irish ones too?

The English Child's Reply.

WE have heard the call from your fair green Isle;
    Our hearts have wept at your saddening tale;
And we long to waken a brighter smile
    By a story of love which shall never fail.

We should like you to come to our Bible-land,
    And share our comforts and blessings too;
We would take you all with a sister's hand,
    And try to teach and to gladden you.

But you're so far off that it cannot be,
    And we have no wings, or to you we'd fly;
So we'll try to send o'er the foaming sea
    Sweet words to brighten each heavy eye,—

Sweet words of Him, who was once so poor,
    That He had not where to lay His head;
But hath opened now the gleaming door
    To the palace of light, where His feast is spread.

There you may enter; He calls each one,—
    You're as welcome there as the greatest king!
Come to Him then, for He casts out none,
    And nothing at all do you need to bring.

He will change your rags for a robe of white,
    An angel-harp, and a crown of gold;
You may dwell for aye in His presence bright,
    And the beaming smiles of His love behold.

We will gladly save from our little store
    Our pennies, our farthings, from day to day,
And only wish we could do far more;
    But for Erin's children we'll always pray.

The Disappointed Carol Singers.

Oh, must we not sing our Christmas hymn,
    And will you not hear our song?
With joyous voice, but with weary limb,
    We have roamed the whole day long!

We have thought of the merry Christmas time
    For many a week before,
And have gleefully learnt our Christmas rhyme
    To carol at your door.

There are no merry larks to wake you now,
    No blackbirds in woody dell;
The nightingale loves not the leafless bough,
    The humming bee sleeps in his cell.

Oh, winter is gloomy and dark enough,
    And must it be silent too?
Are the chorus of winds and the storm-song rough
    The only sweet music for you?

But we are the birds of the winter day,
    When all else is dark and still;
Then, lady, send us not all away,
    And with sorrow our eager hearts fill.

Oh, do not thus wave your beautiful hand,
    And bid us unheard to go;
For the carolling time of our little band
    Comes but once a year, you know.

The Happiest Christmas Day.

SYBIL, my little one, come away,
I have a plan for Christmas Day:
Put on your hat, and trot with me,
A dear little suffering girl to see.

'Tis not very far, and there's plenty of time,
For the bells have not begun to chime;
So, Sybil, over the sparkling snow
To dear little Lizzie let us go.

Dear little Lizzie is ill and weak,
Only just able to smile and speak.
Yesterday morning I stood by her bed;
Now, shall I tell you what she said?

'Christmas is coming to-morrow,' said I.
'I shall be happy!' was Lizzie's reply;
'Happy, *so* happy!' I wish you had heard
How sweetly and joyously rang that word.

'Dear little Lizzie, lying in pain,
With never a hope to be better again,
Lying so lonely, what will you do?
Why will the day be so happy to you?'

Lizzie looked up with a smile as bright
As if she were full of some new delight;
And the sweet little lips just parted to say,
'I shall think of Jesus all Christmas Day!'

How would you like to take her the spray
Of red-berried holly I gave you to-day?
And what if we gave her the pretty wreath too
That Bertha has made with ivy and yew?

The green and the scarlet would brighten the gloom
Of dear little Lizzie's shady room;
And, Sybil, I know she would like us to sing
A Christmas song of the new-born King.

Sybil, my little one, if we do,
It will help us to 'think of Jesus' too;
And Lizzie was right, for that is the way
To have the happiest Christmas Day!

Coming into the Shade.

OUT in the midsummer sunshine,
　　Out in the golden light,
Merrily helping the gardener,
　　Ever so busy and bright,—
With tiny barrow and rake and hoe,
Helena flitted to and fro.

But the midsummer sun rose higher
　　Over the flowery spot;
'I must rest a little now,' she said,
　　'I am so tired and hot.
Oh, let me come to you, and look
At the pictures in your beautiful book.'

Why we should leave the sunny lawn
　　She did not understand,
But cheerily, trustfully, Helena laid
　　In mine, her little brown hand,
And I led her away to a shady room,
To rest in the coolness and the gloom.

For she could not have seen the pictures
　　Out in that dazzling light;
The book was there with its colours fair,
　　But the sunshine was too bright.
But in the shade I could let her look
At the pictures in my beautiful book.

'I have never seen them before,' she said,
　　'I am so glad I came!
And the gardener will manage the flowers, I think
　　Without me, just the same!
And I need not trouble at all, you know,
About my barrow and rake and hoe.'

So page after page was gently turned,
　　As I showed her one by one,
And told her what the pictures meant,
　　Till the beautiful book was done.
And *then*—I shall not soon forget
The loving kiss of my tiny pet.

And *now*—I shall not soon forget
　　The lesson she had taught,
How from the sunshine into the shade
　　God's little ones are brought,
That they may see what He could not show
Among the flowers in the summer glow.

Begin at Once.

BAND OF HOPE SONG.

BEGIN at once! In the pleasant days,
　　While we are all together,
While we can join in prayer and praise,
While we can meet for healthful plays,
　　In the glow of summer weather.
Begin at once, with heart and hand,
And swell the ranks of our happy band.

Begin at once! For we do not know
　　What may befall to-morrow!
Many a tempter, many a foe
Lieth in wait where'er you go,
　　With the snare that leads to sorrow.
Begin at once! nor doubting stand,
But swell the ranks of our happy band.

Begin at once! There is much to do;
　　Oh, do not wait for others!
Join us to-day!—be brave and true;
Join us to-day!—there's room for you,
　　And a welcome from your brothers.
Begin at once! for the work is grand
That God has given to our happy band.

Begin at once! In the strength of God,
　　For that will never fail you!
Under His banner, bright and broad,
You shall be safe from fear and fraud,
　　And from all that can assail you.
Begin at once,—with resolute stand,
And swell the ranks of our happy band.

'That's Not the Way at Sea.'

Reply of Captain Bourchier of the training-ship *Goliath,* when his boys
entreated him to save himself from the burning wreck. 1876.

He stood upon the fiery deck,
　　Our Captain kind and brave!
He would not leave the burning wreck,
　　While there was one to save.
We wanted him to go before,
　　And we would follow fast;
We could not bear to leave him there,
　　Beside the blazing mast.
But his voice rang out in a cheery shout,
　　And noble words spoke he,—
'That's not the way at sea, my boys,
　　That's not the way at sea!'

So each one did as he was bid,
　　And into the boats we passed,
While closer came the scorching flame,
　　And our Captain was the last.
Yet once again he dared his life,
　　One little lad to save;
Then we pulled to shore from the blaze and roar,
　　With our Captain kind and brave.
In the face of Death, with its fiery breath,
　　He had stood,—and so would we!
For that's the way at sea, my boys,
　　For that's the way at sea!

Now let the noble words resound,
    And echo far and free,
Wherever English hearts are found,
    On English shore or sea.
The iron nerve of duty, joined
    With golden vein of love,
Can dare to do, and dare to wait,
    With courage from above.
Our Captain's shout among the flames
    A watchword long shall be,—
'That's not the way at sea, my boys,
    That's not the way at sea!'

Welcome to Winterdyne.

FRANCIE and Willie, welcome to you!
    Alfred and Alice, welcome too!
To an English home and English love
Welcome, each little Irish dove!
Never again we hope to be
Kept apart by an angry sea.
A thousand welcomes, O darlings mine,
    When we see you at Winterdyne!

Welcome all to a warm new nest,
    Just the place for our doves to rest,
Through the oaks and beeches looking down
On the winding valley and quaint old town,
Where ivy green on the red rock grows,
And silvery Severn swiftly flows,
With an extra sparkle and glitter and shine
    Under the woods of Winterdyne.

On a quiet evening in lovely spring,
    In the tall old elms the nightingales sing;
Under the forest in twilight grey,
I have heard them more than a mile away,
Sweeter and louder and far more clear
Than any thrush you ever did hear;

Perhaps, when the evenings grow long and fine,
        They will sing to you in Winterdyne.

Little to sadden, and nothing to fear;
        Priest and Fenian never come here;
Only the sound of the Protestant bells
Up from the valley pleasantly swells,
And a beautiful arch, to church, is made
Under the sycamore avenue's shade;
You pass where its arching boughs entwine,
        Out of the gates of Winterdyne.

Welcome to merry old England! And yet
        We know that old Ireland you will not forget;
Many a thought and prayer will fly
Over the mountains of Wales so high,
Over the forest and over the sea,
To the home which no longer yours must be.
But farewells are over, O darlings mine,
        Now it is Welcome to Winterdyne!

To Jericho and Back.

Suggested by a child's remark, 'What a queer place Jericho must be, if all
the persons and things get there that are *wished* there!'

Once on a time I a visit had paid,
All very pleasant as long as I made
Remarks on the topics I fancied or guessed
Any one present was sure to like best.
Then came the trial of courage and skill;—
(Oh for a talent for gilding the pill!)
Out of my pocket with tremulous thought
A card for collecting was cautiously brought.

What the result, there is no need to tell;
Collectors are often received very well,
Sometimes, alas! it is quite the reverse,
So you take up the work for better, for worse;

Still, I was conscious 'twas better to go
After revealing my errand, and so
Forth in the mist of the evening I wandered,
And on changes of tone and of countenance pondered!

Weary the feet, and closing the day;
Is there not danger of losing the way?
Strange are the hills and the forests around;
Where shall a home-leading pathway be found?
I cannot turn back, and I cannot advance;—
Is it a nightmare, or is it a trance?
Shadowy figures are faintly seen,
Spectral and silent, dimly serene;
Persons and things in range on range,
All familiar, yet all so strange;
Shades of all things that ever annoyed,
All that ever one wished to avoid.

Strange though it be, I need not fear;
'Tis a wonderful region, and how I came here
I cannot explain, but as it is so,
Let me investigate whether or no,
And enumerate some of the objects I find;
No names shall be mentioned, so no one will mind.

Determining thus, I quickly began
Everything round me more closely to scan,
Hoping to make a report of the case
To friends who had never discovered the place;
Having set out on this singular track,
Not in a hurry was I to get back.

Aid unexpected was close to my side,
Soon I perceived an invisible guide,
Only a voice, clear, quiet, and low,
Telling me all that I wanted to know.

People of every age and class
Under review appeared to pass;
Some I recognised perfectly well,
(More of these than I choose to tell!)

Of others I learnt the name and degree
From the bodiless guide who followed me.

There were several sharp little girls
Who had made remarks on chignons and curls,
And dozens and dozens of dreadful boys
With special talents for mischief and noise;
Specimens, too, in greatest variety,
Of every sort of bores of society,—
Boorish bores, and bores polite,
People who stay too late at night,
People who make long morning calls,
People who think of nothing but balls,
People who never a move will make,
People who never a hint can take;
Strong-minded bores, and weak-minded too,
Masculine, feminine, not a few;
People who borrow books to lose,
People who will not wipe their shoes,
People who keep your mind on the rack
Lest some pussy escape from the sack;
Over stupid, and over clever;
People who seem to talk for ever;
People who mutter, and people who drawl,
People who will not talk at all.

There were ledgers and day-books in piles on piles,
And letters and papers in files on files;
Foolscap and parchment, deeds and wills;
And oh, such a mass of unpaid bills!

There was a wonderful heap of slates,
Scribbled all over with sums and dates,
With names of counties and names of towns,
With Latin verbs and German nouns,
Vulgar fractions and multiplication,
And plenty more of the like vexation.
And *finished* was seldom seen;
Many a half-worked cushion and screen,

Many a drawing just half done,
Plenty of things in haste begun;
Soon might Patience and Perseverance
Among this collection effect a clearance.

Now and then throughout my stay
Things arrived in a wholesale way;
Sometimes a house came gliding down,
Sometimes a village or even a town;
Sometimes a borough my eyes would meet,
With candidates, voters, and votes complete;
'But,' whispered my guide, 'the person who sent it
Was never the man who could represent it.'

'The person who sent it! that's not at all clear:
Who has the power to send things here?
What is the power, and how does one use it?
Can any one have it if only they choose it?'
'Every one has it,' responded my guide;
'Oft by yourself has the power been tried,
On yourself too, or you would not be here,
In this region of shadows so dismal and drear.
Only a wish is the power that brings
Hither this medley of persons and things;
Only a wish of the opposite kind
Loosens the spell, as you'll presently find.
Some one has wished you farther away,
That is the reason you came here to-day;
Some one may wish you were speedily near,
Then you no longer may stay with us here.
Watch your companions, you'll see at a glance
A few are awake, but most in a trance.
Thousands are sent who never know it,
Editors sending many a poet,
Children sending half their teachers,
Listeners sending half their preachers.
There are some who send their dearest friends
If they happen to cross their private ends,

Or give advice which is good and true,
If it's not the thing that they *wish* to do;
Or to be a little too quick of sight.'
(If they never came back, it would serve them right!)

Plenty of music went on meanwhile,
Not in the Handel Festival style!
For hither most people agree to despatch
New violins, with players to match,
Old pianos that rattle and jingle,
Or Broadwood grands that make your ears tingle
With polkas and waltzes four hours a day;
All barrel organs, whatever they play;
All German bands that won't play in tune;
People who practise too late or too soon;
Contraltos that groan, and sopranos that squall,
Basses that bellow, and tenors that bawl.
Suddenly, while these melodious strains
Filled up the measure of puzzles and pains,
Everything faded away from my gaze,
Into the deepening darkness and haze;
All the unbearable chaos of sound
Melted away into silence profound.

How I came back, to this day I don't know,
Only I found myself all in a glow,
Hastening into the parlour to see
If I had kept them all waiting for tea.
Welcoming voices said,—'We were afraid
You with some neighbour the evening had staid;
Your presence is wanted to brighten and cheer;
Where have you been? we were wishing you here!'
'Thanks,' cried I; 'you have called me away
From a limbo of dreary shades to-day.
May you never the pathway know
Leading away to JERICHO!
Or if you are sent on that dismal track,
May loving wishes soon summon you back!'

My Nest.

My lodging was on the cold rough ground,
  And my pillow a rocky shelf;
And the Poet's Corner was full of dust,
And bits of stick and dead leaves, just
  An emblem of myself!

But lo! I find that some little birds,
  With busy beak and wing,
Have made for me a cosy nest,
The very sort that I like best,
Where I can lie in pleasant rest,
  And twitter, if not sing!

And the Poet's Corner is swept so clean,
  And made so nice and neat,
That really I should feel quite rude,
If I don't, in common gratitude,
Produce some verses on the spot,
And pour them out all fresh and hot,
  For my little birds so sweet.

Ethelbert's 'Coming Home in the Dark.'

Did I tell you how we went to tea,
All by ourselves, with kind Mrs. B.?
And how we came home in the dark so late,
I think it was nearly half-past eight!
We liked the tea, and all the rest,
But coming home in the dark was best,—
Best of all! oh, it *was* such fun,
The nicest thing we have ever done.
Nurse took Willie, and Bertha took me,—
Bertha is such a great girl, you see;
She sometimes says to us, 'Now, little boys,
Don't you make such a dreadful noise,
You will wake little Sybil with all your riot!'
And then we have to be—oh, so quiet!

She is nearly eight, and ever so tall;
But Willie and I are not very small;
We are six years old, and our birthdays came
Both on one day, the very same.
So people say we are little twins,
And as much alike as two little pins.
And Papa likes having a pair of boys,
Although we make such a dreadful noise;
'Much more amusing,' we heard him say,
'Than a couple of odd ones any day!'
    It was only so very dark down below
Along the lane where the blackberries grow,
For the little stars were out in the sky,
And we laughed to see them, Willie and I,
For they twinkled away, so quick and bright,
I think they were laughing at us that night.
A bright one got up from behind a tree,
And peeped at Bertha and Willie and me;
And round the corner we saw another
Playing at hide-and-seek with his brother,
Popping out from a cloud, and then
Running behind it to hide again.
    And then the kind little Moon came out
To take care of the Stars as they played about;
She looked so quiet and good, we thought
That perhaps they went to her school to be taught,
And to learn from her how to shine so bright;
But Grandmamma told us we did not guess right,
For the Moon goes to school herself to the Sun:
Do you think she meant it only in fun?
    Then all of a sudden the Wind ran by,
And flew up to kiss the Stars in the sky;
He tucked them up, and said good-night,
And drew the curtain round them tight.
That was a great dark cloud, you see,
That hid the Stars from Willie and me.
I think they were sorry to go to bed,
For they did not look tired at all, we said;
And one or two of them tried to peep;

But very soon they were all asleep,
For the Wind kept singing their lullaby,
And we felt quite vexed with him, Willie and I.
    I think the Moon asked if she might not stay
To light us a little bit more of the way,
But he whistled quite loud, and we thought he said,
'No, no, no! you must go to bed!'
The good little Moon did what she was bid,
And under the curtains her pretty face hid;
And then it got darker and darker still;
Nurse said she was setting behind the hill.
So perhaps she was tired, and glad to go;
It's a long way across the sky, you know.
    We were not afraid, but we did not talk
As we came along the avenue walk;
And we did not *quite* like looking back,
For the pretty green trees were all quite black.
But I whispered to Willie that God was there,
And we need not be frightened, for He would take care
    And then all at once we saw the light
In the dining-room window, ever so bright;
And up we came through the little gate,—
Oh, it *was* so nice to come home so late!
And then we gave a famous shout,
For dear Mamma herself came out
To meet us, just as we got to the door;
But she had not expected us home before.
And then we took it by turns to talk,
And tell them about the tea and the walk;
And Papa *did* laugh so,—we wondered why!
At what we told him, Willie and I.

Another manuscript score in her hand. Frances was a musician to the core, and a very finely gifted composer.

Songs.

National Hymn.

Written by request to music by Rossini.

O Lord most high,
Who art God and Father,
Hear Thou our cry,
While Thy children gather!
Lord of Peace, oh hearken,
Though war-clouds darken!
Do Thou our labours bless,
And crown them with success!

Bend from Thy glory now,
Hear each suppliant vow!
And on our children pour
Blessings evermore.
Guarded by Thee,
England shall be
Bright in Thy light,
Strong in Thy might,
Glorious and free!

Hero and saint,
Victors at last,
Bid us not faint,
But follow, follow fast.
Make us, we pray,
Loyal as they,
Faithful and brave,
Our country to save!

When in the grim fight,
Pierceth the dim light,
Through the cleft ranks that shall close no more,

Fearfully flashing,
Awfully crashing,
Death-furrows follow the cannon's roar.
When wounded lie,
Ready to die;
When death is braved,
That life may be saved;
Teach us to show
Mercy with might,
Pardon the foe,
Crown Thou the right!

Father, hear us!
Thou art near us!
Guard and cheer us
By Thy strong hand!
Then Art resplendent,
Labour attendant,
Shall bless our land!

Lord, bless the land we love
God save our Queen!

Scotland's Welcome to H.R.H. Princess Louise.

SWEET Rose of the South! contented to rest
In the fair island home which thy presence has blessed:
From the Highlands resounding, glad welcome shall float,
And the Lowlands re-echo the jubilant note.

Merry England has loved thee and cherished thee long,
Her blessings go with thee in prayer and in song;
Bonnie Scotland has won thee, and lays at thy feet
Love tender and fervent, love loyal and sweet.

Chorus.—Our own bonnie Scotland with welcome shall ring,
While greeting and homage we loyally bring;
The crown of our love shall thy diadem be,
And the throne of our hearts is waiting for thee.

Then come, like the sunrise that gilds with a smile
The dark mountains and valleys of lonely Argyle;
Golden splendour shall fall on the pale northern snow,
And with roselight of love the purple shall glow.

Though the voice that should bless, and the hand that should seal,
Is 'away,' and at rest in 'the land o' the leal,'
May the God of thy father look graciously down,
With blessings on blessings thy gladness to crown.

Chorus.—Our own bonnie Scotland with welcome shall ring,
     While greeting and homage we loyally bring;
     The crown of our love shall thy diadem be,
     And the throne of our hearts is waiting for thee.

Severn Song.

THE Severn flow is soft and fair, as slowly
     The light grows dim;
The sunset glow is soft and full, and holy
     As evening hymn.
We float along beneath the forest darkling,
Blending with song the silence of the hour:
We swiftly glide where rapids bright and sparkling
Bear us beside the ruddy rock and tower.
    O softly, softly row in measured time,
     While nearer, nearer swells the curfew chime.
Now, now again adown the current shooting,
     New joy we hail;
While through the forest thrills the fairy fluting
     Of nightingale.
O sweet and sweeter that hidden lay,
That in the twilight dies away.
Then merrily onward! O merrily row!
And smoothly swift, O Severn, flow!

The Severn flow is swift and strong, as neareth
     The home we love;
The sunset glow has paled and passed, and cleareth
     The heaven above.

The children's eyes will soon be gently closing,
Calm stars arise and shine on earth instead;
And through the night, all peacefully reposing,
Angels of light shall guard each tiny bed.
    O swiftly, swiftly row o'er darkening stream,
     While nearer, nearer shines the home lamp's gleam.
Now, now awake the song of purest thrilling,
      Of home and love;
And call the echoes forth, with music filling
      The rocks above.
Our song is sweetest as falls the day,
For we are on our homeward way:
Then merrily onward! O merrily row!
And smoothly swift, O Severn, flow!

For Charity.

THE sun is burning, O little maiden,
Thou hast sweet water, is it for me?
I am so thirsty, so heavy-laden,
Give me cool water, for charity!
     Sparkling and gleaming,
     The crystal streaming
Seems but awaiting my only plea—
I am so thirsty, so heavy-laden,
Give me cool water, for charity!

O gentle maiden, I thirst no longer,
But sweeter waters thou hast for me:
Then pour them freely, from fountain stronger,
Sweet thoughts of kindness, for charity!
     The world is only
     A pathway lonely,
And hearts are waiting for sympathy;
Then pour them freely from fountain stronger
Sweet thoughts of kindness, for charity!

O little maiden, 'tis thine to brighten,
Like sparkling waters, life's lonely lea;

All grief to soften, all joy to heighten
With love and gladness, for charity!
Thus onward flowing,
All good bestowing,
A stream of blessing thy life shall be,
All grief to brighten, all joy to heighten
With love and gladness, for charity!

The Devonshire Yeoman's Home.

Ten years ago to-day our wedding bells were rung,
When all along the winding lane wild roses hung;
And now the roses cluster on our own white walls,
And down the lane resound our merry children's calls.
There's sunshine on the moor and on the glittering sea,
And sunshine in our hearts as fresh and fair and free;
We would not change our lot for London gold,
For home, our own sweet home, is sweeter now tenfold.

No city seasons come our pleasant year to mar;
The hay—the fruit—the harvest-time are merrier far,
For pictures and for music rare we need but look
Around our home, and listen to the grand old Book.
The hours flow on from morning prayer to evening praise,
With trust that lightens, love that brightens darkest days;
For though ten years have passed, love grows not old,
And home, our own dear home, is dearer now tenfold.

The Dawn of May.

Come away, come away, in the dawn of May,
When the dew is sparkling bright;
When the woods are seen
All in golden green
In the crystal, crystal light.
The sweet perfume of violet bloom,
And hawthorn fragrance rare,
From the cool mossy shade,
Or the warm sunny glade,
Is filling all the air.

Come away, come away, in the dawn of May,
When the lark and the white cloud meet;
When the tuneful breeze,
In the old oak trees,
Is harping, harping sweet.
With joyous thrill and merry trill,
The thrush and blackbird vie,
As they chant loving lays,
And a full song of praise,
To the Lord of earth and sky.

Come away, come away, in the dawn of May,
In the pearly morning-time,
When the cowslips spring,
And the blue-bells ring
Their fairy, fairy chime.
With happy song, we march along,
And carol on our way,
One in heart, one in voice,
Let us all now rejoice
In the sunny dawn of May.

The Tyrolese Spring Song.

THE meadows rejoice in their verdure so bright,
And glisten with pearl drops of dew,
The glaciers are gleaming in radiant light,
The breezes are fitful and few.
From heaven coming down, like a golden-haired child,
Fair Spring o'er the earth has sparklingly smiled,
With flower-twined staff, he goes forth o'er the wild.

The song of the birds and the herdsman's glad lay
Are heard in the morning so bright;
They sing when the bells, at the closing of day,
Awaken the stars of the night.
The swell of the joyous and heart-stirring song
Through mountain and valley is pealing along,
In a tide of rejoicing, all glorious and strong.

Then a fount of emotion awakes in the heart,
    And the spirit is mightily stirred,
The Tyrolese longs from his roof to depart
    To wander and roam as he will;
When the meadows rejoice in their emerald glow,
The sons of the mountain forth joyously go,
The world in its beauty and gladness to know.

My Messengers.

I SAID to the merry birds of the woods,
    'Carry a song to the Fair One!'
They twittered and trilled, for they quite understood,
    And flew away blithely to bear one.
Then listen, if, tapping thy window sill,
    They come with their chirping and singing,
O listen! for over forest and hill,
    My message of love they are bringing.

I said to the lilies, 'Carry for me,
    Carry a smile to the Sweetest!'
They nodded and said, 'Our sister is she,
    That loveliest lily thou greetest.
O gather and send us,' they whispered to me,
    'And bid us bloom fragrantly near her,
To waken her smile, rejoicing to be
    Thy message of comfort to cheer her.'

I said to the golden stars of night,
    'O carry my love to the Dearest!
In darkness surrounding with silver light
    The Brightest, the ever Nearest!'
And watchest thou now, my own, my love,
    In weary and lonely sadness?
Look up to the stars in the heaven,
    They bear thee my message of gladness.

God Keep Thee.

O DARK was the day when I left her alone,
　My darling, so gentle, so dear!
O sad, yet O sweet was her silvery tone,
　As she said, with a glistening tear:—
'Oh, must thou go forth in the cold world to-day,
And leave me, to wander so far, far away?
Oh, think of the moments of joy that are flown,
And remember the love that is ever thine own!
　　Oh, Father, I pray, protect him alway,
　　　Protect by night and by day!'
I left thee, indeed, in the cold world to roam,
Yet, darling, my heart stayed behind!
In dreams I come back to the dear little home,
　And unaltered is all that I find.
And then, as I listen, I hear a soft tone
Float up from thy lips to the emerald throne,
'Oh, keep him, and bless him, by night and by day,
And guard him for me while so far, far away.
　　Oh, Father, I pray, protect him alway,
　　　Protect by night and by day!'

The ocean of life with its hurrying swell
　Has drifted me far on its tide,
But only and ever my true heart shall dwell
　In quiet and love at thy side.
And when all the wandering and drifting are o'er,
My rest and my haven, my golden-bright shore,
My joy, and my home, and my heart too, shall be
For ever, belovèd, for ever with thee!
　　Oh, Father, I pray, protect her alway,
　　　Protect by night and by day!

Rose of Roses.

OH, the treasures of the Spring,
　Crimson, blue, and golden!

Scattered from her radiant wing,
   Nothing is withholden.
Myriad blossoms ope each hour,
   Who shall tell the fairest?
But I miss the sweetest flower,
   Rose, of roses rarest.

Oh, the glory of the light,
   Through the noontide beaming!
Oh, the stars of purple light,
   Through the darkness gleaming!
But the star of softest ray,
   Clearest, purest, whitest,
Shineth only far away,
   Star, of stars the brightest!

Oh, the music everywhere!
   Joyous larks are singing,
Rivulets are flowing fair,
   Merry chimes are ringing.
But I miss from day to day
   Music that is dearest,
Even thine, though far away,
   Heart, of hearts the nearest.

Hast Thou a Thought?

WHEN home I came after many a day
Of longing and waiting so far away,
I sought the path in the sunset glow,
Where the bright eyes watched for me long ago.
And the fair night fell as I whispered low,
'Hast thou a thought of the wanderer now?'

Then softly glimmered a sudden light,
And I saw thee lean from the casement bright,
And a name floated forth from a voice so sweet!
No doubting of heart and no lingering of feet!
For I hastened near, and I whispered low,
'Hast thou a thought for the wanderer now?'

Then silently nestled my own sweet bird,
With a joy too deep for a song or word;
And I question no more, for the answer I know!
So I ask not aloud, and I ask not low,
Whether every night, whether every day,
Thou hadst a thought of thy love far away!

My Welcome.

I HAVE waited for thy coming, love,
    As the song-bird waits for spring,
Ere the echo of his merry lay
    Makes the forest arches ring;
But when the spring is gone, love,
    And summer's glory fills,
How musical the hush, love,
    Between the shadowy hills.

I have waited for thy coming, love,
    Yet bring to greet thee near,
Nor laugh, nor words, nor carol gay,
    But stillness and a tear;
But if I know thy heart, love,
    And if thou readest mine,
This welcome is the best, love,
    The truest, fondest sign.

A Wife's Letter.

'Not that I've anything special to say, but only that it comes from me.'—
E. to G., Jan. 11, 1869.

MY OWN!
        You won't expect to hear
    As you have only just departed,
But I'll be better than you fear,
    And write as soon as you have started.
It seems a long and tiresome day;
    I'm merely writing, as you see,

Not that I've anything to say,
   But only that it comes from me.

I watched the carriage out of sight,
   And then came back to do my work;
I could not set the stitches right,
   And so for once the task I'll shirk;
I've put the children's frocks away
   To write a line or two to thee,
Not that I've anything to say,
   But only that it comes from me.

I hope the train will not be late,
   And that it will not freeze or rain,
And oh! if you should have to wait,
   Be sure you don't catch cold again.
I wish this moment on the way
   To overtake you I could be!
Not that I've anything to say,
   But only to be nearer thee.

'Tis six-and-twenty hours almost
   Before I see you, as I've reckoned;
But you'll get this by early post,
   And you'll be home before the second.
I'd like to sit and write all day
   To Some One, if my hands were free,
Not that I've anything to say,
   But only that it comes from me.

Though this is such a stupid letter,
   With love and kisses 'tis impearled;
I know that you will like it better
   Than all the poems in the world.
I trust that all is safe and well,
   Although I am not there to see;
I've nothing else, my Own, to tell,
   But only that this comes from me.

The Husband's Reply.

FIVE minutes all I have to spare,
    But these, my Own, I give to you!
Your precious letter's lying there,
    So full and fond, so dear and true.
I think you'll hardly hope to hear,
    As I shall soon be home again,
But you'll get this at seven, dear,
    I'm due at eight, and *then*—oh *then!*

A hurried word or two assures
    That all is safe and well, my dove.
My notes are not so long as yours,
    Though worth as much in golden love.
So where I've been, and whom I've seen,
    And how, and why, and what, and when,
I'll tell you when we meet, my queen,
    At eight o'clock,—and *then*—oh *then!*

Only for One.

I HAVE a smile my friends to greet,
Hearty and pleasant for all I meet,
        Hidden from none:
But I have a smile that they do not know,
Lit by a deeper, tenderer glow,
And I keep it bright in my heart below,
        Only for one!

I have a song for every ear,
Leaving an echo to soothe and cheer
        When it is done:
But I have a music of truer beat,
Not to be poured at the great world's feet,
Richer and softer and far more sweet,
        Only for one!

I have a love for all who care
Aught of its warmth to claim, or share,
   Free as the sun;
But I have a love which I do not hint,
Gold that is stamped with my soul's imprint,
A wealth of love, both mine and mint,
   Only for one!

One for the Other.

Was it 'only for one,' dear, 'only for one,'
  That the smile, and the song, and the love should be?
Then a smile shall flash, and a song shall flow,
And a deep, deep love shall thrill and glow,
  Only for thee, dear, only for thee!
    For so shall it be,
  One for the other—nevermore lonely,
  One for the other—ever and only.

The blossoms that now at my feet you lay
  Shall be golden fruit for you and me,
When spring and summer have passed away,
And softly falls the autumn day,
  Like the close of a holy melody.
    For so shall it be,
  One for the other—nevermore lonely,
  One for the other—ever and only.

Yes! one for the other, blessing and blessed,
  In the strength of His gladness, calm and bright,
But with more of blessing and love for all,
The smile shall beam, and the song shall fall,
  Touching the shadows around with light,—
    Because it shall be
  One for the other—nevermore lonely,
  One for the other—ever and only!

Thinking Together, or Gravitation.

OF what are you thinking now, dear,
　　Now that good-night is said,
Now that the children's eyes are shut,
　　And the stars shine out instead;
Now that the far church-clock sounds near,
　　For the world is all so still,
And the cottage twinkle has long gone out
　　On the slope of the fir-crowned hill?

Of what are you thinking now, dear?
　　Could a thought-flash reach me here,
The message would not surprise me,
　　But only strengthen and cheer.
For love has told it already,
　　That seer so bold and true!
I know you are thinking of me, dear,
　　For I am thinking of you.

I know you are thinking of me, dear,
　　For the whirl of the day hath ceased,
The circling force is spent at last,
　　And our spirits are released;
And heart to heart hath swiftly turned
　　After the lonely strife,
For each is the centre of each, dear,
　　By the law of our truest life.

We have but one other thought, dear,
　　In these quiet, restful hours,
And that is of Him whose love is twined
　　In a threefold cord with ours.
So you are thinking of me, dear,
　　And I am thinking of you,
And He is thinking of us both:
　　Is it not sweet and true?

There Is Music by the River.

THERE is music by the river,
  And music by the sea,
And music in the waterfall
  That gusheth glad and free.
There is music in the brooklet
  That singeth all alone,
There is music in the fountain
  With its silver-tinkling tone.

But the music of thy spirit
  Is sweeter far to me
Than the melody of rivers,
  Or the anthems of the sea.
Why should I dwell in silence
  When the music is so near
That may overflow my spirit
      So full, so clear!
      Oh! let me listen!

There is music in the forest,
  A myriad-voicèd song;
And music on the mountains
  As the great winds rush along:
There is music in the gladness
  Of morning's merry light,
And in silence of the noontide,
  And in hush of starry night.

But a deeper, holier music
  Is the music of thy soul,
And I think the angels listen
  As its starry echoes roll.
Why should I dwell in silence
  When the music that is thine
May overflow my spirit
      And blend—with mine!
      Oh! let me listen!

'The Shining Light, That Shineth More and More unto the Perfect Day.'

PROVERBS 4:18.

A YEAR ago the gold light
    Sweet morning made for me;
A tender and untold light,
    Like music on the sea.
Light and music twining
    In melodious glory,
A rare and radiant shining
    On my changing story.

To-day the golden sunlight
    Is full and broad and strong;
The glory of the One light
    Must overflow in song;
Song that floweth ever,
    Sweeter every day,
Song whose echoes never,
    Never die away.

How shall the light be clearer
    That is so bright to-day?
How shall the hope be dearer
    That pours such joyous ray?
I am only waiting
    For the answer golden,
What faith is antedating
    Shall not be withholden.

Golden Land.

FAR from home alone I wander
    Over mountain and pathless wave,
But the fair land that shineth yonder
    Claimeth the love that erst it gave.
Golden Land, so far, so nearing!
    Land of those who wait for me!

Ever brighter the vision cheering,
Golden Land, I haste to thee!

On my path a golden sunlight
Softly falls where'er I roam,
And I know it is the one light
Both of exile and of home.
Golden Land, so far, so near,
On my heart engraven clear,
Though I wander from strand to strand,
Dwells my heart in that Golden Land.

Twilight Voices.

(IN ILLNESS.)

WHAT are the whispering voices
That awake at twilight fall?
Do they come from the golden sunset
With their haunting, haunting call?
They tell me of breezy spring-times,
And of dreamy summer eves,
And of snow-wreaths merrily shaken
From the shining ivy leaves.
But the far-off treble changeth
To a tenor tone, and so
I know that the voices tell me
Only of long ago.
I hear you, I hear you,
In the gentle twilight fall
Come to me, come!
With your haunting, haunting call.

What are the tuneful voices
That awake at early dawn?
Do they come from the orient portals
Of the palace of the morn?
They tell of a Golden City
With pearl and jasper bright,

And of shining forms that beckon
 From the pure and dazzling light.
Then a rush of far-off harpings
 Blends with the voices clear,
And I know that the night is passing,
 And I know that the day is near!
I hear you, I hear you,
  Sweet voices of the dawn!
Come to me, come!
 In the early, early morn.

See also pages 386, 419, and 402–403. Such leaflets, pamphlets, and cards were—and are—easy to print and to give to many.

(11) Everlasting Salvation.
(to follow "Final Perseverance.")

734 Isa. 45. 17. "Saved in the Lord with an everlasting salvation."
Tersteegen or Salzburg. 87. 87. D.

1 O What everlasting blessings! God outpoureth on His own!
Ours by promise true & faithful spoken from the eternal throne;
Ours by His eternal purpose ere the universe had place;
Ours the blood-sealed everlasting covenant of glorious grace.

2 With salvation everlasting He shall save us, He shall bless
With the largess of His grace, everlasting righteousness;
Ours the everlasting mercy, all His wondrous dealings prove,
Ours His everlasting kindness finish of everlasting love.

3 In the Lord God Jehovah (resting), everlasting strength have we;
He Himself, our sun, our glory, everlasting light shall be;
Everlasting life it most, purchased by the life laid down,
And our heads, oft bowed & weary, everlasting joy shall crown.

(over.

This is the front of a manuscript F.R.H. wrote, which she assigned as hymn number 734 in the very valuable hymnbook Songs of Grace and Glory, which she was preparing with Rev. Charles Busbridge Snepp. The next page has the completion of this manuscript.

4
We shall dwell with Christ for ever, When the shadows flee away;
In the everlasting glory of the everlasting day;
Mine Thee, beloved Saviour, everlasting blessings belong;
Everlasting adoration, everlasting land of song!

Frances Ridley Havergal. 1871.

This is the back of a sheet with the manuscript F.R.H. wrote. Apparently she wrote this on August 12, 1871 (the date given for this in the definitive Nisbet edition of her Poetical Works, diligently prepared by her sister and niece), and then on August 13 at the bottom of the manuscript she revised the last line of the first stanza. This hymn in Songs of Grace and Glory has the title "Everlasting Salvation," but in the volume of poetry Under the Surface, *which she published later, apparently she changed the title to "Everlasting Blessings." She wrote the words and also composed the music for this hymn. See Volume V of the Havergal edition, Songs of Truth and Love: Music by Frances Ridley Havergal and William Henry Havergal. See also page 421 of this book.*

Hymns.

Prayer Before Church.

LORD, I am in Thy house of prayer,
Oh, teach me rightly how to pray;
Incline to me Thy gracious ear,
And listen, Lord, to what I say.

Give me, O Lord, a praying heart,
And also an attentive ear;
Help me to choose the better part,
And teach me Thee to love and fear.

A Prayer.

LORD, in mercy pardon me
All that I this day have done:
Sins of every kind 'gainst Thee,
O forgive them through Thy Son.

Make me, Jesus, like to Thee,
Gentle, holy, meek, and mild,
My transgressions pardon me,
O forgive a sinful child.

Gracious Spirit, listen Thou,
Enter in my willing heart,
Enter and possess it now,
Never, Lord, from me depart.

O eternal Three in One,
Condescend to bend Thine ear;
Help me still towards heaven to run,
Answer now my humble prayer.

Thoughts.

On entering church when the sunshine streamed through the large window,
so that its outline was completely lost in the overpowering brilliance.

OH, Thou, the Sun of Righteousness,
Whose bright rays every cloud dispel,
E'en yon fair brilliance is far less
Than that wherein Thou aye dost dwell.

Oh, Thou, my precious Saviour, shine
In all Thy radiance on my soul;
Oh, let me know what love is Thine,
Oh, let me reach this long-sought goal.

To me, to me Thy glory show,
Shall ever be my earnest prayer;
Grant me to leave the things below,
And in that perfect bliss to share,

Which to Thy faithful ones is given.
Oh, let Thy glory on me beam,
And let me taste the joys of heaven,
Before the close of life's strange dream.

Soon, Lord, reveal Thyself to me;
How long must I thus sadly wait?
My spirit yearns Thyself to see,
Oh, hear me in Thy mercy great!

'He that Overcometh.'

REVELATION 3:5.

'HE that overcometh in the fight
Shall be clothed in raiment white and pure;
In the ever-blessèd book of life
Shall his name eternally endure.'

'When my Father on His dazzling throne
Sits, with myriad angels all around,
I'll confess his name, to men unknown;
Heaven and earth shall listen to the sound.'

Who, with such a glorious end in view,
Would not in the heavenly conflict join?
Strange that willing soldiers are so few,
Strange so many faint, who once were Thine.

Oh, it is a service blest indeed!
Though the strife be long, the end is sure;
And our Leader gives to all who need
Grace that they may to the end endure.

'Neath Thy standard be my place, O Lord:
Grant me strength and grace, that I ere long
May obtain that rich and full reward.
Then, as conquering I sheath my sword,
Thou, my Captain, shall be all my song.

A Song of Welcome.

(FOR THE ST. NICHOLAS SUNDAY SCHOOL.)

OH God, with grateful hearts we come
    Thy goodness to adore,
While we our Pastor welcome home
    To England's happy shore.

For Thy delivering love we praise,
    And Thy restoring hand,—
Oh spare him yet for long, long days
    To this our little band.

Thy Spirit's fulness on him rest,
    Thy love his sunshine be!
And may he still, while doubly blest,
    A blessing be from Thee.

When the Chief Shepherd shall appear,
    May he receive, we pray,
A crown of glory bright and clear
    That fadeth not away.

'The Lord Is Gracious.'

'The Lord is gracious and full of compassion, slow to anger and of great mercy.'—Psalm 145:8.

THE Lord is gracious—full of grace
To those who seek through Christ His face;
O come then, sinner, taste and see
The fulness *of His love* for thee.

Full of compassion is His heart,
Each weary sigh, each rankling smart
Is known to Him whom we adore,
The Saviour who our sorrows bore.

To anger slow! though every hour
Provoking His destroying power;
How strange, such words of peace to give,
Through Him who died that we might live.

Great mercy! Yet another seal
To all His gracious words reveal;
Great mercy for the greatly stained,
For those who mercy long disdained.

We little know God's thoughts to man,
They are too great for us to scan:
Thou art too high and we too low,
The wonders of Thy love to know.

But crown Thy mercies, Lord, and send
Thy Spirit as our Teacher-Friend;
That we may see, and feel, and praise
The grace and love of all Thy ways!

'O Spirit of Our Triune Lord.'

'The Spirit proceeding from the Father and the Son.'

O SPIRIT of our Triune Lord,
    Known by Thy might, unseen but felt,
Be Thy sweet influence now outpoured,
    With power to rouse, with love to melt.

O Holy One, who dost proceed
   Both from the Father and the Son,
Reveal to us our sin and need,
   And what our Saviour Christ hath done.

O Thou, whose love, exceeding great,
   Sent Thine own Son to bleed and die,
For Thy good Spirit's power we wait,
   Thy glorious grace to testify.

New Year Hymn.

Jesus, blessèd Saviour,
   Help us now to raise
Songs of glad thanksgiving,
   Songs of holy praise.
O how kind and gracious
   Thou hast always been!
O how many blessings
   Every day has seen!
     Jesus, blessèd Saviour,
       Now our praises hear,
     For Thy grace and favour
       Crowning all the year.

Jesus, holy Saviour,
   Only Thou canst tell
How we often stumbled,
   How we often fell!
All our sins (so many!),
   Saviour, Thou dost know;
In Thy blood most precious,
   Wash us white as snow.
     Jesus, blessèd Saviour,
       Keep us in Thy fear,
     Let Thy grace and favour
       Pardon all the year.

Jesus, loving Saviour,
 Only Thou dost know
All that may befall us
 As we onward go.
So we humbly pray Thee,
 Take us by the hand,
Lead us ever upward
 To the Better Land.
  Jesus, blessèd Saviour,
   Keep us ever near,
  Let Thy grace and favour
   Shield us all the year.

Jesus, precious Saviour,
 Make us all Thine own,
Make us Thine for ever,
 Make us Thine alone.
Let each day, each moment,
 Of this glad New-year,
Be for Jesus only,
 Jesus, Saviour dear.
  Then, O blessèd Saviour,
   Never need we fear,
  For Thy grace and favour
   Crown our bright New-year!

Hymn for Ireland.

'The isles shall wait upon Me, and on Mine arm shall they trust.'—ISAIAH 51:5.

FATHER, we would plead Thy promise, bending at Thy glorious throne,
That the isles shall wait upon Thee, trusting in Thine arm alone!
One bright isle we bring before Thee, while in faith Thy children pray
For a full and mighty blessing, with united voice to-day.

Gracious Saviour, look in mercy on this Island of the West,
Win the wandering and the weary with Thy pardon and Thy rest:
As the *only* Friend and Saviour let Thy blessèd name be owned,
Who hast shed Thy blood most precious, and for ever hast atoned!

Blessèd Spirit, lift Thy standard, pour Thy grace, and shed Thy light!
Lift the veil and loose the fetter; come with new and quickening might;
Make the desert places blossom, shower Thy sevenfold gifts abroad;
Make Thy servants wise and stedfast, valiant for the truth of God.

Triune God of grace and glory, be the isle for which we plead
Shielded, succoured with Thy blessing, strong in every hour of need;
Flooded with Thy truth and glory (glowing sunlight from above),
And encompassed with the ocean of Thine everlasting love.

Oh, surround Thy throne of power with Thine emerald bow of peace:
Bid the wailing, and the warring, and the wild confusion cease.
Thou remainest King for ever,—Thou shalt reign, and earth adore!
Thine the kingdom, Thine the power, Thine the glory evermore.

Church Missionary Jubilee Hymn.

'He shall see of the travail of His soul, and shall be satisfied.'—ISAIAH 53:11.

REJOICE with Jesus Christ to-day,
All ye who love His holy sway!
The travail of His soul is past,
He shall be satisfied at last.

Rejoice with Him, rejoice indeed,
For He shall see His chosen seed!
But ours the trust, the grand employ,
To work out this divinest joy.

Of all His own He loseth none,
They shall be gathered one by one;
He gathereth the smallest grain,
His travail shall not be in vain.

Arise and work! arise and pray
That He would haste the dawning day!
And let the silver trumpet sound,
Wherever Satan's slaves are found.

The vanquished foe shall soon be stilled,
The conquering Saviour's joy fulfilled,
Fulfilled in us, fulfilled in them,
His crown, His royal diadem.

Soon, soon our waiting eyes shall see
The Saviour's mighty Jubilee!
His harvest-joy is filling fast,
He shall be satisfied at last!

Thy Father Waits for Thee.

WANDERER from thy Father's home,
    So full of sin, so far away,
Wilt thou any longer roam?
    Oh, wilt thou not return to-day?
Wilt thou? Oh, He knows it all,
    Thy Father sees, He meets thee here!
Wilt thou? Hear His tender call,
    'Return, return!' while He is near.

He is here! His loving voice
    Hath reached thee, though so far away!
He is waiting to rejoice,
    O wandering one, o'er thee to-day.
Waiting, waiting to bestow
    His perfect pardon, full and free;
Waiting, waiting till thou know
    His wealth of love for thee, for thee!

Rise and go! Thy Father waits
    To welcome and receive and bless;
Thou shalt tread His palace gates
    In royal robe of righteousness.
Thine shall be His heart of love,
    And thine His smile, and thine His home,
Thine His joy, all joys above—
    O wandering child, no longer roam!

Will You Not Come?

WILL you not come to Him for *Life?*
    Why will ye die, oh, why?
He gave His life for you, for you!
The gift is free, the word is true!
    Will you not come? oh, why will you die?

Will you not come to Him for *Peace?*
    Peace through His cross alone!
He shed His precious blood for you;
The gift is free, the word is true!
    He is our Peace—oh, is He your own?

Will you not come to Him for *Rest?*
    All that are weary, come!
The rest He gives is deep and true,
'Tis offered now, 'tis offered you!
    Rest in His love and rest in His home.

Will you not come to Him for *Joy?*
    Will you not come for this?
He laid His joys aside for you,
To give you joy so sweet, so true:
    Sorrowing heart, oh, drink of the bliss!

Will you not come to Him for *Love,*
    Love that can fill the heart?
Exceeding great, exceeding free!
He loveth you, He loveth me!
    Will you not come? Why stand you apart?

Will you not come to Him for ALL?
    Will you not 'taste and see'?
He waits to give it all to you,
The gifts are free, the words are true!
    Jesus is calling, 'Come unto Me!'

What Will You Do Without Him?

I COULD not do without Him!
    Jesus is more to me
Than all the richest, fairest gifts
    Of earth could ever be.
But the more I find Him precious—
    And the more I find Him true—
The more I long for you to find
    What He can be to you.

You need not do without Him,
    For He is passing by,
He is waiting to be gracious,
    Only waiting for your cry;
He is waiting to receive you—
    To make you all His own!
Why will you do without Him,
    And wander on alone?

Why will you do without Him?
    Is He not kind indeed?
Did He not die to save you?
    Is He not all you need?
Do you not want a Saviour?
    Do you not want a Friend?
One who will love you faithfully,
    And love you to the end?

Why will you do without Him?
    The word of God is true,
The world is passing to its doom—
    And you are passing too.
It may be no to-morrow
    Shall dawn on you or me;
Why will you run the awful risk
    Of all eternity?

What will you do without Him,
    In the long and dreary day

Of trouble and perplexity,
　　When you do not know the way,
And no one else can help you,
　　And no one guides you right,
And hope comes not with morning,
　　And rest comes not with night?

You could not do without Him,
　　If once He made you see
The fetters that enchain you,
　　Till He hath set you free:
If once you saw the fearful load
　　Of sin upon your soul—
The hidden plague that ends in death,
　　Unless He makes you whole.

What will you do without Him
　　When death is drawing near?
Without His love—the only love
　　That casts out every fear;
When the shadow-valley opens,
　　Unlighted and unknown,
And the terrors of its darkness
　　Must all be passed alone!

What will you do without Him,
　　When the great white throne is set,
And the Judge who never can mistake,
　　And never can forget,—
The Judge whom you have never here
　　As Friend and Saviour sought,
Shall summon you to give account
　　Of deed and word and thought?

What will you do without Him,
　　When He hath shut the door,
And you are left outside, because
　　You would not come before?
When it is no use knocking,
　　No use to stand and wait,

For the word of doom tolls through your heart,
   That terrible 'Too late!'

You *cannot* do without Him
   There is no other Name
By which you ever *can* be saved,
   No way, no hope, no claim!
Without Him—everlasting loss
   Of love, and life, and light!
Without Him—everlasting woe,
   And everlasting night.

But with Him—oh! *with Jesus!*
   Are any words so blest?
With Jesus, everlasting joy
   And everlasting rest!
With Jesus,—all the empty heart
   Filled with His perfect love;
With Jesus,—perfect peace below,
   And perfect bliss above.

Why should you do without Him?
   It is not yet too late;
He has not closed the day of grace,
   He has not shut the gate.
He calls you!—hush! He calls you!
   He would not have you go
Another step without Him,
   Because He loves you so.

He would not do without you!
   He calls and calls again—
'Come unto Me! Come unto Me!'
   Oh, shall He call in vain?
He wants to have you with Him;
   Do you not want Him too?
You cannot do without Him,
   And He wants—even you.

'Forgiven—Even Until Now.'

(Numbers 14:19.)

For New Year's Day 1879.

'Thou hast forgiven—even until now!'
  We bless Thee, Lord, for this,
And take Thy great forgiveness as we bow
  In depth of sorrowing bliss;
While over all the long, regretful past
This veil of wondrous grace Thy sovereign hand doth cast.

'Forgiven until now!' For Jesus died
  To take our sins away;
His Blood was shed, and still the infinite tide
  Flows full and deep to-day.
He paid the debt; we own it, and go free!
The cancelled bond is cast in Love's unfathomed sea.

'Forgiven until now!' For God is true,
  Faithful and just is He!
Forgiving, cleansing, making all things new!
  'Who is a God like Thee?'
O precious blood of Christ, that saves and heals,
While all its cleansing might the Holy Ghost reveals.

Yes, 'even until now!' And so we stand,
  Forgiven, loved, and blessed;
And, covered in the shadow of God's hand,
  Believing, are at rest.
The one great load is lifted from the soul,
That henceforth on the Lord all burdens we may roll.

Yes, 'even until now!' Then let us press
  With free and willing feet
Along the King's highway of holiness,
  Until we gain the street
Of golden crystal, praising purely when
We see our pardoning Lord; forgiven until then!

He Hath Done It!

'I have blotted out, as a thick cloud, thy transgressions, and, as a cloud, thy sins: return unto Me; for I have redeemed thee. Sing, O ye heavens; for the Lord hath done it.'—Isaiah 44:22, 23.

'I know that, whatsoever God doeth, it shall be for ever: nothing can be put to it, nor anything taken from it.'—Ecclesiastes 3:14.

Sing, O heavens! the Lord hath done it!
　　Sound it forth o'er land and sea!
Jesus says, 'I have redeemed thee,
　　Now return, return to Me.'
Oh return, for His own life-blood
　　Paid the ransom, made us free
　　　Evermore and evermore.

For I know that what He doeth
　　Stands for ever, fixed and true;
Nothing can be added to it,
　　Nothing left for us to do;
Nothing can be taken from it,
　　Done for me and done for you,
　　　Evermore and evermore.

Listen now! the Lord hath done it!
　　For He loved us unto death;
It is finished! He has saved us!
　　Only trust to what He saith.
He hath done it! Come and bless Him,
　　Spend in praise your ransomed breath
　　　Evermore and evermore.

O believe the Lord hath done it!
　　Wherefore linger? wherefore doubt?
All the cloud of black transgression
　　He Himself hath blotted out.
He hath done it! Come and bless Him,
　　Swell the grand thanksgiving shout
　　　Evermore and evermore.

Asking.

LUKE 11:13

O HEAVENLY Father, Thou hast told
Of a Gift more precious than pearls and gold:
A Gift that is free to every one,
Through Jesus Christ, Thy only Son:
　　For His sake, give it to me.

Oh, give it to me! for Jesus said,
That a father giveth his children bread,
And how much more Thou wilt surely give
The Gift by which the dead shall live!
　　For Christ's sake, give it to me.

I cannot see, and I want the sight:
I am in the dark, and I want the light;
I want to pray, and I don't know how;
Oh, give me Thy Holy Spirit now!
　　For Christ's sake, give it to me!

If Thou hast said it, I must believe
It is only 'ask' and I shall receive;
If Thou hast said it, it must be true,
And there's nothing else for me to do!
　　For Christ's sake, give it to me.

So I come and ask, because my need
Is very great and real indeed.
On the strength of Thy word I come and say,
Oh, let Thy word come true to-day!
　　For Christ's sake, give it to me!

Love for Love.

1 JOHN 4:16.

KNOWING that the God on high,
　　With a tender Father's grace,
Waits to hear your faintest cry,
　　Waits to show a Father's face,—
Stay and think!—oh, should not you
Love this gracious Father too?

Knowing Christ was crucified,
      Knowing that He loves you now
Just as much as when He died
      With the thorns upon His brow,—
Stay and think!—oh, should not you
Love this blessèd Saviour too?

Knowing that a Spirit strives
      With your weary, wandering heart,
Who can change the restless lives,
      Pure and perfect peace impart,—
Stay and think!—oh, should not you
Love this loving Spirit too?

Nothing to Pay.

NOTHING to pay! Ah, nothing to pay!
Never a word of excuse to say!
Year after year thou hast filled the score,
Owing thy Lord still more and more.
      Hear the voice of Jesus say,
'Verily thou hast nothing to pay!
Ruined, lost art thou, and yet
I forgave thee all that debt.'

Nothing to pay! the debt is so great;
What will you do with the awful weight?
How shall the way of escape be made?
Nothing to pay! yet it must be paid!
      Hear the voice of Jesus say,
'Verily thou hast nothing to pay!
All has been put to My account,
I have paid the full amount.'

Nothing to pay; yes, nothing to pay!
Jesus has cleared all the debt away;
Blotted it out with His bleeding hand!
Free and forgiven and loved you stand.
      Hear the voice of Jesus say,
'Verily thou hast nothing to pay!
Paid is the debt, and the debtor free!
Now I ask *thee,* lovest thou ME?'

Nothing to pay.

Nothing to pay, Ah, nothing to pay;
Never a word of excuse to say!
Year after thou hast filled the score,
Owing thy Lord still more and more.
Hear the voice of Jesus say,
"Verily thou hast nothing to pay!
Ruined and lost art thou, and yet
I forgave thee all that debt.

Nothing to pay, nothing to pay!
Hear the voice of Jesus say,
Verily thou hast nothing to pay!
Finished and lost art thou and yet,
I forgave thee all that debt

Nothing to pay! the debt is so great;
What will you do with the awful weight?
How shall the way of escape be made?
Nothing to pay! it must be paid!
Hear the voice of Jesus say,
"Verily thou hast nothing to pay!
All has been put to my account,
I have paid the full amount

Nothing to pay, yes, nothing to pay!
Jesus has cleared all the debt away;
Blotted it out with His bleeding hands,
Free and forgiven and loved you stand;
Hear the voice of Jesus say,
"Verily thou hast nothing to pay!
Paid is thy debt, and thou art free!
Now, I pray thee, to love me..."

April 1879

upon New Year

Two pages from F.R.H.'s Manuscript Book Nº IX. This was one of her last poems.

A Merrie Christmas.

"A Merrie Christmas" to you!
For we "serve the Lord with mirth";
And we carol forth glad tidings
Of our holy Saviour's birth.
So we keep the olden greeting
With its meaning deep & true,
And wish "a merrie Christmas,
And a Happy New Year to you!"

Oh yes, "a merrie Christmas;
With blithest song & smile,
Bright with the thought of Him Who dwelt
On earth a little while,
That we might dwell for ever
Where never falls a tear.
So "a merrie Christmas" to you,
And a happy, happy year!

Oct. 15.

Boswell.

Another page from her Manuscript Book Nº IX, her last Manuscript Book.

Christmas Verses.

A Merrie Christmas.

'A MERRIE Christmas' to you!
　　For we serve the Lord with mirth,
And we carol forth glad tidings
　　Of our holy Saviour's birth.
So we keep the olden greeting
　　With its meaning deep and true,
And wish 'a merrie Christmas'
　　And a happy New Year to you!

Oh, yes! 'a merrie Christmas,'
　　With blithest song and smile,
Bright with the thought of Him who dwelt
　　On earth a little while,
That we might dwell for ever
　　Where never falls a tear :
So 'a merrie Christmas' to you,
　　And a happy, happy year!

A Happy Christmas.

A HAPPY Christmas to you!
　　For the Light of Life is born,
And His coming is the sunshine
　　Of the dark and wintry morn.
The grandest orient glow must pale,
The loveliest western gleams must fail :
　　　　But His great Light,
　　　　So full, so bright,
Ariseth for thy heart to-day;
His shadow-conquering beams shall never
　　pass away.

A happy Christmas to you!
For the Prince of Peace is come,

And His reign is full of blessings,
    Their very crown and sum.
No earthly calm can ever last,
'Tis but the lull before the blast :
        But His great peace
        Shall still increase
In mighty, all-rejoicing sway;
His kingdom in thy heart shall never pass away.

Our Saviour Christ Was Born.

    OUR Saviour Christ was born
That we might have the rose without the thorn;
    All through His desert life
He felt the thorns of human sin and strife.
    His blessed feet were bare
To every hurting brier; He did not spare
One bleeding footstep on the way
He came to trace for us, until the day
The cruel crown was pressed upon the Brow,
That smiles upon us from His glory now.

    And so He won for us
Sweet, thornless, everlasting flowers thus!
    He bids our desert way
Rejoice and blossom as the rose to-day.
    There is no hidden thorn
In His good gifts of grace; He would adorn
The lives that now are His alone,
With brightness and with beauty all His own.
Then praise the Lord who came on Christmas Day
To give the rose and take the thorns away.

Christmas Gifts.

'Thou hast received gifts for men.'—PSALM 68:18.

    CHRISTMAS gifts for thee,
        Fair and free!

Precious things from the heavenly store,
Filling thy casket more and more;
Golden love in divinest chain,
That never can be untwined again;
Silvery carols of joy that swell
Sweetest of all in the heart's lone cell;
Pearls of peace that were sought for thee
In the terrible depths of a fiery sea;
Diamond promises sparkling bright,
Flashing in farthest reaching light.

Christmas gifts for thee,
Grand and free!
Christmas gifts from the King of love,
Brought from His royal home above;
Brought to thee in the far-off land,
Brought to thee by His own dear hand.
Promises held by Christ for thee,
Peace as a river flowing free,
Joy that in His own joy must live,
And love that Infinite Love can give.
Surely thy heart of hearts uplifts
Carols of praise for such Christmas gifts!

Christmas Mottoes.

UNTO you the Child is born,
On this blessèd Christmas morn.
Unto you, to be your Peace;
Unto you, for He hath found you;
Unto you, with full release
From the weary chains that bound you;
Unto you, that you may rise
Unto Him above the skies.

THE wilderness shall rejoice,
And the wintry waste shall sing,

At the wakening herald voice
  Of the coming of the King.
So the sparkling Christmas snow
  Is dearer than summer light;
For He whom we love came down below
  In the hush of a Christmas night.
May thy Christmas morning break
  Holy and bright and calm;
And may all thy life for His dear sake
  Be a joyful Christmas psalm.

Is it a wintry night?
  Watch! for the heavenly light
Shineth, O mourner, around and above!
  Tidings of joy to thee
  Float on the minstrelsy!
Rise up and welcome the Son of His love.

'Behold, thy King cometh unto thee.'—Zechariah 9:9.

Cometh in lowliness,
  Cometh in righteousness,
Cometh in mercy all royal and free!
  Cometh with grace and might,
  Cometh with love and light;
Cometh, belovèd! He cometh to thee!

Bright be thy Christmas tide!
  Carol it far and wide,
Jesus, the King and the Saviour, is come!
  Jesus thy guest will be;
  O let Him dwell with thee!
Open thy heart for His palace and home.

WHAT do the angels sing?
What is the word they bring?
What is the music of Christmas again?
Glad tidings still to thee,
Peace and good-will to thee,
Glory to God in the highest! Amen.

OH, Christmas blessings cannot cease,
Christmas joy is deep and strong!
For Christ is come to be our Peace,
Our Salvation and our Song.

Christmas Gifts.

THE wondrous love and light,
The fulness and the glory,
The meaning and the might
Of all the Christmas story,
May Christ Himself unfold to you to-day,
And bid you go rejoicing on your way.

A HAPPY, happy Christmas
Be yours to-day!
Oh, not the failing measure
Of fleeting earthly pleasure,
But Christmas joy abiding,
While years are swiftly gliding,
Be yours, I pray,
Through Him who gave us Christmas Day!

A BRIGHT and blessed Christmas Day,
With echoes of the angels' song,
And peace that cannot pass away,
And holy gladness, calm and strong,

And sweet heart carols, flowing free!
This is my Christmas wish to thee!

Down the ages hoary
Peals the song of glory,
Peace, and God's good-will!
Other echoes die away,
But the song of Christmas Day
Echoes from the Judean hill,
Ever clearer, louder still.
Oh, may its holy, heavenly chime
Make all thy life a Christmas time!

Christmas Sunshine.

Do the angels know the blessed day,
    And strike their harps anew?
Then may the echo of their lay
    Float sweetly down to you,
And fill your soul with Christmas song
That your heart shall echo your whole life long.

Jesus came!—and came for me!
    Simple words! and yet expressing
Depths of holy mystery,
    Depths of wondrous love and blessing.
Holy Spirit, make me see
All His coming means for me;
Take the things of Christ, I pray,
Show them to my heart to-day.

Oh, let thy heart make melody,
    And thankful songs uplift,
For Christ Himself is come to be
    Thy glorious Christmas gift.

A HAPPY, happy Christmas,
   And a happy, happy year!
Oh, we have not deserved it,
   And yet we need not fear.
For Jesus has deserved it,
   And so, for Jesus' sake,
This cup of joy and blessing
   With grateful hand we take.

THERE is silence high in the midnight sky,
   And only the sufferers watch the night;
But long ago there was song and glow,
   And a message of joy from the Prince of Light,
And the Christmas song of the messenger-throng
The echoes of life shall for ever prolong.

GREAT is the mystery
   Of wondrous grace,
God manifest we see
   In Jesu's face.
O deepest mystery
   Of Love Divine,
God manifest for me,
   And Jesus mine!

WHAT was the first angelic word
That the startled shepherds heard?—
'Fear not!' Beloved, it comes to you
As a Christmas message most sweet and true,
As true for you as it was for them
In the lonely fields of Bethlehem;
And as sweet to-day as it was that night,
When the glory dazzled their mortal sight.

CHRIST is come to be my Friend,
 Leading, loving to the end;
Christ is come to be my King,
 Ordering, ruling everything.
Christ is come! Enough for me,
Lonely though the pathway be.

GIVE me a song, O Lord,
 That I may sing to Thee,
In true and sweet accord
 With angel minstrelsy.
Oh, tune my heart that it may bring
A Christmas anthem to my King.

SWELL the notes of the Christmas Song!
 Sound it forth through the earth abroad!
  Glory to God!
Blessing and honour, thanks and laud!
Take the joy of the Christmas Song!
 Are not the tidings good and true?
  Peace to you,
And God's good-will that is ever new!

CHRIST is come to be thy light,
Shining through the darkest night;
He will make thy pilgrim way
Shine unto the perfect day.
Take the message! let it be
Full of Christmas joy to thee!

Titles of Christ.

Wonderful.

'For unto us a child is born, unto us a son is given; and the government shall be upon His shoulder: and His Name shall be called Wonderful, Counsellor, The Mighty God, The Everlasting Father, The Prince of Peace.'—Isaiah 9:6.

Wonderful! Wonderful!
Ring out the Name, O Christmas chimes!
Wonderful! Wonderful!
Echo the word to farthest climes!
May the splendour of this great Name
Shine and glow with a mighty flame,
Filling thy life with its glorious rays,
Filling thy spirit with Christmas praise.

Counsellor.

Mist and cloud and darkness
    Veil the wintry hour,
But the sun dispels them
    With his rising power.

Mist and cloud and darkness
    Often dim thy day,
But a Christmas glory
    Shines upon thy way.

May the Lord of Christmas,
    Counsellor and Friend,
Light thy desert pathway
    Even to the end.

The Everlasting Father.

O NAME of gentlest grace,
   O Name of strength and might,
Meeting the heart-need of our orphaned race
   With tenderest delight!
Our Everlasting Father! This is He
Who came in deep humility
   A little child to be!

The Mighty God.

THE Christmas bells proclaim
   His glorious name,
   'The Mighty God!'
God manifest indeed,

And yet the Woman's Seed,
   To whom we sing
All glory, praise, and laud!
   Divinest Lord and King.

The Prince of Peace.

O NAME of beauty and of calm!
   O Name of rest and balm,
   Of exquisite delight,
And yet of sovereignty and might!
Let it make music in thy heart to-day,
And bid thee go rejoicing on thy way;
For Jesus is thy Peace, thy Prince of Peace,
Whose reign within thy heart shall evermore increase.

Man of Rest.

'Behold, a son shall be born to thee, who shall be a man of rest.'
—1 Chronicles 22:9.

HAIL, Christmas morn!
For unto us the Son is born,
The Man of Rest!
The weary quest
Is over now, for He who cometh, calleth,
'Come unto Me, and I will give you rest!'
The still voice falleth
On hearts that, listening, are blessed.
And daily shall the blessing flow,
And daily shall the gladness grow,
For we which have believed do enter into rest.

"SATISFIED."

"He shall see of the travail of his soul, and shall be satisfied."—Isa. liii. 11.

REJOICE with Jesus Christ to-day,   Lu. xv. 6.
All ye who love His holy sway!   Ps. cx. 3.
The travail of His soul is past,   Isa. liii. 11.
He shall be satisfied at last.   Isa. xlix. 7, 8.

Rejoice with Him, rejoice indeed,   John iii. 29.
For He shall see His chosen seed!   Isa. liii. 10.
But ours the trust, the grand employ,   1 Cor. iii. 9.
To work out this divinest joy.   Zeph. iii. 17-20.

Of all His own He loseth none,   John xvii. 12.
They shall be gathered one by one;   Isa. xxvii. 12.
He garnereth the smallest grain,   Amos ix. 9.
His travail shall not be in vain!   Heb. ii. 13.

Arise, and work! arise, and pray   2 Pet. iii. 12.
That He would haste the dawning day!   Cant. ii. 18.
And let the silver trumpet sound,   Lev. xxv. 9, 10.
Wherever Satan's slaves are found.   Isa. lxi. 1.

The vanquished foe shall soon be stilled,   Ps. viii. 2.
The conquering Saviour's joy fulfilled—   Jude 24.
Fulfilled in us, fulfilled in them—   John xvii. 13.
His crown, His royal diadem.   Isa. lxii. 3.

Soon, soon our waiting eyes shall see   Matt. xxvi. 64.
The Saviour's mighty Jubilee!   1 Thess. i. 10.
His harvest joy is filling fast;   Isa. ix. 3, marg.
He shall be satisfied at last.   Ps. cxxvi. 6.

FRANCES RIDLEY HAVERGAL.

See pages 273–274 of this book. Maria V.G. Havergal wrote below this leaflet: "references by F.R.H. This old copy from her study."

references by J. R. H. This old copy from her study.

4

Soon will a New Year's Day
Break o'er the heavenly skies!
Soon will its Day-Star glow,
Soon will its Day-Spring lead
That perfect, endless, Day!

Sing, then, the Saviour's love,
My "Everlasting Light"!
Sing, for I soon shall be
Walking with Him in white,
Throughout that perfect Day!

Sing, for how sweetly near
Cometh that Day at times!
Sing, for e'en *now* its songs
Blend with the welcome chimes
Of this my glad New Year!

Sing, then! Yea, *always* sing!
Singing keeps Heaven in sight!
Wouldst thou be full of Christ?
Sing of Him, day and night,
Through all this glad New Year!

EDWIN C. WRENFORD.

NAIRN.

London: S. W. PARTRIDGE & Co. Edinburgh: J. TAYLOR, 31 Castle Street.

Price 6d. per dozen.

THE CHRISTIAN'S WATCHWORD

FOR

1878.

"In the Light."

"Walk in the light, as He is in the light."—1 ST JOHN i. 7.

SING for the Old Year dead!
Sing for the New Year born!
Sing for the nightless days,
Clear as the shining morn,
Through all the glad New Year!

Sing for the glad New Year,
Circling its path of light!
Sing, for this New Year's Day,
Ending my soul's long night,
Heralds a glad New Year!

2

Sing, for the Morning Star,
Greeting my heart, hath sped,
Veiled in the Day-Spring's light,—
Light that shall, growing, spread
Through all the glad New Year!

Sing, for the Sun hath risen,
Clothed in His fervent might,—
JESUS, with healing wings,
JESUS, the world's true Light,—
Gilding my glad New Year!

Sing, for now evermore
Brightly that Sun shall reign!
Light of eternal day,
How can *He* wax and wane,—
Sun of my glad New Year?

Seasons may wax and wane,
Days may be short or long,—
Filled with *His* "marvellous light,"
Mine shall be clear and strong
Through all this glad New Year!

Sing, for in strength it shines,
Shadowless light of God!
Bright, then, my path shall be,
Bright as by angels trod,
Through all the glad New Year!

3

Sing, though the heavens be dark,
Waves of affliction roll,
Or even death be near,
Wrapping in gloom my soul,
During the glad New Year!

Sing, for above the gloom,
Turning my night to day,
Grandly the Sun will shine,
Chasing my griefs away,—
Clouds of my glad New Year!

Bringing my heart to Him,
Telling Him all its sin,
Telling Him all my thoughts,
Light shall, without, within,
Brighten the glad New Year!

This, then, my joy shall be,—
Living each day in light,
Walking with Him in love,
Faith shall increase to sight
Through all the glad New Year!

Sing, then, the Old Year dead!
Sing, too, the New Year born!
Sing of my soul's night past!
Sing of her glorious morn!
Through all the glad New Year!

This poem by Edwin Charles Wrenford was found among Havergal manuscripts and papers.

New Year Verses.

A Happy New Year to You.

New mercies, new blessings, new light on thy way;
New courage, new hope, and new strength for each day;
New notes of thanksgiving, new chords of delight,
New praise in the morning, new songs in the night;
New wine in thy chalice, new altars to raise;
New fruits for thy Master, new garments of praise;
New gifts from His treasures, new smiles from His face;
New streams from the fountain of infinite grace;
New stars for thy crown, and new tokens of love;
New gleams of the glory that waits thee above;
New light of His countenance full and unpriced;—
All this be the joy of thy new life in Christ!

Another Year.

Another year is dawning!
    Dear Master, let it be,
In working or in waiting,
    Another year with Thee.

Another year of leaning
    Upon Thy loving breast,
Of ever-deepening trustfulness,
    Of quiet, happy rest.

Another year of mercies,
    Of faithfulness and grace;
Another year of gladness
    In the shining of Thy face.

Another year of progress,
    Another year of praise;

Another year of proving
  Thy presence 'all the days.'

Another year of service,
    Of witness for Thy love;
Another year of training
    For holier work above.

Another year is dawning,
    Dear Master, let it be,
On earth, or else in heaven,
    Another year for Thee!

Faithful Promises.

Isaiah 41:10.

New Year's Hymn.

Standing at the portal
    Of the opening year,
Words of comfort meet us,
    Hushing every fear;
Spoken through the silence
    By our Father's voice,
Tender, strong, and faithful,
    Making us rejoice.
Onward then, and fear not,
    Children of the day!
For His word shall never,
    Never pass away!

I, the Lord, am with thee,
    Be thou not afraid!
I will help and strengthen,
    Be thou not dismayed!
Yea, I will uphold thee
    With my own right hand;
Thou art called and chosen
    In my sight to stand.

Onward then, and fear not,
  Children of the day!
For His word shall never,
  Never pass away!

For the year before us,
  Oh, what rich supplies!
For the poor and needy
  Living streams shall rise;
For the sad and sinful
  Shall His grace abound;
For the faint and feeble
  Perfect strength be found.
Onward then, and fear not,
  Children of the day!
For His word shall never,
  Never pass away!

He will never fail us,
  He will not forsake;
His eternal covenant
  He will never break!
Resting on His promise,
  What have we to fear?
God is all-sufficient
  For the coming year.
Onward then, and fear not,
  Children of the day!
For His word shall never,
  Never pass away!

New Year's Wishes.

WHAT shall I wish thee?
  Treasures of earth?
Songs in the spring-time,
  Pleasure and mirth?
Flowers on thy pathway,
  Skies ever clear?

Would this ensure thee
  A Happy New Year?

What shall I wish thee?
  What can be found
Bringing thee sunshine
  All the year round?
Where is the treasure,
  Lasting and dear,
That shall ensure thee
  A Happy New Year?

Faith that increaseth,
  Walking in light;
Hope that aboundeth,
  Happy and bright;
Love that is perfect,
  Casting out fear;—
These shall ensure thee
  A Happy New Year.

Peace in the Saviour,
  Rest at His feet,
Smile of His countenance
  Radiant and sweet,
Joy in His presence,
  Christ ever near!—
This will ensure thee
  A Happy New Year!

A Happy New Year.

A HAPPY New Year! Oh such may it be!
Joyously, surely, and fully for thee!
Fear not and faint not, but be of good cheer,
And trustfully enter thy happy New Year!

Happy, so happy! Thy Father shall guide,
Protect thee, preserve thee, and always provide!

Onward and upward along the right way
Lovingly leading thee day by day.

Happy, so happy! Thy Saviour shall be
Ever more precious and present with thee!
Happy, so happy! His Spirit thy Guest,
Filling with glory the place of His rest.

Happy, so happy! Though shadows around
May gather and darken, they flee at the sound
Of the glorious Voice that saith, 'Be of good cheer!'
Then joyously enter thy happy New Year!

New Year Mottoes.

'From this day will I bless you.'—HAGGAI 2:19.

'FROM this day'
He shall bless thee!
What shall then distress thee?
'From this day'
He will never leave thee;
What shall grieve thee?
Christ, thy mighty Friend,
Loveth to the end
'From this day!'

'Be glad and rejoice, for the Lord will do great things.'—JOEL 2:21.

THE Lord *hath* done great things for thee!
All through the fleeted days
Jehovah hath dealt wondrously;
Lift up thy heart and praise!
For greater things thine eyes shall see,
Child of His loving choice!
The Lord *will* do great things for thee;
Fear not, be glad, rejoice!

WONDROUSLY
The Lord *hath* dealt with thee!
  Wondrous mercy all the way,
  Wondrous patience every day,
  Wondrous pardon, wondrous feeding,
  Wondrous help and wondrous leading
    Through the bygone year.

  Wondrously
The Lord *shall* deal with thee!
  Wondrous tenderness and grace,
  Wondrous shining of His face,
  Wondrous faithfulness and power,
  Wondrous love, shall twine each bower
    Through the coming year!

CROWN the year with Thy goodness, Lord!
  And make every hour a gem
  In the living diadem,
    That sparkles to Thy praise.

Crown the year with Thy grace, O Lord!
  Be Thy fresh anointings shed
  On Thy waiting servant's head,
    Who treads Thy royal ways.

Crown the year with Thy glory, Lord!
  Let the brightness and the glow
  Of its heavenly overflow
    Crown Thy beloved's days!

STRONG and loving is thy Friend!
  Trust Him for the untried year!
He shall lead thee to the end,
  Ever gracious, ever near.
As the everlasting hills
  Thou shalt find His faithfulness;
As the crystal mountain-rills.

'And on the east side toward the rising of the sun shall they of the standard of the camp of Judah pitch throughout their armies: and Nahshon the son of Amminadab shall be captain of the children of Judah.'—NUMBERS 2:3.

TOWARD the rising of the sun
Now thy standard raise!
Let thy New Year's halt be one
In the Camp of Praise.
Then the wilderness shall be
Fruitful, fair, and glad for thee.

ANOTHER year of patient toil,
A few sheaves won from rocky soil,
May seem not much to thee;
But all thy work is with the Lord,
And thine exceeding great reward
Thy God Himself shall be.

PRAISING together for all the way,
Now let us welcome our New Year's Day,
Rejoicing together in faith and love,
Hoping together for rest above.

ETERNITY with Jesus
Is long enough for rest;
Thank God that we are spared to work
For Him whom we love best!

'The Lord bless thee, and keep thee: The Lord make His face shine upon thee, and be gracious unto thee: The Lord lift up His countenance upon thee, and give thee peace.'—NUMBERS 6:24–26.

THE threefold blessing Israel heard
Three thousand years ago,

God grant it may on thee to-day
  In power and fulness flow;
That Light and Peace in grand increase
  All through the year may glow.

Lord Jesus, keep our dear one
  All through the year;
By day and night Thy presence bright
  Be ever near;
And Thy sweet word be always heard
  To guide and cheer.

'I will sing of mercy and judgment.'—Psalm 101:1.

One year less
Of wisely-ordered loss,
Of sorrow and of weariness,
  Conflict and cross.

One year more
Of mercies ever new,
Of love in never-failing store,
  Faithful and true.

'He it is that doth go before thee; He will be with thee, He will not fail thee.'
  —Deuteronomy 31:8.

The Lord thy God!
He it is that goes before thee,
His the banner waving o'er thee,
  Bright and broad!
When the fiercest foes assail thee,
He it is that will not fail thee,
  The Lord thy God!

'The righteous, and the wise, and their works, are in the hand of God.'—ECCLESIASTES 9:1.

THE future! who may lift the veil
And read its yet unwritten tale?
But sorrow and joy alike we leave
    In the Hand that doeth all things well,
And calmly from that Hand receive
    All that each coming year may tell.
We would not ask of life or death,
It shall be as the Master saith.

Now Thy loving Spirit
    On our lives outpour;
Make us know Thee better,
    Make us love Thee more.
Take us now, we pray Thee,
    Make us all Thine own;
Keep us Thine for ever,
    Keep us Thine alone!

'NOT as the world giveth
    Give I to you!'
Saith the Redeemer,
    Faithful and True.
May He enrich thee,
    This New Year's Day,
With gifts from His treasure
    That pass not away.

THIS New Year Thou givest me,
    Lord, I consecrate to Thee,
        With all its nights and days:
Fill my hand with service blest,
Fill my heart with holy rest,
        And fill my life with praise.

A BRIGHT New Year, and a sunny track
　　Along an upward way,
And a song of praise on looking back,
　　When the year has passed away,
And golden sheaves nor small nor few!
This is my New Year's wish for you!

ANOTHER year for Jesus!
　　How can I wish for you
A greater joy or blessing,
　　O fellow-worker true?
Is the work difficult?
　　Jesus directs thee.
Is the path dangerous?
　　Jesus protects thee,
Fear not, and falter not,—
　　Let the word cheer thee!—
All through the coming year
　　He will be with thee!

HAPPY, because He loves thee!
　　Happy, because He lives!
Bright with that deepest gladness
　　Which only Jesus gives.
Happy, because He guides thee,
　　Because He cares for thee;
Happy, ever so happy,
　　Thus may thy New Year be!

FOR the weariest day
　　May Christ be thy stay!
For the darkest night
　　May Christ be thy light!
For the weakest hour
　　May Christ be thy power!
For each moment's fall
　　May Christ be thy All!

Easter Echoes.

ARISE, for He is risen to-day,
    And shine, for He is glorified;
Put on thy beautiful array,
    And keep perpetual Easter-tide.

THE white flowers, freed
From snowy sepulchres, may speak
    In angel-tone to thee,—
    'Oh, fear not ye!
The Saviour whom ye seek
    Is risen indeed!'

IN the likeness of His death
    We were planted,
Therefore, by His Spirit's breath
    Resurrection-life is granted;—
Resurrection beauty glowing,
Resurrection power outflowing,
Resurrection gladness cheering,
Resurrection glory nearing.

'SHALL rise again!'
His word shall be
Enough for thee,
O mourning heart, so full of pain!
Yet see
The promise sealed.
By loveliest miracles. Each wakening flower
Of fell or field,
Is fair new proof of resurrection power.

FAR on the mountain height
They grew;
Each vivid tint
A new
And fair imprint
Of the once piercèd Feet,
A token sweet
(Sent very tenderly),
That Jesus lives and loves and cares for me.

OH, let me know
The power of Thy resurrection!
Oh, let me show
Thy risen life in clear reflection!
Oh, let me soar
Where Thou, my Saviour Christ, art gone before!
In mind and heart
Let me dwell always, only, where Thou art.

Birthday Poems.

ACROSTICS.

Cecilia Havergal.

C HRIST hath called thee, Christ hath blest,
E verlasting life is thine;
C losely cleaving, thou shalt rest
I n His glorious love divine.
L et Him teach thee what He will,
I n thee day by day fulfil
A ll His sweet and blessèd will.

H e is come to claim His throne,
A nd thy life is all His own;
V oices of this passing earth,
E choes of its praise or mirth,
R each not, when the heart hath heard
G olden music of His word.
' A ll for Jesus' henceforth be!
L ive for Him who died for thee.

Edith Havergal.

E ARLY chastening, early blessing!
D arkest cloud hath brightest bow!
I n the night of pain distressing,
T hine hath been the joy to show
H ow God is a Sun and Shield.

H eir thou art by His good pleasure,
A ll thy title Spirit-sealed!
V iew thy grand and royal treasure—
E very gift in Love's full measure,
R iches of His grace, so great,
G lory's far exceeding weight,—
A ll in Christ for ever thine!
L ight and Life and Love Divine!

For E. P. S.

F RANCIE, may thy childhood be
A s a blossom-laden tree,
S howing promise full and free.

W ILLIE, be thy life a song,
H oly, happy, sweet, and long,
S welling through a world of wrong.

A LFRED, be a fragrant flower,
H ailing either sun or shower,
S weetest in its fading hour.

A LICE, in thy baby measure,
E ver be thy parents' treasure,
S howering golden love and pleasure.

Mizpah.

MESSAGES FOR ABSENT FRIENDS.

ONLY a leaf, yet it shall bear
　　A wealth of love, of mintage true!
Only a simple earnest prayer,
　　That silently goes up for you;
Yet you and I may never know
What blessings from that prayer may flow.

　　'GRACE, mercy, peace.'
Triple blossom, rainbow-hued,
Fresh and fragrant, heaven-bedewed,
Brightening desert solitude,
Springing from the Love Divine,
Love that ever shall entwine
With our own, with yours and mine.

UPON the same bright morning star
Our gaze may meet, though severed far :
The Star of Bethlehem to-day
Shines brightly on our wintry way;
And, gazing on its radiance clear,
Our hearts may meet, and we are near!

As the sounding shell conveys
　　The murmur of the sea,
So let this tiny token raise
　　Some memory of me;
For loving thought of prayer and praise
　　Fail not to rise for thee.

THOUGH the circling flight of time may find us
    Far apart, or severed more and more,
Yet the farewell always lies behind us,
    And the welcome always lies before.
Meanwhile God is leading, surely, slowly,
    Through the shadows with a hand of love,
To the house where, 'mid the myriads holy,
    Only welcomes wait us both above.

Birthday Mottoes.

MAY the tale the years are telling,
        Always be
Like an angel-anthem swelling
Through thy spirit's quiet dwelling,
Till the glory all-excelling
        Dawn for thee!

MANY a happy year be thine,
        If our Father will!
He has traced the fair design,
He will fill it, line by line,
    Working patiently, until
Thy completed life shall shine,
Glorious in the life divine.

MANY and happy thy birthdays be!
    In the light of heaven arrayed;
With the rainbow arching every cloud
    When the pathway lies in shade;
And full and far may the blessing flow,
    That thy future life is made.

LOVE would strew upon thy way
    Fairest, freshest flowers to-day;
Love would daily, hourly shed
    Brightest sunbeams on thy head.

So she prays: that heavenly grace
 Be thy flower-awakening dew,
And the brightness of His face
 Gild thy life with sunshine true.

'Upward, still upward' thy pathway be,
Into the sunshine grand and free;
Leaving the mists and clouds below,
Gaining the pure and stainless snow.
Upward, still upward! Thy faithful Guide
Always close at His pilgrim's side,
Leading thee on from height to height,
Nearer and nearer the stars of light.

Birthday blessings, fullest, sweetest,
 Fall on thee to-day!
Earthly pleasure, fairest, fleetest,
 Will not, cannot stay;
But the true and heavenly treasure
 Cannot pass away :
May its richest, grandest measure
 Gild thy natal day!

The Love of God the Father,
 The Grace of God the Son,
The joy of God the Holy Ghost,—
 A blessing three in one,
Be yours aboundingly, I pray,
For this and every coming day!

Leaning, resting, trusting, loving,
 Enter thy new year!
For the Lord who lives to love thee
 Will be always near,
Shielding, guiding, caring, blessing!—
 What hast thou to fear?

WE pray Thee for our dear one!
　　May a sunny birthday prove
The portal of long happy years,
　　All radiant with Thy love.
And we praise Thee for our dear one!
　　For all the mercies past,
And for all the blessing that shall flow
　　While life itself shall last.

A HOLY, happy birthday
　　And a happy, happy year!
Ah, we have not deserved it,
　　And yet we need not fear.
For Jesus has deserved it!
　　And so, for Jesus' sake,
This cup of joy and blessing
　　With grateful heart we take.

I HAVE no birthday gifts to bring,
　　But I will crave a Royal dower,
The sevenfold largesse of the King.

His Peace be thine, His Love unknown;
　　His own deep Joy, His Strength and Power,
His Grace abounding, be thine own!

His Rest be thine, sweet rest to-day,
　　Rest while the swift years pass away,
And then His Glory thine for aye!

To M. V. G. H.

ON HER BIRTHDAY.

THE blessing of the trusting one,
　　Who knows her faithful Friend;
The blessing of the waiting one,
　　Who trusts Him to the end;

The blessing of the watching one,
　　Whose eyes are on the Lord;
The blessing of the chastened one,
　　That marvellous reward!—
These sweetest birthday blessings be
　　Abundantly bestowed on thee!

　　Blessing and blest
　　　　May thy new year be,
　　Brightest and best
　　　　Of the years to thee,
　　Awaiting the rest
　　　　Of eternity!

M. L. C.'s Birthday Crown.

Only just a line to say,
Miriam, on this summer day,
What my spirit's love would breathe,
While thy birthday crown I wreathe.

Crown! How many a mingled thought
By that little word is brought!
Yet may each enlinkèd be
In a birthday wish for thee.

One who wears a crown should reign
Sovereign over some domain;
Held by thee, love's fairy sway
Still may every heart obey.

First we think of royal gems,
Coronets and diadems;
'Twere an idle wish, I ween,
Be thou happy as a Queen!

To another crown we turn,
While our loving hearts would burn,
Worn by Him who on the tree,
Miriam, hath died for thee.

By that thorn-enwoven crown.
By the life for thee laid down,
May thy every fleeting year
Bring thee to His love more near!

Then the crown of golden light,
Worn by those who walk in white,
May that be thy blest reward
In the presence of thy Lord!

To John Henry C — on His Third Birthday.

BLESSINGS on thee, darling boy,
Peace and love and gentle joy!
May the coronal they twine
Through the dream of life be thine!

Little hast thou known of life,
Of its sorrow, of its strife,
Thine not yet dark Future's blast,
Thine not yet a shadowy Past.

While we reck of coming years,
Strangely mingling hopes and fears,
What are sober thoughts to thee,
In the tide of birthday glee!

Thou art beautiful and bright,
Daily wakening new delight,
Would that we the prize could hold,
Always keep thee three years old!

No, not always; thou may'st be
Something brighter yet to see,
Noble-hearted, lofty-souled,
When more years have o'er thee rolled.

Love is watching round thee now,
Tracing sunbeams on thy brow;
Never be her mission done
To thy father's only son!

Yet a higher, deeper love
Watcheth o'er thee from above
Then thy fount of motive be
Love to Him who loveth thee.

Darling, may thy years below
Like a strain of music flow,
Ever sweeter, purer, higher,
Till it swell the angel choir.

Be thy life a star of light,
Glistening through earth's stormy night,
Shining then with glorious ray
Through the One Eternal Day!

For Elizabeth Clay's Birthday.

'My presence shall go with thee,
    And I will give thee rest!'
A promise sweetly tender,
    Soothing the anxious breast.

He knows the lonely spirit,
    And all its hidden woe;
He knows the weary yearnings
    No earthly friend can know.

His presence shall go with thee,
    And His upholding hand
Thy orphaned footsteps guiding
    All through the stranger's land.

Encompassed by that Presence
    Thou wilt not be alone,
And thou may'st safely rest thee
    'Neath the shadow of His throne.

When spring-time's emerald glory
    Bids hill and valley smile,
And thou once more regainest
    The white cliffs of our isle,

Shall I not hear thee whisper,
In accents calmly blest—
'His presence *hath* been with me,
And He *hath* given me rest'?

'Coming of Age.'

(J. H. S.)

WHAT do we seek for him to-day, who, through such golden gates
Of mirth and gladness, enters now where life before him waits?
'Mid light and flowers the feast is spread, and young and old rejoice,
And motto texts speak out for all, with earnest, loving voice.

The threefold blessing Israel heard three thousand years ago,
Oh! grant it may on him to-day in power and fulness flow;
For, faithful and unchangeable, each word of God is sure,
Though heaven and earth shall pass away, His promises endure.

The Angel of the Covenant, redeeming from all ill
Both son and father, bless the lad, and every prayer fulfil;
Nor only bless, but make him, too, a blessing, Lord, from Thee :
With length of days, oh, satisfy; let him Thy glory see.

Through all the journey of his life, Thy presence with him go;
Rest *in* Thee here, and *with* Thee there, do Thou, O Lord, bestow.
Oh, keep him faithful unto death, then grant to him, we pray,
The crown of glory and of life, that fadeth not away.

So shall the father's soul be glad for him he holds so dear,
A son whose heart is truly wise in God's most holy fear;
And hallowed be our festal joy with gratitude and praise;
Forget not all His benefits, whose kindness crowns our days.

Then glory in the highest be to Him, our Strength and Song;
May every heart uplift its part, in blessings deep and long.
Through Him who died that we might live, our thanks to God ascend,
The King of kings, and Lord of lords, our Saviour and our Friend.

To the Rev. C. B. Snepp.

I HAVE no hymn, my brother,
   Upon your desk to lay,
No song of holy gladness
   To bring to you to-day;

To 'Songs of Grace and Glory'
   No verses sweet and new!
I write not for ten thousand,
   I only write for you.

For oh, my heart is singing
   A song of quiet praise
To Him who has preserved you,
   Upholding all your ways.

To Him who knows our sorrows,
   Who knew the orphan's heart,
And sent a friend to cheer it,
   And act a brother's part.

So I come before my Father,
   My hands in faith uplift,
To fill your cup with gladness
   And every perfect gift.

And may His loving-kindness
   Crown all with grace for grace
Till in the coming glory
   You stand before His face!

And see with light from heaven
   Clear-shining on thy ways,
Each pilgrimage petition
   Transmuted into praise.

Saturday Night.

TO THE SAME.

LORD, refresh Thy weary servant,
    Send him sweet and quiet rest;
Thou hast made him oft a blessing,
    Let him now be doubly blest.

Let him feel Thy holy presence
    Richly dwelling in his soul,
Every care and every burden
    Bid him on Jehovah roll.

Lord, as he for Thee hath spoken,
    Now to him, oh do Thou speak!
With Thy still small voice of comfort
    Crown the mercies of the week.

May He wake with strength renewed,
    Yet again to work for Thee;
Full of Sabbath joy and blessing
    Let his spirit always be!

"I could not do without Thee."

John vi. 68. "Lord, to whom shall we go?"
Tune 130. Goldbach. 76, 76. D.

I could not do without Thee,
O Saviour of the lost!
Whose wondrous love redeemed me
At such tremendous cost.
Thy righteousness, Thy pardon,
Thy precious blood, must be
My only hope and comfort,
My glory and my plea.

I could not do without Thee,
I cannot stand alone,
I have no strength or goodness,
No wisdom of my own.
But Thou, beloved Saviour,
Art All-in-all to me,

Manuscript in F.R.H.'s hand of the poem on pages 375–376 of this book. At the end, after her signature, she quoted the first part of Isaiah 41:10.

And weakness with its power,
If leaning hard on Thee,
Could not do without Thee.
O Jesus, Saviour dear!
Even when thy eyes are hidden,
I know that Thou art near,
How weary and how lonely were
This thoughtful life around me,
Without the sweet communion,
The secret rest with Thee.

3

I could not do without Thee,
For, oh! the way is long,
And I am often weary,
And sigh replaces song.
How could I do without Thee, O Thou dear!
I do not know the way,
Thou knowest, & Thou leadest,
And wilt not let me stray.

I could not do without Thee,
No other friend could read
The spirit's strange deep longings,
Interpreting its need.
No human heart could enter
Each dim recess of mine,
And soothe, & hush, & calm it,
O blessed Lord, but Thine!

I could not do without Thee,
On life is fleeting fast,
And there an solemn meaning
The river must be passed.
But Thou wilt never leave me,
And though the waves roll high,
I know Thou art with me ever,
And whisper, "It is I."

Frances Ridley Havergal

For there are not for anybody the best of January 1873

Sonnets.

A Waking Thought.

THEN Time will seem as but a pebble cast
    Into the ocean of Eternity,
Breaking for one short moment that pure light,
Which dwells upon its calm expanse of joy,
As into shiv'ring radiance, and shade-like circles.
Soon melting back into primeval brightness,
(Like that which was, when all created essence
Took but the forms of blended light and music,
    In glory of an infinite variety),
Through the translucent crystal of that sea,
It swiftly sinks to rest, within the depths
Of that great heart, like an aye-glistening
And treasured memory of things gone by,
Bearing, deep graven on its pale, clear front,
One word—REDEMPTION!

Life Mosaic.

MASTER, to do great work for Thee, my hand
    Is far too weak! Thou givest what may suit—
    Some little chips to cut with care minute,
Or tint, or grave, or polish. Others stand
Before their quarried marble fair and grand,
    And make a life work of the great design
    Which Thou hast traced; or, many-skilled, combine
To build vast temples, gloriously planned.
Yet take the tiny stones which I have wrought,
    Just one by one, as they were given by Thee,
Not knowing what came next in Thy wise thought.
Set each stone by Thy master-hand of grace,
    Form the mosaic as Thou wilt for me,
And in Thy temple-pavement give it place.

To Helga.

COME down, and show the dwellers far below
   What God is painting on each mountain place!
   Show His fair colours, and His perfect grace,
Dowering each blossom born of sun and snow:
His tints, not thine! Thou art God's copyist,
   O gifted Helga! His thy golden height,
   Thy purple depth, thy rosy sunset light,
Thy blue snow-shadows, and thy weird white mist.
Reveal His works to many a distant land!
   Paint for His praise, oh paint for love of Him!
He is thy Master, let Him hold thy hand,
   So thy pure heart no cloud of self shall dim.
At His dear feet lay down thy laurel-store,
Which crimson proof of thy redemption bore.

Memorial Names.

THE High Priest stands before the Mercy Seat,
   And on his breast bright mingling jewel-flames
   Reflect Shechinah light; twelve patriarch names
Flash where the emerald and sapphire meet
Sardius and diamond. With softer beam,
   From mystic onyx on his shoulders placed,
   Deep graven, never altered or erased,
The same great names, in birthday order, gleam.
May each name written here be thus engraved,
   Set in the place of power, the place of love,
   And borne in sweet memorial above,
By Him who loved and chose, redeemed and saved
   Be each dear name, the greatest and the least,
   Always upon the heart of our High Priest.

Our Red-Letter Days.

My Alpine staff recalls each shining height,
    Each pass of grandeur with rejoicing gained,
    Carved with a lengthening record, self-explained,
Of mountain-memories sublime and bright.
No valley-life but hath some mountain days,
    Bright summits in the retrospective view,
    And toil-won passes to glad prospects new,
Fair sunlit memories of joy and praise.
Grave on thy heart each past 'red-letter day!'
Forget not all the sunshine of the way
By which the Lord hath led thee: answered prayers
And joys unasked; strange blessings, lifted cares,
Grand promise-echoes! Thus thy life shall be
One record of His love and faithfulness to thee.

Luke 9:13.

The Lord commanded, 'Give ye them to eat,'—
    Five loaves and two small fishes all their store
    For hungering crowds. He knew they had no more,
And He had called them to that wild retreat.
They gave it as He gave them, piece by piece,
    Where on the green grass grouped the great and small
    Till all were filled. So not theirs at all
But His, the glory of that grand increase.
Master, I have not strength to serve Thee much,
    The 'half-day's work' is all that I can do,
But let Thy mighty, multiplying touch
    Even to me the miracle renew.
Let five words feed five thousand, and Thy power
Expand to life-results one feeble hour.

The Eternity of God.

42)
43)

1 Tim. 1. 17. "The King eternal, immortal, invisible".
Ps. 90. 2. "From everlasting to everlasting Thou art God".

St Paul 87, 887, 77, 77.

King Eternal and Immortal!
  We, the children of an hour,
Bend in lowly adoration,
Rise in raptured admiration
    At the Whisper of Thy power.
      Myriad ages in Thy sight,
        Are but as the fleeting day;
        Like a vision of the night,
          Worlds may rise and pass away.

All Thy glories are eternal,
    None shall ever pass away;
Truth and mercy all-victorious,
Righteousness and love all glorious,
    Shine with everlasting ray.
      All resplendent, are the light
      Bade primeval darkness fleet;
      All transcendant, through the flight
        Of eternities to be.
Thou art God from everlasting,
    And to everlasting art!
Ere the dawn of shadowy ages,
Dimly guessed by angel sages,
    Ere the beat of seraph-heart, —
      Thou, Jehovah, art the Same,
        And Thy years shall have no end;
        Changeless nature, changeless name,
        Ever Father, God, and Friend.
      God Triune our covenant Friend.

Frances Ridley Havergal. Feb. 11. 4 p.m.

29 lines

See pages 366–367 of this book. See also page 340 for another manuscript of this poem.

In Memoriam.

My Mother's Request.

(SUNDAY MORNING, 8 O'CLOCK.)

THE Sabbath morn dawns o'er the mountain brow,
And lights the earth with glory soft and mild:
Oh, think'st thou, dearest mother, even now
Of me, thy youngest and most wayward child?

For this, my mother, is the sacred hour
When thou didst bid me ever think of thee:
Oh, surely nothing earthly could have power
To break the spell which hallows it to me.

Thy loving look, thy feeble voice, I seem,
Though years have passed, to see and hear again;
Not as the shadowy fancies of a dream,
But as distinct, as vivid now as then.

'When in my Saviour's glorious home I dwell,
Forget not this my last request to thee:
When soundeth forth the early Sabbath bell,
Where'er thou art, my Fanny, think of me!'

Oh, why was this thy dying wish—thy last?
Thou would'st not think that I should e'er forget
My mother's love, that passing years might cast
A cloudy veil, where that bright star did set;

Thou could'st not wish to wake the grief anew
Which Time's dark poppies might have lulled awhile;
'Twas not that tear-drops might again bedew
My cheek for aye, and chase again each smile.

Oh no! were death an endless, joyless sleep,
Thou hadst not bid me on thy memory dwell;

This hour for thee thou hadst not bid me keep,
To grieve thy child, thou lovèdst her too well.

But well thou knew'st I could not think of thee
Without remembering Him with whom thou art,
To whom thou oft didst pray so fervently
That I might give my wandering, wilful heart.

I must remember too the joyful faith
Which filled thy soul e'en in thy dying hour,
And led thee calmly through the vale of death;
There I must ever see its wondrous power.

I could not but fulfil thy last desire,
The last sweet echo of thy loving voice,
Calling my mind each Sabbath morning higher,
Where thou in endless Sabbath dost rejoice.

So if my heart should tempt me to forget
To watch and pray, and Jesu's love to seek,
This quiet hour might break for me the net,
And free my feet afresh each opening week.

Oft when I wavered, slipped, and nearly fell,
Yet stunned and giddy heeded not my fate,
The fatal charm was broken by that bell,
Thy memory oped my eyes ere yet too late.

And oft when sad and hopeless seemed my way,
Its sweet sound told me of the victory
Which thy bright faith hath gained, and then a ray
Of hope hath whispered, 'Such may be for thee.'

Oh, 'twas a mother's love which did devise
This gentle way of helping her child's soul;
Not on earth only, but from yon bright skies
To aid her steps towards the heavenly goal.

Oh, Thou who dwellest with Thy ransomed, where
The one long Sabbath ne'er may darkly close,
By Thy rich mercy grant this earliest prayer,
Which oft for me from her dear lips arose.

Bring me, oh, bring me to Thy house of light,
That there with my loved mother I may dwell,
And e'er rejoicing in Thy presence bright,
May praise Thy love, who doest all things well.

May Dirge.

I WELCOME not thy coming now,
For sorrow darkeneth my brow,
And but for glad hearts wakest thou,
   Fair May.

When, years ago, thou dawnedst bright,
With thy first hours blest my sight
The fairest child that e'er saw light
   Of May.

She grew a gladder, blither thing
Than butterfly on purple wing,
Or happy birds which sweetly sing
   In May.

'Twas she who brought my sunniest hours,
For she was lovelier than the flowers
Which bloom amid thy emerald bowers,
   Bright May.

How oft, when grief had touched my heart,
She chased it with her fairy art;
Thy charms to her thou didst impart,
   Glad May.

But oh! there is a treacherous smile,
Which Spring assumeth to beguile,
And many rue thy sunny wile,
   False May.

A flush in her loved cheek arose,
More rich than ruby tint that glows
In western cloud when evenings close
   In May.

Her dark eye brightly, strangely gleamed,
More beautiful than e'er she seemed;
Oh, who of evil nigh had dreamed
        That May?

But when the snowdrop came again,
I saw that tenderest care was vain;
My Ella passed from all her pain
        In May.

That precious life no skill could save;
I laid her in a quiet grave,
Where now the snowy blossoms wave
        Of May.

Once more they shed their sweet perfume,
As incense o'er my darling's tomb,
Though soon departs their fragile bloom
        With May.

Thou hast my child! Thy sparkling dew
Is glittering on her grave anew;
Soon thou wilt deck her father's too,
        O May!

I cannot live without her here,
For earth is desolate and drear,
E'en when thy morning shineth clear,
        Blithe May.

To cheer me thou canst weave no spell
Deep sadness in my heart doth dwell,
And I must bid my last farewell
        To May.

Speed, speed thy slow return, for when
Once more thou comest, then, oh then,
I shall be with my child again,
        Sweet May!

To F. M. G. on Her Brother's Death.

STAY not the current of thy tears, for they
Must flow, and 'tis a sad relief to weep
For one who, having brightened long the way,
          Now lies in death's long sleep.

A brother's love! I know it is a treasure
Which may by nothing earthly be replaced;
I know that *this* filled up the bounteous measure
          Of joy which thou didst taste.

I know that sadness fills thy youthful heart
E'en to o'erflowing; and it well may seem
That nought to thee remaineth but the smart;
          Of happiness no gleam.

And Jesus knows it. Oh, He did not call
Thy brother from his loving sister's side
Without remembering *thee*, thy sorrows all;
          He knows the heart He tried.

But He would have thee turn thy weeping eye
To gaze on Him, who suffered all for thee,
That the effulgence every tear may dry
          Which beams from Calvary.

All earthly love is as a thread of gold,
Most fair, but what the touch of death may sever:
But *His* a cable sure, of strength untold:
          Oh! His love lasteth ever.

And this sweet love He would on thee bestow,
The fulness of His grace to thee make known,
A glimpse of heaven grant thee here below,
          And thou shouldst be His own.

Thou wilt not sigh, if this one Pearl thou gain,
O'er earthly treasures, costly though they be.
Short is the night of weeping and of pain;
          Endless the joy for thee!

Thy brother striketh now his harp of gold,
And singeth joyously his first 'new song';
The echo of his melody hath rolled
    The aisles of heaven along.

He weareth raiment white, which angel hands
From the full vestry of the Lamb have brought;
With palm and crown, before His throne he stands
    Who him by blood hath bought.

Gladness unspeakable his soul doth fill,
He hath forgotten pain, and grief, and sorrow;
Eternal bliss hath dawned on him, he will
    See no woe-bringing morrow.

He might have passed through many a weary year
Of sickness, trouble, or perplexity,
And as an autumn leaf, all brown and sere,
    Been *shaken* from the tree;

He might have forfeited the heavenly prize,
Had he lived longer on the Tempter's ground:
Then gaze no longer where his body lies
    Beneath the new formed mound.

Yes, look up from the scene of mourning, where
Nought but a dreary blank thine eyes can see:
Thou hast a brother now in heaven, and there
    He waits to welcome thee!

Evelyn.

Dying? Evelyn, darling!
   Dying? can it be?
Spring so joyous all around,
Such a spring, so early crowned,
Heralding all summer glee,
Life for everything but thee!
   Evelyn, darling, dying?
Yet it is no phantom sound,

Though the word is haunting me;
    Thou art lying
Now where life and death do meet,
Thorny path and golden street.
I thought I had no heart to write,
    But the pencil near me lay,
    Which has traced me many a day,
Dipped in colours dark or bright,
Lays I guessed would meet the sight
    Of at least some loving eye,
And perchance be heard again,
    Winning echoes far and nigh,
    Touching chords of sympathy
In the weary souls of men.
And I took it in my hand,
    For it seemed to be relief,
    After this long week of grief,
Just to let the thought expand,
And the word that haunted me
Just to write; though none shall see
What is written, only He
Who is gently leading thee,
    Evelyn, darling, without fears,
Through the vale of death,—and me
    Through the vale of tears.

All so calm;—a hazy veil
    Falling on the golden west;
Silence, like a minstrel pale,
    Preluding the Sabbath rest.
There is night before the dawn
Rise for *us* of Sabbath morn:
Is there any night for *thee*
Ere thine eyes the glory see?
Are the angels, bright and strong,
    Bearing thy free soul away,
Teaching thee the glad new song,
    On the grand star-paven way?
Art thou even now at rest,
    Lying on the Saviour's breast?

Evelyn, darling, is it so?
Would, oh, would that I could know!
I can only wait in sorrow
For the tidings of the morrow.

Evelyn, darling, laid so low!
Only three short months ago
Thou wert full of life and glee,
Round the laden Christmas tree;
Foremost in the carol-singing,
Fun and frolic gaily flinging.
Tallest, fairest of the troop,
  Opening rose on slender stem,
Reigning 'mid the bright-eyed group,
  Queen without a diadem;
In thy robe of snowy sheen,
Decked with silken emerald green.
Few there are who ever knew
  Merrier holidays than thine,
Whether summer breezes blew,
  Or the winter stars did shine.
Evelyn, darling, can it be,
  Was that Christmas tree the last?
How believe it, that for thee
  Christmas holidays are past!
And that summer leaves will wave,
  And the Easter moon will shine,
Over the first household grave,
   First,—and *thine!*

I am not praying,—prayer is hushed,
  God's hand is laid upon my heart;
The earthly hope for ever crushed,
  The heavenly *answered,* not in part,
But fully, perfectly! I prayed
  For life, and He hath given the life
Which triumphs o'er the grave's cold shade;
  For peace, and He hath ended strife
And spoken love. There have been tears

And earnest pleadings through long years;
But He is faithful to His word,
I *know* at last that He has heard.
But not, oh not as I had thought
    In ignorant and selfish love,
The Master calls,—she tarries not,
    For He hath need of her above.
The lambs He gathers with His arm
No grief, no sin, no death can harm,
So safely folded on His breast,
For ever and for ever blest.
Could God Himself give more? His will
Is best, though we are weeping still.

Yet the old cry comes again,
    Evelyn, darling, dying!
Is it true, or is it dreaming?
Is it only ghastly seeming
Of a sorrow far away,
Not to fall for many a day?
    If I saw thee lying,
I might realize it so!
Last I saw thee in the glow
Of thy brightest health and bloom;
Was it only for the tomb?
Then the sorrow grows with this—
    Not a word of fond good-bye,
Not one tender parting kiss,
    Not one glance of loving eye!
Well I know it could not be!
God's appointed way for me
Was assuredly—'Be still,
Wait in silence for His will.'
Father, I have said Amen,
Said it often, now again!
Father, strengthen it and seal!
Let my weary spirit feel
I am very near to Thee,
For Thy hand is laid on me,—

Though the shadows gather deep,
Thou canst calm and aid and keep.

Father, where the shadows fall
Deeper yet, deepest of all,
Send Thy peace, and show Thy power
In affliction's direst hour;
To each mourning heart draw near,
Soothe and bless, sustain and cheer.
Thou *wilt* hear, I know not *how!*
Thou canst help, 'and only Thou.'
This my prayer I leave with Thee.
Father! hear and answer me
For the sake of Him who knows
All our love and all our woes.

Starlight Through the Shadows.

I.

THY dear one is with Jesus now!
  Seeing Him face to face,
Gazing upon His own belovèd brow,
  Watching His smile of grace;
Hearing the Master's voice in all its sweetness,
Knowing Him now in all His own completeness;
  With Jesus now, with Him for ever!
  Never to leave Him—grieve Him never!
Could God Himself give more? His will
Is best, though we are weeping still.

II.

  He knows!
Yes, Jesus knows! just what you cannot tell
  He understands so well!
The silence of the heart is heard,
He does not need a single word,
  He thinks of you;

He watcheth, and He careth too,
He pitieth, He loveth! All this flows
    In one sweet word: 'He knows!'

III.

There shall be no more pain! Not any more!
All weariness, all faint exhaustion o'er,
No quivering nerve, no aching unconfessed,
    No memory of misery to cast
    One shadow from the past
Upon the unshadowed splendour of His rest!
Belovèd! God is leading thee to this,
Preparing thee for thy preparing bliss.

IV.

When thou passest through the waters,
    I will be with thee!
Sure and sweet and all-sufficient
    Shall His Presence be.
All God's billows overwhelmed Him
    In the great Atoning Day;
Now He only leads thee through them,
    With thee all the way.

In Loyal and Loving Remembrance of H.R.H. the Princess Alice.[1]

Two nations mourn! The same great grief is known
    By human hearts on either side the sea,
Mourning with those who yet must mourn alone
    Upon the silent height where only He
Can come and whisper comfort, who hath worn
The lonely diadem of cruel thorn.

[1] Written to accompany a memorial wreath of white roses and palm leaves, painted by the Baroness Helga von Cramm.

Mourning for her whose royal love hath shown
    Secrets of comfort in the darkest days;
Who, like her Master, stooping from a throne
    The suffering or the lost could heal or raise;
Leaving, like Him, example pure and bright,
For court or cottage home a starry light.

Two nations mourn; a hand from each would lay
Fair flowers and simple verse upon her tomb to-day.

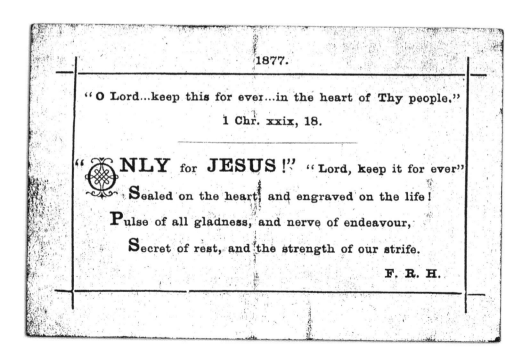

Another small card, printed to give to many. See pages 443 and 565 of this book.

Under the Surface.

I.

On the surface, foam & roar,
Restless heave & passionate dash,
Shingle-rattle along the shore,
Gathering boom & thundering crash.

Under the surface, soft green light,
A hush of peace & an endless calm;
Winds & waves from a choral height
Falling sweet as a far-off psalm.

On the surface, swell & swirl,
Tossing weed and drifting waif,
Broken spars that the mad waves whirl,
As round wreck-watching rocks they chafe.

Under the surface, loveliest forms,
Feathery fronds with crimson curl,
Treasures too deep for the raid of storms,
Delicate coral & hidden pearl.

II

On the surface, lilies white,
A painted skiff with a singing crew,
Sky-reflections soft & bright,
Tremulous scarlet, gold & blue.

Under the surface, life in death,
Slimy tangle & oozy moans,
Creeping things with watery breath,
Blackening roots & whitening bones.

On the surface, a shining reach,
A crystal couch for the moonbeams' rest,
Starry ripples along the beach,
Sunset songs from the breezy west.

Under the surface, glooms & fears,
Treacherous currents cold & strong,
Deafening rush in the drowning ears,—
Have ye rightly read my song?

Frances Ridley Havergal

A fair copy autograph in F.R.H.'s handwriting. See pages 342–343.

99

The Eternity of God.

I Tim. 1. 17. "The King Eternal, Immortal, Invisible".

I

King Eternal and Immortal!
  We, the children of an hour,
Bend in lowly adoration,
Rise in raptured admiration,
  At the whisper of Thy power.
    Myriad ages in Thy sight
    Are but as the fleeting day;
    Like a vision of the night
    Worlds may rise and pass away.

II

All Thy glories are eternal,
  None shall ever pass away;
Truth and Mercy all-victorious,
Righteousness and Love all glorious
  Shine with everlasting ray.
    All resplendent, ere the light
    Bade primeval darkness flee;
    All transcendent, through the flight
    Of eternities to be.

This first page of the fair copy autograph of "The Eternity of God" was found in F.R.H.'s Manuscript Book No VI. See pages 326 and 366–367 of this book.

Under the Surface.

Prelude.

TAKE it, O Father! This new book be Thine,
Filled only with Thy teachings, only filled
For Thee, and for the pilgrims to Thy home.
I know not what bright impulses of song
May come upon my waiting soul, nor when;
Or whether years of silence yet may fall
In still parenthesis as once before;
Or whether tighter tension must be laid
By Thy unerring Hand, that so the tone
May be more true to that immortal key
Which reaches loneliest depth of human heart
With echoes from Thine own. I would not shrink
From suffering, if I may but sing for Thee.
Father, Thou knowest how this gift hath seemed
Thine own direct sweet answer to the prayer
For peace and patience in the silent grief
Thy Hand, Thine own, has portioned out for me.
And I have felt Thy call, not loud, but clear,
To praise Thee with my song, as, it may be,
I had not done had all my heart's desire
Been granted me.

.   .   .   .

Thou knowest how (so often) I have laid
An aching heart upon Thy heart of love,
And wept out all my sorrow, till at last
Thou gavest Thy belovèd sleep. And then
Came singing in the morning some glad thought
That, wafted over land and sea, has put
New songs in silent mouths, and come again
With harvest of rejoicing back to me.

Let not Thy blessing fail! I long for this,
I ask it for the sake of Him whose Name
Is my sure plea. O send it, gracious Lord!
As Thou hast spared me to begin to-day
The seventh small volume of these leaves of life,
So let a sevenfold blessing rest upon
All that shall fill these pages. Give me thoughts,
But quicken them with power; give me words,
But wing them with Thy love; give music too,
But let it ring all beautiful and sweet
With holiness; yea, give to me, if such
Thy holy will, far better and far more
Than heretofore, but only add this gift,
Without which all were worthless and in vain,
Thy Blessing. So the glory and the praise
Shall all be Thine for evermore. Amen.

Under the Surface.

I.

On the surface, foam and roar,
    Restless heave and passionate dash,
Shingle rattle along the shore,
    Gathering boom and thundering crash.

Under the surface, soft green light,
    A hush of peace and an endless calm,
Winds and waves from a choral height,
    Falling sweet as a far off psalm.

On the surface, swell and swirl,
    Tossing weed and drifting waif,
Broken spars that the mad waves whirl,
    Where wreck-watching rocks they chafe.

Under the surface, loveliest forms,
    Feathery fronds with crimson curl,
Treasures too deep for the raid of storms,
    Delicate coral and hidden pearl.

II.

On the surface, lilies white,
   A painted skiff with a singing crew,
Sky-reflections soft and bright,
   Tremulous crimson, gold and blue.

Under the surface, life in death,
   Slimy tangle and oozy moans,
Creeping things with watery breath,
   Blackening roots and whitening bones.

On the surface, a shining reach,
   A crystal couch for the moonbeams' rest,
Starry ripples along the beach,
   Sunset songs from the breezy west.

Under the surface, glooms and fears,
   Treacherous currents swift and strong,
Deafening rush in the drowning ears:
   Have ye rightly read my song?

Autobiography.

AUTOBIOGRAPHY! So you say,
   So do I *not* believe!
For no men or women that live to-day,
Be they as good or as bad as they may,
   Ever would dare to leave
In faintest pencil or boldest ink
All they truly and really think,
What they have said and what they have done,
What they have lived and what they have felt,
   Under the stars or under the sun.
At the touch of a pen the dewdrops melt,
   And the jewels are lost in the grass,
   Though you count the blades as you pass.
At the touch of a pen the lightning is fixed,
   An innocent streak on a broken cloud;
   And the thunder that pealed so fierce and loud,

With musical echo is softly mixed.
                    Autobiography? No!
        It never was written yet, I trow.
            Grant that they try!
            Still they must fail!
            Words are too pale
For the fervour and glow of the lava-flow.
        Can they paint the flash of an eye?
        How much less the flash of a heart,
        Or its delicate ripple and glitter and gleam,
        Swift and sparkling, suddenly darkling,
        Crimson and gold tints, exquisite soul-tints,
        Changing like dawn-flush touching a dream!
                    Where is the art
That shall give the play of blending lights
        From the porphyry rock on the pool below?
Or the bird-shadow traced on the sunlit heights
        Of golden rose and snow?

You say 'tis a fact that the books exist,
Printed and published in Mudie's list,
        Some in two volumes, and some in one—
Autobiographies plenty. But look!
        I will tell you what is done
        By the writers, confidentially!
They cut little pieces out of their lives
        And join them together,
Making them up as a readable book,
        And call it an autobiography,
Though little enough of the life survives.

What if we went in the sweet May weather
To a wood that I know which hangs on a hill,
And reaches down to a tinkling brook,
That sings the flowers to sleep at night,
And calls them again with the earliest light.
Under the delicate flush of green,
        Hardly shading the bank below,
Pale anemones peep between
        The mossy stumps where the violets grow;

Wide clouds of bluebells stretch away,
　　And primrose constellations rise,—
　　　　Turn where we may,
　　Some new loveliness meets our eyes.
The first white butterflies flit around,
Bees are murmuring close to the ground,
　　The cuckoo's happy shout is heard.
　　　　Hark again!
　　Was it echo, or was it bird?
　　All the air is full of song,
A carolling chorus around and above;
From the wood-pigeon's call so soft and long,
To merriest twitter and marvellous trill,
Every one sings at his own sweet will,
True to the key-note of joyous love.

Well, it is lovely! is it not?
But we must not stay on the fairy spot,
　　So we gather a nosegay with care:
　　A primrose here and a bluebell there,
And something that we have never seen,
　　Probably therefore a specimen rare;
Stitchwort, with stem of transparent green,
　　The white-veined woodsorrel, and a spray
　　Of tender-leaved and budding May.
We carry home the fragrant load
In a close, warm hand, by a dusty road;
The sun grows hotter every hour;
Already the woodsorrel pines for the shade
　　　　We watch it fade,
And throw away the fair little flower;
We forgot that it could not last an hour
Away from the cool moss where it grows.
Then the stitchworts droop and close;
There is nothing to show but a tangle of green,
For the white-rayed stars will no more be seen.
Then the anemones, can they survive?
Even now they are hardly alive.
Ha! where is it, our unknown spray?
　　　　Dropped on the way!

Perhaps we shall never find one again.
At last we come in with the few that are left,
 Of freshness and fragrance bereft;
   A sorry display.
   Now, do we say,
'Here is the wood where we rambled to-day;
See, we have brought it to you;
Believe us, indeed it is true.
  This is the wood!' do we say?

So much for the bright and pleasant side.
There is another. We did not bring
All that was hidden under the wing
Of the radiant-plumaged Spring.
   We never tried
To spy, or watch, or away to bear,
Much that was just as truly there.
    What have we seen?
    Hush, ah, hush!
Curled and withered fern between,
And dead leaves under the living green
Thick and damp. A clammy feather,
All that remains of a singing thrush
Killed by a weasel long ago,
In the hungry winter weather.
Nettles in unfriendly row,
And last year's brambles, sharp and brown,
Grimly guarding a hawthorn crown.
A pale leaf trying to reach the light
By a long weak stem, but smothered down,
Dying in darkness, with none to see.
The rotting trunk of a willow tree,
Leafless, ready to fall from the bank;
A poisonous fungus, cold and white,
And a hemlock growing strong and rank
A tuft of fur and a ruddy stain,
Where a wounded hare has escaped the snare,
Only perhaps to be caught again.
No specimens we bring of these,

Lest they should disturb our ease,
And spoil the story of the May,
And make you think our holiday
Was far less pleasant than we say.

Ah no! We write our lives indeed,
But in a cipher none can read,
Except the author. He may pore
The life-accumulating lore
   For evermore,
And find the records strange and true,
Bring wisdom old and new.
But though he break the seal,
No power has he to give the key,
   No licence to reveal.
  We wait the all-declaring day,
  When love shall know as it is known.
Till then, the secrets of our lives are ours and
   God's alone.

Compensation.

O THE compensating springs! O the balance-wheels of life,
Hidden away in the workings under the seeming strife!
Slowing the fret and the friction, weighting the whirl and the force,
Evolving the truest power from each unconscious source.

How shall we gauge the whole, who can only guess a part?
How can we read the life, when we cannot spell the heart?
How shall we measure another, we who can never know
From the juttings above the surface the depth of the vein below?

Even our present way is known to ourselves alone,
Height and abyss and torrent, flower and thorn and stone;
But we gaze on another's path as a far-off mountain scene,
Scanning the outlined hills, but never the vales between.

How shall we judge their present, we who have never seen
That which is past for ever, and that which might have been?

Measuring by ourselves, unwise indeed are we,
Measuring what we *know* by what we can hardly *see*.

Ah! if we knew it all, we should surely understand
That the balance of sorrow and joy is held with an even hand,
That the scale of success or loss shall never overflow,
And that compensation is twined with the lot of high and low.

The easy path in the lowland hath little of grand or new,
But a toilsome ascent leads on to a wide and glorious view;
Peopled and warm is the valley, lonely and chill the height,
But the peak that is nearer the storm-cloud is nearer the stars of light.

Launch on the foaming stream that bears you along like a dart,—
There is danger of rapid and rock, there is tension of muscle and heart;
Glide on the easy current, monotonous, calm, and slow,
You are spared the quiver and strain in the safe and quiet flow.

O the sweetness that dwells in a harp of many strings,
While each, all vocal with love, in tuneful harmony rings!
But O, the wail and the discord, when one and another is rent
Tensionless, broken, or lost, from the cherished instrument.

For rapture of love is linked with the pain or fear of loss,
And the hand that takes the crown must ache with many a cross;
Yet he who hath never a conflict hath never a victor's palm,
And only the toilers know the sweetness of rest and calm.

Only between the storms can the Alpine traveller know
Transcendent glory of clearness, marvels of gleam and glow;
Had he the brightness unbroken of cloudless summer days,
This had been dimmed by the dust and the veil of a brooding haze.

Who would dare the choice, *neither* or *both* to know,
The finest quiver of joy or the agony-thrill of woe?
Never the exquisite pain, then never the exquisite bliss,
For the heart that is dull to that can never be strung to this.

Great is the peril or toil if the glory or gain be great;
Never an earthly gift without responsible weight;
Never a treasure without a following shade of care;
Never a power without the lurk of a subtle snare.

For the swift is not the safe, and the sweet is not the strong;
The smooth is not the short, and the keen is not the long;
The much is not the most, and the wide is not the deep;
And the flow is never a spring, when the ebb is only neap.

Then hush! oh, hush! for the Father knows what thou knowest not,
The need and the thorn and the shadow linked with the fairest lot;
Knows the wisest exemption from many an unseen snare,
Knows what will keep thee nearest, knows what thou could'st not bear.

Hush! oh, hush! for the Father portioneth as He will,
To all His beloved children, and shall they not be still?
Is not His will the wisest, is not His choice the best?
And in perfect acquiescence is there not perfect rest?

Hush! oh, hush! for the Father, whose ways are true and just,
Knoweth and careth and loveth, and waits for thy perfect trust;
The cup He is slowly filling shall soon be full to the brim,
And infinite compensations for ever be found in Him.

Hush! oh, hush! for the Father hath fulness of joy in store,
Treasures of power and wisdom, and pleasures for evermore;
Blessing and honour and glory, endless, infinite bliss;—
Child of His love and His choice, oh, canst thou not wait for this?

The Moonlight Sonata.

INTRODUCTION.

THE ills we see,—
The mysteries of sorrow deep and long,
The dark enigmas of permitted wrong,—
Have all one key:
This strange, sad world is but our Father's school;
All chance and change His love shall grandly overrule.

How sweet to know
The trials which we cannot comprehend
Have each their own divinely-purposed end!
He traineth so
For higher learning, ever onward reaching
For fuller knowledge yet, and His own deeper teaching.

He traineth thus
That we may teach the lessons we are taught;
That younger learners may be further brought,
Led on by us:
Well may we wait, or toil, or suffer long,
For His dear service so to be made fit and strong.

He traineth so
That we may shine for Him in this dark world,
And bear His standard dauntlessly unfurled:
That we may show
His praise, by lives that mirror back His love,—
His witnesses on earth, as He is ours above.

Nor only here
The rich result of all our God doth teach
His scholars, slow at best, until we reach
A nobler sphere:
Then, not till then, our training is complete,
And the true life begins for which He made us meet.

Are children trained
Only that they may reach some higher class?
Only for some few school-room years that pass
Till growth is gained?
Is it not rather for the years beyond
To which the father looks with hopes so fair and fond?

Bold thought, flash on
Into the far depths of Eternity;
When Time shall be a faint star-memory,
So long, long gone!
Only not lost to our immortal sight,
Because it ever bears Redemption's quenchless light.

Flash on, and stand
Among thy bright companions,—spirits blest,
Inhabiting through ages of glad rest
The Shining Land!
Each singing bliss into each other's hearts,—
Outpouring mighty joy that God's full hand imparts.

If sweet below
To minister to those whom God doth love,
What will it be to minister above!
His praise to show
In some new strain amid the ransomed choir,
To touch their joy and love with note of living fire;

With perfect praise,
With interchange of rapturous revelation
From Christ Himself, the burning adoration
Yet higher to raise,
For ever and for ever so to bring
More glory and still more to Him, our gracious King.

Look on to this
Through all perplexities of grief and strife,—
To this, thy true maturity of life,
Thy coming bliss;
That such high gifts thy future dower may be,
And for such service high thy God prepareth thee.

What though to-day
Thou canst not trace at all the hidden reason
For His strange dealings through the trial-season,—
Trust and obey:
And, like the child whose story follows here,
In after life and light all shall be plain and clear.

ALICE'S STORY.

PART I.

The firelight softly glanced upon
Dark braids and sunny curls,
Where, in a many-windowed room,
Yet dim with late November gloom,
Were busy groups of girls.

Some sat apart to learn alone;
Some studied side by side;

Some gathered round a master's chair
In reverent silence; others there
    For readiest answer tried.

For one young name a summons came,
    And Alice quickly rose:
The rapid pen aside is laid;
The call once heard must be obeyed
    At once,—as well she knows.

Yet with no joyous step or smile
    She hastens now away,
A teacher's earnest look to meet,
Whose hand is filled with music sweet,
    As hers shall be one day.

Beside her at the instrument
    A place her teacher takes,
With patient eye, yet keenest ear;
And Alice knows that he will hear
    The slightest fault she makes.

Oh, such a music-task as this
    Was never hers before!
So long and hard, so strange and stern,—
A piece she thinks she cannot learn,
    Though practised o'er and o'er.

It is not beautiful to her,—
    She cannot grasp the whole:
The Master's thought was great and deep,—
A mighty storm, to seize and sweep
    The wind-harp of the soul.

She only plays it note by note,
    With undeveloped heart;
She does not glimpse the splendour through
Each chord, so difficult and new,
    Of veiled and varied art.

Unwonted beat and weird repeat
   She cannot understand;
She stumbles on with clouded brow,—
Her cheek is flushed, and aching now
   The weary little hand.

She looked up in her teacher's face;
   Tears were not far away:
'*Must* I go on till it is done?
Oh, let me change it, sir, for one
   That I can better play.

'I cannot make it beautiful,—
   It has no tune to sing;
And when I am at home, I fear
My friends will never care to hear
   This long and dreary thing.'

He said, 'If you might freely choose,
   My child, what would you learn?'
'Oh, I would have the "Shower of Pearls,"
Or "Soldiers' March," like other girls,
   And quick approval earn;

'Or sweet Italian melodies,
   With brilliant run and shake:
If you would only give me such,
I think that I could please you much,—
   Such progress I should make.'

'Learn this, and it will please me more,'
   Said he, with kindest voice:
'And though 'tis now so hard to play,
Trust me, you will be glad some day
   That I have ruled your choice.'

Tears trembled on the lash, and now
   His face she could not see;
Once more she pleaded, as they fell,
'But I shall never play it well:
   It is too hard for me!'

'One thing I grant,' he said: 'that you
    May fully, freely tell
Your father, who is kind and wise:
And, Alice, what he shall advise,
    Say, will it not be well?'

Again she came, and stumblingly
    The hard sonata played:
Another week had passed away,
With toilsome practice every day,
    Yet small the progress made.

Her father's writing, bold and clear,
    Lay on the instrument:
'Your letter safely came to me,
And now shall answer lovingly
    To my dear child be sent.

'The hardest gained is best retained;
    You learn not for to-day:
I cannot grant your fond request
Your teacher certainly knows best,—
    So trust him and obey.'

The teacher spoke; she listened well,
    No word of his to miss:
'Alice, I want to make of you
An artist, noble, high, and true;
    And no light thing is this.

'There's happier, better work in store
    Than merry tunes to play:
You have a mission to fulfil,—
You do not know it; but I will
    Prepare you as I may.

'Will you believe that I know best,
    And persevere, my child?'
She answered, with a little sigh,
'Yes: I will trust, and I will try';
    And then her teacher smiled.

Part II.

Long has the school been left behind,
    For years have passed away:
We find her now where evening light
Fades not into the darksome night,
    But melts into the day.

There, in an arched and lofty room,
    She stands, in fair white dress;
Where grace and colour and sweet sound
Combine and cluster all around,
    And rarest taste express.

'Tis Alice still, but woman grown
    In hand and head and heart:
And those who now around her throng
Are skilled in music and in song,
    In learning and in art.

It was an evening of delight
    To be remembered long,
With many a reach of vivid thought,
And many a vision artist-wrought,
And—crown of all that friendship brought—
    The eloquence of song.

The North is bright, with lingering light
    To Northern summers given,—
A tender loveliness that stays
When twilight falls upon the days,
    As silence falls in heaven.

'Now, Alice: now the time is come!
    Sweet music you have poured;
But, in this gentle twilight fall,
Give now the very best of all
    That in your heart is stored.

'Give now the Master's masterpiece;
    All silent we will be:

And you shall stir our inmost souls,
While, like a fiery river, rolls
  Beethoven's harmony.'

An instrument was by her side,—
  A new and glad possession,
Whose perfect answering conveyed
Each delicate and subtle shade
  Of varying expression.

She needed no reminding score,
  For memory was true:
And what is learnt in childish years,
Deep graven on the mind appears
  Our life's whole journey through.

And so she only had to let
  The long-known music flow
From happy heart and steady hand,
As with a magic flame-command,
Enkindling in the listening band
  A full responsive glow.

Through shade more beautiful than light,
  Through hush of softest word,
Through calm and silence, still and deep
As angel-love or seraph sleep,
  The opening notes were heard.

THE SONATA.

PART I. (ADAGIO.)

Soft and slow,
Ever a gentle underflow;
Soft and slow,
Murmuring peacefully on below.

A twilight song; while the shadows sleep
                    Dusk and deep,
Over the fountain, under the fern,
                    Solemn and still:
Waiting for moonlight over the hill
To touch the bend of the lulling burn,
                    And make it show
                    As a diamond bow,
Shooting arrows of glancing light
                    In luminous flight
To the gloomy head of the waterfall;
                    Again to break,
                    In silvery flake,
Under the wild and grim rock-wall.
A twilight song, a song of love,
Softer than nightingale, sweeter than dove;
Loving and longing, loving and yearning,
With a hidden flow of electric burning
                    Ever returning;
Melting again in calm repeat,
                    Slow and sweet,
                    Sweet and slow;
While ever the gentle underflow
Murmurs lovingly on below,
In notes that seem to come from far,—
                    From the setting star
                    In the paling west,
                    Faint and more faint,
Like the parting hymn of a dying saint
                    Sinking to rest.

A moment of deep hush; then wakes again
With sudden sparkle of delight,—a new and joyous
        strain.

PART II. (ALLEGRETTO.)

Awake! Awake!
    For life is sweet:
Awake! Awake!
    New hopes to greet.
The shadows are fleeting,
    The substance is sure;
The joys thou art meeting
    Shall ever endure.
Awake! awake!
    For twilight now
That veiled the lake
    Where dark woods bow,
In moonlight resplendent
    Is passing away;
For brightness ascendant
    Turns night into day.
Oh, listen! yet listen!
    The moonlight song
Where still waters glisten
    Is floating along:
A melodious ripple of silver sound
In golden rhythm of light-bars bound,
Linked with the loveliness all around.
    A song of hope,
        That soars beyond
    The farthest scope
        Of a vision fond;
While the loneliest silence of solemn night,
And the depth of shadow beneath our feet,
Only make the song more sweet,—
Only make the sacred light
Yet more tender, yet more bright;
And song and radiance both entwining
In radiant singing and musical shining
        Float on and on
    Till the night is gone,
        Ever for rest
        Far too blest.

Then wake, then wake
    From slumberous leisure!
Arise and take
    Thy truest pleasure!
A life is before thee which cannot decay;
A glimpse and an echo are given to-day
Of glory and music not far away.
Take the bliss that is offered thee:
Hope on, hope ever, and thou shalt be
    Blest for aye!

Once more a pause is made:
While deeper still the silence, deeper yet the shade.

PART III. (PRESTO AGITATO.)

Now in awful tempest swelling,
Fallen hosts anew rebelling,
Battle shout and lava torrent
Mingle in a strife abhorrent.
Fiery cataracts are leaping,
Passion-driven stars are sweeping
In a labyrinth of courses;
Space is torn with clashing forces:
'Tis a fearful new rehearsal
Of old chaos universal.

Hush! and hark! and hear aright,
    And you shall know
      It is not so!
'Tis the roar of chariot wheels,
That nothing hinders, nothing bars,
Whose flint-sparkles are the stars
    Flashing bright;
And the mighty thunder-peals
Are the trampling of its steeds.
    On it speeds,

Crushing wrongs like river-reeds,
By the grandly simple might
          Of Eternal Right.

'Tis a song—a battle song—
          And a shout of victory,
Darting through the conflict strong
      Terror to the enemy.
Rising, while the moon is setting
      That beheld the struggle sore;
Rising still, while not forgetting
      That the battle is not o'er;
Rising, while the day is breaking
      O'er the hills, serene and strong;
Rising, while the birds are waking
      With their myriad-throated song,
Rising! yet with much to do
      Ere the strife be ended!
                    For loud confusion
                    And wild delusion
Are rampant still, and still are blended
With the song of triumph bursting through.
          It rises to fall again;
                    Falls, but to rise;
          Hushed, but to call again
                    Loud to the skies.
          Resounding like thunder
                    In conquering march,
          That reverberates under
                    The resonant arch.

Sternly triumphant o'er wrongful might,
In whirlwind of battle, in tempest of fight,
          See the singers before us,
          In warrior chorus,
              Never despairing,
                    Never yielding:
              Ever preparing
                    And faithfully wielding

Weapons kept bright,
And armour of light;
Shattering barriers that seemed adamantine,
Spurning the depth and scaling the height
While over all the turmoil and fray
Shines, in the dawn that heralds the day
Star-lit, a crown amaranthine.

Yea: a mighty song,
Of joy and triumph strong;
Magnificent in madness,
And glorious in gladness.
Every obstacle is hurled
To an infinite abyss;
Giant standards are unfurled,—
Banners of a far-off world
Calling followers from this;
Calling, calling: shall it be
To noble failure and heroic death?
Lifted with a parting breath,
Is the shout of victory
Failing fast?
Is the only crown at last
Death—death?
No!
'Tis not so!
For light and life
End the war and crown the strife.
Joy to the faithful one full shall be given!
Rising in splendour that never shall set,
The morning of triumph shall dawn on thee yet
When gladness and love for ever have met
In heaven.

———

She ended. For a little space
The music still seemed swelling;
As it were too sweet and rare
Like common sound to leave the air
As a deserted dwelling.

Then, through the flow of loving thanks
　　And murmuring delight,
And marvel at the Master's art,
One rich approval reached her heart
　　More than all else that night.

One who had also freely brought
　　His own high gift of song,
Drew near and spoke: 'For many a year
That marvellous work has been most dear,—
　　Known, loved, and studied long.

' I own, like you, allegiance true,
　　And deemed my insight clear;
But never guessed until to-night
The depths of meaning and the might
　　Of what you rendered here.

' The Master has been much to me;
But more than ever now I see
　　That there is none above him.
You have been his interpreter:
To you it has been given to stir
　　The souls of all who love him.'

Then swift up-flashed a memory,—
　　A long-forgotten day;
A memory of tears once shed,
Of aching hand and puzzled head,
And of the father's word that said,
　　'Trust and obey.'

The lesson learnt in patience then
　　Was lit by love and duty:
The toiling time was quickly past,
The trusting time had fleeted fast,
And Alice understood at last
　　Its mysteries of beauty.

O glad, perpetual harvest-time
After the sowing days!
For all her life rich joy of sound,
And deep delight to loved ones round,
And to the Master,—praise!

CONCLUSION.

Ye read her story.
Take home the lesson with a spirit-smile:
Darkness and mystery a little while,
Then—light and glory,
And ministry 'mid saint and seraph band,
And service of high praise in the Eternal Land!

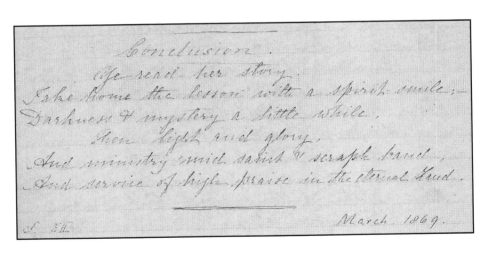

The end of F.R.H.'s fair copy autograph of "The Moonlight Sonata" in her Manuscript Book Nº VI.

The start of "The Sovereignty of God," F.R.H.'s fair copy autograph in her Manuscript Book Nº VI. See page 367.

Our God.

The Infinity of God.

'Too wonderful for me'—PSALM 139:6.

HOLY and Infinite! Viewless, Eternal!
 Veiled in the glory that none can sustain,
None comprehendeth Thy being supernal,
 Nor can the heaven of heavens contain.

Holy and Infinite! limitless, boundless
 All Thy perfections, and power, and praise!
Ocean of mystery! awful and soundless
 All Thine unsearchable judgments and ways!

King of Eternity! what revelation
 Could the created and finite sustain,
But for Thy marvellous manifestation,
 Godhead incarnate in weakness and pain!

Therefore archangels and angels adore Thee,
 Cherubim wonder, and seraphs admire;
Therefore we praise Thee, rejoicing before Thee,
 Joining in rapture the heavenly choir.

Glorious in holiness, fearful in praises,
 Who shall not fear Thee, and who shall not laud?
Anthems of glory Thy universe raises,
 Holy and Infinite! Father and God!

The Spirituality of God.

'God is a Spirit.'—JOHN 4:24.

WHAT know we, Holy God, of Thee,
 Thy being and Thine essence pure?

Too bright the very mystery
   For mortal vision to endure.

We only know Thy word sublime,
   Thou art a Spirit! Perfect! One!
Unlimited by space or time,
   Unknown but through the eternal Son.

By change untouched, by thought untraced,
   And by created eye unseen,
In *Thy great Present* is embraced
   All that shall be, all that hath been.

O Father of our spirits, now
   We seek Thee in our Saviour's face;
In truth and spirit we would bow,
   And worship where we cannot trace.

The Eternity of God.

'The King eternal, immortal, invisible.'—1 TIMOTHY 1:17.

KING Eternal and Immortal!
   We, the children of an hour,
Bend in lowly adoration,
Rise in raptured admiration,
   At the whisper of Thy power.

Myriad ages in Thy sight
   Are but as the fleeting day;
Like a vision of the night,
   Worlds may rise and pass away.

All Thy glories are eternal,
   None shall ever pass away;
Truth and mercy all victorious,
Righteousness and love all glorious,
   Shine with everlasting ray:
      All resplendent, ere the light
         Bade primeval darkness flee;

All transcendent, through the flight
Of eternities to be.

Thou art God from everlasting,
And to everlasting art!
Ere the dawn of shadowy ages,
Dimly guessed by angel sages,
Ere the beat of seraph-heart;
Thou, Jehovah, art the same,
And Thy years shall have no end
Changeless nature, changeless name,
Ever Father, God, and Friend!

The Sovereignty of God.

'Be still, and know that I am God.'—PSALM 46:10.

GOD Almighty! King of nations! earth Thy footstool, heaven Thy throne!
Thine the greatness, power, and glory, Thine the kingdom, Lord, alone!
Life and death are in Thy keeping, and Thy will ordaineth all,
From the armies of Thy heavens to an unseen insect's fall.

Reigning, guiding, all-commanding, ruling myriad worlds of light;
Now exalting, now abasing, none can stay Thy hand of might!
Working all things by Thy power, by the counsel of Thy will,
Thou art God! enough to know it, and to hear Thy word: 'Be still!'

In Thy sovereignty rejoicing, we Thy children bow and praise,
For we know that kind and loving, just and true, are all Thy ways.
While Thy heart of sovereign mercy and Thine arm of sovereign might,
For our great and strong salvation, in Thy sovereign grace unite.

The Essential Blessedness of God.

'Dwelling in the light.'—1 TIMOTHY 6:16.

O GLORIOUS God and King,
O gracious Father, hear

The praise our hearts would bring
   To Thee, who, ever near,
Yet in eternity dost dwell,
Immortal and invisible.

Around Thee all is light,
   And rest of perfect love,
And glory full and bright,
   All human thought above:
Thyself the Fountain infinite
Of all ineffable delight.

O depth of holy bliss,
   Essential and Divine!
What thought can measure this,—
   Thy joy, *Thy* glory,—Thine!
Yet such our treasure evermore,
Thy fulness is Thy children's store.

O Father, Thy great grace
   We magnify and praise;
Called to that blessed place,
   With Thee through endless days
Thy joy to share, Thy joy to be,
Thy glory all unveiled to see!

Thine Is the Power.

Our Father, our Father, who dwellest in light,
We lean on Thy love, and we rest on Thy might;
In weakness and weariness joy shall abound,
For strength everlasting in Thee shall be found:
Our Refuge, our Helper in conflict and woe,
Our mighty Defender, how blessed to know
      That Thine is the Power!

Our Father, Thy promise we earnestly claim,
The sanctified heart that shall hallow Thy Name,
In ourselves, in our dear ones, throughout the wide world,
Be Thy Name as a banner of glory unfurled;
Let it triumph o'er evil and darkness and guilt,
We know Thou canst do it, we know that Thou wilt,
      For Thine is the Power!

Our Father, we long for the glorious day
When all shall adore Thee, and all shall obey.
Oh hasten Thy kingdom, oh show forth Thy might,
And wave o'er the nations Thy sceptre of right.
Oh make up Thy jewels, the crown of Thy love,
And reign in our hearts as Thou reignest above,
      For Thine is the Power!

Our Father, we pray that Thy will may be done,
For full acquiescence is heaven begun;—
Both in us and by us Thy purpose be wrought,
In word and in action, in spirit and thought;
And Thou canst enable us thus to fulfil,
With holy rejoicing, Thy glorious will,
      For Thine is the Power!

Our Father, Thou carest; Thou knowest indeed
Our inmost desires, our manifold need;
The fount of Thy mercies shall never be dry,
For Thy riches in glory shall mete the supply;
Our bread shall be given, our water be sure,
And nothing shall fail, for Thy word shall endure,
      And Thine is the Power!

Our Father, forgive us, for we have transgressed,
Have wounded Thy love, and forsaken Thy breast;
In the peace of Thy pardon henceforth let us live,
That through Thy forgiveness we too may forgive;
The Son of Thy love, who hath taught us to pray,
For Thy treasures of mercy hath opened the way,
      And Thine is the Power!

Thou knowest our dangers, Thou knowest our frame,
But a tower of strength is Thy glorious name;
Oh, lead us not into temptation, we pray,
But keep us, and let us not stumble or stray;
Thy children shall under Thy shadow abide;
In Thee as our Guide and our Shield we confide,
      For Thine is the Power!

Our Father, deliver Thy children from sin,
From evil without and from evil within,
From this world, with its manifold evil and wrong,
From the wiles of the Evil One, subtle and strong;
Till, as Christ overcame, we, too, conquer and sing,
All glory to Thee, our victorious King,
      For Thine is the Power!

Our Father, Thy children rejoice in Thy reign,
Rejoice in Thy highness, and praise Thee again!
Yea, Thine is the kingdom and Thine is the might,
And Thine is the glory transcendently bright;
For ever and ever that glory shall shine,
For ever and ever that kingdom be Thine,
      For Thine is the Power!

F.R.H.'s manuscript of the poem on pages 367–368.

46.

Will lead astray;
We wait the all-declaring day,
150 When love shall know as it is known.
Till then the secrets of our lives are ours
and God's alone.

G. S. Dec. 13.

The One Reality.

Torn veils
Fog-wreaths of doubt in blinding eddies drifted,
Whirlwinds of fancy, counter gusts of thought,
Shadowless shadows where warm lives were sought,
Numb feet that feel not their own tread, uplifted
On clouds of formless wonder, lightning-rifted!
What marvel that the whole world's life should seem,
To helmless intellect, a Brahma-dream,
From which the real and restful is out-sifted!
Through the dim storm a white peace-bearing Dove
Gleams, & the mists roll back, the shadows flee,
The dream is past. A clear calm sky above,
Firm rock beneath; a royal-scrolled tree.
And One, thorn-diademed, the King of love,
The Son of God who gave Himself for me.

F. R. H. Evening Hours. Jan./72. Jan. 1. 1870.

A page from F.R.H.'s Manuscript Book Nº VI. See page 373.

Another fair copy autograph in F.R.H.'s hand, in her Manuscript Book Nº VI.

Our Saviour.

The One Reality.

FOG-WREATHS of doubt in blinding eddies drifted,
    Whirlwinds of fancy, countergusts of thought,
    Shadowless shadows where warm lives were sought,
Numb feet, that feel not their own tread, uplifted
On clouds of formless wonder, lightning-drifted!
    What marvel that the whole world's life should seem,
    To helpless intellect, a Brahma-dream,
From which the real and restful is out-sifted!
    Through the dim storm a white peace-bearing Dove
Gleams, and the mist rolls back, the shadows flee,
    The dream is past. A clear calm sky above,
Firm rock beneath; a royal-scrollèd tree,
    And One, thorn-diademed, the King of Love,
The Son of God, who gave Himself for me.

To Thee.

'Lord, to whom shall we go?'—JOHN 6:68.

I BRING my sins to Thee,
    The sins I cannot count,
That all may cleansèd be
    In Thy once opened Fount.
I bring them, Saviour, all to Thee,
The burden is too great for me.

My heart to Thee I bring,
    The heart I cannot read;
A faithless, wandering thing,
    An evil heart indeed.
I bring it, Saviour, now to Thee,
That fixed and faithful it may be.

To Thee I bring my care,
　The care I cannot flee;
Thou wilt not only share,
　But bear it all for me.
O loving Saviour, now to Thee
I bring the load that wearies me.

I bring my grief to Thee,
　The grief I cannot tell;
No words shall needed be,
　Thou knowest all so well.
I bring the sorrow laid on me,
O suffering Saviour, now to Thee.

My joys to Thee I bring,
　The joys Thy love hath given,
That each may be a wing
　To lift me nearer heaven.
I bring them, Saviour, all to Thee,
For Thou hast purchased all for me.

My life I bring to Thee,
　I would not be my own;
O Saviour, let me be
　Thine ever, Thine alone.
My heart, my life, my all I bring
To Thee, my Saviour and my King!

Confidence.

(Impromptu on the road to Warwick.)

I.

In Thee I trust, on Thee I rest,
O Saviour dear, Redeemer blest!
No earthly friend, no brother knows
My weariness, my wants, my woes.
　　On Thee I call,
　　Who knowest all.
O Saviour dear, Redeemer blest,
In Thee I trust, on Thee I rest.

II.

Thy power, Thy love, Thy faithfulness,
With lip and life I long to bless.
Thy faithfulness shall be my tower,
My sun Thy love, my shield Thy power
In darkest night,
In fiercest fight.
With lip and life I long to bless
Thy power, Thy love, Thy faithfulness.

I could not do without Thee.

I COULD not do without Thee,
O Saviour of the lost!
Whose precious blood redeemed me,
At such tremendous cost.
Thy righteousness, Thy pardon,
Thy precious blood must be
My only hope and comfort,
My glory and my plea!

I could not do without Thee!
I cannot stand alone,
I have no strength or goodness,
No wisdom of my own.
But Thou, belovèd Saviour,
Art all in all to me;
And weakness will be power,
If leaning hard on Thee.

I could not do without Thee!
For oh! the way is long,
And I am often weary,
And sigh replaces song.
How *could* I do without Thee?
I do not know the way;
Thou knowest and Thou leadest,
And wilt not let me stray.

I could not do without Thee,
    O Jesus, Saviour dear!
E'en when my eyes are holden,
    I know that Thou art near.
How dreary and how lonely
    This changeful life would be,
Without the sweet communion,
    The secret rest with Thee!

I could not do without Thee!
    No other friend can read
The spirit's strange deep longings,
    Interpreting its need.
No human heart could enter
    Each dim recess of mine,
And soothe and hush and calm it,
    O blessèd Lord, but Thine!

I could not do without Thee!
    For years are fleeting fast,
And soon, in solemn loneliness,
    The river must be passed.
But Thou wilt never leave me,
    And, though the waves roll high,
I know Thou wilt be near me,
    And whisper, 'It is I.'

'Jesus Only.'

MATTHEW 17:8.

I.

'JESUS only!' In the shadow
    Of the cloud so chill and dim,
We are clinging, loving, trusting,
    He with us, and we with Him;
All unseen, though ever nigh,
'Jesus only'—all our cry.

II.

'Jesus only!' In the glory,
    When the shadows all are flown,
Seeing Him in all His beauty,
    Satisfied with Him alone;
May we join His ransomed throng,
'Jesus only'—all our song!

Is it for me?

'O Thou whom my soul loveth.'—SONG OF SOLOMON 1:7.

Is it for me, dear Saviour,
    Thy glory and Thy rest?
For me, so weak and sinful,
    Oh, shall *I* thus be blessed?
Is it for me to see Thee
    In all Thy glorious grace,
And gaze in endless rapture
    On Thy belovèd Face?

Is it for me to listen
    To Thy belovèd Voice,
And hear its sweetest music
    Bid even me rejoice?
Is it for me, Thy welcome,
    Thy gracious 'Enter in'?
For me, Thy 'Come, ye blessed!'
    For me, so full of sin?

O Saviour, precious Saviour,
    My heart is at Thy feet;
I bless Thee and I love Thee,
    And Thee I long to meet.
A thrill of solemn gladness
    Has hushed my very heart,
To think that I shall really
    Behold Thee as Thou art;

Behold Thee in Thy beauty,
	Behold Thee face to face;
Behold Thee in Thy glory,
	And reap Thy smile of grace;
And be with Thee for ever,
	And never grieve Thee more!
Dear Saviour, I *must* praise Thee,
	And lovingly adore.

Hidden in Light.

WHEN first the sun dispels the cloudy night,
	The glad hills catch the radiance from afar,
	And smile for joy. We say, 'How fair they are,
Tree, rock, and heather-bloom, so clear and bright!'
But when the sun draws near in westering might,
	Enfolding all in one transcendent blaze
	Of sunset glow, we trace them not, but gaze
And wonder at the glorious, holy light.
Come nearer, Sun of Righteousness! that we,
	Whose swift short hours of day so swiftly run,
So overflowed with love and light may be,
	So lost in glory of the nearing Sun,
That not our light, but Thine, the world may see,
	New praise to Thee through our poor lives be won.

He Is Thy Lord.

'So shall the King greatly desire thy beauty; for He is thy Lord, and worship thou Him.'
—PSALM 45:11.

JESUS, belovèd Master, art Thou near?
My heart goes forth to Thee! Thy precious Word
Has flashed a bright yet tender thrill, a touch
Of living light, all through my silent soul.
	I had not looked for it. I was too tired
For earnest search, and could not rise above
A sense of weary pain, that drew a veil
Of mist and lonely gloom before my eyes.

But as I lay and waited for the sleep
That had been asked, the Book beside my hand
Lured me to glance at lightly opening leaves.
Did not Thy loving Spirit guide the glance
That fell upon the unsought word of power:
'*He is thy Lord!*' So simple, yet so strong,
So all-embracing! oh, it was enough
To chase away all mists and glooms of life.

'HE *is thy Lord!*' Thyself, O Saviour dear,
And not another. Whom have I but Thee
In heaven or earth? And whom should I desire?
For Thou hast said, '*So shall the King desire thee!*'
And well may I respond in wondering love,
'Thou art my Lord, and I will worship Thee.'

He IS *thy Lord!*' So certainly! I know
My glad allegiance has been given to Thee,
Because Thine all-compelling love and grace
Have won the citadel which else had stood
Defiant, till God's wrath had laid it low.
So certainly! a fact which cannot change
Because Thou changest not, my glorious Lord.

'*He is* THY *Lord!*' Oh, mine! though other lords
Have had dominion, now I know Thy name,
And its great music is the only key
To which my soul vibrates in full accord,
Blending with other notes but as they blend
With this. Oh, mine! But dare I say it, *I*,
Who fail and wander, mourning oftentimes
Some sin-made discord, or some tuneless string?
It would be greater daring to deny,
To say, 'Not mine,' when Thou hast proved to me
That I am Thine, by promise sealed with blood.

'*He is thy* LORD!' Oh, I am *glad* of this,
So glad that Thou art Master, Sovereign, King!

Only I want Thy rule to be supreme
And absolute; no lurking rebel thought,
No traitor in disguise to pass its bounds.
So glad,—because it is such rest to know
That Thou hast ordered and appointed all,
And wilt yet order and appoint my lot.
For though so much I cannot understand,
And would not choose, has been, and yet may be,
Thou choosest and Thou rulest, THOU, my Lord!
And this is peace, such peace,—I hardly pause
To look beyond to all the coming joy
And glory of Thy full and visible reign:
Thou reignest now—' *He is thy Lord!* ' to-day!

    ' My *Lord!* '   My heart hath said it joyfully.
Nay, could it be my own cold, treacherous heart?
'Tis comfort to remember that we have
No will or power to think one holy thought,
And thereby estimate His power in us,—
' *No man can say that Jesus is the Lord,*
But by the Holy Ghost. '   Then it must be
That all the sweetness of the word, ' Thy Lord,'
And all the long glad echoes that it woke,
Are whispers of the Spirit, and a seal
Upon His work, as yet so faintly seen.

    ' *My Lord, my God!* '   Thou hearest, blessèd Lord,
Thou knowest how, like Mary, I would bend
At Thy belovèd feet, if Thou wert here!
' If Thou wert here? '   But surely Thou *art* here,
And I believe it, though I cannot see.
I should not love Thee now wert Thou not near,
Looking on me in love.   Yea, Thou dost meet
Those that remember Thee.   Look on me still,
Lord Jesus Christ, and let Thy look give strength
To work for Thee with single heart and eye.

Our King.

'Worship thou Him.'—PSALM 45:11.

O SAVIOUR, precious Saviour,
  Whom yet unseen we love;
O Name of might and favour,
  All other names above!
    We worship Thee, we bless Thee,
      To Thee alone we sing;
    We praise Thee, and confess Thee
      Our holy Lord and King!

O Bringer of salvation,
  Who wondrously hast wrought,
Thyself the revelation
  Of love beyond our thought!
    We worship Thee, we bless Thee,
      To Thee alone we sing;
    We praise Thee, and confess Thee
      Our gracious Lord and King!

In Thee all fulness dwelleth,
  All grace and power divine;
The glory that excelleth,
  O Son of God, is Thine:
    We worship Thee, we bless Thee,
      To Thee alone we sing;
    We praise Thee, and confess Thee
      Our glorious Lord and King!

Oh, grant the consummation
  Of this our song above,
In endless adoration,
  And everlasting love:
    Then shall we praise and bless Thee,
      Where perfect praises ring,
    And evermore confess Thee
      Our Saviour and our King!

Ascension Song.

'He ascended up on high.'—EPHESIANS 4:8.

GOLDEN harps are sounding,
Angel voices ring,
Pearly gates are opened—
Opened for the King;
Christ, the King of Glory,
Jesus, King of Love,
Is gone up in triumph
To His throne above.
    All His work is ended,
    Joyfully we sing,
    Jesus hath ascended!
    Glory to our King!

He who came to save us,
He who bled and died,
Now is crowned with glory
At His Father's side.
Never more to suffer,
Never more to die,
Jesus, King of Glory,
Is gone up on high.
    All His work is ended,
    Joyfully we sing,
    Jesus hath ascended!
    Glory to our King!

Praying for His children,
In that blessèd place,
Calling them to glory,
Sending them His grace;
His bright home preparing,
Faithful ones, for you;
Jesus ever liveth,
Ever loveth too.
    All His work is ended,
    Joyfully we sing,

Jesus hath ascended!
Glory to our King!

Advent Song.

THOU art coming, O my Saviour!
   Thou art coming, O my King!
In Thy beauty all-resplendent,
In Thy glory all-transcendent;
   Well may we rejoice and sing!
Coming! in the opening east,
   Herald brightness slowly swells;
Coming! O my glorious Priest,
   Hear we not Thy golden bells?

Thou art coming, Thou art coming!
   We shall meet Thee on Thy way,
We shall see Thee, we shall know Thee,
We shall bless Thee, we shall show Thee
   All our hearts could never say!
What an anthem that will be,
Ringing out our love to Thee,
Pouring out our rapture sweet
At Thine own all-glorious feet!

Thou art coming! Rays of glory,
   Through the veil Thy death has rent,
Touch the mountain and the river
With a golden glowing quiver,
   Thrill of light and music blent.
Earth is brightened when this gleam
Falls on flower and rock and stream;
Life is brightened when this ray
Falls upon its darkest day.

Not a cloud and not a shadow,
   Not a mist and not a tear,
Not a sin and not a sorrow,
Not a dim and veiled to-morrow,
   For that sunrise grand and clear!

Jesus, Saviour, once with Thee,
　　Nothing else seems worth a thought!
Oh, how marvellous will be
　　All the bliss Thy pain hath bought!

Thou art coming! At Thy table
　　We are witnesses for this,
While remembering hearts Thou meetest,
In communion clearest, sweetest,
　　Earnest of our coming bliss.
Showing not Thy death alone,
　　And Thy love exceeding great,
But Thy coming and Thy throne,
　　All for which we long and wait.

Thou art coming! We are waiting
　　With a hope that cannot fail;
Asking not the day or hour,
Resting on Thy word of power
　　Anchored safe within the veil.
Time appointed may be long,
　　But the vision must be sure:
Certainty shall make us strong,
　　Joyful patience can endure!

Oh, the joy to see Thee reigning,
　　Thee, my own belovèd Lord!
Every tongue Thy name confessing,
Worship, honour, glory, blessing,
　　Brought to Thee with glad accord!
Thee, my Master and my Friend,
　　Vindicated and enthroned!
Unto earth's remotest end
　　Glorified, adored, and owned!

66.

Confidence. (Sacred Song.)

I

In Thee I trust, on Thee I rest,
O Saviour dear, Redeemer blest.
No earthly friend, no brother knows
My weariness, my wants, my woes.
On Thee I call,
Who knowest all,
O Saviour dear, Redeemer blest,
In Thee I trust, on Thee I rest.

II

Thy power, Thy love, Thy faithfulness,
With lip & life I long to bless.
Thy faithfulness shall be my tower,
My sun Thy love, my shield Thy power,
In darkest night,
In fiercest fight.
With lip & life I long to bless
Thy power, Thy love, Thy faithfulness.

Sept. 26. 1870.

FH. Published as Song. 1870. Nov.

F.R.H. set this to music by Handel, and the score was published by Hutchings & Romer in London, the primary publishers of her music. See Volume V of the Havergal edition, Songs of Truth and Love: Music by Frances Ridley Havergal and William Henry Havergal. *See also pages 374–375 of this book.*

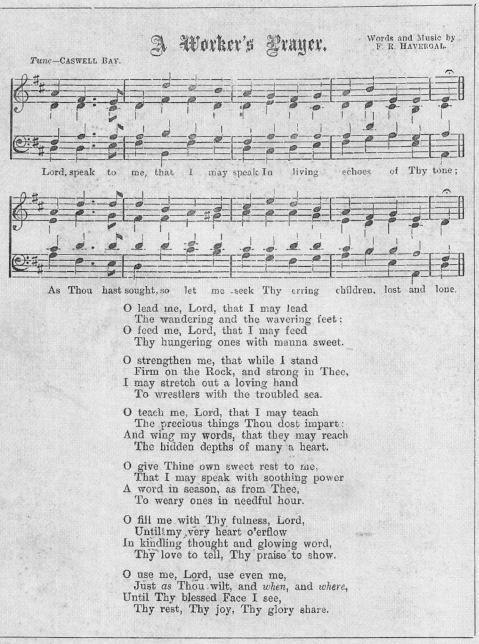

A Worker's Prayer.

Words and Music by
F. R. HAVERGAL.

Tune—CASWELL BAY.

Lord, speak to me, that I may speak In living echoes of Thy tone;

As Thou hast sought, so let me seek Thy erring children, lost and lone.

O lead me, Lord, that I may lead
The wandering and the wavering feet;
O feed me, Lord, that I may feed
Thy hungering ones with manna sweet.

O strengthen me, that while I stand
Firm on the Rock, and strong in Thee,
I may stretch out a loving hand
To wrestlers with the troubled sea.

O teach me, Lord, that I may teach
The precious things Thou dost impart:
And wing my words, that they may reach
The hidden depths of many a heart.

O give Thine own sweet rest to me,
That I may speak with soothing power
A word in season, as from Thee,
To weary ones in needful hour.

O fill me with Thy fulness, Lord,
Until my very heart o'erflow
In kindling thought and glowing word,
Thy love to tell, Thy praise to show.

O use me, Lord, use even me,
Just *as* Thou wilt, and *when*, and *where*,
Until Thy blessed Face I see,
Thy rest, Thy joy, Thy glory share.

1/6 per 100.]   J. & R. Parlane, Paisley

See pages 388–389. Very important, richly valuable scores which Frances composed are found in Volume V of the Havergal edition, Songs of Truth and Love: Music by Frances Ridley Havergal and William Henry Havergal.

Our Work.

'Workers together with Him.'—2 Corinthians 6:1.

'Serve the Lord with gladness: come before His presence with singing.'—
Psalm 100:2.

Have You Not a Word for Jesus?

'O Lord, open Thou my lips; and my mouth shall show forth Thy praise.'—
Psalm 51:15.

Have you not a word for Jesus? not a word to say for Him?
He is listening through the chorus of the burning seraphim!
He is listening; does He hear you speaking of the things of earth,
Only of its passing pleasure, selfish sorrow, empty mirth?
He has spoken words of blessing, pardon, peace, and love to you,
Glorious hopes and gracious comfort, strong and tender, sweet and true;
Does He hear you telling others something of His love untold,
Overflowing of thanksgiving for His mercies manifold?

Have you not a word for Jesus? Will the world His praise proclaim?
Who shall speak if ye are silent? ye who know and love His name.
You, whom He hath called and chosen His own witnesses to be,
Will you tell your gracious Master, 'Lord, we cannot speak for Thee'?
'Cannot!' though He suffered for you, died because He loved you so!
'Cannot!' though He has forgiven, making scarlet white as snow!
'Cannot!' though His grace abounding is your freely promised aid!
'Cannot!' though He stands beside you, though He says, 'Be not afraid!'

Have you not a word for Jesus? Some, perchance, while ye are dumb,
Wait and weary for your message, hoping *you* will bid them 'come';
Never telling hidden sorrows, lingering just outside the door,
Longing for *your* hand to lead them into rest for evermore.
Yours may be the joy and honour His redeemèd ones to bring,
Jewels for the coronation of your coming Lord and King.
Will you cast away the gladness thus your Master's joy to share,
All because a word for Jesus seems too much for you to dare?

What shall be our word for Jesus? Master, give it day by day;
Ever as the need arises, teach Thy children what to say.
Give us holy love and patience; grant us deep humility,
That of self we may be emptied, and our hearts be full of Thee;
Give us zeal and faith and fervour, make us winning, make us wise,
Single-hearted, strong and fearless,—Thou hast called us, we will rise!
Let the might of Thy good Spirit go with every loving word;
And by hearts prepared and opened be our message always heard!

Yes, we have a word for Jesus! Living echoes we will be
Of Thine own sweet words of blessing, of Thy gracious 'Come to Me.'
Jesus, Master! yes, we love Thee, and to prove our love, would lay
Fruit of lips which Thou wilt open, at Thy blessèd feet to-day.
Many an effort it may cost us, many a heart-beat, many a fear,
But Thou knowest, and wilt strengthen, and Thy help is always near.
Give us grace to follow fully, vanquishing our faithless shame,
Feebly it may be, but truly, witnessing for Thy dear Name.

Yes, we have a word for Jesus! we will bravely speak for Thee,
And Thy bold and faithful soldiers, Saviour, we would henceforth be:
In Thy name set up our banners, while Thine own shall wave above,
With Thy crimson Name of Mercy, and Thy golden Name of Love.
Help us lovingly to labour, looking for Thy present smile,
Looking for Thy promised blessing, through the brightening 'little while.'
Words for Thee in weakness spoken, Thou wilt here accept and own,
And confess them in Thy glory, when we see Thee on Thy throne.

A Worker's Prayer.

LORD, speak to me, that I may speak
 In living echoes of Thy tone;
As Thou hast sought, so let me seek
 Thy erring children, lost and lone.

O lead me, Lord, that I may lead
 The wandering and the wavering feet;
O feed me, Lord, that I may feed
 Thy hungering ones with manna sweet.

O strengthen me, that while I stand
   Firm on the Rock and strong in Thee,
I may stretch out a loving hand
   To wrestlers with the troubled sea.

O teach me, Lord, that I may teach
   The precious things Thou dost impart;
And wing my words, that they may reach
   The hidden depths of many a heart.

O give Thine own sweet rest to me,
   That I may speak with soothing power
A word in season, as from Thee,
   To weary ones in needful hour.

O fill me with Thy fulness, Lord,
   Until my very heart o'erflow
In kindling thought and glowing word,
   Thy love to tell, Thy praise to show.

O use me, Lord, use even me,
   Just *as* Thou wilt, and *when*, and *where*;
Until Thy blessèd Face I see,
   Thy rest, Thy joy, Thy glory share.

Our Commission.

'And the Spirit and the Bride say, Come. And let him that heareth say, Come.'
—REVELATION 22:17.

YE who hear the blessèd call
   Of the Spirit and the Bride,
Hear the Master's word to all,
   Your commission and your guide—
'And let him that heareth say,
   Come,' to all yet far away.

'Come!' alike to age and youth;
   Tell them of our Friend above,
Of His beauty and His truth,
   Preciousness and grace and love;

Tell them what you know is true,
Tell them what He is to you.

'Come!' to those who never heard
    Why the Saviour's blood was shed;
Bear to them the message-word
    That can quicken from the dead;
Tell them Jesus 'died for all,'
Tell them of His loving call.

'Come!' to those who do not care
    For the Saviour's precious death,
Having not a thought to spare
    For the gracious words He saith:
Ere the shadows gather deep,
Rouse them from their fatal sleep.

'Come!' to those who, while they hear,
    Linger, hardly knowing why;
Tell them that the Lord is near,
    Tell them Jesus passes by.
Call them *now*; oh, do not wait,
Lest to-morrow be too late!

'Come!' to those who wander far,
    Seeking, never finding, rest;
Point them to the Morning Star;
    Show them how they may be blest
With the love that cannot cease,
Joyful hope and perfect peace.

'Come!' to those who draw in vain
    From the broken cisterns here,
Drinking but to thirst again;
    Tell them of the fountain near.
Living water, flowing still,
Free for 'whosoever will.'

'Come!' to those who faint and groan
    Under some unuttered grief,

Hearts that suffer all alone;
　　Try to bring them true relief.
Tell them 'Jesus wept,' and He
Still is full of sympathy.

'Come!' to those who feel their sin,
　　Fearing to be lost at last,
Mourning for the plague within,
　　Mourning for transgressions past;
Tell them Jesus calls them in,
Heavy laden with their sin.

Such as these are all around,
　　Meeting, passing, every day;
Ye who know the joyful sound,
　　Have ye not a word to say?
Ye who hear that blessed 'Come,'
Sweet and clear, can ye be dumb?

Brothers, sisters, do not wait,
　　Speak for Him who speaks to you!
Wherefore should you hesitate?
　　This is no great thing to do.
Jesus only bids you say,
'Come!' and will you not obey?

Lord! to Thy command we bow,
　　Touch our lips with altar fire;
Let Thy Spirit kindle now
　　Faith and zeal, and strong desire;
So that henceforth we may be
Fellow-workers, Lord, with Thee.

Singing for Jesus.

'With my song will I praise Him.'—PSALM 28:7.

SINGING for Jesus, our Saviour and King,
　　Singing for Jesus, the Lord whom we love;
All adoration we joyously bring,
　　Longing to praise as we praise Him above.

Singing for Jesus, our Master and Friend,
　　Telling His love and His marvellous grace,
Love from eternity, love without end,
　　Love for the loveless, the sinful and base.

Singing for Jesus, and trying to win
　　Many to love Him, and join in the song;
Calling the weary and wandering in,
　　Rolling the chorus of gladness along.

Singing for Jesus, our Life and our Light;
　　Singing for Him as we press to the mark;
Singing for Him when the morning is bright,
　　Singing, still singing, for Him in the dark.

Singing for Jesus, our Shepherd and Guide,
　　Singing for gladness of heart that He gives;
Singing for wonder and praise that He died,
　　Singing for blessing and joy that He lives.

Singing for Jesus, oh, singing with joy!
　　Thus will we praise Him and tell out His love,
Till He shall call us to brighter employ,
　　Singing for Jesus for ever above.

A Silence and a Song.

I AM alone, dear Master—
　　Alone in heart with Thee!
Though merry faces round me
　　And loving looks I see.

There's a hush among the blithe ones,
　　While a pleasant voice is heard,
A truce to all the tournament
　　Of flashing wit and word.

And in that truce of silence,
　　I lay aside my lance,
And through the light and music send
　　One happy upward glance.

I know not what the song may be,
    The words I cannot hear;
'Tis but a gentle melody,
    All simple, soft, and clear.

But the sweetness and the quiet
    Have set my spirit free,
And I turn in loving gladness,
    Dear Master, now to Thee.

I know I love Thee better
    Than any earthly joy,
For Thou hast given me the peace
    Which nothing can destroy.

I know that Thou art nearer still
    Than all this merry throng,
And sweeter is the thought of Thee
    Than any lovely song.

Thou hast put gladness in my heart,
    Then well may I be glad!
Without the secret of Thy love,
    I could not but be sad.

I bless Thee for these pleasant hours
    With sunny-hearted friends,
But more for this sweet moment's calm
    Thy loving-kindness sends.

O Master, gracious Master,
    What will Thy presence be,
If such a thrill of joy can crown
    One upward look to Thee?

'Tis ending now, that gentle song,
    And they will call for me;
They know the music I love best,—
    My song shall be for Thee!

For Thee, who hast so lovèd us,
　　And whom, not having seen,
We love; on whom in all our joy,
　　As in our grief, we lean.

Be near me still, and tune my notes,
　　And make them sweet and strong,
To waft Thy words to many a heart
　　Upon the wings of song.

I know that all will listen,
　　For my very heart shall sing,
And it shall be Thy praise alone,
　　My glorious Lord and King.

The Coming of the Healer.

'They came into the land of Gennesaret. And *when* the men of that place had knowl-
edge of Him, they sent out into all that country round about, and brought unto Him all
that were diseased; and besought Him that they might only touch the hem of His gar-
ment: and as many as touched were made perfectly whole.'—Matthew 14:34–36.

From the watch of lonely mountain prayer, in gathering storm and blast—
From the path no mortal foot could tread, o'er waters wild and vast,
He came, the glorious Son of God, with healing, love, and light,
To the land of far Gennesaret, that lay in shadowy night.

Oh blessèd morning, sunrise true, upon that gloomy shore!
Where they who walked in darkness long, the Light of Life adore.
Oh blessèd coming to the land of Death's usurping sway;
For where those shining footsteps fall, the shadows flee away!

But *when* the Light had touched the hills by slumbering Galilee,
The golden wave must roll afar towards the western sea:
And *when* the men had knowledge of the Holy One of God,
Then they sent out through all the land, and spread His fame abroad.

And *then* they brought the suffering ones, the lonely, or the dear,
And laid them at the Healer's feet, from far away, or near:
Then bent before the Wondrous One, and earnestly besought
That they might only touch the hem around His garment wrought.

He heard the prayer, and gave the will and strength to touch the hem;
And gave the faith, and virtue flowed from Him, and healèd them:
For every one whose feeblest touch thus met the Saviour's power,
Rose up in perfect health and strength in that accepted hour.

O Tender One, O Mighty One, who never sent away
The sinner or the sufferer, Thou art The Same to-day!
The Same in Love, the Same in Power, and Thou art waiting still,
To heal the multitudes that come, yea, 'whosoever will!'

We know Thee, blessed Saviour, who hast 'filled us with good things';
Thou hast arisen on our land, with healing in Thy wings;
Thou hast arisen on our hearts, with light and life Divine;
Now bid us be Thy messengers, bid us 'arise and shine!'

Oh, let Thy Spirit fire our zeal, that we may now 'send out,'
And tell that Thou art come 'in all the country round about,'—
That Thou art waiting now to heal, that Thou art strong to save,
That Thou hast spoilt the Spoiler, Death, and triumphed o'er the grave.

Oh, make us fervent in the quest, that we may bring them in,
The weary and the wounded, and the sufferers from sin;
The stricken and the dying, let us seek them out for Thee,
And lay them at Thy glorious feet, that healèd they may be.

Oh, pour upon our waiting hearts the Spirit of Thy grace,
That we may plead with Thee to show the brightness of Thy face,
Beseeching Thee to grant the will and strength and faith to such
As lie in helpless misery, Thy garment's hem to touch.

And then, Lord Jesus, make them whole, that they may rise and bring
New praise and glory unto Thee, our Healer and our King;
Yea, let Thy saving health be known through all the earth abroad,
So shall the people praise Thy Name, our Saviour and our God.

Another for Christ.

ANOTHER called, another brought, dear Master, to Thy feet!
Oh, where are words to tell the joy so wonderful and sweet!
Oh, where are words to give Thee thanks that Thou indeed hast heard,
That Thou hast proved and sealed anew Thy faithful promise-word!

We prayed so long, with fervent hope and patient faith, that she
With all her early wealth of love might give herself to Thee;
Well knowing that our prayer must be the echo of Thy will,
Itself the earnest and the pledge that Thou wilt all fulfil.

And now the prayer is turned to praise, and with the angel-throng,
Who even now are pouring forth a new and joyful song,
Our hearts ascend, our whispers blend, in deepest thrill of praise,
The happiest Alleluia-hymn that human heart can raise.

Oh, joy to know that Thou hast found Thy fair and weary dove,
Rejoicing o'er the wanderer now, and resting in Thy love,
That *Thou* art glad, that Thou hast seen the travail of Thy soul,
Thy blessèd Name emblazoned on a new and living scroll!

O Master, blessèd Master, it is hard indeed to know
That thousands round our daily path misunderstand Thee so!
Despisèd and rejected yet, no beauty they can see,
O King of glory and of grace, belovèd Lord, in Thee!

Not even as a lovely song of pleasant voice appears
The story of Thy wondrous love in dull and drowsy ears;
'Tis nothing to the passers-by, who coldly turn aside,
That Thou hast poured Thy precious blood, that Thou wast crucified.

O Saviour, precious Saviour, come in all Thy power and grace,
And take away the veil that hides the glory of Thy face!
Oh, manifest the marvels of Thy tenderness and love,
And let Thy Name be blessed and praised all other names above.

Oh, vindicate Thyself, and show how perfect are Thy ways,
Untraceable, because too bright for weak and mortal gaze;
Shine forth, O Sun, and bid the scales of darkening evil fall,
Thou Altogether Lovely One, Thou glorious All-in-all!

Yet conquering Thy word goes forth on all-triumphant way!
'Ye *shall* be gathered one by one,' 'tis true afresh to-day!
And so we hush the yearning cry, 'How long, O Lord, how long?'
A sweet new token Thou hast given to change it into song.

So once again we praise Thee, with Thy holy ones above,
Because another heart has seen Thy great and mighty love;
Another heart will own Thee Lord, and worship Thee as King,
And grateful love and glowing praise and willing service bring.

Another voice to 'tell it out' what great things Thou hast done,
Another life to live for Thee, another witness won,
Another faithful soldier on our Captain's side enrolled,
Another heart to read aright Thy heart of love untold!

'How Wonderful!'

HE answered all my prayer abundantly,
     And crowned the work that to His feet I brought,
     With blessing more than I had asked or thought—
A blessing undisguised, and fair, and free.
I stood amazed, and whispered, 'Can it be
     That He hath granted all the boon I sought?
     How wonderful that He for me hath wrought!
How wonderful that He hath answered me!'
O faithless heart! He *said* that He would hear
     And answer thy poor prayer, and He *hath* heard
And proved His promise. Wherefore didst thou fear?
     Why marvel that Thy Lord hath kept His word?
More wonderful if He should fail to bless
Expectant faith and prayer with good success!

Valiant for the Truth.

'Ye should earnestly contend for the faith which was once delivered unto the saints.'
—JUDE 3.

UNFURL the Christian Standard! lift it manfully on high,
And rally where its shining folds wave out against the sky!
Away with weak half-heartedness, with faithlessness and fear!
Unfurl the Christian Standard, and follow with a cheer!

In God's own name we set it up, this banner brave and bright,
Uplifted for the cause of Christ, the cause of Truth and Right;
The cause that none can overthrow, the cause that must prevail,
Because the promise of the Lord can never, never fail!

Now, who is on the Lord's side, who? come, throng His battle-field;
Be strong, and show that ye are men! come forth with sword and shield!
What peace, while traitorous Evil stalks in false array of light?
What peace, while enemies of Christ are gathering for the fight?

Unfurl the Christian Standard, with firm and fearless hands!
For no pale flag of compromise with Error's legion bands,
And no faint-hearted flag of truce with Mischief and with Wrong,
Should lead the soldiers of the Cross, the faithful and the strong.

Unfurl the Christian Standard, and follow through the strife
The noble army who have won the martyr's crown of life;
Our ancestors could die for Truth, could brave the deadly glow,
And shall we let the standard fall, and yield it to the foe?

But if ye dare not hold it fast, yours only is the loss,
For it *shall* be victorious, this Standard of the Cross!
It shall not suffer, though ye rest beneath your sheltering trees,
And cast away the victor's crown for love of timid ease.

The Lord of Hosts, in whom alone our weakness shall be strong,
Shall lead us on to conquest with a mighty battle song;
And soon the warfare shall be past, the glorious triumph won,
The kingdoms of this world *shall* be the kingdoms of His Son!

A Plea for the Little Ones.

It was Easter Monday morning,
　　A dull and showery day;
We were sorry for the children
　　Who could not run and play.

I heard the sound of singing
　　As I passed along the street—

An unseen tiny chorus
　　Of tiny voices sweet.

Beneath a sheltering doorway,
　　Safe from the April weather
Eight happy little singers
　　Sat lovingly together,

Five crowding on the doorstep
　　With arms entwined, and three
On broken stool or baby chair,
　　Close clustering knee to knee.

They sang about the 'happy land,'
　　So very 'far away,'
And happier faces never shone
　　In any game of play.

And then they sang it all again,
　　And gently rocked each other;
Then said the little leader,
　　'Now let us sing another!'

'Now *I* will say a hymn to you!'
　　(Oh, the sixteen eyes were bright!)
So I said them 'Little Jessie,'
　　As they listened with delight.

JESSIE'S FRIEND.

'Little Jessie, darling pet,
　　Do you want a Friend?
One who never will forget,
　　Loving to the end?
One whom you can tell, when sad,
　　Everything that grieves,
One who loves to make you glad,
　　One who never leaves?

'Such a loving Friend is ours,
　　Near us all the day,

Helping us in lesson-hours,
  Smiling on our play;
Keeping us from doing wrong,
  Guarding everywhere;
Listening to each happy song,
  And each little prayer.

'Jessie, if you only knew
  What He is to me,
Surely you would love Him too,
  You would "come and see."
Come, and you will find it true,
  Happy you will be!
Jesus says, and says to you,
  "Come, oh come, to Me."'

————

'Now tell me who, if you can guess,
  Was little Jessie's Friend?
Who is the Friend that loves so much,
  And loveth to the end?'

I would that you had seen the smile
  On every sunny face;
It made a palace of delight
  Out of that dismal place,

As, reverently yet joyously,
  They answered without fear,
'It's Jesus!' That belovèd Name
  Had never seemed more dear.

And then we talked awhile of Him—
  They knew the story well;
His holy life, His precious death,
  Those rosy lips could tell.

All beautiful, and wonderful,
  And sweet and true it seemed,
Such hold no fairy tale had gained
  That ever fancy dreamed.

So, to be good and kind all day
    These little children tried,
Because they knew *He* was so good,
    Because *He* bled and died.

Blest knowledge! Oh, what human lore
    Can be compared with such!
'Who taught you this, dear little ones?
    Where did you learn so much?'

Again the bright eyes cheerily
    Looked up from step and stool;
They answered (mark the answer well!),
    '*We learnt it all at school!*'

At school, at school! And shall we take
    The Book of books away!
Withhold it from the little ones?
    Leave them at will to stray—

Upon dark mountains, helplessly,
    Without the guiding light
That God entrusts to *us*, until
    They perish in the night?

What was the world before that Book
    Went forth in glorious night?
Availed the lore of Greece and Rome
    To chase its Stygian night?

We send the messengers of life
    To many a distant strand,
And shall we tie the tongues that teach
    The poor of our own land?

Shall husks and chaff, be freely given,
    And not the Bread of Life?
And shall the Word of Peace become
    A centre of mad strife?

Shall those who name the Name of Christ
    His own great gift withhold?

Our Lamp, our Chart, our Sword, our Song,
    Our Pearl, our most fine Gold!

Why would ye have 'no Bible taught'?
    Is it for *fear?* or shame?
Out, out upon such coward hearts,
    False to their Master's name!

If God be God, if truth be truth,
    If Christian men be men,
Let them arise and fight the fight,
    Though it were one to ten!

With battle-cry of valiant faith,
    Let Britain's sons arise,—
'Our children *shall* be taught the Word
    That only maketh wise!'

So, dauntlessly, will we unfurl
    Our banner bright and broad,
The cause of His dear Word of Life,
    Our cause, the Cause of God.

Tell It Out.

'Tell it out among the heathen that the Lord is King.'—Psalm 96:10.
(Prayer-Book Version.)

Tell it out among the heathen that the Lord is King!
    Tell it out, tell it out!
Tell it out among the nations, bid them shout and sing!
    Tell it out, tell it out!
Tell it out with adoration, that He shall increase;
That the mighty King of Glory is the King of Peace.
Tell it out with jubilation, though the waves may roar,
That He sitteth on the water-floods, our King for evermore!
    Tell it out, etc.

Tell it out among the nations that the Saviour reigns!
    Tell it out, tell it out!

Tell it out among the heathen, bid them burst their chains!
   Tell it out, tell it out!
Tell it out among the weeping ones that Jesus lives;
Tell it out among the weary ones what rest He gives;
Tell it out among the sinners that He came to save;
Tell it out among the dying that He triumphed o'er the grave.
   Tell it out, etc.

Tell it out among the heathen Jesus reigns above!
   Tell it out, tell it out!
Tell it out among the nations that His name is Love!
   Tell it out, tell it out!
Tell it out among the highways, and the lanes at home;
Let it ring across the mountains and the ocean foam;
Like the sound of many waters let our glad shout be,
Till it echo and re-echo from the islands of the sea!
   Tell it out, etc.

Sisters.

OH! for a fiery scroll, and a trumpet of thunder might,
 To startle the silken dreams of English women at ease,
Circled with peace and joy, and dwelling where truth and light
 Are shining fair as the stars, and free as the western breeze!

Oh! for a clarion voice to reach and stir their nest,
 With the story of sisters' woes gathering day by day
Over the Indian homes (sepulchres rather than rest),
 Till they rouse in the strength of the Lord, and roll the stone away.

Sisters! Scorn not the name, for ye cannot alter the fact!
 Deem ye the darker tint of the glowing South shall be
Valid excuse above for the Priest's and Levite's act,
 If ye pass on the other side, and say that ye did not see?

Sisters! Yea, and they lie, not by the side of the road,
 But hidden in loathsome caves, in crushed and quivering throngs,
Down-trodden, degraded, and dark, beneath the invisible load
 Of centuries, echoing groans, black with inherited wrongs.

Made like our own strange selves, with memory, mind, and will;
  Made with a heart to love, and a soul to live for ever!
Sisters! Is there no chord vibrating in musical thrill,
  At the fall of that gentle word, to issue in bright endeavour?

Sisters! Ye who have known the Elder Brother's love,—
  Ye who have sat at His feet, and leant on His gracious breast,
Whose hearts are glad with the hope of His own blest home above,
  Will ye not seek them out, and lead them to Him for rest?

Is it too great a thing? Will not *one* rise and go,
  Laying her joys aside, as the Master laid them down?
Seeking His lone and lost in the veilèd abodes of woe,
  Winning His Indian gems to shine in His glorious crown!

An Indian Flag.

THE golden gates were opening
    For another welcome guest;
For a ransomed heir of glory
    Was entering into rest:

The first in far Umritsur
    Who heard the joyful sound,
The first who came to Jesus
    Within its gloomy bound.

The wonderers and the watchers
    Around his dying bed,
Saw Christ's own fearless witness
    Safe through the valley led.

And they whose faithful sowing
    Had not been all in vain,
Knew that the angels waited
    Their sheaf of ripened grain.

He spoke: 'Throughout the city
    How many a flag is raised
Where loveless deities are owned,
    And powerless gods are praised!

'I give my house to Jesus,
    That it may always be
A flag for Christ, the Son of God,
    Who gave Himself for me.'

And now in far Umritsur
    That flag is waving bright,
Amid the heathen darkness,
    A clear and shining light.

A house where all may gather
    The words of peace to hear,
And seek the only Saviour
    Without restraint or fear;

Where patient toil of teaching,
    And kindly deeds abound;
Where holy festivals are kept,
    And holy songs resound.

First convert of Umritsur,
    Well hast thou led the way;
Now, who will rise and follow?
    Who dares to answer, 'Nay'?

O children of salvation!
    O dwellers in the light!
Have ye no 'flag for Jesus,'
    Far-waving, fair, and bright?

Will ye not band together,
    And, working hand in hand,
Set up a 'flag for Jesus,'
    In that wide heathen land?

In many an Indian city,
    Oh, let a standard wave,
Our gift of love and honour,
    To Him who came to save;

To Him beneath whose banner
Of wondrous love we rest;
Our Friend, the Friend of sinners
The Greatest and the Best.

The Lull of Eternity.[1]

MANY a voice has echoed the cry for 'a lull in life,'
Fainting under the noontide, fainting under the strife.
Is it the wisest longing? is it the truest gain?
Is not the Master withholding possible loss and pain?

Perhaps if He sent the lull, we might fail of our heart's desire!
Swift and sharp the concussion striking out living fire,
Mighty and long the friction resulting in living glow,
Heat that is force of the spirit, energy fruitful in flow.

What if the blast should falter, what if the fire be stilled,
What if the molten metal cool ere the mould be filled?
What if the hands hang down when a work is almost done?
What if the sword be dropped when a battle is almost won?

Past many an unseen Maelstrom the strong wind drives the skiff,
When a lull might drift it onward to fatal swift or cliff.
Faithful the guide that spurreth, sternly forbidding repose,
When treacherous slumber lureth to pause amid Alpine snows.

The lull of Time may be darkness, falling in lonely night,
But the lull of Eternity neareth, rising in full calm light;
The earthly lull may be silence, desolate, deep and cold,
But the heavenly lull shall be music sweeter a thousand-fold.

Here, it is 'calling apart,' and the place may be desert indeed,
Leaving and losing the blessings linked with our busy need;
There!—why should I say it? hath not the heart leapt up,
Swift and glad, to the contrast, filling the full, full cup?

---

[1] Sequel to 'A Lull in Life.' See *The Ministry of Song*, p. 199 (Pocket Edition).

[See pages 119–120 of this book.]

Still shall the key-word, ringing, echo the same sweet *'Come!'*
'Come' with the blessèd myriads safe in the Father's home;
'Come'—for the work is over; 'come'—for the feast is spread;
'Come'—for the crown of glory waits for the weary head.

When the rest of faith is ended, and the rest in hope is past,
The rest of love remaineth, Sabbath of life at last.
No more fleeting hours, hurrying down the day,
But golden stillness of glory, never to pass away.

Time with its pressure of moments, mocking us as they fell
With relentless beat of a footstep, hour by hour the knell
Of a hope or an aspiration, then shall have passed away,
Leaving a grand calm leisure, leisure of endless day.

Leisure that cannot be dimmed by the touch of time or place,
Finding its counterpart measure only in infinite space;
Full, and yet ever filling, leisure without alloy,
Eternity's seal on the limitless charter of heavenly joy.

Leisure to fathom the fathomless, leisure to seek and to know
Marvels and secrets and glories eternity only can show;
Leisure of holiest gladness, leisure of holiest love,
Leisure to drink from the Fountain of infinite peace above.

Art thou patiently toiling, waiting the Master's will,
For a rest that never seems nearer, a hush that is far off still?
Does it seem that the noisy city never will let thee hear
The sound of His gentle footsteps drawing, it may be, near?

Does it seem that the blinding dazzle of noonday glare and heat
Is a fiery veil between thy heart and visions high and sweet?
What though 'a lull in life' may never be made for thee?
Soon shall a 'better thing' be thine, the Lull of Eternity!

The Sowers.

In the morning sow thy seed, nor stay thy hand at evening hour,
Never asking which shall prosper—both may yield thee fruit and flower:

Thou shalt reap of that thou sowest; though thy grain be small and bare,
God shall clothe it as He pleases, for the harvest full and fair;
Though it sink in turbid waters, hidden from thy yearning sight,
It shall spring in strength and beauty, ripening in celestial light;
Ever springing, ever ripening;—not alone in earthly soil,
Not alone among the shadows, where the weary workers toil;
Gracious first-fruits there may meet thee of the reaping-time begun;
But upon the Hill of Zion, 'neath the Uncreated Sun,
First the *fulness* of the blessing shall the faithful labourer see,
Gathering fruit to life eternal, harvest of Eternity.

Let us watch awhile the sowers, let us mark their tiny grain,
Scattered oft in doubt and trembling, sown in weakness or in pain;
Then let Faith, with radiant finger, lift the veil from unseen things,
Where the golden sheaves are bending and the harvest anthem rings.

I.

'Such as I have I sow, it is not much,'
    Said one who loved the Master of the field;
'Only a quiet word, a gentle touch
    Upon the hidden harp-strings, which may yield
No quick response; I tremble, yet I speak
For Him who knows the heart, so loving, yet so weak.'

And so the words were spoken, soft and low,
    Or traced with timid pen; yet oft they fell
On soil prepared, which she would never know
    Until the tender blade sprang up, to tell
That not in vain her labour had been spent;
Then with new faith and hope more bravely on she went.

II.

'I had much seed to sow,' said one; 'I planned
    To fill broad furrows, and to watch it spring
And water it with care. But now the hand
    Of Him to whom I sought great sheaves to bring,
Is laid upon His labourer, and I wait,
Weak, helpless, useless, at His palace gate.

Now I have nothing, only day by day
 Grace to sustain me till the day is done;
And some sweet passing glimpses by the way
 Of Him, the Altogether Lovely One;
And some strange things to learn, unlearnt before,
That make the suffering light, if it but teach me more.'

Yet, from the hush of that secluded room,
 Forth floated wingèd seeds of thought and prayer;
These, reaching many a desert place to bloom,
 And pleasant fruit an hundred-fold to bear;
Those, wafted heavenward with song and sigh,
To fall again with showers of blessing from on high.

III.

'What can I sow?' thought one, to whom God gave
 Sweet notes and skilful fingers. 'Can my song
Be cast upon the waters, as they lave
 My feet with grateful echo, soft and long,
Or break in sunny spray of fair applaud?
Shall this be found one day as fruit to Thee, my God?'

He sang, and all were hushed. Oh, sweeter fall
 The notes that pour from fervent fount of love,
Than studied flow of sweetest madrigal!
 He sang of One who listened from above,
He cast the song at His belovèd feet;—
Some said, 'How strange!' And others felt, 'How sweet!'

IV.

Another stood, with basket stored indeed,
 And powerful hand both full and faithful found,
And cast God's own imperishable seed
 Upon the darkly heaving waste around:
Yet oft in weariness, and oft in woe,
Did that good sower store, and then go forth to sow.

The tide of human hearts still ebbed and flowed,
    Less like the fruitful flood than barren sea;
He saw not where it fell, and yet he sowed:
    'Not void shall it return,' said God, 'to Me!'
The precious seed, so swiftly borne away,
A singing reaper's hand shall fill with sheaves one day.

V.

Another watched the sowers longingly,
    'I cannot sow such seed as they,' he said;
'No shining grain of thought is given to me,
    No fiery words of power bravely sped:
Will others give me of their bounteous store?
My hand may scatter that, if I can do no more.'

So by the wayside he went forth to sow
    The silent seeds, each wrapped in fruitful prayer,
With glad humility; content to know
    The volume lent, the leaflet culled with care,
The message placed in stranger hands, were all
Beneath His guiding eye who notes the sparrow's fall.

VI.

An opening blossom, bright with early dew,
    Whose rosy lips had touched the Living Spring
Before the thirst of earth was felt; who knew
    The children's Saviour, and the children's King,
Said, 'What can I sow, mother?' 'Darling boy,
Show all how glad He makes you; scatter love and joy!'

That sparkling seed he took in his small hand,
    And dropped it tenderly beside the flow
Of sorrows that he could not understand,
    And cast it lovingly upon the snow
That shrouded aged hearts, and joyously
Upon the dancing waves of playmates' thoughtless glee.

VII.

'What seed have I to sow?' said one. 'I lie
    In stilled and darkened chamber, lone and low;
The silent days and silent nights pass by
    In monotone of dimness. Could I throw
Into the nearest furrow one small seed,
It would be life again, a blessèd life indeed!'

And so she lay through lingering month and year,
    No word for Him to speak, no work to do;
Only to suffer and be still, and hear
    That yet the Golden Gate was not in view;
While hands of love and skill, this charge to keep,
Must leave the whitening plain, where others now would reap.

––––––––––

Such the sowing; what the reaping? Many a full and precious ear
Waved and ripened, fair and early, for the patient sowers' cheer.
Not without some gracious witness of God's faithfulness and love
Toiled they, waiting for the coming of the harvest-home above;
Word, and prayer, and song, and leaflet, found, though after many days,
Quickening energy and courage, brightening hope and wakening praise.
Yet how many a seed seemed trodden under foot, and left to die,
Lost, forgotten by the sower, never traced by human eye;
Many a worker meekly saying, 'Lord, how thankful will I be,
If but one among a thousand may bring forth good fruit to Thee!'

––––––––––

One by one, no longer
    Gently bid to wait;
One by one, they entered
    Through the Golden Gate.

One by one they fell adoring
    At the Master's feet,
Heard His welcome, deep and thrilling,
'Enter thou!' each full heart filling,
All its need for ever stilling—
    All its restless beat.

Then the gift, the free, the glorious,
　　Life with Him, eternal life,—
Erst bestowed amid the weeping,
And the weary vigil-keeping,
　　And the bitter strife,—

Now in mighty consummation,
　　First in all its fulness known,
Dower of glory all transcendent,
Everlasting and resplendent,
　　Is their own!

All their own, through Him who loved them,
　　And redeemed them unto God!
New and living revelation
Of the marvels of salvation,
Wakes new depths of adoration,
　　New and burning laud.

Now they see their gracious Master,
　　See Him face to face!
Now they know the great transition
From the veiled to veil-less vision,
　　In that bright and blessèd place.

What a change has passed upon them!
　　Made like Him, the Perfect One,—
Made like Him whose joy they enter,
Him, the only Crown and Centre
　　Of the endless bliss begun.

————

But Eternity is long,
　　And its joys are manifold!
Though the service of its song
　　Never falters or grows cold,
Though the billows of its praise
　　Never die upon the shore,

Though the blessèd harpers raise
    Alleluias evermore,
Though the eye grows never dim
    Gazing on that mighty Sun,
Ever finding all in Him,
    Every joy complete in one;—

Yet THE INFINITE is He,
    In His Wisdom and His Might;
And it needs eternity
    To reveal His Love and Light
To the finite and created!
    Archangelic mind and heart
Never with His bliss was sated,
    Never knew the thousandth part
Of the all-mysterious rays
    Flowing from Essential Light,
Hiding in approachless blaze
    God Himself, the Infinite.

Infinite the ocean-joy
    Opening to His children's view;
Infinite their varied treasure,
Meted not by mortal measure—
Holy knowledge, holy pleasure,
Through Eternity's great leisure,
    Like its praises, ever new.

So the blessèd sowers' gladness
    In the free and royal grace
Should be crowned with added glory,
Woven with their earthly story,
    Linked with time and place.

Glad surprise! for every service
    Overflowing their reward!
No more sowing, no more weeping,
Only grand and glorious reaping,
    All the blessing of their Lord.

I.

She who timidly had scattered
    Trembling line or whispered word,
Till the holy work grew dearer,
And the sacred courage clearer,
    Now her Master's own voice heard.

Calling shining throngs around her,
    All her own fair harvest found;
Then, her humble name confessing,
With His radiant smile of blessing,
    All her dower of gladness crowned.

II.

'Welcome thou, whose heavenly message
    Came with quickening power to me!
O most welcome to the portals
Of this home of bright immortals,
    I have waited long for thee!'

'Who art thou? I never saw thee
    In my pilgrimage below,'
Said he, marvelling. 'I will show thee,'
Answered he, 'the love I owe thee,
Full and fervent, for I know thee
    By the starlight on thy brow.

'Words that issued from thy chamber
    Turned my darkness into light;
Guided footsteps, weak and weary,
Through the desert wild and dreary,
    Through the valley of the night.

'Come! for many another waits thee!
    All unfolded thou shalt see,
Through the ecstatic revelation
Of their endless exultation,
    What our God hath wrought by thee.'

III.

Hark! a voice all joy-inspiring
    Peals adown the golden floor,
Leading on a white-robed chorus,
Sweet as flute, and yet sonorous
    As the many waters' roar.

He who sang for Jesus heard it!
    ''Tis the echo of thy song!'
Said the leader. 'As we listened,
Cold hearts glowed and dim eyes glistened,
    And we learned to love and long—

'Till the longing and the loving
    Soared to Him of whom you sang;
Till our Alleluia, swelling,
Through the glory all-excelling,
    Up the jasper arches rang.'

IV.

'Mid the angel-constellations,
    Like a star of purest flame,
Shining with exceeding brightness,
Robed in snowy-glistering whiteness,
    Now a singing reaper came;

Came with fulness of rejoicing
    That belovèd smile to meet:
'Master, lo, I come with singing,
Myriad sheaves of glory bringing
    To Thy dear and blessèd feet.'

Followed o'er the golden crystal
    Glittering hosts with crown and palm;
Joining him whose voice had taught them,
To the praise of Him who bought them,
    In a new and rapturous psalm.

V.

He who humbly watched the sowers,
    Watched the reapers of the Lord;
Sharing all their jubilation,
Hailing every coronation,
    Gladdened by their great reward.

'Seed of others long I scattered,
    Now their harvest joy is mine,
Kindling holy contemplation
Into glowing adoration,
    Into ecstasy divine.'

So he chanted. But the Master
    Beckoned through the shining throng:
While the praises of the choir
Rose into that silence, higher
    Than the highest flight of song.

Great and gracious words were spoken
    Of his faithful service done,
By the Voice that thrills all heaven;
And mysterious rule was given
    To that meek and marvelling one.

VI.

Found the little child rich harvest
    From his tiny seed of love;
Little footsteps followed surely
In the footprints marked so purely,
    Till they met again above.

Aged ones and feeble mourners
    Felt the solace of his smile;
Hastened on with footsteps lighter,
Battled on with courage brighter,
    Through the lessening 'little while,'

Till they too had joined the mansions
    Where the weary are at rest.

Could that little one forget them?
Oh, how joyously he met them
   In this dear home safe and blest!

And the Saviour, who had called him,
   Smiled upon His little one;
On his brow, so fair and tender,
Set a crown of heavenly splendour,
   With the gracious words 'Well done!'

VII.

Yet again a wondrous anthem
   Rang across the crystal sea;
Harps and voices all harmonious,
Nearer, nearer, sweet, symphonious,
   Meet for heaven's own jubilee.

One by one the singers gathered,
   Ever swelling that great song,
Till a mighty chorus thundered,
Till the listening seraphs wondered,
   As its triumph pealed along.

Onward came they with rejoicing,
   Bearing one upon their wings,
With their waving palms victorious,
To the presence-chamber glorious
   Of the very King of kings.

And a whisper, clear and thrilling,
   Fell upon her ravished ear—
'Lo, *thy* harvest song ascending!
Lo, *thy* golden sheaves are bending
   Full and precious, round thee here!

'Nay,' she said, 'I have no harvest,
   For I had no power to sow;
Burdening others, daily dying,
Year by year in weakness lying,
   Still and silent, lone and low.'

Then a flash of sudden glory
    Lit her long life-mystery;
By that heavenly intuition
All the secret of her mission
    Shone, revealed in radiancy.

And she knew the sweet memorials
    Of her hidden life had shed
Glories on the sufferer's pillow,
Calmness on the darkling billow,
    Peace upon the dying bed.

Thousand, thousand-fold her guerdon,
    Thousand, thousand-fold her bliss!
While His cup of suffering sharing,
All His will so meekly bearing,
He was gloriously preparing
    This for her, and her for this!

He that goeth forth and weepeth, seed of grace in sorrow bringing,
Laden with his sheaves of glory, doubtless shall return with singing.

Two pages from F.R.H.'s Manuscript Book Nº VI. See pages 402–403, 492, and 388–389.

65

Accepted.

"Accepted in the Beloved." "Perfect in Christ Jesus."
"Complete in Him."

I

Accepted, perfect and complete,
For God's inheritance made meet,
How true, how glorious and how sweet!

II

In the Belovèd, He by the King
Accepted, though not anything
But forfeit lives had we to bring.

III

And perfect in Christ Jesus made,
On Him our great transgressions laid,
We in His righteousness arrayed.

IV

Complete in Him, our glorious Head,
With Jesus raised from the dead,
And by His mighty Spirit led.

V

O blessèd Lord, is this for me?
Then let my whole life henceforth be
One Alleluia song to Thee!

F.R.H.

Hastings. Sep. 3. 1870.

F.R.H.'s fair copy autograph that she copied in her Manuscript Book Nº VI.

Our Blessings.

'Blessed be the God and Father of our Lord Jesus Christ, who hath blessed us with all spiritual blessings in heavenly places in Christ.'—Ephesians 1:3.

Everlasting Blessings.

'I know that whatsoever God doeth, it shall be for ever.'—Ecclesiastes 3:14.

Oh, what everlasting blessings God outpoureth on His own!
Ours by promise true and faithful, spoken from the eternal throne;
Ours by His eternal purpose ere the universe had place;
Ours by everlasting covenant, ours by free and royal grace.

With salvation everlasting He shall save us, He shall bless
With the largess of Messiah, everlasting righteousness;
Ours the everlasting mercy all His wondrous dealings prove;
Ours His everlasting kindness, fruit of everlasting love.

In the Lord Jehovah trusting, everlasting strength have we;
He Himself our Sun, our Glory, Everlasting Light shall be;
Everlasting life is ours, purchased by The Life laid down;
And our heads, oft bowed and weary, everlasting joy shall crown.

We shall dwell with Christ for ever, when the shadows flee away,
In the everlasting glory of the everlasting day.
Unto Thee, belovèd Saviour, everlasting thanks belong,
Everlasting adoration, everlasting laud and song!

Accepted.

'Accepted in the Beloved.'—Ephesians 1:6. 'Perfect in Christ Jesus.'—Colossians 1:28.
'Complete in Him.'—Colossians 2:10.

Accepted, Perfect, and Complete,
For God's inheritance made meet!
How true, how glorious, and how sweet!

In the Belovèd—by the King
Accepted, though not anything
But forfeit lives had we to bring.

And Perfect in Christ Jesus made,
On Him our great transgressions laid,
We in His righteousness arrayed.

Complete in Him, our glorious Head,
With Jesus raisèd from the dead,
And by His mighty Spirit led!

O blessèd Lord, is this for me?
Then let my whole life henceforth be
One Alleluia-song to Thee!

Fresh Springs.

'All my fresh springs shall be in Thee.'—PSALM 87:7. (*Prayer-Book Version.*)

HEAR the Father's ancient promise!
    Listen, thirsty, weary one!
'I will pour My Holy Spirit
    On Thy chosen seed, O Son.'
Promise to the Lord's Anointed,
    Gift of God to Him for thee!
Now, by covenant appointed,
    All thy springs in Him shall be.

Springs of life in desert places
    Shall thy God unseal for thee;
Quickening and reviving graces,
    Dew-like, healing, sweet and free.
Springs of sweet refreshment flowing,
    When thy work is hard or long,
Courage, hope, and power bestowing,
    Lightening labour with a song.

Springs of peace, when conflict heightens,
    Thine uplifted eye shall see;
Peace that strengthens, calms, and brightens,
    Peace itself a victory.

Springs of comfort, strangely springing,
 Through the bitter wells of woe;
Founts of hidden gladness, bringing
 Joy that earth can ne'er bestow.

Thine, O Christian, is this treasure,
 To Thy risen Head assured!
Thine in full and gracious measure,
 Thine by covenant secured!
Now arise! His word possessing,
 Claim the promise of the Lord;
Plead through Christ for showers of blessing,
 Till the Spirit be outpoured!

Faithful Promises.

NEW YEAR'S HYMN.

ISAIAH 41:10.

STANDING at the portal
 Of the opening year,
Words of comfort meet us,
 Hushing every fear.
Spoken through the silence
 By our Father's voice,
Tender, strong, and faithful,
 Making us rejoice.
  Onward, then, and fear not,
   Children of the Day!
  For His word shall never,
   Never pass away!

I, the Lord, am with thee,
 Be thou not afraid!
I will help and strengthen,
 Be thou not dismayed!
Yea, I will uphold thee
 With My own Right Hand;
Thou art called and chosen
 In my sight to stand.

Onward, then, and fear not,
    Children of the Day!
For His word shall never,
    Never pass away!

For the year before us,
    Oh, what rich supplies!
For the poor and needy
    Living streams shall rise;
For the sad and sinful
    Shall His grace abound;
For the faint and feeble
    Perfect strength be found.
        Onward, then, and fear not,
            Children of the Day!
        For His word shall never,
            Never pass away!

He will never fail us,
    He will not forsake;
His eternal covenant
    He will never break!
Resting on His promise,
    What have we to fear?
God is all-sufficient
    For the coming year.
        Onward, then, and fear not.
            Children of the Day!
        For His word shall never,
            Never pass away!

The Faithful Comforter.

'The Holy Ghost—He is faithful.'—Hebrews 10:15, 23.

To Thee, O Comforter Divine,
For all Thy grace and power benign,
    Sing we Alleluia!

To Thee, whose faithful love had place
In God's great Covenant of Grace,
  Sing we Alleluia!

To Thee, whose faithful voice doth win
The wandering from the ways of sin,
  Sing we Alleluia!

To Thee, whose faithful power doth heal,
Enlighten, sanctify, and seal,
  Sing we Alleluia!

To Thee, whose faithful truth is shown,
By every promise made our own,
  Sing we Alleluia!

To Thee, our Teacher and our Friend,
Our faithful Leader to the end,
  Sing we Alleluia!

To Thee, by Jesus Christ sent down,
Of all His gifts the sum and crown,
  Sing we Alleluia!

To Thee, who art with God the Son
And God the Father ever One,
  Sing we Alleluia! Amen!

Under His Shadow.

(COMMUNION HYMN.)

'I sat down under His shadow with great delight.'—SONG OF SOLOMON 2:3.

SIT down beneath His shadow,
 And rest with great delight;
The faith that now beholds Him
 Is pledge of future sight.

Our Master's love remember,
 Exceeding great and free;
Lift up thy heart in gladness,
 For He remembers thee.

Bring every weary burden,
    Thy sin, thy fear, thy grief;
He calls the heavy laden,
    And gives them kind relief.

His righteousness 'all glorious'
    Thy festal robe shall be;
And love that passeth knowledge
    His banner over thee.

A little while, though parted,
    Remember, wait, and love,
Until He comes in glory,
    Until we meet above;

Till in the Father's kingdom
    The heavenly feast is spread,
And we behold His beauty,
    Whose blood for us was shed!

Covenant Blessings.

'He hath made with me an everlasting covenant, ordered in all things, and sure.'
—2 SAMUEL 23:5.

JEHOVAH's Covenant shall endure,
All ordered, everlasting, sure!
O child of God, rejoice to trace
Thy portion in its glorious grace.

'Tis thine, for Christ is given to be
The Covenant of God to thee:
In Him, God's golden scroll of light,
The darkest truths are clear and bright.

O sorrowing sinner, well He knew,
Ere time began, what He would do!
Then rest thy hope within the veil;
His covenant mercies shall not fail.

O doubting one, the Eternal Three
Are pledged in faithfulness for thee;
Claim every promise, sweet and sure,
By covenant oath of God secure.

O waiting one, each moment's fall
Is marked by love that planned them all;
Thy times, all ordered by His hand,
In God's eternal covenant stand.

O feeble one, look up and see
Strong consolation sworn for thee;
Jehovah's glorious arm is shown,
His covenant strength is all thine own.

O mourning one, each stroke of love
A covenant blessing yet shall prove;
His covenant love shall be thy stay;
His covenant grace be as thy day.

O Love that chose, O Love that died,
O Love that sealed and sanctified!
All glory, glory, glory be,
O covenant Triune God, to Thee!

The Triune Presence.

(BIRTHDAY OR NEW YEAR'S HYMN.)

'Certainly I will be with thee.'—EXODUS 3:12.

'CERTAINLY I will be with thee!' Father, I have found it true:
To Thy faithfulness and mercy I would set my seal anew.
All the year Thy grace hath kept me, Thou my help indeed hast been,
Marvellous the loving-kindness every day and hour hath seen.

'Certainly I will be with thee!' Let me feel it, Saviour dear,
Let me know that Thou art with me, very precious, very near.
On this day of solemn pausing, with Thyself all longing still,
Let Thy pardon, let Thy presence, let Thy peace my spirit fill.

'Certainly I will be with thee!' Blessèd Spirit, come to me,
Rest upon me, dwell within me, let my heart Thy temple be;
Through the trackless year before me, Holy One, with me Abide!
Teach me, comfort me, and calm me, be my ever-present Guide.

'Certainly I will be with thee!' Starry promise in the night!
All uncertainties, like shadows, flee away before its light.
'Certainly I will be with thee!' He hath spoken: I have heard!
True of old, and true this moment, I will trust Jehovah's word.

Fair copy autograph in F.R.H.'s Manuscript Book Nº VI.

Now and Afterward.

'Nevertheless afterward.'—HEBREWS 12:11.
'And afterward receive me to glory.'—PSALM 73:24.

Now and Afterward.

Now, the sowing and the weeping,
    Working hard and waiting long;
Afterward, the golden reaping,
    Harvest home and grateful song.

Now, the pruning, sharp, unsparing;
    Scattered blossom, bleeding shoot!
Afterward, the plenteous bearing
    Of the Master's pleasant fruit.

Now, the plunge, the briny burden,
    Blind, faint gropings in the sea;
Afterward, the pearly guerdon
    That shall make the diver free.

Now, the long and toilsome duty
    Stone by stone to carve and bring;
Afterward, the perfect beauty
    Of the palace of the King.

Now, the tuning and the tension,
    Wailing minors, discord strong;
Afterward, the grand ascension
    Of the Alleluia song.

Now, the spirit conflict-riven,
    Wounded heart, unequal strife;
Afterward, the triumph given,
    And the victor's crown of life.

Now, the training, strange and lowly,
　　Unexplained and tedious now;
Afterward, the service holy,
　　And the Master's 'Enter thou!'

'Tempted and Tried!'

'Tempted and tried!'
　　Oh! the terrible tide
May be raging and deep, may be wrathful and wide!
　　Yet its fury is vain,
　　For the Lord shall restrain;
And for ever and ever Jehovah shall reign.

'Tempted and tried!'
　　There is One at thy side,
And never in vain shall His children confide!
　　He shall save and defend,
　　For He loves to the end,
Adorable Master and glorious Friend!

'Tempted and tried!'
　　Whate'er may betide,
In His secret pavilion His children shall hide!
　　'Neath the shadowing wing
　　Of Eternity's King
His children shall trust and His servants shall sing.

'Tempted and tried!'
　　Yet the Lord shall abide
Thy faithful Redeemer, thy Keeper and Guide,
　　Thy Shield and thy Sword,
　　Thine exceeding Reward!
Then enough for the servant to be as his Lord!

'Tempted and tried!'
　　The Saviour who died
Hath called thee to suffer and reign by His side.
　　His cross thou shalt bear,
　　And His crown thou shalt wear,
And for ever and ever His glory shalt share.

Not Forsaken.

(Answer to an extremely beautiful but utterly melancholy sonnet, entitled 'Forsaken.')

OH, not forsaken! God gives better things
   Than thou hast asked in thy forlornest hour.
   Love's promises shall be fulfilled in power.
Not death, but life; not silence, but the strings
Of angel-harps; no deep, cold sea, but springs
   Of living water; no dim, wearied sight,
   Nor time- nor tear-mist, but the joy of light;
Not sleep, but rest that happy service brings;
And no forgotten name thy lot shall be
   But God's remembrance. Thou canst never drift
     Beyond His love. Would I could reach thee where
The shadows droop so heavily, and lift
     The cold weight from thy life!—And if I care
For one unknown, oh, how much more doth HE!

Listening in Darkness—Speaking in Light.

'What I tell you in darkness, that speak ye in light.'—MATTHEW 10:27.

HE hath spoken in the darkness,
   In the silence of the night,
Spoken sweetly of the Father,
   Words of life and love and light.
Floating through the sombre stillness
   Came the loved and loving Voice,
Speaking peace and solemn gladness,
   That His children might rejoice.
What He tells thee in the darkness,
   Songs He giveth in the night—
Rise and speak it in the morning,
   Rise and sing them in the light!

He hath spoken in the darkness,
   In the silence of thy grief,
Sympathy so deep and tender,
   Mighty for thy heart relief;

Speaking in thy night of sorrow
 Words of comfort and of calm,
Gently on thy wounded spirit
 Pouring true and healing balm.
What He tells thee in the darkness,
 Weary watcher for the day,
Grateful lip and life should utter
 When the shadows flee away.

He is speaking in the darkness,
 Though thou canst not see His face,
More than angels ever needed,
 Mercy, pardon, love, and grace.
Speaking of the many mansions,
 Where, in safe and holy rest,
Thou shalt be with Him for ever,
 Perfectly and always blest.
What He tells thee in the darkness,
 Whispers through Time's lonely night,
Thou shalt speak in glorious praises,
 In the everlasting light!

Evening Tears and Morning Songs.

'Weeping may endure in the evening, but singing cometh in the morning.'
—Psalm 30:5 (*Margin*).

In the evening there is weeping,
 Lengthening shadows, failing sight;
Silent darkness slowly creeping
 Over all things dear and bright.

In the evening there is weeping,
 Lasting all the twilight through;
Phantom shadows, never sleeping,
 Wakening slumbers of the true.

In the morning cometh singing,
 Cometh joy and cometh sight,
When the sun ariseth, bringing
 Healing on his wings of light.

In the morning cometh singing,
　　Songs that ne'er in silence end,
Angel minstrels ever bringing
　　Praises new with thine to blend.

Are the twilight shadows casting
　　Heavy glooms upon thy heart?
Soon in radiance everlasting
　　Night for ever shall depart.

Art thou weeping, sad and lonely,
　　Through the evening of thy days?
All thy sighing shall be only
　　Prelude of more perfect praise.

Darkest hour is nearest dawning,
　　Solemn herald of the day;
Singing cometh in the morning,
　　God shall wipe thy tears away!

Peaceable Fruit.

'Nevertheless, afterward it yieldeth the peaceable fruit of righteousness.'
　　—Hebrews 12:11.

What shall Thine 'afterward' be, O Lord,
　　For this dark and suffering night?
Father, *what* shall Thine 'afterward' be?
Hast Thou a morning of joy for me,
　　And a new and joyous light?

What shall Thine 'afterward' be, O Lord,
　　For the moan that I cannot stay?
Shall it issue in some new song of praise,
Sweeter than sorrowless heart could raise,
　　When the night hath passed away?

What shall Thine 'afterward' be, O Lord,
　　For this helplessness of pain?

A clearer view of my home above,
Of my Father's strength and my Father's love?
    Shall this be my lasting gain?

What shall Thine 'afterward' be, O Lord?
    How long must Thy child endure?
Thou knowest! 'Tis well that I know it not!
Thine 'afterward' cometh, I cannot tell what,
    But I know that Thy word is sure.

What shall Thine 'afterward' be, O Lord?
    I wonder and wait to see,
(While to Thy chastening hand I bow,)
What 'peaceable fruit' may be ripening now,
    Ripening fast for me!

Right!

SCENE I.

THE summer sun was high and strong,
    And dust was on the traveller's feet:
Oh, weary was the stage and long,
    And burning was the early heat!
There was a pause. For Ernest stood
Upon the borders of a wood.
Between him and his home it lay,
Stretching in mystery away:
What might be there he could not tell
Of briery steep, or mossy dell,
Of bog or brake, of glen or glade,
All hidden by the dim green shade.

He had not passed that way before,
    And wonderingly he waited now,
While mystic voices, o'er and o'er,
    Soft whispered on from bough to bough.
Oh, was it only wind and trees
    That made such gentle whisperings?

Or was it some sweet spirit breeze
   That bore a message on its wings,
And bid the traveller that day
Go forward on his woodland way?

How should he know? He had no clue,
   And more than one fair opening lay
Before him, where the broad boughs threw
   Cool, restful shade across the way.
Which should he choose? He could not trace
   The onward track by vision keen;
The drooping branches interlace,
   Not far the winding paths are seen.
Oh for a sign! Were choice not right,
   Was no return, for well he knew
The hours were short, and swift the night;
   Once entered, he must hasten through.

For what hath been can never be
   As if it had not been at all;
We gaze, but never more can we
   Retrace one footstep's wavering fall.
Oh, how we need from day to day
A guiding Hand for all the way!
Oh, how we need from hour to hour
That faithful, ever-present Power!

Which should he choose? He pondered long,
   And with the sounds of bird and bee
He blent an oft-repeated song,
   A soft and suppliant melody:

     'Oh for a light from heaven,
       Clear and divine,
     Now on the paths before me
       Brightly to shine!
     Oh for a hand to beckon!
       Oh for a voice to say,
     "Follow in firm assurance—
       This is the way!"

'Listening to mingling voices,
    Seeking a guiding hand,
Watching for light from heaven,
    Waiting I stand;
Onward and homeward pressing,
    Nothing my feet should stay,
Might I but plainly hear it,—
    "This is the way!"'

Was it indeed an answer given,
    That whisper through the tree-tops o'er him?
Was it indeed a light from heaven
    That fell upon the path before him?
Or was it only that he met
    The wayward playing of the breeze,
Parting the heavy boughs to let
    The sunshine fall among the trees?
Again he listened—did it say,
'This is the onward, homeward way?'
Perhaps it did. He would not wait,
But pressing towards a Mansion Gate
That, yet unseen, all surely stood
Beyond the untried, unknown wood,
And trusting that his prayer was heard,
Although he caught no answering word,
And gazing on with calm, clear eye
The straightest, surest path to spy
(Not seeking out the smooth and bright,
If he might only choose the right),
With hopeful heart and manly tread,
Into the forest depths he sped.

SCENE II.

Hours flit on, and the sunshine fails in the zenith of day;
    Hours flit on, and the loud wind crashes and moans o'er the ridge;
Heavily beateth the strong rain, lashing the miry clay,
    Hoarsely roareth the torrent under the quivering bridge.

Under the shivering pine-trees, over the slippery stone,
    Over the rugged boulder, over the cold wet weed,
Ernest the traveller passeth, storm-beaten, weary and lone,
    Only following faintly whither the path may lead.

Leading down to the valleys, dank in the shadow of death,
    Leading on through the briers, poisonous, keen, and sore;
Leading up to the grim rocks, mounted with panting breath,
    Only to gain a glimpse of sterner toil before.

Faint and wounded and bleeding, hungry, thirsty, and chill,
    Hardly a step before him seen through the tangled brake,
Rougher and wilder the storm-blast, steeper the thorn grown hill,
    Brave heart and bright eye and strong limb, well may they quiver
        and ache!

Was it indeed the *right* way? Was it a God-led choice,
    Followed in faith and patience, and chosen not for ease?
Was it a false, false gleam, and a mocking, mocking voice
    That fell on the woodland pathway, and murmured among the trees?

Oh the dire mistake! fatal freedom to choose!
    Had he but taken a fair path, sheltered, level, and straight,
Never a thorn to wound him, never a stone to bruise,
    Leading safely and softly on to the Mansion Gate!

Was it the wail of a wind-harp, cadencing weird and long,
    Pulsing under the pine-trees, dying to wake again?
Is it the voice of a brave heart striving to utter in song
    Agony, prayer, and reliance, courage and wonder and pain?

             'Onward and homeward ever,
                Battling with dark distress,
             Faltering, but yielding never,
                Still shall my faint feet press.
             Why was no beckoning hand
                Sent in my doubt and need?
             Why did no true guide stand
                Guiding me right indeed?
             Why? They will tell me all
                When I have reached the gate,

Where, in the shining hall,
　　Many my coming wait.

'Oh the terrible night,
　　Falling without a star!
Darkness anear, but light—
　　Glorious light afar!
Oh the perilous way!
　　Oh the pitiless blast!
Long though I suffer and stray,
　　There will be rest at last.
Perhaps I have far to go,
　　Perhaps but a little way!
Well that I do not know!
　　Onward! I must not stay.

'Splinter and thorn and brier
　　Yet may be sore and keen;
Rocks may be rougher and higher,
　　Hollows more chill between.
There may be torrents to cross,
　　Bridgeless, and fierce with foam;
Rest in the wild wood were loss,
　　There will be rest at home.
Battling with dark distress,
　　Faltering, but yielding never,
Still shall my faint feet press
　　Onward and homeward ever!'

Pulsing under the pine-trees, dying, dying,—and gone,—
　　Gone that Æolian cadence, silent the firm refrain;
Only the howl of the storm-wind rages cruelly on:
　　Has the traveller fallen, vanquished by toil and pain?

SCENE III.

Morning, morning on the mountains, golden-vestured, snowy-browed!
Morning light of clear resplendence, shining forth without a cloud;
Morning songs of jubilation, thrilling through the crystal air;
Morning joy upon all faces, new and radiant, pure and fair.

At the portals of the mansion, Ernest stands and gazes back.
There is light upon the river, light upon the forest track;
Light upon the darkest valley, light upon the sternest height;
Light upon the brake and bramble, everywhere that glorious light!

Strong and joyous stands the traveller, in the morning glory now,
Not a shade upon the brightness of the cool and peaceful brow;
Not a trace of weary faintness, not a touch of lingering pain,
Not a scar to wake the memory of the suffering hours again.

Onward by the winding pathway, many another journeyed fast,
Hastening to the princely mansion by the way that he had passed;
Spared the doubting and the erring by those footsteps bravely placed
In the clogging mire, or trampling on the wounding bramble-waste.

Some had followed close behind him, pressing to the self-same mark,
Cheered and guided by the refrain of that singer in the dark;
Some were near him in the tempest, while he thought himself alone,
And regained a long-lost pathway, following that beckoning tone.

Some who patiently, yet feebly, sought to reach that mansion too,
Caught the unseen singer's courage, battled on with vigour new;
Some, exhausted in the struggle, sunk in slumber chill and deep,
Started at that strange voice near them, rousing from their fatal sleep.

Now they meet and gather round him, and together enter in,
Where the rest is consummated and the joys of home begin,
Where the tempest cannot reach them, where the wanderings are past,
Where the sorrows of the journey not a single shadow cast.

Singing once in dismal forest, singing once in cruel storm,
Singing now at home in gladness in the sunshine bright and warm,
Once again the voice resoundeth, pouring forth a happy song,
While a chorus of rejoicing swells the sweet notes full and long:

> 'Light after darkness,
> Gain after loss,
> Strength after suffering,
> Crown after cross.
> Sweet after bitter,
> Song after sigh,

Home after wandering,
　Praise after cry.

'Sheaves after sowing,
　Sun after rain,
Sight after mystery,
　Peace after pain.
Joy after sorrow,
　Calm after blast,
Rest after weariness,
　Sweet rest at last.

'Near after distant,
　Gleam after gloom,
Love after loneliness,
　Life after tomb.
After long agony,
　Rapture of bliss!
Right was the pathway
　Leading to this!'

The Col de Balm.

SUNSHINE and silence on the Col de Balm!
　I stood above the mists, above the rush
　Of all the torrents, when one marvellous hush
Filled God's great mountain temple, vast and calm,
With hallelujah light, a seen though silent psalm;—

Crossed with one discord, only one.　For Love
　Cried out, and would be heard: 'If ye were here,
　O friends, so far away and yet so near,
Then were the anthem perfect!' And the cry
Threaded the concords of that Alpine harmony.

Not vain the same fond cry, if first I stand
　Upon the mountain of our God, and long,
　Even in the glory, and with His new song
Upon my lips, that you should come and share
The bliss of heaven, imperfect still till all are there.

Dear ones! shall it be mine to watch you come
    Up from the shadows and the valley mist,
    To tread the jacinth and the amethyst,
To rest and sing upon the stormless height,
In the deep calm of love and everlasting light?

'Eye Hath Not Seen.'

'You never write of heaven,
    Though you write of heavenly themes;
You never paint the glory
    But in reflected gleams!'
My pencil only pictures
    What I have known and seen:
How can I tell the joys that dwell
    Where I have never been?

I sing the songs of Zion,
    But I would never dare
To imitate the chorus,
    Like many waters, there.
I sketch the sunny landscape,
    But can I paint the sun?
Can that by art, which human heart
    Conceiveth not, be won?

The Laplander, that never
    Hath left his flowerless snows,
Might make another realize
    The fragrance of the rose:
The blind might teach his brother
    Each subtle tint to know,
Of lovely lights and summer sights
    Of shadow and of glow.

To whom all sound is silence,
    The dumb man might impart
The spirit-winging marvels
    Of Handel's sacred art.

But never, sister, never
   Was told by mortal breath
What they behold, o'er whom hath rolled
   The one dark wave of death.

Yet angel-echoes reach us,
   Borne on from star to star,
And glimpses of our purchased home,
   Not always faint and far.
No harp seraphic brings them,
   No poet's glowing word,
By One alone revealed and known—
   The Spirit of the Lord.

Have we not bent in sadness
   Before the mercy-seat,
And longed with speechless longing
   To kiss the Master's feet?
And though for precious ointment
   We had but tears to bring,
We let them flow, and could not go
   Till we had seen our King.

Then came a flash of seeing
   How every cloud should pass,
And vision should be perfect,
   Undimmed by darkling glass.
The glory that excelleth
   Shone out with sudden ray,
We seemed to stand so near 'the land'
   No longer 'far away,'—

The glisten of the white robe,
   The waving of the palm,
The ended sin and sorrow,
   The sweet eternal calm,
The holy adoration
   That perfect love shall bring,
And, face to face, in glorious grace,
   The beauty of the King!

Oh, this is more than poem,
    And more than the highest song;
A witness with our spirit,
    Though hidden, full and strong.
'Tis no new revelation
    Vouchsafed to saint or sage,
But light from God cast bright and broad
    Upon the sacred page.

Our fairest dream can never
    Outshine that holy light,
Our noblest thought can never soar
    Beyond that word of might.
Our whole anticipation,
    Our Master's best reward,
Our crown of bliss, is summed in this—
    'For ever with the Lord!'

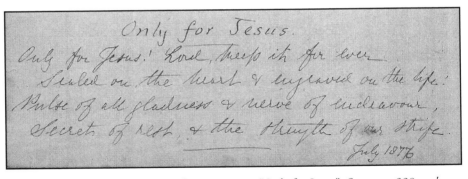

F.R.H.'s manuscript of the single stanza poem "Only for Jesus." See pages 338 and 565 of this book.

The Church Justified.

"This is the name wherewith she shall be called, The Lord our Righteousness." Jer. XXXIII. 16.

I.

Israel of God, awaken! Blessed of
God! arise and shine!
Beaming forth and smitest redeemed,
Rejoice in thy no longer thine!
For the Lord thy God shall restore thee
with a new and glorious Name,
With the garments of Salvation, with
the robe of righteousness.

II.

By the grace of God the fallen, there
art freely justified.
Through the great redemption purchased
by the blood of them who died.
By His life, for thee fulfilling God's
command, bearing shame,
His glorious righteousness, that is
gained of thy God.

III.

Therefore, justified for ever by the faith
which He hath given,

Peace, and joy, & hope abounding, goeth
thy heal-forth to Heaven.
Most firm blotted for ever, when
thy life shall crown & last,
thy firmness then shalt be called,
By which "the Lord our Righteousness."

Christ, the Lord our Righteousness.

2 my Brown,
May 1877.

The Presentation of the Church.

Behold I and the children which God hath given me.

I.

Our Saviour and our King!
Enthroned & crowned above!
Will with encircling gladness bring
The children of His love.

II.

Oh then the brighter far
His glory shall inherit;
Let me return, "Your name to save
To meeting from His fold.

III.

As shall comfort His own
From every shrine & crash,

The Church of Christ.

'Whom He did predestinate, them He also called; and whom He called, them He also justified; and whom He justified, them He also glorified.'
—Romans 8:30.

I. Chosen.
II. Called.
III. Justified.

IV. Sanctified.
V. Joined to Christ.
VI. Presented Faultless.

VII. Glorified.

I.

Chosen in Christ.

'He hath chosen us in Him before the foundation of the world.'—Ephesians 1:4.

O thou chosen Church of Jesus, glorious, blessèd, and secure,
Founded on the One Foundation, which for ever shall endure;
Not thy holiness or beauty can thy strength and safety be,
But the everlasting love wherewith Jehovah lovèd thee.

Chosen—by His own good pleasure, by the counsel of His will,
Mystery of power and wisdom working for His people still;
Chosen—in thy mighty Saviour, ere one ray of quickening light
Beamed upon the chaos, waiting for the Word of sovereign might.

Chosen—through the Holy Spirit, through the sanctifying grace
Poured upon His precious vessels, meetened for the heavenly place;
Chosen—to show forth His praises, to be holy in His sight;
Chosen—unto grace and glory, chosen unto life and light.

Blessèd be the God and Father of our Saviour Jesus Christ,
Who hath blessed us with such blessings all uncounted and unpriced!
Let our high and holy calling, and our strong salvation be,
Theme of never-ending praises, God of sovereign grace, to Thee!

II.

Called.

'Partakers of the heavenly calling.'—HEBREWS 3:1.

HOLY brethren, called and chosen by the sovereign Voice of Might,
See your high and holy calling out of darkness into light!
Called according to His purpose and the riches of His love;
Won to listen by the leading of the gentle heavenly Dove!

Called to suffer with our Master, patiently to run His race;
Called a blessing to inherit, called to holiness and grace;
Called to fellowship with Jesus, by the Ever-Faithful One;
Called to His eternal glory, to the kingdom of His Son.

Whom He calleth He preserveth, and His glory they shall see;
He is faithful that hath called you,—He will do it, fear not ye!
Therefore, holy brethren, onward! thus ye make your calling sure;
For the prize of this high calling, bravely to the end endure.

III.

Justified.

'This is the name wherewith she shall be called, The Lord our Righteousness.'
—JEREMIAH 33:16.

ISRAEL of God, awaken! Church of Christ, arise and shine
Mourning garb and soilèd raiment henceforth be no longer thine!
For the Lord thy God hath clothed thee with a new and glorious dress,
With the garments of salvation, with the robe of righteousness.

By the grace of God the Father, thou art freely justified,
Through the great redemption purchased by the blood of Him who died;
By His life, for thee fulfilling God's command exceeding broad,
By His glorious resurrection, seal and signet of thy God.

Therefore, justified for ever by the faith which He hath given,
Peace, and joy, and hope abounding, smooth thy trial path to heaven:
Unto Him betrothed for ever, who thy life shall crown and bless,
By His name thou shalt be callèd, Christ, 'The Lord our Righteousness!'

IV.

Sanctified.

'Sanctified in Christ Jesus.'—1 CORINTHIANS 1:2.

CHURCH of God, beloved and chosen, Church of Christ, for whom He died,
Claim thy gifts and praise thy Giver!—*'Ye are washed and sanctified.'*
Sanctified by God the Father, and by Jesus Christ His Son,
And by God the Holy Spirit, Holy, Holy Three in One.

By His will He sanctifieth, by the Spirit's power within;
By the loving Hand that chasteneth fruits of righteousness to win;
By His truth and by His promise, by the Word, His gift unpriced,
By His own blood, and by union with the risen life of Christ.

Holiness by faith in Jesus, not by effort of thine own,—
Sin's dominion crushed and broken by the power of grace alone,—
God's own holiness within thee, His own beauty on thy brow,—
This shall be thy pilgrim brightness, this thy blessèd portion now.

He will sanctify thee wholly; body, spirit, soul shall be
Blameless till thy Saviour's coming in His glorious majesty!
He hath perfected for ever those whom He hath sanctified;
Spotless, glorious, and holy is the Church, His chosen Bride.

V.

Joined to Christ.

'Head over all things to the Church, which is His body.'—EPHESIANS 1:22, 23.

JOINED to Christ in mystic union,
    We Thy members, Thou our Head,
Sealed by deep and true communion,
    Risen with Thee, who once were dead—
Saviour, we would humbly claim
All the power of this Thy name.

Instant sympathy to brighten
    All their weakness and their woe,

Guiding grace their way to lighten,
    Shall Thy loving members know;
All their sorrows Thou dost bear,
All Thy gladness they shall share.

Make Thy members every hour
    For Thy blessèd service meet;
Earnest tongues, and arms of power,
    Skilful hands, and hastening feet,
Ever ready to fulfil
All Thy word and all Thy will.

Everlasting life Thou givest,
    Everlasting love to see;
They shall live because Thou livest,
    And their life is hid with Thee.
Safe Thy members shall be found,
When their glorious Head is crowned!

VI.

Presented Faultless.

'Behold I and the children which God hath given Me.'—HEBREWS 2:13.

OUR Saviour and our King,
    Enthroned and crowned above,
Shall with exceeding gladness bring
    The children of His love.

All that the Father gave
    His glory shall behold;
Not one whom Jesus came to save
    Is missing from His fold.

He shall confess His own
    From every clime and coast,
Before His Father's glorious throne,
    Before the angel host.

'O righteous Father, see,
In spotless robes arrayed,
Thy chosen gifts of love to Me,
Before the worlds were made.

'By new creation Thine;
By purpose and by grace,
By right of full redemption Mine,
Faultless before Thy face.

'As Thou hast lovèd Me,
So hast Thou lovèd them;
Thy precious jewels they shall be,
My glorious diadem!'

VII.

Glorified.

'The God of all grace, who hath called us unto His eternal glory by Christ Jesus, .
. . to Him be glory.'—1 PETER 5:10, 11.

SOVEREIGN Lord and gracious Master,
Thou didst freely choose Thine own,
Thou hast called with mighty calling,
Thou wilt save, and keep from falling;
Thine the glory, Thine alone!
Yet Thy hand shall crown in heaven
All the grace Thy love hath given;
Just, though undeserved, reward
From our glorious, gracious Lord.

From the martyr and apostle
To the sainted baby boy,
Every consecrated chalice
In the King of Glory's palace
Overflows with holy joy.
Sovereign choice of gift and dower,
Differing honour, differing power,—
Yet are all alike in this,
Perfect love and perfect bliss.

In those heavenly constellations,
     Lo! what differing glories meet;
Stars of radiance soft and tender,
Stars of full and dazzling splendour,
     All in God's own light complete;
          Brightest they whose holy feet,
          Faithful to His service sweet,
          Nearest to their Master trod,
          Winning wandering souls to God.

Oh the rapture of that vision!
     (Every earthly passion o'er),
Our Redeemer's coronation,
And the blissful exaltation
     Of the dear ones gone before.
          Grace that shone for Christ below
          Changed to glory we shall know;
          And before His unveiled face
          Sing the glory of His grace.

Hymn
43
42

The Infinity of God.

Ps. 139. 9. "Too wonderful for me."

Sternberg 11.10, 11.10.

1 Holy and Infinite! Viewless, Eternal!
   Veiled in the glory that none can sustain!
None comprehendeth Thy Being supernal,
   Nor can the Heaven of heavens contain.

2 Holy and Infinite! Limitless, boundless,
      All Thy perfections & powers & praise! ff
Ocean of mystery! awful and soundless,
      All time unsearchable indament & ...

3 King of Eternity! what of revelation
      could the created & finite sustain,
But for Thy marvellous manifestation,
      Godhead incarnate in weakness & pain!

4 Therefore archangels and angels adore Thee,
      Cherubim wonder & seraphs admire;
Therefore we praise Thee, rejoicing before Thee,
      Joining in rapture the heavenly choir.

5 Glorious in holiness, fearful in praises,
      Who shall not fear Thee, & Who shall not laud?
Anthems of glory. Thy universe raises,
      Holy and Infinite! Father & God!

Frances Ridley Havergal. 1872

(Feb. 23. between 9 & 10 p.m.)

The overlaying of a piece of paper onto the other paper was done by F.R.H. This working draft manuscript in F.R.H.'s handwriting was part of her work on the hymnbook Songs of Grace and Glory, *and this was published as hymn number 42 in that volume. Apparently Frances cut and pasted different manuscript pages here. See page 365 of this book.*

1

The Message of an Eolian Harp.

"Goodbye, my mother!"
The brownhaired boy, with merry reverence,
Turned from the window where she leant, to meet
His holiday companions, blithely bound
With bat & ball for healthy English sport.
She watched his lithesome form, so slight yet strong,
Till, passing from the gate, he waved his cap,
And vanished. Then she sighed.

      Beside her sat
A friend of years. A different portrait each
Who knew her would have drawn, for different traits
Shone out in turn as sympathetic gleams
Fell on them or flashed out. And few could tell
The colour of her ~~this~~ eyes, or grey or brown,
Because the hue was lost in light, or shade;
Nor if her mouth were large or small, because
The play of thought made visible was there,
Like shifting rainbows on white foam. Her hair
Was dark, & she was rather tall; and this
Was all in which most people would agree.
Not always sigh for sigh or smile for smile

This is the first page of the first poem in F.R.H.'s Manuscript Book № VI.

Lights and Shadows of Spring-time.

The Message of an Æolian Harp.

              'GOOD-BYE, my mother!'
The brown-haired boy, with merry reverence,
Turned from the window where she leant, to meet
His holiday companions, blithely bound,
With bat and ball for healthy English sport.
She watched his lithesome form, so slight yet strong,
Till, passing from the gate, he waved his cap
And vanished. Then she sighed.
                      Beside her sat
A friend of years. A different portrait each
Who knew her would have drawn, for different traits
Shone out in turns as sympathetic gleams
Fell on them or flashed out. And few could tell
The colour of her eyes, or grey or brown,
Because the hue was lost in light or shade;
Nor if her mouth were large or small, because
The play of thought made visible was there,
Like shifting rainbows on white foam. Her hair
Was dark, and she was rather tall: and this
Was all in which most people would agree.
    Not always sigh for sigh or smile for smile
She gave; for now and then fine tact of heart
Suggests an opposite as best response,
Completing by contrasting, like a scarlet flower
With soft green leaves. So with her rippling voice,
Like waters that now murmur low, now leap
In spray-like laughter, Beatrice replied
To Eleanor's slow sigh:
                  'When he comes home,
How full of cricket stories he will be!
'Tis most amusing when he gives accounts,
Sparkling with boyish wit, yet earnestly,

As if an empire hung upon the match:
Only one needs a glossary of terms!
How well he knows the interest with which
You hear! I mark, he intersperses all
With rough pet names, shy veils of tenderness
For his dear mother. Eleanor, I think
Your Hubert has not merely head and hand,
As all his comrades know, but true heart too,
As you alone know fully. Well for him
That he has such a heart to meet his own,
And well for you; for 'tis a blessèd gift,
Not shared by all alike—the power to love;
And not less blessèd for proportioned pain,
Its fiery seal, its royal crown of thorns.'
 ' So seems it, Beatrice, to you, who find
No lurking danger in its concentration,
Because you have so many near and dear.
Not so to me. I tremble when I think
How much I love him; but I turn away
From thinking of it, just to love him more;—
Indeed, I fear, too much.'
       ' Dear Eleanor,
Do you love him as much as Christ loves us?
Let your lips answer me.'
        ' Why ask me, dear?
Our hearts are finite, Christ is infinite.'
  ' Then, till you reach the standard of that love,
Let neither fears nor well-meant warning voice
Distress you with " too much." For HE hath said—
How much—and who shall dare to change His measure?—
"That ye should love AS *I have lovèd you."*
Oh, sweet command, that goes so far beyond
The mightiest impulse of the tenderest heart!
A bare permission had been much; but He,
Who knows our yearnings and our fearfulness,
Chose graciously to *bid* us do the thing
That makes our earthly happiness, and set
A limit that we need not fear to pass,
Because we cannot. Oh the breadth, and length,

And depth, and height of love that passeth knowledge!
Yet Jesus said, "AS I have lovèd you."'
    'O Beatrice, I long to feel the sunshine
That this should bring; but there are other words
Which fall in chill eclipse. 'Tis written, "Keep
Yourselves from idols." How shall I obey?'
    'Dear, not by loving less, but loving more.
It is not that we love our precious ones
Too much, but God too little. As the lamp
A miner bears upon his shadowed brow,
Is only dazzling in the grimy dark
And has no glare against the summer sky
So, set the tiny torch of our best love
In the great sunshine of the Love of God,
And, though full fed and fanned, it casts no shade
And dazzles not, o'erflowed with mightier light.'
    She watched in hope to see the pale lips curve
More peacefully in answer to her words.
But Eleanor's quick spirit bridged too soon
The gap between one ridge of anxious thought
And that beyond, to see the glen between,
Where pastures green and waters still were spread.
So, answering not her friend's thought, but her own
She said, ''Tis but half true that love is power,
'Tis sometimes weakness.'
                            'Nay! You have not found
It thus at all. See how the bold bright boy,
Wilful and wayward else, will follow prompt
The magnet of your wish, with sudden swerve
From his own bent or fancy.'
                            'That is true,
And oh, so sweet to me! But by the power
I gauge the weakness. Beatrice, your heart
Has ached with longing for some stranger soul
That it might flee from danger to the One,
The Only Refuge; you have felt keen pain
In calling those who will not come to Him
Who waits to give them life; but I, *I* strive
For one far more than all the world to me,—

My boy, my only one, and fatherless,
Just entering the labyrinth of life
Without its only clue, with nothing but
My feeble hand to shield from powers of ill.
    'His mind is opening fast, and I have tried
To show the excellency of the knowledge
Of Jesus Christ our Lord; he listens well,
To please his mother, whom he would not grieve;
But never pulse of interest I feel,
And echoless the name of Jesus falls,
While classic heroes stir him with delight.
My boy, my only one! I taught him words,
When years ago his tiny feet peeped out
From the white nightgown in the nursery hush;
And folding firm the busy little hands,
He lisped "Our Father." But *words* are not *prayer.*
I put the lamp of life in his small hand,
Filling his memory with shining truths
And starry promises. He learnt them all
For love of me, just as he would have learnt
Some uncouth string of barbarous names,
Had I so wished: no more. They are no light
To him, no strength, no joy. O Beatrice,
'Tis this that presses on my weary heart,
And makes it more than widowed. For I know
That he who is not lost, but gone before,
Is only waiting till I come; for death
Has only parted us a little while,
And has not severed e'en the finest strand
In the eternal cable of our love:
The very strain has twined it closer still,
And added strength. The music of his life
Is nowise stilled, but blended so with songs
Around the throne of God, that our poor ears
No longer hear it. Hubert's life is mute
As yet; and what if all my tuning fail!'
    And Eleanor looked up among the clouds
With weary, wistful eyes, while Beatrice
Sent a far-passing glance beyond them all,

Beyond the sunshine too.
                    A sudden smile
Rose from within and overflowed her lips
And made them beautiful. Poor Eleanor
Deemed it the herald of some happy thought,
Some message, it might be, from God to her,
Wrapped in the simple words of friend to friend.
We do not always know it when we have
The privilege to be God's messengers,
Nor who shall be His messengers to us.
Unconsciously a pale responsive smile
Gleamed out to welcome it, and hardly waned
As unexpected change of subject came.
    'I did not tell you, did I, of my gift,
My beautiful Æolian harp?'
                    'Oh no!
I was too full of mine, my boy, and you
Too full of ready sympathy with me.'
    'Nay, do not say " *too* full," that could not be,
Yours is so great a gift, so great a care!
I shall not tire of thinking with you thus,
Until I do not love you, which means never.
But as we turn from gazing on the sea
To lift admiringly a tiny shell,
So you shall turn from your great interest
To hear of my Æolian treasure now.
Say, have you ever seen one?'
                    'Never, dear;
But visible, and almost audible,
Your words shall make it.'
                    'There's not much to see:
Two plain smooth boards, one thick, one very thin,
With seven tensioned strings upon the under,
Just covered by the upper, and a space
That you might lay a finger in between.
Yet one can almost reverence the thing
For very marvel at its spirit tones
And mysteries of music, that we love
But cannot understand.'

'But tell me more,
Dear Beatrice: what is its music like?
Whence comes it? and what does it say to you?'
  ''Tis easier to answer what and whence
Than your third question, for not twice
I hear the same soul-message from its strings.
But I will tell you of the first it brought;
Your heart will follow mine, and trace the under-thought.

I.

'A friend, a kind, dear friend
Gave me this harp, that should be all my own,
That it might speak to me in twilight lone
    When other sounds were fled; that it might send
Sweet messages of calming, cheering might,
Sweet sudden thrills of strange and exquisite delight.

II.

'Upon the strings I laid my hand,
And all were tuned in unison; one tone
Was yielded by the seven, one alone,
    In quick obedience to my touch-command.
It could not be that this was all he meant
Of promised music, when my little harp was sent.

III.

'To win the tones I found the way
In his own letter, mine before the gift:
"You cannot wake its music till you lift
    The closèd sash. Take up and gently lay
Your harp where it may meet the freshening air,
Then wait and listen." This I did, and left it there.

IV.

'I waited till the sun had set,
And twilight fell upon the autumn sea;

I watched, and saw the north wind touch a tree,
Dark outlined on the paling gold, and yet
My harp was mute. I cried, "Awake, O north!
Come to my harp, and call its answering music forth."

V.

'Like stars that tremble into light
Out of the purple dark, a low, sweet note
Just trembled out of silence, antidote
To any doubt; for never finger might
Produce that note, so different, so new:
Melodious pledge that all he promised should come true.

VI.

'It seemed to die; but who could say
Whether or when it passed the border-line
'Twixt sound and silence? for no ear so fine
That it can trace the subtle shades away;
Like prism-rays prolonged beyond our ken,
Like memories that fade, we know not how or when.

VII.

'Then strange vibrations rose and fell,
Like far sea-murmurs blending in a dream
With madrigals, whose fairy singers seem
Now near, now distant; and a curfew bell,
Whose proper tone in one air-filling crowd
Of strong harmonics hides, as in a dazzling cloud.

VIII.

'Then delicately twining falls
Of silvery chords, that quiver with sweet pain,
And melt in tremulous minors, mount again,
Brightening to fullest concords, calm recalls,
And measured pulsings, soft and sweet and slow,
Which emphasizing touch love's quiet under-glow.

IX.

'A silence. Then a solemn wail,
    Swelling far up among the harmonies,
    And shattering the crystal melodies
        To fleeting fragments glisteringly pale,
    Yet only to combine them all anew
By resolutions strange, yet always sweet and true.

X.

'Anon a thrill of all the strings;
    And then a flash of music, swift and bright,
    Like a first throb of weird Auroral light;
        Then crimson coruscations from the wings
    Of the Pole-Spirit; then ecstatic beat,
As if an angel-host went forth on shining feet.

XI.

'Soon passed the sounding starlit march,
    And then one swelling note grew full and long,
    While, like a far-off old cathedral song,
        Through dreamy length of echoing aisle and arch,
    Float softest harmonies around, above,
Like flowing chordal robes of blessing and of love.

XII.

'Thus, while the holy stars did shine
    And listen, these Æolian marvels breathed;
    While love and peace and gratitude enwreathed
        With rich delight in one fair crown were mine.
    The wind that bloweth where it listeth brought
This glory of harp-music,—not my skill or thought.'

She ceased. Then Eleanor looked up,
    And said, 'O Beatrice, I too have tried
    My finger-skill in vain. But opening now
    My window, like wise Daniel, I will set
    My little harp therein, and listening wait
    The breath of heaven, the Spirit of our God.'

Baby's Turn.

Tiny feet so busy in a tiny patter out of sight,
Little hands escaping from protecting doily white,
One in lifted eagerness, and one that grasps the baby chair,—
All impatient! Baby darling, must not sister have a share?

Only just a moment, dearie; coming, coming! don't be vexed!
Only just a moment, darling; then we'll see whose turn is next!
Ah, she knows as well as we do! Baby's turn is come at last;
Now the little mouth may open; gently, gently, not too fast.

Baby's turn! To-day 'tis only for the fruit so nice and sweet,
But a far-away to-morrow hastens on with silent feet;
When the yesterdays of life are clearest in our dimming gaze,
Baby's vision will be filled with brightly realized to-days.

Baby's turn for fair unfolding in the sunny girlhood time,
For the blossom and the breezes, for the carol and the chime;
Baby's turn to wear the crown of womanhood upon her brow,
Heavier but nobler than the fairy gold which glitters now.

Baby's turn to care for others, and to kiss away the tear,
For the joy of ministration to the suffering or the dear,
For the happiness of giving help and comfort, love and life,
Whether walking all alone, or as a blessed and blessing wife.

Baby's turn for this and more, if God should give her length of days;—
For the calmness of experience and the retrospect of praise,
For the silver trace of sorrows glistening in the sunset ray,
For the evening stillness falling on the turmoil of the day.

What though Baby's turn may come for bitter griefs and wearing fears!
Love shall lighten every trial,—love that prays and love that hears.
See! she watches and she wonders till the reverie is o'er;
Did she think she was forgotten? Now 'tis Baby's turn once more!

The Children's Triumph.

THE Sunbeams came to my window,
　　And said, 'Come out and see
The sparkle on the river,
　　The blossom on the tree!'
But never a moment parleyed I
　　With the bright-haired Sunbeams' call!
Though their dazzling hands on the leaf they laid,
I drew it away to the curtain-shade,
　　Where a sunbeam could not fall.

The Robins came to my window,
　　And said, 'Come out and sing!
Come out and join the chorus
　　Of the festival of the Spring!'
But never a carol would I trill
　　In the festival of May;
But I sat alone in my shadowy room,
And worked away in its quiet gloom,
　　And the Robins flew away.

The Children came to my window,
　　And said, 'Come out and play!
Come out with us in the sunshine,
　　'Tis such a glorious day!'
Then never another word I wrote,
　　And my desk was put away!
When the Children called me, what could I do?
The Robins might fail, and the Sunbeams too,
　　But the Children won the day.

The First Smile.

A SMILE, a smile, my darling!
　　After the weeks of pain;
The restless eye, the shaded brow
Lit with a welcome brightness now—
　　The first sweet smile again!

A smile, a smile, my darling!
   Not many days ago
We hailed the first fair snowdrop, white,
Pale, and sweet in the early light,
   After the frost and snow.

More welcome than the snowdrop,
   More gladdening than the sun,
The pale sweet smile that dawned at last,
Although so faint, and fleeting fast,
   Although the only one.

We hail it as the herald
   Of sunny summer days,
Of blessings for our darling boy,
Of peaceful love, and thankful joy,
   And fuller note of praise.

The Sunday Book.

READ to him, Connie, read as you sit,
   Cosy and warm in the great arm-chair,
   Let your hand press lovingly, lightly there,
   Let the gentle touch of your sunny hair
Over his cheek like a soft breeze flit.

Read to him, Connie! The house is still,
   The week-day lessons, the week-day play,
   And the week-day worries are hushed away
   In the golden calm of the Holy Day;
He will listen now if ever he will.

Read to him, Connie, read while you may!
   For the years will pass, and he must go
   Out in the cold world's treacherous flow,
   Danger and trial and evil to know,—
He may drift in the dark, far, far away!

Now he is happy and safe in the nest,
 Teach him to warble the songs of home,
 Teach him to soar but never to roam,
 Only to soar to a starry dome,
Linking with heaven the hearts he loves best.

Read to him, Connie! Read what you love,
 Holy and sweet be your Sabbath choice;
 And the music that dwells in a sister's voice
 Shall lure him to listen while angels rejoice,
As the soft tones blend with the harps above.

Read to him, Connie! Read of the ONE
 Who loves him most, yes, more than you!
 Read of that love, so great, so true,
 Love everlasting, yet ever new;
For who can tell but his heart may be won!

Read to him, Connie! For it may be
 That your Sunday book, like a silver bar
 Of steady light from a guiding star,
 May gleam in memory, clear and far,
Across the waves of a wintry sea.

Amy.

'I have loved you, saith the Lord.'—MALACHI 1:2.

A MY, this thy promise be,
M arvellous and sweet and free,
'Y ea, the Lord hath lovèd thee.'
H e hath loved thee, and He knows
A ll thy fears and all thy foes;
V ictor thou shalt surely be
E ver through His love to thee.
R est in quiet joy on this,—
G reater love hath none than His:
A nd may this thy life-song be,
L ove to Him that loveth thee!

'It Is Well with the Child.'[1]

ONLY one dark December time,
    With chill and gloomy hours;
And *now*—the 'everlasting spring,'
    The 'never-withering flowers.'

Only one week of weary pains,
    With suffering oppressed;
And *now*—the Sabbath that remains,
    God's everlasting rest.

Only one word of earthly speech,
    The sweetest and the first;
And *now*—the songs that angels sing
    From baby lips have burst.

Only one journey, fondly borne
    In arms of tenderest love;
And *now*—no wanderings more for him,
    Safe in the home above.

Yes, safe for ever, safe and blest,
    Where they 'go no more out';
With Jesus, whom he never grieved
    By any sin or doubt.

Not preluded by tearful prayer,
    His happy praise shall swell,
And joy of 'welcome' shall be his
    Who never knew 'farewell.'

---

[1] In memory of J. S., who fell asleep December 6, 1870, aged seven months. The day before his death he fixed his eyes upon his mother with a long gaze of wonderful intelligence and love, and after repeated effort, uttered distinctly the 'one word'—'Mamma!'

At Home To-night.

I.

THE lessons are done and the prizes won,
    And the counted weeks are past;
O the holiday joys of the girls and boys
    Who are 'home to-night' at last!
O the ringing beat of the springing feet,
    As into the hall they rush!
O the tender bliss of the first home kiss,
    With its moment of fervent hush!
So much to tell and to hear as well,
    As they gather around the glow!
Who would not part, for the joy of heart
    That only the parted can know—
        At home to-night!

II.

But all have not met, there are travellers yet
    Speeding along through the dark,
By tunnel and bridge, past river and ridge,
    To the distant, yet nearing mark.
But hearts are warm, for the winter storm
    Has never a chill for love:
And faces are bright in the flickering light
    Of the small dim lamp above.
And voices of gladness rise over the madness
    Of the whirl and the rush and the roar,
For rapid and strong it bears them along
    To a home and an open door—
        Yes, home to-night!

III.

Oh, home to-night, yes, home to-night,
    Through the pearly gate and the open door!
Some happy feet on the golden street
    Are entering now to 'go out no more.'

For the work is done and the rest begun,
    And the training time is for ever past,
And the home of rest in the mansions blest
    Is safely, joyously reached at last.
O the love and light in that home to-night!
    O the songs of bliss and the harps of gold!
O the glory shed on the new-crowned head!
    O the telling of love that can ne'er be told—
O the welcome that waits at the shining gates,
    For those who are following far, yet near;
When all shall meet at His glorious feet
    In the light and the love of His home so dear!
        Yes, 'home to-night!'

NOTE. —These verses, written a few days before Christmas, were suggested by the remark of a young friend, after picturing the merry 'breaking up' of her old schoolfellows,—'They will all be at home to-night.' The thought arose—'Perhaps some of Christ's little ones, who have been learning in His school, may be reaching His home to-night!' And while the third stanza was being written, a telegram came bearing the sad and unexpected tidings that a dear little girl of twelve years old had indeed just reached home, after a short illness, and entered the presence of the Saviour whom she had early learnt to love. The coincidence of the thought with the very hour of her departure, being unconnected with any idea of her illness, was remarkable.

Two Rings.

SHE stood by the western window,
    In the midsummer twilight fair;
And the sunset breeze leaped from the trees
    To lift her heavy hair.

Loving and lingering that good-night,
    Which again and again was said,
As ever a fresh excuse was found
    To 'put off going to bed.'

She took a ring from the table,
    Blue, with a diamond eye;
A forget-me-not that would never fade
    'Neath any wintry sky.

She placed it on her little hand,
　　And danced with sudden glee;
'Look at my ring, my pretty ring!
　　It is mine just now, you see!'

She laughed her merry ringing laugh,
　　I answered with a sigh,
Strange echo to my darling's mirth,
　　Though scarcely knowing why.

Her childish beauty touched my heart,
　　And rose to a vision fair
Of far-off days, when another ring
　　That little hand might wear.

And mine—it might be pulseless then
　　Under the churchyard tree;
So I drew her gently to my side,
　　And took her on my knee.

'It shall be yours, my darling,'
　　I said; 'but not to-day;
It *shall* be yours, my darling,
　　When I am gone away.'

She glanced up quickly in my face,
　　Not sure that she heard aright;
And the shadow that fell in the sweet brown eyes
　　Was sweeter than any light.

Then she bent her head and kissed the ring,
　　With a kiss both grave and long;
Hardly the kiss of a little child,
　　So fervent and so strong.

And hardly the tones of a little child,
　　That spoke so earnestly,—
'Yes; I will always wear it,
　　Mine it shall always be.

'But oh!' (and the eyes, love-brightened,
    Shone with a sudden tear),
'I hope I shall never wear it,
    Never, oh never, dear!'

––––––––

Five summers smoothly passed away,
    And the sixth was drawing nigh,
While herald glory woke the earth,
    And filled the dazzling sky.

An April morning, radiant
    With June-like gleam and glow,
Arose as fair as if the world
    No shade of grief could know.

A tiny packet came for me,
    With many a dark-edged fold,
And safe within it lay a ring,—
    A little ring of gold.

Oh, well I knew its carving quaint
    Of old ancestral days;
Last seen upon a waving hand
    In slanting autumn rays.

O fair young hand, that waved good-bye
    With passing grace and glee!
We knew not that it was farewell,—
    The *last* farewell for me.

The sweet bright spring that touched the earth
    With all-renewing might,
For *her* eternal beauty brought,
    Eternal life and light.

All through the solemn Passion week
    She lay so still and sweet,
A carven lily, white and pure,
    For God's own temple meet;—

Until the day when Jesus died,
    The Saviour whom she knew,
The Shepherd whom she followed home
    The shadowy portal through.

And when the evening gently closed
    That sad and sacred day,
They left the last kiss on her brow,
    And took the ring away.

———————

Two rings are always on my hand,
    The azure and the gold,
And they shall gleam together till
    My tale of life is told.

The Two Rings

A fair copy autograph in F.R.H.'s Manuscript Book Nº VI. See pages 467–470 of this book. This was Frances' niece, Evelyn, the daughter of Henry and Miriam Crane. See also pages 332–336. Evelyn was 15 when she died in April, 1868.

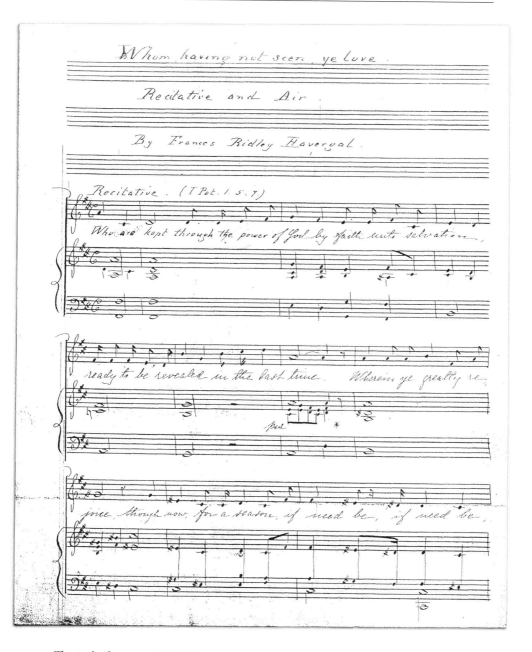

This is the first page of F.R.H.'s manuscript score of "Whom having not seen, ye love."
She was a very finely (and rarely) gifted musician and composer.

Songs.

'Bells Across the Snow.'

O CHRISTMAS, merry Christmas!
    Is it really come again?
With its memories and greetings,
    With its joy and with its pain.
There's a minor in the carol,
    And a shadow in the light,
And a spray of cypress twining
    With the holly wreath to-night.
And the hush is never broken
    By laughter light and low,
As we listen in the starlight
    To the 'bells across the snow.'

O Christmas, merry Christmas!
    'Tis not so very long
Since other voices blended
    With the carol and the song!
If we could but hear them singing
    As they are singing now,
If we could but see the radiance
    Of the crown on each dear brow;
There would be no sigh to smother
    No hidden tear to flow,
As we listen in the starlight
    To the 'bells across the snow.'

O Christmas, merry Christmas!
    This never more can be;
We cannot bring again the days
    Of our unshadowed glee.
But Christmas, happy Christmas,
    Sweet herald of goodwill,

With holy songs of glory
　　Brings holy gladness still.
For peace and hope may brighten,
　　And patient love may glow,
As we listen in the starlight
　　To the 'bells across the snow.'

Singing at Sunset.

DID you hear it at the sunset?
　　Happy, happy thrush!
Carolling and trilling
　　Through the evening hush.
Singing at the sunset,
　　Singing, singing sweet,
Where the shadows and the splendour
　　Softly, softly meet;
Pouring out the full notes,
　　Ringing, ringing loud,
When the gold is on the beeches,
　　And the crimson on the cloud!
　　　Singing at the sunset!
　　　Happy, happy song!

Shall we listen in the sunset,
　　Listen, listen long,
Silent for the glory,
　　Silent for the song?
Singing at the sunset,
　　Angel voices hear,
And the harpings of the harpers
　　Ringing, ringing clear;
Nearing all the gladness,
　　Leaving all the gloom,
When the light is on the River,
　　And the glory on the tomb!
　　　Singing at the sunset!
　　　Happy, happy song!

Heather Lintie.[1]

I.

'Heather Lintie, tell me, pray
Why the Snow-wreath went away?'

'Silent Snow-wreath sat alone,
Till she heard the laughing call
Of the merriest stream of all
   In the land.
Down the steep from stone to stone,
Shyly creeping, smiling, weeping,
   While a sunbeam held her hand,
Snow-wreath found her home ere long,
Silence melted into song.
   Now she flows, but not alone,
    Singing and rejoicing.'

II.

'Heather Lintie, tell me, pray,
Why the Burnie went away?'

'Burnie laughed adown the hill,
Keeping all the flowers awake,
Till she saw the purple lake
   Deep and still.
Down the glen from stone to stone,
Blithely dancing, glinting, glancing,
   Singing on in silver tone,
Burnie found her home ere long,
Silence sweeter far than song;
   Now she flows, but not alone,
    Resting and rejoicing.'

[1] 'Heather Lintie,' a Scotch linnet; 'Burnie,' a little brook.

III.

'Heather Lintie, tell me, pray,
Why you do not fly away?'

 Heather Lintie plumed her wing,
 Sang about a happy nest,
 Made with one who loved her best
  In the spring.
 Where beneath a boulder-stone,
 In the heather all together,
  Warmly nestle all her own.
 Heather Lintie will not roam
 From her sweet and hidden home.
  So she sings, but not alone,
   Loving and rejoicing.

Sunbeam and Dewdrop.

O SUNBEAM, O sunbeam!
 I would be a sunbeam too!
 When the winter chill
 Hushes lark and rill;
 When the thunder-showers
 Bow the weeping flowers;
 When the shadows creep,
 Cold, and dark, and deep,—
We would follow, swift and bright,
Blending all our love and light,
 Chasing winter, grim and hoary,
  Shining all the tears away—
 Turning all the gloom to glory,
  All the darkness into day.

O dewdrop, O dewdrop,
 I would be a dewdrop too!
 When the fatal glow,
 Sultry, still and slow,

Makes the scentless flowers
Droop in withering bowers,
Leaf and shade and bloom
Touched with early doom,—
We would follow, sweet and bright,
Blending life and love and light:
Making what was parched and dreary,
Glad and lovely, fresh and fair,
Softly cheering what was weary,
Sparkling, starlike, everywhere.

Dream-Singing.

I DREAMT that I was singing,
Singing all for thee:
And still the notes went ringing
Far over land and sea.

Went ringing till they found thee,
Though so far away,
And, softly floating round thee,
Made music all the day.

Made music that could cheer thee,
Full of gentle glee;
Then leaving echoes near thee,
Came back again to me.

Came back with love and blessing
On their spirit-wings,
With musical expressing
Of sweet and holy things.

I dreamt that I was singing,
Come again to me!
And all its fairy ringing
No more a dream shall be.

She Waits for Me.

'I WAIT for thee!' I said it in the splendour
  Of golden moons beneath the lonely palms.
'I wait for thee!' An echo, clear and tender,
  Fell from the height across the silver calms.
    For I had waited long,
      And hope was growing weary,
    Though faith and love were strong,
      And lit the path so dreary,—
        Till o'er the coral sea
        My love should come to me,
          'I wait for thee.'

'I wait for thee!' I said it in my dreaming,
  Then fell a hush beyond the hush of night;
And, fairer far than southern waters gleaming,
  A Presence passed in soft celestial light.
    Then calm and sweet and clear,
      A spirit voice came singing,
    Far, far away, yet near,
      Like star-bells' crystal ringing.
        Oh, well my own heart knew
        That voice so clear and true—
          'I wait for thee!'

'She waits for me!' I said it in my weeping,
  For never more she cometh o'er the sea;
She waits for me! A glorious vigil keeping
  Beyond the stars, she waiteth there for me.
    And now I wait awhile,
      Beneath the palm trees lonely.
    And learn once more to smile,
      For she hath gladness only.
        Beside the Crystal Sea,
        Until the shadows flee,
          She waits for me.

New Year's Hymn.
Is. 41.10.

At the solemn portal
Of the opening year,
Words of comfort meet us,
Hushing every fear:
Spoken through the silence
By our Father's voice,
Tender, strong & faithful,
Making us rejoice.
Onward then, & fear not,
Children of the day!
For His word shall never,
Never pass away!

4
He will never fail thee,
He will not forsake!
His eternal covenant
He will never break!
Resting on His promise,
What have we to fear?
God is all-sufficient
For the coming year.
Onward then, & fear not,
Children of the day!
For His word shall never,
Never pass away!

F.R.H. Jan 4th 1873

This is one side of a single-fold sheet manuscript of the "New Year's Hymn" on pages 423–424 of this book. Frances almost surely revised the first line of this poem after this manuscript was written. The other side of the sheet is found on the next page 480.

2

"I the Lord am with thee,
Be thou not afraid!
I will help & strengthen,
Be thou not dismayed!
Yea, I will uphold thee
With my own right hand;
Thou art called & chosen
In my sight to stand.
Onward then, & fear not,
Children of the day!
For His word shall never,
Never pass away!

3

For the years before us,
Oh what rich supplies!
For the poor & needy
Living streams shall rise;
For the sad & sinful
Shall His grace abound;
For the faint & feeble
Perfect strength be found.
Onward then, & fear not,
Children of the day!
For His word shall never,
Never pass away.

A Mountain Cantata.

'That Thy name is near, Thy wondrous works declare.'—Psalm 75:1.

The Mountain Maidens.

(Zella, Dora, Lisetta.)

A CANTATA.

————

Part I.—Sunrise.

(1.) Dawn Chorus.

The stars die out, and the moon grows dim,
   Slowly, softly, the dark is paling!
Comes o'er the eastern horizon-rim,
   Slowly, softly, a bright unveiling.

The white mist floats in the vale at rest,
   Ghostly, dimly, a silver shiver;
The golden east and the purple west
   Flushing deep with a crimson quiver.

The mountains gleam with expectant light,
   Near and grandly, or far and faintly,
In festal robing of solemn white,
   Waiting, waiting, serene and saintly.

————

Lo! on the mountain-crest, sudden and fair,
Bright herald of morning, the rose-tint is there;
Peak after peak lighteth up with the glow
That crowneth with ruby the Alpine snow.

Summit on summit, and crest beyond crest,
The beacons are spreading away to the west;
Crimson and fire, and amber and rose,
Touch with life and with glory the Alpine snows.

(2.) Chorale.

Father, who hast made the mountains,
    Who hast formed each tiny flower,
Who hast filled the crystal fountains,
    Who hast sent us sun and shower:
Hear Thy children's morning prayer,
Asking for Thy guardian care;
Keep and guide us all the day,
Lead us safely all the way.

Let Thy glorious creation
    Be the whisper of Thy power;
New and wondrous revelation
    Still unfolding every hour.
Let the blessing of Thy love
Rest upon us from above;
And may evening gladness be
Full of thanks and praise to Thee.

(3.) Recitative.—*Dora.*

Our pleasant summer work begins. You go,
O merry Zella, with the obedient herd
To upland pastures, singing all the way.
And you, Lisetta, to the sterner heights,
Where only foot of Alpine goat may pass,
Or step of mountain maiden. It is mine
To work at home preparing smooth white cheese
For winter store, and often needed gain.
And mine the joy of welcoming once more
My loving sisters when the evening falls.

(4.) SONG.—*Dora.*

The morning light flingeth
    Its wakening ray,
And as the day bringeth
    The work of the day,
The happy heart singeth;
    Awake and away!

No life can be dreary
    When work is delight;
Though evening be weary,
    Rest cometh at night;
And all will be cheery,
    If faithful and right.

When duty is treasure,
    And labour a joy,
How sweet is the leisure
    Of ended employ!
Then only can pleasure
    Be free from alloy.

[Repeat v. 1.]

(5.) SONG.—*Zella.*

Away, away! with the break of day,
    To the sunny upland slope!
Away, away! while the earliest ray
    Tells of radiant joy and hope.

    With the gentle herd that know the word
        Of kindness and of care,
    While with footsteps free they follow me,
        As I lead them anywhere.

Away, away! with a merry lay,
    And the chime of a hundred bells;
Away, away! with a carol gay,
    And an echo from the fells.

To the pastures high, where the shining sky
　　Looks down on a wealth of flowers;
To the sapphire spots, where forget-me-nots
　　Smile on through lonely hours.

Away, away! while the breezes play
　　In the fragrant summer morn;
Away, away! while the rock-walls grey
　　Resound with the Alpen-horn.

To the crags, all bright in the golden light
　　With floral diadems,
As fresh and fair, as ' rich and rare,'
　　As any royal gems.

Away, away! while the rainbow spray
　　Wreaths the silver waterfalls;
Away, away! Oh, I cannot stay
　　When the voice of the morning calls!

(6.) Recitative.—*Lisetta.*

Adieu, my Dora! Zella dear, adieu!
The quick light tinkle of the goat-bells now
Reminds me they are waiting for my call,
To follow where small flowers have dared to peep
And laugh, beside the glacier and the snow.
I shall not go alone, your love shall go with me.

(7.) Duet.—*Zella and Dora.*

Adieu, adieu till eventide!
　　The hours will quickly pass,
The shadow of the rocks will glide
　　Across the sunny grass.
We shall not mourn the lessening light,
For we shall meet at home to-night.

Adieu, adieu till eventide!
　　The hour of home and rest,

The hour that finds us side by side,
   The sweetest and the best.
For love is joy, and love is light,
And we shall meet at home to-night!

Adieu, adieu till eventide!
   'Tis but a little while!
We would not stay the morning's pride,
   Or noontide's dazzling smile.
But welcome evening's waning light,
For we shall meet at home to-night!

Part II.—Noon.

(8.) SONG.—*Lisetta.*

It is noon upon the mountains, and the breeze has died away,
And the rainbow of the morning passes from the torrent spray,
And a calm of golden silence falls upon the glistening snow,
While the shadows of the noon-clouds rest upon the glen below.

It is noon upon the mountains, noon upon the giant rocks;
Hushed the tinkle of the goat-bells, and the bleating of the flocks;
They are sleeping on the gentians, and upon the craggy height,
In the glow of Alpine noon-tide, in the glory of the light.

It is noon upon the mountains: I will rest beside the snow,
Glittering summits far above me, blue-veined glaciers far below;
I will rest upon the gentians, till the quiet shadows creep,
Cool and soft, along the mountains, waking me from pleasant sleep.

(9.) NOON CHORUS.

Rest! while the noon is high,
   Rest while the glow
Falls from the summer sky
   Over the snow.

Rest! where the Alpen-rose
   Crimsons the height,
Piercing the mountain-snows,
   Purpling the light.

Rest! while the waterfalls,
    Murmuring deep
Far-away lullabies,
    Hush thee to sleep.
        Rest! while the noon, etc.

Rest! where the mountains rise,
    Shining and white;
Piercing the deep blue skies,
    Solemn and bright.
Sleep! while the silence falls,
    Soothing to rest,
Sweetest of lullabies,
    Calming and blest.
        Rest! while the noon, etc.

(10.) RECITATIVE.—*Lisetta.*

Where am I? I was sleeping by the snow
Upon the Alpen-roses in the noon.
But am I dreaming now? The sun is low,
'Tis twilight in the valley, and I hear
No music of the goat-bells. Oh, I fear
It is no dream, but night is coming soon,
And I am all alone upon the height,
And there are small faint tracks, too quickly lost,
That need sure foot and eye in fullest light,
And crags to leap, and torrents to be crossed!
I go! may Power and Love still guard and guide aright.

(11.) SONG.—*Lisetta.*

Alone, alone! yet around me stand
    God's mountains, still and grand!
        Still and grand, serene and bright,
        Sentinels clothed in armour white,
        And helmeted with scarlet light.
           His Power is near,
           I need not fear.

Beneath the shadow of His Throne
Alone, alone, yet not alone!

Alone, alone! yet beneath me sleep
   The flowers His hand doth keep.
      Small and fair, by crag or dell,
      Trustfully closing star and bell,
      Eve by eve as twilight fell.
        His Love is near,
        I need not fear.
Beneath the rainbow of His Throne,
Alone, alone, yet not alone!

Alone, alone! yet I will not fear,
   For Power and Love are near!
      Step by step, by rock and rill,
      Trustfully onward, onward still,
      I follow home with hope and will!
        So near, so near,
        I do not fear!
Beneath the Presence of His Throne,
Alone, alone, yet not alone!

Part III.—Sunset.

(12.) SUNSET CHORUS.

     It is coming, it is coming,
     That marvellous up-summing,
Of the loveliest and grandest all in one:
     The great transfiguration,
     And the royal coronation,
Of the Monarch of the mountains by the priestly Sun.

     Watch breathlessly and hearken,
     While the forest throne-steps darken
His investiture in crimson and in fire;
     Not a herald-trumpet ringeth,
     Not a pæan echo flingeth,
There is music of a silence that is mightier far, and higher.

Then in radiant obedience,
A flush of bright allegiance
Lights up the vassal-summits and the proud peaks all around;
And a thrill of mystic glory
Quivers on the glaciers hoary,
As the ecstasy is full, and the mighty brow is crowned.

Crowned with ruby of resplendence
In unspeakable transcendence,
'Neath a canopy of purple and of gold outspread,
With rock-sceptres upward pointing,
While the glorious anointing
Of the consecrating sunlight is poured upon his head.

Then a swift and still transition
Falls upon the gorgeous vision,
And the ruby and the fire pass noiselessly away;
But the paling of the splendour
Leaves a rose-light, clear and tender,
And lovelier than the loveliest dream that melts before the day.

Oh to keep it, oh to hold it,
While the tremulous rays enfold it!
Oh to drink in all the beauty, and never thirst again!
Yet less lovely if less fleeting!
For the mingling and the meeting
Of the wonder and the rapture can but overflow in pain.

It is passing, it is passing!
While the softening glow is glassing
In the crystal of the heavens all the fairest of its rose.
Ever faintly and more faintly,
Ever saintly and more saintly,
Gleam the snowy heights around us in holiest repose.

O pure and perfect whiteness!
O mystery of brightness
Upon those still, majestic brows shed solemnly abroad!
Like the calm and blessèd sleeping
Of saints in Christ's own keeping,
When the smile of holy peace is left, last witness for their God.

(13.) SONG.—*Dora.*

The tuneful chime of the herd is still,
    For the milking hour is past,
And tinkle, tinkle, along the hill,
    The goat-bells come at last.
But sister, sister, where art thou?
We watch and wait for thy coming now.

The crimson fades from the farthest height,
    And the rose-fire pales away;
And softly, softly, the shroud of night
    Enfolds the dying day.
But sister, sister, where art thou?
We watch and wait for thy coming now.

The cold wind swells from the icy steep,
    And the pine-trees quake and moan;
And darkly, darkly the grey clouds creep,
    And thou art all alone.
O sister, sister, where art thou?
We watch and wait for thy coming now.

(14.) DUET.—*Zella and Dora.*

We will seek thee, we will find thee,
    Though the night-winds howl and sweep!
We will follow through the torrent,
    We will follow up the steep.
Follow where the Alpen-roses
    Make the mountain all aglow,
Follow, follow through the forest,
    Follow, follow to the snow!
And our Alpine call shall echo
    From the rock and from the height,
Till a gladder tone rebounding,
Thine own merry voice resounding,
    Fill us with a great delight.

> Lisetta! Lisetta!
> Hush and hearken! Call again!
> Lisetta! Lisetta!
> Hearken, hearken! All in vain!
>
> We will seek thee, we will find thee,
> In the wary chamois' haunt;
> Toil and terror, doubt and danger,
> Loving hearts shall never daunt!
> We will follow in the darkness,
> We will follow in the light;
> Follow, follow till we find thee,
> Through the noon or through the night.
> We will seek thee, we will find thee,
> Never weary till we hear,
> Over all the torrents' rushing,
> Joyous answer clearly gushing,
> Thine own Alpine echo dear!
> Lisetta! Lisetta!
> Hush and hearken! All in vain!
> Lisetta! Lisetta!
> Hearken, hearken! Call again!

(15.) TRIO.—*Zella, Dora, and Lisetta.*

LISETTA *(pp)*. I am coming!
ZELLA and DORA *(f)*. She is coming!
LISETTA *(p)*. I am coming, wait for me!
ZELLA and DORA *(p)*. She is coming!
LISETTA *(mf)*. I am coming!
ZELLA and DORA *(f)*. Come, oh come, we wait for thee!
> Nearer, nearer comes the echo,
> Nearer, nearer comes the voice,
> Nearer, nearer fall the footsteps,
> Making us indeed rejoice.
LISETTA. I am coming, wait for me!
ZELLA and DORA. Come, oh come, we wait for thee!

ZELLA, DORA, and LISETTA.

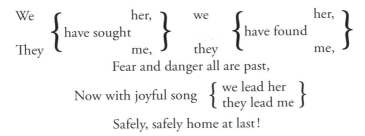

We { have sought her, } we { have found her, }
They { me, } they { me, }
Fear and danger all are past,

Now with joyful song { we lead her
they lead me }

Safely, safely home at last!

(16.) CHORUS—*Finale.*

Safe home, safe home!
Fear and danger all are past,
We are safely home at last!

Oh, the love-light shed around,
    In a rich and radiant flow,
When the lost and loved are found,
    Is the sweetest heart can know.
Fairer than the dawn-light tender,
    Fuller than the noon-tide glow,
Brighter than the sunset-splendour,
    Purer than the moonlit snow.

Now let the wild cloud sweep,
    Let the wild rain pour!
Now let the avalanche leap
    With its long grand roar!
Now let the black night fall
    On the mountain crest!
Safe are our dear ones all
    In our mountain nest.

Safe home, safe home!
Fear and danger all are past,
We are safely home at last!

This was found in F.R.H.'s Manuscript Book № VI. The previous two pages of this Manuscript book are shown on page 419.

Miscellaneous.

A Seeing Heart.[1]

To 'Fanny Crosby.'

SWEET blind singer over the sea,
Tuneful and jubilant! how can it be,
That the songs of gladness, which float so far,
As if they fell from the evening star,
Are the notes of one who never may see
'Visible music' of flower and tree,
Purple of mountain, or glitter of snow,
Ruby and gold of the sunset glow,
And never the light of a loving face?
Must not the world be a desolate place
For eyes that are sealed with the seal of years,
Eyes that are open only for tears?
How can she sing in the dark like this,
What is her fountain of light and bliss?

Oh, her heart can see, her heart can see!
And its sight is strong, and swift and free.
Never the ken of mortal eye
Could pierce so deep and far and high
As the eagle vision of hearts that dwell
In the lofty, sunlit citadel
Of Faith that overcomes the world,
With banners of Hope and Joy unfurled,
Garrisoned with God's perfect Peace,
Ringing with pæans that never cease,
Flooded with splendour bright and broad,
The glorious light of the Love of God.

---

[1] Many sweet hymns by Fanny Crosby have become known, and are warmly appreciated in England and Scotland. In answer to the inquiry, 'Who is Fanny Crosby?' the following beautiful reply was received:—'She is a blind lady, whose heart can *see splendidly* in the sunshine of God's love.' Hence the above greeting to a far-off fellow-minister of song.

Her heart can see, her heart can see!
Well may she sing so joyously!
For the King Himself, in His tender grace,
Hath shown her the brightness of His face:
And who shall pine for a glow-worm light,
When the Sun goes forth in His radiant might?
She can read His law, as a shining chart,
For His finger hath written it on her heart;
She can read His love, for on all her way
His hand is writing it every day.
'Bright cloud' indeed must that darkness be,
Where 'Jesus only' the heart can see.

Her heart can see! her heart can see,
Beyond the glooms and the mystery,
Glimpses of glory not far away,
Nearing and brightening day by day;
Golden crystal and emerald bow,
Lustre of pearl and sapphire glow,
Sparkling river and healing tree,
Evergreen palms of victory,
Harp and crown and raiment white,
Holy and beautiful dwellers in light;
A throne, and One thereon, whose face
Is the glory of that glorious place.

Dear blind sister over the sea!
An English heart goes forth to thee.
We are linked by a cable of faith and song,
Flashing bright sympathy swift along;
One in the East and one in the West,
Singing for Him whom our souls love best,
'Singing for Jesus,' telling His love
All the way to our home above,
Where the severing sea, with its restless tide,
Never shall hinder, and never divide.
Sister! what will our meeting be,
When our hearts shall sing and our eyes shall see!

July on the Mountains.

(ON THE SNOWDON RANGER TRACK.)

THERE is sultry gloom on the mountain brow,
   And a sultry glow beneath.
Oh for a breeze from the western sea,
Soft and reviving, sweet and free,
Over the shadowless hill and lea,
   Over the barren heath!

There are clouds and darkness around God's ways,
   And the noon of life grows hot;
And though His faithfulness standeth fast,
As the mighty mountains, a shroud is cast
Over its glory, solemn and vast
   Veiling, but changing it not.

Send a sweet breeze from Thy sea, O Lord,
   From Thy deep, deep sea of Love;
Though it lift not the veil from the cloudy height,
Let the brow grow cool and the footsteps light,
As it comes with holy and soothing might,
   Like the wing of a snowy dove.

My Window.

UNDER my window my couch is set,
I have gazed through it long, I am gazing yet;
      While on my table lie,
Without one look, each treasured book,
      And the verses planned,
Which will have to be copied by and by,
For the pencil fell from forgetful hand.

Though all that from my couch I see
Is the topmost bough of a leafless tree,

Clear pencilled where the blue
Dies into white as it meets the light
　　From the bright south-east,
I have revelled in my morning view,
My eyes have had a very feast.

Last night I sat without a lamp,
When the clouds broke up their sullen camp,
　　Through the tiny pointed arch,
With its one cross-bar, I watched a star,
　　As on unknown quest,
Just touch the zenith of its march,
And curve its path to the solemn west.

Now all the clouds have fled away,
The Dark has died, and the living Day
　　Has dropped the stars on her shroud;
And as I lie, the shining sky
　　Is so grandly bright,
With so much radiance endowed,
That it trembles with its wealth of light.

A wealth that is enough for me,—
I need not mountain, wood, or sea,
　　In many-tinted sight;
This seven-rayed flow of pure white glow
　　Through the sapphire air,
This calming glory of the Light,
Is so unutterably fair.

It is not idle to employ
Quick-passing moments on a joy,
　　Like these sweet morning rays.
So I do not think, but rest and drink
　　From the crystal river,
While a dewdrop of rejoicing praise
Floats up to Him, the kind Light-Giver!

Candlemas Day.

YES, take the greenery away
That smiled to welcome Christmas Day,
Untwine the drooping ivy spray.

The holly leaves are dusty all,
Whose glossy darkness robed the wall,
And one by one the berries fall.

Take down the yew, for with a touch
The leaflets drop, as wearied much
With light and song, unused to such.

Poor evergreens! Why proudly claim
The glory of your lovely name,
So soon meet only for the flame?

Another Christmas Day will show
Another green and scarlet glow,
A fresh array of mistletoe.

And this new beauty, arch or crown,
Will stiffen, gather dust, grow brown,
And in its turn be taken down.

To-night the walls will seem so bare!
Ah, well! look out, look up, for there
The Christmas stars are always fair.

They will be shining just as clear
Another and another year,
O'er all our darkened hemisphere.

So Christmas mirth has fleeted fast,
The songs of time can never last,
And all is buried with the past.

But Christmas love and joy and peace
Shall never fade and never cease,
Of God's goodwill the rich increase.

'*Now!*'

I.

A NIGHT of danger on the sea,
    Of sleeplessness and fear!
Wave after wave comes thundering
    Against the strong stone pier;
Each with a terrible recoil,
    And a grim and gathering might,
As blast on blast comes howling past,
Each wild gust wilder than the last,
    All through that awful night.

II.

Well for the ships in the harbour now,
    Which came with the morning tide;
With unstrained cable and anchor sure,
    How quietly they ride!
Well for the barque that reached at eve,
    Though watched with breathless fear,
It was sheltered first ere the tempest burst,
    It is safe inside the pier!

III.

But see! a faint and fatal light
    Out on the howling sea!
'Tis a vessel that seeks the harbour mouth,
    As in death-agony.
Though the strong stone arms are open wide,
    She has missed the only way;
'Tis all too late, for the storm drives fast,
The mighty waves have swept her past,
And against that sheltering pier shall cast
    Their wrecked and shattered prey.

IV.

Nearer and nearer the barque is borne,
    As over the deck they dash,
Where sailors five are clinging fast
To the sailless stump of the broken mast,
    Waiting the final crash.
Is it all too late? is there succour yet
    Those perishing men to reach?
Life is so near on the firm-built pier,
    That else must be death to each.

V.

There are daring hearts and powerful arms,
    And swift and steady feet,
And they rush as down to a yawning grave,
In the strong recoil of the mightiest wave,
Treading that awful path to save,
    As they trod a homeward street.
Over the boulders and foam they rush
    Into the ghastly hollow;
They fling the rope to the heaving wreck,
The aim was sure, and it strikes the deck,
    As the shouts of quick hope follow.

VI.

Reached, but not saved! there is more to do,
    A trumpet note is heard;
And over the rage and over the roar
Of billowy thunders on the shore,
    Rings out the guiding word.
There is one chance, and only one,
    All can be saved, but how?
'*The rope hold fast, but quit the mast*
    At the trumpet-signal "NOW!"'

VII.

There is a moment when the sea
    Has spent its furious strength;
A shuddering pause with a sudden swirl,
Gathering force again to hurl
Billow on billow in whirl on whirl;
    That moment comes at length—
With a single shout the '*Now*' peals out,
    And the answering leap is made.
Well for the simple hearts that just
Loosing the mast with fearless trust,
    The strange command obeyed!

VIII.

For the rope is good, and the stout arms pull
    Ere the brief storm-lull is o'er;
It is but a swift and blinding sweep
Through the waters wild and dark and deep,
    And the men are safe on shore—
Safe! though the fiend-like blast pursue,
    Safe! though the waves dash high;
But the ringing cheer that rises clear
    Is pierced with a sudden cry:

IX.

'There are but four drawn up to shore,
    And five were on the deck!'
And the straining gaze that conquers gloom
Still traces, drifting on to doom,
    One man upon the wreck.
Again they chase in sternest race
    The far-recoiling wave;
The rope is thrown to the tossing mark,
But reaches not in the windy dark
    The one they strive to save.

X.

Again they rush, and again they fail,
　　Again, and yet again:
The storm yells back defiance loud,
The breakers rear a rampart proud,
　　And roar, 'In vain, in vain!'

XI.

Then a giant wave caught up the wreck,
　　And bore it on its crest;
One moment it hung quivering there
　　In horrible arrest.
And the lonely man on the savage sea
　　A lightning flash uplit,
Still clinging fast to the broken mast
　　That he had not dared to quit.

XII.

Then horror of great darkness fell,
　　While eyes flashed inward fire;
And over all the roar and dash,
Through that great blackness came a crash,
　　A token sure and dire.
The wave had burst upon the pier,
　　The wreck was scattered wide;
Another '*Now*' would never reach
The corpse that lay upon the beach
　　With the receding tide.

XIII.

God's '*Now*' is sounding in your ears;
　　Oh, let it reach your heart!
Not only from your sinfulness
　　He bids you part;
Your righteousness as filthy rags
　　Must all relinquished be,
And only Jesus' precious death
　　Must be your plea.

XIV.

Now trust the one provided rope,
    Now quit the broken mast,
Before the hope of safety be
    For ever past.
Fear not to trust His simple word,
    So sweet, so tried, so true,
And you are safe for evermore;
    Yes,—even you!

Light at Eventide.[1]

'At evening time it shall be light.'—ZECHARIAH 14:7.

DEAR Lord, Thy good and precious Book seems written all for me;
Wherever I may open it, I find a word from Thee.
My eyes are dim, but this one verse is pillow for the night,
Thy promise that 'At Evening Time it shall be' surely 'light.'

It was not always light with me; for many a sinful year
I walked in darkness, far from Thee; but Thou hast brought me near,
And washed me in Thy precious blood, and taught me by Thy grace,
And lifted up on my poor soul the brightness of Thy face.

My Saviour died in darkness that I might live in light,
He closed His eyes in death that mine might have the heavenly sight;
He gave up all His glory to bring it down to me,
And took the sinner's place that He the sinner's Friend might be.

His Spirit shines upon His Word, and makes it sweet indeed,
Just like a shining lamp held up beside me as I read;
And brings it to my mind again alone upon my bed,
Till all abroad within my heart the love of God is shed.

I've nearly passed the shadows and the sorrows here below;
A little while—a little while, and He will come, I know,
And take me to the glory that I think is very near,
Where I shall see Him face to face and His kind welcome hear.

---

[1] Written to accompany an engraving:—An old man, worn, but peaceful, sitting at his cottage door in evening sunlight, with The Book on his knee.

And now my loving Jesus is my Light at Eventide,
The welcome Guest that enters in for ever to abide;
He never leaves me in the dark, but leads me all the way,—
So it *is* light at Evening Time, and soon it will be Day!

'Yet Speaketh.'

'YET speaketh!' though the voice is hushed that filled
    Cathedral nave or choir, like clearest bell,
With music of God's truth,—that softly thrilled
    The silence of the mourner's heart,—that fell
So sweetly, oh, so sweetly, on the ear
    Of those to whom that voice was dearest of the dear.

'Yet speaketh!' For the echo lingers yet
    Where fifty years ago his voice was heard,
And old men weep, who never can forget
    Their early gladness through his faithful word;
O'er all the waves and storms of life between,
    That voice floats on for them still powerful and serene.

'Yet speaketh!' Glowing hymns, like heavenly breeze,
    That stir us, and our soft Hosannas lift
To Hallelujahs;—holy melodies,
    Enrobed in grand sweet harmonies, a gift
Laid wholly on the altar of his God,
    Without one thought or care for this world's vain applaud:

Deep teachings from the Word he held so dear,
    Things new and old in that great treasure found;
A valiant cry, a witness strong and clear,
    A trumpet with no pale, uncertain sound:—
These shall not die, but live; his rich bequest
To that belovèd Church whose servant is at rest.

'Yet speaketh!' In the memory of those
    To whom he was indeed 'a living song,'[1]

---

[1] A blind girl, who heard two or three of his last sermons, said 'He was a living song to me.' She too, is 'gone home.' [This refers to F.R.H.'s father, William Henry Havergal.]

The voice, that like fair morning light arose,
　　Rings on with holy influence deep and strong;
Rings on, unmingled with another sound,
The sweetest, clearest still among all others found.

'Yet speaketh!' By that consecrated life,
　　The single-hearted, noble, true, and pure,
Which, lifted far above all worldly strife,
　　Could all but sin so patiently endure.
O eloquence! by this he speaketh yet;
　　For who that knew and loved could evermore forget?

'Yet speaketh!' E'en the shadow, poor and dim,
　　Of sun-traced portrait, and the cold, white stone
(All that the stranger-artist guessed of him),
　　Speak to our hearts in gentle spirit-tone,
Vocal with messages of faith and love,
And burning thoughts that fall like swift stars from above.

'Yet speaketh!' There was no last word of love,
　　So suddenly on us the sorrow fell;
His bright translation to the home above
　　Was clouded with no shadow of farewell;
His last Lent evening closed with praise and prayer,
And then began the songs of endless Easter there.

'Yet speaketh!' O my father, now more dear
　　Than ever, I have cried—'Oh, speak to me
Only once more, once more!' But now I hear
　　The far-off whisper of thy melody;
Thou art 'yet speaking' on the heavenly hill,
Each word a note of joy,—and shall we not 'be still'?

For New Year's Day, 1874.

'From glory to glory.'—2 CORINTHIANS 3:18.

'FROM glory unto glory!' Be this our joyous song,
As on the King's own highway we bravely march along!
'From glory unto glory!' O word of stirring cheer,
As dawns the solemn brightness of another glad New Year.

Our own belovèd Master 'hath many things to say';
Look forward to His teaching, unfolding day by day;
To whispers of His Spirit, while resting at His feet,
To glowing revelation, to insight clear and sweet.

'From glory unto glory!' Our faith hath seen the King,
We own His matchless beauty, as adoringly we sing:
But He hath more to show us! O thought of untold bliss!
And we press on exultingly in certain hope to this:—

To marvellous outpourings of His 'treasures new and old,'
To largess of His bounty, paid in the King's own gold,
To glorious expansion of His mysteries of grace,
To radiant unveilings of the brightness of His face.

'From glory unto glory!' What great things He hath done,
What wonders He hath shown us, what triumphs He hath won!
We marvel at the records of the blessings of the year!
But sweeter than the Christmas bells rings out His promise clear—

That 'greater things,' far greater, our longing eyes shall see!
We can but wait and wonder what 'greater things' shall be!
But glorious fulfilments rejoicingly we claim,
While pleading in the power of the All-prevailing Name.

'From glory unto glory!' What mighty blessings crown
The lives for which our Lord hath laid His own so freely down!
Omnipotence to keep us, Omniscience to guide,
Jehovah's Triune Presence within us to abide!

The fulness of His blessing encompasseth our way;
The fulness of His promises crowns every brightening day;
The fulness of His glory is beaming from above,
While more and more we realize the fulness of His love.

'From glory unto glory!' Without a shade of care,
Because the Lord who loves us will every burden bear;
Because we trust Him fully, and know that He will guide,
And know that He will keep us at His belovèd side.

'From glory unto glory!' Though tribulation fall,
It cannot touch our treasure, when Christ is all in all!

Whatever lies before us, there can be naught to fear,
For what are pain and sorrow when Jesus Christ is near?

'From glory unto glory!' O marvels of the word!
'With open face beholding the glory of the Lord,'
We, even we (O wondrous grace!) 'are changed into the same,'
The image of our Saviour, to glorify His Name.

Abiding in His presence, and walking in the light,
And seeking to 'do always what is pleasing in His sight,'
We look to Him to keep us 'all glorious within,'
Because 'the blood of Jesus Christ *is cleansing* from all sin.'

The things behind forgetting, we only gaze before,
'From glory unto glory,' that 'shineth more and more,'
Because our Lord hath said it, that such shall be our way
(O splendour of the promise!) 'unto the perfect day.'

'From glory unto glory!' Our fellow-travellers still
Are gathering on the journey! the bright electric thrill
Of quick instinctive union, more frequent and more sweet,
Shall swiftly pass from heart to heart in true and tender beat.

And closer yet, and closer the golden bonds shall be,
Enlinking all who love our Lord in pure sincerity;
And wider yet, and wider shall the circling glory glow,
As more and more are taught of God that mighty love to know.

O ye who seek the Saviour, look up in faith and love,
Come up into the sunshine, so bright and warm above!
No longer tread the valley, but, clinging to His hand,
Ascend the shining summits and view the glorious land.

Our harp-notes should be sweeter, our trumpet-tones more clear,
Our anthems ring so grandly, that all the world must hear!
Oh, royal be our music, for who hath cause to sing
Like the chorus of redeemed ones, the Children of the King!

Oh, let our adoration for all that He hath done
Peal out beyond the stars of God, while voice and life are one!
And let our consecration be real, and deep, and true;
Oh, even now our hearts shall bow, and joyful vows renew!—

'In full and glad surrender we give ourselves to Thee,
Thine utterly, and only, and evermore to be!
O Son of God, who lovest us, we will be Thine alone,
And all we are, and all we have, shall henceforth be Thine own!'

Now, onward, ever onward, from 'strength to strength' we go,
While 'grace for grace' abundantly shall from His fulness flow,
To glory's full fruition, from glory's foretaste here,
Until His Very Presence crown our happiest New Year!

Finis.[1]

ANOTHER little volume filled with varied verse and song,
Should wake another note of praise, unheard, but deep and strong;
For He who knows my truest need, and leads me day by day,
Has given the music that hath been such solace on my way.

I look up to my Father, and know that I am heard,
And ask Him for the glowing thought, and for the fitting word:
I look up to my Father, for I cannot write alone,
'Tis sweeter far to seek His strength than lean upon my own.

And so the closing verses of my new-filled book shall be
A note of praise, dear Father, sung only unto Thee,—
To Thee, who hast so helped me, to Thee who hast so blessed,
The only Friend who knows my heart, the nearest and the best.

I bless Thee, gracious Father, who hast moulded praise from pain,
And turned a wail* of mourning to a trustful calm refrain,
To many a sorrow giving me an afterward of song,
And wafting it to other hearts in comfort true and strong.

I bless Thee, gracious Father, for Thy pleasant gift to me,
And earnestly I ask Thee that it may always be
In perfect consecration laid at Thy glorious feet,
Touched with Thine altar-fire, and made an offering pure and sweet.

---

[1] Written on the last leaf of a MS. volume.
* At this point in the manuscript F.R.H. crossed out the earlier word and above that added "note" — "and turned a ~~wail~~ note of mourning . . . ." See page 748.

This is the fair copy autograph of the twenty-fifth poem in Loyal Responses (pages 547–548 of this Volume), written in F.R.H.'s "Manuscript Book Nº VIII Begun November. 1873." Frances wrote at the end of the poem, "Dictated during illness, Nov 3. 1874." This fair copy autograph was written in F.R.H.'s hand later, copied from an earlier dictated manuscript. The completion of this poem in the manuscript is found on page 558 of this book.

Loyal Responses.

Consecration Hymn.

'Here we offer and present unto Thee, O Lord, ourselves, our souls and bodies,
to be a reasonable, holy, and lively sacrifice unto Thee.'

TAKE my life, and let it be
Consecrated, Lord, to Thee.

Take my moments and my days;
Let them flow in ceaseless praise.

Take my hands, and let them move
At the impulse of Thy love.

Take my feet, and let them be
Swift and 'beautiful' for Thee.

Take my voice, and let me sing
Always, only, for my King.

Take my lips, and let them be
Filled with messages from Thee.

Take my silver and my gold;
Not a mite would I withhold.

Take my intellect, and use
Every power as Thou shalt choose.

Take my will, and make it Thine;
It shall be no longer mine.

Take my heart, it *is* Thine own;
It shall be Thy royal throne.

Take my love; my Lord, I pour
At Thy feet its treasure-store.

Take myself, and I will be
Ever, *only*, ALL for Thee.

Set Apart.

'Know that the Lord hath set apart him that is godly for Himself.'—Psalm 4:3.

I.

Set apart for Jesus!
Is not this enough,
Though the desert prospect
Open wild and rough?
Set apart for His delight,
Chosen for His holy pleasure,
Sealed to be His special treasure!
Could we choose a nobler joy?—and would we if we might?

II.

Set apart to serve Him,
Ministers of light,
Standing in His presence,
Ready day or night!
Chosen for His service blest,
He would have us always willing
Like the angel-hosts, fulfilling
Swiftly and rejoicingly, each recognised behest.

III.

Set apart to praise Him,
Set apart for this!
Have the blessèd angels
Any truer bliss?
Soft the prelude, though so clear;
Isolated tones are trembling;
But the chosen choir, assembling,
Soon shall sing together, while the universe shall hear.

IV.

Set apart to love Him,
        And His love to know!
Not to waste affection
        On a passing show.
Called to give Him life and heart,
        Called to pour the hidden treasure,
        That none other claims to measure,
Into His belovèd hand! thrice-blessèd 'set apart!'

V.

Set apart for ever
        For Himself alone!
Now we see our calling
        Gloriously shown!
Owning, with no secret dread,
        This our holy separation,
        Now the crown of consecration
Of the Lord our God shall rest upon our willing head![1]

[1] Numbers 6:7.

The Secret of a Happy Day.

'The secret of the Lord is with them that fear Him.'—Psalm 25:14.

I.

Just to let thy Father do
        What He will;
Just to know that He is true,
        And be still.
Just to follow hour by hour
        As He leadeth;
Just to draw the moment's power
        As it needeth.
Just to trust Him, this is all!
        Then the day will surely be

Peaceful, whatsoe'er befall,
    Bright and blessèd, calm and free.

II.

Just to let Him speak to thee
    Through His word,
Watching, that His voice may be
    Clearly heard.
Just to tell Him everything
    As it rises,
And at once to Him to bring
    All surprises.
Just to listen, and to stay
    Where you cannot miss His voice.
This is all! and thus to-day,
    Communing, you shall rejoice.

III.

Just to ask Him what to do
    All the day,
And to make you quick and true
    To obey.
Just to know the needed grace
    He bestoweth,
Every bar of time and place
    Overfloweth.
Just to take thy orders straight
    From the Master's own command!
Blessèd day! when thus we wait
    Always at our Sovereign's hand.

IV.

Just to recollect His love
    Always true;
Always shining from above,
    Always new.

Just to recognise its light
All-enfolding;
Just to claim its present might,
All-upholding.
Just to know it as thine own,
That no power can take away.
Is not this enough alone
For the gladness of the day?

V.

Just to trust, and yet to ask
Guidance still;
Take the training, or the task,
As He will.
Just to take the loss or gain,
As He sends it;
Just to take the joy or pain,
As He lends it.
He who formed thee for His praise
Will not miss the gracious aim;
So to-day and all thy days
Shall be moulded for the same.

VI.

Just to leave in His dear hand
Little things,
All we cannot understand,
All that stings!
Just to let Him take the care
Sorely pressing,
Finding all we let Him bear
Changed to blessing.
This is all! and yet the way
Marked by Him who loves thee best!
Secret of a happy day,
Secret of His promised rest.

The Unfailing One.

'He faileth not.'—ZEPHANIAH 3:5.

I.

HE who hath led will lead
   All through the wilderness;
He who hath fed will feed;
   He who hath blessed will bless;
He who hath heard thy cry,
   Will never close His ear;
He who hath marked thy faintest sigh,
   Will not forget thy tear.
He loveth always, faileth never;
So rest on Him, to-day, for ever!

II.

He who hath made thee whole
   Will heal thee day by day;
He who hath spoken to thy soul
   Hath many things to say.
He who hath gently taught
   Yet more will make thee know;
He who so wondrously hath wrought
   Yet greater things will show.
He loveth always, faileth never;
So rest on Him, to-day, for ever!

III.

He who hath made thee nigh
   Will draw thee nearer still;
He who hath given the first supply
   Will satisfy and fill.
He who hath given thee grace
   Yet more and more will send;
He who hath set thee in the race
   Will speed thee to the end.

He loveth always, faileth never;
So rest on Him, to-day, for ever!

IV.

He who hath won thy heart
    Will keep it true and free;
He who hath shown thee what thou art
    Will show Himself to thee.
He who hath bid thee live,
    And made thy life His own,
Life more abundantly will give,
    And keep it His alone.
He loveth always, faileth never;
So rest on Him, to-day, for ever!

V.

Then trust Him for to-day
    As thine unfailing Friend,
And let Him lead thee all the way,
    Who loveth to the end.
And let the morrow rest
    In His belovèd hand;
His good is better than our best,
    As we shall understand,—
If, trusting Him who faileth never,
We rest on Him, to-day, for ever!

On the Lord's Side.

'Thine are we, David, and on thy side, thou son of Jesse.'—1 CHRONICLES 12:18.

I.

WHO is on the Lord's side?
    Who will serve the King?
Who will be His helpers,
    Other lives to bring?

Who will leave the world's side?
　　Who will face the foe?
Who is on the Lord's side?
　　Who for Him will go?
Response.　By Thy call of mercy,
　　　　By Thy grace divine,
　　　　We are on the Lord's side;
　　　　Saviour, we are Thine.

II.

Not for weight of glory,
　　Not for crown and palm,
Enter we the army,
　　Raise the warrior-psalm;
But for Love that claimeth
　　Lives for whom He died:
He whom Jesus nameth
　　Must be on His side.
Response.　By Thy love constraining,
　　　　By Thy grace divine:
　　　　We are on the Lord's side,
　　　　Saviour, we are Thine.

III.

Jesus, Thou hast bought us,
　　Not with gold or gem,
But with Thine own life-blood,
　　For Thy diadem.
With Thy blessing filling
　　Each who comes to Thee,
Thou hast made us willing,
　　Thou hast made us free.
Response.　By Thy grand redemption,
　　　　By Thy grace divine,
　　　　We are on the Lord's side;
　　　　Saviour, we are Thine.

IV.

Fierce may be the conflict,
   Strong may be the foe,
But the King's own army
   None can overthrow.
Round His standard ranging,
   Victory is secure,
For His truth unchanging
   Makes the triumph sure.
Response. Joyfully enlisting
      By Thy grace divine,
     We are on the Lord's side;
     Saviour, we are Thine.

V.

Chosen to be soldiers
   In an alien land;
'Chosen, called, and faithful,'
   For our Captain's band;
In the service royal
   Let us not grow cold;
Let us be right loyal,
   Noble, true, and bold.
Response. Master, Thou wilt keep us,
      By Thy grace divine,
     Always on the Lord's side,
     Saviour, always Thine!

True-hearted, Whole-hearted.

I.

TRUE-HEARTED, whole-hearted, faithful and loyal,
   King of our lives, by Thy grace we will be
Under Thy standard, exalted and royal,
   Strong in Thy strength, we will battle for Thee!

II.

True-hearted, whole-hearted! Fullest allegiance
 Yielding henceforth to our glorious King;
Valiant endeavour and loving obedience
 Freely and joyously now would we bring.

III.

True-hearted! Saviour, Thou knowest our story;
 Weak are the hearts that we lay at Thy feet,
Sinful and treacherous! yet, for Thy glory,
 Heal them, and cleanse them from sin and deceit.

IV.

Whole-hearted! Saviour, belovèd and glorious,
 Take Thy great power, and reign Thou alone,
Over our wills and affections victorious,
 Freely surrendered, and wholly Thine own.

V.

Half-hearted, *false*-hearted! Heed we the warning!
 Only the whole can be perfectly true;
Bring the whole offering, all timid thought scorning,
 True-hearted only if whole-hearted too.

VI.

Half-hearted! Saviour, shall aught be withholden,
 Giving Thee part who hast given us all?
Blessings outpouring, and promises golden
 Pledging, with never reserve or recall.

VII.

Half-hearted! Master, shall any who know Thee
 Grudge Thee their lives, who hast laid down Thine own?
Nay; we would offer the hearts that we owe Thee,—
 Live for Thy love and Thy glory alone.

VIII.

Sisters, dear sisters, the call is resounding,
    Will ye not echo the silver refrain,
Mighty and sweet, and in gladness abounding,—
    'True-hearted, whole-hearted!' ringing again?

IX.

Jesus is with us, His rest is before us,
    Brightly His standard is waving above.
Brothers, dear brothers, in gathering chorus,
    Peal out the watchword of courage and love!

X.

Peal out the watchword, and silence it never,
    Song of our spirits, rejoicing and free!
'True-hearted, whole-hearted, now and for ever,
    King of our lives, by Thy grace we will be!'

'By Thy Cross and Passion.'

'He hath given us rest by His sorrow, and life by His death.'—JOHN BUNYAN.

I.

WHAT hast Thou done for me, O mighty Friend,
    Who lovest to the end!
Reveal Thyself, that I may now behold
    Thy love unknown, untold,
Bearing the curse, and made a curse for me,
That blessed and made a blessing I might be.

II.

Oh, Thou wast crowned with thorns, that I might wear
    A crown of glory fair;
'Exceeding sorrowful,' that I might be
    Exceeding glad in Thee;
'Rejected and despised,' that I might stand
Accepted and complete on Thy right hand.

III.

Wounded for my transgression, stricken sore,
  That I might 'sin no more';
Weak, that I might be always strong in Thee;
  Bound, that I might be free;
Acquaint with grief, that I might only know
Fulness of joy in everlasting flow.

IV.

Thine was the chastisement, with no release,
  That mine might be the peace;
The bruising and the cruel stripes were Thine,
  That healing might be mine;
Thine was the sentence and the condemnation,
Mine the acquittal and the full salvation.

V.

For Thee revilings, and a mocking throng,
  For me the angel-song;
For Thee the frown, the hiding of God's face,
  For me His smile of grace;
Sorrows of hell and bitterest death for Thee,
And heaven and everlasting life for me.

VI.

Thy cross and passion, and Thy precious death,
  While I have mortal breath,
Shall be my spring of love and work and praise,
  The life of all my days;
Till all this mystery of love supreme
Be solved in glory—glory's endless theme.

The Opened Fountain.

A fountain opened for sin and for uncleanliness . . . Wounded in the house of
My friends.—ZECHARIAH 13:1, 6.

I.

AND I have wounded Thee—oh, wounded Thee!—
  Wounded the dear, dear Hand that holds me fast!
Oh, to recall the word! That cannot be!
  Oh, to unthink the thought that out of reach hath passed!

II.

Sorrow and bitter grief replace my bliss;
  I could not wish that any joy should be;
There is no room for any thought but this,
  That I have sinned—have sinned—have wounded Thee!

III.

How *could* I grieve Thee so! Thou couldst have kept;
  My fall was not the failure of Thy word.
Thy promise hath no flaw, no dire 'except,'
  To neutralize the grace so royally conferred.

IV.

Oh the exceeding sinfulness of sin!
  Tenfold exceeding in the love-lit light
Of Thy sufficient grace, without, within,
  Enough for every need, in never-conquered might!

V.

With all the shame, with all the keen distress,
  Quick, 'waiting not,' I flee to Thee again;
Close to the wound, belovèd Lord, I press,
  That Thine own precious blood may overflow the stain.

VI.

O *precious* blood! Lord, let it rest on me!
  I ask not only pardon from my King,
But cleansing from my Priest. I come to Thee
  Just as I came at first,—a sinful, helpless thing.

VII.

Oh, cleanse me now! My Lord, I cannot stay
  For evening shadows and a silent hour:
Now I have sinned, and *now*, with no delay,
  I claim Thy promise and its total power.

VIII.

O Saviour, bid me 'go and sin no more,'
  And keep me always 'neath the mighty flow
Of Thy perpetual fountain; I implore
  That Thy perpetual cleansing I may fully know.

The Precious Blood of Jesus.

I.

PRECIOUS, precious blood of Jesus,
      Shed on Calvary;
Shed for rebels, shed for sinners,
      Shed for me.

II.

Precious blood, that hath redeemed us!
      All the price is paid;
Perfect pardon now is offered,
      Peace is made.

III.

Precious, precious blood of Jesus,
  Let it make thee whole;
Let it flow in mighty cleansing
  O'er thy soul.

IV.

Though thy sins are red like crimson,
  Deep in scarlet glow,
Jesu's precious blood can make them
  White as snow.

V.

Now the holiest with boldness
  We may enter in,
For the open fountain cleanseth
  From all sin.

VI.

Precious blood! by this we conquer
  In the fiercest fight,
Sin and Satan overcoming
  By its might.

VII.

Precious, precious blood of Jesus,
  Ever flowing free!
O believe it, O receive it,
  'Tis for thee!

VIII.

Precious blood, whose full atonement
  Makes us nigh to God!
Precious blood, our song of glory,
  Praise and laud!

I Remember Thee.

'Thus saith the Lord, I remember thee, the kindness of thy youth, the love of thine espousals.'
—JEREMIAH 2:2.

I.

My Lord, dost Thou indeed remember me,
          Just *me*, the least and last?
     With all the names of Thy redeemed,
     And all Thy angels, has it seemed
As though my name might perhaps be overpassed;
Yet here I find Thy word of tenderest grace,
True for this moment, perfect for my case,—
'Thus saith Jehovah, I remember thee!'

II.

My Lord, dost Thou remember *this* of me,
          The kindness of *my* youth?—
     The tremulous gleams of early days,
     The first faint thrills of love and praise,
Vibrating fitfully? Not much, in truth,
Can I bring back at memory's wondering call;
Yet Thou, my faithful Lord, rememberest all,—
'Thus saith Jehovah, I remember thee!'

III.

My Lord, dost Thou remember this of me,
          My love, so poor, so cold?
     Oh, if I had but loved Thee more!
     Yet Thou hast pardoned. Let me pour
My life's best wine for Thee, my heart's best gold
(Worthless, yet all I have), for very shame
That Thou shouldst tell me, calling me by name,—
'Thus saith Jehovah, I remember thee!'

IV.

My Lord, dost Thou remember this of me,
          The day of Thine own power?

The love of *mine* espousals sweet,
The laying wholly at Thy feet
Of heart and life, in that glad, willing hour?
That love was Thine—I gave Thee but Thine own,
And yet the Voice falls from the emerald throne,—
'Thus saith Jehovah, I remember thee!'

V.

My Lord, dost Thou remember *this* of me?
Forgetting every fall,
Forgetting all the treacherous days,
Forgetting all the wandering ways,
With fulness of forgiveness covering all;
Casting these memories, a hideous store,
Into the crimson sea, for evermore,
And only saying, 'I remember thee!'

VI.

My Lord, art Thou indeed remembering me?
Then let me not forget!
Oh, be Thy kindness all the way,
Thy everlasting love to-day,
In sweet perpetual remembrance set
Before my view, to fill my marvelling gaze,
And stir my love, and lift my life to praise,
Because Thou sayest, 'I remember thee!'

Knowing.

I.

I KNOW the crimson stain of sin,
Defiling all without, within;
But now rejoicingly I know
That He has washed me white as snow.
I praise Him for the cleansing tide,
Because I know that Jesus died.

II.

I know the helpless, hopeless plaint,
'The whole head sick, the whole heart faint';
But now I trust His touch of grace,
That meets so perfectly my case,
So tenderly, so truly deals;
Because I know that Jesus heals.

III.

I know the pang of forfeit breath,
When life in sin was life in death;
But now I know His life is mine,
And nothing shall that cord untwine,
Rejoicing in the life He gives,
Because I know that Jesus lives.

IV.

I know how anxious thought can press,
I know the weight of carefulness;
But now I know the sweet reward
Of casting all upon my Lord,
No longer bearing what He bears,
Because I know that Jesus cares.

V.

I know the sorrow that is known
To the tear-burdened heart alone;
But now I know its full relief
Through Him who was acquaint with grief,
And peace through every trial flows,
Because I know that Jesus knows.

VI.

I know the gloom amid the mirth,
The longing for the love of earth;
But now I know the Love that fills,
That gladdens, blesses, crowns, and stills,

That nothing mars and nothing moves,—
I know, I know that Jesus loves.

VII.

I know the shrinking and the fear,
When all seems wrong, and nothing clear;
But now I gaze upon His throne,
And faith sees all His foes o'erthrown,
And I can wait till He explains,
Because I know that Jesus reigns.

Trusting Jesus.

I.

I AM trusting Thee, Lord Jesus,
    Trusting only Thee;
Trusting Thee for full salvation,
    Great and free.

II.

I am trusting Thee for pardon;
    At Thy feet I bow,
For Thy grace and tender mercy,
    Trusting now.

III.

I am trusting Thee for cleansing
    In the crimson flood;
Trusting Thee to make me holy
    By Thy blood.

IV.

I am trusting Thee to guide me;
    Thou alone shalt lead!
Every day and hour supplying
    All my need.

V.

I am trusting Thee for power;
 Thine can never fail!
Words which Thou Thyself shalt give me,
  Must prevail.

VI.

I am trusting Thee, Lord Jesus:
 Never let me fall!
I am trusting Thee for ever,
  And for all.

Looking unto Jesus.

I.

Looking unto Jesus!
 Battle-shout of faith,
Shield o'er all the armour,
 Free from scar or scathe.
Standard of salvation,
 In our hearts unfurled,
Let its elevation
 Overcome the world!

II.

Look away to Jesus,
 Look away from all;
Then we need not stumble,
 Then we shall not fall.
From each snare that lureth,
 Foe or phantom grim,
Safety this ensureth:
 Look away to Him.

III.

Looking into Jesus,
        Wonderingly we trace
Heights of power and glory,
        Depths of love and grace.
Vistas far unfolding
        Ever stretch before,
As we gaze, beholding
        Ever more and more.

IV.

Looking up to Jesus,
        On the emerald throne!
Faith shall pierce the heavens
        Where our King is gone.
Lord, on Thee depending,
        Now, continually,
Heart and mind ascending,
        Let us dwell with Thee.

Shining.

I.

ARE you *shining* for Jesus, dear one?
        You have given your heart to Him;
But is the light strong within it,
        Or is it but pale and dim?
Can *everybody* see it,—
        That Jesus is all to you?
That your love to Him is burning
        With radiance warm and true?
Is the seal upon your forehead,
        So that it *must* be known
That you are 'all for Jesus,'—
        That your heart is all His own?

II.

Are you shining for Jesus, dear one?
    You remember the first sweet ray,
When the sun arose upon you
    And brought the gladsome day;
When you heard the gospel message,
    And Jesus Himself drew near,
And helped you to trust Him simply,
    And took away your fear;
When the darkness and the shadows
    Fled like a weary night,
And you felt that you could praise Him,
    And everything seemed bright.

III.

Are you shining for Jesus, dear one,
    So that the holy light
May enter the hearts of others,
    And make them glad and bright?
Have you spoken a word for Jesus,
    And told to some around,
Who do not care about Him,
    What a Saviour *you* have found?
Have you lifted the lamp for others,
    That has guided your own glad feet?
Have you echoed the loving message,
    That seemed to you so sweet?

IV.

Are you shining for Jesus, dear one,—
    Shining for Him all day,
Letting the light burn always
    Along the varied way?
Always,—when those beside you
    Are walking in the dark?
Always,—when no one is helping,
    Or heeding your tiny spark?

Not idly letting it flicker
    In every passing breeze
Of pleasure or temptation,
    Of trouble or of ease?

V.

Are you shining for Jesus, dear one,—
    Shining just everywhere,
Not only in easy places,
    Not only just here or there?
Shining in happy gatherings,
    Where all are loved and known?
Shining where all are strangers?
    Shining when quite alone?
Shining at home, and making
    True sunshine all around?
Shining abroad, and faithful—
    Perhaps among faithless—found?

VI.

Are you shining for *Jesus,* dear one,
    Not for yourself at all?
Not because dear ones, watching,
    Would grieve if your lamp should fall?
Shining because you are walking
    In the Sun's unclouded rays,
And you cannot help reflecting
    The light on which you gaze?
Shineth because it shineth
    So warm and bright above,
That you *must* let out the gladness,
    And you *must* show forth the love?

VII.

Are you shining for Jesus, dear one?
    Or is there a little sigh
That the lamp His love had lighted
    Does not burn clear and high?

Is the heavenly crown that waits you,
    Still, still without a star,
Because your light was hidden,
    And sent no rays afar?
Do you feel you have not loved Him
    With a love right brave and loyal,
But have faintly fought and followed
    His banner bright and royal?

VIII.

Oh, come again to Jesus!
    Come as you came at first,
And tell Him all that hinders,
    And tell Him all the worst;
And take His sweet forgiveness
    As you took it once before,
And hear His kind voice saying,
    'Peace! go, and sin no more!'
Then ask for grace and courage
    His name to glorify,
That never more His precious light
    Your dimness may deny.

IX.

Then rise, and, 'watching daily,'
    Ask Him your lamp to trim
With the fresh oil He giveth,
    That it may not burn dim.
Yes, rise and shine for Jesus!
    Be brave, and bright, and true
To the true and loving Saviour,
    Who gave Himself for you.
Oh, shine for Jesus, dear one,
    And henceforth be your way
Bright with the light that shineth
    Unto the perfect day!

Growing.

I.

UNTO him that hath, Thou givest
  Ever 'more abundantly.'
Lord, I live because Thou livest,
  Therefore give more life to me;
Therefore speed me in the race;
Therefore let me grow in grace.

II.

Deepen all Thy work, O Master,
  Strengthen every downward root,
Only do Thou ripen faster,
  More and more, Thy pleasant fruit.
Purge me, prune me, self abase,
Only let me grow in grace.

III.

Jesus, grace for grace outpouring,
  Show me ever greater things;
Raise me higher, sunward soaring,
  Mounting as on eagle-wings.
By the brightness of Thy face,
Jesus, let me grow in grace.

IV.

Let me grow by sun and shower,
  Every moment water me;
Make me really hour by hour
  More and more conformed to Thee,
That Thy loving eye may trace,
Day by day, my growth in grace.

V.

Let me then be always growing,
    Never, never standing still;
Listening, learning, better knowing
    Thee and Thy most blessèd will.
Till I reach Thy holy place,
Daily let me grow in grace.

Resting.

'This is the rest wherewith ye may cause the weary to rest; and this is the refreshing.'
—Isaiah 28:12.

I.

RESTING on the faithfulness of Christ our Lord;
Resting on the fulness of His own sure word;
Resting on His power, on His love untold;
Resting on His covenant secured of old.

II.

Resting 'neath His guiding hand for untracked days;
Resting 'neath His shadow from the noontide rays;
Resting at the eventide beneath His wing,
In the fair pavilion of our Saviour King.

III.

Resting in the fortress while the foe is nigh;
Resting in the lifeboat while the waves roll high;
Resting in His chariot for the swift glad race;
Resting, always resting in His boundless grace.

IV.

Resting in the pastures, and beneath the Rock;
Resting by the waters where He leads His flock;
Resting, while we listen, at His glorious feet;
Resting in His very arms!—O rest complete!

V.

Resting and believing, let us onward press,
Resting in Himself, the Lord our Righteousness;
Resting and rejoicing, let His saved ones sing,
Glory, glory, glory be to Christ our King!

Filling.

'Filled with all the fulness of God.'—EPHESIANS 3:19.

I.

HOLY Father, Thou hast spoken
    Words beyond our grasp of thought,—
Words of grace and power unbroken,
    With mysterious glory fraught.

II.

Promise and command combining,
    Doubt to chase and faith to lift;
Self renouncing, all resigning,
    We would claim this mighty gift.

III.

Take us, Lord, oh, take us truly,
    Mind and soul and heart and will;
Empty us and cleanse us throughly,
    Then with all Thy fulness fill.

IV.

Lord, we ask it, hardly knowing
    What this wondrous gift may be;
But fulfil to overflowing,—
    Thy great meaning let us see.

V.

Make us in Thy royal palace
　　Vessels worthy for the King;
From Thy fulness fill our chalice,
　　From Thy never-failing spring.

VI.

Father, by this blessèd filling,
　　Dwell Thyself in us, we pray;
We are waiting, Thou art willing,
　　Fill us with Thyself to-day!

Increase Our Faith.

'Lord, increase our faith.'—LUKE 17:5.

I.

INCREASE our faith, belovèd Lord!
　　For Thou alone canst give
The faith that takes Thee at Thy word,
　　The faith by which we live.

II.

Increase our faith! So weak are we,
　　That we both may and must
Commit our very faith to Thee,
　　Entrust to Thee our trust.

III.

Increase our faith! for there is yet
　　Much land to be possessed;
And by no other strength we get
　　Our heritage of rest.

IV.

Increase our faith! On this broad shield
　　'*All*' fiery darts be caught;
We must be victors in the field
　　Where Thou for us hast fought.

V.

Increase our faith, that we may claim
　　Each starry promise sure,
And *always* triumph in Thy name,
　　And to the end endure.

VI.

Increase our faith, O Lord, we pray,
　　That we may not depart
From Thy commands, but *all* obey
　　With free and loyal heart.

VII.

Increase our faith—increase it still—
　　From heavenward hour to hour,
And in us gloriously ' fulfil
　　The work of faith with power.'

VIII.

Increase our faith, that never dim
　　Or trembling it may be,
Crowned with the ' perfect peace' of him
　　' Whose mind is stayed on Thee.'

IX.

Increase our faith, for Thou hast prayed
　　That it should never fail;
Our stedfast anchorage is made
　　With Thee, within the veil.

X.

Increase our faith, that unto Thee
    More fruit may still abound;
That it may grow 'exceedingly,'
    And to Thy praise be found.

XI.

Increase our faith, O Saviour dear,
    By Thy sweet sovereign grace,
Till, changing faith for vision clear,
    We see Thee face to face!

'Nobody Knows but Jesus.'

I.

'NOBODY knows but Jesus!'
    'Tis only the old refrain
Of a quaint, pathetic slave-song,
    But it comes again and again.

II.

I only heard it quoted,
    And I do not know the rest;
But the music of the message
    Was wonderfully blessed.

III.

For it fell upon my spirit
    Like sweetest twilight psalm,
When the breezy sunset waters
    Die into starry calm.

IV.

'Nobody knows but Jesus!'
    Is it not better so,

That no one else but Jesus,
    My own dear Lord, should know?

V.

When the sorrow is a secret
    Between my Lord and me,
I learn the fuller measure
    Of His quick sympathy.

VI.

Whether it be so heavy,
    That dear ones could not bear
To know the bitter burden
    They could not come and share!

VII.

Whether it be so tiny,
    That others could not see
Why it should be a trouble,
    And seem so real to me:

VIII.

Either and both, I lay them
    Down at my Master's feet,
And find them, alone with Jesus,
    Mysteriously sweet.

IX.

Sweet, for they bring me closer
    To the dearest, truest Friend;
Sweet, for He comes the nearer,
    As 'neath the cross I bend;

X.

Sweet, for they are the channels
 Through which His teachings flow;
Sweet, for by these dark secrets
 His heart of love I know.

XI.

'Nobody knows but Jesus!'
 It is music for to-day,
And through the darkest hours
 It will chime along the way.

XII.

'Nobody knows but Jesus!'
 My Lord, I bless Thee now
For the sacred gift of sorrow
 That no one knows but Thou.

He Is Thy Life.

I.

Jesus, Thy life is mine!
Dwell evermore in me;
 And let me see
That nothing can untwine
 My life from Thine.

II.

Thy life in me be shown!
Lord, I would henceforth seek
 To think and speak
Thy thoughts, Thy words alone,
 No more my own.

III.

Thy love, Thy joy, Thy peace,
Continuously impart
          Unto my heart;
Fresh springs, that never cease,
          But still increase.

IV.

The blest reality
Of resurrection power,
          Thy Church's dower,
Life more abundantly,
          Lord, give to me!

V.

Thy fullest gift, O Lord,
Now at Thy feet I claim,
          Through Thy dear name!
And touch the rapturous chord
          Of praise forth poured.

VI.

Jesus, my life is Thine,
And evermore shall be
          Hidden in Thee!
For nothing can untwine
          Thy life from mine.

Enough.

I.

I AM so weak, dear Lord, I cannot stand
          One moment without Thee!
But oh! the tenderness of Thine enfolding,
And oh! the faithfulness of Thine upholding,

And oh! the strength of Thy right hand!
    That strength is enough for me!

II.

I am so needy, Lord, and yet I know
    All fulness dwells in Thee;
And hour by hour that never-failing treasure
Supplies and fills, in overflowing measure,
My least, my greatest need; and so
    Thy grace is enough for me!

III.

It is so sweet to trust Thy word alone:
    I do not ask to see
The unveiling of Thy purpose, or the shining
Of future light on mysteries untwining:
Thy promise-roll is all my own,—
    Thy word is enough for me!

IV.

The human heart asks love; but now I know
    That my heart hath from Thee
All real, and full, and marvellous affection,
So near, so human; yet divine perfection
Thrills gloriously the mighty glow!
    Thy love is enough for me!

V.

There were strange soul-depths, restless, vast, and broad,
    Unfathomed as the sea;
An infinite craving for some infinite stilling;
But now Thy perfect love is perfect filling!
Lord Jesus Christ, my Lord, my God,
    Thou, Thou art enough for me!

All.

I.

GOD'S reiterated 'ALL!'
   O wondrous word of peace and power!
Touching with its tuneful fall
   The rising of each hidden hour,
           All the day.

II.

Only *all* His word believe,
   All peace and joy your heart shall fill,
All things asked ye shall receive:
   This is Thy Father's word and will,
           For to-day.

III.

' *All* I have is thine,' saith He.
   ' *All* things are yours,' He saith again;
All the promises for thee
   Are sealed with Jesus Christ's Amen,
           For to-day.

IV.

He shall *all* your need supply,
   And He will make *all* grace abound,
*Al*ways *all* sufficiency
   In Him for *all* things shall be found,
           For to-day.

V.

All His work He shall fulfil,
   All the good pleasure of His will,
Keeping thee in *all* thy ways,
   And with thee always, ' *all* the days,'
           And to-day!

Only.

I.

ONLY a mortal's powers,
    Weak at their fullest strength;
Only a few swift-flashing hours,
    Short at their fullest length.

II.

Only a page for the eye,
    Only a word for the ear,
Only a smile, and by and by
    Only a quiet tear.

III.

Only one heart to give,
    Only one voice to use;
Only one little life to live,
    And only one to lose.

IV.

Poor is my best, and small:
    How could I dare divide?
Surely my Lord shall have it all,
    He shall not be denied!

V.

All! for far more I owe
    Than all I have to bring;
All! for my Saviour loves me so!
    All! for I love my King!

VI.

All! for it is His own,
    He gave the tiny store;
All! for it must be His alone;
    All! for I have no more.

VII.

All! for the last and least
    He stoopeth to uplift:
The altar of my great High Priest
    Shall sanctify my gift.

My Master.[1]

'I love my master; .... I will not go out free. And he shall serve him for ever.'
—Exodus 21:5, 6.

I.

I LOVE, I love my Master,
    I will not go out free,
For He is my Redeemer,
    He paid the price for me.

II.

I would not leave His service,
    It is so sweet and blest;
And in the weariest moments
    He gives the truest rest.

III.

I would not halve my service,
    His only it must be,—
His *only,* who so loved me
    And gave Himself for me.

---

[1] See the poem on the same text, written on the same day as Frances' poem, by her sister Ellen, on pages 1097–1101 of this book.

IV.

My Master shed His life-blood
      My vassal life to win,
And save me from the bondage
      Of tyrant self and sin.

V.

He chose me for His service,
      And gave me power to choose
That blessèd, 'perfect freedom'
      Which I shall never lose:

VI.

For He hath met my longing
      With word of golden tone,
That I shall serve for ever
      Himself, Himself alone.

VII.

'Shall serve Him' hour by hour,
      For He will show me how;
My Master is fulfilling
      His promise even now!

VIII.

'Shall serve Him,' and 'for ever';
      O hope most sure, most fair!
The perfect love outpouring
      In perfect service there!

IX.

Rejoicing and adoring,
      Henceforth my song shall be:
I love, I love my Master,
      I will not go out free!

Perfect Peace.

In illness.

I.

Like a river glorious
    Is God's perfect peace,
Over all victorious
    In its bright increase.
Perfect—yet it floweth
    Fuller every day;
Perfect—yet it groweth
    Deeper all the way.
    Chorus. Stayed upon Jehovah,
            Hearts are fully blest,
           Finding, as He promised,
            Perfect peace and rest.

II.

Hidden in the hollow
    Of His blessèd hand,
Never foe can follow,
    Never traitor stand.
Not a surge of worry,
    Not a shade of care,
Not a blast of hurry
    Touch the spirit there.
    Chorus. Stayed upon Jehovah,
            Hearts are fully blest,
           Finding, as He promised,
            Perfect peace and rest.

III.

Every joy or trial
    Falleth from above,
Traced upon our dial
    By the Sun of Love.

We may trust Him solely
　　All for us to do;
They who trust Him wholly,
　　Find Him wholly true.
　　Chorus. Stayed upon Jehovah,
　　　　　　Hearts are fully blest,
　　　　　Finding, as He promised,
　　　　　Perfect peace and rest.

'I Am with Thee!'

I.

'I am with thee!' He hath said it
　　In His truth and tender grace;
Sealed the promise, grandly spoken,
With how many a mighty token
　　Of His love and faithfulness.

II.

He is with thee!—In thy dwelling,
　　Shielding thee from fear of ill;
All thy burdens kindly bearing,
For thy dear ones gently caring,
　　Guarding, keeping, blessing still.

III.

He is with thee!—In thy service
　　He is with thee 'certainly,'
Filling with the Spirit's power,
Giving in the needing hour
　　His own messages by thee.

IV.

He is with thee!—With thy spirit,
　　With thy lips, or with thy pen;

In the quiet preparation,
In the heart-bowed congregation,
   Nevermore alone again!

V.

He is with thee!—With thee always,
   All the nights and all the days;
Never failing, never frowning,
With His loving-kindness crowning,
   Tuning all thy life to praise.

VI.

He is with thee!—Thine own Master,
   Leading, loving to the end;
Brightening joy and lightening sorrow,
All to-day, yet *more* to-morrow,
   King and Saviour, Lord and Friend.

VII.

He is with thee!—Yes, for ever,
   Now, and through eternity;
Then with Him for ever dwelling,
Thou shalt share His joy excelling,
   Thou with Christ, and Christ with thee!

Trust and Distrust.

I.

DISTRUST thyself, but trust His grace;
   It is enough for thee!
In every trial thou shalt trace
   Its all-sufficiency.

II.

Distrust thyself, but trust His strength;
   In Him thou shalt be strong:

His weakest ones may learn at length
    A daily triumph-song.

III.

Distrust thyself, but trust His love;
    Rest in its changeless glow:
And life or death shall only prove
    Its everlasting flow.

IV.

Distrust thyself, but trust alone
    In Him, for all—for ever!
And joyously thy heart shall own
    That Jesus faileth never.

Without Carefulness.

'I would have you without carefulness.'—1 Corinthians 7:32.

I.

Master! how shall I bless Thy name
    For Thy tender love to me,
For the sweet enablings of Thy grace,
    So sovereign, yet so free,
That have taught me to obey Thy word
    And cast my care on Thee!

II.

They tell of weary burdens borne
    For discipline of life,
Of long anxieties and doubts,
    Of struggle and of strife,
Of a path of dim perplexities
    With fears and shadows rife.

III.

Oh, I have trod that weary path,
 With burdens not a few,
With shadowy faith that Thou would'st lead
 And help me safely through,
Trying to follow and obey,
 And bear my burdens too.

IV.

Master! dear Master, Thou didst speak,
 And yet I did not hear,
Or long ago I might have ceased
 From every care and fear,
And gone rejoicing on my way
 From brightening year to year.

V.

Just now and then some steeper slope
 Would seem so hard to climb,
That I *must* cast my load on Thee;
 And I left it for a time,
And wondered at the joy at heart,
 Like sweetest Christmas chime.

VI.

A step or two on wingèd feet,
 And then I turned to share
The burden Thou hadst taken up
 Of ever-pressing care;
So what I would not leave with Thee
 Of course I had to bear.

VII.

At last Thy precious precepts fell
 On opened heart and ear,
A varied and repeated strain
 I could not choose but hear,

Enlinking promise and command,
　　Like harp and clarion clear:

VIII.

'No anxious thought upon thy brow
　　The watching world should see;
No carefulness! O child of God,
　　For *nothing* careful be!
But cast thou *all* thy care on Him
　　Who always cares for thee.'

IX.

Did not Thy loving Spirit come
　　In gentle, gracious shower,
To work Thy pleasure in my soul
　　In that bright, blessèd hour,
And to the word of strong command
　　Add faith and will and power?

X.

It was Thy word, it was Thy will—
　　That was enough for me!
Henceforth no care shall dim my trust,
　　For all is cast on Thee;
Henceforth my inmost heart shall praise
　　The grace that set me free.

XI.

And now I find Thy promise true,
　　Of perfect peace and rest;
I cannot sigh—I can but sing
　　While leaning on Thy breast,
And leaving everything to Thee,
　　Whose ways are always best.

XII.

I never thought it could be thus,—
    Month after month to know
The river of Thy peace without
    One ripple in its flow;
Without one quiver in the trust,
    One flicker in its glow.

XIII.

Oh, Thou hast done far more for me
    Than I had asked or thought!
I stand and marvel to behold
    What Thou, my Lord, hast wrought,
And wonder what glad lessons yet
    I shall be daily taught.

XIV.

How shall I praise Thee, Saviour dear,
    For this new life so sweet,
For taking all the care I laid
    At Thy belovèd feet,
Keeping Thy hand upon my heart
    To still each anxious beat!

XV.

I want to praise, with life renewed,
    As I never praised before;
With voice and pen, with song and speech,
    To praise Thee more and more,
And the gladness and the gratitude
    Rejoicingly outpour.

XVI.

I long to praise Thee more, and yet
    This is no care to me:
If Thou shalt fill my mouth with songs,
    Then I will sing to Thee;

And if my silence praise Thee best,
  Then silent I will be.

XVII.

Yet if it be Thy will, dear Lord,
  Oh, send me forth, to be
Thy messenger to careful hearts,
  To bid them taste and see
How good Thou art to those who cast
  All, all their care on Thee!

Thy Reign.

'Righteousness, and peace, and joy in the Holy Ghost.'—ROMANS 14:17.

I.

THY reign is righteousness;
  Not mine, but Thine!—
A covering no less
Than the broad, bright waves of Thy great sea,
  That roll triumphantly
From line to pole, and pole to line;
  A reign where every rebel thought
  In sweet captivity
To Thine obedience is brought.

II.

Thy reign is perfect peace;
  Not mine, but Thine!—
A stream that cannot cease,
For its fountain is Thy heart. O depth unknown!
  Thou givest of Thine own,
Pouring from Thine and filling mine.
The 'noise of war' hath passed away;
  God's peace is on the throne,
Ruling with undisputed sway.

III.

Thy reign is joy divine!
Not mine, but Thine,
Or else not any joy to me!
For a joy that flowed not from Thine own,
Since Thou hast reigned alone
Were vacancy or misery.
O sunshine of Thy realm, how bright
This radiance from Thy throne,
Unspeakable in calmest light!

IV.

Thy reign shall still increase!
I claim Thy word,—
Let righteousness and peace
And joy in the Holy Ghost be found,
And more and more abound
In me, through Thee, O Christ my Lord;
Take unto Thee Thy power, who art
My Sovereign, many-crowned!
Stablish Thy kingdom in my heart.

Tried, Precious, Sure.

JESUS CHRIST

'The Same yesterday, and to-day, and for ever.'—HEBREWS 13:8.
'A stone, a tried stone, a precious corner stone, a sure foundation.'—ISAIAH 28:16.

I.

THROUGH the yesterday of ages,
Jesus, Thou hast been The Same;
Through our own life's chequered pages,
Still the one dear changeless name.
Well may we in Thee confide,
Faithful Saviour, proved and 'TRIED!'

II.

Joyfully we stand and witness
    Thou art still to-day The Same;
In Thy perfect, glorious fitness,
    Meeting every need and claim.
Chiefest of ten thousand Thou!
Saviour, O most 'PRECIOUS,' now!

III.

Gazing down the far for ever,
    Brighter glows the one sweet Name
Stedfast radiance, paling never,
    Jesus, Jesus! still The Same.
Evermore 'Thou shalt endure,'
Our own Saviour, strong and 'SURE!'

Just When Thou Wilt.[1]

I.

JUST when Thou wilt, O Master, call!
Or at the noon, or evening fall,
Or in the dark, or in the light,—
Just when Thou wilt, it must be right.

II.

Just when Thou wilt, O Saviour, come,
Take me to dwell in Thy bright home!
Or when the snows have crowned my head,
Or ere it hath one silver thread.

III.

Just when Thou wilt, O Bridegroom, say,
'Rise up, my love, and come away!'

[1] Dictated in illness.

Open to me Thy golden gate
Just when Thou wilt, or soon, or late.

IV.

Just when Thou wilt—Thy time is best—
Thou shalt appoint my hour of rest,
Marked by the Sun of perfect love,
Shining unchangeably above.

V.

Just when Thou wilt!—no choice for me!
Life is a gift to use for Thee;
Death is a hushed and glorious tryst,
With Thee, my King, my Saviour, Christ!

The fair copy autograph of the last poem in Loyal Responses, in F.R.H.'s Manuscript Book Nº VIII. See also page 508 for the first part of "Perfect Peace."

Verses on Texts.

Isaiah 7:4.

'Be quiet; fear not.'

THOU layest Thy hand on the fluttering heart,
    And sayest, 'Be still!'
The silence and shadow are only a part
    Of Thy sweet will.
Thy Presence is with me, and where Thou art
    I fear no ill.

Deuteronomy 28:12.

'The Lord shall open unto thee His good treasure, the heaven to give the rain unto thy land in his season, and to bless all the work of thine hand.'

HIS love is the key and His glory the measure
    Of grace all-abounding and knowledge and light:
To thee shall be opened this infinite treasure,
    To thee, the unsearchable riches of Christ.

2 Chronicles 32:8.

'With him is an arm of flesh; but with us is the Lord our God to help us, and to fight our battles. And the people rested themselves upon the words of Hezekiah king of Judah.'

UPON Thy word I rest,
    So strong, so sure;
So full of comfort blest,
    So sweet, so pure.
The word that changeth not, that faileth never!
My King! I rest upon Thy word for ever.

Psalm 37:7.

'Rest in the Lord ("Be silent to the Lord," margin), and wait patiently for Him.'

REST, and be silent! For, faithfully listening,
    Patiently waiting, thine eyes shall behold
Pearls in the waters of quietness glistening,
    Treasures of promise that He shall unfold.
Rest, and be silent! for Jesus is here,
Calming and stilling each ripple of fear.

Esther 8:8.

'Write ye also for the Jews, as it liketh you, in the king's name, and seal it with the king's ring: for the writing which is written in the king's name, and sealed with the king's ring, may no man reverse.'

FOR He hath given us a changeless writing,
    Royal decrees that light and gladness bring;
Signed with His name in glorious inditing,
    Sealed on our hearts with His own signet ring.

2 Corinthians 10:5.

'Casting down imaginations, and every high thing that exalteth itself against the knowledge of God, and bringing into captivity every thought to the obedience of Christ.'

LET every thought
    Be captive brought,
Lord Jesus Christ, to Thine own sweet obedience!
    That I may know,
    In ebbless flow,
The perfect peace of full and pure allegiance.

Matthew 11:26.

'Even so, Father: for so it seemed good in Thy sight.'

AND if it seemeth good to Thee, my Father,
　　Shall it seem aught but good to me?
Thy will be done! Thou knowest I would rather
　　Leave all with Thee.

Ezekiel 20:12.

'Moreover also I gave them my sabbaths, to be a sign between me and them, that they might know that I am the Lord that sanctify them.'

THE token of His truth and care, the gift that He hath blessed,
The pledge of our inheritance, the earnest of His rest;
The diamond hours of holy light, the God-entrusted leisure:
Oh for a heart to prize aright this rich and heavenly treasure!

Psalm 43:3.

'O send out Thy light and Thy truth: let them lead me; let them bring me unto Thy holy hill, and to Thy tabernacles.'

THY light and truth forth-sending
　　From Thy own radiant side,
　　Be Thou our Guard and Guide!
On Thee alone depending,
No darkness can affright;
Thy shield of Truth and Light,
Clear-flashing through the night,
　　Is all-defending.

Psalm 147:11.

'The Lord taketh pleasure in them that fear Him, in those that hope in His mercy.'

O MYSTERY of grace,
That chooseth us to stand before Thy face,
To be Thy 'special treasure,'
Thy portion, Thy delight, Thine own;
That taketh pleasure
In them that fear Thy Name, that hope alone
In Thy sweet mercy's boundless measure!

Genesis 12:2.

'And I will make of thee a great nation, and I will bless thee, and make thy name great; and thou shalt be a blessing.'

THY Spirit's fulness on him rest,
Thy love his sunshine be,
And may he still, while doubly blest,
A blessing be from Thee.
Be his the everlasting name
Inscribed by Thy own hand,
That he the promised home may claim
In Thine own Holy Land.

Genesis 5:24.

'Enoch walked with God: and he was not; for God took him.'

OH may'st thou walk! from hour to hour
Of every passing year,
Keeping so very near
To Him whose power is love, whose love is power.
So may'st thou walk! in His clear light,
Leaning on Him alone,
Thy life His very own,
Until He takes thee up to walk with Him in white.

Ezekiel 33:10, Isaiah 53:6.

'Therefore, O thou son of man, speak unto the house of Israel; Thus ye speak, saying, If our transgressions and our sins be upon us, and we pine away in them, how should we then live?'

'All we like sheep have gone astray; we have turned every one to his own way; and the Lord hath laid on Him the iniquity of us all.'

ON Thee, the Lord
    My mighty sins hath laid;
And against Thee Jehovah's sword
    Flashed forth its fiery blade.
The stroke of justice fell on Thee,
    That it might never fall on me.

Job 11:17.

'And thine age shall be clearer than the noonday; thou shalt shine forth, thou shalt be as the morning.'

FEAR not the westering shadows,
    O children of the day!
For brighter still and brighter
    Shall be your homeward way.
Resplendent as the morning,
    With fuller glow and power,
And clearer than the noonday,
    Shall be your sunset hour.

Isaiah 44:22, 23.

'I have blotted out, as a thick cloud, thy transgressions, and, as a cloud, thy sins: return unto Me; for I have redeemed thee.

'Sing, O ye heavens; for the Lord hath done it: shout, ye lower parts of the earth: break forth into singing, ye mountains, O forest, and every tree therein: for the Lord hath redeemed Jacob, and glorified Himself in Israel.'

O MOUNTAIN heights, break forth and sing
    In colour-music fair and sweet!
O forest depths, awake and bring
    Your delicate odours to His feet.

Sing, for the Lord hath done it!
Proclaim Redemption, for He won it!
Let Easter hallelujahs rise from every living thing!

Song of Solomon 5:16.

'Yea, He is altogether lovely.'

THERE is One, so fair, so bright,
So good, so gracious! Love, and Life, and Light,
Are His rich titles. Oh, for Him I long,
To be my Hope, my Joy, my Strength, my Song!
Earth's shadow melts in conquering light away
Before the rising Daystar's earliest ray.

Song of Solomon 2:14.

'Let me hear Thy voice: for sweet is Thy voice.'

HAST thou not heard within some sacred pile,
When hushed the swelling choir, through vaulted aisle
A sweet low echo lingering of the song,
As would angelic harps the sound prolong?
So through the silent chambers of my soul,
In calmest melody *His* sweet words roll.

1 Timothy 6:12.

'Lay hold on eternal life, whereunto thou art also called.'

A LIFE is before thee which cannot decay,
A glimpse and an echo are given to-day
Of glory and music not far away.
Take the bliss that is offered thee,
     And thou shalt be
     Safe and blest for aye.

A Covenant.

Now, Lord, I give myself to Thee;
 I would be wholly Thine,
As Thou hast given Thyself to me,
 And Thou art wholly mine.
Oh, take me,—seal me as Thine own,
 Thine altogether—Thine ALONE!

Only for Jesus.

ONLY for Jesus! Lord, keep it for ever
 Sealed on the heart and engraved on the life!
Pulse of all gladness and nerve of endeavour,
 Secret of rest, and the strength of our strife.

Chosen Lessons.

'Him shall He teach in the way that He shall choose.'—PSALM 25:12.

IN the way that He shall choose
 He will teach us;
Not a lesson we shall lose,
 All shall reach us.

Strange and difficult indeed
 We may find it,
But the blessing that we need
 Is behind it.

All the lessons He shall send
 Are the sweetest,
And His training, in the end,
 Is completest.

Hitherto and Henceforth.

HITHERTO the Lord hath helped us,
　　Guiding all the way;
Henceforth let us trust Him fully,
　　Trust Him all the day.

Hitherto the Lord hath loved us,
　　Caring for His own;
Henceforth let us love Him better,
　　Live for Him alone.

Hitherto the Lord hath blessed us,
　　Crowning all our days;
Henceforth let us live to bless Him,
　　Live to show His praise.

Rhymed Mottoes for the Members of the Open-Air Mission.

'Occupy till I come.'—LUKE 19:13.

'OCCUPY till I return':
Let us, Lord, this lesson learn;
May our every moment be
Faithfully filled up for Thee.

————

'Be not far from me.'—PSALM 22:11.

BE not far from me, we pray:
'I am with thee all the day';
This Thy answer, strong and clear!
Master, Thou art *always* near.

'He is faithful that promised'—HEBREWS 10:23.

> THOU art faithful; praise Thy name,
> Thou art evermore the same;
> Thou hast promised; oh, how blest
> On Thy royal word to rest!

———————

'He that winneth souls is wise.'—PROVERBS 11:30.

> 'HE that winneth souls is wise'
> In the Master's gracious eyes;
> Well may we contented be
> To be counted fools for Thee.

———————

'Redeeming the time.'—COLOSSIANS 4:5.

> So may we redeem the time,
> That with every evening chime
> Our rejoicing hearts may see
> Blood-bought souls brought back to Thee.

———————

'Lay up His words in thine heart'—JOB 22:22.

> LET us, by Thy Spirit stirred,
> In our hearts lay up Thy word.
> Daily, Lord, increase our store,
> Fill our treasures more and more.

Advent Thoughts.

'Behold, the Bridegroom cometh!'—MATTHEW 25:6.

> O HERALD whisper falling
>   Upon the passing night,
> Mysteriously calling
>   The Children of the Light!

He cometh; oh, He cometh!
   Our own belovèd Lord!
This blessèd hope up-summeth
   Our undeserved reward.

He cometh! Though the hour,
   Nor earth nor heaven may know,
Sure is the word of power,
   'He cometh!' Even so!

———

'Look up, and lift up your heads; for your redemption draweth nigh.'—LUKE 21:28.

ADVENT shadows gather deep,
   Wars and desolations,
Troubled wakings, troubled sleep,
   Rushing of the nations.
Advent glory, grand and clear,
   Herald flashes flingeth;
And the Judge who draweth near,
   Full salvation bringeth.

TRUSTING JESUS.

———o———

I AM trusting Thee, Lord Jesus,
  Trusting only Thee!
Trusting Thee for full salvation,
   Great and free.

I am trusting Thee for pardon,
  At Thy feet I bow;
For Thy grace and tender mercy,
   Trusting now.

I am trusting Thee for cleansing,
  In the crimson flood;
Trusting Thee to make me holy,
   By Thy blood.

6d. per 100.   PAISLEY: J. AND R. PARLANE.

2

I am trusting Thee to guide me,
  Thou alone shalt lead,
Every day and hour supplying
   All my need.

I am trusting Thee for power,
  Thine can never fail;
Words which Thou Thyself shalt give me,
   Must prevail.

I am trusting Thee, Lord Jesus,
  Never let me fall!
I am trusting Thee for ever,
   And for all.

        FRANCES RIDLEY HAVERGAL.

This printed card was found among F.R.H.'s papers, easy and inexpensive to print and give to many. J. & R. Parlane and C. Caswell printed several or many such cards and leaflets by F.R.H.

1877.

"He that winneth souls is wise". Prov. 11. 30

He that winneth souls is wise..."
In the Master's gracious eyes;
Will every one contented be
To be counted fools for Thee

1878.

"Redeeming the time". Col. 4. 6

So may we redeem the time,
That with every morning chime
Our upspring hearts may see
More lost souls brought back to Thee

1879.

"Lay up His words in thine heart". Job 22. 22

Let us, by Thy Spirit stirred,
In our hearts lay up Thy word,
Daily, Lord, inscribe me there,
Fill our treasures more and more

---

48. Rhymed Annual Mottoes for the Members of the Open-Air Mission

1874.

"Occupy till I come". Luke 19. 13

Occupy till I return:
Yet this, Lord, this lesson learn;
Thou, in every moment be
Faithfully filled up for Thee

1875.

"Be not far from one". Psa. 22. 11

Be not far from me, we pray;
"I am with you all the day;"
This Thy answer, strong and clear!
Master, Thou not always near.

1876.

He is faithful that promised. Heb. 10. 23

Thou art faithful; Praise Thy name,
Thou art evermore the same;
Thou hast promised; Oh how blest
Are Thy royal word to rest.

See pages 566–567 of this book.

VI.

Yes, we have a word for Jesus! we will bravely
   speak for Thee,
And Thy bold and faithful soldiers, Saviour, we
   would henceforth be:
In Thy name set up our banners, while Thine own
   shall wave above,
With Thy crimson Name of Mercy, and Thy golden
   Name of Love.
Help us lovingly to labour, looking for Thy
   present smile,
Looking for Thy promised blessing, through the
   brightening "little while."
Words for Thee in weakness spoken, Thou wilt
   here accept and own,
And confess them in Thy glory, when we see Thee
   on Thy throne.

Frances Ridley Havergal.

"O LORD, OPEN THOU MY LIPS; AND MY MOUTH

SHALL SHEW FORTH THY PRAISE."

Psalm li. 15.

"HAVE YOU NOT A WORD FOR JESUS?"

A QUESTION

FOR ALL WHO LOVE HIM.

I.

Have you not a word for Jesus? not a word to
   say for Him?
He is listening through the chorus of the burning
   seraphim!
HE IS LISTENING; does He hear you speaking of
   the things of earth,
Only of its passing pleasure, selfish sorrow, empty
   mirth?
He has spoken words of blessing, pardon, peace,
   and love to you,
Glorious hopes and gracious comfort, strong and
   tender, sweet and true;
Does He hear you telling others something of His
   love untold,
Overflowings of thanksgiving for His mercies
   manifold?

PAISLEY: J. AND R. PARLANE.   *1s. 6d. per 100*

II.

Have you not a word for Jesus? Will the world
   His praise proclaim?
Who shall speak if ye are silent? ye who know
   and love His name.
You, whom He hath called and chosen His own
   witnesses to be,
Will ye tell your gracious Master, "Lord, we
   cannot speak for Thee!"
"Cannot!" though He suffered for you, died
   because He loved you so!
"Cannot!" though He has forgiven, making
   scarlet white as snow!
"Cannot!" though His grace abounding is your
   freely promised aid!
"Cannot!" though HE stands beside you, though
   HE says, "Be not afraid!"

III.

Have you not a word for Jesus? Some, perchance,
   while ye are dumb,
Wait and weary for your message, hoping *you* will
   bid them "come";
Never telling hidden sorrows, lingering just outside
   the door,
Longing for *your* hand to lead them into rest for
   evermore.
Yours may be the joy and honour His redeemed
   ones to bring,
Jewels for the coronation of your coming Lord and
   King.
Will you cast away the gladness thus your Master's
   joy to share,
All because a word for Jesus seems too much for
   you to dare?

IV.

What shall be our word for Jesus? Master, give it
   day by day;
Ever as the need arises, teach Thy children what to
   say.
Give us holy love and patience; grant us deep
   humility,
That of self we may be emptied, and our hearts be
   full of Thee;
Give us zeal and faith and fervour, make us
   winning, make us wise,
Single-hearted, strong and fearless,—Thou hast
   called us, we will rise!
Let the might of Thy good Spirit go with every
   loving word;
And by hearts prepared and opened be our message
   always heard!

V.

Yes, we have a word for Jesus! Living echoes we
   will be
Of Thine own sweet words of blessing, of Thy
   gracious "Come to Me."
Jesus, Master! yes, we love Thee, and to prove our
   love, would lay
Fruit of lips which Thou wilt open, at Thy blessed
   feet to-day.
Many an effort it may cost us, many a heart-beat,
   many a fear,
But Thou knowest, and wilt strengthen, and Thy
   help is always near.
Give us grace to follow fully, vanquishing our
   faithless shame,
Feebly it may be, but truly, witnessing for Thy
   dear Name.

A single-fold leaflet, one of several leaflets published in her day, printed very inexpensively and given out readily to friends and strangers. The note at the top of the first page is in Frances' handwriting. See pages 387–388 of this book.

'Under His Shadow.'

An Interlude.

THAT part is finished! I lay down my pen,
  And wonder if the thoughts will flow as fast
Through the more difficult defile. For the last
  Was easy, and the channel deeper then.
My Master, I will trust Thee for the rest;
Give me just what Thou wilt, and that will be my best.

How can *I* tell the varied, hidden need
  Of Thy dear children, all unknown to me,
Who at some future time may come and read
  What I have written! All are known to Thee.
As Thou hast helped me, help me to the end;
Give me Thy own sweet messages of love to send.

So now, I pray Thee, keep my hand in Thine,
  And guide it as Thou wilt. I do not ask
To understand the wherefore of each line;
  Mine is the sweeter, easier, happier task
Just to look up to Thee for every word,
Rest in Thy love, and trust, and know that I am heard.

Zenith.

I.

WE watched the gradual rising of a star,
  Whose delicate, clear ray outshone the crowd;
  Gleaming between the rifts of parting cloud,
Brighter above each dusky-veiling bar.
The fairy child, the glimpse of girlish face,
Rising to woman's dower of fairest, fullest grace.

And still she rose, and still she calmly shone,
 Walking in brightness ever-brightening still;
 Gladdening, attracting at her queenly will,
With starlike influence. The years wore on,
And Isabel, the star, the pearl, the flower,
Could not but know her gift, the secret of her power.

'Never so lovely as to-night,' they said,
 Again and yet again! There came a night
 When many owned afresh the royal might
Of beauty, as she came with snowfall tread,
And summer smile, and simple maiden dress,
Crowned only with the light and her own loveliness.

And the next day she was a little tired;
 And the next night the rose had somewhat paled.
 The fair pearl glistened, yet it somewhat failed
Of the past gleam, the radiance all-admired.
From the soft emerald of the wind-waved grass,
How soon the diamond sparkle of the dew must pass!

And the next week the sunbeams vainly sought
 An entrance, where their merry rival lay
 Fevered and weary; while, from day to day,
The quick pulse wasted what short slumber brought
Of slow renewing. So the dark mist fell,
And hid the starry fire that all had loved so well.

Again she shone, when from that dark mist freed,
 But with that singular radiance never more;
 The brightening upward path so quickly o'er,
The solemn westward curve begun indeed!
The unconscious zenith of her lovely light
For ever left behind on that gay triumph-night!

II.

Ho! for the Alps! The weary plains of France,
 And the night-shadows, leaving far behind,
 For pearl horizons with pure summits lined,—
On through the Jura-gorge, in swift advance

Speeds Arthur, with keen hope and buoyant glee,
On to the mountain land, home of the strong and free!

On! to the morning flush of gold and rose;
   On! to the torrent and the hoary pine;
   On! to the stillness of life's utmost line;
On! to the crimson fire of sunset snows.
Short starlit rest, then with the dawn's first streak,
On! to the silent crown of some lone icy peak!

'Twas no nerve-straining effort, then, for him
   To emulate the chamois-hunter's leap
   Across the wide rock-chasm, or the deep
And darkly blue crevasse with treacherous rim,
Or climb the sharp arête, or slope of snow,
With Titan towers above, and cloud-filled gulfs below.

It was no weariness or toil to count
   Hour after hour in that weird white realm,
   With guide of Alp-renown to touch the helm
Of practised instinct, rocky spires to mount,
Or track the steepest glacier's fissured length,
In the abounding joy of his unconquered strength.

But it was gladness none can realize
   Who have not felt the wild Excelsior thrill,
   The strange exhilarate energies that fill
The bounding pulses, as the intenser skies
Embrace the infinite whiteness, clear and fair,
Inhaling vigorous life with that quick crystal air.

That Alpine witchery still onward lures,
   Upward, still upward, till the fatal list
   Grows longer of the early mourned and missed;
Leading where surest foot no more ensures
The life that is not ours to throw away
For the exciting joys of one brief summer day.

For there are sudden dangers none foreknow;
   The scarlet-threaded rope can never mock
   The sound-loosed avalanche, frost-cloven rock,
Or whirling storm of paralyzing snow.

But Arthur's foot was kept; no deathward slips
Darkened the zenith of his strength with dire eclipse.

So year by year, as his rich manhood filled,
    He revelled in health-giving mountain feats;
    Spurning the trodden tracks and curious streets,
As fit for old men, and for boys unskilled
In Alpine arts, not strong nor bold enough
To battle with the blast and scale the granite bluff.

One glowing August sun went forth in might,
    And smote with rosy sword each snowy brow,
    Bright accolade of grandeur! Now, oh now
Amid that dazzling wealth of purest light,
His long ambition should be crowned at last,
And every former goal rejoicingly o'erpast.

For ere the white fields softened in the glow,
    He stood upon a long-wooed virgin-peak,
    One of the few fair prizes left to seek;
Each rival pinnacle left far below!
He stood in triumph on the conquered height:
And yet a shadow fell upon his first delight.

For well he knew that he had surely done
    His utmost, and that never summer day
    Could bring a moment on its radiant way
Like the first freshness of that conquest, won
Where all had lost before. A sudden tear
Veiled all the glorious view, so grand, so calm, so clear!

III.

An hour of song! of musical delight
    To those whose quick, instructed ear could trace,
    Through complex harmonies, the artistic grace,
The finest shades of meaning, and the might
Of order and of law. Nor less to those
Who loved it as we love the fragrance of the rose.

And Cecil stood, with all the added ease
    Of ripe experience and of sure success;
    With all her glad instinctive consciousness
Of natural gift that could not fail to please;
With all her rich maturity of tone,
Like sun-glow of the South on purple clusters thrown.

She sang rejoicing in her song,—each bar
    A separate pulse of pleasure. Were there none
    To listen and applaud, or only one,
As freely she had poured it. For a star
Shines, not because we watch it! Only blaze
Of artificial light reserves its measured rays.

Yet who, that ever tasted, does not know
    The witchery of any phase of power,
    Ascendency unsought, magnetic dower
Of influence? And Cecil found it so,
And though but vaguely conscious of her might,
Lived in her own strong spell, a glamour of delight.

Nor only joy of power and joy of song
    To fill the singer's chalice were combined
    But sympathetic influences of mind
Acting, re-acting, as the charmèd throng
Followed the wave of her swift magic wand,
Yet lured her ever on to fair heights still beyond.

And so the song passed to its dying fall,
    As the electric interchanges crossed.
    What marvel that the closing chord was lost
In rush of quick applause and fond recall!
And Cecil rose once more, and poured again,
From fuller-gushing fount, the doubly welcomed strain.

Higher and higher rose the glorious song,
    Deeper and deeper grew the silence round;
    All unrestrained the free, full notes resound,
In splendid carol-gladness, holding long
Unwearied listeners in chains unseen,
As willing captives led by their victorious queen.

Tribute of wondering smile was freely paid,
    And then, as subtle modulation wrought
      Soft shadows in the sunny strain, some brought
   The deeper homage of a tear, and, swayed
Beyond confession, strove in vain to hide
The unconquerable rush of sweet emotion's tide.

Then once again the clear tones rose and swelled,
    While flashed the singer's eye with inward fire,
      And still the spirit of the song soared higher
   Until the closing cadence, as she held
All hearts entranced, till like a sunset ray,
The last, long, sweet note thrilled, and softly died away.

And all was over! Ah, she had not guessed
    That she had touched the zenith of her song,
      That gradual declining, slow and long
   Must mark the path now trending to the west!
No boundary line is seen, and yet we cross
In one veiled hour, from gain, to sure though lingering loss.

She often sang again. But oftener fell
    Apologies of unaffected truth.
      There was more effort, yet less power, in sooth;
   The ringing tone less like a golden bell.
Not quite in voice of late. 'I'll do my best!
Do not expect too much;—I think my voice needs rest.'

So one by one the songs no more were seen
    That called for grandest tone and clearest trill.
      And when she sang, though old friends loved it still,
   The stranger wondered what the spell had been.
And then they spoke of how she *used* to sing!
Passing, or passed away is every earthly thing.

IV.

A silent house beneath a dome of stars,
    A deeply-shaded lamp, a lonely room;
      A fire whose fitful whispers through the gloom
   In rhythmic cadence leapt athwart the bars:

A broad, worn desk; a broad, worn, bending brow;
Yet a bright eye beneath, full of strange brightness now.

A rapid hand, that wrote swift words of flame,
    Far-glowing words to kindle other fires;
      Words that might flash along Time's mystic wires,
   And thrill the ages with a deathless name;
Barbed words, that fasten where they fall, and stay
Deep in the souls of men, and never pass away.

Little recked Theodore of fame that night
    And less of gold. The current was too strong
      For such vain barques to launch. It swept along
   Whither he hardly knew; the impulse bright
Passing at every turn some opening view,
Some echoing mountain height, some vista far and new.

Lost memories trooped in amid the crowd
    Of happiest images; ethereal forms
      Of weirdly prescient fancy, spectral swarms,
   Before him in oppressive beauty bowed,
And beckoned him, with gleaming hands, to grasp
Their fleeting loveliness in firm and joyous clasp.

And inward music rose, and wreathed around
    Each thought that shaped itself to outline clear;
      The royal chimes rang on, more sweet, more near,
   With every gust. He caught the silver sound,
And cast its fairy mantle o'er the flow
Of his melodious lines, in all their fiery glow.

Such times are but the crystallizing hours
    That make the rainbow-bearing prism. They change
      Long-seething soul-solutions into strange
   And startling form;—new properties and powers,
And beauties hardly dreamt, yet latent there,
The poet-touch evokes, strong, marvellous, and fair.

For there are long, slow overtures before
    Such bursts of song;—much tension unconfessed,
    Much training and much tuning,—years compressed,
  Concentrated in ever-filling store;
Till thoughts, that surged in secret deep below,
Rise from volcanic fount in sudden overflow.

  Much living to short writing! such the law
    Of living poems, that have force to reach
    Depths that are sounded by no surface-speech,
  And thence the sympathetic waters draw
With golden chain of many a fire-forged link,
Gently, yet mightily, up to the pearly brink.

  Was it the stillness of the lonely night
    That set his spirit free, with wizard hand,
    Opening the gates of more than fairyland?
  Oft had he known the pulse of poet-might,
But never quite the free, exultant power
In which he revelled now through that enchanted hour.

  Was it not rather that the harvest-time,
    After the sowing and the watering long,
    Was fully come; the golden sheaves of song
  Falling in fulness, and that royal chime
Pealing the harvest-home of wealth unseen,
Where the remaining years might only come and glean?

  At length the last page lay beneath the light,
    From wavering erasure free, and wrought
    Too perfectly for any after-thought.
  He rose, threw up the sash, and on the night,—
The brilliant, solemn night,—looked forth and sighed,
And felt the immediate ebb of that unwonted tide.

  For it was over! and the work was done
    For which his life was lived! unconscious yet!
    The blossom fell because the fruit was set;
  The standard furled because the field was won.
And with the energy, the gladness passed,
And left him wearied out and sorrowful at last.

For only work that is for God alone
   Hath an unceasing guerdon of delight,
   A guerdon unaffected by the sight
Of great success, nor by its loss o'erthrown.
All else is vanity beneath the sun,
There may be joy in *doing*, but it palls when *done*.

V.

Once more. A battle-field of mental might,
   A broad arena for the utmost skill
   Of world-famed gladiators, echoing still
With praise or cruel blame, beyond the sight
Of each day's keen spectators, to the verge
Of widest continents and ocean's farthest surge.

A great arena, whence the issues flow
   Not only through an empire but a world,
   Moulding the centuries; wherein are hurled
Thunders whose ultimate havoc none can know,
Striking not names but nations:—such the scene
Of conflict and renown, long entered by Eugene.

Many a time his weighty sword he threw
   Into the scale of victory, and swayed
   The critical turns, the great events that made
The era's history. For well he knew
Each subtle art of eloquence, combined
With rarest gifts of speech, and native powers of mind.

His patriotism earned a noble meed
   Of trust and honour, more than any fame,
   And sweeter. Yet some thought his hard-won claim
Not meetly recognised. Perchance indeed
The shadow crossed his own thought, as he found
Less kingly orators with heavier laurels crowned.

At length a contest of long doubtful end
   Drew to a climax, and his soul was stirred,

And every generous faculty was spurred
To utmost energy. For he could spend
His very self upon the cause that seemed
Clear justice and clear right; or rather, so he deemed!

For there are few who care to analyze
The mingled motives, in their complex force,
Of some apparently quite simple course.
One disentangled skein might well surprise.
Perhaps a 'single heart' is *never* known
Save in the yielded life that lives for God alone,—

And that is *therefore* doubted, as a dream,
By those who know not the tremendous power
Of all-constraining love! So in that hour
Of fierce excitement, 'mid the flashing gleam
Of measured glaive, I will not dare to say
That Eugene's purest zeal no party claim might sway.

Still, all combined to bid the eagle soar
Beyond the common clouds, the shifting mists
Of every-day debate, the very lists
Of strong opponents strengthening him the more.
As the strong pinion finds the opposing breeze
The very means of rising over land and seas.[1]

So Eugene rose in his full manly strength,
Reining at first the fiery courser in,
That with calm concentration he might win
The captious ear;—reserve of power at length,
At the right moment from the wise curb freed,
Triumphantly burst forth with grand impetuous speed.

And as the great speech mounted to a pause
Some foes were silenced, some were wholly gained,
And all were spellbound, stilled, and marvel-chained,
And, more than all the clatter of applause,
The cause was won! 'Eugene was at his best
To-night!' So much they knew! They did not know the rest!

---

[1] See Duke of Argyle's 'Reign of Law.' [Apparently this is *The Reign of Law* by George Douglas Campbell, Duke of Argyll (1823–1900), London: Alexander Strahan, 1867.]

For they who watched with envy or delight
   The moment of his zenith, little knew
   It was the moment of his setting too;
For fell paralysis drew near that night.
Never again Eugene might proudly stand
And sway the men who swayed the sceptre of his land.

VI.

A simple Christmas Day at home! And yet
   It was the very zenith of two stars
   That rose together through the cloudy bars,
In bright perpetual conjunction met.
A day whose memory should never cease,—
A Coronation Day of Love and Joy and Peace.

The culmination of two lives that passed
   Through many a chance and change of chequered years,
   Each shining for the other, hopes and fears
Centred within their home! And now at last
They gazed upon a clear, calm sky around,
And rested in their love, that day serenely crowned.

Bernard and Constance had no wish beyond
   Each other's gladness, and the fuller good
   Of those belovèd ones who blithely stood
Around the Christmas fire,—the fair and fond,
The strong and merry; sons and daughters grown
In closest unity,—rich treasures all their own.

Bright arrows of full quiver! still unshot
   By ruthless bow of Time and scattered wide,
   Still in the sweet home-bundle tightly tied,
Though feathered for the flight from that safe spot.
Flight when? and whither? Ah me! who might say
What should befall before another Christmas Day!

Closer they clustered in the twilight fall,
   And talked of pleasant memories of the year,
   And then of pleasant prospects far and near;
Each name responding at each gleeful call.

The merry mention of a dear name there
Had never yet been hushed by any empty chair.

But, most of all, the gladness and the pride
  Circled around the eldest brother's name;
  His first success, his rising college fame,
 Made merriest music at that warm fireside;
And in the parent-hearts deep echoes thrilled,
As the repeated chord proclaimed fond hopes fulfilled.

No dim presentiment of sorrow fell
  Upon that zenith hour of happiness,
  Perhaps the brightest that could ever bless
 A merely earthly lot; the purest well
Of natural joy, unselfish, undefiled,
Up-springing to the day, while heaven above it smiled.

And so the evening hours sped swiftly by,
  And Christmas carols closed the happy time,
  And Christmas bells, in sweet wind-wafted chime,
 Stole softly through the shutters. Not a sigh
With music of the gay good-night was blent,
No discord in that full, harmonious content.

What then? Bernard and Constance wakeful lay
  A long, long while, unwilling each to tell
  That, as the midnight tolled, it seemed the knell
 Of the great gladness of that Christmas Day.
'Oh, what if it should prove too bright to last,
Clear shining that precedes the wild and rainy blast!'

And they were right. It *could* not come again!
  Sickness, and scattering, and varied woe,
  Yet nothing but the lot of most below,
 Soon marred the music of that perfect strain.
And though the westering path had many a gleam,
That zenith-joy was but an oft-remembered dream.

VII.

A soft spring twilight. Cherry blossoms white
    Whispered about the summer they were told
    Was coming, when the beech trees would unfold
Their horny buds, and chestnuts would be dight
In great green leaves. 'What will become of us?'
They wondered! And they shivered as they questioned thus.

For the east wind came by, with curfew bell
    Upon his wings, and touched them stealthily,
    Shrivelling the tender leaves. And silently
In their sweet white array the blossoms fell.
Ah for the zenith of the cherry tree!
Yet *is* it past, although the snowy glories be?

Wait for the shining of the summer day;
    Wait for the crimson glow amid the green;
    Wait for the wealth of ruby ripeness, seen
After the fitful spring has passed away.
Wait till the Master comes, with His own hand
To find His pleasant fruit in clusters rich and grand.

Yes, soft spring twilight! And a bowing head,
    A kneeling form amid the shadows grey;
    A heart from which the hopes had passed away,
That made life exquisite as the blossoms shed
Around that open window;—and a throb
Of dull grey pain, that rose, and forced one low deep sob.

Only the zenith of his youth had passed,
    And scarcely that. Yet perhaps the saddest time
    Is while the echo of the matin chime
Has hardly died away in silence vast;
Sadder to realize the noonday height,
Than the slow-gathering shades of long impending night.

It did not seem that there could ever be
    Another zenith, different, and bright
    With grander hopes, and far more glorious light
Than all the spells of syren minstrelsy,

And all the love and gladness that entwined
The merry paths of youth, for ever left behind.

    For Godfrey had no special powers to spur
        To emulation in the great world-race,
        No special gifts or aims;—the open space
    A possible joy had filled—the dream of her
Who might have been and yet was not to be
Queen of his life! and now—the dark-draped throne was free!

    Free! Yet Another claimed that empty throne,
        And in the twilight He was drawing near,
        'Mid all those shadows of dim grief, and fear,
    And sense of vanity. The King unknown,
Unrecognised as yet, was come to reign,
And yet to crown the life that owned its life was vain.

    And while the spring airs trembled through the trees,
        The gracious Wind that bloweth where it lists
        Dispersed the fallacies, the world-breathed mists
    That hid unseen realities. That Breeze
Unveiled the mysteries of hidden sin,
And let the all-searching Light flash startlingly within.

    Then the vague weariness was roused indeed,
        And passed away for ever, as he saw
        The nearer lightnings of the holy law
    Through suddenly deepening darkness; then the need
More of a Saviour than mere safety dawned
In lurid daybreak, as he glimpsed the gulf that yawned

    Close at his feet—those careless feet that trod
        So merrily a harmless-seeming course
        Of merely useless pleasure, by the force
    Of custom, and yet never came to God,
Never yet stepped upon the Living Way
That only leads to life and everlasting day.

    Again that holy Breeze swept by in might,
        And fanned each faint desire to stronger flame;

He said, 'O bid me come to Thee!' He came,
Just as he was, that memorable night.
And lo! the King, who waited at the door,
Entered, to save, to reign, and to go out no more.

And then he saw those awful lightnings fall
Through the cleft heavens upon a lonely Tree
That stood upon a mount called Calvary,
And knew that stroke had spent the fiery ball:
And then the earthquake closed the gulf below,
While he stood all unscathed, safe from the overthrow.

'Stood,' said I? Nay, in wonder and in love
As on that more than vision Godfrey gazed,
He fell at his Deliverer's feet, and praised
With a new sweetness, sweet as harps above,
The glorious One, whose royal grace had saved
The aimless wanderer, who never grace had craved.

Far in the night this wondrous watch he kept
With the unslumbering Shepherd, while a joy,
The first he ever knew without alloy,
Filled all his soul with light. At last he slept,
Wrapped in this strange new peace, whose steady beam
Made all his past life seem a sinful, troubled dream.

What then? It was no zenith, though the star
Of life shone out at radiant height, that dimmed
Each previous gleam to gloom that barely rimmed
The shifting clouds, with something, that, from far
Might have been fancied light, yet only made
The darkness more discerned, the spirit more afraid.

Rather, it was the rising! the first hour
Of the true shining, that should rise and rise
From glory unto glory, through God's skies,
In strengthening brightness and increasing power.
A rising with no setting, for its height
Could only culminate in God's eternal light.

The feeble glimmer of the former days,
　　The hope, the love, the very glee, that paled
　　Just at their seeming zenith, and then failed
　Of fuller sparkling,—all the scattered rays
Were caught up and transfigured, in the blaze
Of the new life of love, and energy, and praise.

　　The joy of loyal service to the King
　　　Shone through them all, and lit up other lives
　　　With the new fire of faith, that ever strives,
　Like a swift-kindling beacon, far to fling
The tidings of His victory, and claim
New subjects for His realm, new honour for His Name.

　　And so the years flowed on, and only cast
　　　Light, and more light, upon the shining way,
　　　That more and more shone to the perfect day;
　Always intenser, clearer than the past;
Because they only bore him on glad wing
Nearer the Light of Light, the Presence of the King.

　　Who recks the short recession of a wave
　　　In the strong flowing of a tide? And so
　　　Without a pang could Godfrey leave below
　Successive earthly zeniths, while he gave
A glad glance upward to the rainbow Throne,
And joyously pressed on to nobler heights alone.

　　Or if awhile a looming sorrow-cloud
　　　He entered, still he found the Glory there,
　　　Shechinah-brightness resting still and fair
　Within the holy curtains, as he bowed
Before the Presence on the Mercy-seat;
Then forth he came with sound of golden bells most sweet.

　　And then the music floated on the wind,
　　　A constant carol of glad tidings told,
　　　Of how the lives the One Life doth enfold
　Are ever with that Life so closely twined,
That nought can separate, below, above,
And life itself is one long miracle of love.

At last the gentle tone was heard, that falls
In all-mysterious sweetness on the ear
That long has listened, longing, without fear,
Because so well it knows the Voice that calls;
Though only once that solemn call is heard,
While angel-songs take up the echoes of the word.

'Friend, go up higher!' So he took that night
The one grand step, beyond the stars of God,
Into the splendour, shadowless and broad,
Into the everlasting joy and light.
The Zenith of the earthly life was come;
What marvel that the lips were for the moment dumb!

What then? Eye hath not seen, ear hath not heard!
Wait till thou too hast fought the noble strife,
And won, through Jesus Christ, the crown of life!
Then shalt thou know the glory of the word,
Then as the stars for ever—ever shine,
Beneath the King's own smile,—perpetual Zenith thine!

The Thoughts of God.

THY thoughts, O God! O theme Divine!
Except Thy Spirit in my darkness shine,
And make it light,
And overshadow me
With stilling might,
And touch my lips that I may speak of Thee,—
How shall I soar
To thoughts of Thy thoughts? and how dare to write
Of Thine?

Thou understandest mine
Far off and long before.
Thou searchest, knowest, compassest! Thy hand is laid
Upon me. Whither shall I flee
From Omnipresence and Omniscience? If I fly
To heaven, Thou art there: and if I lie
In the unseen land,

Behold, Thou art there also! If I take
The wings of morning, and my dwelling make
In the uttermost parts of the great sea,
Even there Thy hand shall lead me, Thy right hand
Shall hold me. If I say
Surely the night
Shall cover me, it shall be light
About me. Yea, the shade
Of darkness hideth not from Thee,
Night shineth as the day;
The darkness and the light are both alike to Thee.

Thee I will praise: for I am fearfully
And wonderfully made.
My substance was not hid from Thee
When I was made in secret, curiously wrought
And yet imperfect. Then
Thine eyes did see me. In Thy book
Were all my members written, when
Not one of them was into being brought.
Such knowledge is too wonderful for me,
Too excellent, too high. Yet 'tis but one
Keen ray of Thy great sun
Touching an atom in a dusty nook!

One ray! while others traverse depths profound
Of possible chaos; and illume
The boundless bound
Of space; and vivify worlds all unguessed,
To whom
Our farthest eastern spark,
Caught by the mightiest telescope that ever pierced the dark,
Is farthest west.

One ray! while others overflow
The countless hosts of angels with celestial blaze;
With still diviner glow,
Flooding each heart with adoration sweet;
And yet too glorious for the gaze
Of seraphim, who cover face and feet

With burning wings,
While through the universe their 'Holy, holy,' rings.

Only one ray! Yet doth it come
So close to us, so very near,
Our inmost selves enfolding,
Discerning, penetrating,—we, beholding
Its terrible brightness, well might fear,
But for the glow
Of known and trusted Love that pulseth warm below
And so
The psalm ariseth, strong and clear,
'How precious are Thy thoughts to me, O God!
How great their sum!'
Uncounted, marvellous, and very deep and broad,
Unsearchable and high!
Infinity
Of holiest, mightiest mystery,
That never sight
Or tongue of mortal seer
Could see or tell,
That never flight
Of flame-like spirits that in strength excel
Hath reached! The very faith that brings us near
Reveals new distances, new depths of light
Unfathomed,—seas of suns that never eye
Created, hath beheld or ever can behold!
What know we of God's thoughts? One word of gold
A volume doth enfold.
They are—'Not ours!'
Ours? what are they? their value and their powers?
So evanescent, that while thousands fleet
Across the busy brain,
Only a few remain
To set their seal on memory's strange consistence.
Of these, some worthless, some a life-regret,
That we would fain forget;
And very few are rich and great and sweet;

And fewer still are lasting gain,
And these most often born of pain,
Or sprung from strong concussion into strong existence.

What else? Even in their proudest strength so weak,
So isolated and so rootless,
So flowerless and so fruitless;—
We think, and dare not do,—we think, and cannot speak!
A thought alone is less than breath,
Only the shudder of a living death,
A thing of scorn,
A formless embryo in chaos born,
It must be seized with resolute grasp of will,
With swiftness and with skill,
And moulded on life's anvil, ere it glow
With any fire or force;
And wrought with many a blow
And welded in the heat by toiling strength
With many another, ere it go at length
The humblest mission to fulfil.
And then its tiny might
Is not inherent, but alone dependent
Upon the primal source
And spring of power, First, Sole, Supreme, Transcendent!

What else? So circumscribed in flight!
Like bats in sunshine, striking helpless wings
Against the shining things,
That to their dazzled sight
Appear not; hindered everywhere
By unseen obstacles with puzzling pain.
Or like the traveller, toiling long to gain
An Alpine summit, white and fair,
With far-extending view; but still withheld,
And to the downward track with fainting step compelled
By an intangible barrier; for the air
Is all too rare,
Too keenly pure
For valley-dweller to endure.

For thus our thoughts rebound
From the Invisible-Infinite, on every side
        Hemmed ever round
By the Impassable, that never mortal pinion
    Hath over-soared, that mocks at human pride,
    Imprisoned in its own supposed dominion.

        What else? So mingled, so impure;
    So interwoven with the threads of sin,
        Visible or invisible as the sight
            Is purged to see them in God's light;
So subtle in their changeful forms, now dark, now bright;
    Such mystery of iniquity within,
That we must loathe our very thoughts, but for the cure
        He hath devised,—the blessed Tree
    The Lord hath shown us, that, cast in, can heal
    The fountain whence the bitter waters flow.
            Divinest remedy
            Whose power we feel,
    Whose grace we comprehend not, but we know.

    What else? So fallible, so full of errors,—
    No certainty! In aught unproved and new,
    Treading volcanic soil o'er smothered terrors;
    Spectral misgivings rising to the view,
            As each step crushes through
Some older crust of truth assumed. And this is all
            That human thoughts can do,
    Leaning on human strength and reason solely;
        Now wrong, now right, now false, now true,
            As may befall!
    And even the truest never reaching wholly
            Truth Absolute,
        That still our touch eludes,
        And vanishes in deeper depths when man intrudes
            Within her awful solitudes,
            Where many a string is mute
            And many awanting, all the rest
            Imperfectly attuned at best,—

We can but wait for truth of tone,
For truth of modulation and expression,
         With lowliest confession
Of utter powerlessness, content
To trust His thoughts and not our own,—
Until the Maker of the instrument
Shall tune it in another sphere,
By His own perfect hand and ear.

Now turn we from the darkness to the light,
From dissonance to pure and full accord!
'My thoughts are not as your thoughts, saith the Lord,
Nor are your ways as My ways. As the height
Of heaven above the earth, so are My ways,
    My thoughts, to yours;—out of your sight,
               Above your praise.'
              O oracle most grand!
Thus teaching by sublimest negative
What by a positive we could not understand,
              Or, understanding, live!
              And now, search fearlessly
The imperfections and obscurity,
              The weakness and impurity,
Of all our thoughts. On each discovery
Write, 'NOT as ours!' Then, in every line,
              Behold God's glory shine
In humbling yet sweet contrast, as we view
His thoughts, Eternal, Strong, and Holy, Infinite, and True.

And now, what have we of these thoughts of God,
         So high, so deep, so broad?
What hath He given, and what are we receiving?
              A revelation
              Dim, pale, and cold
Beside their hidden fire, yet gorgeously enscrolled
         Upon His wide Creation.
         He would not all withhold,
His children in the silent darkness leaving;

Nor would He overwhelm our heart
And strike it dumb;
And so He hath enfolded some
In fair expressions for the eye and ear
Though faint, yet clear;
Such as our powers may apprehend in part.
Thus hath He wrought
The dazzling swiftness of the thought
That veiled itself for mortal ken in light.
And thus the myriad-handed might
Of that from which the million-teeming ocean fell,
No greater toil to Him,
From silent depth to surfy rim,
Than the small crystal drop which fills a rosy shell.
And thus the Infinite Ideal
Of perfect Beauty, (only real
In Him and through Him, pure conception
Too exquisite for our perception,)
He hath translated, giving us such lines
As we can trace,
In mountain grandeur and in lily grace,
In sunset, cloudland, or soul-moulded face,
Such alphabets and signs
As we, His little ones, may slowly, softly read,
Supplying thus a deep, true spirit-need.

What know we more? One thought He hath expressed
In that great scheme
Of which we, straining, catch a glimpse or gleam
In light or shadow;—scheme embracing all,
Star-system cycles and the sparrow's fall;—
Scheme all-combining, wisest, grandest, best.
We call it Providence. And each may deem
Himself a tiny centre of that thought;
For how mysteriously enwrought
Are all our moments in its folds of might,
Our own horizon ever bounding
And yet not limiting, but still surrounding
Our lives, while reaching far beyond our quickest sight.

O thought of consummated harmony!
Each life is one note in that symphony,
Without which were its cadence incomplete:
Yet each note complex, formed of many a reed;
And each reed quivering with vibrations passing count,
  And each vibration blending
   In mystic trinities ascending
   Through weird harmonics that recede
Into the unknown silences, or meet
In dashing thrills unanalyzed, and mount
In tangled music, yet all plain and clear
    Unto the Master's ear.
O thought of consummated melody
And perfect rhythm! though its mighty beat
  Transcend angelic faculty,
    And though its mighty bars
May be the fall of worlds, the birth of stars,
  Its measure—all eternity—
    One echo, calm and sweet,
Our clue to this great music of God's plan,
Sounds on in ever-varying repeat—
Glory to God on high, peace and goodwill to man!

What have we more? Scan we the blinding blaze
   Of the refulgent rays
Outpourèd from the Very Fount of Light?
One thought of God in undiluted splendour
   Flashed on our feeble gaze,
Were never borne by mortal sight.
   He knew it, and He gave,
    In mercy tender,
All that the soul unwittingly doth crave,
  All that it can receive. He robed
In finite words the sparkles of His thought,
   The starry fire englobed
In tiny spheres of language, shielding, softening thus
The living, burning glory. And He brought
   Even to us

This strange celestial treasure that no prayer
   Had asked of Him, no ear had heard,
No heart of man conceived. He laid it there,
Even at our feet, and said it was His Word.
     O mystery of tender grace!
       We find
   God's thoughts in human words enshrined,
God's very life and love with ours entwined.
All wonderingly from page to page we pass,
Owning the darkening yet revealing glass;
      In every line we trace,
       In fair display,
  Prismatic atoms of the glorious bow
  Projected on the darkest cloud that e'er
O'ergloomed the world that God had made so fair,
The rainbow of His covenant; each one
Reflecting perfectly a sevenfold ray,
       Shot from the sun
     Of His exceeding love,
     Strong and serene above,
Upon a tremulous drop of tearful life below.

One thought, His thought of thoughts, awakes our song
Of endless thanks and marvelling adoration
More than aught else. For Providence, Creation,
All He hath made and all He doth prepare,
      Thoughts grand and wise, and strong,
      Thoughts tender and most fair,
Are pale beside the glory of Salvation,
Redemption's gracious plan and glorious revelation:—
    The focus where all rays unite;
Each attribute arrayed in sevenfold light,
   Each adding splendour to the rest.
      The meeting blest
Of His great love and foreseen human woe
Struck forth a mighty fire, that sent a glow
Throughout the universe;—an overflow
   To the dim confines that none know

Save He who traced them; lit up gloriously
The farthest vistas of Eternity;
And, flooding heaven itself with radiance new,
Revealed the heart of God, all-merciful, all-true.

Thus are the thoughts of God made known to men.
    Yet is all revelation bounded
    First by its vehicle, and then
    By its reception. Unseen things
    Remain unfathomed and unsounded,
        And hidden as the springs
    Of an immeasurable sea,
    Because His thought, sublime and great,
    No language finds commensurate
       With its infinity;
And when compressed in any finite mould,
'Tis but a fraction that the mind of man
       Receiveth. For we hold
        But what we span,
        We only see
What feeble lenses and weak sight may scan.
And thus a double lessening, double veiling
Of the unimagined glory of a thought of Him
    Who dwells between the cherubim!
       First, suffering and paling
    By its necessitate transition
From Infinite to Finite, for that all expression
    Is by its nature finite; then the vision
    Which angels might receive straightway,
        Unshorn of any ray,
        And hold in full possession,
        Must enter by the portal
    Of faculties sin-paralyzed and mortal;
And in the human breast's low-vaulted gloom
       It finds no room
       For any high display.

This is no guess-work. It is even so
With our poor thoughts. For they are always more

Than any form or language can convey.
We know
Things that we cannot say;
We soar,
Where we could never map our flight.
We see
Flashes and colourings too quick and bright
For any hand to paint. We meet
Depths that no line can sound. We hear
Strange far-off mental music, all too sweet,
Too great for any earthly instrument;
Gone, if we strive to bring it near.

For who that knows
The sudden surging and the startling throes
Of subterranean soul-fires with no vent,
That seek an Etna all in vain;—
Or the slow forming of some grand, fair thought,
With exquisite lingering outwrought,
Only to melt before the touch of effort or of pain:—
(Like quivering rose-fire 'neath a filmy veil
In mountain dawn,
That grows all still and pale
When the transparent silver is withdrawn.)
Oh! who that knows but owns the meagre dower
Of poor weak language married to thought's royal power—
Oh! who that knows but needs must own,
If it be thus
Even with us,
Groping and tottering alone
Around the footstool of His throne,
With limited ideas and babe-like powers,
What must it be with Him, whose thoughts are not as ours!
And now
We only bow,
And gaze above
In raptured awe and silent love;

For mortal speech
Can never reach
A word of meetly-moulded praise,
For one glimpse of the blessèd rays,
Ineffable and purely bright,
Outflowing ever from the Unapproachèd Light.

———————

They say there is a hollow, safe and still,
A point of coolness and repose
Within the centre of a flame, where life might dwell
Unharmed and unconsumed, as in a luminous shell,
Which the bright walls of fire enclose
In breachless splendour, barrier that no foes
Could pass at will.

There is a point of rest
At the great centre of the cyclone's force,
A silence at its secret source;—
A little child might slumber undistressed,
Without the ruffle of one fairy curl,
In that strange central calm amid the mighty whirl.

So, in the centre of these thoughts of God,
Cyclones of power, consuming glory-fire,—
As we fall o'erawed
Upon our faces, and are lifted higher
By His great gentleness, and carried nigher
Than unredeemèd angels, till we stand
Even in the hollow of His hand,—
Nay, more! we lean upon His breast—
There, there we find a point of perfect rest
And glorious safety. There we see
His thoughts to usward, thoughts of peace
That stoop to tenderest love; that still increase
With increase of our need; that never change,
That never fail, or falter, or forget.
O pity infinite!
O royal mercy free!

O gentle climax of the depth and height
Of God's most precious thoughts, most wonderful, most strange!
  'For I am poor and needy, yet
The Lord Himself, Jehovah, *thinketh upon me!*'

The Ministry of Intercession.

THERE is no holy service
  But hath its secret bliss:
Yet, of all blessèd ministries,
  Is one so dear as this?
The ministry that cannot be
  A wondering seraph's dower,
Enduing mortal weakness
  With more than angel-power,
The ministry of purest love
  Uncrossed by any fear,
That bids us meet at the Master's feet,
  And keeps us very near.

God's ministers are many,
  For this His gracious will,
Remembrancers that day and night
  This holy office fill.
While some are hushed in slumber,
  Some to fresh service wake,
And thus the saintly number
  No change or chance can break.
And thus the sacred courses
  Are evermore fulfilled,
The tide of grace by time or place
  Is never stayed or stilled.

Oh, if our ears were opened
  To hear as angels do
The Intercession-chorus
  Arising full and true,
We should hear it soft up-welling
  In morning's pearly light,

Through evening's shadows swelling
    In grandly gathering might,
The sultry silence filling
    Of noontide's thunderous glow,
And the solemn starlight thrilling
    With ever deepening flow.

We should hear it through the rushing
    Of the city's restless roar,
And trace its gentle gushing
    O'er ocean's crystal floor:
We should hear it far up-floating
    Beneath the Orient moon,
And catch the golden noting
    From the busy Western noon,
And pine-robed heights would echo
    As the mystic chant up-floats,
And the sunny plain resound again
    With the myriad-mingling notes.

Who are the blessèd ministers
    Of this world-gathering band?
All who have learnt One Language,
    Through each far-parted land;
All who have learnt the story
    Of Jesu's love and grace,
And are longing for His glory
    To shine in every face.
All who have known the Father
    In Jesus Christ our Lord,
And know the might and love the light
    Of the Spirit in the Word.

Yet there are some who see not
    Their calling high and grand,
Who seldom pass the portals,
    And never boldly stand
Before the golden altar
    On the crimson-stainèd floor,
Who wait afar and falter,
    And dare not hope for more.

Will ye not join the blessèd ranks
   In their beautiful array?
Let intercession blend with thanks
   As ye minister to-day!

There are little ones among them,
   Child-ministers of prayer,
White robes of intercession
   Those tiny servants wear.
First for the near and dear ones
   Is that fair ministry,
Then for the poor black children,
   So far beyond the sea.
The busy hands are folded,
   As the little heart uplifts
In simple love, to God above,
   Its prayer for all good gifts.

There are hands too often weary
   With the business of the day,
With God-entrusted duties,
   Who are toiling while they pray,
They bear the golden vials,
   And the golden harps of praise,
Through all the daily trials,
   Through all the dusty ways.
These hands, so tired, so faithful,
   With odours sweet are filled,
And in the ministry of prayer
   Are wonderfully skilled.

There are ministers unlettered,
   Not of Earth's great and wise,
Yet mighty and unfettered
   Their eagle-prayers arise.
Free of the heavenly storehouse!
   They hold the master-key
That opens all the fulness
     Of God's great treasury.
They bring the needs of others,
   And all things are their own,

For their one grand claim is Jesu's name
　　Before their Father's throne.

There are noble Christian workers,
　　The men of faith and power,
The overcoming wrestlers
　　Of many a midnight hour;
Prevailing princes with their God,
　　Who will not be denied,
Who bring down showers of blessing
　　To swell the rising tide.
The Prince of Darkness quaileth
　　At their triumphant way,
Their fervent prayer availeth
　　To sap his subtle sway.

But in this Temple-service
　　Are sealed and set apart
Arch-priests of intercession,
　　Of undivided heart.
The fulness of anointing
　　On these is doubly shed,
The consecration of their God
　　Is on each low-bowed head.
They bear the golden vials
　　With white and trembling hand
In quiet room or wakeful gloom
　　These ministers must stand,—

To the Intercession-Priesthood
　　Mysteriously ordained,
When the strange dark gift of suffering
　　This added gift hath gained.
For the holy hands uplifted
　　In suffering's longest hour
Are truly Spirit-gifted
　　With intercession-power.
The Lord of Blessing fills them
　　With His uncounted gold,
An unseen store, still more and more,
　　Those trembling hands shall hold.

Not always with rejoicing
   This ministry is wrought,
For many a sigh is mingled
   With the sweet odours brought.
Yet every tear bedewing
   The faith-fed altar fire
May be its bright renewing
   To purer flame, and higher.
But when the oil of gladness
   God graciously outpours,
The heavenward blaze with blended praise
   More mightily upsoars.

So the incense-cloud ascendeth
   As through calm crystal air,
A pillar reaching unto heaven,
   Of wreathèd faith and prayer.
For evermore the Angel
   Of Intercession stands
In His Divine High Priesthood,
   With fragrance-fillèd hands,
To wave the golden censer
   Before His Father's throne,
With Spirit-fire intenser,
   And incense all His own.

And evermore the Father
   Sends radiantly down
All-marvellous responses,
   His ministers to crown;
The incense-cloud returning
   As golden blessing-showers,
We in each drop discerning
   Some feeble prayer of ours,
Transmuted into wealth unpriced,
   By Him who giveth thus
The glory all to Jesus Christ,
   The gladness all to us!

'Free to Serve.'

SHE chose His service. For the Lord of Love
Had chosen her, and paid the awful price
For her redemption ; and had sought her out,
And set her free, and clothed her gloriously,
And put His royal ring upon her hand,
And crowns of loving-kindness on her head.
She chose it. Yet it seemed she could not yield
The fuller measure other lives could bring ;
For He had given her a precious gift,
A treasure and a charge to prize and keep,
A tiny hand, a darling hand, that traced
On her heart's tablet words of golden love.
And there was not much room for other lines,
For time and thought were spent (and rightly spent,
For He had given the charge), and hours and days
Were concentrated on the one dear task.

But He had need of her. Not one new gem,
But many, for His crown ;—not one fair sheaf,
But many, she should bring. And she should have
A richer, happier harvest-home at last,
Because more fruit, more glory, and more praise,
Her life should yield to Him. And so He came,
The Master came Himself, and gently took
The little hand in His, and gave it room
Among the angel-harpers. Jesus came
And laid His own hand on the quivering heart,
And made it very still, that He might write
Invisible words of power—'Free to serve !'
Then through the darkness and the chill He sent
A heat-ray of His love, developing
The mystic writing, till it glowed and shone
And lit up all her life with radiance new,—
The happy service of a yielded heart.
With comfort that He never ceased to give,
Because her need could never cease, she filled
The empty chalices of other lives,

And time and thought were thenceforth spent for Him
Who loved her with His everlasting love.

Let Him write what He will upon our hearts
With His unerring pen. They are His Own,
Hewn from the rock by His selecting grace,
Prepared for His own glory. Let Him write!
Be sure He will not cross out one sweet word
But to inscribe a sweeter,—but to grave
One that shall shine for ever to His praise,
And thus fulfil our deepest heart-desire.
The tearful eye at first may read the line
'Bondage to grief!' but He shall wipe away
The tears, and clear the vision, till it read
In ever-brightening letters, 'Free to serve!'
For whom the Son makes free is free indeed.

Nor only by reclaiming His good gifts,
But by withholding, doth the Master write
These words upon the heart. Not always needs
Erasure of some blessèd line of love
For this more blest inscription. Where He finds
A tablet empty for the 'lines left out,'
That 'might have been' engraved with human love
And sweetest human cares, yet never bore
That poetry of life, His own dear hand
Writes 'Free to serve!' And these clear characters
Fill with fair colours all the unclaimed space,
Else grey and colourless.
                                    Then let it be
The motto of our lives until we stand
In the great freedom of Eternity,
Where we '*shall* serve Him' while we see His face,
For ever and for ever 'Free to serve.'

Coming to the King.

2 CHRONICLES 9:1–12.

I CAME from very far away to see
    The King of Salem; for I had been told

Of glory and of wisdom manifold,
And condescension infinite and free.
How could I rest, when I had heard His fame,
In that dark lonely land of death from whence I came?

I came (but not like Sheba's Queen), alone!
No stately train, no costly gifts to bring;
No friend at court, save One, that One the King!
I had requests to spread before His throne,
And I had questions none could solve for me,
Of import deep, and full of awful mystery.

I came and communed with that mighty King,
And told Him all my heart; I cannot say,
In mortal ear, what communings were they.
But wouldst thou know, go too, and meekly bring
All that is in thy heart, and thou shalt hear
His voice of love and power, His answers sweet and clear.

O happy end of every weary quest!
He told me all I needed, graciously;—
Enough for guidance, and for victory
O'er doubts and fears, enough for quiet rest;
And when some veiled response I could not read,
It was not hid from Him,—this was enough indeed.

His wisdom and His glories passed before
My wondering eyes in gradual revelation;
The house that He had built, its strong foundation,
Its living stones; and, brightening more and more,
Fair glimpses of that palace far away,
Where all His loyal ones shall dwell with Him for aye.

True the report that reached my far-off land
Of all His wisdom and transcendent fame;
Yet I believèd not until I came,—
Bowed to the dust till raised by royal hand.
The half was never told by mortal word;
My King exceeded all the fame that I had heard!

Oh, happy are His servants! happy they
 Who stand continually before His face,
 Ready to do His will of wisest grace!
My King! is mine such blessedness to-day?
For I too hear Thy wisdom, line by line,
Thy ever-brightening words in holy radiance shine.

Oh, blessèd be the Lord thy God! who set
 Our King upon His throne. Divine delight
 In the Belovèd crowning Thee with might,
Honour, and majesty supreme; and yet
The strange and Godlike secret opening thus,—
The kingship of His Christ ordained through love to us!

What shall I render to my glorious King?
 I have but that which I receive from Thee;
 And what I give, Thou givest back to me,
Transmuted by Thy touch; each worthless thing
Changed to the preciousness of gem or gold,
And by Thy blessing multiplied a thousand-fold.

All my desire Thou grantest, whatsoe'er
 I ask! Was ever mythic tale or dream
 So bold as this reality,—this stream
Of boundless blessings flowing full and free?
Yet more than I have thought or asked of Thee,
Out of Thy royal bounty still Thou givest me.

Now I will turn to my own land, and tell
 What I myself have seen and heard of Thee,
 And give Thine own sweet message, 'Come and see!'
And yet in heart and mind for ever dwell
With Thee, my King of Peace, in loyal rest,
Within the fair pavilion of Thy presence blest.

'Surely in what place my Lord the King shall be, whether in death or life,
even there also will thy servant be.'—2 SAMUEL 15:21.

'Where I am, there shall also My servant be.'—JOHN 12:26.

Reality.

'FATHER, WE KNOW THE REALITY OF JESUS CHRIST.'—
Words used by a workman in prayer. [1]

REALITY, reality,
  Lord Jesus Christ, Thou art to me!
From the spectral mists and driving clouds,
From the shifting shadows and phantom crowds;
From unreal words and unreal lives,
Where truth with falsehood feebly strives;
From the passings away, the chance and change,
Flickerings, vanishings, swift and strange,
    I turn to my glorious rest on Thee,
    Who art the grand Reality.

    Reality in greatest need,
  Lord Jesus Christ, Thou art indeed!
Is the pilot real, who alone can guide
The drifting ship through the midnight tide?
Is the lifeboat real, as it nears the wreck,
And the saved ones leap from the parting deck?
Is the haven real, where the barque may flee
From the autumn gales of the wild North Sea?
    Reality indeed art Thou,
    My Pilot, Lifeboat, Haven now!

    Reality, reality,
  In brightest days art Thou to me!
Thou art the sunshine of my mirth,
Thou art the heaven above my earth,
The spring of the love of all my heart,
And the Fountain of my song Thou art;

---

[1] At another prayer meeting on the same day a young Christian who had been witnessing for this 'reality' among those who called religion a 'phantom' and a 'sham' prayed earnestly, 'Lord Jesus, let Thy dear servant write for us what Thou art—Thou living, bright Reality!' And, urging His plea with increasing vehemence, he added, 'and let her do it *this very night.*' That 'very night' these verses were flashed into my mind; while he was 'yet speaking,' they were written and *dated.* Does not this show the 'reality of prayer?'

For dearer than the dearest now,
And better than the best, art Thou,
　　Belovèd Lord, in whom I see
　　Joy-giving, glad Reality.

　　Reality, reality,
　Lord Jesus, Thou hast been to me.
When I thought the dream of life was past,
And 'the Master's home-call' come at last;
When I thought I only had to wait
A little while at the Golden Gate,—
Only another day or two,
Till Thou Thyself shouldst bear me through,
　　How real Thy presence was to me
　　How precious Thy Reality!

　　Reality, reality,
　Lord Jesus Christ, Thou art to me!
Thy name is sweeter than songs of old,
Thy words are better than 'most fine gold,'
Thy deeds are greater than hero-glory,
Thy life is grander than poet-story;
But Thou, Thyself, for aye the same,
Art more than words and life and name!
　　Thyself Thou hast revealed to me,
　　In glorious Reality.

　　Reality, reality,
　Lord Jesus Christ, is crowned in Thee.
In Thee is every type fulfilled,
In Thee is every yearning stilled
For perfect beauty, truth, and love;
For Thou art always far above
The grandest glimpse of our Ideal,
Yet more and more we know Thee real,
　　And marvel more and more to see
　　Thine infinite Reality.

　　Reality, reality
　Of grace and glory dwells in Thee.

How real Thy mercy and Thy might!
How real Thy love, how real Thy light!
How real Thy truth and faithfulness!
How real Thy blessing when Thou dost bless!
How real Thy coming to dwell within!
How real the triumphs Thou dost win!
 Does not the loving and glowing heart
 Leap up to own how real Thou art?

 Reality, reality!
 Such let our adoration be!
Father, we bless Thee with heart and voice,
For the wondrous grace of Thy sovereign choice.
That patiently, gently, sought us out
In the far-off land of death and doubt,
That drew us to Christ by the Spirit's might,
That opened our eyes to see the light
 That arose in strange reality,
 From the darkness falling on Calvary.

 Reality, reality,
 Lord Jesus Christ, Thou art to me!
My glorious King, my Lord, my God,
Life is too short for half the laud,
For half the debt of praise I owe
For this blest knowledge, that 'I know
The reality of Jesus Christ,'—
Unmeasured blessing, gift unpriced!
 Will I not praise Thee when I see
 In the long noon of Eternity,
 Unveiled, Thy 'bright Reality!'

Far More Exceeding.

καθ᾽ ὑπερβολὴν εἰς ὑπερβολὴν.—2 Corinthians 4:17.

'From glory unto glory!' Thank God, that even here
The starry words are shining out, our heavenward way to cheer!
That e'en among the shadows the conquering brightness glows,
As ever from the nearing Light intenser radiance flows.

'From glory unto glory!' Shall the grand progression fail
When the darkening glass is shattered as we pass within the veil?
Shall the joyous song of 'Onward!' at once for ever cease,
And the swelling music culminate in monotone of peace?

Shall the fuller life be sundered at the portal of its bliss,
From the principle of growth entwined with every nerve of this?
Shall the holy law of progress be hopelessly repealed,
And the moment of releasing see our sum of glory sealed?

The tender touch of moonlight, with an orbit quickly run,
The lustre of the planet, circling slowly round the sun,
The mighty revolutions of its million-heated blaze,
'From glory unto glory' lead our far-expanding gaze.

Then onward, ever onward, through the unexplored abyss
(Dark barrier between the suns of other worlds and this),
Until the measure-unit mocks the grasp of human thought,
And space and time commingle while the clue is feebly sought.

Till, in that wider ocean, deep calleth unto deep,
Star-glories with attendant worlds, forth-flashing as they sweep
Around their unseen centre, that point of mystic power,
In unimagined cycles, where an age is but an hour.

Then! onward and yet onward! for the dim revealings show
That systems unto systems in grand succession grow,
That what we deemed a volume but one golden verse may be,
One rhythmic cadence in the flow of God's great poetry.

That what we deemed a symphony was one all-thrilling bar,
Through aisles of His great temple resounding full and far;
That what we deemed an ocean was a shallow by the shore!
Then! onward yet, in eagle flight, through the Infinite we soar—

'From glory unto glory,' till the spirit fails; and then
Illimitable vistas still opening to our ken,
Mysterious immensities of order and of light,
Stretch far beyond our farthest thought, as thought beyond our sight.

But the starting-point in heaven shall be no 'glory of the moon,'
No planet gleam, no stellar fire, no blaze of tropic noon;

From 'glory that excelleth' all that human heart hath known,
Our 'onward, upward,' shall begin in the presence of the Throne.

'From glory unto glory' of loveliness and light,
Of music and of rapture, of power and of sight,
'From glory unto glory' of knowledge and of love,
Shall be the joy of progress awaiting us above.

'From glory unto glory' that ever lies before,
Still wondering, adoring, rejoicing more and more,
Still following where He leadeth, from shining field to field,
Himself the goal of glory, Revealer and Revealed!

'From glory unto glory' with no limit and no veil,
With wings that cannot weary and hearts that cannot fail;
Within, without, no hindrance, no barrier as we soar;
And never interruption to the endless 'more and more'!

For infinite outpourings of Jehovah's love and grace,
And infinite unveilings of the brightness of His face,
And infinite unfoldings of the splendour of His will,
Meet the mightiest expansions of the finite spirit still.

———————

O Saviour, hast Thou ransomed us from death's unknown abyss,
And purchased with Thy precious blood such everlasting bliss?
Art Thou indeed preparing us, with love exceeding great,
And preparing all this glory in such 'far exceeding weight'?

Then let our hearts be surely fixed where truest joys are found,
And let our burning, loving praise, yet more and more abound;
And, gazing on the 'things not seen,' eternal in the skies,
'From glory unto glory,' O Saviour, let us rise!

'The Splendour of God's Will.'

IN the freshness of the spring-time,
    In the beauty of the May,
When the swift-winged breezes carolled,
    And the lambs were all at play,

And the birds were blithe and busy,
    Upon her couch she lay.

Like a lily bruised and drooping,
    Before its early flower
Had fully opened to the sun,
    Or reached a noontide hour:
Broken and yet more fragrant
    For the heavy-beating shower.

It was not the first spring-time
    Passed without one glad sight
Of a starry primrose growing,
    Or a brooklet swift and bright,
And without one bounding footstep
    On a field with daisies white.

It was not the first spring-time—
    And it might not be the last
In weariness and suffering
    Thus to be slowly passed;
For when the young feet cannot move
    Months do not travel fast.

And yet she saw what others
    Have never sought or seen,
A splendour more than spring-light
    On fair trees waving green,
And more than summer sunshine
    On Ocean's silver sheen.

Her pencil, tracing feebly
    Words that shall echo still,
Perchance some unknown mission
    May joyously fulfil:—
'I think I just begin to see
    The *splendour* of God's will!'

O words of golden music
    Caught from the harps on high,

Which find a glorious anthem
   Where we have found a sigh,
And peal their grandest praises
   Just where ours faint and die!

O words of holy radiance
   Shining on every tear,
Till it becomes a rainbow,
   Reflecting, bright and clear,
Our Father's love and glory
   So wonderful, so dear!

O words of sparkling power,
   Of insight full and deep!
Shall they not enter other hearts
   In a grand and gladsome sweep,
And lift the lives to songs of joy
   That only droop and weep?

For her, God's will was suffering,
   Just waiting, lying still!
Days passing on in weariness,
   In shadows deep and chill;
And yet she had begun to see
   The Splendour of God's Will!

And oh, it is a splendour,
   A glow of majesty,
A mystery of beauty,
   If we will only see;
A very cloud of glory
   Enfolding you and me.

A splendour that is lighted
   At one transcendent flame,
The wondrous Love, the perfect Love,
   Our Father's sweetest name;
For His very Name, and Essence,
   And His Will are all the same!

A splendour that is shining
    Upon His children's way;
That guides the willing footsteps
    That do not want to stray,
And that leads them ever onward
    Unto the perfect day.

A splendour that illumines,
    Th' abysses of the Past
And marvels of the Future,
    Sublime and bright and vast;
While o'er our tiny Present
    A flood of light is cast.

No twilight falls upon it,
    No shadow dims its ray,
No darkness overcomes it,
    No night can end its day;
It hath unending triumph
    And everlasting sway.

Blest Will of God! most glorious,
    The very fount of grace,
Whence all the goodness floweth
    That heart can ever trace—
Temple whose pinnacles are love,
    And faithfulness its base.

Blest Will of God! whose splendour
    Is dawning on the world,
On hearts in which Christ's banner
    Is manfully unfurled,
On hearts of childlike meekness,
    With dew of youth impearled.

O Spirit of Jehovah,
    Reveal this glory still!
That many an empty chalice
    Sweet thanks and praise may fill,
When, like this 'little one,' they see
    'The Splendour of God's Will':

That faith may win the vision
    That hers hath early won,
And gaze upon the splendour,
    And own the cloudless sun,
And join the seraph song of love,
    And *sing*—'Thy Will be done!'

The Two Paths.

VIA DOLOROSA AND VIA GIOJOSA.

(Suggested by a Picture.)

My Master, they have wronged Thee and Thy love!
They only told me I should find the path
A Via Dolorosa all the way!
Even Thy sweetest singers only sang
Of pressing onward through the same sharp thorns,
With bleeding footsteps, through the chill dark mist,
Following and struggling till they reach the light,
The rest, the sunshine of the far beyond.
The anthems of the pilgrimage were set
In most pathetic minors, exquisite,
Yet breathing sadness more than any praise.
Thy minstrels let the fitful breezes make
Æolian moans on their entrusted harps,
Until the listeners thought that this was all
The music Thou hadst given. And so the steps
That halted where the two ways met and crossed,
The broad and narrow, turned aside in fear,
Thinking the radiance of their youth must pass
In sombre shadows if they followed Thee;
Hearing afar such echoes of one strain,
The cross, the tribulation, and the toil,
The conflict, and the clinging in the dark.
What wonder that the dancing feet are stayed
From entering the only path of peace!
Master, forgive them! Tune their harps anew,
And put a new song in their mouths for Thee,
And make Thy chosen people joyful in Thy love.

Lord Jesus, Thou hast trodden once for all
The Via Dolorosa,—and for *us!*
No artist-power or minstrel-gift may tell
The cost to Thee of each unfaltering step,
Where love that passeth knowledge led Thee on,
Faithful and true to God, and true to us.
    And now, belovèd Lord, Thou callest us
To follow Thee, and we will take Thy word
About the path which Thou hast marked for us.
Narrow indeed it is! Who does not choose
The narrow track upon the mountain-side,
With ever-widening view, and freshening air,
And honeyed heather, rather than the road,
With smoothest breadth of dust and loss of view,
Soiled blossoms not worth gathering, and the noise
Of wheels instead of silence of the hills,
Or music of the waterfalls? Oh, why
Should they misrepresent Thy words, and make
'Narrow' synonymous with 'very hard'?
    For Thou, Divinest Wisdom, Thou hast said
Thy ways are ways of pleasantness, and all
Thy paths are peace; and that the path of him
Who wears Thy perfect robe of righteousness,
Is as the light that shineth more and more
Unto the perfect day. And Thou hast given
An olden promise, rarely quoted now,[1]
Because it is too bright for our weak faith:
'If they obey and serve Him, they shall spend
Days in prosperity, and they shall spend
Their years in pleasures.' All because *Thy* days
Were full of sorrow, and Thy lonely years
Were passed in grief's acquaintance—all for us!
    Master, I set my seal that Thou art true!
Of Thy good promise not one thing hath failed,
And I would send a ringing challenge forth,
To all who know Thy name, to tell it out,
Thy faithfulness to every written word,

[1] Job 26:9

Thy loving-kindness crowning all the days,—
To say and sing with me : ' The Lord is good,
His mercy is for ever, and His truth
Is written on each page of all my life! '
Yes! there *is* tribulation, but Thy power
Can blend it with rejoicing. There *are* thorns,
But they have kept us in the narrow way,
The King's highway of holiness and peace.
And there *is* chastening, but the Father's love
Flows through it ; and would any trusting heart
Forego the chastening and forego the love ?
And every step leads on to ' more and more,'—
From strength to strength Thy pilgrims pass, and sing
The praise of Him who leads them on and on,
From glory unto glory, even here!

Sunday Night.

REST him, O Father! Thou didst send him forth
With great and gracious messages of love ;
But Thy ambassador is weary now,
Worn with the weight of his high embassy.
Now care for him as Thou hast cared for us
In sending him ; and cause him to lie down
In Thy fresh pastures, by Thy streams of peace.
Let Thy left hand be now beneath his head,
And Thine upholding right encircle him,
And, underneath, the Everlasting arms
Be felt in full support. So let him rest,
Hushed like a little child, without one care,
And so give Thy belovèd sleep to-night.

Rest him, dear Master! He hath poured for us
The wine of joy, and we have been refreshed.
Now fill *his* chalice, give him sweet new draughts
Of life and love, with Thine own hand ; be Thou
His ministrant to-night ; draw very near
In all Thy tenderness and all Thy power.
Oh speak to him! Thou knowest how to speak
A word in season to Thy weary ones,

And he is weary now. Thou lovest him—
Let Thy disciple lean upon Thy breast,
And, leaning, gain new strength to 'rise and shine.'

    Rest him, O loving Spirit! Let Thy calm
Fall on his soul to-night. O holy Dove,
Spread Thy bright wing above him, let him rest
Beneath its shadow; let him know afresh
The infinite truth and might of Thy dear name—
'Our Comforter!' As gentlest touch will stay
The strong vibrations of a jarring chord,
So lay Thy hand upon his heart, and still
Each overstraining throb, each pulsing pain.
Then, in the stillness, breathe upon the strings,
And let Thy holy music overflow
With soothing power his listening, resting soul.

Precious Things.

I.

OH what shining revelation of His treasures God hath given!
Precious things of grace and glory, precious things of earth and heaven.
Holy Spirit, now unlock them with Thy mighty golden key,
Royal jewels of the kingdom let us now adoring see!

II.

'Unto you therefore which believe, He is precious,'—1 PETER 2:7.

Christ is precious, oh most precious, gift by God the Father sealed;
Pearl of greatest price and treasure, hidden, yet to us revealed;
His own people's crown of glory, and resplendent diadem;
More than thousand worlds, and dearer than all life and love to them.

III.

'Behold, I lay in Zion a chief corner stone, elect, precious.'—1 PETER 2:6.

Marvellous and very precious is the Corner Stone Elect;
Though rejected by the builders, chosen by the Architect;

All-supporting, all-uniting, and all-crowning, tried and sure;
True Foundation, yet true Headstone of His temple bright and pure.

IV.

'Ye know that ye were not redeemed with corruptible things, . . . but with the precious blood of Christ, as of a lamb without blemish and without spot.'—1 Peter 1:18, 19.

Now, in reverent love and wonder, touch the theme of deepest laud,
Precious blood of Christ that bought us and hath made us nigh to God!
His own blood, O love unfathomed! shed for those who loved Him not;
Mighty fountain always open, cleansing us from every spot.

V.

'How precious also are Thy thoughts unto me, O God! how great is the sum of them!'
—Psalm 139:17.

Oh, how wonderful and precious are Thy thoughts to us, O God!
Outlined in Creation, blazoned on Redemption's banner broad;
Infinite and deep and dazzling as the noontide heavens above;
Yet *more* wonderful to usward are Thy thoughts of peace and love.

VI.

'Whereby are given unto us exceeding great and precious promises, that by these ye might be partakers of the divine nature.'—2 Peter 1:4.

Then, exceeding great and precious are Thy promises Divine;
Given by Christ, and by the Spirit sealed with sweetest 'All are thine!'
Precious in their peace and power, in their sure and changeless might,
Strengthening, comforting, transforming; suns by day and stars by night.

VII.

'To them that have obtained like precious faith with us through the righteousness of God, and our Saviour Jesus Christ.'—2 Peter 1:1.

Precious faith our God hath given; rich in faith is rich indeed!
Fire-tried gold from His own treasury, fully meeting every need:
Channel of His grace abounding; bringing peace and joy and light;
Purifying, overcoming; linking weakness with His might.

VIII.

'The precious ointment upon the head, that ran down upon the beard, even Aaron's beard; that went down to the skirts of his garments.'—Psalm 133:2.

Precious ointment, very costly, of chief odours pure and sweet,
Holy gift for royal priesthood, thus for temple-service meet;
Such the Spirit's precious unction, oil of gladness freely shed,
Sanctifying and abiding on the consecrated head.

IX.

'How excellent (*marg.* precious) is Thy loving kindness, O God! therefore the children of men put their trust under the shadow of Thy wings.'—Psalm 36:7; Isaiah 54:8, 10.

Who shall paint the flash of splendour from the opened casket bright,
When His precious loving-kindness beams upon the quickened sight!
Priceless jewel ever gleaming with imperishable ray,
God will never take it from us, though the mountains pass away.

X.

'It cannot be valued with the gold of Ophir, with the precious onyx, or the sapphire. No mention shall be made of coral or of pearls: for the price of wisdom is above rubies.'—Job 28:16, 18.

Far more precious than the ruby, or the crystal's rainbow light,
Valued not with precious onyx or with pearl and sapphire bright,
Freely given to all who ask it, is the wisdom from above,
Pure and peaceable and gentle, full of fruits of life and love.

XI.

'Blessed of the Lord be his land for the precious things of heaven, for the dew, and for the deep that coucheth beneath, and for the precious fruits brought forth by the sun, and for the precious things put forth by the moon, and for the chief things of the ancient mountains, and for the precious things of the lasting hills, and for the precious things of the earth.'—Deuteronomy 33.13–16.

Nor withhold we glad thanksgiving for His mercies ever new,
Precious things of earth and heaven, sun and rain and quickening dew;
Precious fruits and varied crowning of the year His goodness fills,
Chief things of the ancient mountains, precious things of lasting hills.

XII.

'If thou take forth the precious from the vile, thou shalt be as My mouth.'
—JEREMIAH 15:19.

Such His gifts! but mark we duly our responsibility
Unto Him whose name is Holy, infinite in purity;
Sin and self no longer serving, take the precious from the vile,
So His power shall rest upon thee, thou shalt dwell beneath His smile.

XIII.

'The precious sons of Zion, comparable to fine gold.'—LAMENTATIONS 4:2.

Sons of Zion, ye are precious in your heavenly Father's sight,
Ye are His peculiar treasure, ye His jewels of delight;
Sought and chosen, cleansed and polished, purchased with
transcendent cost,
Kept in His own royal casket, never, never to be lost.

XIV.

'That the trial of your faith, being much more precious than of gold that
perisheth, though it be tried with fire, might be found unto praise and honour
and glory at the appearing of Jesus Christ.'—1 PETER 1:7.

Precious, more than gold that wasteth, is the trial of your faith,
Fires of anguish or temptation cannot dim it, cannot scathe!
Your Refiner sitteth watching till His image shineth clear,
For His glory, praise, and honour, when the Saviour shall appear.

XV.

'Precious in the sight of the Lord is the death of His saints.'—PSALM 116:15.

Precious, precious to Jehovah is His children's holy sleep;
He is with them in the passing through the waters cold and deep;
Everlasting love enfolds them softly, safely to His breast,
Everlasting love receives them to His glory and His rest.

XVI.

'He showed me that great city, the holy Jerusalem, descending out of heaven from God, having the glory of God: and her light was like unto a stone most precious; even like a jasper stone, clear as crystal.'—REVELATION 21:10, 11.

Pause not here,—the Holy City, glorious in God's light, behold!
Like unto a stone most precious, clear as crystal, pure as gold;
Strong foundations, fair with sapphires, sardius and chrysolite,
Blent with amethyst and jacinth, emerald and topaz bright.

XVII.

'A city which hath foundations, whose builder and maker is God.'—HEBREWS 11:10.

Glorious dwelling of the holy, where no grief or gloom of sin
Through the pure and pearly portals evermore shall enter in:
Christ its Light and God its Temple, Christ its song of endless laud!
Oh what precious consummation of the precious things of God!

'Afterwards.'

(FROM F. R. H. TO K. T.)

'THERE is no "afterward" on earth for me!'
　　Beloved, 'tis not so!
That God's own 'afterwards' are pledged to thee,
　　Thy life shall show.

No 'afterward' indeed of great things wrought,
　　By willing hands and feet;
No sheaf is thine, from wider harvests brought,
　　With singing sweet.

Fair flowing years of ease and laughing strength,
　　With cloudless morning skies,
Sweet life renewed, and active work at length,
　　His love denies.

But living fruit of righteousness to Him
　　His chastening shall yield,
And constant 'afterwards,' no longer dim,
　　Shall be revealed.

Is it no 'afterward' that in thy heart
    His *love* is shed abroad?
And that His Spirit breathes, while called apart,
    The *peace* of God?

That *joy* in tribulation shall spring forth
    To greet His visits blessed,
Whose wisdom wakes the south wind or the north,
    As He sees best!

Shall not *longsuffering* in thee be wrought,
    To mirror back His own?
His *gentleness* shall mellow every thought,
    And look, and tone.

And *goodness!* In thyself dwells no good thing,
    Yet from thy glorious Root
An 'afterward' of holiness shall spring—
    Most precious fruit!

The trial of thy *faith* from hour to hour
    Shall yield a grand increase;
He shall fulfil the work of faith with power
    That cannot cease.

And all around shall praise Him as they see
    The *meekness* of thy Lord.
Thus, even here and now, how blest shall be
    Thy sure reward!

This pleasant fruit it shall be thine to lay
    At thy Belovèd's feet,
The ripening clusters growing day by day
    More full and sweet.

If at His gate He keeps thee waiting now
    Through many a suffering year,
Watch for His daily 'afterwards,' and thou
    Shalt find them here:

Till, as refinèd gold, in thee shall shine
    His image, no more dim;

Then shall the endless 'afterward' be thine
Of rest with Him.

'Vessels of Mercy, Prepared unto Glory.'

ROMANS 9:23.

VESSELS of mercy, prepared unto glory!
   This is your calling and this is your joy!
This, for the new year unfolding before ye,
   Tells out the terms of your blessèd employ.

Vessels, it may be, all empty and broken,
   Marred in the Hand of inscrutable skill;
(Love can accept the mysterious token!)
   Marred but to make them more beautiful still
JEREMIAH 18:4.

Vessels, it may be, not costly or golden;
   Vessels, it may be, of quantity small,
Yet by the Nail in the Sure Place upholden,
   Never to shiver and never to fall.
ISAIAH 22:23, 24.

Vessels to honour, made sacred and holy,
   Meet for the use of the Master we love,
Ready for service all simple and lowly,
   Ready, one day, for the temple above.
2 TIMOTHY 2:21.

Yes, though the vessels be fragile and earthen,
   God hath commanded His glory to shine;
Treasure resplendent henceforth is our burthen,
   Excellent power, not ours but Divine.
2 CORINTHIANS 4:5, 6.

Chosen in Christ ere the dawn of Creation,
   Chosen for Him, to be filled with His grace,
Chosen to carry the streams of salvation
   Into each thirsty and desolate place.
ACTS 9:15.

Take all Thy vessels, O glorious Finer,
   Purge all the dross, that each chalice may be
Pure in Thy pattern, completer, diviner,
   Filled with Thy glory and shining for Thee.

PROVERBS 25:4.

Seulement pour Toi.

[Written for and sung by some Swiss peasants at a Sunday afternoon Bible reading, July 23rd, 1876.]

Que je sois, O cher Sauveur,		*O that I be—May I be, O dear Saviour,*[1]
Seulement à Toi!	Hosea 3:1*	*Only (wholly) to Thee (Thine)!*
Soit l'amour de tout mon cœur	Matt. 22:37	*Be the love of all my heart*
Seulement pour Toi.		*Solely for Thee.*
Je reviens à mon Père	John 14:6	*I come back to my Father*
Seulement par Toi,		*Only through Thee,*
Ma confiance entière	Psalm 118:8	*My confidence entire*
Sera en Toi,		*Wants to be (will be) in Thee,*
Seulement en Toi.		*Only in Thee.*
Le péché Tu as porté	I Peter 2:24	*The sin, Thou hast carried (borne)*
Seul, seul pour moi;		*Alone, alone for me;*
Et Ton sang Tu as versé		*And Thy blood Thou hast shed*
Seul, seul pour moi.		*Alone, alone for me.*
Toute gloire, toute joie	Rev. 5:12	*All glory, all joy,*
Sera pour Toi;		*Will be for Thee;*
L'espérance et la foi	Acts 4:12	*The hope and faith*
Seront en Toi,		*Will be in Thee,*
Seulement en Toi.		*Only in Thee.*
Aujourd'hui, O cher Seigneur,	II Cor. 6:2	*Today, O dear Lord,*
Acceptes-moi!	Ephesians. 1:6	*Accept me!*
Tu es seul mon grand Sauveur,	Isaiah 19:20	*Thou alone art my great Saviour,*
Tu es mon Roi.	Psalm 44:4	*Thou alone art my King.*
Tous mes moments, tous mes jours	II Cor.	*All my moments, all my days*
Seront pour Toi!	5:15	*Will be for Thee!*
Jésus, gardes-moi toujours	Isaiah 27:3	*Jesus, keep me always*
Seulement pour Toi,		*Only for Thee,*
Seulement pour Toi.		*Only for Thee.*

[1] English translation by David Chalkley.

*Note: In the posthumously published *Under His Shadow*, these Scripture references were given on these lines.

Que je chante et que je pleure Seulement pour Toi!	Psalm 21:13	*O that I sing and that I weep Only for Thee!*
Que je vive et que je meure Seulement pour Toi!	Romans 14:8	*Let me live and let me die Only for Thee!*
Jésus, que m'as tant aimé Mourant pour moi,	Galatians 2:20	*Jesus, how Thou hast loved me, Dying for me,*
Toute mon éternité Sera pour Toi, Seulement pour Toi.	I Thess. 4:17	*All my eternity Will be for Thee, Only for Thee.*

A Song in the Night.

[Written in severe pain, Sunday afternoon, October 8th, 1876, at the Pension
Wengen, Alps.]

I TAKE this pain, Lord Jesus,
From Thine own hand,
The strength to bear it bravely
Thou wilt command.

I am too weak for effort,
So let me rest,
In hush of sweet submission,
On Thine own breast.

I take this pain, Lord Jesus,
As proof indeed
That Thou art watching closely
My truest need:

That Thou, my Good Physician,
Art watching still;
That all Thine own good pleasure
Thou wilt fulfil.

I take this pain, Lord Jesus,
What Thou dost choose
The soul that really loves Thee
Will not refuse.

It is not for the first time
    I trust to-day;
For Thee my heart has never
    A trustless 'Nay!'

I take this pain, Lord Jesus,
    But what beside?
'Tis no unmingled portion
    Thou dost provide.

In every hour of faintness,
    My cup runs o'er
With faithfulness and mercy,
    And love's sweet store.

I take this pain, Lord Jesus,
    As Thine own gift,
And true though tremulous praises
    I now uplift.

I am too weak to sing them,
    But Thou dost hear
The whisper from the pillow,—
    Thou art so near!

'Tis Thy dear hand, O Saviour,
    That presseth sore,
The hand that bears the nail-prints
    For evermore.

And now beneath its shadow,
    Hidden by Thee,
The pressure only tells me
    Thou lovest me!

The Voice of Many Waters.

FAR away I heard it,
    Stealing through the pines,
Like a whisper saintly,

Falling dimly, faintly,
    Through the terraced vines.

Freshening breezes bore it
    Down the mountain slope;
So I turned and listened,
While the sunlight glistened
    On the snowy cope.

Far away and dreamy
    Was the Voice I heard;
Yet it pierced and found me,
Through the voices round me—
    Song without a word.

All the life and turmoil,
    All the busy cheer
Melted in the flowing
Of that murmur, growing,
    Claiming all my ear.

What the mountain-message,
    I could never tell;
Such Æolian fluting
Hath no language suiting
    What we write and spell.

Rather did it enter
    Where no words can win,
Touching and unsealing
Springs of hidden feeling,
    Slumbering deep within.

Voice of many waters
    Only heard afar!
Hushing, luring slowly,
With an influence holy,
    Like the Orient Star.

———————

Follow where it leadeth,
   Till we stand below,
While the noble thunder
Wins the hush of wonder,
   Silent in its glow.

Light and sound triumphant
   Fill the eye and ear;
Every pulse is beating
Quick unconscious greeting
   To the vision near.

Rainbow-flames are wreathing
   In the dazzling foam,
Fancy far transcending,
Power and beauty blending
   In their radiant home.

All the dreamy longing
   Passes out of sight,
In a swift surrender
To the joyous splendour
   Of this song of might.

Self is lost and hidden
   As it peals along;
Fevered introspection,
Paler-browed reflection
   Vanish in the song.

For the spirit, lifted
   From the dulling mists,
Takes a stronger moulding,
As the sound enfolding,
   Bears it where it lists.

Voice of many waters!
   Must we turn away
From the crystal chorus
Now resounding o'er us
   Through the flashing spray!

Far away we hear it,
  Floating from the sky;
Mystic echo, falling
Through the stars, and calling
  From the thrones on high.

There are voices round us,
  Busy, quick, and loud;
All day long we hear them,
We are still so near them,
  Still among the crowd.

Yet athwart the clamour
  Falls it, faint and sweet,
Like the softest harp-tone,
Passing every sharp tone
  Down the noisy street.

To the soul-recesses
  Cleaving then its way,
Waking hidden yearning,
Unwilled impulse turning
  To the Far Away.

Far away—and viewless,
  Yet not all unknown—
In the murmur tracing
Soft notes interlacing
  With familiar tone.

So we start and listen!
  While the murmur low
Falleth ever clearer,
Swelleth fuller, nearer
  In melodious flow.

Voice of many waters
  From the height above
Hushing, luring slowly
With its influence holy,
  With its song of love!

Following where it leadeth,
   Pilgrim feet shall stand,
Where the holy millions
Throng the fair pavilions
   In the Glorious Land.

Where the sevenfold 'Worthy!'
   Hails the King of kings,
Blent with golden clashing
Of the crowns, and flashing
   Of cherubic wings;

Rolls the Amen Chorus,
   Old, yet ever new;
Seal of blest allegiance,
Pledge of bright obedience,
   Seal that God is true.

Through the solemn glory
   Alleluias rise,
Mightiest exultation,
Holiest adoration,
   Infinite surprise.

There immortal powers
   Meet immortal song,
Heavenly image bearing,
Angel-essence sharing,
   Excellent and strong.

Strong to bear the glory
   And the veil-less sight,
Strong to swell the thunders
And to know the wonders
   Of the home of light.

Voice of many waters!
   Everlasting laud!
Hark! it rushes nearer,
Every moment clearer,
   From the Throne of God!

The Key Found.

THERE is a strange wild wail around, a wail of wild unrest,
A moaning in the music, with echoes unconfessed,
And a mocking twitter here and there, with small notes shrill and thin,
And deep, low, shuddering groans that rise from caves of gloom within.

And still the weird wail crosses the harmonies of God,
And still the wailers wander through His fair lands, rich and broad;
Grave thought-explorers swell the cry of doubt and nameless pain,
And careless feet, among the flowers, trip to the dismal strain.

They may wander as they will in the hopeless search for truth,
They may squander in the quest all the freshness of their youth,
They may wrestle with the nightmares of sin's unresting sleep,
They may cast a futile plummet in the heart's unfathomed deep:

But they wait and wail and wander in vain and still in vain,
Though they glory in the dimness and are proud of very pain;
For a life of Titan struggle is but one sublime mistake,
While the spell-dream is upon them, and they cannot, will not wake.

Awake, O thou that sleepest! The Deliverer is near!
Arise, go forth to meet Him! Bow down, for He is here!
Ye shall count your true existence from this first, blessèd tryst,
For He waiteth to reveal Himself, the Very God in Christ.

For the soul is never satisfied, the life is incomplete,
And the symphonies of sorrow find no cadence calm and sweet,
And the earth-lights never lead us beyond the shadows grim,
And the lone heart never resteth till it findeth rest in Him.

Do ye doubt our feeble witness? Though ye scorn us, come and see!
Come and hear Him for yourselves, and ye shall know that it is He!
Ye shall find in Him the Centre, the Very Truth and Life,
Resplendent resolution of the endless doubt and strife.

Ye shall find a perfect fitness with your highest, deepest thought,
In Him, the fair Ideal, that so long ye vainly sought,
In Him the grand Reality ye never found before,
In Him the Lord that ye must love, the God ye must adore.

Ye shall find in Him the filling of the 'aching void' within;
In Him the instant antidote for anguish and for sin;
In Him the conscious meeting of the soul's unuttered need;
In Him the *All* that ye have sought, the goal of life indeed.

As the light is to the eye, with its sensitive array
Of delicate adjustments with their finely balanced play,
With its instinct of perception, and its craving for the light,
So is Jesus to the spirit, when He gives the inward sight.

As the full and clear translation of some characters of fate,
With their sibylline enfoldings, of dim mysterious weight,
And a haunting terror lest the real be darker than the guessed!
So is Jesus to the questions and enigmas of the breast.

As the key is to the lock, when it enters quick and true,
Fitting all the complex wards that are hidden from the view,
Moving all the secret springs that no other finds or moves,
So is Jesus to the soul, when His saving power He proves.

As the music to the ear, when the mightiest anthems roll,
With its corridors conveying every echo to the soul,
With its exquisite discernment of vibration and of tone,—
So is Jesus to the heart that is made for Him alone.

No need to prove the sunshine when the eye receives the light!
When the cipher is deciphered, we know the clue is right;
The key is known by fitting the strange intricate wards;
And the ears must own the music when they recognise the chords.

No need to prove a Saviour, when once the heart believes,
And the light of God's own glory in Jesus Christ receives!
No need for weary puzzle, with heart-lore strange and dim,
When we find our dark enigmas are simply solved in Him!

We cannot doubt our finding the very Key indeed,
When Jesus fills up every void, responds to every need,
When all the secrets of our hearts before Him are revealed,
And all the mystery of life, alone with Him, unsealed.

We cannot doubt, when once the ear of listening faith has heard,
With all-responsive thrill of love, the music of His word!
He gives the witness that excels all argument or sign,—
When we have heard it for ourselves we *know* it is Divine!

And then, oh, then the wail is stilled, the wandering is o'er,
The rest is gained, the certainty that never wavers more;
And then the full, unquivering praise arises glad and strong,
And life becomes the prelude of the everlasting song!

(HER LAST BIRTHDAY.)

SEULEMENT POUR TOI.

Seulement pour Toi.

Que je sois, O cher Sauveur,
Seulement à Toi!
Soit l'amour de tout mon cœur
Seulement pour Toi.
Je reviens à mon Père
Seulement par Toi,
Ma confiance entière
Sera en Toi,
Seulement en Toi.

Le péché Tu as porté
Seul, seul pour moi;
Et Ton sang Tu as versé
Seul, seul pour moi.
Toute gloire, toute joie
Sera pour Toi;
L'espérance et la foi
Seront en Toi
Seulement en Toi.

Aujourd'hui, O cher Seigneur,
Acceptes-moi!
Tu es seul mon grand Sauveur,
Tu es mon Roi.
Tous mes moments, tous mes jours
Seront pour Toi!
Jésus, gardes-moi toujours
Seulement pour Toi,
Seulement pour Toi.

Que je chante et que je pleure
Seulement pour Toi!
Que je vive et que je meure
Seulement pour Toi!
Jésus, qui m'as tant aimé
Mourant pour moi,
Toute mon éternité
Sera pour Toi,
Seulement pour Toi.

FRANCES RIDLEY HAVERGAL.

LONDON: S. W. PARTRIDGE & CO., 9, PATERNOSTER ROW.

Fins-Hauts. Sunday July 23. 1876.
Written for & sung les villages at a Bible Reading

F.R.H. placed this printed copy in her Manuscript Book Nº VIII. See pages 626–627. She wrote: Fins-hauts. Sunday July 23. 1876. Written for & sung by villagers at a Bible reading

An Easter Prayer

Oh let me know
The power of Thy Reserection;
Oh let me show
Thy risen life in calm and clear reflection.
Oh let me soar
Where Thou, my Saviour Christ art gone before;
In mind and heart
Let me dwell always, only, where Thou art.

Oh let me give
Out of the gifts Thou freely givest;
Oh let me live
With life abundantly because Thou livest;
Oh make me shine
In darkest places for Thy light is mine;
Oh let me be
A faithful witness for Thy truth and Thee.

Oh let me show
The strong reality of Gospel story;
Oh let me go
From strength to strength, from glory unto glory;
Oh let me sing
For very joy because Thou art my King
Oh let me praise
Thy love and faithfulness through all my days.

F.R.H.'s fair copy autograph, very late in her life, found in her last Manuscript Book,
Nº IX. See pages 641–642.

Closing Chords.

What Thou Wilt.

Do what Thou wilt! Yes, only do
    What seemeth good to Thee :
Thou art so loving, wise, and true,
    It must be best for me.

Send what Thou wilt ; or beating shower,
    Soft dew, or brilliant sun ;
Alike in still or stormy hour,
    My Lord, Thy will be done.

Teach what Thou wilt ; and make me learn
    Each lesson full and sweet,
And deeper things of God discern
    While sitting at Thy feet.

Say what Thou wilt ; and let each word
    My quick obedience win ;
Let loyalty and love be stirred
    To deeper glow within.

Give what Thou wilt ; for then I know
    I shall be rich indeed ;
My King rejoices to bestow
    Supply for every need.

Take what Thou wilt, belovèd Lord,
    For I have all in Thee !
My own exceeding great reward,
    Thou, Thou Thyself shalt be !

Hope.

WHAT though the blossom fall and die?
    The flower is not the root;
The sun of love may ripen yet
    The Master's pleasant fruit.

What though by many a sinful fall
    Thy garments are defiled?
A Saviour's blood can cleanse them all;
    Fear not! thou art His child.

Arise! and, leaning on His strength,
    Thy weakness shall be strong;
And He will teach Thy heart at length
    A new perpetual song.

Arise! to follow in His track
    Each holy footprint clear,
And on an upward course look back
    With every brightening year.

Arise! and on thy future way
    His blessing with thee be!
His presence be thy staff and stay,
    Till Thou His glory see.

Fear Not.

ISAIAH 43:1–7.

LISTEN! for the Lord hath spoken!
    'Fear thou not,' saith He;
'When thou passest through the waters,
    I will be with thee.

'Fear not! for I have redeemed thee;
    All My sheep I know!
When thou passest through the rivers,
    They shall not o'erflow.

'Fear not! by thy name I called thee,—
     Mine thy heart hath learned;
When thou walkest through the fire,
     Thou shalt not be burned.

'Thou art Mine! oh, therefore fear not!
     Mine for ever now!
And the flame shall never kindle
     On thy sealèd brow.

'Thou art precious, therefore fear not,
     Precious unto Me!
I have made thee for My glory,
     I have lovèd thee.'

The Scripture Cannot Be Broken.

JOHN 10:35.

UPON the Word I rest,
     Each pilgrim day;
This golden staff is best
     For all the way.
What Jesus Christ hath spoken,
     Can*not* be broken!

Upon the Word I rest,
     So strong, so sure,
So full of comfort blest,
     So sweet, so pure!
The charter of salvation,
     Faith's broad foundation.

Upon the Word I stand!
     That cannot die!
Christ seals it in my hand,
     He cannot lie!
The word that faileth never!
     Abiding ever!

Chorus. The Master hath said it! Rejoicing in this,
    We ask not for sign or for token;
    His word is enough for our confident bliss,—
    'The Scripture *cannot* be broken!'

'He Suffered.'

'He suffered!' Was it, Lord, indeed for me,
    The Just One for the unjust, Thou didst bear
    The weight of sorrow that I hardly dare
To look upon, in dark Gethsemane?
'He suffered!' Thou, my near and gracious Friend,
    And yet my Lord, my God! Thou didst not shrink
    For me that full and fearful cup to drink,
Because Thou lovedst even to the end!
'He suffered!' Saviour, was Thy love so vast
    That mysteries of unknown agony,
    Even unto death, its only gauge could be,
Unmeasured as the fiery depths it passed?
Lord, by the sorrows of Gethsemane,
Seal Thou my quivering love for ever unto Thee!

Behold Your King.

'Behold, and see if there be any sorrow like unto My sorrow.'—Lamentations 1:12.

Behold your King! Though the moonlight steals
    Through the silvery sprays of the olive tree,
No star-gemmed sceptre or crown it reveals,
    In the solemn shade of Gethsemane.
        Only a form of prostrate grief,
        Fallen, crushed, like a broken leaf!
Oh, think of His sorrow! that we may know
The depth of love in the depth of woe.

Behold your King! Is it nothing to you,
    That the crimson tokens of agony
From the kingly brow must fall like dew,

Through the shuddering shades of Gethsemane?
Jesus Himself, the Prince of Life,
Bows in mysterious mortal strife;
Oh, think of His sorrow! that we may know
The unknown love in the unknown woe.

Behold your King, with His sorrow crowned,
Alone, alone in the valley is He!
The shadows of death are gathering round,
And the Cross must follow Gethsemane.
Darker and darker the gloom must fall,
Filled is the Cup, He must drink it all!
Oh, think of His sorrow! that we may know
His wondrous love in His wondrous woe.

NOTE.—After F.R.H.'s MS. copy of 'Adoration,' written Dec. 31, 1866, she adds:—'I find this is exactly my hundredth poem, beginning from my No. 2 MS. book, and not reckoning juvenile pieces before I left school. I am not sorry that "Adoration" happens to close the round number as well as the year 1866. I should like the same subject, only better treated, to *close* my verse-writing for *life*. One would wish one's last poem to be some expression of praise to the Crucified One.'

It is a remarkable coincidence that 'Behold your King,' and 'He Suffered,' are the *closing* poems in F.R.H.'s book, written in pencil, 1879.

An Easter Prayer.

OH let me know
The power of Thy resurrection;
Oh let me show
Thy risen life in calm and clear reflection;
Oh let me soar
Where Thou, my Saviour Christ, art gone before;
In mind and heart
Let me dwell always, only, where Thou art.

Oh let me give
Out of the gifts Thou freely givest;
Oh let me live
With life abundantly because Thou livest;

Oh make me shine
In darkest places, for Thy light is mine;
Oh let me be
A faithful witness for Thy truth and Thee.

Oh let me show
The strong reality of gospel story;
Oh let me go
From strength to strength, from glory unto glory,
Oh let me sing
For very joy, because Thou art my King;
Oh let me praise
Thy love and faithfulness through all my days.

Easter Dawn.

It is too calm to be a dream,
Too gravely sweet, too full of power,
Prayer changed to praise this very hour!
Yes, heard and answered! though it seem
Beyond the hope of yesterday,
Beyond the faith that dared to pray,
Yet not beyond the love that heard,
And not beyond the faithful word
On which each trembling prayer may rest,
And win the answer truly best.

Yes, heard and answered! sought and found!
I breathe a golden atmosphere
Of solemn joy, and seem to hear
Within, above, and all around,
The chime of deep cathedral bells,
An early herald peal that tells
A glorious Easter tide begun;
While yet are sparkling in the sun
Large raindrops of the night storm passed,
And days of Lent are gone at last.

Written in pencil the early dawn of her last Easter Day, April 1879.

Unfinished Fragments.

THE Master will guide the weary feet,
 Choosing for each, and choosing aright
The noontide rest in the summer heat:
 For some the glory of Alpine height,
For some the breezes fresh and free
And the changeful charm of wave and sea;
For some the hush and the soothing spells
Of harvest fields and woodland dells;
For some it may be the quiet gloom
Of the suffering couch in shaded room.
Master, *our* Master, oh let it be
That our leisure and rest be still with Thee,
With Thee and *for* Thee each sunny hour.

 . . . .

In pencil, May 1879.

'ARISE, depart! for this is not your rest!'
 The Voice fell strangely on the sleeping fold,
 As fell the starlight's quivering gold
Upon the dusky lake's untroubled breast,
And yet the Shepherd's hand had led them there,
And made them to lie down amid the pastures fair.

'Arise ye, and depart!' The morning rays
 Lit up the emerald slope and crystal pool,
  Sweet sustenance for many days,
 And quiet resting places, calm and cool.
They knew not why, nor whither, yet they went!
His own hand put them forth, and so they were content.

And so they followed Him, they could not stay
 When He had risen, the Shepherd good and fair.

 . . . .

In pencil, May 1879.

Most Blessed For Ever.[1]

PSALM 21:6.

THE prayer of many a day is all fulfilled,
　　Only by full fruition stayed and stilled;
You asked for blessing as your Father willed,
　　Now He hath answered: 'Most blessed for ever!'

Lost is the daily light of mutual smile,
　　You therefore sorrow now a little while;
But floating down life's dimmed and lonely aisle
　　Comes the clear music: 'Most blessed for ever!'

From the great anthems of the Crystal Sea,
　　Through the far vistas of Eternity,
Grand echoes of the word peal on for thee,
　　Sweetest and fullest: 'Most blessed for ever!'

*'And they sung as it were a new song before the
throne.'*—REVELATION 14:3.

---

[1] Written on her beloved father's death, but now chosen as the closing chord of F.R.H.'s songs on earth.

Note: The published "NOTE" on page 641 of this book was published on page 838 of the definitively fine Nisbet edition of *The Poetical Works of Frances Ridley Havergal*, after the end of "Behold Your King." That NOTE was likely written by Maria V. G. Havergal, or possibly her niece Frances Anna Shaw. In the second paragraph of that NOTE, "F.R.H.'s book" referred to her last Manuscript Book Nº IX. See pages II–III and 645 of this book.

44

"He Suffered."

"He suffered!" Was it, Lord, indeed for me,
The Just One for the unjust; Thou didst bear
The weights of sorrow that I hardly dare
To look upon, in dark Gethsemane?
"He suffered!" Thou, my near & gracious Friend,
And yet my Lord, my God! Thou didst
not shrink
For me that full & fearful cup of wrath to drink
Because Thou lovedst even to the end!
"He suffered!" Saviour, was Thy love so vast
That mysteries of unknown agony,
Even unto death, it only agony could be,
Unmeasured as the fiery depths its passed?
Lord, by the sorrows of Gethsemane
Seal Thou my quivering love for ever
unto Thee.

March 6. 1879

One of her last poems, dated March 6, before her death June 3, 1879. See page 640.

F.R.H. kept Manuscript Books of her poems, writing out a fair copy autograph of a poem after she had finalized it (though occasionally she made later changes). This is the first page of her five-page Index near the end of her Manuscript Book Nº VIII, the largest of her Manuscript Books that have been found, having 282 hand-numbered pages, and poems dated from December 10, 1873 to January 24, 1878. Her Manuscript Book Nº IX, begun February 24, 1878, was her last one, having 54 hand-numbered pages.

Index to First Lines.

———

Note: This single verse of six lines was the hymn number 538 in the definitive 1880 edition of *Songs of Grace and Glory* edited by Charles Busbridge Snepp and Frances Ridley Havergal (published approximately six months after F.R.H. died and six months before Rev. Snepp died):

> O Jesus, make Thyself to me
> A living, bright reality;
> More present to faith's vision keen
> Than any outward object seen;
> More dear, more intimately nigh,
> Than e'en the sweetest earthly tie!

Charlotte Elliott, 1860

In an earlier edition of *Songs of Grace and Glory* (an edition of words only, published by W. Hunt & Co., London, 1872), this single verse hymn was given this attribution: J. Taylor, Edinburgh, card, 1860. In the final, definitive edition of *Songs of Grace and Glory* (with both words and music) published by James Nisbet & Co. in 1880, this was the attribution for this single-verse hymn 538: Charlotte Elliott, 1860. In F.R.H.'s essay on Charlotte Elliott's hymns (see page 714 of Volume II of the Havergal edition), she quoted this verse (with the title "Jesus Known" at the top of the verse) and then wrote, "It is pleasant to find that the long-questioned authorship of this helpful verse is now known." We can be very confident that F.R.H. had solid reason to attribute this to Charlotte Elliott. Though this is not completely certain now, likely this verse was a seed in Frances before she wrote "Reality" (on pages 608–610 of this book).

Lines by the REV. F. JEFFERY.

TO F. R. H., AFTER READING "UNDER THE SURFACE."

How restless seems man's outward life,
    Like billows of the sea,
With every jarring wind at strife,
    From dangers never free !

.   .   .   .   .

Yet, safe beneath its storm-lashed face,
    See ocean's treasures lie ;
So rests the heart secured by grace
    In deep tranquillity.

.   .   .   .   .

The summer sun lit up the bay,
    No breath its bosom curled,
When youth and pleasure launched away
    Upon their ocean world.

Foul slimy monsters lurk within,
    Below those waters fair ;
And so the smiling life of sin
    Hides death and fell despair.

                              F. J.

December 13, 1875.

This was published in the Appendix of Memorials of Frances Ridley Havergal *by Maria V. G. Havergal (the first item in Volume IV of the Havergal edition). F.R.H. wrote this reply to his poem:*

Rightly you have read my song!
    Who in Jesus liveth,
'Neath life's turmoil strange and strong,
    Knows the peace He giveth.

Peace that overflows our days,
    Silently victorious;
Peace that blossoms into praise,
    Hidden, yet most glorious.

                F.R.H., December 16, 1875.

Poems Not Found in the Nisbet Edition of

The Poetical Works of
Frances Ridley Havergal

and

Notes about Havergal's Poems

POEMS NOT PUBLISHED IN NISBET'S *POETICAL WORKS*

These poems—written by F.R.H. but not published in Nisbet edition of *The Poetical Works of Frances Ridley Havergal*—are given in this order:

Then these are given next :

50

Winter Light. (Song.)

I

O the dark time of the year!
All the glow of radiant June-light,
All the fervour of the noon-light,
  Morning glory, evening clear,
Rainbow hues, & sparkling dews,
    What are they
If one whom I love is far away!
    O the dark time,
  O the sad time of the year!

II

  O the bright time of the year!
All the shadow of the low cloud,
Gloom & greyness of the snow-cloud,
  Early twilight, dim & drear,
Slowest flight of darkest night
    What are they!
For one whom I love will come today!
    O the bright time,
  O the glad time of the year!

Dec 23.

R. A.

F.R.H.'s fair copy autograph of "Winter Light" in her Manuscript Book № VI. See page 700 of this book.

After the definitively fine edition of Nisbet's *Poetical Works*, (N.P.W.), this is a presentation of poems by F.R.H. that were not included in that volume. These include poems by F.R.H. published in other books but not included in Nisbet's *Poetical Works*, and poems found in Manuscript Books and on loose, separate pieces of paper. Unless the certainty of authorship for a poem is specified otherwise (i.e. "likely by" or "not by"), each of these poems was written by Frances Ridley Havergal.

After that, noteworthy textual differences found among the manuscripts of poems are presented.

UNPUBLISHED POEMS AND DIFFERING TEXTS AMONG THE EXTANT MANUSCRIPTS.

There are extant and available today six Manuscript Books of poems by F.R.H., having fair copy autographs of many of her poems in her handwriting. We can infer that there were nine of these bound volumes, because she was writing poems in the "Manuscript Book Nº IX" (left with nearly two-thirds of the pages blank, unused) at the end of her life. The Manuscript Books numbered III, IV, VII, VIII, and IX are now located in the Worcestershire County Council Records Office in Worcester, England, deposited in the 1970's by Cynthia Havergal, a great-granddaughter of F.R.H.'s brother Henry East Havergal, and by Vernon Graham Havergal Shaw, a grandson of F.R.H.'s sister Ellen Prestage Havergal Shaw. The Manuscript Book Nº VI was given—along with other very valuable family items—by Frances' sister Maria Vernon Graham Havergal to the Church Missionary Society in 1886, and this is now located in the C.M.S. Archives in the University of Birmingham (England) Library. The Manuscript Books have these lengths (approximations are caused by Index pages, title pages, etc.): Nº III has approximately 100 pages, Nº IV has approximately 90 pages, Nº VI has approximately 185 pages, Nº VII has approximately 100 pages, Nº VIII has approximately 285 pages, and Nº IX has 58 pages, with nearly twice as many more pages left blank (114 blank pages, if I counted correctly). Apparently Frances would wait until she had finalized a poem (we know of poems that she first wrote on envelopes or other pieces of paper available at the time) before she would copy it in a Manuscript Book (rough drafts were seldom placed in these Manuscript Books), although she would occasionally change details later in her fair copy autographs on the pages of these Manuscript Books. The copies she made in these Manuscript Books are beautiful to read. Years ago I heard or read a fine musician (a concert pianist, I think) say that he had handled and examined a bound volume containing a number of original manuscripts of Mozart Piano Concertos copied out in Mozart's own hand, and another time I heard a conductor speak of one time in Vienna when he was handed the manuscript score of the Op. 68 "Pastoral" Symphony in Beethoven's own handwriting. To have handled and examined the original manuscripts of so many of F.R.H.'s poems, many other manuscript letters and other items in her handwriting, and her last study Bible (so diligently marked, referenced, annotated by her) has been a true privilege to me.

A number of poems have details in the manuscript copies that differ from the texts of the same poems published while F.R.H. lived or after she died. Although many or most of the finalized copies are no longer extant or available to be examined now, very great deference should be given to the texts of the published poems. Nearly always, the published text should be regarded as the finalized text which Frances intended to be published. In the books published while she lived, she oversaw the publication and would have finalized the texts herself as she meant them to be. For an example, her fair copy autograph of the Consecration Hymn had for the sixteenth line, "Every power as Thou dost choose," but we can be very confident—without a later draft available now— that Frances herself finalized and published that as "Every power as Thou shalt choose." For the books published posthumously, her sister Maria and their niece (F.R.H.'s god-daughter) Frances Anna Shaw had all or nearly all the original materials at that time, both rough drafts and fair copy autographs: these two ladies not only had the definitive sources but also had great, intimate familiarity with Frances' works and life, and great deference should be given to the finalized texts they published after Frances died. An example of this is "The Scripture Cannot Be Broken" written very late in her life: the rough draft (initially quite different from the finalized text, later revised) and the fair copy autograph were attached on page 49 of the Manuscript Book Nº IX (see pages XXVI–XXVII near the front of this book), but the published text (on pages 639–640 of this book) can be trusted as F.R.H.'s finalized text, because of the trustworthiness of Maria and Frances Anna, who had materials and knowledge not available to us now. Their preparation of the Nisbet edition of *The Poetical Works of Frances Ridley Havergal* is definitive and trustworthy.

In these transcriptions of manuscript poems that were not published, even in small details an effort was made to copy closely what Frances wrote; thus, for example, details of punctuation (often missing punctuation at the ends of lines) which might make no sense here were copied as she wrote on the manuscript, details which very likely she would have changed if she published them.

Most—not all—of the extant poems by F.R.H. not published in Nisbet's *Poetical Works* were found in the six extant Manuscript Books. We do not know

now what was done with the three missing Manuscript Books (N°'s I, II, and V), and there may have been other poems in them not published and now lost: we do not know. Maria wrote near the end of Chapter IV of her *Memorials of Frances Ridley Havergal* (apparently—from the context—referring to the time period of 1854–1855), "Her [F.R.H.'s] manuscript book contains twenty-five original German and English poems . . . ." The location of her poems in German has not been found, if still extant at all, and only two poems by her in French have been found, the wonderfully rich "Seulement pour Toi" and an unfinished poem "Qui veut venir?" (see pages 626–627 and page 663 of this book), though she was utterly fluent in French.

Besides the poems in German of which Maria wrote, are there other poems by F.R.H. not yet found and included here? I think that likely there are, though earnest, diligent effort was made to be thorough and to try to find everything that could be found. If an item is still safely intact, but no one knows where that item is nor how to find it, if it is unavailable, is that item really extant? Though I do not know this with absolute certainty, I think that approximately 99% or more of all that is extant has been found and included here in this edition. Please see the Post Script to the Bibliography, on page 1178 of this book. There is such a large, truly rich gold-mine in the poems we have now, that concern about any missing, lost ones seems inappropriate. Thanks be to God for this wonderful treasure He has provided.

Among the manuscripts of F.R.H.'s poems, small, insignificant or inconsequential differences (for example, details of punctuation and other unimportant differences) are not mentioned, but a number of differences from the published poems were found to be worthy of mention and are presented in the section entitled "Noteworthy Textual Differences Found among the Manuscripts of Poems." The appearance is that F.R.H. often wrote down first drafts (which were usually or nearly always identical or nearly identical to her final drafts) on various pieces of paper, for example, on the back of an envelope or such, and that she waited until she was ready to finalize the text before she copied poems into the Manuscript Book that she was using at that time. Her handwriting in the Manuscript Books is very attractive, beautiful, and these copies in the Manuscript Books are remarkably clean, with comparatively very few changes or additions made by her: she apparently—very likely—regarded a poem as finalized when she wrote it out in a Manuscript Book, and any changes are very uncommon. Please see also the comments and quotations on her poetry on pages XIX-XXIII near the front of this book.

David Chalkley

In Volume II of this edition (*Whose I Am and Whom I Serve Prose Works of Frances Ridley Havergal*), F.R.H.'s prose volume *The Royal Invitation* has an exceptional section that is a complete poem. In the Eighteenth Day of *The Royal Invitation*, F.R.H. used the first stanza from her poem "I could not do without Thee" (pages 375–376 of this book) and then the thirteen stanzas of her poem "What will you do without Him?" (pages 276–278 of this book), with changes. This poem (and all of *The Royal Invitation*) was prepared and published by Frances, and because it is a unique adaptation of the two poems, it is given here just as she did it in that book.

EIGHTEENTH DAY.

––––––––

Without Christ.

"At that time ye were without Christ."—Ephesians 2:12.

John 6:68	I COULD not do without Thee,
Luke 19:10	O Saviour of the lost!
1 Peter 1:18, 19	Whose precious blood redeemed me,
Revelation 5:9	At such tremendous cost.
Romans 3:22	Thy righteousness, Thy pardon,
Ephesians 1:7	Thy precious blood—must be
Hebrews 6:19	My only hope and comfort,
Galatians 6:14	My glory and my plea.
Psalm 73:23	I could not do without Him!
Song. 5:10	Jesus is more to me
Philippians 3:8	Than all the richest, fairest gifts
Matthew 13:44	Of earth could ever be.
1 Peter 2:7	But the more I find Him precious,
Psalm 18:2	And the more I find Him true,
Psalm 34:8	The more I long for you to find
John 1:46	What He can be to you.
Hosea 13:9	You need not do without Him,
Matthew 20:30	For He is passing by;
Isaiah 30:18	He is waiting to be gracious,
Isaiah 30:19	Only waiting for your cry.

2 Cor. 6:17	He is waiting to receive you,—
Isaiah 43:1	To make you all His own!
Hosea 11:8	Why will you do without Him,
Hosea 14:2	And wander on alone?
Hosea 13:10	Why will you do without Him?
Titus 3:4	Is He not kind indeed?
Romans 5:8	Did He not die to save you?
John 4:14	Is He not all you need?
Acts 5:31	Do you not want a Saviour?
John 15:14	Do you not want a Friend?
Hosea 2:20	One who will love you faithfully,
John 13:1	And love you to the end?
Jeremiah 4:30	Why will you do without Him?
Matthew 24:35	The Word of God is true;
1 John 2:17	The world is passing to its doom,
Psalm 144:4	And you are passing too.
James 4:14	It may be, no to-morrow
Proverbs 27:1	Shall dawn for you or me;
Proverbs 29:1	Why will you run the awful risk
Isaiah 33:14	Of all eternity?
Hosea 9:5	What will you do without Him
Eccles. 12:1	In the long and dreary day
Isaiah 59:9, 10	Of trouble and perplexity,
Hosea 2:6	When you do not know the way;
Hosea 13:9, 10	And no one else can help you,
Jeremiah 2:17	And no one guides you right,
Jeremiah 2:25	And hope comes not with morning,
Job 7:4	And rest comes not with night?
Romans 7:24	You could not do without Him,
John 8:33, 34	If once He made you see
2 Peter 2:19	The fetters that enchain you
Romans 8:2	Till He hath set you free;
Psalm 38:4	If once you saw the fearful load
Ezekiel 33:10	Of sin upon your soul,—
Jeremiah 17:9	The hidden plague that ends in death,
Jeremiah 17:14	Unless He makes you whole!

Jeremiah 12:5	What will you do without Him
Eccles. 12:3	When death is drawing near,
Song. 8:6, 7	Without His love—the only love
1 John 4:18	That casts out every fear;
Jeremiah 13:16	When the shadow-valley opens,
Job 8:13, 14	Unlighted and unknown,
Job 10:21, 22	And the terrors of its darkness
Psalm 23:4	Must all be passed alone?
Revelation 6:17	What will you do without Him
Revelation 20:11	When the great White Throne is set,
Romans 2:16	And the Judge who never can mistake,
Hosea 7:2	And never can forget,—
2 Cor. 5:10	The Judge, whom you have never here
Matthew 7:23	As Friend and Saviour sought,
Romans 14:12	Shall summon you to give account
Matthew 12:36	Of deed, and word, and thought?
Matthew 25:11	What will you do without Him
Revelation 3:7	When He hath shut the door,
Hebrews 3:19	And you are left outside, because
John 5:40	You would not come before;
Luke 13:25	When it is no use knocking,
Hebrews 12:17	No use to stand and wait,
Revelation 22:11	For the word of doom tolls through your heart,
Luke 16:26	That terrible 'Too late'?
John 14:6	You cannot do without Him!
1 Timothy 2:5	There is no other name
Acts 4:12	By which you ever *can* be saved,—
Ephesians 2:12	No way, no hope, no claim!
Mark 8:36	Without Him—everlasting loss
John 3:36	Of love, and life, and light!
Matthew 25:41	Without Him—everlasting woe,
Matthew 8:12	And everlasting night.
Song. 4:8	But with Him—oh! *with Jesus!*—
John 17:24	Are any words so blest?
Isaiah 35:10	With Jesus—everlasting joy
1 Thess. 4:17	And everlasting rest!

Psalm 107:9	With Jesus—all the empty heart
Ephesians 3:19, 20	Filled with His perfect love!
Isaiah 26:3	With Jesus—perfect peace below,
Psalm 16:11	And perfect bliss above!
Jeremiah 5:31	Why should you do without Him?—
Revelation 3:20	It is not yet too late;
2 Cor. 6:2	He has not closed the day of grace,
Matthew 7:13	He has not shut the gate.
Mark 10:49	He calls you!—hush!
John 6:67	He calls you!—He would not have you go
Hosea 2:14	Another step without Him,
John 15:13	Because He loves you so.
Ezekiel 33:11	Why will you do without Him?
John 7:37	He calls and calls again—
Matthew 11:28	'Come unto Me! Come unto Me!'
Isaiah 65:1, 2	Oh, shall He call in vain?
Matthew 23:37	He wants to have you with Him;
Psalm 13:1, 2	Do you not want Him too?
1 John 5:12	You cannot do without Him,
Jeremiah 31:3	And He wants—even you!

In the same volume, *The Royal Invitation*, the Twenty-fourth Day is F.R.H.'s hymn "Will You Not Come?" (page 275 of this book). Frances quotes the poem identically the same, but in *The Royal Invitation* she gives a Scripture reference beside each line of the poem, as she did with "I did this for thee! What hast thou done for Me?" (pages 64–65 of this book). She wrote in her Prefatory Note to *Loyal Responses*, "almost every line has been either directly drawn from Holy Scripture, or 'may be proved thereby.'" Many—not all—of her poems could have Scripture noted beside the lines. This Twenty-fourth Day of *The Royal Invitation* is given as an example, prepared and published by Frances herself.

TWENTY-FOURTH DAY.

———

Will You Not Come?

"Thou hast received gifts for men; yea, for the rebellious also."—Psalm 68:18.

John 5:40	WILL you not come to Him for life?
Ezekiel 33:11	Why will ye die, oh why?
John 10:11	He gave His life for you, for you!
Romans 6:23	The gift is free, the word is true!
2 Cor. 5:20	Will you not come? oh, why will you die?
Acts 10:36	Will you not come to Him for peace—
Colossians 1:20	Peace through His cross alone?
1 Peter 1:19	He shed His precious blood for you;
Romans 5:15, 18	The gift is free, the word is true!
Ephesians 2:14	He is our Peace! oh, is He your own?
Jeremiah 6:16	Will you not come to Him for rest?
Matthew 11:28	All that are weary, come!
Isaiah 11:10	The rest He gives is deep and true;
Isaiah 28:12	'Tis offered now, 'tis offered you!
Hebrews 4:3, 9	Rest in His love, and rest in His home.
Matthew 13:44	Will you not come to Him for joy,—
John 16:24	Will you not come for this?
Philippians 2:7, 8	He laid His joys aside for you,
John 15:11	To give you joy, so sweet, so true!
Romans 15:13	Sorrowing heart, oh, drink of the bliss!
Ephesians 3:19	Will you not come to Him for love—
Psalm 107:9	Love that can fill the heart,
Ephesians 2:4	Exceeding great, exceeding free?
Revelation 1:5	He loveth you, He loveth me!
Romans 5:8	Will you not come? Why stand you apart?

John 4:14	Will you not come to Him for *all?*
Psalm 34:8	Will you not "taste and see"?
Isaiah 30:18	He waits to give it all to you;
Matthew 7:7, 8	The gifts are free, the words are true!
John 7:37	Jesus is calling, "Come unto Me!"

This next poem was a translation by Théodore Monod into French of F.R.H.'s poem "Will You Not Come?", the Twenty-fourth Day of *The Royal Invitation*. Two handwritten copies were found among Havergal manuscripts and papers: one manuscript was written in Monod's hand, with an explanation at the bottom written in English (original writing of Revd Tho^r Monod   translation of F.R.H.), and another manuscript was the same text written in F.R.H.'s hand (at least, this second copy looks like her handwriting). This very likely was Théodore Monod (1836–1921), a French evangelical pastor fluent in French and English, the nephew of Adolphe Monod. See page 147 of this book. This is a very free (not at all precise) translation into French of F.R.H.'s poem.

24e jour.

Venez!

"Tu as reçu des dons pour les hommes; oui, et même pour les rebelles."

Ps. 68:18 (Version anglaise).

Venez! car Jésus est la vie!
C'est pour vous qu'il voulut mourir:
Son Esprit descendra dans votre âme ravie . . . .
Venez a lui! . . . . pourquoi périr?

Venez, car une paix profonde
De sa croix découle vers nous;
Son sang fut répandu pour le péché du monde . . . .
Cette paix, la possédez-vous?

Venez, car l'existence est dure,
Pleine de labeur et de fiel;
Le repos qu'il vous offre est un repos qui dure,
Dans sa grace, puis dans son ciel.

Venez, car il donne la joie
Acquise au prix de ses douleurs,
Par rayon de soleil que d'en haut—il envoie,
Resplendissant parmi nos pleurs.

Venez, car il est l'amour même,
Un fleuve, un océan d'amour;
Oh! Ne le fuyez point! Comme il m'aime il
vous aime . . . .
Approchez-vous à votre tour.

Venez, car il met toute chose
Dans la main vide de la foi;
Sur sa fidélité que chacun se repose:
N'a-t-il pas dit: "Venez a moi!"

original writing of Rev. Th. Monod
translation of F.R.H.

The next poem was written by Th. Monod, and the manuscript appears to be the same handwriting as the previous one which was specifically noted to be in Monod's hand.

Le Sauveur.

J'ai trouvé, j'ai trouvé la voie
Qui conduit au repos du coeur,
J'ai trouvé la paix et la joie
En Jésus le libérateur.
O mes compagnons de misère
Ensemble invoquons son secours:
Il n'attends que notre prière,
Le Sauveur qui sauve toujours.

Par son sang, sa miséricorde
Efface nos iniquités;
Par son Esprit qu'il nous accorde
Il guérit nos infirmités;

Et plus le mal est inurable[1]
Et plus les fardeaux semblent lourds,
Plus Il se montre secourable
Le Sauveur qui sauve toujours.

Hélas! ma trop longue ignorance
Ne connaissait auparavant,
Dans la lutte ou dans la souffrance,
Qu'un Sauveur qui sauve souvent;
Mais de ma pauvre et triste vie
J'ai vu se transformier le cours,
Depuis mon coeur se confie
Au Saveur qui sauve toujours.

Il est ma force et ma victoire,
L'Ami qui me guide en tout lien,
Il et ma lumière et ma gloire,
Il est mon frère, Il est mon Dieu;
Soit que je vive ou que je meure
Il est mon unique secours . . . .
En me sauveras d'heureuse heure,
O Sauveur qui sauve toujours!

Th. Monod.

F.R.H. was utterly fluent in French. Her sister Maria wrote, "By F.R.H.'s request, *Bruey* is translated into French by Mlle. Tabarié, under the name of *Lilla* (published by J. Bonhoure, 48 Rue de Lille, Paris). F.R.H. was pleased with its lively and idiomatic rendering, making it a pleasant book for the schoolroom."[2]　　Frances' two poems in French ("Seulement pour Toi" and the unfinished "Qui veut venir?") show her fine gifts to write poetry in French, and these manuscripts by Monod further indicate her interest in this. We also know from Maria[3] of "Les choses précieuses," very likely a French translation of Frances' "Precious Things" on pages 619–623 of this book, translated possibly by Frances or by another (we do not know).

---

[1] inurable: word unclear in manuscript

[2] *Letters by the Late Frances Ridley Havergal* edited by Maria V. G. Havergal (London: James Nisbet & Co., 1886, page 182), Maria's note for Frances' letter dated May 6, 1872. See page 198 of Volume IV of the Havergal edition. *Bruey* was a prose volume she wrote for children.

[3] *The Autobiography of Maria Vernon Graham Havergal* (London: James Nisbet & Co., 1887), page 213. See page 545 of Volume IV of the Havergal edition.

Manuscript in Théodore Monod's handwriting. See pages 673–674 of this book. At the bottom another wrote, "original writing of Revd Tho^r Monod translation of F.R.H."

The following poems were found in *Letters by the Late Frances Ridley Havergal* (London: James Nisbet & Co., 1886, edited by Maria V. G. Havergal), not published in *The Poetical Works of Frances Ridley Havergal* (London: James Nisbet & Co., 1884, edited by Maria V. G. Havergal and Frances Anna Shaw).

Letter in Rhyme.

1855.

My very dear friend, I fear you will be
Quite out of all patience with poor little me.
For seeming neglect, I must forthwith atone,
And meekly my humble repentance make known
By scribbling at once my epistle in rhyme,
More akin to the ludicrous than the sublime.
So little I've been with the Muses of late,
And so fearfully thick is becoming my pate,
That even a letter—of lines very few,
'Tis a dubious case, if I ever get through,
For want of a rhyme or a suitable word,
To insert where a gap in the metre is heard.
Not that the Muses will have much to do
With any epistle I scribble to you.
I shall not invoke their capricious assistance,
And keep from Parnassus respectable distance,
And only apply to my own special friend,
The goddess of scribble, at whose shrine I bend,
Both gladly and oft, for she never refuses
Her aid, like the fickle and spiteful old Muses!
A little epitome seems to be due,
Dear Janey (considering our friendship), to you,
Of all the events which since I wrote last,
Like shadows, though pleasant and bright ones, have past;
Well, first on the list, on the thirtieth of June
Our hearts with St. Nicholas' bells were in tune;
Both joyous and grateful indeed they might be,
For my father (the jewel!) came home from the sea.

Returned, yes he is, but not as he went,
With dim seeing eye and his forces all spent;
For sight hath been found by the glorious Rhine,
And his books are reopened—so long a sealed mine.
So after we got up a capital dinner,
Plum-pudding and beef, at which each little sinner
Who claimed to belong to St. Nicholas' school,
Came smiling and cheering till each bench was full.
And now I transcribe, without any fear,
"The Welcome" we sang my father to cheer.

Song of Welcome to Rev. W. H. Havergal.

O God, with grateful hearts we come
    Thy goodness to adore,
While we our pastor welcome home
    To England's happy shore.

For Thy delivering love we praise,
    And Thy restoring hand!
Oh, spare him yet for long, long days
    To this our little band.

Thy Spirit's fulness on him rest,
    Thy love his sunshine be!
And may he still, while doubly blest,
    A blessing be from Thee.

When the Chief Shepherd shall appear,
    May he receive, we pray,
A crown of glory, bright and clear,
    That fadeth not away.

Next day I depart in infinite glee,
My heart's dearest jewel, my brother, to see,
With a couple of sisters to take care of me.
A perfect Elysium Hereford is,
A fairyland palace of pleasure and bliss;

Like some rainbow winged fay every hour flies past,
Only one is e'er mournful, and that is the last.
In this chalice of crystal, brimful of delight,
Full many ingredients mingled, but quite
The chief of them all (after Frank's conversation)
Was the music,—enchanting in my estimation,
Beethoven and Mendelssohn, Handel and Spohr,
Mozart and Corelli, with many names more,
Their harmony poured through voices and fingers,
Around me the echo most sweetly still lingers
More marvellous yet than a musical dream,
Flowed for hours together that glorious stream;
Each day as in music so happily passed,
I fancied more beautiful yet than the last,
Until when I left (with immense lamentation)
I was just in a state of complete saturation,—
The spirit of music seemed then to pervade
My very existence. That spirit has made
A firm resolution spring up within me,
That a decent musician some day *I will* be.
An army of socks in transparent condition
With which to combat, was my own special mission,
With neckties united[1] and with shirts to affright
My latent intentions my letters to write.
This being the case, I shall hope and expect
That you will not accuse me of wilful neglect,
Since darning and visiting, walking and all,
But music especially held me in thrall.
Some ten days ago, spite of Frank's hearty grumbles
At losing his sisters, we came to the Mumbles—
For sea air is better than potion or pill,
To cure or prevent every species of ill.
This side Mumbles Head is dreary indeed,
No sands and no shells and no lovely seaweed,
No rocks which are fit to sketch or to climb.
An expanse of grey mud which is truly sublime
At low tide before you, and shingle at high,
Is the pleasant alternative greeting your eye;

---

[1]The word "united" in the original book may be or likely is a mistake, likely meant to be "untied." No copy in F.R.H.'s handwriting has been found to confirm this.

And being so sheltered the water is quiet,
And hasn't a notion of making a riot.
But over the Head 'tis a different thing,
There a jubilant chorus the waves ever sing;
They seem to rejoice in their glorious might,
Their snowy plumes waving with gleeful delight.
Full many a trophy they bring from the deep,
Where forests untrodden the calm waters sleep;
Fair flowers of ocean of tropical hue,
Which glow on the sands bright with clear briny dew.
While meadow or woodland or wild heathy hill
Invite us to ramble and wander at will.
Church matters seem here in a pitiful state,
Which pains me and grieves me here to relate.
Two ting tangs set up a most pitiful chime
For church, at no very particular time.
You enter, and straight have a very fair notion
Of the nearest approach to perpetual motion.
The comma, the sole punctuation they use,
For the clergyman has not a moment to lose,—
He dashes away like a torrent of water,
And finishes all in an hour and a quarter.
The church has been whitewashed, but right long ago,
As the cracks and the dinginess amply doth show
About the same time, that a strange petrifaction
Confined the incumbent to mere Sunday action.
So many abuses in this place are rife,
The only church things giving token of life,
Are the singing within and the nettles without,
Both equally rampant, without any doubt.
But Janey, dear friend, I must hasten away,
For dinner will never allow of delay;
Entreating forgiveness for silence again,
And imploring a letter ere long from your pen,
I only will add that I ever shall be
What I now am, your fervently loving

FANNIE.

Letters by the Late Frances Ridley Havergal, (London: James Nisbet & Co., 1886), original book pages 5–10; pages 147–148 of Volume IV of the Havergal edition.

Who Shall Be First?

'Tis nearly forty years since our first flower
Awoke beneath the fair spring's early shining;
'Tis more than twenty since a winty hour
Filled up the wreath of home, the sixth young bud entwining.

That wreath, long woven, is unbroken yet,
Not one of all its opening buds hath faded,
Not one gem fallen from that coronet;
Oh, "who shall be the first" to shine in light unshaded?

F. R. H. LATE 1856 OR EARLY 1857.

Letters, page 12; page 149 of Volume IV of the Havergal edition. This refers to the six children of William Henry and Jane Head Havergal. The "first flower" was Miriam (Jane Miriam Havergal Crane, 1817–1898). Next were Henry (Henry East Havergal, 1819–1875); Maria (Maria Vernon Graham Havergal, 1821–1887); Ellen (Ellen Prestage Havergal Shaw, 1823–1886), Frank (Francis Tebbs Havergal, 1829–1891), and the "sixth young bud" Fan (Frances Ridley Havergal, 1836–1879).

Peace.

A Carol for the Children of St. Nicholas Sunday School.

Children, come! with grateful voice
Let us one and all rejoice:
War departs, and Peace descends;
Enemies are turned to friends.

War departs! each tuneful bell
Pealeth forth its welcome knell;
Battle shout and cannon's roar
Shall be heard again no more.

Peace descends on rainbow wing!
Thousand blessings may she bring;
Plenty, joy, and love to all,
Parents, children, "great and small."

Ne'er again may England know
What it is to have a foe;
Ever may the olive green
Shade the throne of England's Queen.

Children, come! your voices raise,
Chant the gladsome hymn of praise;
Thanking Him who reigns above,
Prince of Peace, and God of Love!

F. R. H. 1856.

Letters, page 14; pages 149–150 of Volume IV of the Havergal edition.

A City Rector's Letter to His Parishioners.

November 9, 1859.

My dear parishioners and friends,
    While heartily I greet you,
I must regret to say that now
To duty's stern behest I bow,
And to a small parochial row
    I feel constrained to treat you.

Allow me to remind you first,
    That some few years ago,
Our worthy friend John Wheeley Lea,
(To which Esquire should added be)
The schools erected, which you see
    When through the Butts you go.

An eligible mistress found,
    And all things else in train,
We trusted that the poor would prize
The boon aright, while kind supplies
From ready friends would soon arrive;
    We trusted—but in vain!

The children came and brought their pence,
    But pennies won't supply
The coals to fill those Tudor grates,
Brooms, dusters, door-mats, books and slates,
Insurance, wear and tear and rates,
    And salaries so high.

Though filthy lucre be a snare,
    We can't quite do without it;
And as this evil still is rife,
My precious darling little wife
Has nearly sacrificed her life,
    In teasing you about it.

For each two pounds collected, she
    One pair of boots wears out,
For every five a dress; and then,
'Tis true, though sad, for every ten
She goes and gets laid up again,
    For perhaps a month about.

Then, when at last the work is done
    And each subscription paid,
Your Rector finds himself—but nay,
I spare you—of myself I say
As little as I duly may,
    Not thus the cause I aid.

My friends, it ought not so to be,
    Your duty is most clear;
I pray let 1860 bring
Sweet charity on *golden* wing,
In every bosom may she nestle,
With every world-bound spirit wrestle,
    And make a glad New Year!

F. R. H.

Letters, pages 21–22; pages 151–152 of Volume IV of the Havergal edition.

In a letter dated March 20, 1879, Frances wrote of an earnest conversation and time of prayer with "O.P." She quoted a verse which has not been found anywhere else among her writings, and she introduced it with these words:

> My verse seemed just to express his desire:

> "Reign over me, Lord Jesus!
>   Oh make my heart Thy throne;
> It shall be Thine for ever,
>   It shall be Thine alone!"

Letters by the Late Frances Ridley Havergal edited by Maria V. G. Havergal (London: James Nisbet & Co., 1886), original book page 325, page 238 of Volume IV of the Havergal edition.

To Nurse Carveley.

> I have no photograph to give,
> And so I do not ask for yours;
> But I've a picture that will live
> As long as memory endures.
> The faithful word, the pleasant face,
> The skilful hand, the watchful eye,
> The "sunshine in a shady place,"—
> This photograph will never die!

F. R. H. May 29, 1878.

Letters, page 296; page 230 of Volume IV of the Havergal edition. This was written two days before the death of F.R.H.'s step-mother, Caroline Ann (Cooke) Havergal. Sarah Carveley was a professional nurse, attending Mrs. Havergal in her final illness. A year later, she would be summoned to attend F.R.H. in her final illness.

On one of her trips to Switzerland, F.R.H. wrote this poem about one of her mountain guides, in the first section of *Swiss Letters and Alpine Poems* (London: James Nisbet & Co., 1881), original book page 91, page 301 of Volume IV of the Havergal edition, F.R.H.'s letter of July 14, 1869. Before and after the poem, F.R.H. is quoted in the letter:

Jos. Dévouassoud has been four days' excursions with us, and he asked us to write him a testimonial in his book, so I wrote:

> CAREFUL and gentle, respectful and steady,
> Always obliging and watchful and ready;
> Pleasantly telling, as children say,
> All about everything on the way;
> Good for the glaciers, strong for the steeps;
> Mighty for mountains, and lithesome for leaps;
> Guide of experience, trusty and true,
> None can be better than Dévouassoud!

I gave him a free translation which pleased him amazingly.

The very small volume *Treasure Trove* (London: James Nisbet & Co., 1886? date uncertain) is a compilation of extracts from un published letters and from Bible notes by F.R.H., sections for 31 mornings and 31 evenings, compiled by her niece and god-daughter, Frances Anna Shaw. The morning sections were extracts from letters, and the evening sections were Bible notes. A poem of 24 lines immediately after the title page of *Treasure Trove* is very likely by F.R.H. In the Preface to *Treasure Trove*, a brief "unpublished fragment by F.R.H." is given, and the Ninth Evening and the Seventeenth Morning are poems: these three were not found in any other volumes of F.R.H.'s poems, were definitely written by F.R.H., and are given here (*Treasure Trove* is given on pages 893–921 of Volume II of the Havergal edition.).

This next poem was published between the title page and the Preface in *Treasure Trove*. Though not explicitly identified to be by F.R.H., this is very likely a poem by her.

> O Jesus Christ, my Master,
>   I come to Thee to-day;
> I ask Thee to direct me
>   In all I do or say.
> I want to keep my promise,
>   To be Thy servant true;
> I come to Thee for orders,

Dear Lord, what shall I do?
    I want a heart not heeding
        What others think or say;
    I want an humble spirit
        To listen and obey.
To serve Thee without ceasing,
        Tis but a little while,
My strength, the Master's promise;
        My joy, the Master's smile.
O precious Lord and Master,
        I want to hear Thy voice,
Enduing me with power
        And bidding me rejoice;
That while Thou still dost tarry,
        I faithful may be found;
With lamp all trimmed and burning,
        I wait the trumpet's sound.

Next is an unpublished fragment by F.R.H. in the Preface to *Treasure Trove*:

    "O brother,
Save by the rainbow arch of prayer to One
Who draws our dewdrop longings up, to pour
Their sparklets with His own rich blessing shower,
My voice may never reach thee."

Ninth Evening.

O come to Me, ye weary,
    And lean upon My breast!
O come, ye heavy laden,
    And I will give you rest!
Take but My yoke upon you,
    And learn of Me, your Lord,
For I am meek and lowly
    In heart, as well as word.
And then your souls shall surely
    Find rest from every care,
For My yoke is very easy,
    And My burden light to bear.
                    F.R.H., 1854.

SEVENTEENTH MORNING.

DESPISED, rejected, wounded now,
    Bowed 'neath a cross of shame,
With visage marred, with bleeding brow,
    Know ye the sufferer's name?

O Man of Sorrows!—Is this He
    Who human form should wear,
And with transgressors numbered be,
    Our mighty sins to bear?

O Son of God, who unto death
    Hast loved, so lovèd me,
Henceforth be all my life and breath
    Devoted unto Thee.

F. R. H.

Finally, in the Preface to *Treasure Trove*, there is a four-line stanza not identified and not found in any other volumes of Havergal's poems. These four lines may be by F.R.H. or by her sister, Ellen P. Shaw, who wrote the Preface to this volume compiled by her daughter.

"The white-robed Alleluia flowers
    Which spring from 'neath the sod
Are voiceless—yet each leaflet gives
    Glory and praise to God."

Late in her life F.R.H. began to set to music the 31 poems of *Loyal Responses*, not yet having set all of them when she died (other scores by F.R.H. were posthumously fitted to the poems not newly set to music by her before her death). Her sister Maria published posthumously *Loyal Responses: The Last Melodies of Frances Ridley Havergal with Other Poems and Tunes* (London: Hutchings & Romer, 1881). After the 31 poems, another 9 scores composed by Frances were published in this book, among "The Last Melodies" she wrote. One of these was entitled "Now" and the words for this were adapted from F.R.H.'s poem "Now!" (see the fourteen stanzas on pages 498–502 of this book). This new poem adapted from the original one was very likely or almost surely by F.R.H., and set to music composed by her late in her life.

"Now."   Words and Music by Frances Ridley Havergal.

Five sailors were clinging to the broken mast of a sinking ship in Dublin Bay. A rope was thrown to them. At the trumpet signal "Now !" they were to loose their hold of the mast, and trust themselves to the rope. Four did so, and were hauled safe to shore. The fifth hesitated to let go, and was lost !

> 1. God's "Now" is sounding in your ears,
>   O let it reach your heart !
>   From ev'ry trust but Christ alone
>   He bids you part.
>
> Chorus. There is one hope, and only one !
>   You can be sav'd, but how?
>   The rope hold fast, but quit the mast
>   At the trumpet signal, "NOW !"
>
> 2. Your righteousness as filthy rags
>   Must all relinquished be,
>   And only Jesu's precious death
>   Must be your plea.
>
> 3. Trust now the one provided rope,
>   Quit now the broken mast !
>   Before the hope of safety be
>   For ever past.
>
> 4. Fear not to trust His simple word,
>   So sweet, so tried, so true !
>   And you are safe for evermore,
>   Yes, even you !

51

"Now."

Five sailors were clinging to the broken mast of a sinking ship in Dublin Bay. A rope was thrown to them. At the trumpet signal "Now!" they were to loose their hold of the mast, and trust themselves to the rope. Four did so, and were hauled safe to shore. The fifth hesitated to let go, and was lost!

1. God's "Now" is sound-ing in your ears, O let it reach your heart!

From ev-'ry trust but Christ a-lone He bids you part.

CHORUS.

There is one hope, and on-ly one! You can be sav'd, but how?

The rope hold fast, but quit the mast At the trum-pet sig-nal, "NOW!"

2. Your righteousness as filthy rags
Must all relinquished be,
And only Jesu's precious death
Must be your plea.

3. Trust now the one provided rope,
Quit now the broken mast!

Before the hope of safety be
For ever past.

4. Fear not to trust His simple word,
So sweet, so tried, so true!
And you are safe for evermore,
Yes, even you!

This is the original page 51 of Loyal Responses: The Last Melodies of Frances Ridley Havergal *with Other Poems and Tunes (London: Hutchings & Romer, 1881). All of this original book is given on pages 1170–1241 in Volume V of the Havergal edition.*

Next are items found in F.R.H.'s Manuscript Books.

Items in Manuscript Book № III

The Manuscript Book № III has this written on the cover: III   Odds' & Ends. 1858 to [This is how the title on the front cover ends.] No title page was written in the Manuscript Book № III. The first unpublished item in this Manuscript Book is "A Fit of Depression." An "o" was written beside the title to this poem, and next is an explanation of the "x" and "o" designations by Frances in the poems written in this Manuscript Book № III.

o A Fit of Depression.

An "o" is written next to—to the left of—the title of this poem. We do not know what this meant, but this was a specific notation for Frances (possibly indicating inclusion or exclusion in a collection—we do not know). An "o" was written to the left of the title in her fair copy autograph of "Cascade" (found on pages 86–88 of this book) and to the left of the title of "Psalm 145.8" (found on page 270 of this book). An "x" is written to the left of the title of "The Gem-Wreath" (on pages 106–112) and to the left of the title of "Coming Summer. 1859." (on pages 44–46). Frances marked all the poems in the Manuscript Book № III with an x or an o ("I did this for thee" had an x to the left of the first line). This practice was not continued in the Manuscript Books № IV, VI, VII, and VIII, and was only partially used in the Manuscript Book № IX (no o's, but x's beside several poems). These Manuscript Books were clearly for F.R.H.'s use, and abbreviations and other short-cut indications were written for her own reminders or use.

List of Items with x or o in Manuscript Book № III

TITLE OF POEM	MARKING BY F.R.H.	LOCATION IN THIS VOLUME
"Cascade"	o	pages 86–88
"The Gem-Wreath"	x	pages 106–112
"Johnnie's Birthday"	o	pages 316–317
Psalm 145:18	o	page 270
"As thy days, so shall thy strength be."	x	pages 71–72

TITLE OF POEM	MARKING BY F.R.H.	LOCATION IN THIS VOLUME
"I did this for thee, What hast thou done for me?"	x	pages 64–65
"The Maidens of England"	o	pages 145–146
"A Fit of Depres- sion"[1]	o	page 693
Love Rhapsody of E.P.H. 1856"[2]	o	pages 694–696
"Peace"[3]	o	pages 681–682
"The Lorely"	o	pages 171–172
"Coming Summer. 1859."	x	pages 44–46
"Sunbeams in the Wood"	x	pages 40–41
"For Miriam L. C.'s Birthday"	o	pages 315–316
"Tis fully known to One, by us yet dimly seen"	x	page 119
"My Teacher"	x	pages 29–31
The Tyrolese Spring Song"	o	pages 252–253
"Constance de V"	x	pages 88–98
"Faith & Reason"	x	pages 115–117
"Pray for me." "An- swer to a Request"	o	pages 141–142

[1] This poem was apparently never published, and is given in this section of "Poems Not Found in Nisbet's *Poetical Works*."

[2] This poem was apparently never published, and is given in this section of "Poems Not Found in Nisbet's *Poetical Works*."

[3] This poem was found in *Letters by the Late Frances Ridley Havergal*, page 14, page 149 of Volume IV of the Havergal edition.

TITLE OF POEM	MARKING BY F.R.H.	LOCATION IN THIS VOLUME
"Answer to a remark of A.J.S." "No, not a Star	x	pages 146–147
John 6.68 "To whom, O Saviour shall we go"	x	pages 62–63
"Early Faith"	x	pages 47–48
Isaiah 33.17	x	pages 65–66
Thanksgiving I Thessalonians 5:18	x	pages 17–18
"Christ's Recall"	x	pages 61–62
"The Things which are behind"	x	page 75
"What I do thou knowest not now but thou shalt know hereafter."	x	pages 16–17
"A Waking Thought"	o	page 323
"More Music !"	x	page 100
"For Denmark ho"	o	page 172
"Inscription in a copy of 'Life's Morning' "	o	page 226
"This same Jesus"	x	pages 68–70
"Lines upon the mottoes for J. H. Shaw's birthday"	o	page 318
"My Welcome Song"	o	page 256
Rest quotation by Augustine	x	pages 32–33
"Be not weary."	x	pages 28–29
"Finis"	x	pages 80–82

A Fit of Depression.

THERE is an emptiness in all on earth,
All, all is vanity! The song of mirth
Rings hollow in mine ear. Each joyous smile
Seems sickly or untrue, And even while
My own loved music soothes my soul, it seems
Not real, but echoes from the land of dreams.
Laughter ? it fleetly passeth in a sigh!
Gladness ? a flower that bloometh but to die!
Joy ? there is none, it is a beauteous fable.
Love ? may have been ! but is it? Who is able
To love indded an object all of earth,
Which bears the mark of death e'en from its birth?
Hope? What hath she to feed on? Year by year
Unfoldeth, some more bright and some more drear,
Till thought is weary. Goodness? Like the bow
In cloud and wave its soft bright colours glow.
You long to grasp the loveliness so nigh,
But it eludes you, till the fair hues die
And leave the earth and sky in tenfold gloom.
Oh there is nought to long for but the tomb!
Nought, said I? There is One, so fair, so bright,
So good, so gracious! Love and Life and Light
Are His rich titles. Oh, for Him I long
To be my Hope, my Joy, my Strength, my Song!
Earth's Shadow melts in conquering light away
Before the rising Daystar's earliest ray.

1856.

The fair copy autograph of "A Fit of Depression" was written on two facing pages, the last five lines written on the right-side page. Approximately two-thirds of the right-side page (Manuscript Book page 25) had no handwriting, but apparently two printed leaflets (? or other objects) were attached (glued ? likely) to the bottom two-thirds of page 25 and then later cut out, leaving two rectangular boxes of removed paper. The next page—the other, back side of page 25—is the first page of "Love Rhapsody of E.P.H. 1856," which filled four pages (26–29) and part of page 30. Because the two items attached to page 25 were cut out, approximately two-thirds of page 26 are missing, two blank, rectangular boxes. We have the first six lines of this "Love Rhapsody," then the next 14 lines are missing, and then the rest of the poem is given. This is the only example of this found in any of the manuscripts. Though we do not know, F.R.H. may have had another copy of this poem, and sacrificed the beautiful copy here for the two attached items removed from page 25, or possibly another person cut out these two places.

The author of this poem is very likely or almost certainly F.R.H. E.P.H. (Frances' sister, Ellen Prestage Havergal) was engaged to Giles Shaw in 1855 and married him February 5, 1856. The fact that this poem is copied by Frances here in her Manuscript Book is strong reason to think that Frances herself is the author. No poem by any other author was copied out in any of F.R.H.'s Manuscript Books. There is another example of a poem by Frances that was written about—and in the voice of—Ellen: "A Wife's Letter" was written by Frances, though clearly presented as the communication of Ellen to Giles (see pages 256–257 of this book, followed by the next poem written in the voice of the husband, "The Husband's Reply" on page 258). Frances also wrote a poem which is said in the place of—with the voice of—her father, William Henry Havergal, "A City Rector's Letter to His Parishioners" (see pages 682–683). Another indication that Frances is the author of the "Love Rhapsody of E.P.H." is that Ellen wrote a number of poems (see pages 1091–1098), none of them copied in Frances' extant Manuscript Books.

Love Rhapsody of E.P.H. 1856.

AWAKE my lyre! Long, long, have been thy slumbers
Nor harmony nor discord from thy wire
Have poured their wild and strangely fitful numbers
What art thou dreaming? Wake and tell, O Lyre!
Long have the stars in glorious ranks been marching
Oft has the moon relit her silver fire

[Lines 7–20 are missing on the page.]

Perchance some unknown loveliness were there
Which might, O precious one, with thee compare
Could yon bright worlds unfold to our rapt gaze
The untold radiance of their nearer blaze,—

Some wand of magic might in blissful vision,
Show glories of the fabled realms Elysian,—
Then, then upon Apollo's wings I'd rise,
Then should my song re-echo through the skies;
In strains not all unworthy I might tell
What wondrous excellence in thee doth dwell.
But flights like those alas are not for me
I can but seek low similes for thee.

   Hast thou not seen some dreary mountain steep
Where no birds carol and no flow'rets sleep
Gain music, life and beauty from the fall
Of gleaming waters o'er the rocky wall?
Thou art a bright cascade of pure delight
Soothing the ear and gladdening the sight.

   Hast thou not seen in shadowy forest aisle
Through the green roof a golden sunbeam smile,
And light the path below and search the bowers,
And wake the loveliness of hidden flowers,
Laden with rainbow sparks like thoughts of joy?
Thou art a golden beam without alloy.

   Hast thou not marked the emerald's chastened light
Not gaudy topaz, diamond dazzling bright
So softly pure, on which the eye loves best
In weakness and in weariness to rest?
A jewel thou of more than emerald worth
And emerald beauty, fairest gem of earth.

   Hast thou not heard within some sacred pile
When hushed the swelling choir, through vaulted aisle
A sweet low echo lingering of the song
As would angelic harps the sound prolong?
So through the silent chambers of my soul,
In calmest melody thy sweet words roll.

   Hast thou not watched the royal rose unfold
(More rich than those which Orient thrones behold)
Her gorgeous robes which while perfume they cast
Seem each day more resplendent than the last?
Such are thy graces, every day more glowing
While from a ceaseless fount new charms are flowing.

The nightingale's enhancing lay of eve;
The veil of beauty which the moonbeams weave;
The fragrance of the lily's pearly bell;
The sweetness of the wild bee's honey cell;
The calming power of Evening's first faint star;
The radiance of the comet path afar;
The whiteness of the peaceful mountain snow,
Gleaming o'er burning plains and vales below,
The untold brilliance of the sparry halls,
From mortal sight shut in by Ocean walls;
The joyous brightness of the suntipped waves;
The freshening coolness of the fount which laves
In shade and silence buds that shun the light,
The summer sun's glad warmth and ardent might;
The ruby glories of the western sky;—
All these as wingèd dreams before me fly,
And in each one an emblem faint I see,
Of something far transcending all in thee!
A fairy vision Fancy deems she paints
Fairer than all combined; but see, she faints,
Her pencil falls to earth ere yet begun
Her might task. Ne'er may that task be done,
For nought can image thee! Sweet Poesie, adieu!
Thy rainbow hand alas, I find is powerless too!

Janry 1856

Items in Manuscript Book Nº IV

The Manuscript Book Nº IV has nothing written on the cover. There is a title page, hand-written, which says this:

Nº IV.
Odds & Ends.
from Nov to May 1867.

That was written in F.R.H.'s hand, and below in another's hand this is written:
F.R.H's Autograph M.S.S.

Arithmetical Enigma.

5/12 of the square of 3/5 of a score,
1/8 of a dozen & 1/2 of one more,
2/5 of 1/4 of 5/9 of eighteen,
Of 25, 20, & 12 take the mean,
4/15 of 5/6 of 9/10 of one-third
Of 120, will give you a word
Which in *literal* truth, I will fearlessly state
Must form the foundation of everything great.

N.B. The initials of the above numbers form
the answer.

Frances wrote by hand two copies of her "Arithmetical Enigma," another one on page 20 of her Manuscript Book N⁰ IV, and this one on a loose piece of paper. This was very likely or almost surely written in 1866: In her Manuscript Book N⁰ IV, she dated the poem immediately before this ("Light in Shade or A Proverb Reversed" later re-named by Frances "No Thorn Without a Rose") March 26, 1866, and the poem after this ("Thy Will Be Done") was dated by her July 10, 1866. This is her hand-written copy on a loose piece of paper. See pages 704–706 of Volume III of the Havergal edition.

The fact that two manuscript copies of this poem in her handwriting were found, one written in her Manuscript Book, demonstrates that she regarded this as a finalized poem to be kept and included. As explained on the next page, both copies had the mistake of 1/8 instead of the correct 1/3, almost surely a simple oversight as F.R.H. copied the poem.

Arithmetical Enigma

5/12 of the square of 3/5 of a score,
1/3 of a dozen and 1/2 of one more,
2/5 of 1/4 of 5/9 of eighteen,
Of 25, 20, and 12 take the mean,
4/15 of 5/6 of 9/10 of one-third
Of 120, will give you a word
Which in <u>literal</u> truth, I will fearlessly state,
Must form the foundation of everything great.

———————————

N.B.[1] The initials of the above numbers form the answer.

[1] N.B.: *nota bene*—Latin, " note well."

Note: Two manuscripts of this "Arithmetical Enigma" in F.R.H.'s handwriting were found. In both of the manuscripts, Frances mistakenly wrote 1/8 at the beginning of line 2, and she almost certainly meant 1/3. (When I did the arithmetic, 1/8 makes the answer to line 2 seven and a half. Later I realized that she almost certainly meant to write 1/3. Haydn once wrote above a mistake in a manuscript score he composed, "written in my sleep.") Possibly Maria V. G. Havergal and Frances Anna Shaw did not realize the mistake, could not solve the Enigma, and thus might have thought that it should not be published.

The arithmetic is simple (very accessible to children), but the words to make the poem, and the ideas, are brilliant.

The answer to this Arithmetical Enigma can be found with the first line of this poem in the Index to First Lines, on page 1130 of this book. A detailed solution to this can be found on page 706 of Volume III of the Havergal edition.

David Chalkley

Items in Manuscript Book № VI

The front cover of the Manuscript Book № VI has this written by Frances' sister, Maria Vernon Graham Havergal:

<u>One</u> of F.R.H.'s MSS. Books
"Tell it out." page 149.
"A Workers Prayer" – 150.
Bequeathed to the
C.M.S. Library.
(special <u>care</u>.)   M.V.G.H.

On the inside of the front cover of this Manuscript Book № VI, Frances had written this:

№ VI.
Begun November. 1869.

This was all that F.R.H. wrote for the title at the front of her Manuscript Book № IX.

The next four poems, "Winter Light,"[1] "To a Barrister," "An Evening on the Bréven," and the one stanza by "Sabrina," were all found in F.R.H.'s Manuscript Book № VI, and very likely never published until now.

Winter Light.   (Song.)

I.

O the dark time of the year!
All the glow of radiant June light,
All the fervour of the moon-light,
      Morning glory, evening clear,
      Rainbow hues, and sparkling dews,
            What are they
If one whom I love is far away!
      O the dark time,
O the sad time of the year!

II.

O the bright time of the year!
All the shadow of the low cloud,
Gloom and greyness of the snow-cloud,
      Early twilight, dim and drear,
      Slowest flight of darkest night
            What are they!
For one whom I love will come today!
      O the bright time,
O the glad time of the year!

————

At the bottom right Frances wrote the date "Decr. 23."

This was found in F.R.H.'s Manuscript Book № VI begun November, 1869. On the facing left-side page of the manuscript book is the poem "The Husband's Reply" which was dated January 3. "Winter Light" was very likely written on December 23, 1869. See page 664 of this book.

[1] I think that if Beethoven, Schubert, Mendelssohn, Schumann, Brahms, Busoni, or Rachmaninoff had been fluent in English and had seen "Winter Light," they would have set this to music. Much more can be said of this poem. D.C.

To a Barrister.

That "lawyers" are "sly ware" we may doubt,
　　Not knowing the tricks of the trade;
A pleasanter anagram may you find out
　　How "wealth" from "the law" may be made.

This was found on page 52 of the Manuscript Book № VI begun November, 1869, and very likely never published until now. Immediately before this was the poem "Afterward" which was dated January 4, 1870; immediately after this was the poem "The Heather Lintie" which was dated January 12, 1870.

An Evening on the Bréven.

Fine view, don't you think so & quite worth the ascent.
Why, there's our hotel! don't you see it? down there!
And there's the bureau where our luggage was sent!
I hope I shall find my portmanteau all square!

No,—stupid! you're looking too much to the right!
Here's the glass, now you'll find it,—just there, don't you see!
That's Mont Blanc, I suppose. Dear me, what a height!
It's quite high enough on the Bréven for me.

Yes, very fine view, perhaps the finest we've done.
'Go higher & wait for the sunset?' My dear!
To go without dinner is very poor fun,
And there's nothing but goats' milk & mutton up here.

You forget, we shall miss table d'hôte if we stop!
We have looked at the view & so why should we stay?
Besides, it's a desperate pall to the top,
And the mules go no further than this, so they say.

Hallo! let us see! here's the visitors' book!
Here's a party of Joneses, most likely the same!
Just fancy! here's Robinson's signature, look!
And, sure enough, Tom & his bride! there's the name!

You shall sign for us both, here's a pretty good pen.
Well, now, are you ready? don't let us be late.

I shall order champagne, I am thinking, & then
No more of that foreigners' stuff that I hate!

So down they went to their table d'hôte.
We sailed in a slightly different boat;
Up from the glooming, up to the glowing,
Pressing against the morning tide
If descending, forth hotel ward flowing.
   And now we stand above,
Only we two on the mountain side,
Only a goat-bell tinkling below
Home with the splendours of eventide
Above with the glory of Alpine snow
   In the presence of that great white throne.

   It is coming, it is coming.
   That marvellous upsumming
Of the loveliest and grandest all in one:
   The great transfiguration,
   And the royal coronation
Of the Monarch of the mountains by the priestly Sun.

   Watch breathlessly & hearken
   (While the forest throne steps darken,)
His investiture in crimson and in fire;
   Not a herald trumpet ringeth,
   Not a pæan echo flingeth,
There is music of a silence that is mightier far, and brighter.

   Then, in radiant obedience,
   A flush of bright allegiance
Lights up the vassal summits and the proud peaks all around;
   And a thrill of mystic glory
   Quivers on the glaciers hoary,
As the ecstasy is full and the mighty brow is crowned.

   Crowned with ruby of resplendence,[1]
   In unspeakable transcendence,
'Neath a canopy of purple & of gold outspread;
   With rock-sceptres upward pointing,

---

[1] F.R.H. originally wrote "Crowned with transcendance," and later changed the word to "resplendance."

While the glorious anointing,
Of the consecrating sunlight is poured upon his head.

Then a swift and still transition
Falls upon the gorgeous vision,
And the ruby & the fire pass noiselessly away,
But the paling of the splendour
Leaves a rose-light, clear & tender
And lovelier than the loveliest dream that melts before the day.

Oh to keep it, oh to hold it,
While the tremulous rays enfold it!
Oh to drink in all the beauty, and never thirst again!
Yet less lovely if less fleeting!
For the mingling & the meeting
Of the wonder and the rapture can but overflow in pain.

It is passing, it is passing.
While the softening glow is glassing
In the crystal of the heavens all the fairest of its rose.
Ever faintly and more faintly,
Ever saintly and more saintly,
Gleam the snowy heights around us in holiest repose.

O pure and perfect whiteness!
O mystery of brightness
Upon those still majestic brows shed solemnly abroad!
Like the calm & blessed sleeping
Of saints in Christ's own keeping
When the smile of holy peace is left, last witness for their God.

Only we two on the mountain side,
And a hundred gone away!
Only we two for the wondrous sight
Of the sunset on Mont Blanc tonight,
From the rocky Bréven's lonely height.
Only we two could stay!

Only we two for the pageant new
In the glory of the dawn

And the morning on the mountains spread
And the rose-crown on the Monarch's head:
For the tables d'hôte below are full
   And the lamps are bright and the wines are good
Where the snowish host are gone!

Note. The first view of Mont Blanc from the Chamouni side is that from the
Bréven, which commands the whole range of aiguilles and glaciers, while the
Monarch himself shows his grandest and broadest exposure of eternal snows.
Little idea can be found of the height or majesty from the valley, a certain eleva-
tion is necessary for this. There is a tiny mountain view at Mampre, not far from
the summit of the Bréven, with accommodation, primitive indeed, but suffi-
cient may be had. We went up on a magnificent evening in July, 1871, & had a
sunset & a sunrise all to ourselves, for, though about 100 visitors had been there
that day, not one remained for what is perhaps the grandest display of colouring
in all Europe. They all went down to table d'hôte in Chamouni.

June 6.

Our Own Fireside. Sept./72.

    This ends F.R.H.'s manuscript of this poem with her "Note."

Three notes on "An Evening on the Bréven": 1. This poem was found in the
"Manuscript Book № VI begun November, 1869." This Manuscript book was
part of a collection of very important items given by Maria V. G. Havergal in
1887 to the Church Missionary Society. This collection of items was deposited
as part of the Church Missionary Society archives in the University of Birming-
ham. The "Note" after the poem was written in F.R.H.'s hand immediately after
the last line of the poem. She dated this June 6. This would have been June 6,
1872. The preceding poem in the Manuscript book was "Peaceable Fruit" dated
May, 1872. She also wrote at the left bottom, "Our Own Fireside. Sept./72.",
indicating the publication of this poem in the magazine *Our Own Fireside* (pub-
lished by Rev. Charles Bullock, a former Curate under F.R.H.'s father and a
close family friend).
2. In the last line of the poem, the third word ("snowish") is uncertain, barely
legible.
3. As clearly shown later in the "Note" after the poem, the frivolous nature and
preference for champagne and table d'hôte in the first six stanzas were the words
and way of other visitors, not of Frances and the one with her.

David Chalkley June 9, 2005

The next two poems by F.R.H., "London Super Mare" and "An Educated Topsy," are remarkable, very unusual poems by her. These two poems and "The Confession List" (found in the Manuscript Book № VII and soon to follow these two poems) form what seems to me a unique group in all of F.R.H.'s extant works. On first reading, one could think that these contradict so much that we know about her, but she is thoroughly Frances in these three poems. These poems are a brilliant example of parody. Frances had a fine sense of humor, a real gift, but in these poems she is not being humorous primarily, but parodying situations that were very profoundly false and destructive. One who does not know F.R.H. well can read these poems and think she is humorous here, but she was earnestly serious about profound matters. Though parody is so often associated with mockery and derision, parody can be compassionate and full of light to warn and teach, not always acidic and cruel, and "London Super Mare," "An Educated Topsy," and "The Confession List" are rich examples of this. Parody is a means of conveying truth, of showing what is really the situation, of communicating truth. This is not nervous energy (to "blow off steam" however brilliantly) nor eccentricity, but an effective and brilliant presentation to warn and expose, and to help readers see the profound truth of the matter.

Please read the comments on "The Confession List" on pages 726–730 of this book. These three poems ("The Confession List," "London Super Mare," and "An Educated Topsy") by F.R.H. seem to be examples where God took a gift (here, parody, His creation) so distorted by Satan and sin, and showed how this can be full of His truth and love, to His glory and others' help and enrichment.

"London Super Mare" was found in the Manuscript Book № VI, and also a published copy among Havergal manuscripts and papers. The published copy was printed on pages numbered 457 to 459, on large double-columned pages which may be a newspaper or magazine (only the published text of "London Super Mare" was found, apparently cut out from the periodical or book). At the end of the published copy, the author's full name is printed. The fair copy autograph in the Manuscript Book № VI is dated "Novr 23. 1871."

Far more attention will be given now to the poem "An Educated Topsy." A published copy of this was found among Havergal manuscripts and papers, and though this is not a certainty, this published copy seems to be privately printed. At the end of the published copy, the date November 26, 1873 is given, and below the date this is printed: "For copies for gratuitous distribution address the General Secretary of the National Education Union, 69, Corporation Street, Manchester." No name is given at all for the author in this published copy. Another printed copy of "An Educated Topsy" was found among Havergal papers, a different printing from the published copy, and the handwritten, underlined word "proof" was written at the top of the first page. At the end of this printed "proof" copy the same date was printed, November 26, 1873, and the initials "F. R. H." are printed across from the date, after the last line of the poem. No manuscript in Frances' hand of "An Educated Topsy" has been found, but there is no doubt that she wrote this poem. Whether Maria V. G. Havergal and her niece, Frances Anna Shaw, did not find this poem before they finished the Nisbet edition of *The Poetical Works of Frances Ridley Havergal* (unlikely) or did not think this poem— and also other poems—worthy or appropriate to include in the volume (far more likely), we do not know.

Frances wrote "An Educated Topsy" to show the inconsistency, hypocrisy, and falseness of opposition to Bible instruction in the public schools. This poem has the same truth and truthful end as "A Plea for the Little Ones" but a very different way to say it. She was involved in the effort in Birmingham, England. The *Birmingham Post* was on the side of the National Education League, supporting secularization of the schools and removal of Bible instruction. The *Daily Gazette*, siding with the National Education Union, opposed this secularization, advocating the free instruction of the Bible within the public schools. Rejecting the secularization of public schools and riddance of the Bible from them, Frances' desire was that the children be taught the truth of the Bible and brought to saving faith in Christ. Again for emphasis, her poem "A Plea for the Little Ones" (pages 398–402 of this book) means the same truth as this poem. Frances wrote this in a letter dated May 6, 1872 (found in *Letters by the Late Frances Ridley Havergal*, on pages 180–183 of the original book, pages 197–198 of Volume IV of the Havergal edition), quoting four verses from "A Plea for the Little Ones."

> I have just written a lively little missionary song and tune, "Tell it out," which is being taken up wonderfully quickly. I will send it to you by book post, and you can make any use you like of it. I enclose you my "Plea for the Little Ones," of which I think not less than half a million must have been in type in the last three weeks, such numbers of newspapers and magazines having inserted it. I feel very strongly (on the exclusion of the Bible from Board schools), and it is a perfectly inexplicable thing to me how men who profess to believe and value the Bible, can join hands with "infidels" and "heretics" in desiring its exclusion from Government schools; it is to me "a wonderful and horrible thing" indeed. The last verses in my Plea are:—

> > Shall those who name the Name of Christ
> > His own great gift withhold?
> > Our Lamp, our Chart, our Sword, our Song,
> > Our Pearl, our most fine Gold!

Why would ye have "no Bible taught"?
   Is it for fear? or shame?
Out, out upon such coward hearts,
   False to their Master's name!

With battle-cry of valiant faith,
   Let Britain's sons arise,—
"Our children shall be taught the Word
   That only maketh wise!"

So, dauntlessly, will we unfurl
   Our banner bright and broad:
The cause of His dear Word of Life
   Our cause,—the cause of God.

Miss Janet Grierson in her biography *Frances Ridley Havergal Worcestershire Hymnwriter* gives more details about the context in which the poem was written and published.

> The importance of encouraging children to join the Union [the "Christian Progress Scripture Reading and Prayer Union"] is also stressed, and she expresses the hope that schools will become a recruiting ground for it. This point has a bearing on another cause in which Frances played an active part, namely the burning issue of whether or not religious teaching should be permitted in the Board Schools set up as a result of the 1870 Elementary Education Act.
>
>   . . . .
>
> Birmingham [England] had for some years been the home of the National Education League, and with the *Birmingham Post* on its side, the League in 1872 began to campaign for purely secular education. It was supported in this policy by the Central Nonconformist Committee which had its headquarters in Birmingham. With the backing of such powerful figures as the highly regarded Congregational minister Dr. R. W. Dale and the Unitarian Radical Joseph Chamberlain, the local School Board succeeded in 1873 in inaugurating a system which excluded religious instruction from the timetable of its schools. If religious instruction were to be given on school premises, it must be by clergy or others not involved in the secular instruction, and payment had to be made for the privilege of using classrooms.
>   Opposition to this policy came at first from the National Education Union which had the support of the *Daily Gazette*, and of course this was the side to which Frances, with her passionate love of the Bible, devoted her energies. She was appalled by the attitude of so many influential Nonconformists. In 1872 she wrote:

> I feel *very* strongly (on the exclusion of the Bible from Board
> schools), and it is a perfectly inexplicable thing to me how men who
> *profess* to believe and value the Bible, can join hands with "infidels"
> and "heretics" in desiring its exclusion from Government schools; it
> is to me "a wonderful and horrible thing" indeed.

Her poem "Plea for the Little Ones" written in support of the cause was circu-
lated so widely that she was able to write: "I think not less than half a million
must have been in type in the last three weeks, such numbers of newspapers
and magazines having inserted it."

. . . .

["An Educated Topsy" was part of F.R.H.'s involvement to oppose the restrict-
ing—virtual banning—of Bible instruction in the public schools. The effort
to change the rules lasted for years.]

. . . . At the end of 1879 the School Board passed a resolution permit-
ting Bible reading by the Head Teacher in its schools, while the non-sectarian
character of the religious instruction was preserved by the prohibition of any
comment on the reading. Unfortunately Frances did not live to see the tri-
umph of her cause.[1]

The city of Birmingham's dialect name Brummagem was derived an earlier
name Bromwicham; citizens of Birmingham are called "Brummies," and there
is a definite, special Brummie vocabulary, syntax, and accent, which is apparent
in F.R.H.'s depiction of the Topsy. Of course "topsy-turvy" means backwards,
up-side down, disorderly, chaotic, out of control.

---

[1] *Frances Ridley Havergal Worcestershire Hymnwriter* by Janet Grierson (Bromsgrove, Worces-
tershire: The Havergal Society, 1979), pages 136–138 of the original book, pages 1194–1195 of
Volume IV of the Havergal edition.

127

London super Mare

People may think me "quite contrary"
On the subject of London super Mare;
But never a land or water fairy
Found the magical spell to enlighten
My darkened intellects as to Brighton.
    Perhaps it will amuse
    If I stole my views
In a trip and jingle of rhyme & metre
And make their bitterness somewhat sweeter.

One is entertained at the very station
By evident tokens of preparation
For pic and parade, for assembly & ball;
For the luggage on luggage on luggage beats all
That ever I saw disgorged from a train.
    I'm prepared to maintain
    That, on rough calculation,
    There must have been boxes ten
For each of the claimants, including men.
With all one's civility brought to bear
How could one help concluding there

London Super Mare.[1]

People may think me " quite contrary"
On the subject of London Super Mare;
But never a land or water fairy
Found the magical spell to enlighten
My darkened intellects, as to Brighton.
   Perhaps 'twill amuse,
   If I state my views
In a trip and jingle of rhyme and metre,
And make their bitterness somewhat sweeter.

One is entertained at the very station
By evident tokens of preparation
For pier and parade, for assembly and ball;
For the luggage on luggage on luggage, beats all
 That ever I saw disgorged from a train.
 I'm prepared to maintain
  That, on rough calculation,
  There must have been boxes ten
For each of the claimants, including men.
With all one's charity brought to bear,
How could one help concluding there,
That a good deal more than needful wear—
  Namely, of pomps and vanitie,
  As mentioned in the " Catechee,"—
  Within those boxes there must be!

The very idea of invalids
 Coming to Brighton to recruit,
Is *too* absurd; for one must needs
 Have strength to match and nerves to suit
The jumble and chatter, the rumble and clatter,
The bands and the organs, the hoofs and the wheels!
One's frame should be made of whalebones and steels,
And one's nerves should be iron and brass, I declare it,
  Only to bear it!

[1] This is a train station at Brighton, a city on the coast of the English Channel, south of London.

Old Ocean never can get in a word,
He really hasn't a chance to be heard:
So all his grand sayings and mighty orations,
His gentle discourses and sweet salutations,
　　　　Mysterious questions,
　　　　And sudden suggestions,
His whispers of wisdom, his songs of delight,
　　His symphonies rare and sweet,
Are all thrown away to the wild wind's play;
　　for never a human ear they meet
　　　　Who can listen aright
　　　　In the Babel of sound
　　　　And the turmoil around.
　　　　So these are my views,—
That people have not an idea what they lose
　　　　When Brighton they choose.

　　　　Glorious sight
　　　　Of supreme delight,
And exquisite scene to rejoice the heart,—
　　　　Lo, the Parade!
　　　　That casts in the shade
All exhibitions that ever were made
　　　　Of milliners' glory and tailors' art.
Hundreds of empty-brained simpering mignonness,
　　　　With every variety
　　　　Known to society
Of hayricks and pads and astonishing chignons!
　　　　What a display
　　　　In the sunset ray,
Of velvet and satin and sealskin *ad libitum!*
What studies of feathers and specimen furs!
　　　　While many a toilette occurs
　　　　　　So very *outré*,
　　　That *Punch* would rejoice to gibbet 'em.
　　　　I cannot stay
To enumerate every species of swell
　　　　(Not of the sea, be it understood)
　　　　Which on Parade may be viewed,—

Studies, indeed, of abnormal humanity,
Incarnations of masculine vanity,
  Chiefly noodles and dandies and fops:
'Tis time for my muse's concentration,
In deep and blissful concentration
   On the Shops!
   But such a theme,
   With its myriad gleam
   Of treasures untold
   (And all to be sold),
  Is far beyond a poet's dream.
  'Tis not for me to dare aspire
   To gild refinèd gold
  With baser touch of poetic fire.
  I only say, I have been to see,
  But their wonders of sublimity
   Were quite too much for me,
So I limit my pen to humbler theme.

  I found a dear one sojourning here,
  Whom I had not met for many a year;
   So we planned a walk
   For the sake of talk,
  And I thought how pleasant it would be
  The interchange of heart and mind,
   And counsel sweet to find
   By the shining sea.
All a delusion, we soon found *that!*
For anything more than the flimsiest chat
Yoiu must shut yourselves up and shut Brighton out.
   To attempt conversation
   Is mere vexation,
  While painfully threading in and out
  Steering, and tacking, and jostling about,
  In the labyrinth of such a rout.

I did suggest, as an obvious thing,
A stroll on the beach where the wave-bells ring,
As a change from the racket and bustle and noise
Which seem to constitute Brighton joys.

But my little proposal was laughted to scorn
  On that sunny morn:
"Why, nobody thinks of going down there,
  Except in the bathing season,
  When only 'nobodies' want sea-air!"
And soon I discovered a very good reason,
For, search the coast of Britain round
And a shore of less interest could not be found.
A straight high wall in lieu of rocks,
Is the charming background that smiles
In monotonous neatness, for miles;
They have built it just far enough away,
   Just out of reach
   Of the thundering shooks
   And the Titan play
   Of the wild white spray,
  Which dies on the level beach.
  At every step you sink
   In fatiguing shingle,
   With crunch and jingle:
   Never a golden reach
   Of fair smooth sand,
   Laid by the hand
   Of the lulling tide,
  Inviting many a stroll or ride;
 Never a pure and lovely shell,
  Never a crimson frond,
 Witness of all fair forms that dwell
In the marvellous deep below and beyond;
  Never a living flower,
  Never a waif from mermaid's bower,
  Never a living star,
  Never a crystal, never a spar.
When Nature distributed all her treasures,
And all her special seaside pleasures,
  She took it for granted
  They would not be wanted,
  So Brighton was missed,—
  Left out of the list!

Enough: enough
Of all this stuff!
I wander in fancy far away
To scenes of many a summer day,
Beautiful even now
In the pale and wan November ray.
Where Nature lays her cooling hand
On the hot and aching brow,
And quiets the throbbing heart with a touch,
And whispers much
In her own dear musical tone,
Of rest and calm,
And peace and balm,
Till the heart is tuned to her own sweet psalm
And feels no more alone.
Oh, the healing she has brought!
Oh, the cures that she has wrought!
Only engage her as nurse and physician,
And let her fulfil her miraculous mission,
And you will find
That she leaves behind
All the wonders of homœpathy,
All the powers of old allopathy.
Oh, I could tell,
For I know so well
How the unstrung nerves are tuned again,
And the load rolls off from the tired brain,
And strength comes back to the languid frame
And existence hardly seems the same.
Her work is surer far, and shorter,
When out of sight of bricks and mortar;
When all her gentle remedies
Are brought to bear till the work is done,
Instead of seeking the only one
Which belongs to Brighton,—the fine se-air,
With a thousand counteractives there.

Oh, give to me
A *pier*less and paradeless sea,

With a shore as God made it, grand and free,
And not a mere triumph of masonry!
   Give me the rocks of Ilfracombe,
With their witchery of gleam and gloom;
With the crystal pools in the tide-swept cave,
   Where myriad fairy forests wave;
Where the delicate fringes of crimson and green,
   Purple and amber, ruby and rose,
With snowy-gleaming shells between,
And marvellous forms of life are seen,
   While the musical tide still ebbs and flows.
   Where not a step but brings to view
   Something exquisite, something rare,
   Something wonderfully fair,
   Always beautiful, always new.
      But oh, I forgot!
      I really ought not
   To praise such places:
   They are so dull, you know,
   So very exceedingly slow,
So deficient in Brighton gifts and graces.
      Hush: yes, hush!
      I well may blush,
But, nevertheless, I frankly confess
   My heart is wandering still
   At its strange and wayward will.
   Oh, for the glen of the Waters' Meet,
   Where the merry Lyn leaps down
   to that loveliest vale below,
   And hastens to join the channel flow;
   Where the Lynton cliffs, without a frown,
      Majestically crown
   This mingling of sublime and sweet.

   And oh, for the mighty roar
   At the foot of Penmaenmawr!
      Or an autumn storm
      On the greater Orme;
Where the giant breakers hurl their spray
   At the mountain's mighty breast

And the wild wind, mingling in the fray,
Seizes and whirs it high and away
 Over the proud rock's crest;
 While the maddened waves
 Rush into the caves,
With thunder and growl, and rush back again,
As if the assault had been all in vain,—
But only to gather in awful might
For a tenfold struggle of fiercer fight.
Who would have time for a thought of care,
Or a fit of the blues, if standing there?

Or away, away, to the bracing North,
  To the grand old seas
  Of the Hebrides,
 To the sunny Clyde or the silver Forth!
Purple heather above, and shadowy loch below,
Golden glory of furze, and a far-off wreath of snow;
Violet peaks afar, and dark-green pines anear,
And long bright evenings there, when the gas is
 lighted here;
And concert-halls of birdies sweet, with many a blithe
 cascade:—
But of course this *Can't Compare* with an AFTERNOON
 PARADE!

       FRANCES RIDLEY HAVERGAL.

An Educated Topsy

Scene: A dust heap. Topsy harangues Young Birmingham from a wheelbarrow.

Not if I knows it! Catch *me* at it,
 A-stopping in school to learn religion!
Dick! I'm surprised at your asking "Is *that* it?"
 D'ye know a goose from a carrier pigeon?
Young uns, you listen. I'll tell you about it.
Of course *I* know, and durst you doubt it?

AN EDUCATED TOPSY.

———>·◆·◆·◆·<———

Scene: A Dust Heap.   Topsy harangues Young Birmingham from
a wheelbarrow.

———>·◆·◆·◆·<———

Not if I knows it !   Catch *me* at it,
    A-stopping in school to learn religion !
Dick ! I'm surprised at your asking " Is *that* it ? "
    D'ye know a goose from a carrier pigeon ?
Young uns, you listen.   I'll tell you about it.
Of course *I* know, and durst you doubt it ?
You, indeed ! when never a one of you
Is up in Long Division, and none of you
    Likely to get into Rule of Three,
    And *I'm* in Fractions ! *now* d'ye see ?

" What's the Board ? "   Well, really, Jim !
What an ignorant ! hark at him !
The Board aint nothing religious at all,
And has nothing to do with Peter and Paul.
It's only a " Post "* cut up into bits,
Without any feeling of joins or splits,
And sat upon daily by the " Gazette,"
So maybe the weight will crush it yet.
            So I hear;
            But never fear !
    For *I'm* on their side at present,
    As long as they make it pleasant.

It's this.   There's a " Bible Eight;" you know,
    And another lot that keeps their name
    All quiet, but 'taint far off the same ;
It's " Bible Hate," or I guess it's so.
Well, the Bible Eight was beat, out-and-out,
        After a lively bout,
And the other sort have got their way ;
Religious teaching, they think, don't pay,
So those that want it must go without ;
        Because what eight of them think,
        Has got to be done in a twink ;
        And the seven must go to the wall.
        And never say nothing at all.

It's quite astonishing to see
What a mighty soft that Board must be,
        As now pretends
        To be such friends
To that old Book to gain their ends.

* *Post*, the Birmingham League organ.   *Daily Gazette* supports the National Education
    . Union.
[No. O 197.]

*This is the
first page
of a
printed
copy
—not a
printed
proof copy,
but appar-
ently
a final-
ized,
published,
and
distributed
copy—of
"An Edu-
cated
Topsy."
The next
page 718
has the
last page
of a proof
copy.*

When the different sorts come in to teach
The two or three that have kept in reach,
Out of the regular hours by rule.
- *Mine's* a Hindependent school,
But there's half-a-dozen as says they're Church,
And three or four as are called Wesleyans,
And a couple of Irish—very wee uns.
            Oh, it will be rum
                If the ministers come,
And about one apiece is left in the lurch,
What's been kept in to finish a sum!
It would be sure to be rather windy,
And *might* come up to a proper shindy!
    So, young uns, I vote for politics,

I went on a Sunday once or twice,
    When there was nothing else to do;
And the Superintendent spoke so nice,
    With a kind of smile and a pious look,
    And a way of talking about that Book,
Till I really supposed he thought it was true,
And wanted us all to learn it through,
And liked it himself above a bit!
- But, young uns, believe me, that wasn't it;
For he made a speech the very next day
            Exactly the other way!
            A-wanting the town to pay
For all manner of what they call science and knowledge,
And crackjaw things that they learn at college,
But making it out a most a sin
If ever they let the Bible in,
            Or ever forked out a penny
            To teach it to any
As can't afford to pay for themselves;—
    And sure enough there's a pretty many

Now, young uns, I've finished. Lawk-a-day,
There's one of the Board a-coming this way!
What kind of a handkercher will he have got?
I likes a silk with a spot—
            That's the sort to pay!
He knows it's moonshine to teach
The Ten Commandments and all such preach!
Though likely enough he'll have "moral objection"
            To prigging, when *he's* been done,
            And I've been the one
To do it without detection.
            "Moral objections," indeed!
            Now, young uns, you give heed,
And if I don't lighten him all the same,
Why, Brummagem Topsy's not my name!

Nov. 26*th*, 1873.   F. R. H.

This is the last page of a different copy—a printed proof copy—of "An Educated Topsy." The previous page 717 has the first page of a different copy, apparently a finalized, published, and distributed copy—of "An Educated Topsy."

You, indeed! when never a one of you
Is up in Long Division, and none of you
    Likely to get into Rule of Three,
    And *I'm* in Fractions! *now* d'ye see?

"What's the Board?" Well, really, Jim!
What an ignorant! hark at him!
The Board aint nothing religious at all,
And has nothing to do with Peter and Paul.
It's only a "Post"[1] cut up into bits,
Without any feeling of joins or splits,
And sat upon daily by the "Gazette,"
So maybe the weight will crush it yet.
    So I hear;
    But never fear!
For *I'm* on their side at present,
As long as they make it pleasant.

It's this. There's a "Bible Eight"; you know,
    And another lot that keeps their name
    All quiet, but 'taint far off the same;
It's "Bible Hate," or I guess it's so.
Well, the Bible Eight was beat, out-and-out,
    After a lively bout,
And the other sort have got their way;
Religious teaching, they think, don't pay,
So those that want it must go without;
    Because what eight of them think,
    Has got to be done in a twink;
    And the seven must go to the wall,
    And never say nothing at all.

It's quite astonishing to see
What a mighty soft that Board must be,
    As now pretends
    To be such friends
To that old Book to gain their ends.

---

1 *Post*, the Birmingham League organ. *Daily Gazette* supports the National Education Union.

Or else, I do believe,
They're laughing up their sleeve,
With a finger at their nose.
They'll be "*so* glad to have it taught,"—
So as it's only done by those
As choose to do it all for nought;—
And *so* as it's never named in school,
Nor reckoned as any kind of rule;—
And *so* as none of the marks should count
To make up anyone's amount
In any examination;—
And *so* as any lad or lass
That's top of the school in a Bible-class
Should be worse off for the time they've lost
In learning what's not at the public cost
Of the town or of the nation;—
And *so* as the parents writes to say
Whether they wish it or not,
And just exactly what
They considers the right and proper way.

Now, *do* they think I'd stop in school
To learn the Bible out of hours?
By all the powers
I'm no such fool!
And *do* they think I'd go and work,
Sitting and bothering after dark,
At what won't gain me a single mark,
And what five hundred to one will shirk?
And "Parents" indeed! When most of us "growed"
Up the street or down the road!
"Parents" indeed! If the Board can ketch 'em!
Or send the police to fetch 'em
Out of a quiet fight
To say what religion they think is right;
Or out of the ginshops to say
In what particular way
They'd like the Bible explained to Jack,
Or whether Polly and Bess shall be

Church or Baptist or Methodee,
When they can hardly stand, or see
If black is white or white is black!

I shall answer for myself, I guess!
Won't it be jolly fun to 'fess
    My own particular persuasion!
    Now I believe there's no occasion
For extra hours for Bible work,
So I shall state that I'm a Turk.
And then they'll find they've caught a Tartar,
If they expect to make a martyr.
Why shouldn't I? Why, a Turk will fight
For the sort of religion he thinks is right.
But the chapel-folks do more than that,
    And fight like cocks to have none at all!
I've wondered if they *know* what they'r at!
    There's a queer old story about St. Paul,
            That's much the same,
            With a different name,
How hard for a certain master he fought,
And yet all the while he thought
He was serving the other! But, deary me,
    One needn't bother with those old tales,
            We're not such snails
As to creep and crawl through that old Book,
Into which the Board don't want us to look.
            It's 'cute enough, I suppose,
            And very well knows,
What books are best to give us to learn,
And what to forbid, though it dursn't burn!

A Turk, I said. But if that won't do,
I'll be a Mormon, sure as true!
    'Cause *they* won't want me to stay
    When the rest are off to play,
A-reading the Bible! That's the plan,
So let 'em catch me if they can!
Why, just look here, you Bill and Sam,
If there' s a child in Birmingham

(Except what few is desperate steady,
And ever so good and pious a'ready,)
  That's half his wits alive,
  And can't contrive
To dodge the ministers and their talk,
And out of school to walk,
  Not on the sly,
   But right under their nose,
  I don't suppose
  It's either you or I.

Five hours is learning enough for me,
  And after that I'll see
  That I go free!
And it's likely I'll come out in the cold
At half-past eight, because I'm told
There's a Bible lesson for those who wish,
  And they don't expect it
  That we should neglect it!
My eye! but the Board won't hook such fish!

  But I think I'll stay
  For once in a way,
  To see the fun,
  And what will be done
When the different sorts come in to teach
The two or three that have kept in reach,
Out of the regular hours by rule.
Mine's a Hindependent school,
But there's half-a-dozen as says they're Church,
And three or four as are called Wesleyans,
And a couple of Irish—very wee uns.
  Oh, it will be rum
  If the ministers come,
And about one apiece is left in the lurch,
What's been kept in to finish a sum!
It would be sure to be rather windy,
And *might* come up to a proper shindy!
So, young uns, *I* vote for politics,
When it comes to all such jolly tricks.

I went on a Sunday once or twice,
　　When there was nothing else to do;
And the Superintendent spoke so nice,
　　With a kind of smile and a pious look,
　　And a way of talking about that Book,
Till I really supposed he thought it was true,
And wanted us all to learn it through,
And liked it himself above a bit!
But, young uns, believe me, that wasn't it;
For he made a speech the very next day
　　　　Exactly the other way!
　　　　A-wanting the town to pay
For all manner of what they call science and knowledge,
And crackjaw things that they learn at college,
But making it out a'most a sin
If ever they let the Bible in,
　　　　Or ever forked out a penny
　　　　To teach it to any
As can't afford to pay for themselves;—
　　And sure enough there's a pretty many
With nought but a gin-bottle on their shelves.

Now, young uns, I've finished. Lawk-a-day,
There's one of the Board a-coming this way!
What kind of a handkercher will he have got?
I likes a silk with a spot—
　　　　That's the sort to pay!
He knows it's moonshine to teach
The Ten Commandments and all such preach!
Though likely enough he'll have "moral objection"
　　　　To prigging, when *he's* been done,
　　　　And I've been the one
To do it without detection.
　　　　"Moral objections," indeed!
　　　　Now, young uns, you give heed,
And if I don't lighten him all the same,
Why, Brummagem Topsy's not my name!

Nov. 26th, 1873.   F. R. H.

Items in Manuscript Book № VII

The Manuscript Book № VII has nothing written on the front cover. There is a title page, hand-written, which says this:

№ VII
Begun June 30. 1872

This title page is a left-side un-numbered page; facing this left-side title page is a right-side page, numbered 1, with the first page of the poem "Prelude" which Frances published as the opening poem of *Under the Surface.*

This next poem, found on pages 29–30 of F.R.H.'s Manuscript Book № VII, was written in August, 1872, apparently for "F.A.S." who was Frances Anna Shaw (1856–1948), F.R.H.'s niece and god-daughter. This poem apparently was never published until the quotation of it in Miss Janet Grierson's valuable biography, *Frances Ridley Havergal Worcestershire Hymnwriter* (Worcestershire: The Havergal Society, 1979), at the end of Chapter 5, pages 39–40 of the original book, page 1148 of Volume IV of the Havergal edition.

Answer to a request for a poem
"on the bothers of Going to School!"

'Tis a difficult thing
To refuse to sing
When asked by a nephew small;
But more difficult still
To grind in a mill
Without any grain at all.

For what can I write
When my greatest delight
Was exactly this very thing!
When I never did know
The "bother" and woe
That going to school would bring!

What tears I shed
On going to bed
The night that I left for good!

I'd have dried up each tear
If another half year
Had been promised—indeed I would.

So my dear little friend
I would just recommend
(If advice may be allowed)
That you try to find
The silver behind
This dark little morning cloud.

F.A.S.   August.

On pages 40–48 of her Manuscript Book N̲o̲ VII, Frances wrote out six poems, with this title at the top of the first one:

Six Songs
Imitated (not translated) from the German, for
Music by Franz Abt.

The titles and publication of these poems are given individually next:

I "My Messengers" was published in the section of "Songs" in Nisbet's *Poetical Works* (pages 253–254 of this book).

II "The Song of Love" was published in the section of "Miscellaneous Poems" in N.P.W. (pages 165–166 of this book).

III "God Keep Thee" was published in the section of "Songs" in N.P.W. (page 254 of this book).

IV "Rose of Roses" was published in the section of "Songs" in N.P.W. (pages 254–255 of this book).

V "Hast thou a thought?" was published in the section of "Songs" in N.P.W. (pages 255–256 of this book).

VI "The Confession List" was apparently never published in any of Havergal's

books. The text of her fair copy autograph is given next. This is an exception-
ally complex or subtle (more likely subtle, I think) poem by F.R.H., and com-
ments on this poem are given after the text of the poem.

The Confession List.

A MAIDEN went to the church one day,
She meant to confess, and to sing and pray;
She wrote out a list comprising each
	transgression. For Confession!

And when she knelt down to confess them all,
The tears they began from her eyes to fall.
	"I'll make a good resolution,
	If you'll give me now absolution!"

"Before I absolve, I must hear the list,
Not one must be hidden, not one be missed!"

She couldn't, she couldn't just find it!
Didn't know – didn't know – but she
	hoped he <u>wouldn't</u> mind it!

I picked it up, and I read it too!
But what was there is nothing to you!
	So truly had she divined it,
That I might fancy I had signed it.

The list began – "He loves me so!"
The second ran – "He loves me, I know!"
	And this was all this list meant!
	And so on all the list went!
		And so on, and so on, and so on ! etc.

Nov 26./72

"The Confession List" was apparently never published in any of Havergal's
books, although the assumption can be made that this was published with a mu-

sic score composed by Franz Abt. (Hutchings and Romer, important publishers of music scores composed by Frances, published "The Song of Love," words by F.R.H. set to music by Franz Wilhelm Abt. There is another score, "My Messengers" with words by F.R.H. and music by Abt. These scores, and surely others published in the 19th century, are extremely obscure now if still extant.) This is an exceptionally complex or subtle poem by F.R.H., not so immediately clear or obviously accessible (at least for me) as most of the poems and prose pieces she wrote. She was almost surely showing the falseness and absurdity of the Roman Catholic system of confession. One thing is certain: she was not being flippant here, knowing the profound seriousness of this. As a genuine disciple who truly loved the written Word, the Bible, and the Word made flesh, the Lord Jesus Christ, she clearly believed the doctrine of "Solus Christus" (Christ alone), very likeminded to the Reformers Tyndale, Frith, Ridley, Latimer, and others, rejecting the Roman requirement of confession to a priest. I Timothy 2:5 "For there is one God, and one mediator between God and men, the man Christ Jesus." In probing this poem, one dear (and wise) friend said to me that this poem was too obscure and complex, "not Frances at her best," not worthy to be published. In the earnest effort to present everything found, to show Frances as she truly was and not to edit or delete what I or others may not understand or value, this should be included. Beyond thorough completeness to include all that is found, if one sees what Frances was really thinking and saying here, there is true value in this poem. This poem may seem at first glimpse to be unworthy for publication, but there is richness here. Though her sister Maria and her niece Frances Anna Shaw, who so finely prepared Nisbet's *Poetical Works*, declined to include this (and other poems presented in this section), Frances herself thought this was worthy to write out carefully in a fair copy autograph with her other poems (she could have easily rejected the poem, not copied it in her Manuscript Book, and discarded the original draft), and apparently she regarded this as fully worthy to be included with the other five poems in the set of six. Because the German text which Frances imitated has not been found, we do not know how much of Frances' poem is her own words and ideas and how much is a copy or reflection of the German text, but her underlined words "Imitated (not translated) from the German" indicate much involvement by her: very likely this English poem is significantly or mostly Frances, not only the German text that was the impetus or start for her poem.

I have realized two possible interpretations for this poem. One, far less likely to be what Frances really meant here, is that this is stated by a Roman Catholic who at least partially realized and believed Reformation (Protestant) doctrine, and that "He loves me" in the final verse refers to the love of Christ.

That first interpretation is far outweighed and proven unlikely by the much stronger likelihood of this second interpretation: that this poem is a parody to show the falseness of the Roman system of confession. We can know from an abundance of proof that Frances would not have made light of the doctrines of forgiveness and justification by Christ alone, nor made light of a divergence from that truth: this would have been utmostly serious to her, as surely serious as the truth of Christ and the souls of sinners. We can also know that Frances was remarkably gifted to create parody to present her position. Though parody is not so obvious in the extant writings of and accounts about Frances, the poems "London Super Mare" and "An Educated Topsy" (also, like this "The Confession List," not included by her sister and niece in Nisbet's Poetical Works but found among F.R.H.'s manuscripts and papers) strongly demonstrate her gifts to use parody to state truth. "An Educated Topsy" is an especially strong example of Frances' parody to present truth that she knew and wanted others to see and know. In "The Confession List," neither the maiden in the poem nor the narrator in the poem (the "I" in the next-to-last verse) represent Frances at all, but only are means to expose the false system. "The Confession List" is very similar to the poem "Sin's Round" by George Herbert (F.R.H. greatly valued Herbert's poems and almost certainly would have known this poem by him). "Sin's Round" is a parody showing—portraying—the falseness of an unrepentant sinner who keeps on sinning while emptily claiming sorrow (the sinner blasphemously, effectively mocking the truth).

Sin's Round.

Sorry I am, my God, sorry I am
That my offences course it in a ring.
My thoughts are working like a busy flame,
Until their cockatrice they hatch and bring;
And when they once have perfected their draughts,
My words take fire from my inflamèd thoughts.

My words take fire from my inflamèd thoughts,
Which spit it forth like the Sicilian hill. [Aetna, a volcano]
They vent the wares, and pass them with their faults,
And by their breathing ventilate the ill.
But words suffice not, where are lewd intentions;
My hands do join to finish the inventions.

My hands do join to finish the inventions,
And so my sins ascend three storeys high,   [thoughts, words, deeds]
As Babel grew, before there were dissentions.
Yet ill deeds loiter not; for they supply
New thoughts of sinning; wherefore, to my shame,
Sorry I am, my God, sorry I am.

George Herbert (1593–1633)

Just as Herbert so strongly showed the falseness and wickedness of sin (not remotely endorsing that, but effectively exposing and rejecting that), Frances here is exposing the reality of a false system. George Herbert's poem "Sin's Round" is a similar parody, showing—portraying—the falseness of an unrepentant sinner who keeps on sinning while claiming sorrow. Though parody is so often associated with mockery and derision, parody can be compassionate and full of light to warn and teach, not always acidic and cruel, and "The Confession List," "London Super Mare," and "An Educated Topsy" are rich examples of this. This is not nervous energy (to "blow off steam" however brilliantly) nor eccentricity, but an effective and brilliant presentation to warn and expose, and to help readers see the profound truth of the matter. What a false system, to bring one's sins to another sinner for absolution. F.R.H. meant in "The Confession List" what she wrote in the first verse of her poem "I could not do without Thee" (page 375 of this book).

I Could Not Do Without Thee.

I COULD not do without Thee,
    O Saviour of the lost!
Whose precious blood redeemed me,
    At such tremendous cost.
Thy righteousness, Thy pardon,
    Thy precious blood must be
My only hope and comfort,
    My glory and my plea!

I could not do without Thee!
    I cannot stand alone,
I have no strength or goodness,
    No wisdom of my own.

But Thou, belovèd Saviour,
　　Art all in all to me;
And weakness will be power,
　　If leaning hard on Thee.

I could not do without Thee!
　　For oh! the way is long,
And I am often weary,
　　And sigh replaces song.
How *could* I do without Thee?
　　I do not know the way;
Thou knowest and Thou leadest,
　　And wilt not let me stray.

I could not do without Thee,
　　O Jesus, Saviour dear!
E'en when my eyes are holden,
　　I know that Thou art near.
How dreary and how lonely
　　This changeful life would be,
Without the sweet communion,
　　The secret rest with Thee!

I could not do without Thee!
　　No other friend can read
The spirit's strange deep longings,
　　Interpreting its need.
No human heart could enter
　　Each dim recess of mine,
And soothe and hush and calm it,
　　O blessèd Lord, but Thine!

I could not do without Thee!
　　For years are fleeting fast,
And soon, in solemn loneliness,
　　The river must be passed.
But Thou wilt never leave me,
　　And, though the waves roll high,
I know Thou wilt be near me,
　　And whisper, 'It is I.'

At the end of her Manuscript Book Nº VII, Frances attached a printed, published text of a "National Hymn" (see also pages 247–248 of this book). At the bottom right corner of the published text, Frances wrote "July. 1873."

Items in Manuscript Book Nº VIII

The Manuscript Book Nº VIII has nothing written on the front cover. There is a title page, hand-written, which says this:

Manuscript Book, Nº VIII.
Begun November, 1873.

Jer. 1.9 & Ps. 119.49.

No unpublished poems were found in this Manuscript Book Nº VIII.

Items in Manuscript Book Nº IX

The Manuscript Book Nº IX has nothing written on the front cover. There is a title page, hand-written, which says this:

Manuscript Book. Nº IX.
Begun Febr 24. 1878.

———————

"I will direct their work in truth."   Isa. 61.8

No unpublished poems were found in this Manuscript Book Nº IX .

The following four poems ("A Mother's Loss," the four-line Charade by Sabrina, "Qui veut venir?" and "Prepare us for what Thou preparest for us") were written by F.R.H., found on loose pieces of paper among Havergal archival materials, and never published in any of the books by her or by her family after her death.

"A Mother's Loss" was found in a manuscript, on three sides of a single fold separate sheet of paper, written in Frances' hand-writing and signed "F.R.H. April 1852" at the end. Frances was 15 at that time. See pages XXI, XXVII, and XXVIII of this book.

A mother's loss! Oh who may tell
Its anguish, or what power can quell
The deepest grief, most heartfelt woe
Which childhood's sunny hours may know.

Ah! childhood's happy days are past
In mirth and glee; no shades are cast
Upon their bright and happy way
Where sunbeams ere around them play.

No cares have they: the floweret sweet
Springs up to cheer their tiny feet.
Their tears are like the gentle dew
Which brighten still that floweret's hue.

E'en if a cloud appears awhile
To dim their merry gleeful smile,
A rainbow will be painted there
In colours bright and passing fair.

And music dwells in childhood's voice
Which can the weary heart rejoice.
Its merry tones as blithely ring
As birds which welcome early spring.

And joy that fair young head hath drowned
As with a garland circling round,
Bright are the florerets which compose
That wreath of joy untouched by woe.

But brightest of the blossoms there
And fairest of those flowerets fair,
That priceless gift from God above
In mercy sent: a mother's love.

That flower from childhood's bosom severed,
Its sweetest gift is gone for ever.
The wreath of joy! Oh how defaced!
How can <u>that</u> loss e-er be replaced.

Torn is that young and tender heart
When called from mother love to part.
Ah! manhood stern can never know
The depth of this its bitterest woe!

F.R.H. 1852

This one verse was found among Havergal manuscripts and papers. The handwriting looks very much like F.R.H.'s, and this was apparently a Charade not published with the other 18 Charades.

Say, is not my <u>whole</u> a prize,
While my <u>first</u> it gratifies,
And my <u>second</u> 'tis indeed,
Bright with many a dewy bead.

Sabrina.

Note: This was written by F.R.H. Sabrina was a pen name Frances used for this genre of poems she wrote, and this one was presumably misplaced or declined when the Enigmas and Charades were published. Though she wrote items anonymously with no name at all, the Enigmas and Charades are the only example of her using pen names for herself: she signed Sabrina, Zoïde, and her name Fanny R. H. for poems in this genre. See page 148 of this book of the Havergal edition for a handwritten manuscript list by her Enigmas and Charades with these names she used. Only one other Charade (No. 18, the last one published) was four lines, but Frances' signature "Sabrina" at the end conveys that this is a completed Charade.

The manuscript of an Enigma or Charade written by Frances Ridley Havergal.

Qui veut venir?

Qui veut venir à Jesus Christ?
 Qui veut avoir la vie?
Il veut vous sauver aujourd'hui,
Ah venez, venez à Lui
 Laissez la mort, acceptez la vie.

Qui veut venir à Jésus Christ?
 Qui veut avoir la paix?
Il a versé son sang pour nous,
Son precieux Sang — et c'est pour vous!
 Laissez la lutte — Acceptez la paix.
 unfinished.

Frances mentioned that she was preparing her "French hymns" for S. W. Partridge to print, but this "unfinished" one and the profoundly rich "Seulement pour Toi" are the only two poems in French yet found by this researcher. Frances was utterly fluent in French, and likely wrote other poems in French not yet found, possibly or likely not extant now. The manuscript of "Qui veut venir?" was found among Havergal manuscripts and papers, on one side of a loose piece of paper.

Qui veut venir?

Qui veut venir à Jésus Christ?	*Who wants to come to Jesus Christ?*
Qui veut avoir la vie?	*Who wants to have life?*
Il veut nous sauver aujourd'hui,	*He wants to save you today,*
Ah venez, venez à Lui.	*Ah come, come to Him.*
Laissez la mort, acceptez la vie.	*Leave death, accept life.*
Qui veut venir à Jésus Christ?	*Who wants to come to Jesus Christ?*
Qui veut avoir la paix?	*Who wants to have peace?*
Il a versé son sang pour nous!	*He has shed His blood for us,*
Son précieux sang—et c'est pour vous!	*His precious blood—and this is for you!*
Laissez la latte¹—acceptez la paix.	*Leave labor¹—accept peace.*

unfinished

¹ Laissez la latte—"latte" meant slat or board, apparently a washing board where one hand-washed clothes. To leave trying to wash or scrub away your own sins in your own effort so false and to receive Christ's true righteousness by His shed blood: leave labour, accept peace.

To Frances' unfinished poem of two verses are added these third and fourth verses by David Chalkley. (All four verses in English were translated by David Chalkley.)

Qui veut venir à Jésus Christ?	*Who wants to come to Jesus Christ?*
Qui veut avoir l'amour?	*Who wants to have love?*
Acceptez son don, laissez vos labeurs,	*Accept His gift, leave your labors,*
Autant donné, aimant toujours.	*So much given, loving always.*
Laissez toi-même, acceptez Jésus.	*Leave yourself, accept Jesus.*
Qui veut venir à Jésus Christ?	*Who wants to come to Jesus Christ?*
Qui veut la vérité?	*Who wants the truth?*
Jésus est la parole de Dieu.	*Jesus is the Word of God.*
La Vérité venu à nous.	*The Truth come to us.*
Venez à Lui—Jésus Christ est vrai.	*Come to Him—Jesus Christ is true.*

Note: This is an alternate text for line 3 of the third stanza:

Il nous aime plus qu'on ne puisse décrire,	*He loves us more than we can describe,*

"Prepare us for what Thou preparest for us."

"Prepare our selves for what, O Lord,
  Thou dost for us prepare!"
A dying mother taught her child
  To breathe the little prayer:

A God - sent word the mother left,
  A widely - bearing seed;
Heart after heart pours forth her prayer
  Against its hour of need.

Prepare us, Lord, for every task
  Thou givest us to do;
Prepare us for the tangled ways
  We have to struggle through.

Prepare us, lest in happier days
  We try alone to go,
Forgetting then to seek the hand
  We cry for in our woe.

"Experience teaches!" True, but life
  Doth ne'er itself repeat;
Each trial, new in something, proves
  Our training incomplete.

Thou know'st, but feebly can we work,
  But weakly can we bear;
At best we struggle blindly on:
  Our lot and us prepare!

Make us more ready to perceive,
  More strong to do Thy will,
That soul and body Thy commands
  May cheerfully fulfil.

And when, our life - probation o'er,
  We lie too faint for prayer,
O Saviour, speak those gracious words,
  "Thy mansion I prepare."

This printed poem was found among Havergal manuscripts and papers. This was Frances' mother's desire for her, and though we do not know, this poem may have been—likely was—written by F.R.H.

"Prepare us for what Thou preparest for us."

"Prepare ourselves for what, O Lord,
　　Thou dost for us prepare!"
A dying mother taught her child
　　To breathe the little prayer:

A God-sent word the mother left,
　　A widely-bearing seed;
Heart after heart pours forth her prayer
　　Against its hour of need.

Prepare us, Lord, for every task
　　Thou givest us to do;
Prepare us for the tangled ways
　　We have to struggle through.

Prepare us, lest in happier days
　　We try alone to go,
Forgetting then to seek the hand
　　We cry for in our woe.

"Experience teaches!" True, but life
　　Doth ne'er itself repeat;
Each trial, new in something, proves
　　Our training incomplete.

Thou know'st, but feebly can we work,
　　But feebly can we bear;
At best we struggle blindly on:
　　Our lot and us prepare.

Make us more ready to perceive,
　　More strong to do Thy will,
That soul and body Thy commands
　　May cheerfully fulfill.

And when, our life-probation o'er,
　　We lie too faint for prayer,
O Saviour, speak those gracious words,
　　"Thy mansion I prepare."

The previous poem was found among Havergal manuscripts and papers. This was Frances' mother's desire for her, and though we do not know with certainty the authorship, this poem may have been—likely was—written by F.R.H.

In her final illness Frances' mother said to her, "Fanny dear, pray to God to prepare you for all that He is preparing for you." Frances was only 11 when her mother died, but she remembered those words the rest of her life. Her sister Maria wrote in her biography *Memorials of Frances Ridley Havergal* (in Chapter 2), "Only a few weeks before her own death, Frances referred to this: 'The words mamma taught me in 1848 have been a *life prayer with me*. This "preparing" goes on; it is as when gaining one horizon, another and another spreads before you. So every event prepares us for the next that is prepared for us.'"

Frances' mother, Jane Head Havergal, died July 5, 1848. Near the end of Chapter 2 of *Memorials of Frances Ridley Havergal*, her sister Maria quotes these stanzas copied from Frances' "little book of poems" written in her childhood:

> Eye hath not seen, nor ear hath heard,
> 	Neither can man's heart conceive,
> The blessed things God hath prepared
> 	For those who love Him and believe.
>
> 							July 5, 1848.

> Oh! had I the wings of a dove,
> 	Soon, soon would I be at my rest;
> I would fly to the Saviour I love,
> 	And there would I lie on His breast.
>
> 							July 9, 1848.[1]

The preceding poems are almost unquestionably or altogether certainly by F.R.H., with virtually no doubt about the authorship. This next, final poem is very questionable, likely not written by F.R.H. These three stanzas were published in *Life Echoes* (in the section called "Children's Echoes," on original page 105), attributed to F.R.H. and stated 1849 for the year of composition. This poem is not found in *The Poetical Works of Frances Ridley Havergal* nor in Miriam Crane's collection of F.R.H.'s poems *Streamlets of Song for the Young*. This may be a poem by F.R.H., but after serious searching, I infer that this was a mistake in *Life Echoes*. Maria V. G. Havergal prepared *Life Echoes* in 1883, but this was not

[1] This is reminiscent of Psalm 55:6. "Oh that I had wings like a dove! for then would I fly away, and be at rest."

included the next year when she and her niece Frances Anna Shaw so diligent-
ly prepared the definitive edition *The Poetical Works of Frances Ridley Havergal*.
Also the absence of this poem in Miriam's 1887 *Streamlets of Song for the Young*
suggests that this was a mistake in *Life Echoes*. Maria, Frances Anna Shaw, and
Miriam were brilliant, knew F.R.H. well, had access to or possession of the orig-
inal manuscripts, and almost surely would have included this in both the 1884
and 1887 volumes if they thought this was written by F.R.H.   D.C.

> I love the trees, I love the flowers,
>   I love the sunny sky,
> I love to watch in evening hours
>   The day decline and die;
> I love the birds, their merry song
> Is pleasant as they skim along.
>
> I love to see the gentle moon,
>   So lovely and so pale,
> I love to see the distant stars,—
>   How marvellous their tale!
> I love the soft dim light they throw
> Upon this world of ours below.
>
> When on these lovely things you gaze,
>   Would you the secret know
> Of having as great happiness
>   As ere can be below?
> Then you your Father—God must call,
> And say, "My Father made them all."

There were almost surely other poems by F.R.H. not extant today. For example,
Elizabeth Clay in a letter in the Appendix of *Memorials of Frances Ridley Hav-
ergal* told of a poem Frances wrote on the lovely sunset and surrounding scene
where Elizabeth and Frances had been walking. Such poems may have been dis-
carded by F.R.H., or given to others and lost over the years. We don't know. We
know from Maria, near the end of Chapter 4 in *Memorials*, that she wrote po-
ems in German. This is likely, very nearly a complete collection of the poems by
her that are extant.   David Chalkley

"*Yea, let him take 'all'!*"

Take my life, and let it be
Consecrated, Lord, to Thee.

Take my hands, and let them move
With the impulse of Thy love.

Take my feet, & let them be
Swift & beautiful for Thee.

Take my voice and let me sing
Always, only, for my King.

Take my lips, & let them be
Filled with messages from Thee,

Take my silver & my gold,
Not a mite would I withhold

This is F.R.H.'s original fair copy autograph of the Consecration Hymn, found on pages

Take my moments & my days,
Let them flow in ceaseless praise.

Take my intellect, & use
Every power as Thou dost choose

Take my will & make it Thine
It shall be no longer mine

Take my heart! It is Thine own!
It shall be Thy royal throne!

Take my love, my God I pour
At Thy feet its treasure-store

Take myself & I will be
Ever, Only, All, for Thee!

14–15 of her Manuscript Book Nº VIII. See notes on this poem on the following page.

The preceding two pages show the fair copy autograph in F.R.H.'s handwriting of the Consecration Hymn. At the bottom left corner of the right page, she wrote examples of publication (the periodical *The Christian*, leaflets, the hymn book *Songs of Grace and Glory*, etc.). This was February 4, 1874.

Note that there are small differences in this manuscript and the finalized text published by F.R.H. (see page 509 of this book). The title was changed to "Consecration Hymn." The seventh couplet (beginning "Take my moments") was moved to be the second couplet, and in line 2 of the eighth couplet, "dost" was changed to "shalt." Such changes were almost certainly made by Frances herself, in this poem and in others published while she lived. Note: One major exception is another hymn by her, "I did this for thee; what hast thou done for Me?" Frances' text was in the first person, being the words of Christ to His own ("I gave My life for thee," "I spent long years for thee," etc.), and another—not F.R.H.—changed the words to second person, to be spoken by the believer to Christ ("Thou gav'st Thy life for me," "Thou spent long years for me," etc.). Frances was aware of this great alteration, and apparently tolerated it, but she preferred the original text, not the alteration.

Miss Janet Grierson in her valuable biography of F.R.H. wrote that Frances wrote this at Areley House on the edge of Stourport, Worcestershire, where the Rogers family lived, connected by marriage with Frances' sister Miriam Crane.[1] Frances wrote this about the hymn:[2] "Perhaps you will be interested to know the origin of the consecration hymn, 'Take my life.' I went for a little visit of five days. There were ten persons in the house, some unconverted and long prayed for, some converted but not rejoicing Christians. He gave me the prayer, "Lord, give me *all* in this house!" And He just did. Before I left the house every one had got a blessing. The last night of my visit I was too happy to sleep, and passed most of the night in praise and renewal of my own consecration, and these little couplets formed themselves and chimed in my heart one after another, till they finished with, 'Ever, *only*, ALL for Thee!' "

Frances had cards printed with this hymn, with her name as the author omitted and a blank space for a reader's signature. Her sister Maria wrote an account of Frances very near the end of her life:[3] "As she gave the cards, she asked them to make that hymn a test before God, and if they could really do so, to sign it on their knees at home."

[1] *Frances Ridley Havergal: Worcestershire Hymnwriter* by Janet Grierson (Bromsgrove, Worcestershire: The Havergal Society, 1979), pages 147–148 of the original book, page 1200 of Volume IV of the Havergal edition.

[2] *Memorials of Frances Ridley Havergal* by her sister Maria Vernon Graham (London: James Nisbet & Co., 1880), pages 132–133 of the original book, page 37 of Volume IV of this edition.

[3] See the "Memorandum by M.V.G.H." in *Letters by the Late Frances Ridley Havergal* (London: James Nisbet & Co., 1886), original book pages 326–328, pages 238–239 of Volume IV of the Havergal edition.

NOTEWORTHY TEXTUAL DIFFERENCES FOUND AMONG THE MANUSCRIPTS OF POEMS.

Among the manuscripts of F.R.H.'s poems, small, insignificant or inconsequential differences (for example, details of punctuation and other unimportant differences) are not mentioned, but a number of differences from the published poems were found to be worthy of mention and are presented next. One example of an insignificant difference between the manuscript text and the published text is this: a manuscript of the "New Year's Hymn" has this eighth line, "Every day hath seen!", and this was published "Every day has seen!" (see page 271 of this book). The following differences were found more significant and worthy to present.

Items Found in Manuscript Book № III

Below the title of "The Tyrolese Spring Song," Frances wrote as a subtitle within parentheses, "Translation from German." She was utterly fluent in German and French, and nearly so in Italian. To translate a poem from another language into English so that the English translation is a true poem, is a remarkable gift, likely more challenging than writing a new poem in English: not only is utter fluency in the other language a necessity, but one must also be a true poet in English. Though she showed by this translation ability in this way, Frances did not proceed on to translate German hymns, as Catherine Winkworth so very finely and valuably did, though she almost certainly would have been well aware of Winkworth's work in this.

Items Found in Manuscript Book № IV

The text of the poem "Content" in the fair copy autograph is nearly identical to F.R.H.'s finalized, published text (see pages 35–37 of this book), with only minor differences. In the Manuscript Book № IV, there are eight stanzas, with seven regular stanza dividers in her hand: there is no division between the first and second stanzas, as there is an ellipsis in the published text (she may have had another manuscript copy or version, a possible explanation for her published ellipsis after the first stanza). In this manuscript, she wrote "1856." at the end of the first stanza, and in the published text, "1860" is written. In the fourth line of the fifth stanza, she first wrote "On the border of that fairyland?", and later she squeezed the four letters to the underscored border, borderline; she published "On the border-line of that fairy land,—" ending that line with a comma and dash instead of a question mark.

Manuscript: On the <u>borderl</u>ine of that fairyland?
Published poem: On the border-line of that fairy land,—

(Note that usually such minor differences between manuscripts and published texts are not mentioned in this edition. This fourth line was mentioned because other differences in this poem were found worthy to mention.) At the end of the poem, she wrote "Janr 8. 1867." which matches the date of the poem at the front of Nisbet's *Poetical Works.*

Of all who have written of childhood, has any written so well as Frances Ridley Havergal? She was fully and truly an adult, one who so well remembered and understood a child's world. This poem is one of a number that show this.

F.R.H. published "My Sweet Woodruff" in *The Ministry of Song.* The original fair copy autograph on pages 24–25 in the Manuscript Book № IV had these differences from the published text: The original title for this poem was "To Mary C." Later Frances crossed out the first title ~~To Mary C.~~ and above that wrote the finalized title, "My Sweet-Woodruff." (She wrote a hyphen between "Sweet" and "Woodruff.") In the last line of the ninth stanza, Frances underlined the first two words, <u>We both</u> .

Items Found in Manuscript Book № VI

These changes were made by F.R.H. in her fair copy autograph of "Two Rings:" [1] The earlier title "The Two Rings" was changed to be "Two Rings. The finalized poem is found on pages 467–470 of this book. The first word of the second stanza "Merry" was changed to be "Loving." In the third stanza, lines 2 and 3 had been this:

> And danced with sudden glee;
> Look at my ring would never fade,

[1] "Two Rings" refers to F.R.H.'s niece, Evelyn Emily Crane. See also pages 332–336 of this book, and page 28 of Volume IV of the Havergal edition.

Frances crossed out line 2 and the first four words of line 3, and rewrote them to be this:

> Blue with a diamond eye;.
> A forgetmenot that would never fade,

In the fourth stanza, the last word of line 3 was changed from "thing" to be "ring." In the ninth stanza, the start of line 2 was changed from "Unsure" to be "Not sure."

Frances wrote "A Year Ago. (Song.)" on pages 62–63 of her Manuscript Book N̲o̲ VI. She had first written each of the three stanzas as nine-line stanzas, and later—in each of the three stanzas—she added four new lines between the original fourth and fifth lines, making them thirteen-line stanzas. The published text of this (found on page 262 of this book) is very different: the last 5 lines of each stanza was removed, and in the third stanza, "love" was changed to be "hope" in both places. She dated this July 15, 1870. She wrote at the end "HR" which almost certainly meant Hutchings & Romer. In an advertisement page at the end of a copy of *Memorials of Frances Ridley Havergal* (London, James Nisbet & Co., "Eighteenth Thousand" printing), a list of music scores publshed by Hutchings & Romer names the score "A Year Ago" with words by F.R.H. and music by Blumenthal. The complete text of F.R.H.'s manuscript is given next, notably different from the published poem on page 262. The regular font words were her original text, and the **bold font** words were later added by her to the manuscript.

A Year Ago. (Song.)

A year ago the gold light
    Sweet morning made for me
A tender & untold light,
    Like music on the sea
Light & music twining
    In melodious glory
A rare & radiant shining
    On my changing story
For a year ago I loved you
    As I never loved before;
But I did not know that love would grow
    For ever, more & more,
        For ever — evermore.

Today the glowing sunlight
    Is full & broad & strong;
The glory of the one light
    Must overflow in song:
Song that floweth ever,
    Sweeter every day,
A song whose echoes never,
    Never die away.
For oh ! today I love you
    As I never loved before ;
I did not know that love could grow
    Thus ever, more & more,
        For ever — evermore.

How can the light be clearer
    That is so bright today ?
How can my love be dearer
    Indeed, I cannot say !
I am only waiting
    For the answer golden,
What love is ante dating
    Shall not be withholden.
But I know I yet shall love you
    As I never loved before;
For now I know that love must grow
    For ever, more & more,
        For ever — evermore.

July 15 /70.

HR.   [This was her notation that Hutchings & Romer published
this song (set to music composed by Jacques Blumenthal[1]).]

The poem "Glorified" (on pages 449–450 of this book) was originally entitled
"Grace and Glory" on pages 94–96 of the Manuscript Book № VI. The title
was changed to "Glorified" in her volume of poems *Under the Surface* (under her
oversight, published in 1874).

The poem "Covenant Blessings" (on pages 426–427) was originally entitled
"The Covenant of Grace" on pages 96–98 of the Manuscript Book № VI. The
title was changed to "Covenant Blessings" in her volume of poems *Under the
Surface* (under her oversight, published in 1874).

---

[1] Jacques Jacob Blumenthal (1829—1908), German pianist and composer, later the pianist
to Queen Victoria.

In the section numbered V in "The Sowers" (on page 410), in line 4, the second word was originally "wingéd:" Frances later crossed out "wingéd" and wrote "fiery" above it, on page 106 of the Manuscript Book № VI.

In the un-numbered stanza that begins "All their own, through Him who loved them," in "The Sowers" (on page 412), the third word of line 3 was originally "burning:" Frances later crossed out "burning" and wrote "living" above it, on page 110 of the Manuscript Book № VI. Three lines below that, the third word was originally "rapturous," which Frances later crossed out and wrote "burning" above that.

In the un-numbered stanza that begins "But Eternity is long," in "The Sowers" (on pages 412–413), the fourth word of line 10 was originally "glorious:" Frances later crossed out "glorious" and wrote "mighty" above it, on page 111 of the Manuscript Book № VI.

In the last stanza of the section numbered II. (on page 414), in the next-to-last line, Frances originally wrote "Of their joy and exultation," but later crossed out "joy and" and wrote "endless" above that, on page 114 of the Manuscript Book № VI.

In the last stanza of the section numbered III. (on page 415), in the third line, the second word was originally "the:" Frances later crossed out "the" and wrote "our" above it, on page 115 of the Manuscript Book № VI.

In the fifteenth stanza of "An Evening on the Bréven" (this is the fourth new, complete stanza on page 703), the first word of line 1 and the first word of line 2 had been written "Oh:" Frances later crossed out the h, to be only the single letter O: O~~h~~ This apparently demonstrates a clear difference in her mind between Oh (used two stanzas before this) and O.

The poem "Right!" (on pages 434–440) was originally entitled "A Mistake." Frances crossed out the original title and wrote the new title "Right" (without an exclamation mark nor any punctuation) on page 168 of the Manuscript Book № VI.

In Scene II of "Right," in the second twelve-line stanza (on page 438), F.R.H. wrote the first 8 lines as copied next, and later numbered—and re-ordered—the lines, on pages 175–176 of the Manuscript Book № VI, to be finalized in the order as they were published by her in the volume *Under the Surface*.

5 "Oh the perilous way!
6   Oh the pitiless blast!
7 Long though I suffer & stray
8   There will be rest at last.
1 Oh the terrible night
2   Falling without a star!
3 Darkness anear, but light
4   Glorious light afar.

The last poem in the Manuscript Book N⁰ VI (also published as the last poem in *Under the Surface*) was "Finis." In F.R.H.'s manuscript, the fourth word of line 14 was originally "wail," which she later changed to be "note." The original word "wail" was published in *Under the Surface* in 1874, which suggests that Frances changed the word to "note" after the publication of *Under the Surface*.

And turned a note of mourning to a trustful calm refrain,

Items Found in Manuscript Book N⁰ VII

The title page of the Manuscript Book N⁰ VII is a is a left-side un-numbered page; facing this left-side title page is a right-side page, numbered 1, with the first page of the poem "Prelude" which Frances published as the opening poem of *Under the Surface*.

In the "Prelude" to the volume of poems *Under the Surface* published by Frances in 1874, line 21 has the first three words "Been granted me" and then a period and ellipses, with the resumption of the line "Thou knowest how (so often) I have laid" after the ellipses (see pages 341–342 of this book). The manuscript of this poem shows that Frances originally had written these three lines, which she later removed from the published text. These three lines are here given with the line immediately before and the line immediately after the three lines. In her fair copy autograph, Frances had written an exclamation mark after "so often" in the parentheses, but she removed this from the published text in *Under the Surface*.

I had not done had all my heart's desire
Been granted me, and life had worn the gem
Which had been treasure all too great for me
To bear in safety through the wilderness.
Thou knowest how (so often!) I have laid

Items Found in Manuscript Book № VIII

On pages 4–5 of F.R.H.'s Manuscript Book № VIII, she wrote out a copy of "Will ye not come to Him?" This is different from the (nearly—not quite—identical) texts of the poem on page 275 and on pages 672–673 of this book.

F.R.H. wrote these three different texts or versions of this poem: "Will ye not come to Him?" given next from her fair copy autograph in the Manuscript Book № VIII; "Will You Not Come?" published Nisbet's *Poetical Works of Frances Ridley Havergal* and found on page 275 of this book; and "Will You Not Come?" which she published in *The Royal Invitation* (the Twenty-fourth Day, an exceptional section of poetry in that mostly prose book), found on pages 672–673 of this book. This text given next was the one she published in the hymnbook *Songs of Grace and Glory* (Frances edited the music of that hymnal, more than 1,100 tunes, with Charles Busbridge Snepp the editor of the words and leader of the project, a true labor of love by them both). This text of hymn 1041 of *Songs of Grace and Glory*, given next, is the text copied out by Frances on pages 4–5 of her Manuscript Book № VIII.

Given next is F.R.H.'s fair copy autograph of this, on pages 4–5 of her Manuscript Book № VIII, and then after that the finalized text which she published in the hymnbook *Songs of Grace and Glory*.

A fair copy autograph in F.R.H.'s handwriting, in her Manuscript Book No VIII.

Tis offered now, 'tis offered you!
Rest in His love, & rest in His home.
Will ye not come &c — — for rest.
Will ye not come to Him for joy?
Will ye not come for bliss?
He laid His joys aside for you,
To give you joy, so sweet, so true!
Sorrowing heart, oh drink of the bliss!
Will ye not come &c — — for joy.
Will ye not come to Him for love,
Love that can fill the heart!
Exceeding great, exceeding free!
He loveth you, He loveth me!
Will ye not come? Why stand ye apart?
Will ye not come &c — — for love.
Will ye not come to Him for all?
Will ye not "taste & see"?
He waits to give it all to you,
The gifts are free, the words are true!
Jesus hath said it — "Come unto Me."
Will ye not come &c — — to Him?

Dec. 15.

See also pages 275–278, 668–671, and 672–673, 749, and 752–753 of this book.

Will ye not come to Him?

("Gospel Solo.")

Will ye not come to Him for *life?*
    Why will ye die, oh why?
  He gave His life for you, for you!
 The gift is free, the word is true!
Will ye not come ? oh, why will ye die?
     Refrain: Will ye not come? Will ye not come?
         Will ye not come to Him, to Him?
      Oh, come, come, come, to Him!
        Come unto Jesus, oh, come for *life.*

Will ye not come to Him for *peace*,
    Peace through His cross alone?
  He shed His precious blood for you;
 The gift is free, the word is true!
He is our Peace, oh is He your own?
        Will ye not come? Will ye not come?
         Will ye not come to Him, to Him?
      Oh, come, come, come, to Him!
        Come unto Jesus, oh, come for *peace.*

Will ye not come to Him for *rest?*
    All that are weary, come:
  The rest He gives is deep and true,
 'Tis offered now, 'tis offered you;
Rest in His love, and rest in His home.
        Will ye not come? Will ye not come?
         Will ye not come to Him, to Him?
      Oh, come, come, come, to Him!
        Come unto Jesus, oh, come for *rest.*

Will ye not come to Him for *joy?*
    Will ye not come for this?
  He laid His joys aside for you,
 To give you joy, so sweet, so true!
Sorrowing heart, oh drink of the bliss! ·
        Will ye not come? Will ye not come?
         Will ye not come to Him, to Him?
      Oh, come, come, come, to Him!
        Come unto Jesus, oh, come for *joy.*

Will ye not come to Him for *love*,
  Love that can fill the heart?
Exceeding great, exceeding free!
He loveth you, He loveth me!
Will you not come ? why stand ye apart?
      Will ye not come? Will ye not come?
        Will ye not come to Him, to Him?
    Oh, come, come, come, to Him!
      Come unto Jesus, oh, come for *love*.

Will ye not come to Him for ALL?
  Will ye not "taste and see"?
He waits to give it all to you,
The gifts are free, the words are true!
Jesus hath said it, "Come unto Me."
      Will ye not come? Will ye not come?
        Will ye not come to Him, to Him?
    Oh, come, come, come, to Him!
      Come unto Jesus, oh, come to HIM.

LUCIUS.   [H. P. 293.]

CHORUS.

1041   Matt. xi. 28.   *"Come unto Me."*
        Tune LUCIUS.   8 6, 8 8 9, 8 8 6 9.

1 WILL ye not come to Him for *life*?
    Why will ye die, oh why?
  He gave His life for you, for you!
  The gift is free, the word is true!
  Will ye not come? oh, why will ye die?
    Will ye not come? Will ye not come?
    Will ye not come to Him, to Him?
  Oh, come, come, come to Him!
    Come unto Jesus, oh, come for *life*.

2 Will ye not come to Him for *peace*,
    Peace through His cross alone ?
  He shed His precious blood for you ;
  The gift is free, the word is true!
  He is our Peace, oh is He your own ?
    Will ye not come, etc. . . . for *peace*?

3 Will ye not come to Him for *rest*?
    All that are weary, come :
  The rest He gives is deep and true,
  'Tis offered now, 'tis offered you ;
  Rest in His love, and rest in His home.
    Will ye not come, etc. . . . for *rest*?

PART II.

4 Will ye not come to Him for *joy* ?
    Will ye not come for this ?
  He laid His joys aside for you,
  To give you joy, so sweet, so true !
  Sorrowing heart, oh drink of the bliss !
    Will ye not come, etc. . . . for *joy*?

5 Will ye not come to Him for *love*,
    Love that can fill the heart?
  Exceeding great, exceeding free !
  He loveth you, He loveth me !
  Will you not come ? why stand ye apart?
    Will ye not come, etc. . . . for *love* ?

6 Will ye not come to Him for ALL ?
    Will ye not "taste and see" ?
  He waits to give it all to you,
  The gifts are free, the words are true !
  Jesus hath said it, " Come unto Me."
    Will ye not come, etc. . . . to HIM .

              Frances Ridley Havergal, 1873.

This copy of the hymn was published in Songs of Grace and Glory, *edited by* Charles Busbridge Snepp *(words) and F.R.H. (music, more than 1,100 tunes).*

On pages 14–15 of the Manuscript Book № VIII, Frances wrote out the fair copy autograph of the hymn that begins, "Take my life and let it be Consecrated, Lord, to Thee." A facsimile copy of this is given on pages 740–741, the two facing pages immediately before this section of textual differences between manuscripts and published poems. She wrote this on February 4, 1874.

In her hand-written copy, she wrote the title "Yea, let him take all!" (her title written in quotation marks). This was a quotation of II Samuel 19:30, which Frances quoted at the top of the Eighth Day of *My King* (see page 29 of Volume II of the Havergal edition). She published this as the First Day of *Loyal Responses* with the title "Consecration Hymn" (see page 509 of this book). A few other differences were found, and the text of her original manuscript is given next. (The missing punctuation is copied here the same as her handwritten manuscript.) Like all the poems published by her, we can very confidently assume that the changes in the published texts were made by Frances herself.

Note the small differences in this manuscript and the finalized text published by F.R.H. The title was changed to "Consecration Hymn." The seventh couplet (beginning "Take my moments") was moved to be the second couplet, and in line 2 of the eighth couplet, "dost" was changed to "shalt." These changes were almost certainly made by Frances herself, in this poem, and also such changes in other poems that were published while she lived.

Yea, let Him take all!

Take my life, and let it be
Consecrated, Lord, to Thee.

Take my hands, and let them move
With the impulse of Thy love.

Take my feet, and let them be
Swift and beautiful for Thee.

Take my voice and let me sing
Always, only, for my King.

Take my lips, and let them be
Filled with messages from Thee.

Take my silver and my gold,
Not a mite would I withhold

Take my moments and my days,
Let them flow in ceaseless praise.

Take my intellect, and use
Every power as Thou dost choose

Take my will and make it Thine
It shall be no longer mine

Take my heart! it *is* Thine own!
It shall be Thy royal throne!

Take my love, my Lord I pour
At Thy feet its treasure-store

Take myself and I will be
Ever, Only, All, for Thee!

Feb^r 4.

This was February 4, 1874. She published this, with changes, as the First Day of *Loyal Responses* in 1878.

Frances wrote this next text in her fair copy autograph (on page 169 of the Manuscript Book N° VIII): She mistakenly entitled the poem Genesis 5:22. This was printed as Genesis 5:24 with a different first word (the manuscript "So" was changed to "Oh") in Nisbet's *Poetical Works* (see page 562 of this book).

So may'st thou walk! from hour to hour
Of every passing year,
Keeping so very near
To Him whose power is love, whose love is power.

So may'st thou walk! in His clear light,
Leaning on Him alone,
Thy life His very own,
Until He takes thee up to walk with Him in white.

The poem "Only" was published by F.R.H. in 1878, as the Twenty-third Day in her fifth "Royal" book *Loyal Responses*. This text was finalized and published by Frances herself, and that is the definitive text of that poem, "Only," found on pages 544–545 of this book. In the Manuscript Book № VIII, on pages 177–178, the earlier handwritten fair copy autograph by Frances is different in these details given next.

The title was "Only, yet All."

The first 2 lines had these words:
  "Only a woman's powers, [later finalized "Only a mortal's powers"]
    Only a little strength," [later finalized "Weak at their fullest strength"]

Line 10 had these words: "Only one mind to use." Later Frances crossed through "mind" and wrote above that "voice" which was the finalized text.

Line 13 had these words: "The inventory is small," later finalized and published as "Poor is my best, and small."

The poem "The Secret of a Happy Day" was published by F.R.H. in 1878, as the Third Day in her fifth "Royal" book *Loyal Responses*. This text was finalized and published by Frances herself, and that is the definitive text of that poem, "The Secret of a Happy Day," found on pages 511–513 of this book. The first verse of that poem had been earlier written as the first of six *New Year Mottoes*, with different details in the last three lines, and in the Manuscript Book № VIII, on page 226, the earlier handwritten fair copy autograph by Frances has the text that is given next.

> Just to let thy Father do
>   What He will;
> Just to know that He is true,
>   And be still;
> Just to follow hour by hour
>   As He leadeth;
> Just to draw the moment's power,
>   As it needeth.
> Just to trust Him! this is all!
>   So thy opening year shall be
> Happy, whatsoe'er befall,
>   Bright and blessèd, calm and free.

The poem "The Unfailing One" was published by F.R.H. in 1878, as the Fourth Day in her fifth "Royal" book *Loyal Responses*. This text was finalized and published by Frances herself, and that is the definitive text of that poem, "The Unfailing One," found on pages 514–515 of this book. The first verse of that poem had been earlier written as the third of six brief Birthday poems, a different verse, and in the Manuscript Book № VIII, on page 231, the earlier handwritten fair copy autograph by Frances has the text that is given next.

> He who hath led, will lead;
>   He who hath blessed, will bless;
> He who hath fed, will feed;
>   Can He do less?
> He fainteth not, He faileth never,
>   So rest on Him, today, for ever !

In the section of Christmas verses named "Titles of Chist" in Nisbet's *Poetical Works* (pages 293–295 of this book), the poem "The Everlasting Father" is placed before "The Mighty God," although F.R.H.'s manuscript follows the order of Isaiah 9:6: "For unto us a child is born, unto us a son is given, and the government shall be upon his shoulder, and his name shall be called Wonderful, Counsellor, The mighty God, The everlasting Father, The Prince of Peace."

On pages 248–249 of F.R.H.'s Manuscript Book № VIII (by far the largest, longest of the six Manuscript Books now extant), Frances wrote "Two Advent Cards." These would have been two brief poems for cards anticipating our Lord's return (similar to Christmas cards and Easter cards), cards such as C. Caswell & Co. and Marcus Ward & Co. printed with verses by Havergal. The second of these two poems was published in the section of "Verses on Texts" ("Advent shadows gather deep," page 568 of this book). The first of these two Advent Card poems was not published in Nisbet's *Poetical Works*, but a slightly different text was published in a little known, richly valuable volume that Frances herself prepared for publication late in her life, *Echoes from the Word*, published posthumously by Charles Bullock. The published text of this first Advent Card poem is found on page 801, but there are differences from the manuscript text, which is given next.

Frances first wrote for the title:

"Behold, He cometh!" Rev. 1.7

Afterward, she changed the title to be this:

"Behold, the Bridegroom cometh!" Mat. 25.6

> O herald whisper falling
>   Upon the passing night,
> Mysteriously calling
>   The Children of the Light!
>
> He cometh; oh He cometh!
>   Our own belovèd Lord!
> This blessed hope up-summeth
>   Our undeserved reward.
>
> He cometh! Though the hour
>   Nor earth nor heaven may know,
> Sure is the word of power,
>   "He cometh!" Even so!

In line 7, she very likely meant to place an accent over the second e of blessed (blessèd). She later changed line 5 to be this: "Behold, the Bridegroom cometh," published by her in *Echoes from the Word*.

In her fair copy autograph of the poem "The Voice of Many Waters," F.R.H. drew a double line at three places in the poem, clearly intended by her to be section dividers: between the seventh and eighth stanzas, between the fourteenth and fifteenth stanzas, and between the twenty-first and twenty-second stanzas. The first and third section dividers were observed in Nisbet's *Poetical Works*, but not the second section divider. We do not know whether this was an oversight in N.P.W. or whether F.R.H. later removed the middle section divider.

Items Found in Manuscript Book № IX

On the original page 33 of her Manuscript Book № IX, Frances clearly indicated that this should be the sixth stanza of "Mizpah," though only the first five stanzas were published (on pages 311–312 of this book):

VI

A little while, though parted,
Remember, wait, & love
Until He comes &ᶜ &ᶜ &
(from "Under His Shadow") [F.R.H.'s manuscript page 33]

This would have been the last two stanzas of "Under His Shadow" found on page 426 of this book.

As noted in the preface on page 666, there are important differences between the rough draft, the fair copy autograph, and the finalized, published text of "The Scripture cannot be broken." Because of the diligence and brilliance of Maria Vernon Graham Havergal and Frances Anna Shaw, and the original materials and vast knowledge available to them, we can trust the texts they prepared for the definitive, very fine Nisbet edition of *The Poetical Works of Frances Ridley Havergal.* The published version (on pages 639–640 of this book) can be trusted as F.R.H.'s finalized text. Given next are the texts of her rough draft (few rough drafts of F.R.H.'s poems are extant today) and also her fair copy autograph. Photographs of these two manuscripts are found on pages XXXV–XXXVI of this book. The finalized, published text matches precisely the revisions made on the rough draft, which apparently were made by Frances after she wrote out her fair copy autograph of this poem.[1] This was written in April, 1879.

Rough draft:

The Scripture cannot be broken.

Upon the Word I rest,
Each pilgrim day;
This golden staff is best
For all the way.
What Jesus Christ Himself hath sealed and spoken,
Can not betray or bend, Cannot be broken!

Upon the Word I rest,
So strong, so sure,

---

[1] Note: This was first written as a single stanza on II Chronicles 32:8, one of her "Verses on Texts" written in 1877, a different text, found on page 559 of this book.

So full of comfort blest,
    So sweet, so pure!
The changeless charter of our great salvation,
For faith and hope and joy our broad foundation.

Upon the Word I rest,
    So strong, so sure,
So full of comfort blest,
    So sweet, so pure!
The changeless charter of our great salvation,
For faith and hope and joy our broad foundation.

Upon the Word I stand!
    That cannot die!

Christ seals it in my hand,
    He cannot lie!
The Word that faileth not, that changeth never!
O Christ! We rest upon Thy word for ever!

 Chorus.
The Master hath said it! Rejoicing in this,
    We ask not for sign or for token;
His word is enough for our confident bliss—
    "The Scripture <u>cannot</u> be broken!"

Fair copy autograph:

The Scripture cannot be broken.

Upon the Word I rest,
    Each pilgrim day;
This golden staff is best
    For all the way.
What Jesus Christ Himself hath sealed and spoken,
Can <u>not</u> betray or bend, Can<u>not</u> be broken!

Upon the Word I rest,
    So strong, so sure,
So full of comfort blest,
    So sweet, so pure!

The changeless charter of our great salvation,
For faith and hope and joy our broad foundation.

Upon the Word I rest,
So strong, so sure,
So full of comfort blest,
So sweet, so pure!

The changeless charter of our great salvation,
For faith and hope and joy our broad foundation.

Upon the Word I stand!
That cannot die!
Christ seals it in my hand,
He cannot lie!
The Word that faileth not, that changeth never!
O Christ! We rest upon Thy word for ever!

Chorus. The Master hath said it! Rejoicing in this,
We ask not for sign or for token;
His word is enough for our confident bliss—
"The Scripture cannot be broken!"

On three sides of a single-fold separate piece of paper (not pages in a Manuscript Book), F.R.H. wrote the manuscript of "I could not do without Thee," which she published in *Under the Surface* (see pages 375–376 of this book). Frances originally wrote this slightly different text in the last stanza, which she later changed for the published text:

I could not do without Thee!
For life is fleeting fast,
And then in solemn loneliness
The river must be passed.
But Thou wilt never leave me,
And though the waves roll high,
I know Thou wilt be with me,
And whisper, "It is I."

The Manuscript Books were used by Frances to keep carefully written copies of her poems after she—apparently—thought they were finalized or nearly finalized. The rough draft and fair copy autograph of "The Scripture cannot be broken" are exceptional now (this was so near the end of her life), because there are so few rough drafts of her poems now extant. The manuscript of "Faith and Reason" is another exceptional example and glimpse into the changes Frances made before the finalized text of a poem. Given next is the text from her fair copy autograph of "Faith and Reason," which can be compared to her final text which she published in her first book, *The Ministry of Song* (pages 115–117 of this book). Most of her fair copy autographs of poems in her Manuscript Books are little or no different from the finalized texts she published, but one can infer that this is a glimpse, and that she made other changes and additions in the rough drafts of various poems, though few rough drafts remain extant now. From brief examples we know, she could begin a poem – write down her first draft – on an envelope or a piece of paper handy at the time.

In this particular example, Frances added a new half-page, attached to the gutter edge of the Manuscript Book Nº III, page 64, on which she added later lines on each side of the half-page. Although most or nearly all of her rough drafts have not been found, yet from an extensive exposure to the extant manuscript copies, one can infer—without proof nor certainty—that for most of her poems, there were not often major differences between Frances' first drafts and her final copies, many poems having comparatively small differences or no differences at all. "The Scripture cannot be broken" and "Faith and Reason" seem to be exceptional in the significance of later changes by Frances' in her poems. Remarkable (radical, large, difficult) revisions exemplified in Beethoven's manuscript scores were apparently seldom or never done in F.R.H.'s works.

Faith and Reason.

Reason unstrings the harp to see
    Wherein the music dwells;
Faith pours a hallelujah song,
    And heavenly rapture swells.
While Reason strives to count the drops
    That lave our narrow strand,
Faith launches o'er the mighty deep
    To seek a better land.

One is the foot that slowly treads
    Where darkling mists enshroud;

The other is the wing that cleaves
    Each heaven-obscuring cloud.
Reason the eye which sees but that
    On which its glance is cast;
Faith is the thought that blends in one
    The Future and the Past.

In hours of darkness Reason waits
    Like those in days of yore,
Who rose not from their night-bound place
    On Egypt's veilèd shore:

But Faith more firmly clasps the hand
    Which led her all the day,
And when the longed-for morning dawns;
    Is farther on ~~the~~ her way.

Faith is the snowy sail spread out
    To catch the freshening breeze;
And Reason is the labouring oar
    That smites the wrathful seas.
~~While~~ By Reason's alchymy in vain
~~An~~ Is golden treasure planned,
Faith meekly wears a priceless crown
    Won by no mortal hand.

Reason the telescope that scans
    A universe of light;
And faith the angel who may dwell
    Amid those regions bright.
Reason, a lonely towering elm,
    May fall before the blast;
Faith, like the ivy on the rock,
    Is safe in clinging fast.

While Reason like a Levite waits
    Where priest and people meet;
Faith, by a new and living way,
    Hath gained the mercy-seat.

While Reason but returns to tell
    That this is not our rest,
Faith, like the weary dove, hath sought
    A gracious Saviour's breast.

[Here Frances drew a double-line demarcation, indicating the end of one section of the poem and the start of a new section. In her manuscripts, single-line demarcations indicated the end of one stanza and the start of the next stanza, and double lines meant the break between sections of a poem. She discarded this section divider in the finalized, published text of this poem.]

Yet both are surely precious gifts
    From Him who leads us home,
Though in the wilds Himself hath trod
    A little while we roam.
~~Yet~~ And linked within the soul that knows
    A living loving Lord,
Faith strikes the keynote, Reason then
    Fills up the full-toned chord.

Faith is the upward-pointing spire
    ~~From~~ O'er Life's great temple springing,
From which the chimes of Love float forth
    Celestially ringing;
While Reasons stands below upon
    The consecrated ground,
And like a mighty buttress clasps
    The wide foundation round.

Faith is the bride that stands enrobed
    In white and pure array,
Reason the handmaid who may share
    The gladness of the day.
Faith leads the way and Reason learns
    To follow in her train,
Till step by step the goal is reached
    And death is glorious gain.

Oakhampton
    March 13.   [1859]

Finally, for lack of other space to place this after nearly all the pages have been typeset, here is a 10-line verse by F.R.H., found very late in the work on this book. In her biography *Frances Ridley Havergal Worcestershire Hymnwriter*, Miss Janet Grierson gave this brief poem by F.R.H. Frances wrote this to a school-fellow, Emily Budd, likely written in 1851.

> A fortnight exactly in bed I have been,
> With as ugly a face as I ever have seen,
> And the druggist, I think must have full work to make
> All the pills and the medicine which now I must take.
> In bed I must be, and keep perfectly quiet,
> And carefully shun all excitement and riot.
> And now if in verse to this note you'll reply,
> With many good wishes, I'll bid you goodbye;
> No longer will I on your patience transgress
> So believe me, dear Emmy, your loving Frances.

Frances Ridley Havergal Worcestershire Hymnwriter by Janet Grierson (Bromsgrove, Worcestershire: The Havergal Society, 1979), page 44. See page 1150 of Volume IV of the Havergal edition.

Again, for lack of other space to place this after nearly all the pages have been typeset, here is one other verse: In the October prose text for F.R.H.'s *Royal Gems and Wayside Chimes* (found on page 861 of this book), F.R.H. gives this one stanza, not saying who wrote it. Her practice was to give the name of another poet, but to leave quotations of her own poetry unattributed. This verse is very likely a single stanza written by F.R.H.

> I want "The old, old Story,"
>   How Jesus set us free:
> Or the riven "Rock of Ages,"
>   Or else "Abide with me":
> Or what we used to sing at night,
>   "Nearer, my God, to Thee!"

Note: On page 302, at the end of line 5 of the top stanza, the word in F.R.H.'s fair copy autograph (on page 227 in her Manuscript Book Nº VIII) is "feeding," not "feeling." The word "feeling" was a mistake in Nisbet's *Poetical Works*, and has been corrected here.

Final Details: These next six verses, definitely written by F.R.H., were not published in the Nisbet edition of *The Poetical Works of Frances Ridley Havergal*:

1. "He knows! Yes, Jesus knows just what you can not tell" is found on page 821 of Volume I of the Havergal edition, the Fourth Sunday after Easter in *Echoes from the Word*.

2. "Heir thou art by His good pleasure" is found on page 826 of Volume I, Trinity Sunday in *Echoes from the Word*, and on page 983, Nov. 6 in *Red Letter Days*.

3. "I should not love Thee now wert Thou not near" is found on page 906 of Volume I of the Havergal edition, March 16 in *Red Letter Days*. Part of this verse is found in the last verse of "He Is Thy Lord" on page 380.

4. "Now I know Thy Name, Its mighty music is the only key" is found on page 906 of Volume I, March 17 in *Red Letter Days*. This is an adaptation by F.R.H. of part of the fifth stanza of "He Is Thy Lord" on page 379 of this book.

5. "For words are cold, dead things" is found on page 976 of Volume I, October 16 in *Red Letter Days*. The first four lines of this are found in the fourth verse of "Finis" on page 181 of this book, but the last four lines were written later and published in only *Red Letter Days* alone.

6. The verse for November 22 in *Red Letter Days* (found on page 988 of Vol. I) is a revision of the last two verses of "Colossians 3:2" (found on page 132).

7. In F.R.H.'s late poem "Love for Love" (written February 12, 1879, also called "Stay and Think"), she wrote the first line to be this: "Knowing that the God on high." This was her first line in two fair copy autographs in her handwriting, one on page 39 of her Manuscript Book № IX, and the other on a separate sheet of paper (see page 838 of Volume I). This was the first line published in Nisbet's *Poetical Works* (on page 281 of this book) and in *Echoes from the Word* (page 825 of Vol. I). This first line was changed in *Royal Gems and Wayside Chimes* (on page 862 of Vol. I) to be this: "Knowing that our God on high."

8. At the end of her long poem "Right," all three of the last verses are a quotation of the "chorus of rejoicing" (introduced in the last line of the last verse before the three-verse "chorus"). Nisbet's Poetical Works only gave quotation marks for the last two verses, not for all three of the last verses, but this was only a small mistake in the remarkably fine N.P.W. F.R.H. in her fair copy autograph of this poem (on page 180 of her Manuscript Book No VI) definitely wrote a beginning double quotation mark before the first line of the verse "Light after darkness," clearly and unmistakeably meaning that all three verses were within

quotation marks, and that all three verses were the "chorus of rejoicing." This has been corrected (on page 440 of this book).

Addendum: Found very late in the work on the Havergal edition, the poem "Janet's Bridal" is found on pages 916–917 of this book. This poem was found in a handwritten copy among F.R.H.'s papers. The handwriting generally looks like F.R.H.'s handwriting, except the two s's of "kissing" in the first line of the third stanza (F.R.H. did not usually write two s's in the old-fashioned way—a "long s" followed by a "short s"—as done in this handwritten copy). Frances may have written (authored) this poem, though presumably she did not. We do not know. There are parts of this poem that very much look like F.R.H.'s thought and composition. The lack of punctuation and finalizing details is copied here as in the handwritten copy.

Addendum: Found very late in this work, there were small changes of individual verses between F.R.H.'s manuscript on an envelope and the finalized, published verses. The details for this are placed on pages 930–931 near the end of this book.

Addendum: Please see the note on "reality" on page 659 of this book.

Addendum: Found after the Havergal edition was finished, three fragments of poetry were published on pages 122–125 of *Gems from Havergal Poetry* Selected by Frances A. Shaw (London: Nisbet & Co., Ltd., 1912). This very small book has excerpts from various poems by F.R.H., selected by her niece and goddaughter, Frances Anna Shaw, who had unique, full access to F.R.H.'s manuscripts and papers, and who also prepared for publication the sterling and definitive Nisbet edition of *The Poetical Works of Frances Ridley Havergal* (London: James Nisbet & Co., 1884). The second and third of these three fragments were published in the section of "Closing Chords" in Nisbet's *Poetical Works* (found on page 643 of this book), but the first of the three fragments has not been found anywhere else. That fragment (only four lines) is given next:

> As the music to the ear, when the mightiest anthems roll,
> With its corridors conveying every echo to the soul,
> With its exquisite discernment of vibration and of tone,—
> So is Jesus to the heart that is made for Him alone.

The second fragment began "The Master will guide the weary feet," and the third fragment (two stanzas) began "'Arise, depart ! for this is not your rest!'" Both are found on page 643. David Chalkley, September 6, 2014,.

273 : "JESUS DELIVERS ME NOW."

———o———

1   Hearken, beloved ones, and join in our song,
      Seal it on heart and on brow,
    Sound out the watchward, and pass it along,
      " Jesus delivers me now."

    CHORUS—Jesus delivers me now,
              Jesus delivers me now,
              Able to save me and faithful to keep,
              Jesus delivers me now.

2   What though 'neath sin's heavy crimson-dyed load,
      Conscience may tremble and bow,
    Speak but this word, and pass free on your road,
      " Jesus delivers me now."   Chorus.

3   Should the world tempt you with glory or gain,
      Satan's dread yoke to allow :
    Fear not his fury, repeat the glad strain,
      " Jesus delivers me now."   Chorus.

4   Or should the tears of affliction and grief,
      Water each pilgrimage vow,
    Cling to your God with the words of belief
      " Jesus delivers me now."   Chorus.

5   Then when the gates of the valley of death,
      Sin would with terrors endow,
    Pass up the watchward, and be your last breath,
      " Jesus delivers me now."

    CHORUS—Jesus delivers me now,
              Jesus delivers me now,
              Lead on to glory thou shadow of death,
              Jesus delivers me now.

                                            F.R.H.

no not hers

Maria V. G. Havergal wrote by hand, "no not hers" with certainty. F.R.H. seems an attractive person (or target) for attributions of things she never wrote nor said.

This photograph of Ellen Prestage (Havergal) Shaw on the left, Maria V.G. Havergal on the right, and Frances in the middle, was taken in 1854, when F.R.H. was 17.

Janet's Bridal.

And so I am going to be married!
On this gladdest merriest day
They are gathering roses for the
      bridal
Oh what will the neighbours say!
I have but a knot of blue ribbons
No jewels to deck my hair,
But I have a chaplet of bluebells
That Donald has sent me to wear
Blue bells, fairy like blue bells
Were offered to flowers for me

2nd

How fragrant my favourite trees
And the clematis (steeped) in dew
The mavis is joyfully singing
He carols the woodland through
And Mary & Alice are coming
And Isabel with flowers I see
To strew on the dear little
      footpath
As far as the hawthorne tree;
Blithely over the mountain
They gather from near & far

3

The sunbeams are brightening the
      heather green
And the butterflies white & blue
So joyfully flutter this morning
And am I not joyful too
Our home will be over the
      heather
A smile from the hawthorne tree
Oh I shall be happy with Donald
And he will be happy with me.
Happy ever so happy
Our Westland home will be

Addendum: Found very late in the work on the Havergal edition, this poem was found in a handwritten copy among F.R.H.'s papers. The handwriting generally looks like F.R.H.'s handwriting, and she did—though not usually—write the way of the two s's in "kissing" in the first line of the third stanza (there is at least one other example where F.R.H. wrote two s's in the old-fashioned way—a "long s" followed by a "short s"—as done in this handwritten copy). Frances may have written (authored) this poem, though presumably she did not. We do not know. There are parts of this poem that very much look like F.R.H.'s thought and composition. The lack of punctuation and finalizing details is copied here as in the handwritten copy.

Janet's Bridal

And so I am going to be married
On this gladdest merriest day
They are gathering now for the bridal
Oh what will the neighbours say!
I have but a knot of blue ribbons
No jewels to deck my hair
But I have a chaplet of blue bells
That Donald has sent me to wear
Blue bells, fairylike blue bells
Which opened at dawn for me

2nd

How fragrant my favourite roses
And the clematis[1] steeped in dew
The mavis[2] is joyfully singing
He carols the woodland through
And Mary & Alice are coming
And laden with flowers I see
To strew on the dear little foot path
As far as the hawthorn tree;
Blithely over the mountain
They gather from near & far

3

The sunbeams are kissing the roses
And the butterflies white & blue
So joyfully flutter this morning
And am I not joyful too
Our home will be over the heather
A mile from the hawthorn tree
Oh I shall be happy with Donald
And he will be happy with me!
Happy ever so happy
Our lowland home will be

[author unknown, possibly but not presumably by F.R.H.]

---

[1] clematis: long-stemmed, climbing woody vines with beautiful flowers

[2] mavis: an Old English name for the Song thrush This bird sings a distinctive song with repeated musical phrases.

The Statement "What would Jesus do?"

At the end of "Our Great Example," the Second Day of *Morning Bells* (see page 220 of Volume III of the Havergal edition). F.R.H. gave these two verses:

"If washed in Jesus' blood,
    Then bear His likeness too!
And as you onward press,
        Ask, 'What would Jesus do?'

"Give with a full, free hand,
    God freely gave to you!
And check each selfish thought
        With, 'What would Jesus do?' "

At the end of "Much More than This," the Twelfth Day of *Morning Bells* (page 230 of Volume III), she gave this one verse:

"Be brave to do the right,
    And scorn to be untrue;
When fear would whisper 'yield!'
    Ask, 'What would Jesus do?' "

We do not know who wrote these verses: possibly F.R.H., possibly another person, we don't know now. *Morning Bells* was published by F.R.H. in 1875.

At the end of the second paragraph of "The Bright and Morning Star," the Second Day of *Morning Stars* (published in 1879, page 261 of Volume III), Frances wrote this sentence: "When we stop and say to ourselves, 'what would Jesus do?' it is like looking up at the star to see which way to go."

Finally, there is a fourth detail that shows that F.R.H. knew and valued this statement: In *Lilies and Shamrocks* edited by Frances' sister Maria, a section of letters by F.R.H. to young Nony Heywood and to Nony's mother in 1879, there is a paragraph by the editor, Maria, that includes these sentences: "Dear Nony was so pleased with the motto 'For Jesus' sake only,' she said she wished she had it printed to put up on her wall by her other motto, 'What would Jesus do?' " (See page 426 of Volume III, and also page 414 of Volume IV of this edition.)

This was years before Charles Sheldon's book *In His Steps*, published in 1896 with the subtitle "What Would Jesus Do?" Sheldon's book was a social gospel that Frances would have rejected as false doctrine against Scripture, though she truly loved and obeyed the truth in James 1:27 and Luke 10:25–37. In 1893 Laura Anna Barter (later Mrs. Snow) published *Marjory; or, What would Jesus do?* (London: S. W. Partridge, 1893). S. W. Partridge published works by F.R.H. while she lived. Apparently F.R.H. is, at this time, the earliest example found of this statement "What would Jesus do ?" This is not any claim that the statement "What would Jesus do?" began with F.R.H. We don't know the beginning of this statement (which is similar to the Latin phrase *imitatio Dei*, "imitation of God," known for centuries), but these are noteworthy details.

This is a glimpse of how widely known and read *Morning Bells* was: Nisbet often (not always, very inconsistently) gave the printing numbers of books on the title pages, and these details have been found in research (see page 1629 of Volume IV of the Havergal edition):

> *Morning Bells* 176th Thousand, with the Nisbet address of
> 21 Berners Street, London

> *Morning Bells* 181st Thousand, with the Nisbet address of
> 22 Berners Street, London

Apparently Nisbet changed their street address from 21 Berners Street to 22 Berners Street between 1906 and 1908. This is given in an essay near the end of Volume IV of the Havergal edition.

"READY NOT TO DO" TWO POEMS QUOTED BY F.R.H.

Frances Ridley Havergal wrote this in a letter in October, 1875 (see page 50 of Volume IV of the Havergal edition):

> For myself, I have not been ill, though often poorly, since my last relapse in June; but I decidedly do not get strong, and am not nearly so strong as before my illness, even under these most favourable circumstances of bracing air, and nobody that *must* be seen, and nothing that *must* be done; so I am hardly likely to get any stronger at Leamington. I can do a little, write an hour or two, see one or two people, sing one song, go to church once on Sunday and subside all the rest of the day; but that is the length of my tether. I came upon some verses which seem just to express it.

> "I am not eager, bold, or strong,
> All that is past;
> I am ready *not* to do
> At last, at last.

My half day's work is almost done,
            'Tis all my part;
    I give my patient God
            A patient heart."

    For I am quite satisfied to do *half-day's* work henceforth, if He pleases; and well I may be when I have plenty of proof that He can make a *half-hour's* work worth a whole day's if He will: yes, or half-a-minute's either!

Where Frances found these verses is not known now (possibly she found a different version of the poem published, or possibly she quoted this part from memory with changes—changed consciously or not consciously—in her memory); in research for this edition, this next poem was found in a bound volume of a periodical for October to December of 1865, with this title and these details on the title page: *Littell's Living Age* Conducted by E. Littell, Third Series, Volume XXXI. From the Beginning, Vol. LXXXVII. October, November, December, 1865. Boston: Littell, Son, and Company. In that book, this poem "Rest" was found on page 494, after the end of an article, chapter, or section entitled "Eyre, the South-Australian Explorer." The statement after the title "Rest" was published with the poem here.

Rest.

    The following lines were found under the pillow of a soldier who was lying dead in a hospital near Port Royal, South Carolina:—

1. I lay me down to sleep,
        With little thought or care
    Whether my waking find
        Me here, or there.

2. A bowing, burdened head,
        That only asks to rest,
    Unquestioning, upon
        A loving breast.

3. My good right hand forgets
        Its cunning now—
    To march the weary march
        I know not how.

4. I am not eager, bold,
        Nor strong—all that is past;
    I am ready not to do
        At last, at last.

5. My half day's work is done,
        And this is all my part;
    I give a patient God
        My patient heart,

6. And grasp his banner still,
        Though all its blue be dim;
    These stripes, no less than stars,
        Lead after him.

This is similar to the truth in a poem by Georgiana M. Taylor that F.R.H. quoted in two places: as the hymn number 1068 in *Songs of Grace and Glory* (set to Frances' hymntune "Phebe"), and at the end of the Eighteenth Day of *Royal Commandments*.

Given next is *Songs of Grace and Glory* hymn number 1068 (only the first and third stanzas in S.G.G.), Tune Phebe. 7 7, 7 6. D.

Matthew 17:8. *"Jesus only."*

1. Oh to be nothing,—nothing!
     Only to lie at His feet,
   A broken—emptied—vessel,
     Thus for His use made meet;
   Emptied—that He may fill me,
     As to His service I go;
   Broken,—so that unhindered
     Through me His life may flow.

2. Oh to be nothing, nothing!
     Only as led by His hand;
   A messenger at His gateway,
     Only waiting for His command.
   Only an instrument ready
     His praises to sound at His will;
   Willing, should He not require me,
     In silence to wait on Him still.

3. Oh to be nothing,—nothing!
     Though painful the humbling be,
   Though it lay me low in the sight of those
     Who are now perhaps praising me.
   I would rather be nothing,—nothing,
     That to Him—be their voices raised,
   Who alone—is the Fountain of blessing,
     Who alone—is meet to be praised.

Georgiana M. Taylor, 1869.

[Note: The first of these three verses was the first verse in *Songs of Grace and Glory* hymn number 1068 (found on page 972 of Volume V of the Havergal edition), and was also the first verse at the end of the Eighteenth Day of *Royal Commandments* (found on page 143 of Volume II). The second of these three verses was the second verse at the end of the Eighteenth Day of *Royal Commandments*. The third of these three verses was the second verse in the S.G.G. hymn number 1068 (set to F.R.H.'s hymntune "Phebe"). See also F.R.H.'s poem "Jesus Only" on pages 376–377 of this book]

Friends in thine hour of need may fail;
Foes may for a while prevail;
Father and mother may forsake:
Fear not, my God will undertake.

Rest all thy matters in His Hands;
Run thou the way of His commands;
Refresh thyself daily at His springs;
Repose thyself safe beneath His wings.

Him the Almighty Father, true and kind,
Him Thy Redeemer bearing thee in mind,
Him the Free Spirit in thy soul enshrined,
Him Three in One thou All-in-all shalt find.

W. H. Ridley
Aug. 24ᵗ 1861

This poem was found in a signature Album of F.R.H. (for guests or friends to sign and write notes). This entry was written by Frances' godfather, Rev. William H. Ridley, a friend and former pupil of William Henry Havergal.

Friends in thine hour of need may fail;
Foes may for a while prevail;
Father and Mother may forsake;
Fear not, thy God will undertake.

Rest all thy matters in His hands;
Run thou the way of His commands;
Refresh thyself daily at His springs;
Repose thyself safe beneath His wings.

Him the Almighty Father, true and kind,
Him thy Redeemer bearing thee in mind,
Him the True Spirit in thy soul enshrined,
Him Three in One thou All-in-all shalt find.

W. H. Ridley
Aug. 24th 1861

Whose I am

Jesus, Master, Whose I am,
Purchased Thine alone to be,
By Thy Blood, O spotless Lamb,
Shed so willingly for me,
Let my heart be all Thine own,
Let me live to Thee alone.

Other lords have long held sway;
Now, Thy name alone to bear,
Thy dear voice alone obey,
Is my daily, hourly prayer.
Whom have I in heaven but Thee?
Nothing else my joy can be.

Jesus, Master! I am Thine;
Keep me faithful, keep me near;
Let Thy presence in me shine
All my homeward way to cheer.
Jesus! at Thy feet I fall,
Oh, be Thou my All in all.

Whom I serve

Jesus, Master, Whom I serve,
Though so feebly and so ill,
Strengthen hand and heart and nerve
All Thy bidding to fulfil;
Open Thou mine eyes to see
All the work Thou hast for me.

Lord, Thou needest not, I know,
Service such as I can bring;
Yet I long to prove and show
Full allegiance to my King.
Thou an honour art to me,
Let me be a praise to Thee.

Jesus, Master! wilt Thou use
One who owes Thee more than all?
As Thou wilt! I would not choose,
Only let me hear Thy call.
Jesus! let me always be
In Thy service glad and free.

Just when Thou wilt, O Master, call!
Or at the noon, or evening fall,
Or in the dark, or in the light, —
Just when Thou wilt, it must be right.

Just when Thou wilt, O Saviour, come,
Take me to dwell in Thy bright home!
Or when the snows have crowned my head,
Or ere it hath one silver thread.

Just when Thou wilt, O Bridegroom, say,
"Rise up, my love, and come away."
Open to me Thy golden gate,
Just when Thou wilt, or soon, or late.

Just when Thou wilt — Thy time is best —
Thou shalt appoint my hour of rest,
Marked by the sun of perfect love,
Shining unchangeably above.

Just when Thou wilt! — nor sooner fear,
Life is a gift to use for Thee;
Death is a hushed and solemn tryst,
With Thee, my King, my Saviour, Christ!

3 poems by Frances Ridley Havergal 1836-1879

1997 Incunabula. These three poems were copied by hand, then photocopied many times to give to others, when the mustard seed of this project had grown possibly two or three feet tall. Thanks be to God.

Index to First Lines of Poems after the Nisbet Edition of *Poetical Works.*

Note: This Index gives only the first lines of poems <u>after</u> the Nisbet edition of *The Poetical Works of Frances Ridley Havergal* (pages i to 659 of this book). The Index to First Lines of that definitive volume (Nisbet's *Poetical Works*) is found on pages 647–659 of this book, and that will have very nearly all the poems by F.R.H. This Index gives the first lines of the poems by F.R.H. not found in Nisbet's *Poetical Works* (pages 661–767).

[1] Note: The poems that begin with "Oh" are intentionally listed here with "O" (without the h), though the full "Oh" is given in the texts of the poems.

The First Epistle general of JOHN.

CHAPTER I. *A.D. 90.*

THAT which was from the [a] beginning, which we have heard, which we have seen [c] with our eyes, which we have looked upon, and our hands have [d] handled, of the Word of life;

2 (For the life was manifested, and we have seen it, and bear witness, and shew unto you that eternal life, [f] which was with the Father, and was manifested unto us;)

3 That which we have seen and heard declare we unto you, that ye also may have fellowship [i] with us: and truly our fellowship [i] is with the Father, and with his Son Jesus Christ.

4 And these things write we unto you, that [n] your joy may be full.

5 This then is the message which we have heard of him, and declare unto you, that God is light, [r] and in him is no darkness at all.

6 If we say that we have fellowship with him, and walk in darkness, we lie, and do not the truth:

7 But if we walk [t] in the light, as he is in the light, we have fellowship one with another, and the blood [u] of Jesus Christ his Son cleanseth us from all sin.

8 If we say that we have no sin, [v] we deceive ourselves, and the truth is not in us.

9 If we confess [x] our sins, he is faithful and just to forgive us our sins, and to cleanse [y] us from all unrighteousness.

10 If we say that we have not sinned, we make him a liar, and his word is not in us.

CHAPTER II.

MY little children, these things write I unto you, that ye sin not. And if any man sin, we have an advocate [f] with the Father, Jesus Christ the righteous:

2 And he is the propitiation [g] for our sins: and not for our's only, but also for the sins of the whole world.

3 And hereby we do know that we know him, if we keep [h] his commandments.

4 He that saith, I know him, and keepeth not his commandments, is a liar, and the truth is not in him.

5 But whoso keepeth his word, in him verily is the love [l] of God perfected: hereby know we that we are in him.

6 He that saith he abideth [m] in him, ought himself also so to walk, [n] even as he walked.

7 Brethren, I write no new commandment unto you, but an old commandment, which ye had from the beginning. The old commandment is the word which ye have heard from the beginning.

8 Again, a new [q] commandment I write unto you; which thing is true in him and in you, because the darkness [r] is past, and the true light now shineth.

9 He that saith he is in the light, and hateth his brother, is in darkness [s] even until now.

10 He that loveth his brother abideth in the light, and there is none [y] occasion of stumbling in him.

11 But he that hateth his brother is in darkness, and walketh [u] in darkness, and knoweth not whither he goeth, because that darkness hath blinded his eyes.

12 I write unto you, little children, because your sins are forgiven you for his name's [t] sake.

---

13 I write unto you, fathers, because ye have known him [b] that is from the beginning. I write unto you, young men, because ye have overcome the wicked one. I write unto you, little children, because ye have known the Father. [e]

14 I have written unto you, fathers, because ye have known him that is from the beginning. I have written unto you, young men, because ye are strong, [g] and the word of God abideth [h] in you, and ye have overcome [i] the wicked one.

15 Love [k] not the world, neither the things that are in the world. If [m] any man love the world, the love of the Father is not in him.

16 For all that is in the world, the lust [o] of the flesh, [o] and the lust of the [p] eyes, and the [q] pride of life, is not of the Father, but is of the world.

17 And [s] the world passeth away, and the lust thereof: but he that doeth the will of God abideth for ever.

18 Little children, it is the last [w] time: and as ye have heard [w] that antichrist shall come, even now are there many antichrists; whereby we know that it is the last time.

19 They went out from us, but they were not of us; for [x] if they had been of us, they would no doubt have continued with us: but they went out, that they might be made manifest [z] that they were not all of us.

20 But ye have an unction [a] from the Holy One, and ye know [c] all things.

21 I have not written unto you because ye know not the truth, but because ye know it, and that no lie is of the truth.

22 Who is a liar, but he that [d] denieth that Jesus is the Christ? He is antichrist, that denieth the Father and the Son.

23 Whosoever [f] denieth the Son, the same hath not the Father: [but] he that acknowledgeth the Son, hath the Father also.

24 Let [i] that therefore abide in you, which ye have heard from the beginning. If that which ye have heard from the beginning shall remain in you, ye also shall continue in the Son, and in the Father.

25 And this is the promise that he hath promised us, even eternal [k] life,

26 These things have I written unto you concerning them that seduce you.

27 But the anointing which ye have received of him abideth in you, and ye need not that any man teach you: but as [p] the same anointing teacheth [p] you of all things, and is truth, and is no lie, and even as it hath taught you, ye shall abide in [p] him.

28 And now, little children, abide in him; that, when he shall appear, we may have [r] confidence, and not be ashamed before him at his coming.

29 If ye know that he is righteous, [s] ye know that every one that doeth righteousness is born of him.

CHAPTER III.

BEHOLD, what manner of love [v] the Father hath bestowed upon us, that we should be called the sons [w] of God: therefore the world [w] knoweth us not, because it knew him not.

2 Beloved, now are we the sons [z] of

173

Made in the USA
Monee, IL
08 May 2020